GREAT PEOPLE, GREAT COUNTRY

NIGERIA THE BEAUTIFUL

East or West, Home is the Best

BY

JUBRIL OLABODE AKA (DMS, MBA AVIATION, PH.D)

(Alias Bode Endurance)

Order this book online at www.trafford.com
or email orders@trafford.com

Most Trafford titles are also available at major online book retailers.

© Copyright 2010 Jubril Olabode Aka (DMS, MBA Aviation, Ph.D).
All rights reserved. No part of this publication may be reproduced, stored in a retrieval system, or transmitted, in any form or by any means, electronic, mechanical, photocopying, recording, or otherwise, without the written prior permission of the author.

Note for Librarians: A cataloguing record for this book is available from Library and Archives Canada at www.collectionscanada.ca/amicus/index-e.html

Printed in Victoria, BC, Canada.

ISBN: 978-1-4269-1831-5 (Soft)
ISBN: 978-1-4269-1830-8 (Hard)

Library of Congress Control Number: 2009939675

Our mission is to efficiently provide the world's finest, most comprehensive book publishing service, enabling every author to experience success. To find out how to publish your book, your way, and have it available worldwide, visit us online at www.trafford.com

Trafford rev. 01/27/2010

 www.trafford.com

North America & international
toll-free: 1 888 232 4444 (USA & Canada)
phone: 250 383 6864 ♦ fax: 812 355 4082

MAP OF

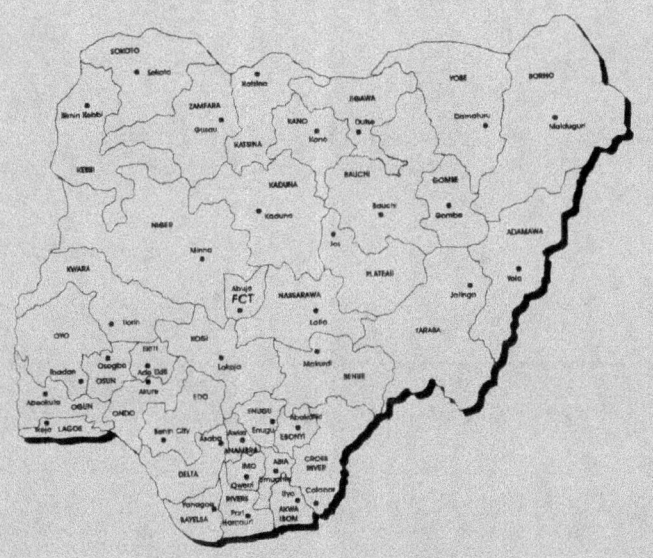

NIGERIA

MISSION STATEMENT

Some people see Nigeria's cup as half empty, but I see it optimistically as more than three quarters full with EFCC, ICPC, NEEDS and Seven-Point Agenda fully operational.

Some pessimists wrongly see Nigeria as the most corrupt nation in the world, but with more than two decades of residency in America, and partially in Europe, I have not seen any country, which is entirely free of corruption, discriminatory practices and election rigging. Bernard Madoff of New York, USA was arrested in December 2008 for committing $50 billion fraud, which is one of the highest ever in the world. He is not a Nigerian.

Many people see Nigeria as the most difficult to rule, but I see Nigerians as the smartest, highly intelligent, highly educated and most blessed compared with many other countries. Nigeria could be the easiest to rule if the leaders are transparent and exemplary.

Nigerian great people and great leaders are not perfect, but the country is moving forward. Let pessimists remove the specks in their eyes before telling Nigeria about the dust in her eyes.

East or West, Home is the Best. Nigeria is our sweet home. There is no other place we can call our home. Nigeria is the best!

Dr. Jubril Olabode Aka (DMS, MBA Aviation, Ph.D).
Texas, USA.

GOD/ALLAH BLESS NIGERIANS!

CONTENTS

Mission Statement vii	
Dedication	xiii
Nigerian Mission Poem	xv
Prologue	xvii

Chapter One   Fathers of Nigerian Nationhood and
                            Independence   1
  Sir Shaihu Usman Dan Fodio (1754-1817)   1
  Sir Herbert Samuel Heelas Macaulay
     (November 14, 1864 – May 7, 1946)   5
  Dr. Benjamin Nnamdi Azikiwe
     (November 16, 1904 - May 11, 1996)   8
  Chief Obafemi Awolowo (March 9, 1909 – May 9, 1987)   14
  Alhaji Sir Ahmadu Bello (June 12, 1910 – January 15, 1966) 23
  Sir Abubakar Tafawa Balewa
     (December 1912 – January 15, 1966)   26

Chapter Two   Successors of Fathers of Nigerian Nationhood
                            and Independence   29
  General Johnson Thomas Umunnakwe Aguiyi Ironsi
     (March 3, 1924 – July 29, 1966)   29
  General Yakubu Danyumma Gowon   33
  General Murtala Ramat Mohammed
     (November 8, 1938 – February 13, 1976)   37
  General Olusegun Obasanjo   41
  President Shehu Usman Aliyu Shagari   48
  General Mohammadu Buhari   52
  General Ibrahim Badamosi Babangida   55
  Chief Ernest Adegunle Oladeinde Shonekan   61
  General Sani Abacha (September 20, 1943 – June 8, 1998)   64
  General Abdulsalami Abubakar   68
  President Umaru Musa Yar'adua   71
  Mallam Aminu Kano (1920 – April 17, 1983)   76
  Senator Joseph Serwuan Tarka (July 10, 1932 – 1980)   79
  Chief Samuel Ladoke Akintola
     (July 6, 1910 – January 15, 1966)   82

Dr. Michael Iheonukara Okpara
    (December 19, 1920 – December 17, 1984)   86
Chief Chukwuemeka Odumegwu Ojukwu   89
General Shehu Musa Yar'adua
    (March 5, 1943 – December 8, 1997)   97
Alhaji Chief Moshood Kashimawo Olawale Abiola
    (August 24, 1937 – July 7, 1998)   99

Other Leaders: 103
  Alhaji Lateef Kayode Jakande.
  Dr. Augustus Taiwo 'Tai' Solarin
  Brigadier General Mohammed Buba Marwa.
  Lt. General Donaldson Oladipo Diya.
  Mrs. Patricia Olubunmi Foluke Etteh.
  Alhaji Abdul Ganiyu 'Gani' Fawehinmi
  Alhaji Abubakar Rimi.
  Professor Wole Soyinka.
  Chief Anthony Enahoro.
  Alhaji (Dr.) Umaru Dikko.
  Prince Bola Ajibola
  Chief Augustus Meredith Adisa Akinloye
  Chief Otunba Theophilus Owolabi Shobowale 'T.O.S.' Benson
  Chief Richard Akinjide

Chapter Three:	Nigeria In Perspective From Independence (1960)	114
Chapter Four:	Nigeria's Hope Is Rising	164
Chapter Five:	The Greatness of Nigerian People and Leadership	185
Chapter Six:	Who Should Be Leaders in Nigeria	225
Chapter Seven:	Nigeria's Fast Economic Growth and Impediments	279
Chapter Eight:	Reducing the Menace of Unemployment	326
Chapter Nine:	War Against Corruption	356
Chapter Ten:	Political Stability and Tolerance	404
Chapter Eleven:	State Secularity and Religious Tolerance	438
Chapter Twelve:	Impressive International Relations	466
Chapter Thirteen:	The Need to Eliminate Discrimination	499
Chapter Fourteen:	Unity in Diversity	514

Chapter Fifteen:	Nigerian Patriotism	529
Chapter Sixteen:	Annulment of June 12, 1993 Presidential Election	539
Chapter Seventeen:	Optimism About Nigerian Future	547

Appendix
   Acknowledgements   585
   Map of Nigeria   605
   The Nigerian National Anthem   607
   The National Pledge   608
   The Nigerian Coat of Arms   608
   Nigerian State and Capital State Title   609
   Nigeria is Born Again (Poem)   611
   Great Igbesa Families   618
   In Memoriam!   620

About the Author   623

Bibliography   626

Jubril Olabode Aka & Children   628

DEDICATION

DEDICATED TO: My Children: Bunmi, Layide, Femi & Makayla. This book titled, "Great People, Great Country, Nigeria, The Beautiful" is dedicated to all my children: Ms. S. Olubunmi Aka in UK, Ms. Z. Olayide Aka in UK, Mr. I. Olufemi Aka in UK and Miss Makayla Tokunbo Aka in USA.

The happiness about seeing these children succeeding in their various spheres of life endeavours, gives me the inspiration to write this book about their fatherland (Nigeria), rising fast to become one of the world's economic superpower, giant nations before the end of the third decade of the twenty-first millennium.

I thank God Almighty for giving me above mentioned four wonderful and lovely children. All of them are exceptionally brilliant with wonderful accomplishments that make me happy and proud of them.

Ms. S. Olubunmi Aka holds B.Sc. Mechanical Engineering and Master's Degree In Geographical Information Systems while Ms. Z. Olayide Aka and Mr. I. Olufemi Aka hold college degrees in Computer Science. The baby girl of the family, Miss Makayla Tokunbo Aka is in the first grade (2008-2009 school year) with extraordinary brilliance.

The book assures them about Nigeria's socio-economic and political reforms, the rapid progress and developments going on in Nigeria as well as enormous available opportunities that can make them proud of a new, baptized Nigeria that has emerged in recent years.

To all my children, the sky is the limit like US President Barack Obama, 2009. I wish all of them God's Enormous Blessings (amen).

NIGERIAN MISSION POEM

<u>NIGERIA THE BEAUTIFUL, OUR NOBLE HOMELAND!</u>

1

Nigeria, Our Country, Our Noble Fatherland, Is Our Homeland.
Nigeria, The Beautiful, The Resourceful, Is Our Nativeland.
There Is No Other Place We Can Call Our Own Homeland.
East Or West, Home Is The Best; Nigeria, Our Home Is The Best.
God/Allah Bless Nigeria; Our Black And Beautiful Homeland.

2

Nigerians Are Great Lovers Of Nigeria; Nigerians Are Patriots.
Nigerians Are The Faithfuls, Ready To March Forward With Nigeria
And Nigerian Great Leaders To The Promised Land – The El Dorado.
East Or West, Home Is The Best; Nigeria, Our Home Is The Best.
God/Allah Bless Nigeria; Our Black And Shining Homeland.

3

Always Put Nigeria First And Work In Nigeria's Best Interest.
Contribute To Nigeria's Development Socio-economically & Politically.
Promote Nigeria's Image To Be Best Among Comity of Nations.
East or West, Home Is The Best; Nigeria, Our Home Is The Best.
God/Allah Bless Nigeria; Our Black And Sweet Homeland.

4

Maintain Nigeria's Polity Unheated, With Due Process And Rule Of Law.
Promote Nigeria's Tolerance In Diversity Of Ethnicity, Religion And Tradition.
To Become The Greatest In Unity, Oneness, Indivisibility And Prosperity.
East Or West, Home Is The Best; Nigeria, Our Home Is The Best.

God/Allah Bless Nigeria; Our Black And Lovely Homeland.

5

Nigeria's Economic Resources Of Oil, Gas, Bitumen, Iron Ore Etc;
Should Be Protected, WellHarnessed And Judiciously Managed.
Stop Nigeria's Brain Drain And Illegal Emigration To Europe & America,
For Green Pastures And Golden Fleece Are Abundant In Nigeria.
God/Allah Bless Nigeria; Our Black And Joyous Homeland.

6

Stop Economic & Financial Sabotage – Fraud, Corruption & Treasury Looting.
Stop Capital Flight, Money Laundering & Illegal Oil Bunkering.
Stop Sex Discrimination, Violence, Arson, Militancy & Election Malpractices.
For Nigeria's Image May Suffer & Drown To The Lowest Ebb.
God/Allah Bless Nigeria; Our Black And Gracious Homeland.

7

Uplift The Masses Empathically And Exemplarily; Failure Is Not An Option.
While Living, Strive To Bequeath A WorldClass Nigeria To Posterity;
Because You May Never Pass Through This Way Again.
East Or West, Home Is The Best; Nigeria, Our Home Is The Best.
God/Allah Bless Nigeria; Our Black And Blessed Homeland.

By
Dr. Jubril Olabode Aka (DMS, MBA Aviation, Ph.D.)

PROLOGUE

PURPOSE AND IMPORTANCE OF THIS BOOK

This book titled "Great People, Great Country, Nigeria The Beautiful" embodies intensive and extensive research work into the antecedents of Thirty-eight (38) Nigerian leaders whose records are readily available, beginning from the Fathers of Nigerian Nationhood and Independence down to President Umaru Musa Yar'Adua. Nigerian great leaders' list is inexhaustible.

The prominent names include; Sir Usman dan Fodio, Sir Herbert Samuel Heelas Macaulay, Dr. Benjamin Nnamdi Azikiwe, Chief Obafemi Awolowo, Sir Ahmadu Bello, Sir Abubakar Tafawa Balewa, General Johnson Thomas Umunnakwe Aguiyi Ironsi, General Yakubu Gowon, General Murtala Ramat Mohammed, General Matthew Olusegun Aremu Okikiolakan Obasanjo, Alhaji Shehu Usman Aliyu Shagari, General Mohammadu Buhari, General Ibrahim Badamosi Babangida, Chief Ernest Adegunle Oladeinde Shonekan, General Sani Abacha, General Abdulsalami Abubakar, Mallam Umaru Musa Yar'Adua, Mallam Aminu Kano, Senator Joseph Serwuan Tarka, Chief Samuel Ladoke Akintola, Dr. Michael Iheonukara Okpara, Chief Chukwuemeka Odumegwu Ojukwu, General Shehu Musa Yar'Adua, Alhaji Chief Moshood Kashimawo Olawale Abiola, Alhaji Lateef Kayode Jakande, Dr. Tai Solarin, General Marwa, General Diya, Mrs. Olubunmi Etteh, Alhaji Gani Fawehinmi (SAN), Professor Wole Soyinka, Alhaji Abubakar Rimi, Chief Anthony Enahoro, Dr. Umaru Dikko, Prince Bola Ajibola, Chief Adisa Akinloye, Chief T.O.S. Benson and Chief Richard Akinjide (SAN).

This book affords the author, Dr. Jubril Olabode Aka (DMS, MBA Aviation, Ph.D) the greatest pleasure to see Nigeria in the best light, full of hope to become one of the greatest economic giant nations before the end of the third decade of the twenty-first century. I consider the goal achievable unequivocally sooner than later, judging from the enormous blessings of Nigeria by God/Allah with great wealth of human, material and mineral resources as well as the emergence of new leadership since the advent of the Fourth Republic whose members are heavenly bent to make Nigeria flourish with gold and honey.

The assertion that Nigeria can become one of the ten greatest economically developed powers in the world by the year 2020 is further ascertained to be fully realizable as a result of:

1. Nigeria's strict adherence to democratic governance and reforms.
2. The establishment of the Economic and Financial Crimes Commission (EFCC) headed by the Iron Lady, Chairperson Farida Waziri who replaced the Iron Man, Mallam Ribadu. She is empowered to monitor and ensure that Nigerian resources are managed judiciously without fraud or corruption. She proved everybody wrong about the deeprooted beliefs that Mallam Ribadu was indispensable and that nobody could match his excellence as Chairman of the EFCC. May God/Allah give Nigeria more women like FARIDA (amen).
3. The incorporation of the Independent Corrupt Practices and Other Related Offences Commission (ICPC), chairmanned by Justice Emmanuel Ayoola which has been a thorn in the flesh of fraudulent and corrupt politicians and other Nigerians, working hand in hand and complementarily with the EFCC.
4. The tremendous influx of foreign and local investments into the economy of Nigeria.
5. The realization by the Presidency, the Legislature, the Judiciary and the generality of Nigerians that Nigeria has the potentiality to make it happen and that teaming up and working hard will make the dream achievable sooner than later.

With all the organs of government working perfectly without "business as usual", the achievement of Nigerian economic prosperity becomes accomplishable sooner than later. Nigeria has also outstandingly improved her international image beyond expectation after earning a pariah status from the comity of nations and ostracized by the international community from 1993-1998, for human rights abuses, fraud, corruption, money laundering and assassinations of political opponents by military killer squads allegedly organized by the dictatorial regime of General Sani Abacha.

Nigerians who can be found in all nooks and corners of the world in academia and all professions are very smart, very intelligent and usually far outclass their hosts in various countries, whether developed, developing or underdeveloped. Their Godgiven versatility to succeed in any given situation where other nationals have failed is beyond comprehension.

If one comes across Nigerians in Europe, America, Asia etc. working on menial jobs such as sales clerks, taxi drivers, petrol, gasoline attendants, security guards, dietary aides, etc., one may not believe that such Nigerians would have their photocopies of minimum of Master's or Doctorate Degree certificates at the back of their pockets or in their wallets and purses. Nigerians are specially gifted and hardworking overseas.

Above mentioned Nigerian qualities and many others not mentioned are inspirational to my writing this book. Having studied and worked in the USA and UK for over two decades and met many Nigerians in the class rooms at graduate, postgraduate and doctoral levels, it is easier for me to assess how Nigerians compare favorably and excel their colleagues from their host countries and those from other countries.

This book is designed to make the world read, realize and appreciate a lot about Nigeria's greatness and her readiness to compete and retain a position of one of the best ten countries economically before the end of the third decade of this century.

Nigeria, the nation of over 140 million people infested with three decades of dictatorship, recovered and changed tremendously within six years of toeing the paths of the world's most civilized and developed democracies and economies. The changes have been steadfast, consistent, conscientious and beneficial with unparalleled strides.

The period of dictatorship was perilous, the last five years (1993-1998) being the most devastating. It was marked with human rights abuses, fraud, corruption, other economic and financial crimes, economic chaos and rise in crimes. Hence, Nigeria was declared a pariah state and ostracized by the world community.

Remarkably, within six years out of eight of Obasanjo Administration, Nigeria became the world's beloved country, a model for other African countries and the peace and power broker in Africa. Nigerian President Obasanjo was bestowed the Chairmanship of African Union and the Chairperson In Office of the Commonwealth. Cardinal Arinze, a Nigerian, became one of the leading candidates considered for the Papacy to succeed Pope John Paul II in early 2005. The Archbishop of Lagos Diocese, Anthony Olubunmi Okojie was promoted to Cardinal. After establishing democratic governance effective May 29, 1999, Nigeria was able to host international conferences of Heads of Governments of the Commonwealth and the Continent of Africa. Nigeria became a trusted nation and has remained like that.

Nigeria occupies a unique position in the world as the greatest concentration of black people on the planet. Statistically, one out of every ten black people in the world is a Nigerian. Nigeria is a member of Organization of Petroleum Exporting Countries (OPEC) and ranks as one of the seven largest producers of petroleum in the world and one of the five largest suppliers of petroleum to the United States of America. In addition to being an oil production giant in the universe, Nigeria is a prospective world leader in exploration of gas, bitumen, iron ore, phosphate and some other solid minerals like gold, zinc and tantalite.

Nigerian ExPresident Obasanjo fought fraud and corruption relentlessly in Nigerian society and won respect and commendation from world leaders thus making Nigeria a role model for most developing countries. His successor, President Umaru Musa Yar'Adua continued to do an excellent job with emphasis on due process and the rule of law. He continued the fight against fraud, corruption, illegal oil bunkering, militancy and other crimes cautiously but Nigerians felt that he was too slow.

In the first time in Nigerian history, Nigerian leaders and fathers of Nigerian Independence, Dr. Nnamdi Azikiwe, the Owelle of Onitsha, first President of Nigeria; Chief Obafemi Awololwo, first Premier of Western Nigeria; Sir Ahmadu Bello, the Sardauna of Sokoto, first Premier of Northern Nigeria; and Sir Abubakar Tafawa Balewa, first Prime Minister of Nigeria, worked tirelessly together and achieved Nigerian Independence in 1960. Nigerian unity in diversity achieved independence for Nigerians and posterity. Hence, in unity, Nigerians can move mountains that are immovable, cross all rivers that are impassable, level all bumps in their paths and fasttrack their movement to the Promised Land in togetherness.

In similar fashion, in 2005, Obasanjo Administration unprecedentedly achieved independence from unsustainable foreign debt of over $30 billion, which was characterized with economic enslavement and neocolonization. The foreign debt with the major part corruptly contracted, plagued Nigeria for about two decades (1985-2005).

Unbelievably, Nigerians were united in condemning the debt and they determinately solved the debt issue together. It is recalled that ExPresident Obasanjo was solidly supported by the entire nation (apart from few skeptics and pessimists) on his pursuits for foreign debt cancellation. He visited many foreign capitals to solicit for debt relief from many Heads of Governments from 1999 to 2005. Pessimists and skeptics criticized him for junketing the globe, but he persisted until he was able to successfully prove them wrong.

In solidarity with Obasanjo's effortful, selfless and patriotic campaign for debt relief, a powerful delegation of most distinguished members of the legislative leadership visited Washington D.C., London, Paris, Rome, etc. in April 2005 to present Nigeria's case for debt cancellation. Many Nigerian organizations also demonstrated publicly in their quest for foreign debt relief.

The prayers of all Nigerians were answered unprecedentedly on June 30, 2005, when the Paris Club granted Nigeria a debt cancellation of $18 billion and promised more. Also, the G8 nations meeting in Gleneagles, Scotland, United Kingdom, promised expansion of aid to Nigeria as well as about $50 billion aid to African countries for national development. That was in addition to $40 billion debt relief to impoverished developing countries, which included some countries in Africa.

Nigerians in particular and Africans generally must remember that good things happen when good people lead. Praise God/Allah, Hallelujah. It was BRAVO' to ExPresident Obasanjo of Nigeria, the Legislature and all Nigerians for a job well done in solidarity. Working together worked wonders for all Nigerians. You all helped to paint a brighter future for Nigerian posterity; God/Allah Bless All Nigerians!

Nigerian economy is being transformed with great improvement in respect of foreign reserve increased to above $60 billion, inflation rate reduced to about ten percent, the gross domestic product (GDP) increased from one percent to seven percent and interest rate reduced to thirteen percent from between nineteen percent and twenty-five percent. Nigeria has provided congenial business climate for local and foreign investments and has struggled to encourage industrial harmony. It has improved on infrastructural development and above all, enhanced safety and security of persons and possessions.

This book helps to remind the world that Nigeria has been baptized, is born again and has regained its good name and image as well as established an enviable position for herself and posterity within the international community. The tough lessons of the past dictatorial era are great lessons for the leadership and the followership in Nigeria chanting loudly together, "At Last, We Are Free; Never Again; Never Again."

This book introduces Nigeria, the greatest concentration of black people in the world, as a democracy effective May 29, 1999, representing the Fourth Republic. It enhances the image of Nigeria to the world, highlights its wealth of resources, differentiates it from its dictatorial past and makes its potentials attractive for local and foreign investments and tourism. It asks many interesting questions from Nigerian elites and pleads for their behaviour modification in the best interest of Nigeria.

The book draws attention to the crackdown on corruption, unprecedented foreign debt cancellation and economic reforms going on in the best interest of the nation and pleads for cooperation and understanding, but cautions that the government must always carry the people along using dialogue, consultation, diplomacy and effective communication strategies.

It must be realized that the best medication may kill the patient if improperly applied and too much fertilizer may kill a plant instead of nurturing it. It pleads for tolerance regarding religious, ethnic, socio-economic and political issues and differences. It also calls for exemplary leadership so that the citizens can fully reap the dividends of democracy.Nigerians should forgive and forget the past wrongs and work together to promote a progressive nation. But where in the world have economic reforms fully succeeded, benefited and raised the generality of the masses when the interest rate is double digit? That is food for thought for presidential economic and financial leaders, advisers and experts. The best economies have been achieved at between 1% and 5% interest rate.

The book also draws the attention of the opposition groups to the wonderful advantages of peaceful conflict resolution and the need for cooperation with government. When it is absolutely necessary, government policies and not personalities may be criticized in the best interest of Nigeria without heating the polity. Opposition just for the sake of it without offering valuable suggestions is not good for Nigeria.

The opposition, the civil society groups and labour movements cannot indulge in calling for mass destructive action all the time without having exhausted all diplomacy and efforts of consultation and conciliation. Nigeria cannot progress, achieve, develop or advance if it is constantly slapped in the face with destruction and disruption instead of seriously negotiating the policies and assisting Nigeria's movement forward. It emphasizes the three R's of good governance—Responsibility, Responsiveness and Reconciliation—and implores government to live up to the best examples of democratic governance. It provides twelve commandments as guides for best conflict resolution practices for the benefit of all.

The book highlights the genesis of Nigerian problems from independence up-to-date and encourages all stakeholders to always put Nigeria first. It examines how the January 15, 1966 coup d'état, the retaliatory one of July 29, 1966 and subsequent ones created mistrust, divisionism, misadministration of resources, mediocrity, anarchical tendencies and the evils of dictatorship, which wrecked the country for about forty years after independence.

It deliberates on the effects of the civil war (1967-1970), the setbacks for the Igbos in particular and Nigeria generally, and it encourages the Igbo Nationality about the desirability to unite, speak with one voice and present a united front to convince other ethnicities to yield the presidency to them as soon as practicable.

The book wonders why the changes envisaged on January 15, 1966, were nonviolent, peaceful and constitutional; perhaps Nigerian history today would have been different without all the killings, mistrust, setbacks and sufferings of over forty years.

Seeing that all major political parties rigged in their strongholds during the past elections, it advises the government to combat election rigging with utmost seriousness. It pleads for understanding, patience and tolerance and explains that politicians from all the political parties in Nigeria accusing their opponents of election rigging are pots calling the kettles black. In what part of the world are elections never rigged? Is it in the Eastern or Western Block of the world? Election riggings are a worldwide problem in all countries without exception. Nigeria should continue to improve on its electoral system without bitterness in the best interest of one Nigeria.

The book deals with the enormous advantages of a strong, united, indivisible Nigeria and warns Nigerians not to repeat the mistakes of the past. It reminds government about transparency, responsibility, responsiveness, exemplariness and good governance to make a difference in the people.

The book commends the foresight of the government and its relentless efforts to eliminate fraud, corruption and economic and financial crimes from Nigerian society. The Fourth Republic of Obasanjo continuing with Yar'Adua remains the first period that any government administration in Nigeria has relentlessly confronted elite crimes without looking back in Nigerian history.

To be more successful, relevant laws in the constitution should be reviewed and strengthened to eliminate loopholes that make elite criminals delay prosecution and get off the hook using legal technicalities. The book advises that law enforcement should be equitable, fair and just and without preferential treatment—no sacred cows and no untouchables. All Nigerians should be regarded as equal before the law. There should be emphasis for due process and the rule of law.

The book talks about the need to eradicate discrimination in respect of age, class, sex and religion as well as fight child abuse including child labour. It also examines Nigerian foreign policy of nonalignment in world politics with Africa as centrepiece where Nigeria represents the peace and power broker in Africa.

The book examines the thorny question about the search for the right leadership for the country. It examines a lot of suggestions made by individuals and groups as well as the Northern Governors' Forum and opinions from the South-East and South-West of Nigeria. In order to appease the various contending ethnicities vying for the presidency, the kingmakers may act discretionally to zone the presidency, even though zoning is considered undemocratic, limits competition and could debar the best candidates from becoming president. Zoning strategy cannot permanently solve Nigerian leadership succession problems, but continuing education, enlightenment campaigns and emphasis on Nigerianism rather than regionalism or ethnicism will achieve lasting results remarkably. Succeeding generations may not have the patience to handpick leaders through zoning. Hence, they need the best examples from their predecessors to always choose the best candidates to lead.

If the zoning system will ensure peace, harmony, unity and stability, it could apply until people become properly informed about the demerits in the zoning system. After 40 years of independence, any state or region that cannot present the best candidates to face healthy competitions for the position of the presidency may as well forget it. Any system or policy that robs the best candidate of the presidency is inversely discriminatory and it should be discouraged. According to Ronald Reagan, the Fortieth President of the USA, "We must act today in order to preserve tomorrow."

The book examines the activities of pessimists, the justification for such mindset but assures them of hope and help around the corner for a stable, better united, transparent Nigerian society and a prosperous nation in the making. It would need the support of all to build Nigeria to an appreciable level of actualizing her dream.

The book renders farreaching opinions about the Nigerian Civil War (1967-1970), its causes, its genesis to the end and the period of rehabilitation, reconstruction and reconciliation. All opinions expressed in the book are honest, nonprejudicial and not meant to be judgmental or condemn any participant or group on either side of the civil war.

The author commends Obasanjo Administration because his regime exerted tremendous efforts to correct a lot of the wrong past for which his administration will be remembered eternally. History will judge. In spite of supervening constraints, the regime confronted fraudulent and corrupt Nigerian elites unprecedentedly and relentlessly, and as such, Obasanjo Administration deserved commendation.

ExPresident Obasanjo's personality, as a revered institution should be preserved, and if anything was wrong, his Ministers, Advisers, Aides, Associates and government functionaries who were given positions of trust but failed should be primarily held responsible and accountable. Heads of Governments don't see everything and don't know everything. There is great history behind his accomplishments while he was the Nigerian President. Honour must be given to whom honour is due. He achieved remarkable and invaluable successes in the arena of Nigerian foreign debt cancellation as a result of socio-economic and political reforms which he brilliantly initiated.

The great Nigerian nation was plagued for over three decades by dictatorship and terrible misadministration. It would therefore take some time to get out of the accumulated problems of misrule socio-economically and politically. The consolation is that the country is moving forward on the right path. Nigerians should rally round and move Nigeria forward as well as move forward in solidarity with Nigeria.

It summarizes arguments of pessimists and optimists about Nigeria's present and the future; and it draws a lot of very interesting conclusions. A lot of questions agitating the minds of Nigerians are critically analyzed; and the book advises for patience and calmness so that Nigerians may start to witness the glorious dawn.

The book empathizes with the efforts of the government over high interest rate and suggests that it should be lowered from double digit figures because with most successful world economies, the rate is lower than five percent. The book highlights that the influence of lobbyists and special interest groups and individuals may make it difficult for government to achieve its objective of low interest rate, which is the main key and opener to successful socio-economic and political reforms. If elites act as their brothers' and sisters' keepers in the best economic interest of Nigeria and Nigerians, low interest rate will be achieved sooner than later.

It warns that the government cannot wait for inflation to bring down the rate of interest without employing open market operations. Waiting is like asking the tail to wag the dog or putting the horse at the back of the cart to push or pull the cart. Socio-economic and political reforms cannot fully realize the desired objectives under double digit, high interest rate.

This book makes important and interesting reading for youths especially students and graduates who are aspiring to leadership. It makes references to the mistakes of many leaders and the repercussions suffered, as well as provides useful guides for youths to avoid leadership pitfalls. It emphasizes that youths are the cream of the crop and golden dreams of our society and appeals to Nigerian society to motivate the youths with gainful opportunities that can make them the best they can be. The youths represent the future in our midst and Nigeria's great future will largely depend upon their background and qualities. The leadership of today cannot eat their cake and have it in the future if corruption continues pathologically with economic and financial crimes thriving like bonfire.

The author, relying on over two decades of experience with the standing of Nigerian and international students, finds it difficult to comprehend why anybody could describe Nigerian college or university graduates as unemployable. That is cheap talk, untruth, over exaggeration, a "holier than thou" attitude and an unjustified denigration of Nigerian graduates and their institutions of higher learning.

The book advises the Minister of Education, the Vice Chancellors of Nigerian universities, Nigerian educators, elders and leaders of Nigeria to always give Nigerian problems a positive solution approach because one cannot successfully solve a problem by first condemning it outright. Remember, it is a bad workman who quarrels with his tools.

Quoting from the Holy Book, "He also brought me up out of the horrible pit, out of the miry clay, and set my feet upon a rock, and established my steps. He has put a new song in my mouth to praise our God, many will see it and fear, and will trust in the Lord." (Psalm 40:23). The quoted revelation is true of Nigerian situations after three decades of brutal dictatorship, human rights abuses, corruption, money laundering, killings with socio-economic and political precariousness under successive military dictators (1966-1999) followed by fullfledged westernized type of democratic governance effective May 29, 1999.

The book highlights that there is nothing wrong if you are honestly fighting for Nigeria peacefully and intelligently with honest criticisms without exhibiting bitterness. If you are fighting for Nigeria and not for selfish reasons, you can succeed only by being partners in progress and not using irreconcilable confrontation and attacks upon attacks on the Will of God/ Allah that is moving Nigeria forward. The cooperation of all Nigerians is indispensable for the forward march. Those who may refuse to cooperate may be given all the freedom they deserve but they must be watched closely not to be able to jeopardize Nigeria's most precious democracy, unity, indivisibility and prosperity. Nigeria is not perfect but that is human.

In recognition of the dignity of life and humanity and to assure ideals in governing human beings in this millennium, the book appeals to the African Union (AU), the Commonwealth of Nations, the European Union (EU), the United Nations (UN), the United States of America, Russia and China to outlaw dictatorships, military takeover of government and any unconstitutional takeover of government in the world. Governments that are not fully democratic within three years should be warned, ostracized and sanctioned by the world community.

Leaders of countries that do not put on human face in governance resulting in human rights violations should be sanctioned. Hobnobbing with dictators and despotic rulers selectively for political and economic benefits is hypocritical and immoral; the UK and US should show examples by stopping it. The world should be bold enough to tell countries that violate human dignity continuously by pretending to be protected by their faith, custom, tradition or religion to change to modernity and civility.

It is observed that some member countries of the United Nations (UN) apply the death penalty and amputation of human limbs indiscriminately for petty offences. They must be called to civilized order of modern society or they will think that they are always right to kill or amputate the limbs of their people who offend. The Holy Bible says, "Let whoever has never sinned cast the stone at the accused," and nobody could because human beings have all sinned, yet the world acquiesces at indiscriminate, barbaric executions and amputations of human beings' limbs in some countries.

Poor people are executed or hanged for minor crimes, and the limbs of criminals of petty thieves of a couple of dollars are amputated while the rulers and leaders steal millions of dollars which they stash in private bank accounts in European and American countries with impunity. Let those rulers and leaders who apply, pass and carry out these amputation sentences in the countries involved swear by the Holy Books that they have never stolen anything in their lives to justify why they still have their own limbs intact.

The author plans that from time to time; nonpartisan political volunteer individuals and groups will be assembled to organize debates and consultations on national issues of topical interest to Nigerian citizenry. It will require going from state to state interacting with the people at local and state levels. There will be guest speeches to students in order to build an understanding set of students who can be great future leaders of Nigeria. Youth development will be a priority.

The volunteer group will be opportuned to meet government and political leaders to discuss the way forward of the country without taking sides politically but purely advising. The group will be registered as a nonprofit organization and memberships will be drawn from all over Nigeria with headquarters in Abuja or Lagos and branches spread to all the state capitals. The members will involve the Nigerian local population in 'waste to wealth programmes', entrepreneurship and modern agricultural practices to ensure mass food production.

The author sees that Nigerian potentialities are very impressive and that sooner than later, Nigeria will become one of the few nations to rank as possessing the greatest socio-economic and political influence on the globe.

He emphasizes that an attitude of 'business as usual' is antithetical to uninterrupted economic growth and development; and he wishes Nigerian elites to engage in 'behaviour modification' in the best interest of Nigeria. Always remember that Nigeria is our country and our home; there is no other place like home; East or West, home is the best and there is no other country we can call our own. Nigeria Is Our Home!

God/Allah Bless Nigeria!

CHAPTER 1

FATHERS OF NIGERIAN NATIONHOOD AND INDEPENDENCE

(1) SIR SHAIHU USMAN DAN FODIO (1754-1817)

He was also known as Shaikh Ibn Fodio or Shehu Usman dan Fodio or Shehu Uthman Dan Fuduye. He was a Fulani mystic born in Gobir in 1754 and died in 1817. He was a great philosopher, a revolutionalist, a reformer, an Islamic Scholar/Educator and a prolific writer of great repute and talents. He was the founder of Sokoto Caliphatehis dynasty. His father was Sir Muhammadu Fodio and one of his children was Muhammed Bello, the grandfather of Alhaji Sir Ahmadu Bello, the Sultan of Sokoto, and First Premier of Northern Region of Nigeria (1957-1966).

He was a teacher of Maliki School of Law and the Qadiriyyah Order of Sufism. His reformist tendencies made him prone to persistent repression from the local authorities as a result of which he left his birthplace, Gobir in 1802 and went into exile with his followers. While he was in exile, his reformist ideas increased tremendously and later developed into a political movement and social revolution, which spread like wildfire through the nooks and corners of Nigeria and Cameroon. His reformation became an instrument that was widely received and echoed across West African nations like an ethnic Fula led Jihad movement.

Sir Usman Dan Fodio was less interested in the pomp and pageantry of rulership so, he passed the rulership of Sokoto Empire to his son, Muhammed Bello while he continued to make contacts with other Islamic religious reformists and Jihad leaders throughout Africa to spread his teachings. He was a prolific writer of hundreds of books on religion, government, society, culture and tradition. He was very critical of Muslim elites about their greed, heavy taxation, their irreligious tendencies and unconscionable violation of the standards of Sharia Law.

He did everything possible to promote learning, education, literacy and scholarship among men and women. In essence, many of his daughters became scholars and great writers. His followers considered him as a Mujaddid, one who is a divinely inspired reformer of Islam. In his honour, the Usmanu Dan Fodio University, Sokoto and many roads are named after him to immortalize his name.

On June 20, 2004, the grand dubar marking the bicentennial of the Sokoto Caliphate was celebrated at the Shehu Kangiwa Square, Sokoto. While speaking at the ceremony, Fourth Republic ExPresident Olusegun Obasanjo described late Sheikh Uthman Dan Fodio as an organizational strategist, an administrative genius and a reformer who believed in dialogue, persuasion, openness, focus, truth, justice and social engagement as well as the welfare of his people. He was said to have preached peace, love, compassion and tolerance.

Sir Dan Fodio became a revered religious thinker having been educated in classical Islamic Science, Philosophy and Theology by his Instructor, Jibril Ibn Umar, a North African Muslim Alim who gave him all the ideas of religious Muslim reformist. He created a religious community in Degel, his hometown, hoping that Degel would be a religious model town where he stayed writing, teaching and preaching for twenty (20) years.

In 1802, Yunfa, the ruler of Gobir who was one of Dan Fodio's students, turned against him, revoked the autonomy of Gobir and allegedly planned the assassination of Dan Fodio and his followers. As a result, they fled to Gudu, a grassland locality where he appealed for help from the Fulani nomads who inhabited the place.

The Jihad activities of Dan Fodio inspired some West African Jihads such as (a) Massina Empire founded by Seku Amadu, (b) Toucouleur Empire founded by El Hadj Umar Tall, who married the granddaughter of Dan Fodio, (c) Adamawa Empire founded by Modibo Adama and (d) Wassoulou Empire founded by Samori.

While he was in Gudu, Dan Fodio was proclaimed the Amir alMuminin. The title made him the leader of the faithful, which gave him the power of a religious and political leader who was authorized to declare and pursue Jihad as well as, able to raise army and become the commander. Soon after, widespread uprising began by inhabitants who felt oppressed and overtaxed. The call for Jihads soon spread to Kano, Katsina, Zaria, Borno, Gombe, Adamawa, Nupe and Ilorin as well as other places where there were Fulani Alims.

After the Fulani War, Usman Dan Fodio emerged as the Commander of the Fulani Empire, which was the largest state south of the Sahara in Africa. His son, Muhammed Bello and his brother, Abdullahi were conducting the Jihads as well as maintained the administration of the empire. Dan Fodio established a government that was grounded in Islamic Law until he retired in 1811 to continue his writings about righteous conduct of the Muslim belief.

When Dan Fodio died in 1817, he was succeeded by his son, Muhammed Bello as Amir alMuminin and thus became the ruler of Sokoto Caliphate. His brother, Abdullahi became the Emir of Gwandu and he took charge of the Western Emirates Nupe and llorin. Hence, all the Hausa States and parts of Nupe, llorin and Fulani outposts in Bauchi and Adamawa came under the rulership of one politicoreligious Islamic System. Up till the British conquest of the empire during the early twentieth millennium, there were twelve (12) caliphs under the Empire of Usman Dan Fodio.

He vehemently criticized and condemned the practices of corruption, injustice, oppression, human rights abuses, heavy taxation as well as obstruction created by the law system in the business and trade going on in the Hausa States.

Sir Usman dan Fodio

Sultan of Sokoto, Amir alMuminin

Reign	1804-1815
Born	1754
Birthplace	Gobir
Died	1817
Place of death	Sokoto

Buried	Hubare, Sokoto.[1]
Successor	*Eastern areas (Sokoto)*: Muhammed Bello, son. *Western areas (Gwandu)*: Abdullahi dan Fodio, brother.
Wives	Maimuna Aisha Hauwa Hadiza
Offspring	23 children, including: Muhammed Bello Nana Asmau Abu Bakr Atiku
Dynasty	Sokoto Caliphate
Father	Muhammadu Fodio (Legal and Religious teacher

Sir Usman dan Fodio

(2)
SIR HERBERT SAMUEL HEELAS MACAULAY
(November 14, 1864 – May 7, 1946)

He was born in Lagos (Nigeria) on November 14, 1864. He was the grandson of Bishop Samuel Ajayi Crowder who was the first African Bishop of the Niger Territory. His father was Rev. Thomas Babington Macaulay, prominent missionary and educator who was the founder of the first secondary school in Nigeria. He was a nationalist of many great skills as a politician, engineer, journalist and musician. He was considered by many Nigerians of his contemporary as the founder of Nigerian nationalism.

He attended the Christian Missionary School in Lagos and worked as a clerk at the Department of Public Works, Lagos in 1881 after which he proceeded to England on government scholarship in 1890 and studied Civil Engineering in Plymouth, England from 1891 to 1894. When he returned to Nigeria, he worked for the British Crown as Land Inspector and resigned his position in 1898 as a result of discriminatory practices by the whites and increasing dissatisfaction about Nigeria continuing as a British Colony. He resigned and became a Private Surveyor in Lagos (Nigeria).

He was one of Nigeria's foremost nationalists strongly opposed to British rule of Nigeria and anxious for the achievement of Nigerian Independence. The British colonists had often maintained that they were governing in the best interest of the people with "the true interest of the natives at heart". Responding, Herbert Macaulay wrote, "The dimension of the 'true interest of the natives at heart' are algebraically equal to the length, breadth and depth of the whiteman's pocket".

He went further to prove his case in 1908 when he exposed European corruption in how the Nigerian Railways finances were mishandled by the whites. Pursuant to that, he seriously complained about inappropriate land grabbing by the British colonists from the natives without compensation. Hence, in 1919, he made a presentation before the British Privy Council in London and successfully argued the cases for the Nigerian chiefs and landowners whose lands were forcibly acquired by the colonists without reparations. His efforts compelled the colonial government to pay reparations to the chiefs and landowners whose lands were acquired by force.

In 1915, he agitated against the payment of water rates. As leader of Lagos Auxiliary of the Antislavery and Aborigines Protection Society, he led opposition against the colonial authority's plans towards effecting land tenure reforms in Lagos and entire Yorubaland.

In retaliation, Herbert Macaulay was jailed twice on trumped up charges by the British colonial authorities. His struggles which were in the best interest of the people, made him very popular. As a follow up, he founded and launched a political party on June 24, 1923 called Nigerian National Democratic Party (NNDP), which represented the first Nigerian political party and won all the seats during the elections of 1923, 1928 and 1933.

In 1931, the British colonists improved relations with Herbert Macaulay and the governor often held conferences with Herbert Macaulay in attendance to curry and secure his support on all issues and avoid opposition. The colonist governor's strategy worked effectively and Macaulay abandoned reforms, became a conservative and supported the British rule.

In 1944, Herbert Macaulay founded and led the National Council of Nigeria and Cameroon (NCNC) in conjunction with Dr. Benjamin Nnamdi Azikiwe who became the party's Secretary General. The main objective of the party was to work hard to achieve Nigerian Independence. Unfortunately, Herbert Macaulay fell ill in Kano in 1946 and died soon after returning to Lagos. As a result, Dr. Nnamdi Azikiwe assumed the leadership of the party and later became the first Nigerian President on the platform of the NCNC and its coalition with the Northern Peoples Congress (NPC).

In memory and appreciation of the pioneering efforts of Herbert Macaulay toward achieving 'Nigerian Independence and Nationhood', some prominent streets were named after him and his portrait adorns Nigerian currency note of one naira denomination, which was replaced with one naira coin.

Sir Herbert Macaulay

(3)
DR. BENJAMIN NNAMDI AZIKIWE
(November 16, 1904 - May 11, 1996)

Dr. Nnamdi Azikiwe, the Owelle of Onitsha was the First Premier of Eastern Nigeria and he became Governor-General and later became the First President of Nigeria. He was born on November 16, 1904 in Zungeru, Northern Nigeria to Onitsha, Igbo parents of Eastern Nigeria. His father was ObedEdom Chukwuemeka Azikiwe, a clerk with British Army Regiment who was forced out of the job out of sheer discrimination. He was very charismatic.

He was a very practical and pragmatic leader of great intellect, with great sense of responsibility. He was an eloquent speaker. He suffered the inequities of colonialism and discrimination at the early age. He was very fluent in speaking Hausa, Igbo and Yoruba languages. He was an allmade Nigerian in one. He was a great Nigerian nationalist.

Dr. Azikiwe was also known and called Zik of Africa. He attended the Roman Catholic Missionary Society's Anglican Mission, Onitsha; the Wesleyan (Methodist) Boys High School, Lagos and Hope Waddell Training Institute in Calabar for his early education. At 21, in 1925, he travelled to the USA and enrolled with Storer College at Harper Ferry as well as did intensive correspondence course in American Law and Procedure through LaSalle Law School, Chicago and passed both with honours. To make ends meet, he moved from job to job, discriminated against, and faced racial taunts. He often became home sick but he continued to struggle to achieve success.

He matriculated to Howard University, Washington DC in 1926 but moved to Lincoln University, Pennsylvania in 1927 and graduated in Political Science. In 1930, he was back to Lincoln University where he earned the Master's of Arts Degree in Political Science with honours. In 1932, he joined the University of Pennsylvania on Scholarship and earned the Master of Science Degree in Anthropology in 1934.

Zik of Africa was offered to pursue the Doctoral Degree at London University by Professor Bronislaw Malinowski but he chose to proceed to Gold Coast (Ghana) where he was employed as Editor of the African

Morning Post by I.T. WallaceJohnson of Sierra-Leone for three years. He was charged for publishing 'treasonable article' but the charge was overturned on appeal.

In February 1937, at the age of 33, he returned to Nigeria full of vigour, enthusiasm and passion to be of great influence that resulted in independence for Nigeria. Zik in coordination with Chief Awolowo, Ahmadu Bello, Abubakar Tafawa Balewa and many other Nigerian leaders of the late 1950's, were able to wrest power from the colonists and the British authorities, and Nigeria became a free nation on October 1st, 1960.

Dr. Azikiwe became Nigerian Governor-General from 1960 to 1963 and was the first President of Nigeria from October 1, 1963 to January 15, 1966. He established the West African Pilot newspaper and became the leader of the Nigerian People's Party from 1978 to 1983. He lost two bids to be Nigerian President during the elections of 1979 and 1983 against exPresident Shagari of the Second Republic of Nigeria.

In 1944, he was the cofounder of the National Council for Nigeria and the Cameroons (NCNC) with Sir Herbert Heelas Macaulay as leader and he became the Secretary-General of the political party. The party was subsequently called National Council for Nigerian Citizens (NCNC). In 1946, he took over the leadership of NCNC when Sir Herbert Macaulay died. The party was a dominant party in Eastern Nigeria and he led the party until 1960.

Between 1947 and 1951, he was member of the Nigerian Legislative Council and became opposition leader of Western House of Assembly from 1952 to 1953. From 1954 to 1959, he was Premier of Eastern Nigeria and President of Nigerian Senate from 1959 to 1960. He was Governor-General from 1960-1963 and First President of Nigeria from October 1, 1963 to January 15, 1966. His positions of Governor-General and President respectively were honourific without executive powers, which were exercised by the Northern Peoples Congress (NPC) represented by Sir Abubakar Tafawa Balewa as Prime Minister (1960-1966).

Zik used his publications effectively to attack racial prejudices and actively promoted nationalist fervor in the colonies of African continent. He became a thorn in the flesh of the colonists and became dissatisfied with the status quo especially in 1947 when he was a member of the

Legislative Council of Nigeria. A new constitution for Nigeria was drafted in 1951 in which he played one of the major roles.

Zik of Africa had extensive business interest which made him rich in the 1950's. He was alleged to have withdrawn $5.6 million government fund and deposited it in the collapsing African Continental Bank in which he was a shareholder to prevent the bank's collapse as revealed in the Times Magazine of 1956. He was found guilty of improper conduct in 1957 by the British Tribunal. His action was to save a situation in the best interest of the Eastern Nigerian economy, completely different from those Nigerian young leaders who stole Nigerian money and laundered it in billions and millions into private bank accounts in Europe and America.

It is recalled that in October 2008, the USA and UK governments provided over $700 billion each to bail out their collapsing banks, insurance and mortgage companies. Other European countries followed suit to stabilize their economic situations. But in 1957, when Dr. Nnamdi Azikiwe procured just $5.6 million to stabilize the African Continental Bank to accomplish the same USA and UK objectives of 2008, he was indicted, prosecuted and found guilty by the colonially sponsored British Tribunal. That was double standard, discriminatory and a height of hypocrisy.

Under pressure, Zik dissolved his state legislature and called for fresh elections. Despite the indictment, he was reelected as Premier because the electorate supported his action, which they considered, was in the best interest of their people to save the collapsing African Continental Bank.

Initially, Zik was alleged to have supported the secessionist course of Eastern Nigeria during the Civil War (1967-1970) but he switched his support to reunification in 1969 when he crossed to Nigerian side and was received with pomp and pageantry, honour and dignity, befitting a former head of government and First President of Nigeria.

In 1978, after the lifting of ban on political parties, he formed the Nigerian People's Party which was strongest in the Eastern Region, the Mid-West and some parts of Western Nigeria, but that was not sufficient to overtake the Northern People's Congress (NPC). He then formed an alliance with the NPC, which resulted in a coalition government headed by Alhaji Shehu Shagari as president and (Dr.) Alex Ekwueme as Vice President from 1979 to 1983.

Zik laid the foundation stone of the University of Nsukka, which opened in 1960. He was hardworking, patriotic and loved by majority of Nigerians. He strongly believed in forming coalitions and compromises to achieve peace, national unity and stability. He had roads, Nnamdi Azikiwe University, Akwa and Nnamdi Azikiwe International Airport, Abuja named after him in appreciation of his great statesmanship to his fatherland, Nigeria. His portrait appears on 500.00 Nigerian currency notes in his honour.

He died on May 11, 1996 and he received state burial. Places named after Dr. Azikiwe include: Nnamdi Azikiwe International Airport, Abuja; Nnamdi Azikiwe University, Akwa; Nnamdi Azikiwe Stadium, Enugu; Nnamdi Azikiwe Street, Lagos; Zik Avenue, Enugu; Azikiwe Hall, University of Ibadan; Zik's Flat, University of Nigeria, Nsukka etc.

At death, Zik of Africa was described by the New York Times as a person who "towered over the affairs of Africa's most populous nation, attaining the rare status of a truly national hero who came to be admitted across the regional and ethnic lines dividing his country." He was a mentor to Kwame Nkruma who later became the President of Ghana.

About ten years after the death of Zik, Igbo political thugs and rioters were alleged to have burnt down his house and property situated in his state of origin. Those responsible for the arson must have benefited from his lifelong struggles to achieve Nigerian Independence and Nationhood. Such arson committed on the property of Zik of Africa after his death for about ten years was abominable, uncivilized and not forgivable. Those who were responsible directly and remotely for the arson, vandalization and utterly condemnable disrespect to the greatest among the dead, should pray for forgiveness to avoid the wrath of God.

Dr. Jubril Olabode Aka (DMS, MBA Aviation, Ph.D.)

Dr. Benjamin Nnamdi Azikiwe

1st President of Nigeria
In office
October 1, 1963 – January 16, 1966

Preceded by   None (position created)

Succeeded by   Johnson AguiyiIronsi

3rd Governor-General of Nigeria
In office
November 16, 1960 – October 1, 1963

Preceded by   James Robertson

Succeeded by   None (position abolished)

1st President of the Senate of Nigeria
In office
January 1, 1960 – October 1, 1960

Preceded by   None (position created)

Succeeded by   Dennis Osadebey

Born	November 16, 1904(19041116) Zungeru, Nigeria
Died	May 11, 1996 (aged 91) Enugu, Nigeria
Political party	National Council of Nigeria and the Cameroons; Nigerian People's Party
Religion	Christianity[1]

(4)
CHIEF OBAFEMI AWOLOWO
(March 9, 1909 – May 9, 1987)

Chief Awolowo, popularly called Awo, the sage, and the immortal was born at Ikenne, Ogun (Gateway) State of Nigeria on March 9, 1909. He became the political leader of the Yoruba nationality of the Western Region of Nigeria. He was a Christian and a Lawyer of great repute. He founded Egbe Omo Oduduwa, the Trade Union Congress of Nigeria, the Action Group (AG) political party and the Unity Party of Nigeria (UPN).

As a young man, he was very active in the practice of journalism and trade unionism. He edited 'The Nigerian Worker' and many other publications. He served as Secretary of the Nigerian Motor Union. He earned a Bachelor's Degree in Commerce and travelled to London, United Kingdom and obtained a law degree.

He became the first indigenous Premier of Western Region of Nigeria from 1952 to 1960 and became the Leader of Opposition in the Federal Parliament from 1960 to 1963 while Dr. Benjamin Nnamdi Azikiwe was the Governor-General and Sir Abubakar Tafawa Balewa was the Prime Minister of Nigeria.

As Premier of Western Nigeria, he strongly and judiciously pursued the channelization of resources earned into free education, health care, employment generation and infrastructural development of Western Region of Nigeria. His priority was the elimination of illiteracy; execute poverty alleviation programmes; improve people's standard of living; enhance people's life expectancy; encourage food security; generate full employment; ease transportation and ensure progress and development of the people of Western Nigeria.

Providentially, he achieved his objectives and became the 'man of the people', dearly wanted to be leader and President of Nigeria, but political stratagem of Nigerian elites from within and outside his region of ethnicity, kept him away from the presidency.

He introduced free primary education for all in Western Region beginning from the middle of 1950's and he established secondary modern schools, technical colleges, health centres and industrial estates. In the 1950's, he established the first television service in Africa for Western Nigeria as well as developed and pursued rural electrification and pipe borne water projects, which he financed with proceeds from cocoa export trade. He had great foresight and he was a great exemplary leader who made his people achieve great things.

While Chief Obafemi Awolowo was accomplishing those goals, his colleagues in the North and East, just like dogs in the manger, were mocking him and blocking his chances to succeed instead of emulating him and doing the right things for their own people. His antagonists within the federal government blocked and starved him of his region's monetary allocation in order to frustrate, stop and derail him from achieving his administration's laudable goals and golden objectives.

In contrast to Chief Awolowo, there were serious complaints that other regional leaders who led Nigeria for over 35 years failed to help their own people. They ran the country's finances aground and infested the country with fraud, corruption, money laundering, capital flight, looting of the treasury and stashing Nigeria's government money in their private bank accounts in Europe, America, Asia and other African countries. They bastardized the nation's economy, increased unemployment astronomically and generated youth militancy and violent crimes to anarchical levels.

He had great foresight and he was a great people's person, very much endeared to the people because of his empathy, compassion and great service to them. His people were always ready to die for him. His successes as leader and the effects of the booming economy of the Western Region made him very popular among his people. He lived; he helped his people and he let them live. Western Region of Nigeria was regarded as the first and most progressive region in Africa during his leadership.

Chief Awolowo's successes of superior politics and fastpaced developmental ideas with accomplishments made him to be disliked by many of the remaining Nigerian regional leaders out of sheer jealousy. It was believed that the colonists and the leaders of the North, ruled by the Northern People's Congress (NPC), who were under the great influence of the British Government (the colonists) were apprehensive of the combined intelligence, education, accomplishments and influence of both Chief Obafemi Awolowo and Dr. Nnamdi Azikiwe who were very eager and restless to achieve Nigerian Independence. The North seemed less prepared to dump British colonists and rulers whose citizens still remained in the northern public and private sectors and establishments longer than was necessary after Nigerian Independence of October 1, 1960.

Hence, the colonists did everything possible in their own selfish interests to sow, perpetrate and perpetuate divisionism, misunderstanding, dispute, and nurturing leadership, ethnic, religious and political mistrusts amongst Nigerian leaders of North versus West and North plus East versus West. The colonists employing 'divide and rule' policies and strategies were successful in their ploys because Nigerian leaders and people focused more on what divided them instead of spending quality time to emphasize on what united them and then harmonize their differences to achieve Nigerian unity, indivisibility, stability, progress and development.

Shortly before independence on October 1, 1960, Chief Obafemi Awolowo agreed to lead his Action Group (AG) party at federal level leaving his deputy, Chief Samuel Ladoke Akintola as Premier of Western Region of Nigeria. The adventure fetched him the Leader of Opposition for refusing to join the coalition of government of unity propounded and formed by the Northern and Eastern political leaders.

As Chief Obafemi Awolowo could not beat the Northern and Eastern leaders' alliance in the elections that followed, he should have joined the coalition for the right reasons, as his deputy Chief Akintola did, judging from the events of calamities and sufferings that befell the Yoruba race thereafter.

As a result of Chief Awolowo's refusal to join the coalition, the coalition leaders in government applied political stratagem, which jeopardized the opportunities of the entire Yoruba race in the sharing of the national cake with equity, justice and fairplay. The physical and psychological torture, which he underwent in the hands of his antagonists who were rated less qualified than he was, surpassed any description. To catch a monkey, you may have to act like a monkey. He did not! When you are not sure of winning a fight, it is best to avoid a confrontation and not start one! He did not!

It is worthy to reiterate the old adage and wise 'dictum' which says, "If you cannot beat them, you may reasonably join them for the right reasons" to avoid a plethora of unpleasant reprisals, sufferings and consequences which set the Yoruba race backward for decades and almost destroyed the Yoruba Nationality. Chief Awolowo suffered terribly, physically, emotionally and psychologically as a result of torture by his political opponents in the government.

While Chief Samuel Ladoke Akintola, Premier of Western Nigeria who was deputy leader to Chief Obafemi Awolowo, saw the benefits of political affiliation with the Northerners as the Easterners did, and pursued the course for the good of Action Group party and Yoruba race, Chief Awolowo decided otherwise and went into opposition at the detriment of himself, his political career, his people and the stability of Western Nigeria. He suffered a lot of humiliations as a leader but he never gave up.

If families cannot settle their internal differences, then, they risk the dangerous interference from outsiders who care less or nothing about them but want them hurt, humiliated and regressed. That was the plight of the Yoruba leaders and people between 1960 and 1966. They should have nobody to blame but themselves first and foremost.

A serious irreconcilable disagreement between Chief Awolowo and Chief Akintola (his deputy), led to serious constitutional crises and fighting in the Western House of Assembly. A state of emergency was declared by the federal government resulting in the detention of some Yoruba leaders and parliamentarians. At the end of it, Chief Akintola formed a new political party called Nigerian National Democratic Party (NNDP), which won the election of 1964 purported to be massively rigged.

Hence, the group called 'Agbekoya' staged massive political uprisings and widespread killings of supporters of Chief Akintola's party and committed uncontrollable arson codenamed 'WETIE' against Chief Akintola's government supporters. When your antagonists are hellbent to burn you with fire, always make sure that you do not rub your body with oil. Chief Awolowo, Chief Akintola and other Yoruba leaders did not heed that precious Yoruba counsel. They should have resorted to internal settlement of their problems before they got out of hand.

Soon after 1964, Chief Awolowo and many of his lieutenants were charged and imprisoned for treasonable felony for conspiring with some Ghanaian authority members under President Kwame Nkrumah of Ghana to overthrow the Federal Government of Nigeria headed by President (Dr.) Nnamdi Azikiwe and Prime Minister Sir Abubakar Tafawa Balewa.

In the elections that followed in 1964, Chief Akintola's party, NNDP of Western Nigeria formed a coalition with the Northern People's Congress (NPC) to become NPC-NNDP, while the remnants of Chief Awolowo's party (Action Group) formed an alliance with the National Council of Nigerian Citizens (NCNC). The election was won by NPC–NNDP amid serious accusations of widespread riggings, and violence ensued especially in many parts of Western Nigeria.

Incomprehensively, there was no coup d'etat between 1960 and 1964 when the Easterners were in alliance in government with the Northerners – NCNC and NPC, but as soon as Chief Akintola, a Yorubaman of Western Nigeria allied with the Northerners (NPC-NNDP) and they won election in 1965, young Igbo military officers staged a coup d'etat and killed Northern and Western leaders and military officers with impunity. They safeguarded their Igbo leaders and military officers. That was tribalistic, wicked, barbaric and treasonable.

The political instability that followed, resulted in the Ifeajuna/ Nzeogwu coup d'etat of January 15, 1966, which overthrew the government by assassinating Prime Minister, Sir Abubakar Tafawa Balewa; Premier of Northern Nigeria, Sir Ahmadu Bello; Premier of Western Nigeria, Chief Samuel Ladoke Akintola and many civilian leaders and military heads of Northern and Western Regions who represented Hausa and Yoruba ethnicities respectively. The coup conspirators and killers spared civilian leaders and military heads of Eastern Nigeria (Igbo) ethnicity. As a result, the bloody coup d'etat was regarded sectional, discriminatory, tribalistic and insulting to the intelligence and integrity of the Northerners (Hausas) and Westerners (Yorubas).

To add more insult to the injury, General Aguiyi Ironsi an Igboman of Eastern Nigeria who was made Military Head of State did not try, convict and execute the coupists who went about boasting about their cruel assassinations and overthrow of the democratically elected government of Nigeria, the First Republic. Above all, General Aguiyi Ironsi planned to introduce a unitary system of government, which was despised by the Northerners (Hausas) and Westerners (Yorubas), but would unduly favour his kinsmen, the Easterners (Igbos).

Hence, the Northern military officers planned the massive retaliatory coup d'etat of July 29, 1966, which killed General Aguiyi Ironsi, and his government was overthrown. At that juncture, Lieutenant Colonel Yakubu Gowon emerged as Military Head of State assisted by Lt. Colonel Murtala Mohammed as his deputy. There were serious riots against the Easterners (Igbos) in the North and they had to leave their properties in other parts of the country to go to Eastern Region, which Lt. Colonel Chukwuemeka Odumegwu Ojukwu later declared as secessionist Biafra.

In the meantime, Chief Obafemi Awolowo was pardoned, released from Calabar Prison and made the Finance Minister and Civilian Deputy Head to General Gowon, the Military Head of State of Nigeria. Chief Awolowo visited the Biafran enclave and tried to broker peace with the secessionists leaders in vain. He remarked that if the Easterners succeeded in breaking away, the Westerners would follow suit and secede from Nigeria.

As Minister of Finance, Chief Awolowo ensured that Nigerian money was changed immediately the secessionist soldiers occupied the Mid-Western Region, vandalized the banks and removed all the money to their enclave, ready to use it to purchase weapons to continue the war. Changing of Nigerian currency at that time was an economic strategy against the secessionists that broke the camel's back. The currency change action was quick, swift, effective and was a decisive blow. It helped to speed up the end of the civil war and ended the sufferings and deaths of innocent people.

Soon after the end of the civil war, he resigned and started to prepare for elective office of Nigerian President. He founded the Unity Party of Nigeria (UPN) in 1979 to succeed the defunct Action Group (AG) party. He contested against Alhaji Shehu Aliyu Shagari, the presidential candidate of the National Party of Nigeria (NPN) and lost in 1979 by about 400,000 votes.

He complained about massive election rigging but the Military Head of State General Olusegun Obasanjo, a Christian and a Yorubaman from the same Ogun State like Chief Obafemi Awolowo, handed over the Nigerian Presidency to Alhaji Shehu Aliyu Shagari, a Muslim and a Northerner from Sokoto State. The Supreme Court decision also favoured Shagari as the winner. In 1983, after President Shagari's first term in office, Chief Obafemi Awolowo recontested the presidency against him and allegedly lost by over four million votes.

Chief Awolowo was the first Nigerian to voluntarily resign from the position of Minister of Finance and Civilian Deputy Head of State. Such posts made many other occupants to become billionaires fraudulently and filthy wealthy corruptly with various foreign private bank accounts hidden in Switzerland, Britain, USA, Canada, Japan, China and other African countries; but he resigned honourably. Many of his contemporaries were very greedy and selfish, but Chief Obafemi Awolowo, the sage, was exemplary and exceptional.

There were untruths circulating in some quarters that the Ifeajuna/Nzeogwu coup d'etat of January 15, 1966 was intended to release Chief Obafemi Awolowo from prison and install him as Head of State of Nigeria. That was a fabrication to win the sympathy of the Yorubas of Western Nigeria for the bloody and cruel assassinations of civilian and innocent military officers of Yoruba nationality by Igbo young military officers during the coup.

Above all, why was he not released between January 15, 1966 and July 29, 1966 when General Aguiyi Ironsi an Igboman became Military Head of State as a result of the discriminatory January 15, 1966 coup d'etat, which was generally called Igbo coup d'etat? It has never happened in the annals of Nigeria that an Igboman or a Yorubaman will allow the other to enjoy an opportunity without a cutthroat competition.

In 2007-2008, Chief Obafemi Awolowo's statue in Ibadan was removed and allegedly replaced with something else by the new political leadership who must have benefited from the free primary education and other invaluable programmes, which Chief Awolowo initiated when he was Premier of Western Nigeria. In civilized communities worldwide, the statues of great leaders are never desecrated but kept honoured and sanctified forever.

Those leaders who desecrated Awo's statue hardly looked back as necessary for guides to chart a path for a great future having learnt nothing from the mistakes of the past. Chief Awolowo will be remembered eternally for the establishment of free primary education, free health care, establishment of Secondary modern schools and technical colleges, employment generation, investment generation, improving the quality of lives of Yorubas and for his exemplary leadership. He was second to none during his lifetime.

In his memory and in recognition of his gracious life accomplishments, so many roads, schools, colleges and the Obafemi Awolowo University, llelfe were named after him in his honour. His portrait adorns Nigerian onehundred naira note. Majority of Yorubas never believed that he died or that he could die because of his accomplishments for the people.

Dr. Jubril Olabode Aka (DMS, MBA Aviation, Ph.D.)

Chief Obafemi Awolowo

Premier of Western Nigeria
In office
October 1, 1959 – October 1, 1960

Succeeded by   Samuel Akintola

Born	March 6, 1909 (19090306) Ikenne, Ogun State
Died	May 9, 1987 (19870510) Ikenne
Political party	Action Group
Profession	Lawyer
Religion	Christian

(5)
ALHAJI SIR AHMADU BELLO
(June 12, 1910 – January 15, 1966)

Sir Ahmadu Bello was the First Premier of Northern Region of Nigeria from 1954 until January 15, 1966 when he was cruelly assassinated by Ifeajuna/Nzeogwu coup d'etat. He played prominent roles in conjunction with Sir Abubakar Tafawa Balewa, First Prime Minister of Nigeria to secure a great place for the Northern Region within independent Nigerian Nationhood. He was a contemporary of Dr. Nnamdi Azikiwe, First President of Nigeria and Chief Obafemi Awolowo, First Premier of Western Region of Nigeria in the joint struggle for Nigerian Independence of October 1, 1960. He was the leader of Northern People's Congress (NPC) which won the 1959 and 1964 parliamentary federal elections.

Sir Ahmadu Bello was born on June 12, 1910 in Rabbah of old Sokoto State. He was heir to the Sokoto Emirate and great grandson of Sultan Bello, founder of Sokoto and descendant of revered Sir Usman Dan Fodio. He was educated at Sokoto Provincial School, Katsina Teachers' Training College and in 1948, he proceeded to England on scholarship and studied local government administration which gave him a lot of savvy in the process of governance.

He was a teacher at the Sokoto Middle School and in 1934, he became the district head of his birthplace, Rabbah and four years later, he became the divisional head of Gusau. He made an unsuccessful bid to become the Sultan of Sokoto in 1938, but received the honourary title of Sardauna of Sokoto.

After his education in England, he represented Sokoto Province in Northern Regional House of Assembly in the elections of 1952. Later, he became a member of the regional executive council taking the portfolio of Minister of Works. He became Minister of Works, Local Government and Community Development successively in the Northern Region of Nigeria.

He became the Premier of Northern Region of Nigeria in 1954 and he led his Northern People's Congress (NPC) to win majority seats in the federal parliamentary elections of 1959 prior to Nigerian Independence. His Party (NPC) forged an alliance with the National Council of Nigeria and Cameroons (NCNC) led by Dr. Nnamdi Azikiwe to form the first indigenous Nigerian government which achieved independence from the United Kingdom.

Alhaji Ahmadu Bello, leader of the majority party in the government chose to remain as Premier while his deputy leader in the NPC, Sir Abubakar Tafawa Balewa became the executive Prime Minister and (Dr.) Nnamdi Azikiwe was the Governor-General and later, the First President of Nigeria honourifically while executive powers remained with the Prime Minister.

He succeeded immensely in the unification of the diverse people of Northern Nigeria under one umbrella before his assassination and the overthrow of the Nigerian government on January 15, 1966 carried out by Ifeajuna/Nzeogwu coup d'etat. The coup was considered sectionally, discriminatorily and ethnically motivated and as such, the Northerners retaliated massively on July 29, 1996 against the Easterners.

In his memory and in recognition of his accomplishments, many roads and the Ahmadu Bello University, Zaria were named after him and his portrait adorns Nigerian money of two hundred naira notes.

Sir Ahmadu Bello

Premier of Northern Nigeria
In office
1954 – 1966

Succeeded by	Hassan Katsina
Born	June 12, 1910 Rabbah, Sokoto State.
Died	January 14, 1966
Political party	Northern People's Congress
Religion	Muslim

Dr. Jubril Olabode Aka (DMS, MBA Aviation, Ph.D.)

(6)
SIR ABUBAKAR TAFAWA BALEWA
(December 1912 – January 15, 1966)

Sir Abubakar Tafawa Balewa was born in Bauchi in December 1912 and was assassinated on January 15, 1966 during the Ifeajuna/Nzeogwu coup d'etat, which overthrew the Nigerian government, which he led as the First Prime Minister of Nigeria. As a local leader, he was very vocal in promoting the course of Nigerian Independence and the formation of the Organization of African Unity (OAU). He was a great nationalist who was very humble and well respected internationally especially within African continent.

He was the son of a Bagen Muslim District Head in Bauchi Divisional District of Lere. He attended Koranic School in Bauchi and acquired his teaching certificate from Katsina College. He was sponsored on northern government scholarship to the University of London School of Education for a year and when he returned, he was appointed Inspector of Schools during the colonial era.

In 1946, he was elected to the colony's Northern House of Assembly and to the Legislative Assembly in 1947. He was very vocal in promoting the interests of Northerners, and in coordination with Sir Ahmadu Bello, the Sardauna of Sokoto; the Northern People's Congress (NPC) was formed under the leadership of Sir Ahmadu Bello while Sir Abubakar Tafawa Balewa was the Deputy Leader.

In 1952, Sir Abubakar Tafawa Balewa was the Minister of Works and later served as Minister of Transport. In 1957, his party (NPC) negotiated and concluded a coalition with the National Council of Nigerian Citizens (NCNC) and he became the First Prime Minister of postcolonial Nigeria with Dr. Azikiwe as Governor-General. He retained his position when Nigeria gained independence on October 1, 1960 and he was reelected as Prime Minister in 1964 until January 15, 1966 while Dr. Nnamdi Azikiwe was Nigerian President from October 1, 1960 to January 15, 1966.

His government declared a 'State of Emergency' on Western Nigeria and imprisoned Chief Awolowo and his lieutenants for treasonable felony. He concluded an alliance with the NNDP, Chief Akintola's party of Western Nigeria and won the election of 1964, which enabled him to continue as Prime Minister until his assassination during the Ifeajuna/Nzeogwu coup d'etat. It was alleged that his dead body was found on the roadside in Lagos after about five days of his being assassinated. That was sad and unfortunate especially when those Igbo military officers and their coconspirators who committed the assassinations were not tried and punished for treason, murder and overthrow of democratically elected government of Nigeria. Capital punishment for the January 15, 1966 coup plotters and their collaborators could have served as a deterrence for the coups d'etat of July 29, 1966; 1975; 1976; 1983, 1985, 1990 and 1993.

He acted remarkably as peace and power broker in African countries. In January 1960, Queen Elizabeth II of United Kingdom knighted him and he received a honourary doctorate degree from the University of Sheffield, England in May 1960.

In honour and remembrance of First Nigerian Prime Minister Abubakar Tafawa Balewa, many roads were named after him as well as the Abubakar Tafawa Balewa University, Bauchi. His portrait adorns the Nigerian currency note of fivenaira denomination.

Dr. Jubril Olabode Aka (DMS, MBA Aviation, Ph.D.)

Sir Abubakar Tafawa Balewa

Prime Minister of Nigeria
In office
October 1, 1960 – January 15, 1966

Succeeded by	None
Born	1912 Bauchi, Nigeria
Died	January 15, 1966
Political party	Northern People's Congress
Religion	Islam

CHAPTER 2

SUCCESSORS OF FATHERS OF NIGERIAN NATIONHOOD AND INDEPENDENCE

(1) GENERAL JOHNSON THOMAS UMUNNAKWE AGUIYI IRONSI (March 3, 1924 – July 29, 1966)

He succeeded Dr. Benjamin Nnamdi Azikiwe, First President of Nigeria who was overthrown in a military coup d'etat spearheaded by Ifeajuna/Nzeogwu when the First Prime Minister of Nigeria, Sir Abubakar Tafawa Balewa was assassinated with Sir Ahmadu Bello, First Premier of Northern Nigeria and Premier of Western Region of Nigeria, Chief Samuel Ladoke Akintola and many others on January 15, 1966.

He was born on March 3, 1924 at Umuahia, Abia State and was assassinated at Lalupon, Oyo State, Nigeria with his host, Lt. Colonel Adekunle Fajuyi during the so called retaliatory coup d'etat of July 29, 1966.

At the age of eight (8), he stayed with his sister, Mrs. Anyamma Johnson whose husband was Sierra-Leonean diplomat in Umuahia. Subsequently, Aguiyi Ironsi took the last name of his brother-in-law who was his father figure and mentor. At twenty-two (22) years of age, he enlisted into the Nigerian Army.

He received military training at Eaton Hall, England where he became a commissioned officer in June 1949. On his return to Nigeria, he was made the Aid-de-camp of John Macpherson, who was the Governor-General of Nigeria. He led the fifth battalion of the Nigerian Army to Kivu and Leopoldville Provinces of Congo during Congo crisis of 1960's in response to the request of the United Nations Secretary-General, Dag Harmmarskjold to Nigerian Federal Government to help with peacekeepers.

As Lt. Colonel, Ironsi performed brilliantly beyond expectations in Congo and he became the Commander of the United Nations Operations in Congo. He returned to Nigeria in 1964. On February 9, 1965, the NPCNCNC coalition government led by Dr. Nnamdi Azikiwe as President and Sir Abubakar Tafawa Balewa as Prime Minister appointed Ironsi as General Officer Commanding of the Nigerian Army after the departure of the British General Officer Commanding.

The military coup d'etat of January 15, 1966 allegedly staged by Igbo young military officers killed Northern and Western Nigerian civilian and military leaders and overthrew the democratically elected federal government. Hence, General Aguiyi Ironsi took over as Military Head of State from Acting Interim President Nwafor Orizu. Unfortunately, the civilian and military leaders of Eastern Region of Nigeria were spared selectively while leaders of other ethnicities were eliminated by assassination. Hence, the coup d'etat of Ifeajuna/Nzeogwu was regarded as sectionally, discriminatorily and tribally motivated. The Northerners, therefore considered that a retaliatory coup d'etat was inevitable and should be carried out soonest against Igbo military officers to wrest governmental power from them.

General Aguiyi Ironsi did not prosecute, convict and execute the coupists who allegedly were his Igbo kinsmen of Eastern Nigeria. The Northerners and Westerners of Nigeria were not pleased with his leaving the coup plotters unpunished. He also issued the Decree No.1, which was about to abrogate the regional setting and replace it with a unitary type of administration, which was bound to favour his Igbo kinsmen, more than other Nigerian ethnicities. Hence, the country was bound to explode as a result of dissatisfaction of the majority comprising of Northerners and Westerners of Nigeria.

As a result of general dissatisfaction about Ironsi's discriminatory steps, which were considered tribalistic, northern military officers allegedly led by General Murtala Muhammed and General Theophilus Danjuma staged the retaliatory coup d'etat on July 29, 1966. General Aguiyi Ironsi and his host, Lt. Colonel Adekunle Fajuyi were assassinated at Lalupon, Oyo State and the military government of Ironsi was successfully toppled.

It was reported that Ironsi was repeatedly questioned about his complicity in the assassination of northern leaders during the January

15, 1966 coup, before he was killed. Although Adekunle Fajuyi was not the target, he was considered as one of those tagged as progressives in the military who did not fully condemn the January 15, 1966 coup d'etat led by Major Chukwuma Kaduna Nzeogwu, an Igboman from Okpanam near Asaba, Delta State.

Lt. Colonel Yakubu Gowon succeeded General Ironsi. If General Ironsi had acted promptly and decisively on available intelligence report, he could probably have foiled the coup against him and he could have saved his own life and the lives of many others.

The great lesson to learn from this episode is that Nigerians should always try to solve their problems using peaceful means because the application of violence begets violence, which often leads to chains of violence and eventual destruction.

General Johnson Aguiyi Ironsi

2nd President of Nigeria

Preceded by   Nnamdi Azikiwe

Dr. Jubril Olabode Aka (DMS, MBA Aviation, Ph.D.)

Succeeded by	Yakubu Gowon
Born	March 3, 1924 (19240303) Umuahia, Abia State, Nigeria
Died	July 29, 1966 Lalupon, Nigeria
Nationality	Nigerian
Political party	*None (military)*

(2)
GENERAL YAKUBU DANYUMMA GOWON

General Gowon became the Military Head of State (1966 1975) in succession to General Aguiyi Ironsi who was assassinated in the military coup d'etat of July 29, 1966. The coup was said to be retaliatorily carried out by Northern Nigeria military officers to avenge the Ifeajuna/ Nzeogwu coup of January 15, 1966. As at then, Gowon was a Lt. Colonel. He was not the most senior to succeed Ironsi but events showed that he was the most acceptable to lead and take over the reins of government. His seniors fled for fear of being targets of assassination. He was popularly known as 'Jack' in the military.

He was born on September 19, 1934 at Kanke, Local Government area of Plateau State. His parents, Nde Yohanna and Matwok Kurnyang were Christian Missionaries of Church Missionary Society (CMS). They moved to Zaria and General Yakubu Gowon spent his early education and youthful life in Zaria.

He enlisted into the Nigerian Army in 1984 and was commissioned as Second Lieutenant on October 19, 1955 at the age of 21. As at January 15, 1966, when he became the Military Head of State, he was a Lieutenant Colonel, a Christian, a Northerner but not a Fulani or Hausa and not of the Islamic faith which placed him in a neutral position at that most troubled time in the annals of Nigeria. It was difficult for his seniors to convincingly claim neutrality and be more acceptable. In fact, his so called military seniors fled for their lives and were in hiding.

He was young at 33, humble, energetic, charismatic, empathic and compassionate. Hence, providentially, he became the most suitable and most acceptable to lead the country. His deputy was Lt. Colonel Murtala Mohammed, who was said to be the real leader of the counter coup d'etat of July 29, 1966.

General Gowon stopped Ironsi's Decree No. 34, which proposed the abolition of the federal system of governance for a unitary type. He tried in vain to persuade the Igbos, many of whom were massacred in the Northern Region, not to go back to the Eastern Region as requested by the Military Governor of Eastern Nigeria, Lt. Colonel

Chukwuemeka Odumegwu Ojukwu (an Igboman) who orchestrated the secessionist tendencies.

Lt. Colonel Ojukwu contended that he could not take orders from Lt. Colonel Gowon and that the Nigerian State could no longer protect the lives of Igbos and as such, Igbos reserved their rights to create a state of their own in which their lives could be preserved and their rights respected.

Nigerian government led by General Gowon could not accept a secession without a fight. To avoid war, 'Aburi Accord' was reached in Accra, Ghana between 4th and 5th of January 1967, but was given different interpretations by both contending sides in terms of restructuring Nigeria into a confederation. Hence, 'Aburi Accord' could not stand. As a follow up, Ojukwu seized federal assets in the East, which included the Delta Region that was yielding oil revenue to the federal government.

Strategically, Gowon divided Nigeria into 12 states on May 5, 1967, which included three states of Rivers State, South Eastern State and East Central State in Ojukwu's enclave. The creation of states was a strategic blow to Ojukwu's intention to control the whole oil rich region located in areas inhabited by minorities who were non-Igbos and would not want to be continuously dominated by secessionist Igbo leaders of Biafra.

Majority of non-Igbos did not support the secession and many Igbos doubted that it would succeed. However, three notable minority leaders were given portfolios by the secessionist government. Lt. Colonel Phillip Effiong was Chief of Defence Staff, Chief N. U. Akpan was Secretary to the government and Chiefs Bassey and Graham Douglas were absorbed within the executives of the secessionist administration.

In reaction to Gowon's state creation of May 5, 1967, Chief Ojukwu formally declared a secession of the Eastern Region on May 30, 1967 and named it 'Republic of Biafra'. His action triggered a police action to arrest the secessionist leaders but it later degenerated into civil war (1967-1970) after the secessionist army crossed over into the Mid-Western Region, over ran it, looted all the money in the banks there to their enclave and started to march toward Lagos through Ore Junction, Ondo State. The war resulted into thousands of soldiers dead and about two million people were displaced and many others were dead.

The Eastern Region was blockaded which allegedly resulted in starvation and there were complaints of atrocities, such as rape, looting and excessive force which the Nigerian government leadership denied; but regarded as unfortunate products of war which both Gowon government and Ojukwu secessionist backers should have avoided by solving Nigerian problems using peaceful means. Secession and/or anarchy cannot lead to solution of problems of Nigeria.

It was unfortunate that the secessionists bombed Lagos, occupied the Mid-Western Region, looted the banks there, started to march through Ore, Ondo State to Lagos, and thereby lost some support of Yorubas and Mid-Westerners who initially sympathized with their course. All that happened before Nigerian Government shifted from police action to arrest the secessionist leaders to declaring fullscale war. Prominent Commanders of the war were Brigadier Benjamin Adekunle, nicknamed scorpion and his successor General Olusegun Obasanjo.

The whole Nigerian Civil War (1967-1970) and violent actions before, during and after it, were avoidable and therefore condemnable. General Gowon fought the war humanly and ended it with no victor, no vanquished declaration followed by committed efforts of 'Reconciliation, Reabsorption, Reconstruction and Rehabilitation'.

Unfortunately, those leaders who chose war instead of peace at the detriment of innocent lives have not been fully accountable for their mistakes. Nigeria should never have a repetition of the past costly and deadly mistakes whereby innocent poor people were plunged into war by the elites who had their families safe in other African countries, Europe and America. Nigerians should stop being fooled by the elites who use them to commit violence.

In 1972, Gowon Administration promulgated the indigenisation decree, which limited foreign participation in specific sectors of Nigerian economy to encourage and expand local investments. He gave workers the Udoji Award and oil exploration started in earnest during his regime.

On June 25, 1975, his deputy, General Murtala Mohammed while Gowon was attending an OAU summit in Kampala, Uganda, overthrew General Gowon. He proceeded to Britain and studied for Ph.D. in Political Science at Warwick University, Coventry, United Kingdom.

In February 1976, Lt. Colonel Bukar Dimka, one of the suspects in the assassination of General Murtala Mohammed, Nigerian Head of State was alleged to have implicated General Gowon in his coup attempt. Hence, General Gowon was stripped of his rank, his pension stopped and he was declared wanted. During President Shagari's Administration (1979-1983), General Gowon was pardoned with Chief Ojukwu; his rank and pension were reinstated and he became free to return to his fatherland, Nigeria. On his return to Nigeria, he formed a nondenominational religious group named 'Nigeria Prays'.

General Yakubu Gowon

3rd President of Nigeria

In office

August 1, 1966 – July 29, 1975

Preceded by	Johnson AguiyiIronsi
Succeeded by	Murtala Mohammed
Born	September 19, 1934 (19340919) Kanke, Plateau State, Nigeria
Religion	Christian

(3)
GENERAL MURTALA RAMAT MOHAMMED
(November 8, 1938 – February 13, 1976)

He was the Military Head of State of Nigeria from July 29, 1975 until February 13, 1976 when he was assassinated in an attempted military coup d'etat, which failed. He vehemently opposed the Ifeajuna/Nzeogwu coup d'etat of January 15, 1966, which assassinated many Northern and Western Nigeria civilian and military leaders while their Eastern Nigeria counterparts in government and the military were safeguarded by their kinsmen who staged the coup. Hence, General Murtala Mohammed who was a Northerner like many others who felt insulted and injured traditionally, nursed a retaliation to avenge the killings of their leaders of HausaFulani ethnicity by Igbo tribe military officers during the coup d'etat of January 15, 1966.

On July 29, 1966, the retaliatory/counter coup succeeded to assassinate General Aguiyi Ironsi and many others of Igbo ethnicity. He intended to effect a secession of the Northern Region of Nigeria but he was advised that he could not do that successfully for economic reasons. He was reminded that Nigeria's wealth of resources was concentrated in the South West, Mid-West, South-South and South-East regions while the expansive Northern Region had very little to maintain and sustain itself to ensure its survival if it seceded from the rest of Nigeria.

He could have been Military Head of State of Nigeria from July 29, 1966, but Lt. Colonel Yakubu Gowon who was his military senior as well as neutral and more acceptable to lead Nigeria, was more favoured to lead as Head of State. As a result, Murtala Mohammed had to wait for nine (9) years until July 29, 1975 before he succeeded to overthrow General Yakubu Gowon.

During the Nigerian Civil war (1967-1970), he was General Officer Commanding (GOC) of the 2nd Division of the Nigerian Army. He made three costly attempts to cross into the secessionist enclave but he was beaten back twice with heavy casualities because the retreating secessionist forces blew up their endside of the Niger Bridge of the Mid-Western Sector of the war. He successfully chased the secessionist soldiers out of the Mid-West Region where his army was charged of committing various atrocities.

His army crossed over into the secessionist enclave during the third attempt, but suffered another disaster at Abagana where a homemade roadside bomb blew up the tanks of his army's supply vehicles. He was blamed repeatedly from Army Headquarters for his intransigence that caused costly material and human losses. He offered to quit or go on a long vacation in England, United Kingdom. He returned to Nigeria after the war and he was given back his post in the Nigerian Army.

General Yakubu Gowon, the Military Head of State was overthrown by General Murtala Mohammed on July 29, 1975 while Gowon was attending an Organization of African Unity (OAU) meeting in Kampala, Uganda. General Murtala Mohammed became the Military Head of State assisted by General Olusegun Obasanjo as Chief of Staff Supreme Headquarters and General Theophilus Danjuma as Chief of Army Staff.

As Military Head of State, General Mohammed scrapped the 1973 census and reverted to 1963 figures for official purposes. He dismissed over 10,000 civil servants and many officers from parastatals for old age, health, idleness, incompetence, backlog of disciplinary cases, fraud, corruption etc. He also demobilized over 10,000 soldiers from the Nigerian Army. Twelve (12) out of twenty-five (25) ministerial appointments of the Federal Executive Council (FEC) were given to civilians. The FEC was secondary to the Supreme Military Council (SMC). Military Governors administered the policies decided by the SMC but they were not members of the Supreme Military Body. News broadcasting became a federal monopoly; staterun universities and newspapers came under federal control.

In order to control inflation, he developed the Third National Development Plan, reduced money supply and encouraged the expansion of the private sector. In terms of foreign policy, he believed in the policy of 'Nigeria First', and maintaining a policy of neutrality instead of nonalignment in international affairs as was in the past.

He supported the Soviet backed Popular Movement for the Liberation of Angola citing South Africa's intervention in support of their rival, National Union for the Total Independence of Angola. As a result, the United States of America was angry because the country was in favour of the withdrawal of Cuban troops from Angola as well as the Soviet Military Advisers.

An abortive coup d'etat was staged by Lt. Colonel Buka Suka Dimka on February 13, 1976 when General Mohammed's car was ambushed and he was assassinated when he was going to his office at the Dodan Barracks, Lagos. Lt. Colonel Dimka implicated many senior military officers who were arrested and executed. He alleged that he discussed the coup plot with General Gowon in the United Kingdom when he visited London. As a result, General Gowon was stripped of his rank while his pension was stopped but President Shagari (1979-1983) pardoned him and restored his full rank and pension.

General Murtala Mohammed was succeeded by his deputy and Chief of Staff, Supreme Headquarters, General Olusegun Obasanjo. In his honour, the government named the Murtala Mohammed International Airport, Ikeja (Lagos) after him as well as many roads in Nigeria. His portrait adorns Nigerian currency note.

General Murtala Ramat Mohammed

Mohammed (left) with Bolaji Akinyemi (right)

Dr. Jubril Olabode Aka (DMS, MBA Aviation, Ph.D.)

4th President of Nigeria
In office
July 29, 1975 – February 13, 1976

Preceded by	Yakubu Gowon
Succeeded by	Olusegun Obasanjo
Born	November 8, 1938(19381108) Nigeria
Died	February 13, 1976 Lagos, Nigeria
Nationality	Nigerian
Political party	*(None)*
Religion	Muslim

(4)
GENERAL OLUSEGUN OBASANJO

General Matthew Olusegun Aremu Okikiolakan Obasanjo was born at Owu, Abeokuta, Ogun (Gateway) State of Western Nigeria on March 5, 1937. He is a Christian, a Yorubaman of Owu, Egba ethnicity. ExPresident Olusegun Obasanjo was Nigerian leader for two periods as Military Head of State of Nigeria from February 13, 1976 to October 1, 1979 and as civilian Nigerian President from May 29, 1999 to May 29, 2007. He was the longest reigning Head of Nigerian Government in the annals of great nation, Nigeria.

He enlisted into the Nigerian Army in 1958 and was trained in Aldershot, UK. He took over the command of the Nigerian Army, which completed the secessionist war from Brigadier Benjamin Adekunle (the Scorpion). He received the surrender note from the Commander of the Secessionist Army, Phillip Effiong after Owerri was overrun by Nigerian Federal Forces in 1970.

When General Yakubu Gowon was overthrown on July 29, 1975, General Obasanjo became Chief of Staff Supreme Headquarters while General Theophilus Danjuma was Chief of Army Staff. When Lt. Colonel Buka Suka Dimka's aborted coup d'etat assassinated the Head of State, General Murtala Mohammed, the coup plotters were not successful to eliminate General Obasanjo and General Danjuma both of whom succeeded in restoring normalcy and announced the failure of the coup. General Obasanjo became the Military Head of State in succession to General Murtala Mohammed who was assassinated.

The coup plotters were able to seize the Lagos Radio Station for a brief period and made an announcement, which was shortlived because Obasanjo and Danjuma were able to gain control and they reestablished security in Lagos. As Military Head of State, General Obasanjo promised to continue the programmes laid down to end military rule and restore civilian administration on October 1, 1979.

A Second Republic Constitution modeled after the governmental system of the United States of America (USA) was adopted in 1979 which established the Presidency (Executive), the Senate, the House of

Representatives and an Independent Judiciary. General and presidential elections were conducted in 1979 and General Obasanjo handed over to civilian President Shehu Aliyu Shagari who was declared winner by the electoral commission. The result was contested in the court and the Supreme Court declared that Alhaji Shagari won the election. Thus, General Obasanjo became the first Military Head of State to willingly relinquish power to a civilian administration.

During his reign as Military Head of State, General Obasanjo encouraged agriculture and production of food toward selfsufficiency. He floated the slogan, "Buy Made In Nigeria Goods" and he banned the importation of luxury items to save foreign exchange. He encouraged local manufacturing and provided tax incentives to foreign and local investors. General Obasanjo retired to his Ota Farm, Ogun State after handing over the presidency to Alhaji Shehu Aliyu Shagari on October 1, 1979.

President Shagari who succeeded General Obasanjo was overthrown by General Mohammadu Buhari, his General Officer Commanding on December 31, 1983. In 1985, General Buhari was overthrown by General Ibrahim Badamosi Babangida who left office for an Interim Administrator, Chief Ernest Shonekan in 1993. In November 1993, the Interim Administrator was overthrown by General Sani Abacha who became Military Head of State.

During the regime of General Sani Abacha (1993-1998), General Obasanjo was alleged to be too vocal in condemning his activities. As a result, he was arrested on trumped up charges of conspiring with others to overthrow the government of General Sani Abacha. He was arrested with many others including his former deputy, General Shehu Musa Yar'Adua who died in prison because agents of the military regime allegedly injected HIV/AIDS virus into his body forcibly. The same fate was planned for General Obasanjo but God saved him.

Miraculously, General Sani Abacha died suddenly, and his captives whom he planned would not come out alive from prison, were released from prison in 1998 by General Abdulsalami Abubakar. General Obasanjo was among those who gained freedom.

Providentially, General Obasanjo was presented to the electorate in 1999 and he won the presidential election on the platform of People's Democratic Party (PDP) and he started another administration as

Nigerian Civilian President effective May 29, 1999 for two terms of four years each. May 29, the day civilian administration began after 16 years of military dictatorship was commemorated as 'Democracy Day' and declared a public holiday.

There was a proposal for a third term for the presidency which required constitutional amendment, but it did not go through because of the controversies, which it generated. Mallam Umaru Musa Yar'Adua as President of Nigeria succeeded him (President Obasanjo) on May 29, 2007.

As Military Head of State from 1976 to 1979 and as civilian President of Nigeria from 1999 to 2007, President Obasanjo recorded outstanding successes some of which are listed below as 125 for history to note.

1. He received the 'Instrument of Surrender' during the Civil War (1967-1970) from General Phillip Effiong, and took part in the reconstruction, rehabilitation, reabsorption and reconciliation era.
2. He was the architect of the indigenisation decree that empowered Nigerians into the corporate world.
3. He was the champion of Operation Feed the Nation as well as Operation 'Buy Nigeria Made Products' to encourage local manufacturing and exportation of goods and services.
4. He assembled 50 wise men in 1979 to provide the Nigerian Constitution for transition to civilian rule.
5. He was the first military ruler to handover to civilian administration in 1979 of Shagari's 2nd Republic.
6. He was the first to transition from civilian to civilian administration on May 29, 2003 for his second term, and he successfully handedover on May 29, 2007 to Yar'Adua's Administration.
7. He achieved the restoration of the dignity and respect for Nigeria in the Comity of Nations, which was jeopardized during preceding military regime between 1993 and 1998 when Nigeria was tagged a pariah state for human rights abuses as well as financial and economic crimes, which resulted in Nigeria being ostracized from International Community.
8. Ensured salary increases for workers.

9. Increased pensioners' wages beyond subsistence level, and thus raised their standard of living and enhanced their life expectancy.
10. The ample evidence of hopelessness and despair characterized of the military regimes of over three decades was replaced with enthusiasm, hope and faith in brighter prospects for democratic Nigeria.
11. Oil and gas prospecting dwarfed the total activities in the previous 30 years and with greater prospects in the ensuing years.
12. Agricultural production was increasing year after year with greater emphasis on nonoil products prospecting.
13. Nigeria was in the forefront in the execution of the programmes of AU, NEPAD, ECOWAS and her presence was felt strongly in the Commonwealth of Nations and the United Nations. Nigeria became the peace and power broker in Africa relating to incidents in Liberia, Sudan, Congo, Rwanda, Sao Tome & Principe, Zimbabwe, Guinea Bissau, Cameroon, Togo and others.
14. Economic and financial crimes and frauds were vigorously fought. Many cases of corruption were prosecuted contrary to none being recorded in four decades prior to Obasanjo Admini stration. He established the EFCC and ICPC to fight corruption and fraud.
15. Maintaining and enhancing peaceful neighbourliness with Republic of Cameroon through diplomacy and dialogue to solve the deepening border dispute arising from the judgement rendered by the International Court of Justice on October 10, 2002. He did not plunge the country into war with Cameroon which could have been disastrous for two neighbouring brotherly African countries.
16. Recovery of a lot of Nigerian money stolen and stashed away in foreign banks in Europe and America by former Military Head of State, General Sani Abacha and his cronies. His tough fight against corruption and his socio-economic and political reforms were remarkable, unique and deterrent.

17. Nigeria achieved the strongest friendly ties with South Africa, Egypt, Ghana, Liberia, Senegal, Benin Republic, other African countries, the Commonwealth countries, China and other Asian countries, the Americas (North and South) and the whole world without exception.
18. His administration approved the establishment of many private colleges and universities which brought education closest to the people. To encourage Nigerians, he enrolled into Nigerian Open University System to demonstrate that position, wealth and age cannot be barriers to continue with education toward attaining university and professional degrees for selfdevelopment. He was exemplary.
19. Inflation and interest rates were reduced reasonably; the Gross Domestic Product (GDP) increased annually beyond 7 percent and foreign reserve rose above $50 billion. The economy was sound.
20. ExPresident Obasanjo assumed the Commonwealth Chairperson In Office as well as the Chairmanship of the African Union.
21. He restored acceptable investment and business climate to Nigeria as well as the confidence of local and foreign investors.
22. He was fully committed to Nigerian unity, oneness and indivisibility.
23. He was a pioneer founder of the Transparency International for the benefit of Nigeria and the world.
24. He accomplished the cancellation of $18 billion out of the foreign debt of Nigeria and paid off the balance of $12 billion progressively, and made Nigeria to be almost foreign debtfree unprecedentedly.
25. Most importantly, President Obasanjo did not hand over to any of the corrupt politicians who had problems with the EFCC and ICPC. He was succeeded by Mallam Umaru Yar'Adua who believed in the rule of law, due process, transparency and servant/service leadership.
26. On Wednesday, January 7, 2009, he graduated and had Postgraduate Degree In Theology from National Open University of Nigeria, Study Centre, Abeokuta. Hence, he demonstrated exemplarily that age, position, wealth and power

should not limit anybody's ability for advanced continuing education.

27. As Nigerian Father/Architect/Innovator of 'Modern Mechanised Farming and Nation-wide Telecommunications', he will be remembered eternally for the tremendous and unparalleled benefits derivable daily from his unique initiatives of modern farming and telecommunications in Nigeria.

General Oluṣẹgun Ọbasanjọ

12th President of Nigeria
In office
May 29, 1999 – May 29, 2007

Vice President	Atiku Abubakar
Preceded by	Abdulsalami Abubakar
Succeeded by	Umaru Yar'Adua

5th President of Nigeria
In office
February 13, 1976 – October 1, 1979

Vice President	Shehu Musa Yar'Adua
Preceded by	Murtala Mohammed
Succeeded by	Shehu Shagari

3rd Vice President of Nigeria
In office
July 29, 1975 – February 13, 1976

President	Murtala Mohammed
Preceded by	J.E.A. Wey
Succeeded by	Shehu Musa Yar'Adua
Born	March 5, 1937 (19370305) Abeokuta, Ogun State, Nigeria
Political party	People's Democratic Party
Spouse	Lynda Obasanjo (exwife, deceased), Stella Obasanjo (deceased)
Religion	Christianity

(5)
PRESIDENT SHEHU USMAN ALIYU SHAGARI

He was in office as Second Republic President from October 1, 1979 to December 31, 1983. He was born in Shagari Village, Sokoto on February 25, 1925 to the family of Magaji Aliyu and Mariamu.

He was Secretary of Sokoto branch of the Northern People's Congress (NPC) between 1951 and 1956 and he represented Sokoto West constituency between 1954 and 1958 in the Federal House of Representatives. ExPresident Alhaji Shehu Usman Aliyu Shagari is a Northerner of Fulani extraction. He holds the title of Turakin Sukkwato in the Sokoto Caliphate. He was a school teacher before he joined party politics.

Alhaji Shagari attended Kaduna College and became a science teacher at Zaria Middle School and later taught Science, History and Geography at Sokoto Middle School. Thereafter, he was made the Headmaster of Argungu Primary School. Around 1946, Alhaji Shagari with others started the Youth Social Circle supported by dignitaries like Ahmadu Bello, Ibrahim Gusau, Mallam Ahmadu Dabbaba etc.

In 1948, there was a merger of nascent political groups which consolidated into Northern People's Congress (NPC). In 1958, Alhaji Shagari became the Parliamentary Secretary of Prime Minister Alhaji Abubakar Tafawa Balewa. He became the Minister of Economic Development in 1960, Minister of Internal Affairs in 1962 and Minister of Works and Survey in 1965.

The Ifeajuna/Nzeogwu coup d'etat of January 15, 1966 stopped his ministerial career and he went back to Sokoto to continue his farm work and later became a Councilor for the Sokoto Native Authority. After the end of the civil war in 1970, the Military Head of State, General Yakubu Gowon appointed him as Economic Affairs Minister and later made him the Minister of Finance.

After Generals Gowon and Mohammed were overthrown as Military Heads of State on July 29, 1975 and February 13, 1976 respectively, Head of State General Olusegun Obasanjo instituted a Constitutional

Conference in preparation for transition to civil rule in 1979. The members of the body were selected, nominated and others elected to the conference.

The conference later metamorphosed into political alignments, which became some of the political parties that contested the 1979 national elections. The National Party of Nigeria (NPN) concept was born at the conference and it fielded Alhaji Shehu Shagari as its presidential candidate. He won the election, succeeded General Olusegun Obasanjo and thus became the Second Republic President of Nigeria.

President Shehu Shagari was said to be humble, God/Allah fearing and transparent. He followed the motto of his ruling political party (NPN) to its letters – 'One Nation, One Destiny', and he made education, housing, agriculture, industries and transportation as his administration's main goals. He constructed Shagari Estates, the Delta Steel Complex, Ajaokuta Steel Complex and Steel Rolling Mills. He launched road network programmes throughout the country and executed the green revolution programme, which fostered mechanized farming resulting in largescale agricultural production.

Alhaji Shehu Shagari established an Economic Stabilization Programme to stem inflationary tendencies and stimulate economic growth. He limited import licences to essential scarce items, reduced government spending and raised customs duties. All his efforts to stabilize the economic situation were not as successful as expected because of the decline in world oil price, which was the main stay of Nigerian economy.

His administration problem was compounded by the alleged corrupt practices of his ministers and government officials. There were accusations of electoral fraud during the 1983 elections, which caused political violence. There was religious intolerance, which caused riots.

His General Officer Commanding (GOC), General Mohammadu Buhari overthrew Alhaji Shagari on December 31, 1983. Overthrowing democratically elected government by military officers who turned dictators did not provide solutions to Nigerian problems because empirically, they did worse than the civilian leaders whom they overthrew.

It was revealed that General Aguiyi Ironsi, Military Head of State (January 15, 1966 – July 29, 1966) and President Shehu Shagari (October

1, 1979 – December 31, 1983) received hints about the plans to topple them, but they were overtrusting and did not take preemptive actions that could have stopped their overthrow. It was also possible that General Yakubu Gowon, Military Head of State (July 29, 1966 July 29, 1975) had an idea that he might be overthrown and perhaps did not act quickly to preempt it. Hopefully, future leaders will not overtrust any of their immediate subordinates who are overambitious.

Enugu State exgovernor, Dr. Chimaroke Nnamani told Alhaji Shehu Shagari, Turakin Sokoto, "You are an exemplary figure and represent a clear subjugation to the 'Will of God'. You represent nonaggressive pursuit of political power. You represent man surrendering to the destiny and the 'Will of God'. You represent the good in our society which we want back".

Alhaji Shehu Shagari

6th President of Nigeria
In office
October 1, 1979 – December 31, 1983

Vice President	Alex Ekwueme
Preceded by	Olusegun Obasanjo
Succeeded by	Muhammadu Buhari
Born	February 25, 1925 (19250225)) Shagari, Sokoto State, Nigeria
Political party	National Party of Nigeria
Religion	Muslim (Sunni)

(6)
GENERAL MOHAMMADU BUHARI

General Buhari was born on December 17, 1942 in Katsina State. He was Nigeria's Military Head of State from December 31, 1983 to August 27, 1985. He contested for the April 19, 2003 and April 21, 2007 presidential elections respectively on the platform of the All Nigerian People's Party (ANPP), but he was not successful. He contested the presidential election results in court but lost. He is of Fulani ethnicity and of Islamic faith.

He became the Military Head of State of Nigeria on December 31, 1983 after the military coup that overthrew Alhaji Shehu Shagari. His Deputy Head of State was General Tunde Idiagbon who was regarded as the strongman of Buhari Administration. General Buhari instituted 'War Against Indiscipline' which he claimed as his justification to overthrow Shagari's democratically elected government of the Second Republic. He alleged that Shagari's regime was corrupt and the Nigerian Society was undisciplined. His military regime promulgated decree no. 2 and decree no. 4 which restricted the democratic lives of Nigerians' abilities to receive and disseminate information.

Decree no. 2 (State Security, Detention of Persons), gave his military administration, the powers to detain indefinitely without trial, any person(s) suspected to be a threat or security risk to the nation. In addition, he enacted decree no. 4 (Public Officers, Protection Against False Accusation), which gave the government the power to criminalize any unfounded allegations against government officers emanating from the press, no matter how trivial. Many people were clamped into detention and most Nigerians became alienated.

Above all, Buhari's Administration committed suicide when it focused on probing all contracts awarded by past governments including the Ministry of Defence where many military officers committed fraudulent and corrupt acts in the awards of contracts. As a result, most senior military officers involved believed that Buhari and Idiagbon Administration was after them and must therefore be toppled. It was easy to conclude and say that leaders like Buhari and Idiagbon were/

are the best for Nigeria, but in actuality, such great, transparent and disciplined leaders never last long.

Many politicians were clamped into jail indefinitely for corrupt purposes and serious attempts were made to bring back former Minister of Transport during Shagari Administration, Mallam Umaru Dikko who took refuge in London. (Dr.) Umaru Dikko was drugged, crated and was to be loaded into a Nigerian bound standing plane in Stansted Airport, England when the British police busted the operation on a tip off.

It was alleged that during Shagari's Administration, the Minister of Transport, (Dr.) Umaru Dikko had repeatedly snooped on the movements of Buhari, the General Officer Commanding (GOC) and the military and he warned Shagari of the possibility of a coup d' etat to topple him by his GOC, Buhari. In effect, all what happened to (Dr.) Alhaji Umaru Dikko after Shagari was toppled seemed like a payback or retaliation.

General Buhari refused to accept one of the highest Nigerian honours from Obasanjo Administration. His leadership and court case challenging the result of the 2007 presidential election caused the split of his party, All Nigerian People's Party (ANPP). Some top members of his party embraced unity government and so, took part in the unity government of President Umaru Yar'Adua, but Buhari refused to participate and he continued to press the court for the nullification of the presidential election result that brought Yar'Adua into power.

Elites' responses to Nigerian democratic experiment are so complex and whoever wants to lead the country successfully must be ready to accept and appreciate the merits and demerits of democratic principles and practices. Buhari could have succeeded as a Military Head of State in a dictatorial environment, but in a democracy, he will need a lot of patience and accommodation capability for human imperfections and errors.

Since he treasonably truncated the Second Republic of Shagari Administration, a democratically elected government, instead of contributing to sustain it, he should accept his two defeats to become civilian President of Nigeria as an 'Act of Providence'. He looks too controversial to be a successful civilian President of Nigeria without any vindictiveness and chaos.

Dr. Jubril Olabode Aka (DMS, MBA Aviation, Ph.D.)

MAJOR-GENERAL MUHAMMADU BUHARI

7th President of Nigeria
In office
December 31, 1983 – August 27, 1985

Preceded by	Shehu Shagari
Succeeded by	Ibrahim Babangida
Born	December 17, 1942 (19421217) Katsina state, Nigeria
Nationality	Nigerian
Political party	Military/All Nigeria People's Party
Religion	Muslim

(7)
GENERAL IBRAHIM BADAMOSI BABANGIDA

General Ibrahim Badamosi Babangida, popularly known as IBB was Nigerian Military Head of State (August 27, 1985 to August 27, 1993). He was born on August 17, 1941 in Minna, Niger State of Nigeria.

'IBB' is of Gwari ethnicity. He studied at India Military School in 1964, the Royal Armoured Centre from January to April 1966, Advanced Armoured Officers' Course from August 1972 to June 1973, Senior Officers' Course, Command and Staff College, Jaji from January 1977 until July 1977 and the Senior International Defence Management Course, Naval Postgraduate School, USA in 1980.

General Babangida joined the Nigerian Army Officer Corps on December 10, 1962 and served under military government of General Obasanjo in administrative capacity. During the Lt. Colonel Buka Suka Dimka aborted coup d'etat, General Babangida was said to have prevented him from making further announcements about the coup by overtaking the radio station in Lagos.

He was Second Lieutenant 1962; Lieutenant 1966; Captain 1968; Major 1970; Lieutenant Colonel July 9, 1970; Colonel 1973; Supreme Military Council Member from August 1, 1975 to October 1, 1979; Brigadier 1979; Major General 1983 and General 1985.

He took a political position under General Buhari's Government but overthrew him on August 27, 1985. He promised that he would bring an end to human rights abuses and hand over power to civilians on October 1, 1990.

In 1986, he launched the Structural Adjustment Programme (SAP), an austerity programme in order to garner the support of the International Monetary Fund (IMF) and the World Bank by applying their economic conditionalities. In applying IMF and World Bank dictated policies, nobody asked whose interests were being servedNigerian or the foreign agencies who had their own operational and financial interests to protect as well as their biases for profitability, survival and continuity as a business.

General Babangida evolved economic policies of 'SAP' as required by the IMF and the World Bank. He effected the deregulation of the agricultural sector by abolishing marketing boards, elimination of price controls, privatization of public enterprises, devaluation of the naira to aid export earnings and relaxation of restrictions on foreign investments.

Initially, the policies worked but was shortlived because of their unpleasant and captivating effects on the generality of the masses by making the poor poorer, the middle class insecure and disappearing, while the corrupt upper class were benefitting and amassing more wealth. Wages were falling, inflation was rising and there was reduction in public spending. Hence, there was hunger, general discontent and violence. In response, the government made some adjustments of the troubleshooting economic policies but it was getting too late to fully reverse the damages done.

Babangida's government was almost toppled by Major Gideon Orka on April 22, 1990. Orka and his coconspirators seized the Lagos Radio Station transmitters and vehemently rained critiques on the government which they accused of widespread corruption and autocracy. They expelled five of the northern states of Nigeria that were predominantly HausaFulani from the Nigerian Union accusing them of domination and marginalization of the Christians of the Middle-Belt with particular reference to the neutralization of the Langtang Mafia.

Legalization of political parties was approved in 1989 and a national census was conducted in November 1991. Thereafter, the Independent National Electoral Commission (INEC) announced on January 24, 1992 that there would be legislative elections to a bicamera National Assembly and a presidential election later in 1992. As a result, the Social Democratic Party (SDP) and the National Republican Convention (NRC) were formed to contest the elections. The legislative election was held and the SDP won majority of seats in both houses of National Assembly (the Senate and House of Representatives).

On August 7, 1992, the Independent National Electoral Commission (INEC) annulled the first round of presidential elections because of widespread rigging, described as electoral frauds. On January 4, 1993, General Babangida declared interest to contest as a civilian presidential candidate. In April 1993, the SDP nominated Chief Moshood Kashimawo Olawale Abiola as its presidential candidate while Bashir Othma Tofa was put forward to contest on the platform of the National

Republican Convention as its presidential candidate in the election fixed for June 12, 1993.

On June 10, 1993, the Abuja High court issued an injunction order that the presidential election scheduled for June 12, 1993 be postponed. In the process, the Director of Information, Mr. Michael O'Brien of the American Embassy wrote a letter to Nigerian Military Government saying that any postponement of the election would be unacceptable to the USA government.

Such letter was a contempt of the court order, also prejudicial to it and implying that the US Embassy officials could tell Nigerian authorities what they should do and should not do about their internal affairs, as if the country was a protectorate of the USA. Can Nigerian Embassy acceptably write such a letter to the USA government about what bothers on USA internal affairs and say that it is not acceptable to Nigeria?

Is that the best way to maintain good international relations? If there is a court order of injunction in the USA, can any other country's embassy in the world tell the USA to ignore it and care less about the rule of law and due process? The letter really compounded Nigerian political problems arising from the June 12, 1993 presidential election which was nullified on June 23, 1993.

As a result, most members of Nigeria's National Defence and Security Council got offended by the contents of the letter from the USA Embassy and decided that the election be postponed for a week. They decided that the letter from the US Embassy be disregarded saying that it was an interferance in the country's internal affairs. They maintained that Nigeria was not a Banana Republic and that the sovereignty of the country be safeguarded. The part played by the INEC Chairman, Professor Humphrey Nwosu to convince the Military Head of State, General Ibrahim Babangida that the election be held in defiance of court injunction was questionable.

Inspite of the strong dissatisfaction and dissension of the majority of members of the NDSC, the INEC Chairman disregarded the court injunction and went ahead and conducted the presidential election of June 12, 1993. Hence, on June 23, 1993, the election won by Chief Abiola was annulled and INEC was dissolved by the NDSC.

As a result, violence erupted and military coup d'etat seemed imminent. Initially, the decree which annulled the election banned the two presidential candidates, Abiola and Tofa from contesting in a new election that was being arranged. The decree provisions caused civil disobedience which was quickly quashed.

On July 6, 1993, the NDSC issued an ultimatum to the two political parties, SDP and NRC to join in an Interim Administration or would face another election. The government then announced that an Interim Administration would be inaugurated on August 27, 1993. New strikes and lock outs occurred on August 26, 1993 which grounded all economic activities. Hence, General Babangida declared that he would step down and he handed over to the Interim Administrator, Chief Shonekan, but within three months of the handover, he (Abacha) overthrew the Interim Administrator in a palace coup and took over as Military Head of State when General Babangida was in the midst of his visit to Egypt.

During the regime of General Babangida, the membership of Nigeria in the Organization of Islamic Conference (OIC) was raised from observer status to fullfledged one. Christians objected to the raised status of Nigerian membership in the organization. As a result, the John Sagaya Commission was convoked to investigate the status of Nigeria in the OIC. The panel concluded that Nigeria was a full member of the organization and it recommended that Nigeria should withdraw its membership.

It happened that Babangida Administration had turbulence with Nigerian press/media when Mr. Dele Giwa, magazine editor, critic of the administration was assassinated with a letter bomb in 1986. The military leader and two of his security agents were accused of having something to do with the editor's death, but they denied the allegation vehemently.

In 1999, President Obasanjo instituted the Human Rights Violation Investigation Commissison (HRVIC) chairmanned by Justice Chukwudifu Oputa with the responsibility to investigate human rights abuses during the military dictatorship era lasing three decades. Oputa Commission invited General Babangida and his two former Security Chiefs to testify, but he challenged and defied the summons as well as questioned the legality/constitutionality of the commission and its powers to summon him to testify.

In 2001, General Babangida's right not to testify was upheld by the court of appeal which held that the panel did not have the power to summon former rulers of the country. In its final submission, the Oputa Commission commented, "On General Ibrahim Babangida, we are of the view that there is evidence to suggest that he and his two Security Chiefs, Brigadier General Halilu Akilu and Colonel A.K. Togun are accountable for the death of Dele Giwa by letter bomb. We recommend that this case be reopened for further investigation in the public interest."

On August 15, 2006, General Babangida announced his interest to compete for the 2007 presidential election during an interview with the Financial Times. He blamed Nigerian elites for fueling religious and ethnic violence and heating the polity unnecessarily. He picked the nomination form of the People's Democratic Party (PDP) on November 8, 2006. In early December 2006, there was a news flash that he had withdrawn his candidacy because of the "moral dilemma" of running against Katsina Governor Umaru Yar'Adua, the younger brother of the late General Shehu Musa Yar'Adua as well as General Aliyu Mohammed Gusau, considering the closeness of his relationship with the two presidential aspirants.

General Babangida is very charismatic, intelligent, loving, caring, empathic and flexible. He is courteous and hardly wants to say "No" if someone would be hurt or offended by such answer. He loves to please all as much as possible, a philosophy that often backfires. His influence in Nigerian political environment may never die. He is a great nationalist

He provided his loving wife, Hajiya Maryam Babangida with the best medical attention from the best doctors in the USA to save her life from ovarian cancer, but because God/Allah loves her more for eternal peaceful life in Heaven, she passed peacefully to her final resting place with the Lord, God/Allah, the Almighty on Sunday, December 27, 2009 at the age of 61 (November 1, 1948 to December 27, 2009).

In September 1986, Hajiya Maryam Babangida founded and championed the execution of a programme of 'Better Life for Rural Women'. She was exceptionally empathic, humble and exemplary in the way she handled women affairs when she was Nigerian First Lady from 1985 to 1993.

She was a great woman, a great and devoted wife as well as a great mother of remarkably great four children. She left the world in a better shape than she met it. She will be remembered eternally.

May Her Soul Rest In Perfect Peace (amen). Adieu!

General Ibrahim Badamosi Babangida

8th President of Nigeria
In office
August 27, 1985 August 27, 1993

Preceded by	Muhammadu Buhari
Succeeded by	Ernest Shonekan
Born	August 17, 1941 Minna, Niger State, Nigeria
Political party	none (military)
Religion	Islam

(8)
CHIEF ERNEST ADEGUNLE OLADEINDE SHONEKAN
(Interim Administrator)

Chief Shonekan was born on May 9, 1936 in Lagos, the former Federal Capital of Nigeria and main commercial centre of the nation. He was born to an Abeokuta father from Ogun (Gateway) State of Nigeria. He was raised in Lagos, Nigeria.

He attended CMS Grammar School, Lagos and the University of London where he obtained his Law Degree. He joined the UAC in 1964 and received management training from Harvard Business School. He pursued the legal profession at the UAC and became Assistant Legal Adviser, then Deputy Legal Adviser after two years and later promoted to the UAC Board of Directors in 1980. He became the Chairman and Chief Executive Officer of the corporation.

Chief Shonekan, a British trained Nigerian Lawyer became an industrialist and popular politician. His seasoned and business acumen coupled with his revered economic skill and wide contacts endeared him to the nation and the Military Head of State, General Babangida at that time of economic turmoil and political uncertainties.

On January 2, 1993, General Babangida appointed him as Head of Government Affairs. During that time, the Transitional Council was given responsibility to prepare programmes for the transfer of power to civilian administration. The precarious condition of the government finances showing a twenty-eight billion naira deficit in the 1993 budget with little foreign reserve became a big problem and a great challenge to Chief Shonekan as Head of the Transitional Council.

A twoyear economic programme was designed realistically that reduced subsidy on oil production, which created a saving of 65 billion naira. The value added tax was raised and the government embarked on fiscal discipline which eventually created increased suffering for the people in general. The annulment of the June 12, 1993 presidential election won by Chief M.K.O. Abiola added to the national instability, and soon after, the whole country became engulfed in political turmoil.

The call for the resignation of the military government became prominent and loudest. Hence, on August 26, 1993, General Babangida finally decided to step aside and he installed an Interim Administrator to succeed him. General Babangida appointed Chief Shonekan as Interim Administrator/President on August 26, 1993 when he allegedly resigned under pressure for the Interim Administrator to channel the country toward democratic governance.

As a result, Chief Shonekan headed the Third Republic which lasted less than three (3) months (August 27, 1993 to November 17, 1993) because General Sani Abacha staged a palace coup d'etat; obtained Chief Shonekan's resignation forcibly and dismantled the entire democratic arrangement put in place by the Interim Administrator. As a result, Nigeria receded to military rule under General Sani Abacha as Military Head of State.

As Interim Administrator, Chief Shonekan lobbied fervently for foreign debt cancellation which the creditors were seriously considering, but when General Sani Abacha staged the military coup, the idea was dropped and most Western Powers and creditors imposed sanctions against Nigeria.

The Interim Administration was vehemently opposed by the supporters of the winner of the June 12, 1993 presidential election as well as all others who preferred democratic governance to military dictatorship. The civil rights advocates and socio-economic and political activists saw the installation of an Interim Administration as a debacle in the movement toward democracy, the people's welfare and social justice.

Chief Shonekan created a timetable for democratic return, the release of political detainees and the withdrawal of Nigerian troops who were on peacekeeping mission in Liberia as part of ECOMOG troops. He initiated an audit of the Nigerian National Petroleum Corporation (NNPC) and he prepared a bill to ban draconian military decrees.

The great problem of the Interim Administrator was his inability to effectively control the military establishment, which remained his 'Achilles heel'. As a result, his Defence Secretary, General Sani Abacha who was a member of his cabinet since August 26, 1993 toppled him on November 17, 1993 and caused the wrath of the world in general.

Chief Ernest Shonekan

9th President of Nigeria
In office
August 26, 1993 – November 17, 1993

Preceded by	Ibrahim Babangida
Succeeded by	Sani Abacha
Born	May 9, 1936 (19360509)
Religion	Christian

(9)
GENERAL SANI ABACHA
(September 20, 1943 – June 8, 1998)

General Abacha was born in Kano on September 20, 1943 and he died in Abuja on June 8, 1998. He had Muslim faith of Kanuri extraction. He was married to Madam Maryam Abacha and blessed with six sons and three daughters.

He received training at Nigerian and British military colleges and received many promotions in the military and became Brigadier in 1983. He played active roles in the bloodless military coup d'etat, which installed General Buhari on December 31, 1983 as well as the one that removed him on August 27, 1985. He became the Chief of Army Staff in 1985 during General Babangida's Administration. In 1990, General Ibrahim Badamosi Babangida appointed him the Minister of Defence.

General Abacha overthrew the Interim Administrator, Chief Ernest Shonekan on November 17, 1993 in a palace coup d'etat by forcibly getting the Interim Administrator to sign a letter of resignation after less than three (3) months in office. By toppling the Interim Administrator, he receded Nigeria into military dictatorship and cancelled all the transitional efforts directed toward preparing the country for civilian administration.

The disruption of the path to civil governance, which the country preferred to military dictatorship, made him to earn many enemies. He was accused of civil rights abuses when he hanged Ogoni activists, Ken SaroWiwa who was opposed to the exploitation of the Niger Delta oil reserves by multinational oil companies. The Auta tribunal found Ken SaroWiwa and some of his adherents guilty of treason, and so, Abacha executed them by hanging them to death. His regime was sanctioned, made a pariah state and ostracized by international community.

General Abacha imprisoned many dignitaries for treason including Chief M.K.O. Abiola, General Olusegun Obasanjo, General Shehu Musa Yar'Adua, General Oladipo Diya etc. and allegedly planned that they would not come out of prison alive. Professor Wole Soyinka, the Nobel Laureate was charged in absentia for treasonable felony.

Abacha's regime suffered serious setback in popularity as a result of opposition from 'Democracy Advocates', who wanted immediate end of military rulership. He banned political activities in general, applied control over the press/media, fired significant number of members of the military and surrounded himself with military loyalists of about 3,000 soldiers.

He did not object to the operations of ECOWAS and he supported the preparation of Nigerian military in the ECOMOG peacekeeping efforts in Liberia and Sierra-Leone for the restoration of their democratic governance. Some of those who worked with Abacha, like Professor Aluko and Alhaji Lateef Jakande revealed that he had a great personality and that he listened and meant well. Later in his leadership, Abacha must have relied on advice from terrible aides who changed his course toward the destruction of the opposition groups without second thought by applying methods antithetical to democracy and humanity.

He was said to have died of a heart attack on June 8, 1998 while other sources alleged that he died of poison concealed in a viagra product imported with two ladies from Switzerland. General Abdulsalami Abubakar succeeded him.

About $5 billion in foreign assets were allegedly traced to General Abacha as being part of the loot from government treasury. Obasanjo Administration made a deal with Abacha family to return all loots but keep $100 million, which many Nigerians saw as trying to reward a thief. When his son, Mohammed Abacha left prison, he reneged on the deal and maintained that all his father's assets were genuinely acquired.

Unfortunately, the name of Abacha has been used several times by '419 Advance Fee' fraudsters/scammers who dupe their victims by collecting advance fees in order to receive a percentage commission out of Abacha family's money, said to be left in Europe unclaimed. Many unsuspecting victims were duped throughout the world.

When General Abacha hanged activist Ken SaroWiwa on November 10, 1995, the Commonwealth of Nations suspended Nigerian membership as well as applied targeted sanctions on the nation. Nigeria was later declared a pariah state when General Abacha was alleged to have established military assassination squad, which succeeded in killing opponents, suspected of being against the policies of his regime.

General Shehu Musa Yar'Adua who was imprisoned by Abacha was said to have died in prison when a medical agent of Abacha Government forcibly injected HIV/AIDS virus into his blood system. General Obasanjo was said to be lucky to reject such injection successfully when he was in Abacha's jail.

Abacha's killer squad eliminated many political opponents of Abacha by assassination that included Alhaja Kudirat Abiola. Some others were lucky to escape assassination but got wounded like Chief Ibru and Elder Statesman, Senator Abraham Adesanya. Many officers of Abacha Military Regime were tried for murder and attempted murder lasting about a decade while they remained in prison custody without bail.

General Abacha intended to convert into a Civilian President and he offered to contest in an election to achieve that objective. There were overwhelming oppositions to that idea and he must have been very angry because of that. Hence, he orchestrated measures to eliminate all those who opposed his ideas in every possible way including death by his assassination squad.

Great People, Great Country, Nigeria The Beautiful

General Sani Abacha

10th President of Nigeria
In office
November 17, 1993 – June 8, 1998

Preceded by	Ernest Shonekan
Succeeded by	Abdulsalami Abubakar
Born	September 20, 1943(19430920) Kano, Nigeria
Died	June 8, 1998 (aged 54) Abuja, Nigeria
Nationality	Nigerian
Political party	none (military)
Religion	Muslim

Dr. Jubril Olabode Aka (DMS, MBA Aviation, Ph.D.)

(10)
GENERAL ABDULSALAMI ABUBAKAR

General Abdulsalami Abubakar was born in Minna, Niger State on June 13, 1942. He is of Islamic religious faith. He had his early education at Native Authority Primary School, Minna and Provincial Secondary School, Bida. He attended Kaduna Technical Institute and later joined the Nigerian Army. He led Nigerian peacekeeping mission to Lebanon and eventually rose to the exalted position of Chief of Defence Staff. He is married to Alhaja Fati Abubakar and blessed with six children.

After the death of General Sani Abacha on June 8, 1998, General Abubakar was sworn in as Military Head of State on June 9, 1998 and he declared a weeklong of national mourning. He promised to transfer power to civilians in the following year, 1999 after holding elections. The Nigerian new Constitution was adopted on May 5, 1999 and General Abubakar organized general and presidential elections and handed over to President Olusegun Obasanjo on May 29, 1999 which marked the beginning of Fourth Republic of civilian administration, sixteen (16) years after civilian President Shagari of the Second Republic (1979-1983) was overthrown by General Mohammadu Buhari.

General Abubakar was fully appreciated by all and sundries for keeping his promise to transition to civilian rule willingly just like General Obasanjo did on October 1, 1979 when he willingly handed over to President Shagari of the Second Republic. The elections he conducted were also regarded as some of the best and freest in the annals of Nigeria.

As a result, General Abubakar received many awards, which included the Rainbow/Push Coalition Peace Prize, the Economic Community of West African States, International Gold Medal, and the Star Award from Ghana. The former Secretary General of the United Nations, Kofi Annan appointed him to lead the United Nations mission to the Congo Kinshasa (MONUC).

General Abubakar gave a lecture at Chicago State University, Chicago, Illinois, USA where he unexpectedly met opposing encounters for the support he allegedly gave General Abacha when he worked for him as Chief of Defence Staff. He was presumed guilty by association without listening to his defence. He was unfairly prejudged as being part of the human rights abuses for which Abacha was accused.

Some Nigerians who held that he associated with those who killed Chief M.K.O. Abiola, the winner of the 1993 presidential election, sued him in the USA. Chief Abiola died in prison custody on July 7, 1998 on the day that he was to be released, purportedly beaten to death and/or poisoned. The whole episode should be a big lesson to Nigerian leadership and all those aspiring to lead the nation.

General Abdulsalami A. Abubakar

11th President of Nigeria
In office
June 9, 1998 – May 29, 1999

Preceded by	Sani Abacha
Succeeded by	Olusegun Obasanjo
Born	June 13, 1942 (19420613) Minna, Niger State

Dr. Jubril Olabode Aka (DMS, MBA Aviation, Ph.D.)

Political party	none (military)
Spouse	Fati
Children	six
Alma mater	Technical Institute, Kaduna
Occupation	Soldier
Religion	Islam

(11)
PRESIDENT UMARU MUSA YAR'ADUA

Mallam Umaru Musa Yar'Adua was born in Katsina, Katsina State, Nigeria on August 16, 1951 into Fulani aristocratic family by his father who was a former Minister in Lagos during the First Republic. His father held the royal title of Mutawalli (treasury custodian) of Katsina Emirate, a title inherited by President Yar'Adua.

He started his early education at Rafukka Primary School in 1958, Dutsinma Boarding Primary School in 1962, Government College, Keffi (1965-1969), Higher School Certificate from Barewa College (1971), Ahmadu Bello University, Zaria (1972-1975) for B.Sc in Education and Chemistry, and M.Sc. Degree in Analytical Chemistry in 1978 at Ahmadu Bello University, Zaria.

He was employed at Holy Child College, Lagos (1975 and 1976) and lectured at Katsina College of Arts, Science and Technology, Zaria from 1976 to 1979. He was director of many companies from 1983 to 1999. He became the Katsina State Governor on May 29, 1999 to May 28, 2007 and was sworn in as Nigerian Fourth Republic President on May 29, 2007 for the first term of four years on the platform of People's Democratic Party (PDP).

Between 1979 and 1983 of the Second Republic, Mallam Umaru Yar'Adua was a member of the People's Redemption Party and his father was briefly National Vice Chairman of the National Party of Nigeria. His brother, General Shehu Musa Yar'Adua was one of the founding fathers of the People's Democratic Movement (PDM) which metamorphosed into People's Democratic Party (PDP). The two brothers, Shehu and Umaru initially belonged to the PDM which became PDP.

Mallam Umaru Yar'Adua was member of the Constituent Assembly in 1988. He contested the gubernatorial election in 1991 but lost to Saidu Barda of the National Republican Convention (NRC). In 1999, he recontested the governorship election and won during the first and second terms. He was said to be the first governor to declare his assets publicly.

Under Governor Yar'Adua, Katsina was the fifth state to adopt Sharia (the Islamic Law). Amina Lawal was sentenced to death by stoning in Bakori court in Katsina for adultery in 2002. A court in Funtua upheld her death sentence but it was overturned in an appeal a year later.

He was chosen as presidential candidate on December 16-17, 2006 on PDP platform at the convention scoring 3,024 votes from party delegates while his opponent, Rochas Okorocha, his closest rival scored 372 votes. His candidacy was fully supported by the incumbent President Olusegun Obasanjo. He chose Goodluck Jonathan, Governor of Bayelsa State of the South-South regional zone as his running mate.

Mallam Umaru Musa Yar'Adua was perceived as one of the outstanding governors (1999-2007) without any stain in his records. His record was spotless, devoid of any suspicion of corruption. He was the first to declare his assets and published his governorship-audited balance sheet as required by law. President Umaru Musa Yar'Adua acknowledged that he had kidney problems for which he visited his physician in Germany once in a while for medical attention. He assured the nation that his health condition was under control contrary to the rumours constantly peddled by his opponents.

The presidential election held on April 21, 2007 fetched President Yar'Adua a landslide victory of 70% as revealed on April 23, 2007. The result was controversial and criticized by observers as being full of irregularities. The results were contested in the court by two presidential candidates who were former Vice President Atiku Abubakar, representing the Action Congress (AC) and presidential candidate of All Nigerian People's Party (ANPP), General Mohammadu Buhari, former Military Head of State (December 31, 1983 to August 27, 1985).

On assumption of office on May 29, 2007, President Yar'Adua called for a government of national unity, which was initially turned down by the AC and ANPP. In late June 2007, the ANPP without General Buhari and the Progressive People's Alliance (PPA) agreed to be part of the unity government.

In accordance with 1999 Nigerian Constitution, President Yar'Adua publicly declared his assets on June 28. 2007 as 856,452,892 naira in assets and 88,793,269.77 naira in liabilities while about 19 million naira belonged to his spouse, Turai Umaru Yar'Adua.

He reversed some unpopular decisions hurriedly taken by his predecessor within few weeks to his ascension of office like the hike in prices of petroleum products, the increase of Value Added Tax (VAT), sale of government houses and land acquisitions at Abuja, Federal Capital Territory. On July 26, 2007, he swore in his cabinet, which comprised of 39 ministers including 2 nominations from the ANPP.

Petitions were filed by exVice President Atiku Abubakar representing (AC) and General Mohammadu Buhari of (ANPP) to nullify the presidential election held on April 21, 2007 which they claimed was massively rigged. On February 26, 2008, the court rejected the petitions and Atiku and Buhari lodged an appeal appropriately respectively. In November 2008, the Supreme Court ruled in favour of President Yar'Adua.

President Yar'Adua married Turai Umaru Yar'Adua in 1975 and they are blessed with seven children including their daughter, Zainab who married Kebbi State Governor Usman Saidu Nasamu Dakingari. President Yar'Ardua was also married to Hauwa Umar Radda from 1992 to 1997 and they had two children.

President Yar'Adua's Administration strongly believes in enforcing the rule of law and following due process in its operations. The process seems thorough and welcomed by majority of Nigerians provided it does not slow down the fight against corruption as well as the operations of the EFCC and ICPC to recover the loot by politicians and government functionaries who stole from the national treasury. President Yar'Adua strongly believes in service to the nation and he has spread the philosophy of 'servant leader' exemplarily to the people of Nigeria.

Dr. Jubril Olabode Aka (DMS, MBA Aviation, Ph.D.)

President Umaru Musa Yar'Adua

	President of Nigeria
	Incumbent
	Assumed office
	29 May 2007
Vice President	Goodluck Jonathan
Preceded by	Olusegun Obasanjo
	Governor of Katsina
	In office
	29 May 1999 – 29 May 2007
Preceded by	Joseph Akaagerger
Succeeded by	Ibrahim Sherma
Born	16 August 1951
	Katsina, Katsina State, Nigeria

Political party	PDP
Spouse	Turai Umaru Yar'adua
Religion	Muslim

(12)
MALLAM AMINU KANO
(1920 – April 17, 1983)

Mallam Aminu Kano lived a great life, full of compassion for the masses. He was a Muslim politician who organized Islamic Movement in Northern Nigeria against British colonial rule in the 1940s. In his honour and memory, Mallam Aminu Kano International Airport, Kano and Aminu Kano Teaching Hospital, Kano as well as many roads were named after him.

He was born to an Islamic Scholar, Mallam Yusuf, a Mufti at the Alkali Court, Kano. He was educated at Katsina College and the University of London, Institute of Education contemporaneously with Sir Abubakar Tafawa Balewa, First Prime Minister of Nigeria. He was a teacher at Bauchi Training College. At that time, he developed and widened the horizon of his political ambition wide and far beyond his interest in the teaching profession.

He became a member of the Bauchi General Improvement Union and wrote a book titled, "Kano, Under the Hammer of the Native Administration". He became the Secretary of Bauchi Discussion Circle, a forum he used to attack the colonial indirect rule in Nigeria. In 1948, he assumed the leadership of the Teacher Training Centre, Manu, Sokoto as well as the Secretary of the Northern Teachers Association. He utilized the position of his office to enhance the quality of Koranic Schools in Northern Nigeria.

Mallam Aminu Kano joined the membership of 'Jamiyyar Mutanen Arewa', which represented a Northern Nigeria cultural organization, which later evolved into one of the dominant political parties during Nigeria's First Republic. In 1950, he led a splinter group of young radicals from the 'Jamiyyar Mutanen Arewa' and established a political party called the Northern Elements Progressive Union (NEPU).

Prior to the formation of NEPU, an Igbira man and trader, Habib Raji Abdallah had evolved a progressive association called the Northern Elements Progressive Association, Kano, which collapsed in 1949 when Habib Raji Abdallah was arrested and jailed.

Nonetheless, Mallam Aminu Kano assembled a new progressive union comprising of progressive learning teachers and some radical intellectuals like Magaji Dambatta, Abba Maikwaru and Bello Ijumu who in togetherness posed a formidable opposition to the management strategies of the Native Administration of the Northern Region of Nigeria.

In 1951, Aminu Kano's party (NEPU) fairly succeeded in Kano primary elections but his party started to face formidable challenges in two subsequent federal elections when the Northern People's Congress (NPC) led by Sir Ahmadu Bello, the Sardauna of Sokoto was formed with Sir Abubakar Tafawa Balewa as Deputy Leader of the NPC.

In 1954, Sir Aminu Kano lost the contested Federal House of Representatives seat to Alhaji Maitama Sule. In the same wise, he failed to win enough votes to secure a seat to the Northern Regional Assembly in 1955.

In 1959, he won a Kano East parliamentary seat on the platform of NEPU, which was in alliance with the NCNC. He was made the Deputy Chief Whip while he was in the Federal House of Representatives. After the retaliatory military coup d'etat of July 29, 1966, Mallam Aminu Kano was made the Federal Commissioner of Health under General Yakubu Gowon as Military Head of State.

When the Nigerian Military Government headed by General Obasanjo lifted the proscription of political parties in 1978, Mallam Aminu Kano formed the People's Redemption Party, joined by prominent people like Sam Ikoku and labour leader, Michael Imodu. Mallam Aminu Kano was presented as presidential candidate in 1979 federal elections, which he lost, but his party succeeded in winning two gubernatorial seats.

Mallam Aminu Kano strongly challenged what he believed were the autocratic and feudalistic actions of the Native Northern Nigerian Administration including the activities of the ruling elites and Emirs who were mostly of Fulani ethnicity. He had massive support in Kano State because of his background, his lineage from Islamic Clerics and his campaign manifestos and messages, which emphasized egalitarianism, equity, justice and fairplay for all. He was very popular among Talakawas (commoners) and migratory petty traders in Northern Nigeria.

He favoured heavy taxation of the rich and wealthy and he supported equal rights for men and women. He opposed discrimination on basis of sex, ethnicity, religion, and he condemned child abuse.

Alhaji Aminu Kano

Member of House of Representatives (Nigeria)
In office
1959 – 1966

Minister for Health
In office
1967 – 1974

Born	1920 Kano
Died	April 17, 1983
Political party	NEPU, People's Redemption Party
Profession	Teacher Politician
Religion	Muslim

(13)
SENATOR JOSEPH SERWUAN TARKA
(July 10, 1932 – 1980)

Senator Joseph Tarka popularly known as 'JST' was from Gboko, Benue State. He was one of the founding fathers of the United Middle Belt Congress which was a political party dedicated to protect the interests of the Middle Beltans of Nigeria. Under General Yakubu Gowon as Military Head of State, Senator Joseph Tarka served as Minister of Transport and later Communications.

He was dedicated to advocate and achieve autonomy for the Middle-Belt of Nigeria. He faced several political battles. He was young, energetic and very skillful at political campaigns. He was nicknamed the 'smiling snake' because of his big smiles while speaking at campaigns.

He was born at Igbor, Benue State on July 10, 1932 to a former teacher and administrator in Benue State. His father's standing in society helped to strengthen Senator Joseph Tarka's political successes in his state of origin. He attended Senior Primary School, Gboko, Benue Middle School and Bauchi Teachers Training College. He worked as rural science teacher in Katsina and TIV Native Authority and was involved on organizing teachers' union.

He was the leading TIV politician and a leading founder of the United Middle Belt Congress (UMBC) political party. He was instrumental to the creation of the Middle Belt State and was deeply involved in the promotion of minority interests of ensuring egalitarianism, equity, nondiscrimination, justice and fairplay.

He was elected as a member of the House of Representatives in 1954 and became a member of the Public Accounts Committee. In 1957 and 1958, as President of UMBC, he led his party's delegates to the constitutional conference in London to discuss Nigerian Independence. Senator Tarka's party, UMBC allied with Chief Awolowo's Action Group (AG) and became the Vice President of the Action Group.

In 1959, he became the Minister of Commerce in the 'Shadow Government' leading to independence in 1960. When he won reelection in 1959, he became the first TIV legislator to be reelected to the second term. His reelection was attributed to his charisma, his father's reputation and goodwill, and the unflinching support he received from the TIV Progressive Union.

In 1962, he was arrested on charges of treasonable felony including some Action Group leaders but he was later discharged and acquitted for insufficient evidence to sustain his prosecution. After the Ifeajuna/Nzeogwu coup d'etat of January 15, 1966, which ended the First Republic, and the retaliatory coup d'etat of July 29, 1966, Senator Tarka returned to national spotlight. He headed the Ministry of Transport and that of Communication in quick succession. However, he resigned his ministerial office voluntarily after he was accused by one of his kinsmen, Dabor of corruption for which he was never indicted, charged nor tried.

Thus, Senator Tarka was commended as the first federal minister to resign his post on allegation of corruption without any government sanction or official inquiry into the allegations. He went into private business and he was very successful.

In 1978, Tarka switched his political alliance and joined the National Party of Nigeria (NPN), which belonged to those whom he had criticized all his life. He served the NPN as Vice Chairman and got elected as Senator while his son, Simeon Tarka was elected to the House of Representatives. In his remembrance and appreciation of his work, institutions and roads were named after him.

SENATOR JOSEPH TARKA

(14)
CHIEF SAMUEL LADOKE AKINTOLA
(July 6, 1910 – January 15, 1966)

Chief Samuel Ladoke Akintola (SLA) was one of the greatest orators that Nigeria has ever produced. He was a lawyer, born in Ogbomosho, South Western Nigeria. He was the Are Onakakanfo XIII of Yorubaland. He trained as a Lawyer in the United Kingdom and returned to Nigeria in 1949.

He teamed up with other prominent Yoruba leaders of Western Region of Nigeria to form the Action Group (AG) under the leadership of the sage and immortal Chief Obafemi Awolowo, First Premier of Western Region of Nigeria. He was deputy leader of the Action Group (AG) and he was the parliamentary leader of his party (AG) in the Federal House of Representatives. He served as Federal Minister of Health, Minister of Communications and Minister of Aviation respectively.

In 1957, the Action Group (AG) leadership swapped political positions between Chief S.L. Akintola and Chief Obafemi Awolowo. Hence, Chief S.L. Akintola became the Premier of Western Region of Nigeria while Chief Obafemi Awolowo became the party leader in the Federal House of Representatives, its leader of opposition and remained the national leader of the Action Group. The shift in position and division of roles and responsibility soon created irreconcilable problems which led to disaster for the party, the AG leaders, the Yorubas, Western Nigeria in particular and Nigeria in general.

The Action Group (AG) factionalization resulted in several crises and fighting in the Western House of Assembly as well as violence, which engulfed the Western Region of Nigeria. Hence, the federal government led by Prime Minister Abubakar Tafawa Balewa who would have wanted to defeat and break the strong opposition party (AG), quickly declared a 'State of Emergency' on Western Nigeria, arrested and relocated the AG leaders and appointed an Administrator to run the affairs of Western Nigeria.

Chief S. L. Akintola was restored to power in 1963 as Premier of Western Nigeria. He formed a new party called, 'Nigerian National

Democratic Party (NNDP)' which was in alliance with the Northern People's Congress (NPC) that was in control of the Federal Government and remained the sworn enemy of the Action Group leadership of Chief Obafemi Awolowo. The NNDP of Chief Akintola won the general election in 1965 amid allegations of massive election rigging. As a result, there were riots all over the Western Region causing killing of innocent people and destruction of properties uncontrollably.

Yoruba communities of Western Nigeria started to eliminate the Northerners in their midst and the Northerners started to eliminate Yorubas from Northern Nigeria in retaliation. Soldiers and Police Officers were drafted to control the anarchical situation but their efforts did not succeed until there was an 'ArmyTakeOver' of government by the military coup d'etat of January 15, 1966 staged by Ifeajuna/Nzeogwu and their collaborators.

The military coup assassinated Chief Samuel Ladoke Akintola, Premier of Western Nigeria; Alhaji Ahmadu Bello, Premier of Northern Nigeria; Sir Abubakar Tafawa Balewa, First Prime Minister of Nigeria and many other innocent Yoruba and Hausa/Fulani civilian leaders and military officers of Western and Northern Nigeria origin.

The coup d'etat conspirators unwittingly safeguarded civilian leaders and military officers of Eastern Nigeria ethnic origin, which made it very unpopular, sectional, tribal, discriminatory, and thus, plunged the Western and Northern nationalities crying for retaliation to avenge the brutal killings of their leaders by tribal military officers of Eastern Nigeria origin. Hence, a retaliatory/counter coup d'etat became inevitable.

Unfortunately, Ifeajuna, Nzeogwu, their collaborators and mentors did not consider the implications of Igbo military officers going outside their state of origin to brutally assassinate Yoruba and Hausa/Fulani leaders and military officers in their (Yoruba and Hausa/Fulari) homelands. Most regrettably, General Aguiyi Ironsi (an Igboman) who took over as Military Head of State did not pacify the situation but made it worse by not prosecuting the coupists and by issuing decree no. 34 which proposed a unitary system of government detested by the northerners.

Chief S. L. Akintola, popularly known as 'SLA' used to wake up all Yoruba race early every morning with special prayer, greetings and sweetest possible message urging Yorubas to participate in the mainstream politics of the country in order to have their fair share of the national cake and other available opportunities. He would say in Yoruba Language on the morning radio, "Enyin omo iya mi", meaning my brothers and sisters, and he would continue to justify why Yorubas should play a greater role in the federation without antagonism against federal authorities.

His oratory and philosophy seemed too sophisticated for most Yorubas who did not understand his good intentions about why the Westerners should be in harmony and alliance with Northerners. Yorubas miss him and Chief Obafemi Awolowo. One wished that Chief Obafemi Awolowo and Chief Samuel Ladoke Akintola were able to settle their differences in the best interest of the Yorubas and the entire nation with the spirit of give and take. Both of them were outstanding and they outclassed all others of their generation.

Regrettably, their irreconcilable altercation adversely affected them personally, the Yoruba race, and Western Nigeria that was first in Africa became relegated to the bottom three in Nigeria. As a result, every Yoruba person suffered series of humiliations for over three decades until the advent of President Obasanjo (1999-2007). It is advisable that people should desist from starting a quarrel or a fight because nobody can actually predict how it will end.

Chief S. L. Akintola lived a wonderful life and left five great children, family and friends prematurely. His sons, Chief Yomi Akintola and Dr. Bimbo Akintola served as Finance Ministers during the Third Republic. Chief Yomi Akintola was Nigeria's Ambassador to Hungary and his daughterinlaw, Mrs. Dupe Akintola was High Commissioner to Jamaica. His youngest son, late Tokunbo Akintola attended Eton College, England and was the first black student to attend the college.

In his honour and remembrance, Ladoke Akintola University of Technology, Ogbomosho was named after him, as well as many roads in Nigerian cities. Nigerians missed his wisdom and his early morning radio prayer, greetings and messages of encouragement to Yoruba race.

Chief Samuel Ladoke Akintola

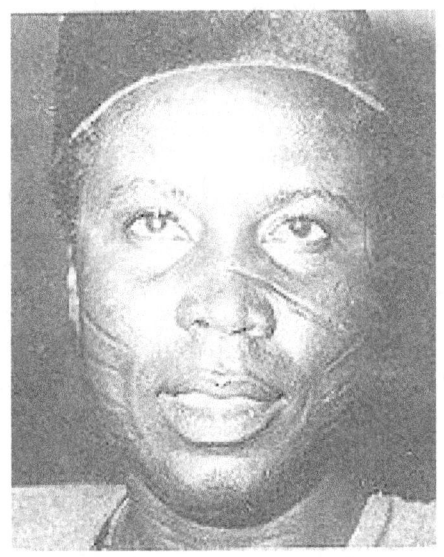

Premier of Western Nigeria
In office
October 1, 1960 – January 15, 1966

Preceded by	Obafemi Awolowo
Succeeded by	None
Born	July 6, 1910(19100706) Ogbomosho, Nigeria
Died	January 15, 1966 (aged 55)
Political party	Action Group
Occupation	Lawyer

(15)
DR. MICHAEL IHEONUKARA OKPARA
(December 19, 1920 – December 17, 1984)

He was a Medical Doctor born in Umuahia, Abia State on December 19, 1920 and he died on December 17, 1984 at the age of sixty-four (64) years.

He was a member of the National Council of Nigeria and the Cameroon's, which later changed to National Council of Nigeria and Citizens (NCNC). He was the second Premier of Eastern Nigeria (October 1, 1959 to January 15, 1966), preceded by Dr. Nnamdi Azikiwe, the First President of Nigeria. Michael Okpara University of Agriculture, Umudike was named after him as well as many streets in honour and appreciation of his leadership.

Dr. Michael Okpara's tenure as Premier of Eastern Nigeria ended on January 15, 1966 when the federal government of Nigeria was overthrown in a military coup d'etat of January 15, 1966. On that day, Igbo military officers led by Ifeajuna and Nzeogwu and their coconspirators of Eastern Nigeria origin, brutally assassinated the Premiers of Northern and Western Nigeria, Sir Ahmadu Bello and Chief Samuel Ladoke Akintola respectively. The coupists spared and safeguarded their Igbo kinsmen from Eastern Nigeria, including Dr. Michael Okpara, Premier of Eastern Region of Nigeria.

Furthermore, the coupists of Eastern Region origin brutally assassinated Sir Abubakar Tafawa Balewa, First Prime Minister of Nigeria, a Northerner, but they spared and safeguarded Dr. Nnamdi Azikiwe, First President of Nigeria, an Igboman of Eastern Nigeria origin like the coupists. They also assassinated many civilian leaders and military officers of Western and Northern Nigeria origin while they spared and safeguarded their counterparts of Eastern Nigeria origin.

That day, January 15, 1966 of the military coup d'etat was the beginning of the mistrust, divisionism, disunity and serious anger among Nigerian ethnicities. If the coup d'etat was bloodless, perhaps the coup d'etat executors might not have created so much anger for retaliation and the inevitability of a counter coup of July 29, 1966. The way the coup was carried out was bloody, sectional, discriminatory, tribalistic, barbaric, cruel and wicked.

General Aguiyi Ironsi, an Igboman, who became the Military Head of State, made Lt. Colonel Chukwuemeka Odumegwu Ojukwu as the Military Governor of the Eastern Region and thus ended the governorship career of Dr. Michael Iheonukara Okpara. Dr. Okpara's greatness coupled with his enormous wisdom was missed by the Easterners in particular and Nigerians in general.

The military officers who took over from Dr. Nnamdi Azikiwe and Dr. Michael Okpara were young and inexperienced. The new leaders did not make use of the talents and wisdom of their civilian predecessors. Hence, they ran into problems that plunged the country into civil war (1967-1970) and left the Easterners in particular and Nigeria in general under perilous military dictatorship for over three decades with all its attendant consequences.

Dr. Michael Iheonukara Okpara

Premier of Eastern Nigeria
In office
October 1, 1959 – January 15, 1966
Preceded by   Nnamdi Azikiwe

Dr. Jubril Olabode Aka (DMS, MBA Aviation, Ph.D.)

Succeeded by	None (Position abolished)
Born	December, 1920 Umuahia, Abia State
Died	December 17, 1984
Political party	National Council of Nigeria and the Cameroons
Profession	Medical Doctor
Religion	Christianity

(16)
CHIEF CHUKWUEMEKA ODUMEGWU OJUKWU

Chief Ojukwu was General and Head of the Secessionist Army of the truncated and unrealized State of Biafra. He is the Nkemba of Nnewi. He was born on November 4, 1933 at Zungeru, Northern Nigeria to Mrs. Bianca Ojukwu and Louis Odumegwu Ojukwu (KBE), former President of African Continental Bank and first President of the Nigerian Stock Exchange who was regarded as a business tycoon and as the first multimillionaire in Nigeria. It was the talk of the town and common knowledge that Chief Ojukwu, the son, was raised and fed with a golden spoon.

Chief Ojukwu attended King's college in Lagos, Epsom College in Surrey, Britain, United Kingdom and later obtained his Master's Degree in History at Lincoln College, Oxford University.

On his return to Nigeria, he joined the Nigerian Army and graduated from the Sandhurst Military Academy, Sandhurst, England. He became a Lt. Colonel and later, the Military Governor of Eastern Nigeria on January 15, 1966. As a result of Ifeajuna/Nzeogwu military coup d'etat, the political career of Dr. Michael Iheonukara Okpara, who was the Premier of Eastern Region of Nigeria, ended abruptly.

He (Chief Ojukwu) was a Lt. Colonel in the Nigerian Armed Forces before the civil war (1967-1970). In the secessionist enclave, he was promoted General contemporaneously, as his former colleagues on the Nigerian side became Generals in the Nigerian Army. Nigeria did not recognize the secessionist army, titles and Biafra, so, it will be safe to refer to the secessionist leader simply as Chief Chukwuemeka Odumegwu Ojukwu without prejudice, and to avoid being drawn into any controversy.

Chief Ojukwu was appointed the Military Governor of Eastern Nigeria after Ifeajuna/Nzeogwu military coup d'etat of January 15, 1966 which assassinated Sir Ahmadu Bello, First Premier of Northern Nigeria; Chief Samuel Ladoke Akintola, Premier of Western Nigeria;

Sir Abubakar Tafawa Balewa, First Prime Minister of Nigeria and many other civilian and military leaders of Northern and Western Nigeria.

While Yoruba and Hausa/Fulani civilian and military leaders were assassinated by the coupists who were regarded as Igbos, the Igbo civilian and military leaders of Eastern Nigeria, regarded as the kinsmen of the coupists were safeguarded like General Aguiyi Ironsi, Dr. Nnamdi Azikiwe, Dr. Michael Okpara etc. Hence, the coup was said to be tribally, sectionally, discriminatorily and ethnically motivated, and the possibility of retaliatory or counter coup became inevitable, real and imminent.

On July 29, 1966, the retaliatory/counter coup, followed by the resentment and indiscriminate assassinations of the Igbos (civilians and military officers) in the North was massive, beyond control and condemnable. The assassinations were described as 'antiIgbo/Christian genocidal pogrom' happening in the Muslim Northern Region.

As a result, Igbo Chiefs assembled at Umuahia and decided to secede and become independent. As at then, the Eastern Region was made up of the Igbo heartland, the Niger Delta (mostly Ijaw) and the Cross River (Effik and Ibibio areas). It was most probable that the Niger Delta and the Cross River leaders were not fully consulted and represented at the meeting of the Igbo Chiefs at Umuahia when the decision to secede was taken, perhaps, there would have been consideration for alternative choices with fewer risks to solve the problems. A less risky alternative decision could have saved everybody concerned, the deaths, pains and sufferings and the refugee problems created by the Civil War (1967-1970).

At that time, Chief Ojukwu, the exuberant leader was too young at 34 but powerful with his control of the armed forces of Eastern Nigeria. It might be difficult for Eastern elders and leaders with different and matured minds to talk for fear of being arrested for disloyalty, betrayal and unpatriotism to the course of Biafra.

The questions to ask are, "what did Dr. Nnamdi Azikiwe say? What did Dr. Okpara and great Igbos of timber and calibre like Justice Nwafor Orizu, Dr. Mbadiwe, Chiefs Jaja and Aja Nwachukwu say? Did anybody suggest alternatives to secession, which carried overwhelming risks? Did those who decide that the Eastern Region should secede properly consider a cost benefit analysis of their decision and possible alternatives?"

At that time, it looked as if the young Igbos of Chief Ojukwu's age and below in Eastern Nigeria were in control, and they were telling others about their invincibility without properly assessing available resources to win against Nigeria; as well as possible reactions from Britain, US, Russia and other African countries.

The 'caveat' is, "Do not start an avoidable war if you are not sure that you can avoid or minimize deaths, pains and sufferings and eventually win, in the best interest of your people in particular and humanity in general. The gains from victory envisaged must outweigh the collateral damages that are inevitable, otherwise, it is not reasonable to start a confrontation, a fight or war."

As demonstrated from their inexperience, the secessionist army bursted into the Mid-Western Region, looted the banks, bombed Lagos and started to march through Ore, Ondo State to Lagos and thus alienated the Yorubas, Mid-Westerners, Niger Deltans and Cross Riverans who initially had sympathy for their course short of secession action.

Above all, it was probable that they were not having enough resources to hold on to their heartland, and yet, they expanded to other regions militarily to complicate their problems. Other regions never wanted to be occupied and dominated, and would resist, fight and defeat them. The secessionist army should not have occupied the Mid-Western and part of South Western Regions in their march to Lagos. They should not have bombed Lagos.

There is a popular saying that when young people are moving forward, they hardly ever look back, and even when they fall, they get up fast and keep moving and eventually run into more problems. But when an elder moves, he/she looks back to assess possible dangers at the back and in the front especially if he/she falls/fails during any time in the process of moving forward.

It is a considered opinion that the first Igbo leaders and elders who were among the 'Fathers of Nigerian Independence and Nationhood' including Dr. Nnamdi Azikiwe; Sir Louis Odumegwu Ojukwu (KBE), Chief Ojukwu's father; Dr. Michael Okpara, Dr. Mbadiwe, Chiefs Aja and Jaja Nwachukwu, Justice Mbanefo, Acting Interim President

Nwafor Orizu and many others would have thought twice before declaring a secession and going to war. The secessionists could have gained more in a peaceful negotiation than the losses suffered during the war. A well-designed costbenefit analysis about the civil war by the secessionist leadership should have provided rational alternative decisions that would have prevented the war.

Those who were involved directly and indirectly in the planning and execution of the coup d'etat of January 15, 1966 should take responsibility for the deaths, pains and sufferings which Igbos and other Nigerians passed through for over four decades from January 15, 1966 to May 29, 1999. Nigerians should start to think deeply about the consequences of their intended actions before they act in order to avoid the costly and deadly mistakes of the past.

The Igbo Chiefs who met in Umuahia and decided about the secession and independence for Eastern Region of Nigeria in 1967, unanimously chose Chief Ojukwu to lead the new country and made him Head of State and General of the People's Army. The new country was named 'Biafra' deduced from the 'Bight of Biafra'. The popular 'Aburi Accord' was reached but it could not be implemented because it was said to be capable of different interpretations in respect of structuring the country as a 'Confederation'. It was possible that the Easterners with highly educated representatives at the conference must have outsmarted the Nigerian side. When people talk about intelligence, the Easterners are second to none in the world. Such intelligence should always be used positively for the benefit of all.

The secessionist army recorded some successes earlier, before Nigeria declared fullscale war. On May 5, 1967, Nigeria, under General Gowon created three (3) states from Eastern Nigeria and twelve as a whole in entire Nigeria. The creation of states encouraged selfdevelopment and reduced the domination of minorities by major ethnicities.

The three (3) states created out of the Eastern Region were: (1) the South East State, (2) East Central State and (3) Rivers State. The creation of the states was a blow to the secessionists because the South-East and the Rivers States were different from the East Central State; the heartland of the Igbos who supported secession while majority of the South-Eastern and Rivers States did not support the secession plan.

On May 30, 1967, Chief Ojukwu reacted to Gowon's creation of states by declaring the secession of Eastern Region and seized federal government assets in the region. He coopted some leaders of the minorities into his cabinet like Bassey, Effiong, Douglas and some others. Lt. Colonel Phillip Effiong who was later promoted 'General' was made the General Officer Commanding the secessionist army.

The secessionist army bursted into the Mid-Western Region occupied it and emptied the money in the banks. They committed various atrocities, marched to Ore, Ondo State and intended to be heading to Lagos. Their warplane bombed Lagos and there were suspicions that secessionist men and loyalists in mufti clothes were already planted in Lagos environs ready to fight. Hence, Nigeria declared a fullscale war, cleared the secessionist army from the Mid-Western Region and closely monitored all suspected secessionist loyalists in Lagos metropolis and other places in the federation.

The Nigerian army proceeded to the secessionist heartland and stronghold from the Northern front and the Mid-Western front with the objective of meeting at the centre of the secessionist enclave. As the secessionist army retreated from the Mid-Western sector, they blew up their endside of bridges to slow down the advance of federal forces. The strategy worked like magic but it was shortlived.

In spite of many losses, the determined federal soldiers overcame one problem after the other, but finally they conquered. The Northern and Western fronts met and disrupted the supply lines of the secessionist army. General Murtala Mohammed made three attempts before his army could cross to the Eastern Region with heavy losses each time especially at Abagana.

The Nigerian currency note was changed soon after the secessionists emptied the money in the Mid-Western banks and removed the money to their enclave. The change of currency notes made it difficult for the secessionists to buy arms and ammunition with stolen Nigerian money. As a result, there was confusion in the secessionist enclave. In addition, inlets and exits of secessionist enclave were blockaded with the probability of essential supplies being cut off or impeded effectively.

Dr. Nnamdi Azikiwe crossed over to Nigeria instead of returning to the secessionist enclave, which was rapidly collapsing. He was welcomed to Nigeria with pomp and pageantry as the First Nigerian President.

The honour and gracious reception he received at the international airport was more than he ever received from his kinsmen whom he helped throughout his lifetime. As the message of his safe arrival into Nigeria was announced, there was spontaneous and incredible jubilation throughout Nigeria from all nooks and corners. People shouted, "Zik of Africa, Zik of Africa".

Chief Ojukwu delivered an 'Ahiara Declaration' on June 1, 1969 at Ahiara Village where he condemned racism and imperialism and blamed Nigeria and United Kingdom for the blockade of his new nation, an act he described as genocidal. As it was glaring that the secession was collapsing, Chief Ojukwu left the Eastern Region of Nigeria to seek refuge in Ivory Coast (Cote d'Ivore) and possibly tried to set up a government in exile.

The General Officer Commanding (GOC) the secessionist army, Lt. Colonel Phillip Effiong who was promoted 'General' by the secessionists military became the Administrator of the enclave on January 10, 1970 after Chief Ojukwu left to Cote d'Ivoire on exile. General Effiong said, "I am also convinced that the suffering of our people must be brought to an end. Our people are now disillusioned and those elements of the old regime, which have made negotiations and reconciliation impossible, have voluntarily removed themselves from our midst. I have therefore instructed an orderly disengagement of troops. I urge General Gowon, in the name of humanity, to order his troops to pause while an armistice is negotiated, in order to avoid the mass suffering caused by the movement of population". He emphasized, "We have always believed that our differences with Nigeria should be settled by peaceful negotiation."

Chief Ojukwu lived in exile for thirteen (13) years. In 1980, President Shagari pardoned Chief Ojukwu at the same time with General Yakubu Gowon to enable them to return to Nigeria from Cote d'Ivoire and England respectively. Chief Ojukwu returned to Nigeria and joined President Shagari's party the National Party of Nigeria (NPN).

In 1983, Chief Ojukwu contested election into the Senate but General Buhari's coup d'etat of December 31, 1983 suspended the 1979 Nigerian Constitution and sacked Shagari's 2nd term in office before it actually started. All the newly elected Senators and House of Representatives Members were also sacked.

During the 2003 presidential election, Chief Ojukwu contested on the platform of the All Progressives Grand Alliance (APGA). He lost to President Olusegun Obasanjo. He challenged the election result in court saying that he won but massive rigging robbed him of becoming the President of Nigeria.

He also contested for the April 21, 2007 presidential election on the platform of All Progressives Grand Alliance (APGA) and lost to President Usman Musa Yar'Adua. He received his military pension on January 14, 2008 and he vehemently complained that he was being referred to as Lieutenant Colonel instead of being called 'General', his rank in the secessionist army, which Nigeria did not recognize.

At the National Peace Forum held during the first week of March 2004 at the International Conference Centre, Abuja, Chief Ojukwu complained about social injustice and canvassed for justice, equity and fairplay in the allocation of Nigeria's resources. He asserted, "Peace must be based on the foundation of truth. In this search for peace, this project cannot afford any part opting out. Nigeria has everything to be the greatest country". He added that the Igbos had no intention to quit the country.

If Nigerian leaders were so magnanimous and merciful to have granted general amnesty, mercy, rehabilitation, reconstruction, reconciliation and reabsorption to the secessionists and their leaders, it would be an act of mercilessness for the secessionists leadership to have denied mercy to executed Banjo, Ifeajuna, Nzeogwu etc. who were pioneers of Eastern Nigerian revolution of 1966.

Those who received pardon and mercy for their tresspasses and iniquities should be capable of giving mercy to those whose backs they climbed and rode to prominence. The secessionist leaders should have granted pardon and mercy to Banjo, Ifeajuna, Nzeogwu and others whose sweat, blood and sacrifice created the secessionist leaders in 1966/67. In effect, the problem for Ndigbo is more from within than from outside. Nigeria does not hate Ndigbo. Nigeria appreciates Ndigbo.

Dr. Jubril Olabode Aka (DMS, MBA Aviation, Ph.D.)

Chief Chukwuemeka Odumegwu Ojukwu

(17)
GENERAL SHEHU MUSA YAR'ADUA
(March 5, 1943 – December 8, 1997)

He was a fine soldier who was well loved by his colleagues. He was a businessman and a politician. He was born in Katsina on March 5, 1943. He was one of the founding fathers of the People's Democratic Movement (PDM) which later metamorphosed into the People's Democratic Party (PDP), the ruling party in Nigeria. His brother, Mallam Umaru Musa Yar'Adua won the Nigerian presidential election and he was sworn in on May 29, 2007.

He had his training at the Royal Military Academy Sandhurst, England, United Kingdom. He actively participated in the Nigerian Civil War (1967-1970). He was the Chief of Staff, Supreme Headquarters, the Deputy to the Military Head of State, General Olusegun Obasanjo (February 13, 1976 – October 1, 1979).

During the regime of General Sani Abacha (1993-1998), General Yar'Adua, General Obasanjo and many others were calling on the Nigerian Military Government to hand over to a democratically elected civilian government and retreat to the barracks. As a result, many agitators for civilian rule were arrested on trumped up charges of treasonable felony for planning to overthrow the Federal Military Government of General Sani Abacha.

Those arrested included General Obasanjo, General Shehu Musa Yar'Adua, Chief Moshood Kashimawo Olawale Abiola and many others – civilians and military officers. A military tribunal tried many of those arrested and gave sentences. General Shehu Musa Yar'Adua was sentenced to life imprisonment. He died in prison on December 8, 1997. It was alleged that Abacha's medical agents injected HIV/AIDS virus forcibly into his body with his hands tied to his back and that the same fate could have befallen General Olusegun Obasanjo who was lucky to refuse injections except from his personal physician.

It was also revealed that a military assassination squad was established by General Sani Abacha to eliminate any of his opponents by assassination. Those shot dead or wounded included Kudirat Abiola whose husband won the June 12, 1993 presidential elections, but was in Abacha's prison. Others who were wounded by gunshots and were lucky to be alive included Chief Ibru and Senator Abraham Adesanya. After the death of Abacha, members of Abacha's military killer squad were arrested, faced prosecution and detained without bail.

GENERAL SHEHU MUSA YAR'ADUA

(18)
ALHAJI CHIEF MOSHOOD KASHIMAWO OLAWALE ABIOLA
(August 24, 1937 – July 7, 1998)

Popularly known and called 'MKO', he was a Yorubaman of the Islamic faith, a professional accountant by training, a business mogul, a publisher, a philanthropist and a rich and very wealthy kind man. He was charismatic and he became a darling of all. He was not a professional politician until he decided to vie for the position of Nigerian President in 1993.

Chief Abiola was born on August 24, 1937 at Abeokuta, Ogun (Gateway) State of Western Nigeria. He worked for ITT Corporation and became its Vice President for Africa and the Middle East. He developed a business empire comprising various industries, which included airline, publishing, agriculture, shipping, bookshops, oil industry, banking etc. He was very wealthy, very charitable and very generous. He was usually emphatic that his wealth could not evaporate because of its enormity.

Chief M.K.O Abiola became the presidential candidate of the controversial presidential election held on June12, 1993 on the platform of Social Democratic Party (SDP) with BabaGana Kingibe as his running mate.

Two days to the election, the Abuja High Court issued an injunction order, received on June 10, 1993 that the proposal to hold the presidential election be suspended. While the military government was considering the implications of the court order, a letter was received from the American Embassy written by Mr. Michael O'Brien, the Director of Information, saying that any postponement was not acceptable to the USA. Majority of members of the National Defence and Security Council (NDSC) headed by General Ibrahim Babangida were infuriated and they pressed for at least a week postponement.

The Chairman of the Independent National Electoral Commission (INEC), Professor Humphrey Nwosu favoured that the election be held as scheduled and he strongly advised the Military Head of State,

General Ibrahim Babangida that the election be conducted as planned. The Attorney General of the Federation, Chief Clement Akpamgbo who found himself in a dilemma suggested that the court order be appealed or probably be quashed with a military decree before any further action to hold the election.

Without cognizance of the court order of injunction, the advice of the Attorney General of the Federation (AGF) and the postponement decision reached by the NDSC, the election was held on June 12, 1993 in defiance of all odds against the decision to go ahead with the presidential election. On June 23, 1993, the NDSC annulled the election, dissolved the INEC and civilian Interim Administrator was to be appointed to transition the country to democratic governance.

Chief M.K.O Abiola was said to have won the presidential election with 8,323,305 votes on the platform of SDP while his opponent, Othma Tofa had 6,073,612 for National Republican Convention (NRC). The annulment of the election caused confusion, violence, chaos, killings, arson and other crimes.

As a result, there was pressure for an end to military dictatorship and the restoration of democratic governance. Hence, the Head of the Military Government, General Ibrahim Badamosi Babangida threw in the towel on August 27, 1993 and passed the torch to Interim Administrator, Chief Ernest Adegunle Oladeinde Shonekan. Chief Shonekan was given the responsibility to transition to democratic administration supported by a cabinet with General Sani Abacha as the Defence Secretary.

Chief Abiola, the presumptive winner of the presidential election of June 12, 1993, his supporters, the Civil Rights Activists and many other organizations did not like the arrangement of handing over the government to an Interim Administrator instead of himself, Chief Abiola.

The matter was further complicated when General Abacha toppled the Interim Administrator on November 17, 1993 and became the de facto president in a palace coup that forced Chief Shonekan to sign a letter of resignation involuntarily. When General Abacha took over as Head of Military Government, he cancelled all the arrangements for transition to civilian administration, which killed all the hopes of

Chief Abiola, his supporters and Nigerian majority who were fedup with military dictatorship.

The emergence of General Abacha as Military Head of State brought chaos, violence, arson and socio-economic and political instabilities. The Comity of Nations applied sanctions on Nigeria and the Commonwealth of Nations suspended Nigerian membership. Chief M.K.O. Abiola, without adequate protection from arrest and detention, unwittingly pronounced himself as Nigerian President and he became vulnerable to all the sufferings and humiliations that befell him from the time of his arrest and detention to the time he died in prison on July 7, 1998.

Chief M.K.O. Abiola and his advisers should have visualized that he would be arrested and detained and thereby lose his freedom, when he declared himself as President of Nigeria. Hence, they should have explored other alternatives including going into exile before taking the risks of confronting a military dictator without any protective arrangement. Who must have advised Chief Abiola to expose himself to such dangers and why did he accept such advice?

Chief M.K.O. Abiola was arrested and charged for treasonable offences and remanded in military custody. It was generally believed that Chief Abiola was too close to the topmost military guys at the corridor of power, and that Military Heads of Government at respective periods were his best friends.

Regrettably, the subhuman ways his case was handled after he won the 1993 presidential election indicated that the relationship the military heads had with him might be purely superficial and business oriented. The aftermath of the relationship makes it difficult for anybody to fully trust anybody under any circumstance. It was a complete betrayal by all concerned. It was hard to believe that people who were so close together could do things that ended in the violent deaths of one another. Such behaviour was unAfrican.

Chief Abiola died on July 7, 1998, the day he was to be released from prison. General Abacha, his captor, died on June 8, 1998. General Abdulsalami Abubakar was the Head of Nigerian Military Government from June 9, 1998 to May 29, 1999. The question in the minds of right thinking people is, "What happened to him?" His safe release from prison could have channeled a new and pleasant history for

Nigeria. Why and how did he die on the day fixed for his release from detention?

It was rumored that Chief Abiola died of a heart attack on July 7, 1998. Some other people said that he was poisoned, but one of the main suspects in the assassination squad organized by General Abacha revealed in the court that Chief Abiola was beaten to death in prison.

If he was lucky to survive and live beyond General Abacha's lifetime, which ended on June 8, 1998, why then did he not live beyond July 7, 1998, the day fixed for his release. His death on that day was extremely, glaringly suspicious. Those who were involved in his death directly and indirectly should seek divine forgiveness to be at peace before they appear on the 'Judgment Day'.

Alhaji Chief Moshood Kashimawo Olawale Abiola

OTHER LEADERS:

There were and/or are other most distinguished Nigerians who played noble leadership roles worthy of acknowledgement in the life of Nigerians pre and post independence existence of the nation.

The list inexhaustively includes:
(1) Alhaji Lateef Kayode Jakande 'alias Baba Kekere': He was born on July 23, 1929 in Lagos. He was the first Civilian Governor of Lagos State of Nigeria. He was also Minister of Works and Housing. He initiated and implemented free education, health care and affordable housing programmes in Lagos State. He was popularly known as the Godson of Chief Obafemi Awolowo, leader of the Yorubas and first Premier of Western Region of Nigeria. Alhaji Lateef Kayode Jakande 'LKJ' will be remembered eternally.
(2) Dr. Augustus Taiwo 'Tai' Solarin (1922-1994): He was born on August 20, 1922 at Ikenne, Remo, Ogun State and he died on June 27, 1994. He was a renowned author, educator, international humanist and activist, a secularist, a social critic and a man of strong convictions who was a thorn in the side of the authorities. He was the proprietor of Tai Solarin University of Education (TASUED), the first Nigerian University of Education, located in Ijagun, Ijebu-Ode, Ogun State of Nigeria. He would be remembered eternally for his love and fights for the masses and the less privileged.
(3) Brigadier General Mohammed Buba Marwa:

He was born in Kaduna on September 19, 1953. He was educated at Pittsburgh University and Harvard University, USA where he bagged Master's Degrees in International Relations and Public Administration respectively. He was Military Administrator (Governor) of Lagos State where he became renowned for outstanding accomplishments for which he would always be remembered by Lagosians. He withdrew his name from being considered for the 2007 presidential election on the platform of the PDP and was later appointed as Nigeria Ambassador on foreign mission.

(4) **Lt. General Donaldson Oladipo Diya:**
He hails from Odogbolu, Ogun State, Western Nigeria. He was Military Vice President of Nigeria from 1994 until 1997 under the de facto military presidency of General Sani Abacha. He was given death penalty by the Military Tribunal that tried many Nigerian dignitaries including President Obasanjo on trumped up charges of planning to overthrow General Sani Abacha.

When Abacha died suddenly in 1998, General Diya was pardoned among many others by General Abdulsalami Abubakar who succeeded Abacha. General Diya could be described as 'Ayorunbo' meaning, 'somebody who crawled stealthily from heaven to earth, from death to life; for escaping from imminent planned death imposed on him by General Abacha'.

(5) **Mrs. Patricia Olubunmi Foluke Etteh:**
She was born on August 17, 1953 to the family of Alabi in Ikire, Osun State of Nigeria. She was the first female Speaker of the Nigerian House of Representatives from June 5, 2007 to October 30, 2007 representing Aiyedade/Isokan/Irewole Constituency of Ikire, Osun State. She was forced out of the Speakership of the House as a result of the usual political machinations and trickery of the menfold.

Most men in positions of leadership in politics in every part of the world whether developed or developing countries got away with inflation of government contracts with impunity, but as a woman, she could not, with a first offence without any official uncontestable indictment.

(6) Abdul-Ganiyu 'Gani' Oyesola Fawehinmi (SAN):
He was born on April 22, 1938 in Ondo, Ondo State of Nigeria. He is a renowned erudite Senior Advocate of Nigeria, author, human rights activist, philantropist, social critic, politician and human and civil rights lawyer.

He was often described as the scourge of irresponsible governments, a thorn in their flesh, champion of the masses' interests and the major cause of high blood pressure for Nigerian dictatorial regimes of three decades (1966-1999). He was incarcerated several times by successive military dictators from 1966-1998.

His popular quote, "Stand up for what is right, even if you are standing alone" is a debatable concept of inflexibility for which Chief Gani Fawehinmi will be remembered eternally. He was the presidential candidate of his party.

The determination of 'What is Right' is complicated by the differences in religion, ethnicity, sociopolitical ideologies, culture, customs, tradition, education, professionalism, perceptuability, skills, moral background and discipline of individuals. In politics, there are no permanent friends but interests, and inflexibility does not work well in a democracy. Opinionation bears inflexibility. A great leader or leadership aspirant should have the capacity to accommodate many others' opinions to be perfectly harmonized democratically for good governance. Hence, sociopolitical activists in Nigeria cannot be right to think that they are always right while others are not. Sometimes, opinionation or inflexibility usually results from lack of or limited exposure/experience and usually as a result of obstinacy or narrow mindedness.

On December 16, 2008, it was published that Chief Gani Fawehinmi (SAN) had refused to accept Nigerian Honour of Order of the Federal Republic (OFR). In his statement, he thanked President Alhaji Umaru Musa Yar'Adua, the Council of State and Nigerians in general who had congratulated him earlier. He remarked that the Nigerian government must have considered his 43 years past activities, crusades and struggles before the decision to give him the award.

His struggles and crusades include: (a) abolition of poverty; (b) unqualified need to preserve, defend and protect fundamental human rights; (c) democratic governance; (d) due process and rule of law; (e) free and qualitative education at all levels; (f) free and qualitative healthcare; (g) strong economy and infrastructural development; and (h) corruptionfree society.

As a result of his struggles, he was subjected to various Nigerian military governments' traumatic travails and persecutions (a) detentions in Ikoyi Prison (3 times), Kaduna, Gombe, Kuje (2 times), Bauchi Prisons etc.; (b) 23 police detentions between 1969 and 1998; (c) 32 arrests; (d) 16 military violent raids of his Law Chamber at Anthony Village, Ikeja, Lagos resulting in removal of his books on the murder of Dele Giwa; (e) bloody shooting of his employees at his chamber by military security agents; (f) nonreturn of his books in spite of Court Orders; (g) seizure of his international passport more than 15 times between 1966-1998; (h) charged to court 18 times for politically motivated criminal offences including treason; jailed once, became prisoner J60 until case was overturned by the Court of Appeal.

He added that he had to go abroad to treat his cancer at the age of 70 years and 8 months because his country (Nigeria), one of the richest with oil revenue was the poorest in providing medical services to the people. He mentioned that corruption was the single, fundamental factor that had retarded the nation's socio-economic development. He also mentioned that Mallam Nuhu Ridadu, the former EFCC Chairman was removed, demoted and persecuted for fighting corruption and stepping on the toes of the 'sacred cows and untouchables' in Nigerian society.

He added that he found it difficult to accept that Nigerian government had the honour to dispense honour because of the breaches of the Nigerian Constitution as highlighted above.

He emphasized that the Nigerian government that covertly and overtly encouraged corruption had no honour in its arsenal of power to dispense honour and consequently, he rejected the 'DISHONOUR of OFR' termed 'HONOUR' given to him by the Federal Government. He added that the masses had found themselves helpless in the doldrum of pain and suffering occasioned by misgovernance of the country.

He added that since May 29, 2007, the beginning of Yar'Adua Presidency, the masses had been groaning in unprecedented poverty for lack of direction. He said that there had been collapsed infrastructures, total paralysis of health sector, nationwide power failure, negative economic effects, pervasive unemployment, increased armed robbery, increasing homelessness, and retrogressive educational programmes and policies. He concluded that there was no hope in sight for the masses and he therefore rejected the 'Award of OFR'.

Undoubtedly, Chief Gani Fawehinmi touched the hearts of all Nigerians and Nigeria's friends all over the world except those who might have perpetrated the above-mentioned atrocities both directly and indirectly. The situation analyzed by him is terrible and one wonders why successive Nigerian governments since 1960 have not made tangible and remarkable difference in the lives of the people.

Usually, the type of leadership you appoint, select or elect will determine the kind of services you get. The lack of technical knowhow, sociopolitical savvy and sagacity in the leadership may be curse against Nigeria's development. Unfortunately, poverty is spreading worldwide in developed, developing and underdeveloped countries without exception. Nigerian problems are humanmade problems arising from human imperfections which presently pervade the whole universe; just like latest fraud of $50 billion allegedly committed by a New Yorker of the Wall Street, Bernard Madoff. Nigeria should change direction, change course immediately to avoid drowning irretrievably or leaders might run the country aground.

Chief Gani Fawehinmi's struggles, crusades and other activities in the best interest of Nigeria and Nigerians are heroic without any iota of doubt, but his conclusion to reject 'Nigerian Honour Award of OFR' is misadvised, falls short of heroism and presupposes that this great Nigerian succumbs to selfdefeatism.

Nigeria with perpetual succession is completely different from the leaders who come and go. Never refuse any good gift or honour from your country, Nigeria because of the shortcomings of the leaders, who mislead but come and will go nomatter how long they want to stay unconstitutionally.

Refusing to take the 'Honour Award of OFR' is like throwing away the gracious innocent baby with the dirty bathwater or refusing to receive the good and honourable message of honour, well-deserved from all Nigerians because of bad messenger(s); and undermining the fact that the "Honour of OFR Award' is from Nigerians and not the ruling elites who need behaviour modifications, but consider 'Gani' and other socio-economic and political activists as their adversaries or thorns in their flesh for telling them the sophisticated truths which they have not grown up to be capable to accept.

General Buhari refused to accept his 'Nigerian Honour Award' from ExPresident Obasanjo; and Professor Chinua Achebe refused to accept his honour award also; but Chief Obafemi Awolowo, leader of the Yorubas, the sage and immortal Awo, first Premier of Western Region of Nigeria, the most persecuted elite politician and leader in the annals of the nation (physically and psychologically tortured), exemplarily accepted his 'Nigerian Honour Award of GFR' delivered by ExPresident Shehu Shagari, his toughest rival and opponent in two presidential election battles (1979 and 1983).

Prior to that, Chief Awolowo lost his presidential bid in 1960 and was imprisoned for treasonable felony and the whole Yoruba race and leadership were traumatized and humiliated for many years. Yet, he took the 'Honour Award GFR' with decency, dignity and gratitude to all Nigerian people. Awo's behaviour in that regard was unprecedented and exemplary. That is a worthy precedent for Nigerians to follow. We are proud of him.

Chief Gani Fawehinmi, Professor Wole Soyinka, Chief Anthony Enahoro and other socio-economic and political activists and critics should focus more on formulating and executing programmes that help the masses in terms of waste to wealth, democracy and power of the people's votes while they keep on asking for improvements in governance by Nigerian leaders without confrontation or violence just like Dr. Martin Luther King Jr. (USA) and Mahatma Gandhi (India). Leaders come and go, but Nigeria will remain for ever. Always believe that with the truth, peace and understanding, we shall overcome sooner than later.

Chapter 13, Rejection of CFR (Second Highest Honour-Professor Achebe) in my book titled, "Blacks Greatest Homeland Nigeria Is Born Again", 2006 made suggestions to Professor Achebe, Chief Gani Fawehinmi, Professor Wole Soyinka and other Nigerians in case they find themselves in the situation of considering whether to accept or reject Nigerian Honour Award. It is wished that they have access to the book available online or at bookshops worldwide in which their names featured prominently.

If anyone is obsessed by elite evils done to Nigeria and Nigerians by the rulership, such person will not be able to have good heart to love his/her country, Nigeria. Chief Gani Fawehinmi and others should summon courage to continue and not relent and/or never quit, because Nigeria's failure is not an option. The future of Nigeria is longer than her past and the number of Nigerians yet unborn is more than the numbers of the past and present Nigerians added together. Nobody should quit from saving Nigeria in spite of odds. May his soul rest in perfect peace (amen).

(7) Alhaji Abubakar Rimi:
He was born in Rimi Village of Sumaila Local Government Area of Kano State in 1940. He attended the University of London where he obtained a Master's Degree in International Relations. He became the first Civilian Governor of Kano State on July 28, 1979. His period of governance was full of accomplishments in respect of spreading social amenities, employing females into his cabinet, engaging in massive adult educational development programmes and establishing

newspaper publishing and giant television station among others.

He became the Minister of Communications in 1983 during Shagari Administration. He played commendable leadership roles in the PRP and PDP political parties respectively and fought relentlessly for the parties and the masses.

(8) Professor Wole Soyinka, Nobel Prize Laureate in Literature in 1986: He was born on July 13, 1934 in Abeokuta, Ogun State. He is a writer, author, poet and most distinguished playwright. He is a sociopolitical activist and critic of Nigerian dictators and governments. He was incarcerated by the successive military dictators who regarded him as a thorn and political adversary to their regimes. He is one of the topmost leaders of PRONACO (Pro-National Conference Organization) and a champion of the call for the convocation of Sovereign National Conference (SNC). He was appointed as a commissioner during the military regime. He was given a Nigerian National Merit Award in December 2008 but he donated the cash award to the Supreme Court of Nigeria.

(9) Chief Anthony Enahoro:

He was born in Uromi, Edo State of Nigeria on July 22, 1923. He was one of the foremost anticolonial activists and he has become the leader of Prodemocracy (PRONACO) organization. He is a most distinguished careerist in the press establishment/realm, politics, the civil service and prodemocracy movement. He was Chairman of National Democratic Coalition (NADECO) that fought General Abacha relentlessly.

He was member of the Western House of Assembly and later became member of federal House of Representatives in 1951 and Minister of Home Affairs in Western Region of Nigeria. He was opposition spokesperson on Foreign Policy and Legislative Affairs in the Federal House of Representatives between 1959 and 1963. He attended the Constitutional Conferences in London that led Nigeria to independence in 1960 and he was said to have moved the motion for Nigerian independence.

(10) Alhaji (Dr.) Umaru Dikko:
He was born in 1936 at Wamba, Northern Nigeria. He was Minister of Transportation (1979-1983) under Shagari Presidency. After General Buhari's coup d'etat that overthrew Alhaji Shehu Shagari on December 31, 1983, Alhaji Dikko fled on exile to London, but kept on criticizing Buhari Military Government.

On July 5, 1984, he was found kidnapped, drugged, crated and labelled 'Diplomatic Luggage' at the Stansted Airport, England, ready to be flown to Lagos, Nigeria. Luckily, the British Police foiled the kidnap on a tip of and rescued him from the crate. After many years in exile in London, Dr. Dikko returned to Nigeria and played roles as Nigerian Senior Statesman and Nationalist.

He was a leading Northern delegate to the National Political Reform Conference (NPRC) charged with the responsibility to review the Nigerian 1999 Constitution; and recommend amendments as appropriate. He was reported to have warned ExPresident Shagari about Buhari coup d'etat when he suspected the activities of the military under General Buhari as the General Officer Commanding (GOC).

(11) Prince Bola Ajibola:
He was born at Abeokuta, Ogun State on March 22, 1934. He was President of World Association of Judges, Attorney General and Minister of Justice, member of International Court of Justice (ICJ), International Law Commission, Permanent Court of Arbitration and Board of Governors Member of World Jurist Association.

He was Nigerian High Commissioner to London and Chairman of the Nigerian/Cameroonian Boundary Adjustment Mixed Commission. Prince Ajibola's antecedents nationally and internationally are various, many, long, eminent and almost countless. He will be remembered eternally for his efforts, which ensured that war between Nigeria and Cameroon to settle their boundary disputes was not an option. Avoiding that war, was one of the greatest achievements of ExPresident Olusegun Obasanjo, and Prince Ajibola deserved a lot of credits for resolving Nigeria/Cameroon border disputes peacefully.

(12) Chief Augustus Meredith Adisa Akinloye:
Popularly known as A.M.A; he was born on August 19, 1916 at Ibadan, Oyo State. He passed to the Lord on September 18, 2007. He read Law at London School of Economics (1946-1948) and became a lawyer, a renowned politician and a high traditional chief, the Seriki of Ibadanland. He was President of Ibadan Peoples Party (IPP) with Adelabu Adegoke as his deputy. He merged IPP with Action Group (AG), led by Chief Obafemi Awolowo.

He became Minister of Agriculture and Natural Resources and later became Chairman of Ibadan City Council. He left Action Group (AG) and teamed up with Chief Samuel Ladoke Akintola's Nigerian National Democratic Party (NNDP) during the Western Region crises.

He served in Balewa's cabinet of the First Republic until the coup d'etat of January 15, 1966 staged by Ifeajuna/Nzeogwu. He was Chairman of the National Party of Nigeria (NPN) while Alhaji Shagari was the President of Nigeria (1979-1983). He went into exile in London for ten years when General Buhari overthrew the government on December 31, 1983. After his return from exile, he served three months in Abacha's jail on trumped up charges of treason to overthrow his regime. He was said to have played vital roles during the election of General Olusegun Obasanjo as President of Nigeria in May 29, 1999. Until his death, Chief Akinloye was a member of the People's Democratic Party (PDP) Board of Trustees.

(13) Otunba Theophilus Owolabi Shobowale 'T.O.S.' Benson:
He was born on July 23, 1917 at Ikorodu, Lagos State. He passed to the Lord on February 13, 2008 at the age of 90, six months short of being 91 on his birthday anniversary of July 23, 2008.

He was Acting Chairman of Lagos Executive Development Board (LEDB), responsible for Lagos residential and industrial estates (1951-1959). He was a delegate to Nigerian Constitution Conference in London in 1953, 1957 and 1958 to achieve Nigerian Independence of 1960. He was one of the stalwarts in the NCNC founded by Herbert Macaulay and Dr. Nnamdi Azikiwe, First President of Nigeria.

He was member of the House of Representatives (1951-1959) and became the Chief Whip. He became the Federal Minister of Information and Broadcasting. He was one of the five (5) men of eminent personalities who championed the course and eventual creation of Lagos State in 1967. He was a renowned sociopolitical activist whose accomplishments would be remembered eternally. He was buried in Ikorodu, Lagos State.

14. Chief Richard Akinjide (SAN):

He is a renowned Nigerian Attorney born in Ibadan, Oyo State in early 1930s. He studied Law in London from 1951 and was called to the English Bar in 1955 and later in Nigeria.

He was a member of the Judicial Systems SubCommittee of the Constitutional Drafting Committee of 1975-1977.

As a member of the National Party of Nigeria in 1979, he helped to provide the legal interpretation of the 'twothird majority' provision in the Nigerian Constitution, which helped Alhaji Shagari to win the legal battle and Presidency in 1979 at the Nigerian Supreme Court. He became legal adviser to his party (NPN) and later, he was appointed the Attorney General and Minister of Justice. He is an eminent legal luminary of the late 20th and early 21st centuries.

GOD/ALLAH BLESS NIGERIA!

CHAPTER 3

NIGERIA IN PERSPECTIVE FROM INDEPENDENCE (1960)

Nigeria is a West African country, a former British colony which attained independence on October 1, 1960. Nigeria was principally regionalized into North, West and East until May 5, 1967 when General Yakubu Gowon, the Military Head of State (1966-1975) created 12 states out of the former three regional groupings in order to encourage selfdevelopment and minimize the incidences of the domination of the minorities by the majority ethnicities.

Nigeria is inhabited by over 140 million people thus becoming the most populous of the fifty-three countries in Africa and the largest concentration of black people in the universe. Statistically, one out of every ten black people in the world is Nigerian.

Nigeria has the largest land area of about 356,669 square miles in West African subregion. She is bordered by the Atlantic Ocean in the south, Republic of Cameroon in the east, Niger and Chad Republics in the north and Republic of Benin in the west.

Nigeria is a renowned member of the Organization of Petroleum Exporting Countries (OPEC), the Commonwealth of Nations, the African Union (AU), the Economic Commission of West African States (ECOWAS), NEPAD, the United Nations (UN) and many other distinguished world bodies. Nigeria is one of the seven largest producers of petroleum products in the world, and one out of five largest suppliers of petroleum products to the United States of America. Nigeria is developing a gas potential to become one of the world's largest producers of gas.

Nigeria's diversification into bitumen production will make her the second largest producer of bitumen in the world next to Venezuela and it is projected to fetch Nigeria over 1.34 trillion naira annually. Bitumen deposits estimated at 42.74 billion metric tons cover about 120 kilometres of the coastal belts of Ogun, Ondo and Edo States of Nigeria.

There are also steel deposits in commercial quantities that rank among the largest in the world. Nigeria is also blessed with naturally fertile land for agriculture, which could make her earn a lot of foreign exchange from cash crops and produce food crops toward selfsufficiency.

Since the beginning of democratic governance on May 29, 1999, Nigeria has been receiving greater attention from world organizations much more than ever before on her socio-economic and political advancement. These are favourable signs for increased foreign investment possibilities in Nigeria. Her staunch adherence to democratic practices is of great interest to the world community after three decades of dictatorship.

Nigeria is structured into six geopolitical zones of South-West, South-South, South-East, NorthWest, NorthCentral and NorthEast made up of 36 States and Abuja as the Federal Capital Territory (Center of Unity). Lagos, former Federal Capital, was classified as the fastest growing city in the world by the United Nations in 2005. Lagos is Nigeria's largest commercial centre. During the National Political Reform Conference, there were agitations for the creation of about six to twelve additional states.

Nigeria is a conglomeration of many groups of varying ethnic, linguistic, religious and cultural diversities. The regional dominant languages include Hausa in the north, Igbo in the southeast and Yoruba in the west. The three main languages are studied at graduate and postgraduate levels at universities and colleges of higher learning. There are over 400 dialects in Nigeria.

The champions and fathers of Nigerian independence of October 1st, 1960 included the Sardauna of Sokoto, Sir Ahmadu Bello, first Premier of Northern Region of Nigeria; Dr. Nnamdi Azikiwe, first

Premier of Eastern Region of Nigeria as well as first President of Nigeria; Sir Abubakar Tafawa Balewa, first Prime Minister of Nigeria; and Chief Obafemi Awolowo, first Premier of Western Region of Nigeria. Nigeria became the Federal Republic of Nigeria on October 1, 1963.

Bello, Zik, Balewa and Awo representing the greatest sons of Nigeria in particular and Africa in general lived exemplary lives, full of dignity, transparency, honesty and firmness. The courses in which they believed were in the best interest of Nigeria. They were second to none. They were contemporaries of Osagiefo of Ghana (former Gold Coast), President Kwame Nkruma; Emperor Haile Selassie of Ethiopia; President Julius Nyerere of Tanzania; President Dauda Jawara of Gambia; Presidents Abdel Nasir and Anwar Sadat of Egypt and many other great Presidents of Africa.

Nigeria witnessed a series of coups d'etat beginning on January 15, 1966, which killed many illustrious military officers and civilian leaders of the Northern and Western Regions while the coup conspirators led by Ifeajuna and Nzeogwu, who were Igbos from Eastern Nigeria spared the lives of military officers and civilian leaders of the Eastern Region of Nigeria.

The aftermath of the coup brought an Igbo Military Officer, Major General Aguiyi Ironsi to power as Military Head of State of Nigeria. The whole episode aroused serious suspicions that the coup was planned, hatched and executed by the Easterners (Igbos) to exterminate top military officers and civilian leaderships of Northern and Western extractions in order to rule the country. Above all, Major General Aguiyi Ironsi, the Head of State, unfolded plans for a unitary system of governance, which might not recognize the federal character of Nigeria in the sharing of opportunities. Such arrangement was his first biggest mistake because the Northerners believed that unitary system of government would definitely favour the Easterners (Igbos) more at the expense of other ethnicities.

In Nigeria then, the Easterners were quite advanced academically and entrepreneurially and would therefore reap the dividends of unitary administration more than any others especially when one of them was the Military Head of State.

The second biggest mistake was that Major General Aguiyi Ironsi did not ensure that Ifeajuna/Nzeogwu coup plotters and their coconspirators, his tribesmen, were prosecuted for treason by a military tribunal when it was crystal clear that they succeeded in overthrowing a democratically elected government by assassinating the Prime Minister, Sir Abubakar Tafawa Balewa, a Northerner; Sir Ahmadu Bello, the Sardauna of Sokoto and Premier of Northern Nigeria; Chief Samuel Ladoke Akintola, Premier of Western Nigeria and many other civilian leaders and top military officers of Northern and Western origins of Nigeria.

The worst part of it was that the coupists were talking freely about what they did and how they did it to the press/media as heroes, which the Northerners thought were acts of mockery, and as such, they started to plan reprisals to avenge the death of their leaders, to wrest power from the Easterners and return it to the North.

The news media of January and February 1966 aggravated the terrible situation and enflamed the anger of the Northerners by portraying the January coup executors as heroes while they denigrated and humiliated the Northerners and Westerners by publishing infuriating stories and pictures of assassinated military and civilian leaders of Northern and Western nationalities.

The pictures of the brutally assassinated leaders with their wounds and blood displayed by the press was not only disrespectful to the dead but also offended against Northern and Western Nigerian cultures, traditions, religion and values. It was a first experience in the annals of Nigeria when young Igbo military officers originating from a different tribe, took up arms and killed the leaders of other Nigerian nationalities while they protected their own ethnic leaders. The propaganda from the press made retaliations inevitable.

The mistrust, divisionism and disunity generated by the coup d'etat would continue as long as young Igbos continue to be fed with untruths about Igbos being hated and marginalized for who they are without honestly reinvigourating them by telling them about the realities of the mistakes of January 15, 1966 coup d'etat, and reassuring them that they can be the best they want to be without anybody being able to stop them.

They must also be constantly reminded about their resourcefulness and unique capabilities and the need to forgive and forget the past. They should be proud of the antecedents of great Igbomen like Zik of

Africa, Dr. Nnamdi Azikwe, the Owelle of Onitsha, one of the fathers of Nigerian independence and first President of Nigeria who was a darling of the Northerners and the Westerners, but like 'Jesus Christ', he was not listened to by the youthful leadership of his own kinsmen during the pre and post civil war era (1967-1970).

Why was the coup tribally/sectionally motivated and bloody? Do the coup collaborators still alive regret their actions about the mistrust and ethnicity perennial problems which their actions have generated? Brigadier Samuel Ademulegun, a Yorubaman who pioneered the Nigerian Army in 1949, commissioned with Aguiyi Ironsi and W.U. Bassey, was assassinated during Ifeajuna/Nzeogwu coup of January 15, 1966. Why was he killed and his Igbo colleagues safeguarded?

Unfortunately, some influential Igbo personalities have been peddling false rumours to pervert the realities and course of history by insinuating that the January 15, 1966 coup of Emmanuel Ifeajuna, Nzeogwu and others was staged to release Chief Obafemi Awolowo from prison and install him as President of Nigeria. That is a new gimmick to connect Yorubas to the coup as a ploy to receive their sympathy for the coup plotters. If that new disturbing fabrication were true, why were Yoruba senior military officers and civilian leaders killed, and why was Chief Obafemi Awolowo not released and installed then, instead of General Aguiyi Ironsi, an Igboman installed as Head of State?

It has not happened in the annals of Nigeria that an Igboman would step aside for a Yorubaman vice versa, without a serious contest for any of Nigeria's topmost positions. For example, in MidJuly 2005, the South-West Senators were alleged to have planned to boycott their committee seats because former Senate President Nnamani allegedly gave more committee chairmanship positions to the South-East (his Igbo kinsmen) and gave less to the South-Westerners (Yorubas) who controlled more states than the South-East. Such problem is avoidable by visionary, nonego centric, tribalistic leadership.

The right leadership would always be just and fair, equitable, transparent, honest, avoid favouritism, discriminatory practices, confusion, and be a uniter and not a divider. Nigerian leaders ought to have learnt enough lessons about sensitive areas where errors of omission or commission can be misinterpreted and costly.

Nigeria's best interest must always be first and foremost in leaders' minds and not ethnicity, religious or tribal considerations dictating decisions. Tribalism was the big problem in 1966, which cost Nigerians three decades of mayhem. Nigeria cannot afford to go back to square one.

Both Yorubas and Igbos believe in healthy competition, which is good for democratic Nigeria. The two nationalities, the Yorubas (West) and the Igbos (East) used to be at each other's throat politically while the biggest region (the North) was solid and unbreakable, but for the Middle Belt people who used to feel that they were being used, manipulated and dominated by the core Northerners before the creation of many states and the six geopolitical zones.

The Middle Belt led by the indomitable Joseph Tarka had shaky and frosty relationship with the core Northerners for feeling that they were being treated as secondclass Northerners politically by the other Northerners – the majority. The unhealthy relationship has subsisted till today, and it has often degenerated into socio-economic, political and ethno-religious confrontations.

As a result of the 1966 coup being regarded as sectionally and ethnicitywise motiviated, a lot of anger and tendencies for retaliations were generated against military officers and civilians of Eastern Nigerian origin. Hence, there was a counter coup, which killed Major General Aguiyi Ironsi and toppled his government on July 29, 1966.

Another biggest mistake that the Head of State, General Aguiyi Ironsi made was that the planning of a counter coup was leaked to him in tape recorded activities, but he did not act in a military fashion by arresting all concerned to save his life and those of others both military and civilian who died on July 29, 1966 and thereafter. He chose to consult with some Northern leaders to intervene and stop the coup plan instead of preempting it himself militarily as Military Head of State. These are lessons for all Nigerians to learn for inaction. "A stitch in time saves nine."

When the law is broken, there should be no sacred cows or untouchables. For that third biggest mistake of inaction or military irresponsiveness, the Military Head of State, General Aguiyi Ironsi, one of the most brilliant and finest military commanders that ever lived, was killed with his host, the Military Governor of Western Region of Nigeria, Lt. Colonel Adekunle Fajuyi, who was not the initial target.

It was rumoured that Lt. Colonel Fajuyi would probably have escaped, but he did not. That was incredible, extreme bravery, loyalty and sacrifice by a Yorubaman to his Igbo boss for which Nigerians regarded him as a martyr.

It is therefore challenging to all Nigerians by asking them for similar consciousness for the sake of Nigerian unity to ensure loyalty to the leadership irrespective of his/her ethnicity by putting Nigeria first in all their thoughts and actions. It can be done. Nigerians must remember that they can only get to the Promised Land quickly in unison, solidarity and togetherness in one strong, united and indivisible nation that all Nigerians can be proud of.

At this juncture, it is important to remind all Nigerians and the entire universe to practise the philosophy of nonviolence of Mahatma Gandhi of India and Dr. Martin Luther King Jr. of the USA in solving human perennial problems of imperfection. If the coupists of 1966 adopted a nonviolence solution to effect changes constitutionally, the course of Nigerian history today would have been different.

Humanity lives forever, and as such, when effecting a change, it must be unequivocal, nondiscriminatory, and done without being in a hurry, but with justice and fairplay and without favouritism. Any mistaken change can create scars and problems that may last for decades and be regretted throughout lifetime.

The counter coup brought into power, Yakubu Gowon, a Lieutenant Colonel as Military Head of State from 1966 to 1975. The new Head of State who originated from the Middle Belt and regarded as of Northern Nigerian origin, was later promoted General.

Appointment of a Head of State is a political appointment, which does not have to go to the most senior, most educated or most professionally qualified person. Hence, at the time of his appointment as Head of State, General Yakubu Gowon was understandably not the most senior or most qualified in the military just like all political appointments in the world. He was 33 years old, young, very charismatic and well liked by Nigerians generally.

At that crucial, insecure, confused and fearspreading time in Nigerian history, General Yakubu Gowon was the most acceptable to lead the country because his superior officers in the military disappeared and were not ready to take over the governance of the country out of sheer fear for their lives. The killings, arson, general confusion and anarchy during the time made their fears real to run for their lives.

The counter coup of July 1966, which was allegedly staged for retaliatory purposes, was deadly to the Easterners both military and civilians, especially those who were residents in the North. Events thereafter led to the Nigerian Civil War from 1967 to 1970, which resulted in the deaths and/or displacement of over two million innocent Nigerians. When two elephants or giants fight, it is the grass under their feet that suffers.

The irony of the Nigerian Civil War was that those who intransigently caused, started, prosecuted and prolonged the war unnecessarily escaped unhurt with their families, wives and children. Many innocent countrymen on both sides who were drafted to fight as well as civilians lost their lives. There were false assurances of invincibility boasted by the secessionists leadership to deceive their own innocent people to continue to fight. Nigerians should stop being fooled more than once.

Usually, elites call you out to create violence for their own selfish interests, and if it is failing, they leave you in the lurch. If they call you out to create violence, arson or fight unconstitutionally, why not let them put their own families and themselves in the foremost front first, so that they will not disappear and leave you there to suffer as soon as they cause the fight, massive disruptive action, riot or war.

Dialogue and compromise could have saved over a million innocent people from the horrors of Nigerian riots, arson, killings and war during and after the civil war. Elites usually incite people into violence, talk and fight war, war and war with others' children while their own children are safe, enjoying life, getting married and graduating in colleges and universities in Europe and America. Nigerians should stop being fooled.

Many publications deliberately equalized the philosophies and activism of nonviolence of Dr. Martin Luther King Jr. of USA and Mahatma Ghandi of India with the secessionist leadership campaign for war between 1967 and 1970. How can the proponents for change through nonviolence and those who preached war and went to war in order to effect human change, be said to be of equal standing?

Personalities who sought peaceful change and got it cannot be compared with others who sought change through war intransigently and got terrible collateral damages. The Nigerian secessionist war caused the loss of many lives and sufferings of more than one million innocent people and over two million were displaced, while Dr. Martin Luther King Jr., through preaching nonviolence, changed American minds of over 300 million people and his preachings improved the lots of many Americans of all races (black, white, brown, etc).

Dr. Martin Luther King Jr. not only foresaw but also told his people that he might not get to the Promised Land with them, that he might be killed, and he never abandoned his people like the secessionsist leadership did. He was assassinated as he predicted, and he died a honourable death in the process, but the whole USA honours him with a public holiday to demonstrate their thanks for his philosophy of human change without violence. His dream and preaching of nonviolence yielded the election of a Blackman, Barack Obama as President of the USA in 2008, symbolizing that with prayers to God/Allah, everything is possible.

On the other hand, the secessionist leadership of Eastern Nigeria abandoned their people in the lurch, deserted and fled with their wives, children and relatives. The war created millions of victims with considerable losses both personal and possessional and no gains except horrors of war, sufferings, hunger, destruction, displacement and setback of three years that left indelible scars of divisionism, distrust, disunity, insecurity and antagonism in the minds of the Igbos in particular and other wellmeaning Nigerians generally.

Warmongers who were making brisk money by buying and selling weapons to their people for war are completely different from preachers and activists of nonviolence. The world has always chosen preachers of peace and nonviolence and rewarded them with Nobel Prizes. Can all Igbo elites during the civil war (1967-1970) honestly raise their hands to God/Allah and swear by the Holy Books that they did not make money and did not get filthy rich at the expense of Ndigbo sufferings, and did not want the war to end because of lucrative returns from trading in weaponry until they fled? Were all the wounded South-Eastern fighters during the civil war rehabilitated by the South-Eastern States' succeeding governments? Is it true that some of the disabled soldiers still alive are begging for alms to eat and survive?

Examining above two scenarios critically, it is not appropriate to place the secessionist leadership on the same level of excellence with Dr. Martin Luther King Jr. of the USA and Mahatma Gandhi of India. Such value judgment was ridiculous, and made those concerned a laughing stock in the eyes of international community. The Igbos, who were the most enterprising Nigerians of all times, lost three years of their lives and suffered terribly, for which up till presently, some of them have not fully regained their rightful places.

During the civil war, the secessionist leadership humiliated their greatest national godfather, one of the greatest African leaders that ever lived, Dr. Nnamdi Azikiwe, the Owelle of Onitsha, the first President of Nigeria. They did not listen to him; they would not listen to Chief Obafemi Awolowo to resolve matters through dialogue and nonviolence; they would not listen to anybody. They disgraced and disowned Dr. Nnamdi Azikiwe and removed him as Chancellor of University of Nigeria, Nsukka, which he founded; but the Yorubas and the Northerners received him with greatest honour when he managed to cross to Nigeria during the war.

Events are unfolding that the Igbo leadership cannot speak with one voice. Their first place in Nigeria up till the beginning of the civil war is becoming the third place. They must settle down in unison and present a formidable front with one topmost leader that Nigeria can trust to be President. They are too divided.

Indiscriminate confrontation with Nigerian leadership is not the right strategy to achieve the presidency. Only regions acting as team players can produce the leader or President of Nigeria. Ndigbo should take that seriously and present their best candidates, men and women of timber and calibre and not fake dreamers to contest future presidential elections.

It is pertinent to quote from the speech of former President J.F. Kennedy of the USA when he was addressing the United Nations in 1961. He reminded the world, "Mankind should put an end to war or war will put an end to mankind." He added, "War is the greatest plague that can afflict humanity; it destroys states; it destroys families. Any scourge is preferable to it." Remember never to be fooled to be incited to create incidences of violence, anarchy or war.

It is observed that Yoruba race is difficult to be pushed around and manipulated to follow people sheepishly more than once as manifested in the 2003 presidential elections. That assertion is confirmable from what Chief Awolowo's Godson, alias Baba Kekere, the renowned, most charismatic, peoples' former Governor of Lagos State, Alhaji Lateef Jakande, said, "I think it was the Alliance for Democracy Party (AD) that really disposed itself of the South-West geopolitical zone and the people's Democratic Party simply cashed in and picked it up."

He explained that the AD party failed to address itself to five laudable cardinal programmes of free education at all levels, free health care, full employment, affordable housing and rural development on which the South-West was built and developed, thereby taking the people for granted, and so, the Yorubas left the AD party enmasse.

In effect, the Yorubas are not sheepish followers. In the same wise, individual Nigerians of all ethnicities should set themselves free from those who use undue influence on them to put them into trouble. Those who incite you to cause trouble cannot save you. When trouble comes, they will desert you as they have always done.

One could also borrow from the tact and diplomacy of ExPresident Obasanjo, which helped to avoid war with neighbouring brotherly African country, the Republic of Cameroon, over the decision of the International Court of Justice on October 10, 2002 regarding the land dispute between the two countries. ExPresident Olusegun Obasanjo mentioned that one of his greatest accomplishments was his decision not to go to war with Cameroon.

Attempts and actions to solve problems by confrontation, fight or war often create more problems than they are meant to solve. Usually, they leave indelible scars, which are never easy to forgive and forget. Nigerian problems are best solved through dialogue, compromise and nonviolence strategies.

ExPresident Obasanjo, through dialogue, diplomacy and compromise with Cameroonian President Biya made Africa and black people all over the world proud by avoiding any of the following war consequences:

(1) A war between Nigeria and Republic of Cameroon

would have caused enormous collateral damages in men, materials and property worth billions of dollars on both sides. Such losses would stagnate or regress the economic situation of both countries and jeopardize the muchdesired socio-economic and political prospects of the continent of Africa. War has disastrous multiplier effects, the end of which is not easily predictable.

(2) The war might become internationalized and assume uncontrolable dimensions with allies from Western and Eastern blocs lying on both sides to complicate the problems of African Union and brotherhood.

(3) There would be sales of weapons by the Western and Eastern powers to both brotherly African countries to kill and destroy themselves. Those Western and Eastern Blocs would make a lot of money and other economic benefits at the misery and expense of two warring brotherly neighbours. There would be unimaginable sufferings in both countries and refugees would infiltrate into other African nations to complicate the economic problems of their host countries.

(4) The war would put the two countries into substantial unsustainable debt and create problems of neocolonialism for the two brotherly nations.

(5) Money that could have been earmarked for economic growth and selfsufficiency would be wasted in purchasing weapons for destructive instead of productive purposes. Mercenaries would have a field day milking on the two neighbouring countries (Nigeria and Cameroon).

(6) War would generate fear, mistrust, hunger, refugee problems, disease, health and safety concerns, housing problems and confusion in warring countries and their allied nations. Africa does not need such socio-economic and political instability that would pervade the entire continent of Africa.

(7) Such war would be a disaster and disappointment for Africans.

(8) In the end, neither of the warring countries would gain

anything but regrets and losses to count with scars and bleedings that may never be forgotten.

There were serious efforts to avoid Nigerian Civil War 1967-1970 by the Federal Government of Nigeria but they all failed to meet the satisfaction of the Eastern Nigerian leadership who recalled all Easterners from other parts of Nigeria and got ready for war.

There was an 'Aburi Accord', which was not implemented. As a result of intransigence, false hope and unreliable claims of invincibility, the Eastern Nigerian leadership declared secession, bombed civilian targets in Lagos and overran the Mid-Western States. They committed terrible atrocities on Mid-Westerners, looted the banks there, removed all the money to their enclave and started to march to Lagos through Ore Junction in Ondo State, where their advance was halted by Federal Forces.

Eventually, the secessionist forces were driven out of Ore and Mid-Western States after severe battles for days during which many lives were lost on both sides. As a result of the money looted from Mid-Western banks, the Nigerian government quickly changed its currency notes to prevent the looters from cashing their loots from Nigerian banks and market.

The Honourable Federal Minister of Finance as at then was the sage, the immortal Chief Obafemi Awolowo who later resigned his appointment, thus becoming the first Nigerian to resign from a federal ministerial appointment that could have made him a multibillionaire with uncountable hidden foreign bank accounts through fraud and corruption, if he were the kind of "jeun, jeun," that is, eat indiscriminately and quench politicians and military men whom Nigeria had.

During the National Peace Forum held in the first week of March 2004 at the International Conference Centre, Abuja, Chief Dim Chukwuemeka Odumegwu Ojukwu, the secessionist leader (1967-70 civil war) was quoted to have said that he believed in one Nigeria. He complained about social injustice and canvassed for the application of justice, equity and fairness in the allocation of the nation's resources adding that the Igbo had no intention to quit the country. He asserted, "Peace must be based on the foundation of truth. In this search for peace, this project cannot afford any part opting out." He added, "Nigeria has everything to be the greatest country."

Chief Ojukwu's statement is classically remarkable and true, but the goal is best achieved through nonviolence, tolerance, cooperation, diplomacy, conciliation, equity, justice and fairplay. The legacy to posterity should be one united, indivisible, peaceful, politically stable and economically prosperous Nigeria.

The presidency must be commended for organizing the National Peace Forum attended by ExPresident Obasanjo, former President Alhaji Shehu Shagari, Chief Ojukwu, Chief Ernest Shonekan, former Head of National Interim Government; Chief Anthony Enahoro, the Sultan of Sokoto, Alhaji Muhammadu Maccido and some other distinguished Nigerians who honestly talked to ensure peace reigned supreme in the country.

Chief Ojukwu, the entire Igbo ethnicity and all right thinking Nigerians had cause to be angry, horrified, apprehensive, feel unsafe and paranoid because of the enormity of the retaliatory killing spree and arsonic actions committed by Northerners against the Igbos soon after July 29, 1966. The retaliation by the Northerners far outweighed what the young Igbo military officers did during their coup d'etat of January 15, 1966. The offensive later culminated into the civil war of 1967-70. The January 15, 1966 coup d'etat by Igbos was avoidable; the civil war was also avoidable. Two wrongs do not make a right.

Unfortunately, the situation degenerated into ethno-religious conflict, which became more deadly and difficult to contain because of incitement from both major religious groups – Muslims and Christians. Why has it been possible for any individuals or groups to directly or indirectly, physically cause, incite or plan ethno-religious and political disturbances, which have resulted in killings and arson since 1966 up to date with impunity?

The Nigerian police should be well equipped to have sophistication and capability to video tape all acts of violence to be able to identify, hunt down, catch, successfully prosecute and convict those who commit arson and killings during riots no matter who they are and no matter how long it takes to bring them to justice one by one.

Whoever has taken part directly and/or indirectly to commit arson and killings during sociopolitical and ethno-religious upheaval will repeat it again and again if not caught and brought to justice in the first instance. What about politicians who keep and finance thugs for their own agenda? When will that stop?

In a new Nigeria, the pattern must change. There must be law and order. Whoever commits the crime must serve appropriate sentence as regulated by law. For once, the Plateau State that suffered a state of emergency for six months served as a serious warning to Kano State, Lagos State, Anambra State, Delta State and others, which were prone to disturbances. Law and order must prevail throughout the country.

If the secessionist leaders were as conciliatory in 1966 and 1967 as Chief Ojukwu was during the National Peace Forum of March 2004, the civil war would have been avoided and the deaths and sufferings of the victims of the war would not have occurred. Also, if there were no seniority struggle between Yakubu Gowon, the Head of State and Odumegwu Ojukwu, the secessionist leader who was not prepared to take orders from Gowon whom he considered his junior colleague in the military, perhaps the civil war would have been avoided.

When the fate of the country fell into the hands of two young military officers at about thirty-five years of age, Gowon and Ojukwu, who were at opposite ends of the continuum pulling the country in opposite directions with elders cut off and unable to rescue the country, one knows that it was only God/Allah that spared Nigeria.

Chief Obafemi Awolowo, the Federal Finance Minister resigned from Gowon's cabinet while Dr. Nnamdi Azikiwe managed to get out of the secessionist enclave and came to Nigerian side. Both men who were fathers and architects of Nigerian independence and statehood must have been frustrated about the way both young military men were riding the country and perhaps never listened to elders.

Personal interest should have given way to national interest to place the country on the right course. Nigerians must be full of prayers never to have a repetition of the events that threw the country into abyss and darkness for four decades.

The coup d'etat of January 15, 1966 was totally wrong. The retaliatory coup on July 29, 1966 which resorted to the killings of innocent Igbos in the north was too much, equally wrong and condemnable. The calling back home of the Igbos from all over the country to the Eastern region was for their safety, and nobody should blame Chief Ojukwu for that, but praise him. The declaration of secession was not the best alternative solution to the problem. The decision was misguided and wrong.

A better deal that ensured full reparations could have been negotiated to avoid the civil war (1967-1970), which claimed over two million displaced and/or killed victims. The right diplomacy, conciliation and compromise could have fetched benefits for the Igbos and other ethnicities that died or suffered during the civil war. Nigerians must be guided to know that two wrongs do not make a right, and why not withdraw from a fight or stop it when it is not beneficial or when your defeat is glaring! It is not wise to continue a losing battle.

To lead Nigeria, there must be serious consideration for maturity, sound academic or professional education, relevant resource management experience, decency, transparency, integrity and other leadership qualities and exemplariness.

Young military officers incessantly staged coups d'etat to rule Nigeria and make it better, but they made it worse. Proverbially, if a young person decides to act as leader or elder, his/her age, inexperience and level of maturity may act as impediment for his/her success. So, the young Nigerians who aspire to be president should sit down and learn first, gain the level of education, experience and maturity needed. Money or wealth does not make a successful Nigerian President or leaders. Thousands of 'Honourary Doctoral University Degrees' will not be sufficient to lead Nigeria successfully.

ExGovernor Kalu of Abia State boasted repeatedly to meet other presidential aspirants dollar for dollar in 2007 to secure his nomination. By using party delegates, how would he be able to stop corruption if he became president? To be a successful president, one must know right from wrong, talk and act presidential and close any foreign bank account that offends against the Nigerian constitution. Nigeria cannot have a controversial person as president or vice president. Nigerians should stop selling their conscience for bribes from politicians who give them money with the left hand and take it back in many folds corruptly with the right hand.

Unfortunately and regrettably, the Nigerian Civil War coupled with the suffering of victims was unduly prolonged as confirmed by Lt. Colonel Phillip Effiong, the General Officer Commanding the secessionist army who later became the Administrator of the secessionist enclave on January 10, 1970 when Chief Ojukwu fled to Cote d'Ivoire.

Lt. Colonel Phillip Effiong who was promoted General by the secessionist army authorities said, "I am also convinced that the suffering of our people must be brought to an end. Our people are now disillusioned and those elements of the old regime, which have made negotiations and reconciliation impossible, have voluntarily removed themselves from our midst. I have therefore instructed an orderly disengagement of troops. I urge on General Gowon, in the name of humanity, to order his troops to pause while an armistice is negotiated, in order to avoid the mass suffering caused by the movement of population."

He added, "We have always believed that our differences with Nigeria should be settled by peaceful negotiation." He sent a delegation to the Nigerian government to negotiate peace on the basis of Organization of African Unity (OAU) resolution, which the secessionists' leadership previously flouted. It is worthy to consider and learn from the examples of stakeholders of Plateau State, the Home of Peace and Tourism, which passed through six months of state of emergency.

It is hoped that the surviving secessionist leadership will tell the truth to the young Igbos born after 1960. It was never that the Igbos were hated by the Yorubas or the Hausas as they are made to believe wrongly, but that Igbo young military officers took up weapons and killed Yoruba and Hausa military and civilian leaders as a result of their inordinate ambition to rule Nigeria, while they shielded and protected their own Igbo leaders who included Dr. Azikiwe, Dr. Okpara, General Aguiyi Ironsi, Chief Ojukwu and many others.

The simple hypothetical question is, "When people from other tribes wake up, plan, assassinate leaders of other tribes, protect their own ethnic leadership, and they continue to boast about what they do and how they do it on newspaper front pages as heroes, what does any reasonable person think will be the consequences in Nigerian nation that is tribal conscious? That was what Nigeria witnessed nationally for the first time in Nigerian history on January 15, 1966. Before then, the Igbos, Hausas and Yorubas moved together and one could hardly notice any difference. The coup plotters of January 15, 1966 and their collaborators were the architects of Nigeria's misfortunes since 1966 up till present time.

Before January 1966, Dr. Nnamdi Azikiwe won many parliamentary elections in Yoruba heartland. He was even more respected in Yorubaland than any of Yoruba leaders including Chief Obafemi Awolowo. There was nothing the Igbos wanted at that time which they never got.

Unfortunately, the coupists of January 15, 1966 who later transitioned into the secessionist enclave for fear of continued reprisals just destroyed all the great things and respect for the Igbos at that time. After the first coup, hardly any Igboman has won elections outside the Igbo heartland like Zik of Africa? Zik had supporters in all Nigerian constituencies. He represented the greatest among Nigerian nationalists.

One of the most glorious days for Nigeria during the civil war was when the Owelle of Onitsha, Dr. Nnamdi Azikiwe, an Igboman, first President of the Federal Republic of Nigeria, left the eastern enclave, abandoned the secessionists and crossed over to Nigeria. He was met with overwhelming ovation and enthusiasm. The shouts of Zik of Africa rended the air unabatingly at the airport of disembarkation and all over Nigeria. There was joy everywhere in Nigeria.

It was a misnomer to say or feel that Nigerians did not love the Igbos who were regarded as some of the most enterprising people in the country. The cause of the biggest problem for Nigerian unity was the Ifeajuna/ Nzeogwu coup of January 15, 1966, which killed northern and western leaders but spared those from the east. That was a terrible pill for any Northern or Western Nigerian to swallow because each Nigerian ethnicity has its pride to protect. Above all, the way the coupists were handled suggested a pat on their backs by Aguiyi Ironsi's government and eastern leaders for a job well done that resulted in chain reactions of retaliations by the Northerners.

In anybody's humble and reasonable assessment, if the January 15, 1966 coup did not happen the way it did, Nigeria's course of history would be different and devoid of so much suspicion, anger, divisionism tendencies and disunity among the general population and the leadership of Nigeria. The war was ended in the spirit of 'no victor, no vanquished' to ensure the success of the process of reconciliation, rehabilitation and reconstruction. The Nigerian leadership declaration of general amnesty coupled with the payment of all benefits to the Igbos was magnanimous. All Nigerians should forget and forgive, move on and stand in brotherhood.

Borrowing from Chief Joshua Dariye, ExGovernor of Plateau State after reinstatement from six months state of emergency, he appealed to his people to rally round, forgive one another and work together, He explained, "The most important thing every Plateau man must say today is, 'I am sorry.' All of us must forgive and forget unconditionally. Government comes and government goes, but we should not destroy Plateau State, our baby. The state is greater than all of us." In the same vein, Nigerians should

forgive and forget; they should not destroy Nigeria, their country, their fatherland, and their native land. Nigeria is greater than any or all Nigerians put together.

What did the coup d'etat of January 15, 1966 accomplish besides bad blood, mistrust, hatred, suffering, death and divisionism? The first coup collaborators who are still alive should tell Nigerians about the benefit of the January 15, 1966 coup. The change, which they wanted to make, should have been bloodless and constitutional. The coup was barbaric and condemnable.

General Yakubu Gowon (retired) as Head of State was the people's darling leader, especially during the 'Udoji Salaries Award' that paid workers substantial arrears of salaries. During his tenure, petroleum was discovered in commercial quantities and Nigeria became a member of the Organization of Petroleum Exporting Countries (OPEC) in 1971. There was a popular saying then, "There are not many bad leaders, just advisers." The statement as well as its origin was not explained. General Gowon was toppled in July 1975 in a bloodless coup when he was attending OAU meeting in Kampala, Uganda and was succeeded by General Murtala Mohammed, his Northern kinsman.

One greatest thing that is unique about the Igbos and the Yorubas is that they will think twice before they overthrow their kinsmen. While in Britain, General Gowon occupied himself with doctoral degree studies and became the first Nigerian Head of State to have acquired the doctoral degree discipline under classroom setting. All Nigerians doff their hats for Dr. Yakubu Gowon who passed through and fulfilled the requirements of doctoral academic discipline in Public Administration.

Remarkably, General Yakubu Gowon created twelve (12) states to reduce feelings of domination, occupation and exploitation of minorities by the majority. The strategy helped to win and end the war by separating the South-South from Eastern Region, and it encouraged selfdevelopment.

General Murtala Mohammed as Head of State, assisted by General Olusegun Obasanjo, demobilized the military, trimmed down the civil service, created new states and ensured strict discipline within the civil service, the parastatals and other government agencies. Within his short period of tenure, General Murtala Mohammed restored sanity within the government public service system.

It was rumoured that he would go in disguise to government offices and parastatals as mystery shopper to detect idle workers and officers who were not fully productive as well as those who had poor customer service. Such workers and officers were subjected to immediate retirement from the public service.

It was said that he would join customer lines at post offices without being detected to identify postal clerks whose customer services were below standard. Clerks performing below expectations were discharged on the spot. He retired a lot of public officers for various offences during his short reign. Workers and management feared him, and they all straightened up in all nooks and corners of Nigeria. Idleness was gone; there was punctuality and regular attendance at work; and there was improved responsiveness in government services.

Nobody was ever sure of his next place of visit, so everybody worked normally as he or she should do. It was difficult then for public officers to be idle or absent from work without any prior, proven and genuine authorization. The use of fake medical reports to cover absences at work, which was very common, stopped. He properly cleaned the public service and set standards, which were strictly followed until he was assassinated in February 1976.

General Murtala Mohammed was assassinated by his own Northern kinsmen in the military who were tried and convicted by the military tribunal and later executed by the Supreme Military Council. Interestingly, the first chairman of the military tribunal was alleged to be one of the ringleaders of the coupists as revealed by the main suspect.

Hence, the tribunal chairman was removed, replaced, tried, convicted and executed.

If Aguiyi Ironsi, Head of State (January 15 to July 29, 1966) had prosecuted and sentenced his kinsmen who staged the January 1966 coup as General Obasanjo did in 1976, Nigerian history today would have been different. Perhaps there would have been no retaliatory coup of July 29, 1966, no mass killings of the Igbos in the North, no secession, no civil war and no dictatorships with attendant dehumanizations that plagued Nigeria for four decades. All those evils that befell Nigeria might have been avoided, deterred or minimized.

General Mohammed was succeeded by his deputy Lieutenant General Olusegun Obasanjo (1976-1979), who later became Fourth Republic civilian President of the Federal Republic of Nigeria from May 29, 1999 to May 28, 2007 for two terms of four years each. He concentrated on preparing the nation for civilian administration in accordance with a draft constitution which was promulgated in 1979.

He supervised the general election of 1979, which ushered in the Second Republic. The presidential election of 1979 ended controversially with a choice between Alhaji Shehu Shagari, a Northerner and Muslim on one hand, and on the other hand was Chief Obafemi Awolowo, a Westerner and a Christian of the same Ogun State and religion like the Head of State, General Olusegun Obasanjo.

Despite the fact that Chief Obafemi Awolowo and General Obasanjo, the Head of State were of the same ethnicity and practised the same Christian religion, General Obasanjo relinquished the rein of government to Alhaji Shehu Shagari, a Northerner and a Muslim. Any other Head of State who was tribalistic or a religiously discriminatory bigot would have found excuses to deny Alhaji Shehu Shagari the presidency.

If confronted with the same situation as Head of State, only God/Allah knows what a Northerner or Easterner would have done differently from what General Obasanjo, a Westerner and Christian, did by handing over power to a Northerner in 1979. General Obasanjo put Nigeria first above his ethno-religious and regional considerations. How many Hausas and Igbos could be just and fair to do what this Yorubaman, General Obasanjo, did for Nigerian unity? That is food for thought for all Nigerians.

Fourteen years later in 1993, a Yorubaman (Westerner) won election to the presidency when a Northerner was Military Head of State. In that case, the election was annulled and an Interim Administrator was appointed to take over. The Westerner, Chief Abiola who won the presidential election, was later imprisoned, and he died in prison suspiciously on the day he was scheduled to be released, July 7, 1998. That was one of the greatest disservices and cruelty to humanity and Yorubas in particular.

Those who conspired to commit such abomination should seek God/Allah's eternal forgiveness. It was too sad. It was a collective responsibility, and all those involved should atone and be forgiven for the sake of one Nigeria and her redemption, which Chief Moshood Abiola stood for throughout his lifetime. He was the greatest philanthropist that ever lived. May his soul rest in perfect peace (amen).

According to Chief Alex Akinyele in Daily Champion News of Tuesday, August 30, 2005, the June 12, 1993 presidential election annulment was reluctantly carried out by General Babangida, Head of State (1985-1993). The cancellation was allegedly influenced irresistibly by Yoruba Monarchs, Emirs, the Military and Clerics. The excuses are untenable.

Did any of those who participated directly and/or indirectly in the annulment regret the events that followed and take responsibility for the blood of the dead, the sufferings of the imprisoned, the human rights violations, the widespread corruption, Nigeria's pariah status and her ostracization by the world community from 1993 to 1998? Nigerians should say, "Never again." Let us forgive and forget and move forward. The period was a time of malevolent dictatorship, sadism, fear and state terrorism for Nigeria.

When will the elite Nigerians start to think about themselves more as Nigerians as well as who is best for Nigerians to be president instead of emphasizing their ethnic or regional nationalities or religious affiliation? A Nigerian's place of birth should not act as the limitation for his or her ability to vie for the exalted office of president if he/she is qualified. The legislature should pass a nondiscrimination law to stop discriminatory acts in Nigeria.

General Obasanjo could have found excuses to cancel the result of the 1979 election, appoint an interim administrator or install Chief

Obafemi Awolowo, a Yorubaman with impunity without caring about the feelings of the people. He never applied any of those wrong solutions but he put Nigeria first and did the right thing unlike what happened on June 23, 1993.

That was the second greatest sacrifice a Yorubaman did for Nigeria in the spirit of one Nigeria by putting Nigeria above his ethnicity interest. The first greatest sacrifice by a Yorubaman was when the former governor of Western Region, Lt. Colonel Adekunle Fajuyi gave up his life while trying to protect that of former Head of State, General Aguiyi Ironsi, an Igboman. Nigerians must do a rethinking in the best interest of one Nigeria and be their brothers' keepers irrespective of differences in ethnicity, religion or political affiliation.

The 1979 national election saw Alhaji Shehu Shagari as victor with a dispute, which was decided by the court. Former Attorney General of the Federal Republic of Nigeria, Richard Akinjide (SAN), a legal luminary, used the twothirds trump card in the Supreme Court and won the case for Alhaji Shehu Shagari.

Nigeria being a big country, there will usually be one dispute or the other, but mature minds will always prevail. Hence, aggrieved parties should always follow due process and rule of law to solve their disputes constitutionally.

Alhaji Shehu Shagari was Second Republic President of Nigeria from 1979 to 1983. During his reign as Nigerian President, he ran the presidency through a coalition type of government. He was said to be kind and well loved by the people for his simplicity and charisma.

One of the most vocal or loquacious honourable ministers of Shagari Administration was the Minister of Transport, Alhaji Umaru Dikko who was alleged to have said that the Nigerian people were not hungry because nobody had started to pick food from dumpsters during Nigeria's biting economic recession.

The alleged statement made everybody angry, but the former minister denied it twenty years later in 2003 when he had the opportunity to refer to it. He said that the Nigerian press misquoted him. Since leaving London for Nigeria, Alhaji Umaru Dikko had been able to serve Nigeria honourably in exalted positions of elder statesmen with distinction. He was a lead delegate to the National Political Reform Conference (NPRC) of February to July 2005.

The Enugu State former Governor, Dr. Chimaroke Nnamani was attributed to have said the following about Second Republic President, Alhaji Shehu Shagari, Turakin Sokoto, "You are an exemplary figure and represent a clear subjugation to the Will of God. You represent nonaggressive pursuit of political power. You represent man surrendering to the destiny and the Will of God. You represent the good in our society which we want back."

After winning the presidential election in 1983 to begin his second term in office, Alhaji Shehu Shagari was toppled by his kinsman in the military, Major General Muhammadu Buhari, the presidential candidate of the ANPP during the 2003 and 2007 presidential elections. He overtrusted his General Officer Commanding (GOC) who toppled him. He could have preempted the coup d'etat if he had acted on some suspicious movements in the military barracks, which had been leaked to him. Similar mistakes of overtrusting cost General Aguiyi Ironsi his life on July 29, 1966. If the coups d'etat were preempted, Nigerian history would be different today.

On December 31, 1983 General Buhari became the Head of State after toppling Alhaji Shehu Shagari thus putting an end to the Second Republic. The Nigerian constitution was suspended and the political appointees of Alhaji Shehu Shagari as well as many politicians were placed in prison custody.

General Buhari fought corruption, fraudulence and money laundering. He operated a government of zero tolerance for foreign exchange malpractices and seriously restricted importation of luxury goods and services. General Buhari and his Deputy, General Tunde Idiagbon brought economic and financial criminals under their feet and put terrible fears in their faces. Politicians were dumped into prisons until they proved their assets and returned their ill-gotten gains.

The politicians and activists of 1999-2008 who portrayed themselves bold, talking and critical of every direction of government democratic dispensation had their mouths shut like packs of cowards or as a consequence, were placed in incarceration indefinitely and forgotten there. There was needed socio-economic and political discipline and accountability throughout all nooks and corners of the country, and out of sheer fears for punishment, all acts of criminality were stopped or became minimal.

If progressive activists like former Kaduna State Governor, Balarabe Musa was completely contained, silenced, incarcerated and could not utter a word, who else could? If elder statesman Alhaji Umaru Dikko, former Transportation Minister (1979-1983) was kidnapped in London (UK), drugged, crated and was about to be bundled into a waiting Nigerian aircraft to be delivered to General Buhari in Nigeria as cargo, who else would not fear? It was a reign of terror against corrupt politicians and general indiscipline.

Professor Tam DavidWest, a member of Buhari Administration, was full of praises for Buhari's accomplishments and lately saw nothing good in Nigerian tertiary institutions and their products. Where was his empathy with good value judgment? Many of his outbursts are questionable.

It was very difficult then to openly criticize Buhari Administration of double standard in the handling of fifty-three loaded boxes allegedly seized by the Department of Customs that were ordered released and delivered to the owner in Northwestern Nigeria allegedly without paying applicable customs duties. At that time, people travelling into the country with more that two boxes were usually questioned at the ports of arrival for infringing the law restricting importation of goods and for foreign exchange control violations.

In a relentless effort to make politicians accountable, Buhari Administration pursued the former Minister of Transportation, Alhaji Umaru Dikko to London where he fled and took refuge after the military takeover of Shagari Administration. Buhari Administration was alleged to have planned and executed the kidnapping, drugging and crating of Alhaji Umaru Dikko, former Minister of Transport, in order to bring him to Nigeria to face trial for alleged corrupt practices.

However, the attempt failed because British Security Agents acting on a tipoff stormed the aircraft at Stansted Airport, England that was to bring Alhaji Dikko to Nigeria. The situation created frosty relations between Nigeria and Great Britain for some years because the British government regarded the kidnapping, drugging and crating of Alhaji Umaru Dikko as an act of international terrorism committed on British soil by Nigerian military government, which the British government regarded as illegitimate, because it was not democratic but military and dictatorial.

Buhari Administration was criticized for interfering with the Hajj Operations, which aroused the displeasure of the Muslims. Above all, Buhari Administration nurtured good intentions to get rid of corrupt practices in Nigeria in order to be able to utilize Nigeria's available resources for sustainable development in the best interest of Nigeria.

Politics should not be a 'do or die game.' In politics there are no permanent enemies but permanent interests. It seems as if General Buhari looks too fine and honest but bitter to be a successful professional politician under democratic dispensation because politics is said to be dirty and he is not.

Chief Obafemi Awolowo, the political archrival of Alhaji Shehu Shagari was granted the highest Nigerian honour award by Shagari Administration under similar situation as existed between General Buhari and ExPresident Obasanjo, but Chief Awolowo took his award with dignity while General Buhari rejected it and refused to attend the award ceremony. The award and honour turned down by General Buhari belonged to Nigeria and was from Nigerians and not any individual leadership.

It is hoped that in the choice of future leaders for Nigeria, there will be serious consideration for leadership qualities such as maturity, experience, temperament, accessibility, character, humility, charisma, socio-economic and political savvy and sagacity. Other necessary qualities include: sound moral judgment and academic and professional education which can be utilized quickly by the leader to get the nation out of the woods during difficult times.

The criterion of being a military officer as the only qualification for consideration to be president cannot fully help the democratic experiment in Nigeria's quest for the right leadership that will lead the nation to the Promised Land. Military training alone may not fully prepare any officer for desired democratic leadership. They are two different areas – militarism, democracy.

Military professionalism provides the right discipline to be the best president, but there must be additional orientation toward democratic best practices and experience, coupled with sound education and training in human and financial resources management, and best democratic leadership practices.

There is always retributive justice administered by God/Allah for what people do. When General Buhari overthrew the government of his kinsman Alhaji Shehu Shagari, he could not know that he himself would be overthrown by his own kinsman, General Babangida in 1985 within twenty months. There are Yoruba proverbs, which say, "When you point your finger at someone, the remaining four fingers will be pointing at you, and when you throw a ball at the wall, it bounces back at you." Whatever a person does, rightly or wrongly, against his fellow man, there is always a payback by God/Allah.

No matter how anyone criticizes Buhari's Administration as a dictator, he should be scored highly for trampling fraudulent and corrupt politicians as well as government functionaries under feet. He put them in incarceration indefinitely until they disgorged their loot. He also pursued those who ran overseas and succeeded in putting Shagari's Minister of Transport, Alhaji Umaru Dikko, in a cage to be transported home from London to come and answer to corruption charges. The kidnapping was foiled at Stansted Airport.

Under democratic setting, General Buhari will not be able to do all that he did in dictatorial governance. Presently, Nigerians are well travelled, better educated and would not tolerate any violation of their human rights. A leader that will succeed in Nigeria under democratic experiment must have the right temperament to accept and endure human imperfections and press/media attacks. Whoever is interested to become President of Nigeria should take note that governance under a democracy is more difficult than under a military or dictatorial setting.

In August 1985, General Buhari was overthrown by his kinsman, General Ibrahim Badamosi Babangida who had the vision of preparing the country for civilian administration.

The Babangida Administration was allegedly not well disposed to newspaper editors who were critical of the administration. The conflict was so pronounced to the extent that the newspaper editors accused the government of complicity in the assassination of Mr. Dele Giwa, one of the newspaper editors with a letter bomb. The problem still remains unresolved up till today.

In 1989, Babangida Administration adopted a constitution that was fashioned in the United States Federal System for transition to democratic government. The 1989 constitution provided for a president, a bicameral legislature and an independent judiciary.

Two parties, the Republican National Convention and the Social Democratic Party emerged, and a presidential election, which saw Chief Moshood Abiola a Yorubaman as winner, was annulled by Babangida Administration on June 23, 1993. Later, Babangida Administration ended after the installation of an interim administration in 1993 headed by Chief Ernest Shonekan.

Unfortunately, the interim administration was uprooted and hijacked by General Sani Abacha who installed himself as Military Head of State of Nigeria. General Babangida must have been under serious pressure and threats to quit when he did. The overall decision generated national calamities. The events that followed should never again be allowed in Nigeria.

On Friday, July 22, 2005 while responding to Vanguard reporter's question, General Babangida exclaimed that Dele Giwa's death was tragic and unfortunate but that those who were linking his regime with it were operating from two regrettable perspectives – ignorance and mischief. He explained that the former Deputy Director of State Security Service, BrigadierGeneral A. K. Togun (rtd.) revealed persistent efforts of security agents to probe the letter bomb episode but encountered frustrating noncooperation from those whose contributions were crucial to the investigation.

He added that the Pastor Chris Omeben, exDeputy InspectorGeneral of Police, a man of God, who handled the investigation, highlighted the frustrations encountered in his book that revealed the whole truth about the investigations conducted on Dele Giwa's death.

He declared that it was inappropriate to accuse leaders of governments of all things that happened during their regimes. He queried the sanity of blaming every sudden and unnatural death on the government in power. He reiterated that it was idiotic to think that because there was a government in place, it must know about all such deaths. He explained that his administration appreciated the deep national passion elicited by the death of Dele Giwa and offered to help in the burial arrangements, but his regime's gesture was rebuffed by those concerned.

General Sani Abacha ruled the country from 1993 to 1998. He was described as pathologically ruthless, cruel and brutal, an apotheosis of evil, human rights abuser and nemesis of dictatorship. He was said to be usually darkgoggled and rarely or never smiling.

Some of his aides and advisers revealed at his death that they operated within the whims and caprices of their boss, General Sani Abacha. When General Abacha died on June 8, 1998 unexpectedly, it was revealed that people jubilated and danced in the streets proclaiming, "Never again should the dark days of Abacha ever return; never again should the years of the locusts ever return."

What is equally disturbing is the billions of Nigerian government money of about $5 billion that General Abacha was alleged to have stashed away in foreign private bank accounts. Such money could have been utilized for investment purposes to establish small and medium scale industries in Nigeria to generate employment and thereby create economic stabilization, enhance the standard of living and extend the life expectancy of Nigerians.

Regrettably, some of Abacha's advisers, aides, associates and friends who rejoiced at his death, curried his favours when he was alive, and they used him to intimidate and exterminate their own opponents. They showered false praise on him out of sheer hypocrisy, and they deceived him by saying that they wanted him to stay on in office and become an elected civilian president.

They told him that he was the best and that he was doing a good job when Nigerians were really suffering, dying of human rights abuses, hunger, poverty and assassination for opposing the maladministration of his dictatorship. As soon as his death was officially announced, those who were benefiting from his dictatorship changed gear and joined the new government to escape reprisals from Nigerians.

During the regime of General Gowon, there was a popular saying, "There are not many bad leaders, just advisers." General Sani Abacha did not do all those wrong things by himself, but when he died, most aides, advisers and friends who assisted him, advised him, dined and wined with him and carried out all the nefarious operations which were adjudged to be human rights violations, disowned him and evaporated as if they were never accomplices.

General Sani Abacha did not carry all the stolen government money to foreign private bank accounts by himself, and no close aide or adviser complained during his lifetime. His closest advisers used him selfishly and misled him for their personal benefits. Soon after his death was announced, many of his cronies denounced him and joined the government that succeeded him.

In one of the publications of *Nigeria Today* in 2000, an eminent Economics Professor Aluko was quoted to have said that General Sani Abacha was misunderstood. The Professor was the Chairman, National Economic Intelligence Committee during Abacha regime. He described General Abacha as a disciplined 'large-hearted' leader who was misunderstood by some members of the elites.

He was reported to have confessed that he had pretty 'bad impressions' of Abacha which stemmed from the initial impressions he formed of the army and the police soon after leaving Oxford University. He said that his impressions changed soon after interaction with General Sani Abacha.

He commended General Abacha as the most disciplined who travelled out and returned same day. He said that he was surprised by Abacha's intellect and curiosity. He added that Abacha could take one on some minute details discussed a few years back which could have escaped some other persons dealing with such vast subjects. What a great appraisal of one's boss!

As Chairman, National Economic Intelligence Committee, what did he know about the truth or falsehood of Abacha stashing $5 billion of Nigeria's money in his private bank accounts overseas as well as the high level of economic and financial crimes, fraud, corruption and human rights violations which resulted in the ostracization of Nigeria by the Comity of Nations?

What valuable advisement was given to save Nigeria from economic and financial maladministration and human rights abuses which so embarrassed the whole world to the extent that the Comity of Nations sanctioned and ostracized Nigeria? What did the advisers and Abacha's close aides know that they were not telling the world? Was everybody else in the world wrong about Abacha regime except his government officials, advisers, aides, relatives and friends? Did Professor Aluko not smell any rat?

In contrast to what above adviser said about General Abacha, he was alleged to have complained that Obasanjo's Administration operated a bastardized economy, which was being left in the hands of foreigners at the expense and detriment of Nigerians.

It was added that Professor Aluko lambasted the government at all levels for being wasteful and corrupt and that government officials were junketing around the world like locusts. Is the pot calling kettle black or people in glass houses throwing stones?

One thing that is seriously disturbing is that Nigerian activists, critics, militants, academicians and professionals who were appointed to political offices in order to straighten up what they used to criticize, did not perform better than those officials whom they used to condemn in spite of their academics and professionalism which Nigerians thought would enable them to make a difference.

It is human to protect one's job and be loyal to one's boss, but that does not mean that it would be right for government officials or advisers not to tell the country all about what they knew and advised against when they were in advisory capacity to the government, especially if things went so bad as they were under General Abacha.

If General Abacha travelled out and returned the same day for which he was allegedly commended, how did he open up all the foreign bank accounts, and did all the money laundering by himself without the knowledge and help of his aides? He could not have stashed $5 billion in foreign private bank accounts without any of his closest associates' assistance.

Academics or professionalism is supposed to train, test and certify a person as having attained reasonable, acceptable and high level of perfection, sensitivity and value judgment. How logical is it to hypothesize, "There are not many bad leaders but bad advisers with bad advisement."

If the leader, president or head of state is bad and is impervious to good advice, a good adviser quits for everybody to know that the problem is the Head of State or the President that is bad and not taking good advice. If advisers continue to quit, the bad President or Head of State will think twice and change direction in the best interest of the country.

According to rumours, the former Minister of Finance, Mrs. (Dr.) Ngozi Okonjo-Iweala recommended some reorganization and rationalization in her ministry in order to curb economic and financial crimes as well as stop excessive deficit budgeting, its implementation and manipulation. It was added that she could have resigned if she was not taken seriously by the presidency. As soon as she was redeployed to become the Minister of Foreign Affairs, she quitted.

Advisers are supposed to be technical experts and professionals in their own fields, and if they cannot be heard or able to influence policy decisions and their implementation, why stay on? What is the incentive for advisers to stay in office if policy decisions and their execution are different from their expert advisement?

If Chief Obafemi Awolowo quitted as Commissioner of Finance during Gowon regime, any adviser, aide or government functionary of merit should be able to quit when dissatisfied during Abacha regime. Why stay in office and pretend nothing is wrong? Is it, "If you can't beat them, join them?" In Nigeria that is undergoing reforms and baptism, there is no room for acquiescence, connivance and conspiracy to commit economic and financial crimes with impunity as witnessed between 1966 and 1999.

The challenge to all advisers and other top officials during General Sani Abacha's regime was for them to tell Nigerians that they did not smell any rat, that everything was fine and that the whole world was lying about the misdeeds of Abacha regime. The world has heard that Abacha was large-hearted and misunderstood, but misunderstood about what?

In the *Daily Independence* publication of November 25, 2003, it was reported that Alhaji Abubakar who was detained in the USA for allegedly conspiring with Abacha's son to loot public funds had agreed to transfer about $300 million (40,566 billion naira) to the coffers of Nigerian Government from foreign account.

Also, the former Petroleum Minister, Mr. Dan Danzia Etete under General Abacha was allegedly being investigated for money laundering of $100m, $20m, $19m, 5.5m Dutch marks, $17.5m, 1.1m francs and $68m respectively. It was reported that he confirmed that he held the accounts in Geneva, Switzerland with the approval of his boss (Abacha) for certain government operations which he believed would not be fair to disclose.

The number of prominent Nigerians killed and/or imprisoned and the amount of money, allegedly classified as part of Abacha's loot, recovered from foreign banks and returned to Nigerian government was substantial evidence to support the world's outcry that Abacha's regime was not large-hearted, but corrupt and abusive of human rights.

In *This Day News* of March 10, 2004, the former Minister of Transport in General Abacha's regime, Chief Ebenezer Babatope, was quoted to have regretted his participation in the government of General Abacha whom he described as the 'maximum ruler' between 1993 and 1998. He was also quoted to have said, "I will carry the responsibility of participating in that government to my grave."

Chief Babatope was said to have agreed that there was repression everywhere and added that there was grand sadism in Abacha's administration. The whole world saw it and declared Nigeria a pariah state and ostracized Nigeria. Yet, some previously trusted Nigerians and Abacha's advisers who were benefiting from other's sufferings did not see anything wrong in Abacha regime.

In the *Sunday Punch* of March 7, 2004, it was reported that General Shehu Musa Yar'Adua, former Chief of Army Staff, Supreme Headquarters confirmed in his prison notes that HIV/AIDS virus was injected into his body with his hands tied to his back by Abacha's Chief Medical Personnel while Abacha's Chief Security Officer allegedly supervised the injection activity.

That horrifying experience of forcefully injecting General Shehu Musa Yar'Adua with a deadly virus which was infectious, contagious and deadly was just one of many criminal cases of human rights violations during Abacha's dictatorial regime.

What about the assassination of Alhaja Kudirat Abiola and the attempted murders of Senator Adesanya and Chief Ibru by Abacha's military killer squad? Were those incidents secret to all advisers, aides and associates of Abacha's Administration? Why did they not condemn or speak out about such evil acts? Is that large-heartedness according to Professor Aluko?

This Day News of March 26, 2004 published a global corruption report released by Transparency International which placed former Nigerian Military Head of State, General Sani Abacha as the fourth most corrupt leader in contemporary world history with $5 billion of Nigerian money, stolen and stashed away in foreign banks.

The report named former President Suharto of Indonesia as first with between $15 billion and $35 billion stolen; then Ferdinand Marcos of the Philippines who came in second with between $5 billion and $10 billion stolen; followed by Zaire's Mobutu Sese Seko who looted about $5 billion just a bit above General Sani Abacha's loot. Was Abacha misunderstood or misrepresented? Did all Abacha's advisers, aides and associates not smell a rat of wrong doings and financial impropriety? Their acquiescence and activities were coconspirational to all the human rights abuses, fraud, corruption and economic and financial crimes committed during Abacha regime.

In a similar interview, late Honourable Wada Nas, former Special Duties Minister under General Sani Abacha, held the same views as Professor Aluko and pretended that he had no idea about the gross financial administration anomalies and other crimes committed during General Abacha's regime.

In responding to press questions, late Hon. Wada Nas of Federal House of Representatives and staunch supporter of the presidential candidature of General Buhari of the ANPP during the 2003 presidential elections, confirmed that his former boss, General Abacha was misunderstood.

The whole international community and its agencies could not have erroneously condemned General Abacha unanimously, if there were no traces of wrong doings. Abacha's smoke was spreading throughout the whole world; yet, his cronies were selfdenying the existence of any fires.

Such fervent denials were neither smart nor brilliant in spite of overwhelming evidence. General Abacha was misunderstood for what? That assertion was untenable because the whole world seeing the glaring evidences of Abacha's atrocious activities could not be wrong in their assessment of Abacha's Administration while only General Abacha himself, his closest advisers and his aides saw nothing wrong in General Abacha's ways of governance from 1993 to 1998.

Late Honourable Wada Nas described General Sani Abacha as somebody he would like to deal with because he found him very courageous and very straightforward. He listened and his yes was yes and his no was no.

What Abacha's regime adopted was old fashioned, mechanistic style of leadership which bullied, harassed, ruled by iron hands, killed, tortured, committed human rights abuses, stole and stashed Nigerian government money in foreign private bank accounts. His rulership was antithetical to modern leadership styles which are scientific, innovative, imaginative, humane, responsive, responsible, accountable, empathic, effective, efficient, communicative, inspirational, harmonious, transparent, motivational and exemplary.

To substantiate the purported intrinsic qualities of General Abacha, late Hon. Wada Nas made references to the case of helpless teachers who wanted to go on strike because they had not been paid for six months. Late Hon. Wada Nas said that he went to General Abacha to explain the situation of the teachers and General Abacha replied, "Let them go on strike. We are going to do what we can do, according to what we have." He also described Abacha's rejection of IMF conditions as a very good act of courage.

The first example quoted by late Hon. Wada Nas above was not an act of courage but an act of insensitivity to the teachers' dehumanization and sufferings with their families for not being paid their salaries for six months' work in the classrooms teaching children designated as future leaders of this great country.

The challenging question is whether General Abacha or Hon. Wada Nas had ever worked for six months without salaries, and if so, what sufferings did they go through with their families? Where in the civilized world can the President, Prime Minister or Head of State tell teachers who have not been paid for six months to go on strike if they wanted to do so without demonstrating any empathy? If it happens, such head of government will be called upon to resign. Did Honourable Wada Nas and Professor Aluko realize that the amount of government money stashed away in foreign private bank accounts by General Sani Abacha and his cronies was more than sufficient to pay the salaries and other benefits of the teachers concerned for more than 100 years, and the balance could be used for investment to generate employment? Is that large-heartedness?

Secondly, the rejection of the IMF guidelines or conditionalities was not an act of courage because of its possible backfiring effect. The rejection could be an act of brazen lack of knowledge of the workings of international business, the monetary and fiscal operational systems, as well as micro and macroeconomic implications of an outright rejection of the IMF guidelines, which Hon. Wada Nas wrongly claimed was an act of courage.

What did Nigeria gain from the purported rejection of the application of IMF guidelines compared with what Nigeria could have lost if General Abacha embraced IMF conditions? It is simple logic that if Nigeria wants to be wealthy, prosperous and economically viable, it will have to move with those countries, agencies and financial institutions with supereconomic power. When and where does a poor man or woman move with the poor and becomes rich in modern history? IMF guidelines or conditionalities are the gateways to wealth and prosperity but they must be applied with caution, appropriately and in a way that carries the people along beneficially.

There is nothing wrong with Nigeria borrowing money from local and/or international financial institutions for national developmental projects provided the money borrowed is fully utilized for the purpose of national development, and projects embarked upon are completed instead of abandoned.

The problem with Nigeria is that money borrowed for development often finds itself into private pocket corruptly, and projects embarked upon are abandoned as uncompleted by contractors after they have been fully paid as a result of connivance with corrupt and fraudulent government functionaries. Due processes in contract awards, mobilisation payment and progressive payments according to workinprogress are never strictly followed as a result of fraud and corruption by government functionaries.

If money borrowed for Nigeria is productively utilized, the completed projects may become viable and profitable sources of income for Nigeria, but if the borrowed money is mismanaged, it will become a liability and a debt burden, which will be difficult to settle. Unfortunately, Nigerian elites who should know better indulge in passing the buck by blaming the IMF, World Bank and other financial agencies instead of condemning those who mismanaged the money borrowed for Nigeria. What were the economic achievements between 1993 and 1998, Mr. Chairman, National Economic Intelligence Committee? Was there any economic intelligence report about all the money stolen and stashed in foreign private bank accounts? Nigerians and the world want to know!

It is insinuational to say that Nigeria has surrendered her government and economy to western powers in the name of reforms. What Nigeria calls reforms are simple best economic and financial management practices which are vehicles to economic and sociopolitical prosperity. Nigeria should start to be represented by the best and most qualified people from their states and localities and not those who are not qualified academically/professionally but are just living on borrowed influence of yesteryears. It must be acknowledged that what was best yesterday may not be good enough for today or tomorrow because the world is changing fast and leaders must update themselves to be functionally effective, efficient and relevant.

Nigerians should be proud for successfully hosting international conferences like COJA, CHOGM and some others in 2003 and thereafter. It is not unlikely that pessimists and those with little knowledge in international relations and business, would undermine the accomplishments and classify the events under luxurious projects.

Such events often tremendously boost national image, and provide trusted business and political enabling environment for foreign investments, which eventually generate employment, enhance economic growth and improve the standard of living of the people. Sooner than later, economic contraction will become a thing of the past in Nigeria. The international trust generated, resulted in unprecedented debt relief and gigantic aid package for Nigeria by Paris Club and the G8 nations in July 2005.

Second Republic Vice President, Chief (Dr.) Alex Ekwueme was said to have described late General Sani Abacha, Nigerian military dictator (1993-1998) as a nationalist during the 50th birthday ceremony of Governor Sam Egwu of Ebonyi State on Monday, June 28, 2004. It was reported that he described General Abacha as the only leader that believed in equity and fair play among the six geopolitical zones in Nigeria. It does not sound true. Former Vice President Ekwueme may have been misquoted.

Compliment is all right for the dead as a great sign of respect, but it must not be illdriven or illtimed. Events that led General Sani Abacha to siphon $5 billion of Nigerian money into foreign private bank accounts, killed many opponents, and overthrew Chief Shonekan's transitional civilian administration were not acts of nationalism. That he committed serious human rights abuses as well as economic and financial crimes against his country, Nigeria which resulted in imposition of sanctions and ostracization of Nigeria from the World Community, do not add up to nationalism.

There was report that when General Shehu Musa Yar'Adua was in prison, he had HIV/AIDS virus forcibly injected into his body by General Abacha's Medical Agent, which later resulted in his death. Many opponents also died mysteriously during Abacha's regime, and some murder cases as well as assassination attempts attributed to his regime's officials were tried in Nigerian courts.

ExPresident Obasanjo was said to have mentioned that when he was at the guesthouse in prison, his medical doctor (Dr. Ajuwon) advised him to insist that only he, his personal doctor (Dr. Ajuwon) should take his blood sample. If he was not forewarned about not letting others take his blood sample, perhaps those who injected HIV/AIDS virus into General Shehu Yar'Adua's body would have succeeded in injecting the same deadly virus into General Obasanjo's blood system to eliminate him during the dictatorial regime of General Sani Abacha (1993-1998).

Are the perpetrators of these evil acts still within the Nigerian society? May God/Allah forbid! These serious crimes against Nigerians and Nigeria committed by General Abacha's regime are antithetical to nationalism. Many wise people cannot reconcile the statement of calling Abacha a nationalist with Nigerian Second Republic Vice President, Alex Ekwueme that we used to know.

Nigerians who travelled overseas during Abacha's regime were often suspected of one thing or the other and subjected to unusually rigorous searches and humiliation. Many Nigerians sought asylum in Britain and America. Nigerian residents overseas were ashamed to say that they were from Nigeria because of the atrocities committed by the overzealous and uncontrollable officials of Abacha's Administration.

It is recalled that the Western Nigerian proclamation of 1966/67, given by Chief Obafemi Awolowo that if the Eastern Region was allowed to secede, then the West would not stay, helped to keep the country of Nigeria together. His forewarning also helped to regulate the civil conduct of the war (1967-70) and minimized the number of collateral damages. If similar premonitions were given to Abacha Administration as well as the 'chop and quench' politicians and government functionaries who assisted him from 1993-1998, he would not have overstepped his bounds to the maximum.

In 1994/95, General Abacha as Nigerian Head of State convoked a National Constitutional Conference, which was allegedly boycotted by the Westerners of Nigerian geopolitical zone. If a whole region (West) quitted the National Constitutional Conference leaving only Northern and Eastern Regions, the product of such conference was doomed to fail.

The Constitutional Conference made some recommendations that were purely cosmetic and would not solve Nigerian problems.

(1) The recommendation for the establishment of positions of President, Vice President, Prime Minister and Deputy Prime Minister in one government is unwieldy, an unnecessary duplication of topmost positions in order to please some people. Such duplication of offices and responsibilities is an invitation to clash of responsibilities, interest, confusion and chaos in governance. Where in the civilized, developed world does such governmental structure exist and operate successfully without confusion, envy and chaos resulting from clash of interest, responsibility, power and authority?

(2) The recommendation for rotational presidency, vice presidency, governorship and other positions as recommended in the 1994/95 NCC document is persuasive but cosmetic, undemocratic and a system of exclusionism. The resultant effect is that the best candidates may be excluded because of their state of origin or ethnicity. It could breed reverse discrimination.

If the country is laying a solid, lasting foundation for posterity, rotation of top offices on ethnicity/tribal consideration is not the best decision. If you are planning shortterm to please some elites, rotation of offices may be acceptable for this generation, but if you are including posterity in your plan longterm, Nigerians must accept, adopt and adapt to what the civilized world is practising. When will Nigerians start to look for the best person to govern instead of paying all attention to ethnicity, religion, state or region of origin of who is to lead the country?

Rotational governance is an elitist compromise programme organized by few elites who are looking for their turn to be president, governor, etc. when they realize that they are not the most qualified for the positions they are aspiring to. If you do not elect the best people to govern, you cannot expect or get the best government services. The elites are recommending governance for their convenience and not government of best services for the citizenry.

Where in the developed and civilized world is rotational presidency or governance written into the constitution? The masses of Nigeria want best services without caring about the religion, sex or ethnicity of the officeholder if he/she can perform best.

On the other hand, the elites who are few and creating the problems are simply anxious about their turn and time to govern rightly or wrongly, purely because of their ethnicity, religion or state of origin irrespective of whether they are the most qualified or not. For how long can government of convenience for elites only, continue into the future?

(3) The recommendation that any political party that has ten percent of votes cast at the National Assembly election should be part of the emerging government as an allparty, unity government is persuasive but cosmetic. It will not establish a strong government, and in reality, the interparties antagonism being avoided would emerge eventually and destabilize the government.

The result of an election may require the establishment of an allparty, unity government if result is close and problems are sensed about going it alone by the winning party. This recommendation does not have to be written into the national constitution.

Election is not a win or die issue, and Nigerians, especially the elites, should know that their party of interest couldn't win all the time. The act of losing an election should not be reason for antagonism, destructive actions, chaos, anarchical tendencies, treasonable actions and calls for actions that could create ungovernableness.

General Abacha promised to promulgate the provisions of the 1994/95 National Constitutional Conference into law on October 1, 1998 after more than two years delay even though the conference was allegedly boycotted by old Western Region of Nigeria. Invariably, such constitution would not have lasted. It must be remembered that General Abacha planned to transition from military to civilian administration with himself converting from military head of state to Nigerian civilian president for a fiveyear single term as contained in the 1994/95 National Constitutional Conference (NCC) recommendations.

If General Abacha did not die untimely on June 8, 1998 with all his atrocities continuing for additional five years, only God/Allah knows how many citizens who opposed him would have escaped assassinations from his special killer squad. It was so bad that the international community declared Nigeria a pariah state and ostracized Nigeria.

As long as Abacha's cronies were not the ones being persecuted during his regime, but were milking at the expense of others, they felt it was all right and the persecutor of others was a hero. That is selfish, ungodly and not in the spirit of God/Allah. Where is empathy and conscientiousness in elites who are thinking about themselves alone and not what is best for Nigeria and the generality of Nigerians.

Some of the elites even believe that 'money and bribing' the electorate and party delegates at conventions will get them the presidency without the necessary leadership qualifications. If the delegates and the electorate elect elites into office because of money and bribery, state of origin, religion or ethnicity, what kind of quality services can be expected during their tenure in office?

Voters, as you lay your beds, so you lie on them. If you take bribes before a candidate is elected, what justification do you have to complain if he/she does not perform? First and foremost, the elected person who paid bribe to win will first think about how to recover the money used as bribe before he/she can think about good services for the electorate. He or she will corruptly recover the money in so many folds. That is the reality of life.

The political opposition leadership should be manned by highly qualified professionals who would show as much love for the country by offering invaluable suggestions that move the country forward without chaos and negativities. Both the government and the opposition must put Nigeria first in all their dealings. The challenging questions are: "What sort of Nigerian are you? Are you an honest critic of your government?" If yes, offer suggestions for policy adjustment and stop pessimism in the best interest of Nigeria. Remember, "Whoever sees no good thing in others is naturally not a good person himself or herself."

It is not too difficult for optimists to understand that presently, Nigeria is being channeled in the right direction. There may be need for adjustments to eliminate human imperfections, but it is not wise to throw away the baby being washed while getting rid of the dirty water, which results from cleaning the baby. Those who want to plant violence should stay in the forefront with their families to fully reap the fruits of violence.

It would be act of cowardice for socalled revolutionary leaders to fly out of Nigeria with their wives, children and relatives and thus leave innocent people in the lurch. Nigerians are living witnesses to what happened between 1967 and 1970 during the civil war. There are no fools in Nigeria anymore but highly intelligent people who would ask questions before they follow anybody to do evil that can hurt their beloved country.

Civilized and exemplary personalities do not say inciteful words in civilized communities where there is full accountability for what people say or do without exception – no sacred cows and no untouchables. Let Nigeria be the best example of the world by translating its diversity into unity and strength, understanding, hope, empathy, cooperation and all becoming their brothers' and sisters' keepers.

Nigerians can do it starting from the Presidency, the Legislature, Judiciary, the Governors, states and local leaders down to the followership. If there is any dirty linen in Nigeria, it cannot be washed in the United States of America. State Governors and leaders who travel overseas should watch how they portray Nigeria in bad light in the attempt to promote their personal political ambitions. Nigerian problems will best be solved by Nigerians using Africanness. Americans and Europeans never come to Nigeria to talk bad, mock or put down their countries as some elite Nigerians come to do in the USA.

In the Daily Independent Online of November 21, 2003, the former Governor of Ondo State, Chief Adebayo Adefarati in an exclusive interview said, "Abacha was another terrible leader. He was a maximum leader really. Well, you know what really happened during his time. Many eminent personalities were killed. I think he was another bad leader by any standard."

Why did General Abacha's advisers and aides not advise against all those happenings, or they just turned their faces the other way and pretended nothing was happening? The politics of hate, divisionism, name-calling, slandering, fabrication, falsehood, dysfunctionalization and incitement to break the law is not in the best interest of Nigeria. Nigerians should always apply due process, rule of law and constitutionality to settle national issues in a way that does not inflame, heat or hurt the polity of Nigerian nation.

On November 5, 2003, it was reported by *Vanguard* that Mrs. Bianca Buchmann, who was at the German Business Delegation, was said to have questioned the investment drive of the government on the face of huge capital flight of $170 billion from the country by Nigerians the previous year.

The former Chief Economic Adviser (CEA) to the President, who later became the Governor of Central Bank of Nigeria, Professor Charles Soludo responded that Nigerians had started to repatriate home their money in foreign banks with a record flow of about $3 billion since 1999. That pace is not good enough to catch up speedily with the desired rate of economic development in Nigeria.

In the same vein, on November 11, 2003, the former Director General of Economic and Financial Crimes Commission (EFCC), Mr. Emmanuel Akomoye mentioned that the EFCC was worried about $170 billion stashed abroad by Nigerians. He added that even if the money was from legitimate means, Nigerians should not have such large sum of money stashed abroad when government representatives were junketing globally seeking investment funds. He enlightened that Nigerians could repatriate part of their money back home for investment. He explained that his Commission had not received any mandate from the government to investigate the owners of the funds and their sources.

In his own contribution, the Ex-Speaker of the House of Representatives, Alhaji Aminu Masari; during the opening of a three day meeting of Inter-Government Action Group against money laundering, called for broad based legislation which would outlaw not only money laundering but also siphoning public funds from Africa to developed economies of the world.

Former House Speaker Masari who was represented by the Deputy Speaker, Honourable Austen Okpara said that some of the huge money deposits by Nigerians in offshore banks might be legitimate, but a good percentage of it would undoubtedly be as a result of public corruption. He implored the legal experts to deliberate on the issue so that the recommended legislation might capture a broader good governance standpoint and eliminate plundering of public funds. The Ex-Chairman of the EFCC, Alhaji Nuhu Ribadu emphasized that the conference should provide a harmonized legislation for the West African subregion to make it impossible for trans-border financial criminals to hide in any part of the subregion.

In his own contribution, Dr. Bello Lafiaji, former Chairman of Nigeria Drug Law Enforcement Agency (NDLEA) clarified that Nigerian money launderers had run to neighbouring countries to take refuge. He stressed that Nigeria had addressed the scourge of drug traffickers substantially using effective interdiction efforts, hence, they were on the run to neighbouring countries with less strict laws on drugs than Nigeria.

He added that the Financial Action Task Force (FATF) had approved the nation's antimoney laundering law and had asked the Federal Government to submit an implementation plan toward delisting Nigeria from the list of noncooperating countries territories.

The sudden death of General Sani Abacha brought in General Abdulsalami Abubakar as Head of State who was described as a complete gentleman by the former Governor of Ondo State, Adebayo Adefarati. The exgovernor said that General Abdulsalami Abubakar came in briefly and conducted an election, which was described as one of the best in the history of Nigeria.

The election conducted by General A. Abubakar ushered in General Olusegun Obasanjo on May 29, 1999. The event that brought in General Matthew Okikiolakan Aremu Olusegun Obasanjo was miraculous and incomprehensible because late Head of State, General Sani Abacha had already condemned President Obasanjo to life imprisonment commuted to 15 years and many others including General Shehu Musa Yar'Adua and General Oladipo Diya for trumped up conspiracy in a coup d'etat to oust him from office. General Obasanjo came from the prison cell to become the President and CommanderinChief of Nigerian Armed Forces. That is one of the greatest and rarest miracles in the history of the world far beyond human comprehension because General Abacha intended that General Obasanjo and many others would not get out of prison alive.

General Obasanjo could be described as 'Ayorunbo' meaning the person from heaven, the survivor. Nigerians should thank God/Allah, the Almighty, and the Omnipotent, for recalling late General Sani Abacha unexpectedly, suddenly, untimely and unannounced in order to save the lives of so many great Nigerians. If Abacha had notice about his death, he would have sent so many people to their graves, their Maker (God/Allah) before his demise out of sheer desperation. God/Allah is greater than all human beings nomatter how powerful, wealthy or influencial they may be.

The period of governance of Nigeria between May 29, 1999 and May 28, 2003 by the Presidency, the Legislature and the Judiciary under a new 'Democratic 1999 Nigerian Constitution' was devoted to a learning process of how to develop a formidable foundation of democracy for Nigeria that had witnessed military dictatorship for about three decades.

The beginning of the year 1999 started just after a period between 1993 and 1998 when Nigeria and Nigerians had passed through their darkest years in history when everybody was swearing, "Never again! Never again!" The arrival of 1999 met Nigerians in a frustrated mode of 'business as usual', period of fear, mistrust, human rights abuses, human trafficking, illegal immigration, corruption and frauds, economic and financial crimes, stealing and stashing of Nigerian money in foreign banks by elites, killings, cultism, gangsterism, economic downturn and instability, high unemployment rate, hyperinflation, disunity and divisionism.

There were ethnic rivalries, industrial disharmony, personal and possessional insecurity, serious international disrepute for Nigeria, 419 advance fee frauds, increasing trans-border crimes and Nigeria's ostracization by the international community. The image of Nigeria was at its lowest ebb in the annals of Nigeria as at 1998.

As a result, Nigerians used to be subjected to extra scrutiny at international airports at that time. All those overwhelming national problems were bequeathed to Obasanjo Administration with a new democratic constitution. The tail end of 2002 was full of activities in preparation for the Senatorial, House of Representatives and Presidential elections. There were fears that the elections would be marred with violence and military coups d'etat as it used to be, with skepticism about successful transition from civilian to civilian administration, which was alien to Nigeria since 1960.

Before May 29, 2003, political opponents of reelected President Obasanjo called for mass action to render the country ungovernable, and they even cursed that the inauguration ceremony scheduled for May 29, 2003 would not happen because of their disagreement with the conduct of the elections, which did not favour them. It is normal to be angry if one loses an election but that is not a licence for treasonable talks or actions.

At this juncture, Nigerians should be reminded, "There is never any general or presidential election in the world that is completely free from problems and malpractices naturally because of human imperfections." The panacea to improve on the system, as Nigeria moves forward, is to place reliance on election tribunals and courts, which are equipped to take care of election malpractices.

We are all living witnesses to the 'USA Presidential Election 2000' where all aggrieved persons went to court without threats to bring their nation down. That was exemplariness; that was civilization; that was nationalism; that was patriotism; that was statesmanship; that was civility demonstrated.

Nigerian politicians, elites and leaders should learn from US exemples and stop playing crude politics showing their fake indispensability, as if Nigeria and Nigerians should not exist if they are not the ones ruling the country. The usual call for mass destructive action and ungovernableness if anyone loses election, is arrogance and ignorance. Nigeria existed before all the present politicians and will live beyond any of them notwithstanding their individual power, wealth, societal influence or political affiliation.

Whenever there are election problems, Nigerians like civilized communities in the world should utilize election tribunals or courts where there are guidelines for due legal process which must be followed to avoid violence, disruptions and anarchical tendencies of the past which created many victims.

It must also be remembered that violence never perfectly solves any human or political problems without leaving indelible scars and prolonged mindset for retaliations. Great people of the world who would be remembered eternally like Dr. Martin Luther King Jr. of the USA, Mahatma Gandhi of India and the Nobel Peace Laureates became real by evolving nonviolence and peaceful means to solve human, socio-economic and political problems. Nigerian leaders and general population should emulate these good standards from civilized world communities.

Former Sole Administrator of Plateau State, Major General Chris Alli (retired), shared his experience with aviation correspondents on Thursday, November 18, 2004 when he returned to Lagos after heading six months state of emergency in Plateau State. He confirmed that the six months state of emergency translated the people's fears into comfort. He added that his experiment demonstrated that Nigerians' interests could be handled and dealt with without violence and that Nigerians preferred peaceful coexistence.

In a reconciliatory tone, Chief Joshua Dariye, Plateau State former Governor after being reinstated, appealed to his people to rally round, forgive one another and work together. He added, "The most important thing every Plateau man must say today is, 'I am sorry'. All of us must forgive and forget unconditionally. Government comes and government goes, but we should not destroy Plateau State. The state is greater than all of us." Chief Dariye's statement must apply to all Nigerians. It is a great lesson to hear former warring factions coming together to speak in tones of reconciliation.

Nigerians should be reminded once again that if the Ifeajuna/ Nzeogwu coup d'etat of January 15, 1966, masterminded by some Igbo military officers of Eastern Nigeria origin, were bloodless, peaceful and nonviolent, perhaps the retaliations, acrimony, divisionism, mistrust, economic instability and subsequent military coups d'etat generated from 1966 up to 1999 might not have happened. If inevitably those problems would occur, they would not be as pronounced as they are today. The inevitable questions are, "What legacies shall Nigerians, the living, bequeath to the unborn Nigerians? What sort of Nigerians are you?"

Let Nigerians ask themselves whether they learned their lessons and 'never again' to allow the mistakes of Nigerian past to be repeated. Change! Change! Change 'business as usual'. Put Nigeria first.

May God/Allah grant Nigerians the serenity to accept those things (incidences, events and occurrences), which they cannot change!

May God/Allah grant Nigerians the courage to change those things (incidences, events and occurrences), which they can change!

May God/Allah grant Nigerians the technical savvy and political sagacity, economic and financial management wizardry coupled with Heavenly Wisdom to understand and fully appreciate the differences between those hypotheses of change, its intricacies and implications.

With any change being introduced, the leadership needs to observe more haste, less speed – 'festina lente' and above all, carry the people along. That is what democracy is all about. There must be a meeting of minds between the leadership and the followership in order to achieve the best results desired for the nation.

The best ideas may be too sophisticated for the people and eventually frustrate them instead of helping them if not applied systematically and appropriately. The application of too much fertilizer to grow a plant may kill it; overdose of the best medication may kill; drinking or eating too much may become harmful. Proportionality, consistency, assertiveness, empathy and transparency in governance will help achieve the desired objectives.

Nigeria needs the best reforms for national prosperity, but they must be applied with the right judgment, at the right time and in the right situation. Socio-economic and political reforms must be backed up by effective researchability to be fully successful and achieve desired result.

A former State Governor from South-East said that he knew what Nigerians wanted, when it seemed that he did not know nor understand what he wanted for himself. It is constant research work on citizens' behaviour that can tell you what the people want.

The Government surely wants the best for the people, and it is making tireless efforts to achieve the best. More efforts should be geared toward effective communication of reform policies to secure the people's understanding and ensure their full participation in governance. Increased level of researchability by the Presidency and the Legislature will help.

So far, Nigeria is moving in the right course, better than ever before and all hands, both government and the opposition, should be on deck to steer the 'Ship of State' to the Promised Land. Why would any Nigerian want to hurt the country and risk the future of his great, great grandchildren? Always place Nigeria first above all considerations irrespective of ethnicity, religion or political leaning.

Nigerian situation is not worse than what happened in the United Kingdom and the United States of America during their periods of development, judging from the long periods of wars they fought and the heavy collateral damages they suffered. The US and the UK eventually overcame their fears and wars and have become the greatest democratic model countries. It will be recalled that the UK passed through years of dictatorship when all kinds of wrongs against humanity were committed.

The consolation for Nigeria is that, it is presently moving in the right direction to greatness following the democratic path and leaving no stones unturned and no rivers uncrossed. The debt relief and gigantic aid packages granted to Nigeria in July 2005 unprecedentedly by Paris Club and the G8 nations respectively demonstrate that the world approves Nigeria's reforms, the drive for corruptfree society and her socio-economic and political progress. The world appreciates Nigeria's forward march.

If Nigerians believe that the Nigerian Messiah has not come, at least the miracles of 1998, the relentless efforts of cleaning Nigerian society from fraud and corruption; the cancellation of $18 billion from foreign debt; the solid foundation being laid for posterity's socio-economic and political advancement; the increase in foreign investment; the dividends of democracy; the respect, love, care and patronage of the nation by international community etc. show light that the Nigerian Messiah was either in our midst or is around the corner watching, guarding and guiding the 'Ship of Nigerian State.'

On Tuesday, November 20, 2007, one hundred and thirteen expatriates including seven Americans were granted Nigerian citizenship and they received Nigerian citizenship certificates to that effect. Also, on Tuesday, August 5, 2008, one hundred and seventy (170) foreign nationals received certificates of Nigerian citizenship. It is a sign that great things are happening in Nigeria. That is the beginning of greater things to come to Nigeria.

GOD/ALLAH BLESS NIGERIA!

CHAPTER 4

NIGERIA'S HOPE IS RISING

Nigeria with above 140 million people, the highest concentration of Black People in the world, is enormously blessed with abundant human, material and natural resources. Nigeria can be described as God/Allah's own Black People's country because of her wonderful blessings by God/Allah with enormous natural resources and her daily protection from natural disasters, which are prevalent in many other countries.

In Nigeria, there is no winter, no heatwave, no iceberg, no volcanoes, no hail storms, no devastating wild fires, and no tormentous tornadoes or thunderstorms. There is no deadly flood; no land, mud, sand or rock slides that kill thousands of people at a time and wipe out human settlements like Tsunamis. Above all, there is no colour discrimination in a country of over 140 million people like you have in Europe and America.

Nigerian problems are manmade and not from natural courses. What a wonderful black people's country in the great African continent where people do not have to worry seasonally about devastating deadly effects of natural disasters! Nigerians must start to appriciate the blessings and mercies of God/Allah on the country.

On the 43rd anniversary of Nigeria's Independence, President Olusegun Obasanjo described and affirmed Nigeria's past situation as "period of harsh realities". He commended the courage of Nigerians by saying, "In spite of harsh realities, we did not despair; in spite of gloom, we did not lose hope; in spite of frustration, we did not give up."

He added, "We looked up even when things were down; we counted our blessings even when things were bleak; and we persistently looked forward in the face of setbacks. We were surrounded by so much darkness, yet we saw light."

He assured Nigerians about the focus on the goal of rebuilding Nigeria. He said, " If the transition to democratic rule in 1999 was the new dawn, we can now with confidence say that the new day has indeed broken."

President Olusegun Obasanjo also affirmed, "It was difficult to argue against the pessimism predicated on the circumstances that we met Nigeria in May 1999. Things were so bad that the pessimists saw no chance of positive action, and many of them were predicting the demise of the nation." He added, "Our structure was rotten, to put it mildly. Our social system was in disarray after suffering years of maladministration, and our national psyque traumatized by tyrannical rule."

The encouraging words of Mr. President confirmed, " A new Nigeria is born or more explicitly, Nigeria is born again with the advent of the new administration effective May 29, 2003." He reiterated, "So it is time for us to rise and put all impediments aside and work." He repeatedly called on Nigerians to change behaviour of "business as usual."

It is fair to say that the civilian government from May 29, 1999 to May 28, 2007 inherited gigantic problems, which needed a lot of time to solve. Also the Presidency, the Legislature and the Judiciary were faced with, and operating new 1999 constitution, full of new systems of democratic governance for which they had to spend the first term of four years learning and experimenting to correct the anomalous effects of maladministration of the past military and dictatorial regimes.

There were bickerings, infightings, mistakes, resistance to change and misunderstandings between the Presidency and the Legislature, but all what happened could be allowed as expected during a learning process. Therefore, the period of civilian administration from May 29, 1999 to May 28, 2007 helped all stakeholders to acquire relevant experience for planning and setting standards of structure for a solid foundation for Nigeria beginning from May 29, 2007.

Nigerians represent one of the best groups of people in the world in terms of smartness, academics and professionalism and God/Allah has blessed Nigeria with enormous natural wealth. Nigerian leaders must keep the wealth of resources in Nigeria for the prosperity of the people instead of stashing Nigerian money in foreign private bank accounts for the benefit of Europeans and Americans when enduring Nigerians are still in want of basic facilities to sustain an appreciable standard of living.

The wonderful qualities inherent in Nigerians derived from their sound upbringing, culture and traditions make it easier for Nigerians to be led, if leaders are exemplary, transparent and responsive. If Nigerians are told to modify behaviour by the leadership who demonstrate glaring sincerity, and if the followership are properly motivated by an exemplary leadership to change "business as usual", they will respond positively in the best interest of their nation.

The Nigerian elitecreated problems seem gigantic and overwhelming but they are childplay if critically compared, itembyitem, oneonone, with the enormity of same or similar problems that are inherent in developed countries establishments. These problems were imported to African countries because judging from their nature; they are alien and contrary to African culture, noble tradition and values. If Nigerian President continues to fight and battle them relentlessly, they will be stamped out to the advantage of the generality of Nigerians and the Black Peoples of the world.

An analysis of levels of happiness in 65 countries in the world by the "World Values Survey" shows Nigeria has the highest percentage of happy people followed by Mexico, Venezuela, El Salvador and Puerto Rico while Russia, Armenia and Romania have the fewest. New Zealand ranked 15 for overall satisfaction, USA 16th, Australia 20th and Great Britain 24th.

The survey was a worldwide investigation of sociocultural and political change conducted every four years by an international network of social scientists. If you are not convinced about the evaluation that Nigeria could come first, please visit developed and industrialized countries of the world, ask people questions and not just look at all the gold that glitters.

On May 29, 2003, ExPresident Olusegun Obasanjo of the Federal Republic of Nigeria called on fellow Nigerians locally and internationally to join him to thank and praise God /Allah for witnessing the milestone event of civilian to civilian transitional governance which had eluded the country for over three decades from 1966 to 1998.

He pledged that his embarkation on a political journey toward sustainable democracy in a truly united nation would continue. He referred to himself and the entire leaders in his government, as the leadership the people could trust. He described his leadership vision for Nigeria as "a united Nigeria, a strong Nigeria, a prosperous Nigeria, a peaceful Nigeria, a just Nigeria, indeed a great Nigeria; Nigeria of God's ordained destiny."

He commended all Nigerians for their patience from the "the darkest episode of our history" transitioning to the "dawn of hope." He referred to the difficult periods of the nation as "numerous bumps" which would be taken care of in their "leadership strides." He envisioned a "Nigerian nation that gets stronger and society that would no longer be in despair but with a much brighter future."

He reiterated his appreciation of the Legislature which he described as "steering the ship of the nation over largely uncharted waters" because of the newness of democratic system of governance as enshrined in the 1999 Constitution of the Federal Republic of Nigeria. He dwelled on "better prospects of law making" and higher degree of harmony between the Executive and the Legislature, which he described as "sine qua non" for effective and efficient governance of Nigeria.

He appreciated the support of other world governments that have welcomed Nigeria back into the folds of comity of nations after Nigeria's ostracization as a result of charges of human rights violations allegedly committed during the preceding military dictatorial administration of General Sani Abacha. He added that Nigeria's honour had been fully restored with due respect after having continued to discharge obligations consistent with policies regulated by the world assembly.

He thanked foreign investors already patronizing the country and extended invitations to new ones. He alluded to the imperfections of humanity to appeal to all those who were aggrieved as a result of the 2002/03 general and presidential elections and assured that postelection reviews by election tribunals would correct anomalies and stand Independent National Election Commission (INEC) in good stead as well as strengthen the nation's democratic principles, policies and practices.

He promised the nation that he would provide transparent, quality and exemplary leadership to all Nigerians irrespective of their political persuasion or affiliation. He requested from all Nigerians, hard work, cooperation, solidarity, understanding and mutual respect for the peaceful running and advancement of the nation.

He reminded all Nigerians yearning for democracy after many years of undemocratic military regime about the sigh of relief, which greeted the "new dawn" with a collective cry of "Never Again, Never Again" to military dictatorship when civilian administration was installed on May 29, 1999.

He explained that even though he had no magic wand to achieve instant transformation of the nation, he asserted, "Fundamentally, Nigeria can be saved and must be rescued and saved by all Nigerians without exceptions because Nigeria is the only place we can call our own country." He contended that any retrogression would be a sign of failure of leadership. He reiterated that the overriding consideration of progressive action would be to rationalize the nation's social system and make it wholesome.

He envisaged that hopelessness and despair would be replaced by enthusiasm, hope and faith and brighter prospects for the citizenry. He mentioned that efforts to truncate anticorruption law were unsuccessful, and its good and effective impact was being felt on costs of government contracts, supplies and purchases. He described corruption as antithetical to development and promised to fight corruption to a standstill.

He added that the Independent Corrupt Practices and Related Offences Commission (ICPC) had brought thirty-nine cases of corruption to court for prosecution within four years compared with none at all in the preceding regimes of over three decades. As at August 2005, ICPC and EFCC had overwhelming numbers of cases to prosecute.

He ruled out the use of intimidation and coercion rather than persuasion, adherence to due process and the rule of law, emphasizing that Nigerians cherish freedom of speech, political expression and association. He confirmed that there were no political prisoners in Nigeria or Nigerian asylum seekers, which was reminiscent with the preceding military regime. He mentioned that Nigeria was no longer regarded as a pariah state by the world community, but a respected nation which had continued to attend and host international events such as the All Africa Games and Commonwealth Heads of Government Conferences.

While reiterating the dividends of continuity, stability and progress, he stressed, "The period from May 29, 1999 to May 28, 2003 was devoted to laying the foundation for the rebirth of Nigeria." He emphasized that there was considerably a lot to be done to achieve the ultimate goal of a truly reborn and truly great nation. He listed a lot of priority areas on which his administration intended to intensify and consolidate progress, which included infrastructure, power supply, healthcare, education, agriculture, industry, political reforms and foreign policy.

He hinted that it appeared a new paradigm was evolving for a new world order. He added that the assumptions of the post World War II order, which gave hope, confidence and security to all nations, big and small was undergoing significant changes. He warned Africans to take note of the trends of those changes and prepare adequately and appropriately, or else, the marginalization that Africa had suffered might become "complete de linkage." He reiterated that in spite of help from outside the nation's borders, Nigerians should not forget to be "masters of their fate, captains of their destiny and architects of their own fortune."

The solution of the nation's problems cannot be left to the President and his advisers alone; all stakeholders must be involved. It must be remembered that the best experts, best advisers, best technocrats and best professionals are human beings with normal human imperfections who have their own personal problems, personal interests, personal agenda, personal biases, personal impulses and constraints which would normally influence their reports, research, recommendations and advisement.

In real life situation, experts as human beings are fallible and also, their opinions have never yielded 100% result of expectations. Hence, in applying expert advice, opinions or recommendations as well as IMF or World Bank guidelines or conditionalities, there must be research and questions asked for justification to achieve success.

There must be appropriateness, proportionality, good timing, effective communication, good presentation and explanation of policy direction as well as empathy during implementation of policies in order to carry the people along. Policy implementation objective must be geared toward eliminating the sufferings of the citizenry – the masses in particular.

Sometimes, an expert opinion may be too sophisticated for Nigerian situation and would fail if applied prematurely. It must also be remembered that "Enterprise Nigeria" is the business of all and not only the privileged few elites in Nigeria. In socio-economic and political issues, best results are achieved if the leadership in particular and people generally ensure that national interests take precedence over personal, group or sectional interests. In a democracy, the people must be carried along in policy decision-making and implementation.

If any leader is in doubt about any expert advice, do not hesitate to talk to market women from Lagos, Ijebu-Ode, Onitsha, Agboh, Aba, Abeokuta, Kano, etc as well as traditional rulers, labour leaders, private sector operators, etc. for complementary advice that can produce complimentary results. These people are more peopleoriented and they know a lot more about solving human, socio-economic and political problems than most bookworms who have never lived among the masses to understand their problems.

Book knowledge alone without a lot of local and international experience cannot provide the right panacea for Nigerian problems. Unfortunately, expertise covered with human flesh has never solved any problem with perfection, yet most experts often feel they know everything because of their book knowledge. They do not. Sometimes, research reports and intelligence reports may be distorted to favour given situation. Sometimes, expert recommendations may be commercialized or issued as coverup. Nothing is perfect.

Expertise without the right commitment and sincerity of purpose cannot yield the best results. It must also be understood that the degree of commitment and sincerity of individuals whether an expert or not will be situationally dictated. Therefore, those people in authority positions must be adequately motivated to function properly.

The big problem Nigeria has had since independence in 1960 up to date is wrong advisement. There was a popular saying during the regime of General Yakubu Gowon as Head of State, which goes thus, "There are not many bad leaders, just advisers."

Presidential advisers and aides have enormous responsibilities to tell the President the truth in all situations and not only curry favours by telling him only what he would like to hear. When advisers deliberate with the President and everybody comes out laughing all the time, then most probably, somebody must be hiding something.

Loyalty is extremely important but the right advisement, right policies and their proper implementation in a way that would make the President 'the beloved leader' of this great nation would be much more important. For example, the wrong advisement from the Intelligence Community of the greatest country on the planet is known to have caused more confusion, more deaths, more terrorism and prolonged avoidable war in the Middle East. A great adviser can change the toughest minds if he comes up with honest facts and figures and proves his points.

ExPresident Obasanjo passionately appealed to all Nigerians for behaviour modification, to speed up the accomplishment of set goals and objectives during his tenure. He made references to the pessimism of some people who regarded him as a loner in his belief that Nigerians could change for better. Such pessimists need complete reeducation on modern human resource management especially case studies on attitude building to remodel their thoughts and understanding of humanity.

In present Nigeria, all people must be ready to listen and change without exception especially the leadership. Listening is an essential part of effective communication. Anybody, high or low, who is still fraudulent or corrupt, or doing something wrong or working against Nigerian national interest is definitely not listening nor changing.

In the *Guardian News* of Tuesday, August 20, 2003, a statement credited to the former Senate President, Adolphus Wabara reads, "But Mr. President has changed. I think he listens more now." To achieve effective governance, the entire leadership of the country must listen and change wherever necessary; then the people will follow automatically, and they will listen, trust and change from 'business as usual.'

Listening is an indispensability to achieve effective communication updown, bottomup. Whoever does not listen or change for better must be purged and replaced no matter his or her influence or connections in government or society because Nigeria can no longer accept failures or afford any retrogressions.

Unprecedentedly, President Obasanjo accomplished the cancellation of $18 billion out of the foreign debt of Nigeria and paid off the balance of $12 billion progressively and made Nigeria to be foreign debtfree. Look at how developed countries manipulate brain drain from Nigeria and other African countries.

Nigerians who are educated with Nigerian money and become highly qualified are lured overseas to be paid less than indigenes of their host countries. In fact, being a brain drain overseas is better than remaining unemployed in Nigeria and wasting away in one's own home country just because her wealth of resources have been mismanaged with impunity and laundered overseas into private secret bank accounts.

Invariably, the money of about $521 billion that could have been used for investment to generate employment in Nigeria was allegedly stolen and stashed in overseas banks with impunity by the elites who were regarded as sacred cows and untouchables between 1960 and 1998. Nigeria still has enormous natural resources, which have not been tapped or realized. Nigeria's national wealth should be protected and judiciously utilized for national development.

ExPresident Obasanjo listed some social negative tendencies militating against some Nigerians such as: fraud, corruptibility, ethnicity, lack of patriotism, lawlessness, inefficiency, diminished sense of justice and lack of mutual respect for one another. He added that the ultimate solution for combating the social ills would be selfless and relentless sacrifice from all Nigerians to the nation.

He emphasized, "Instead of asking, what's in it for me, we ask, what's in it for Nigeria." He concluded his address by calling on all Nigerians to board the "Nigeriacraft with him, to keep it at a cruising level that is beyond turbulence and at an optimum cruising speed in the direction of Nigerian dreams."

Nigeria has set a standard of zero tolerance for corruption, which both Nigerians and foreigners should strictly adhere to or face the consequences. There will be no more sacred cows or untouchables nor selective or discriminatory prosecution of cases. All Nigerians and foreigners who engage in businesses in Nigeria have been duly warned. "To be forewarned is to be forearmed." Nigeria today is committed to transparency, responsibility, accountability and incorruptibility and will not tolerate indiscipline, blackmail or intimidation.

Nigerians ought to blame some of the legislators for scandals about corrupt practices that leaked in the legislative houses in early 2005, but they must also remember to blame themselves and change the system that forces any elected representative to borrow millions of money to spend by bribing the electorate before he or she can win an election in Nigeria. Also, the system forces politicians to rely on godfathers to get money to spend or rig elections into victory.

There is corruption in advanced, developed and civilized countries of Europe and America, but it is not widespread and crude nor practised with impunity as it is in Nigeria. The system itself corrupts Nigerians as well as the legislators. It must be reviewed. In fact, Nigerians who have been pointing accusing fingers are not saints, but everybody must change from 'business as usual.'

So, instead of Nigerian legislators resorting to defensiveness and vindictiveness by fighting back with impeachment proposals to undo the presidency for leaking their corrupt practices, they should research into the causes of the scandals of corruption, one of which is campaign financing, and pass appropriate campaign finance legislation. Such law should take away the burden of heavy indebtedness of borrowing millions of naira to finance elections.

If according to information, one of Abia State politicians contributed 100 million naira in part to finance the 1999 presidential election, what do Nigerians expect if he or she is given an office? The first thing he/she would do in office would be to make a plan to recover his/her contribution in so many folds. In Anambra State, some leaders described politics as business like unavoidable money exchange bribery game. It should not be so, and it is not.

With three levels of governance, the Federal, State and Local Council, it looks as if it is only the Federal Government that is effectively fighting corruption, which should not be the case. Do people still have to bribe to collect drivers' licences, car tags or plate numbers, etc. at local councils? The whole of Nigeria and all Nigerians should fight corruption in all forms. Are policemen still collecting 20 naira as bribe from bus conductors? It must be stopped at all costs.

The system must enable the citizenry to report cases of corruption whether small or big to authorities for quick prosecution. Are the systems watching members of the ICPC and CFCC to ensure that none of them can be corrupted or compromised? It is a good start, and Nigerians generally must be commended for their vision to rid Nigerians of corrupt practices. The world is full of praises for the government of Nigeria.

If the electorate receives a bribe worth millions of naira with the right hand before a candidate is elected, and on getting to office, the elected person corruptly takes the money back with the left hand in so many folds, who is wrong or right? The whole Nigerian people need complete reorientation, which must start from the leadership and flow down to the followership without exception.

Corruption must be preached against in churches and mosques; on land, air and water with flyers initiated by government and conspicuously displayed in all localities. The opposition, civil society groups, the NLC, the NGOS, the private and public sectors functionaries and the generality of Nigerians should be partners in progress in the operation to clean Nigeria of corrupt elements.

The President, Legislature, Judiciary, Governors, Local Council Chairpersons and government functionaries, elders and leaders at federal, state and local government levels as well as private sector leadership should take the lead in this crusade. It is a task that must be done.

Unfortunately and unreasonably, some Nigerian elites who are fond of opposing and criticizing the government just to be noticed, made a great deal of mountain out of mole hills about the 7 billion naira presidential library to be established in Ogun (Gateway) State with funds to be donated by individuals and groups from the private sector.

It is recalled that the thirty-ninth, fortieth, forty-first and forty-second Presidents of the USA, Jimmy Carter, Ronald Reagan, George H.W. Bush and Bill Clinton respectively as well as previous Presidents of the USA established presidential libraries funded by private generous donors. The forty-third President George W. Bush announced in September 2005 of his intention to establish his presidential library in Texas, USA, and that it would be funded by the private sector. It is therefore difficult to see what is unusual or wrong about the presidential library as long as it is not funded with taxpayers' money.

Presidential library is an educational and nonprofit making establishment. Some respected legal luminaries threatened and dissipated energy to challenge the project in court. There is nothing wrong to test its constitutionality in court with all sincerity and patriotism without imputing motives and heating Nigerian polity unnecessarily. Nigerians' time is precious, and elites should stop wasting it by crying foul when none exists. Obasanjo's presidential library cannot cost up to 10 percent of any of the USA presidential libraries. Elites should devote attention on how to help the masses instead of being provocative for nothing.

Nigerians must fully recognize that Nigeria binds them together, and they should emulate the Americans who place their country, the USA, above all other interests and considerations. America is first for all Americans. All Nigerians, irrespective of ethnicity, religion, political affiliation and social groups, wish the best for their country in different forms and approaches. Nigerians love their country undoubtedly and without any qualifications. They must harmonize their diversity to achieve the best results for the country. It is the only country we can proudly call our own.

In the pursuit of peace and stability, Nigeria and other African countries should limit the internationalization of the solution to their problems to Africanness. Undue influence and interference from the Western Bloc and their agencies may usually create more problems than are meant to be solved because their own national interests and biases will usually take precedence in whatever advice or solution they offer to solve Blackman's problems.

For example: The IsraeliPalestinian confrontations will be easier to solve if other nations do not lie on either side telling the Israelis and Palestinians what to accept, what not to accept, what to do and how to do it in recognition of their own national interests and biases. Also, the Iraqi conflicts, war, insurgency and problems will be easier to solve by her nationals if some other nations and militant groups do not take sides in their own national and group interests, biases and ideologies telling Iraqi nationalities what to accept, what not to accept, what to do and how to go about it.

The same situation goes with the Kashmirean problem where Pakistan and India who are nuclear power neighbours lie on opposite sides with their armies disputing who owns what part of Kashmir. The people of Kashmir who Pakistan and India are claiming want peace and not war, development and not destruction, safety and not insecurity, long life and not untimely death.

They want food, health, education, development, basic necessities of life, water, housing, socio-economic and political stability but not destabilization, fear, uncertainties, destruction of life and properties and war which envelope them daily as a result of the dispute between Pakistan and India.

In effect, the Kashmireans are not the primary nor major problems to peace but those other countries who line up with either India or Pakistan on opposing sides dictating where some Kashmireans belong and where the others do or do not belong.

The Israelis and Palestinians, India and Pakistan should learn from Nigeria's and Cameroon's commendable efforts to settle their dispute over Bakassi Peninsula and some other border territories without going to war nor endangering the daily lives of the people on both sides of the border of Nigeria and Cameroon. The world must learn from the peaceful approach to dispute resolution adopted by the Federal Republic of Nigeria and the Republic of Cameroon. It is a great credit to Africa in particular and the Blacks in general. ExPresident Obasanjo of Nigeria and President Biya of Cameroon deserve Nobel Peace Prizes for their exemplary handling of the territorial dispute with peace.

It is therefore better for Nigerians as well as African nationalities not to start a conflict knowing fully well that it is difficult to accurately predict how a conflict, violence or war will end with its consequences if it is started. Always remember that any Nigerian or African problem will solve easily if it is approached with Africanness, peace, understanding, good conscience, tolerance and patriotism. Always be your brothers' and sisters' keepers.

<u>Some Realities About Life.</u>

By the end of this millennium, December 31, 2099, practically all living Nigerians of today would have passed to the greater world beyond. In effect, as at December 31, 2099, Nigeria would be inhabited by entirely new sets of generations of people and leaders. All Nigerians of today will be history only to be remembered by the individual legacies they bequeath to posterity.

The question that you should start to ask yourselves now is, "What legacies are you leaving behind to future Nigerians, your succeeding generations yet unborn? From now on, let Nigerians start to search their minds and hearts and begin to lay the formidable foundation of prosperity for their future generations with honesty, peace, unity, incorruptibility, acts of legality, accountability, transparency, responsibility, responsiveness, economic wealth, exemplary leadership qualities, impeccability and godliness.

Whoever you are today, start to think and take actions as to how you want to be remembered perhaps like the sage and immortal Chief Obafemi Awolowo, first Premier of Western Region of Nigeria (Yorubaman), who initiated and executed free educational and developmental programmes successfully in the mid1950's for which he will be remembered eternally.

What about other Nigerian nationalists who were the fathers of Nigerian Independence like Zik of Africa, Dr. Nnamdi Azikiwe, first President of Nigeria; Sir Ahmadu Bello, the Sardauna of Sokoto, first Premier of Northern Nigeria; Sir Abubakar Tafawa Balewa, first Prime Minister of Nigeria and many others who championed Nigerian nationhood in 1950s and 1960s.

Do you want to be remembered as ExPresident Obasanjo who became the first Nigerian President who battled frauds, corruption, economic and financial crimes of elites, sacred cows and untouchables; restored Nigeria's name, image, dignity and respect among international community and relentlessly pursued policies that will ensure Nigeria's economic survival, prosperity as well as the sustenance and protection of Nigeria's hardwon democracy?

General Obasanjo was the first military Head of State to peacefully hand over power to a civilian elected President, Alhaji Shehu Shagari, and President Obasanjo was the first civilian Nigerian leader to transition from civilian to civilian administration successfully. Unprecedentedly, ExPresident Obasanjo secured foreign debt cancellation of $18 billion for Nigeria, had promises for more debt relief in July 2005 as well as gigantic aid package for the country from Paris Club and G8 countries.

ExPresident Obasanjo's reputation in Africa, the Commonwealth and the United Nations was unique and unparalleled. He reinstated and uplifted Nigeria on the world map within a record time beyond comprehension. Each time we saw him on American television speaking in the African Union, the Commonwealth or United Nations, we

(Nigerians) in the Diaspora, used to proudly acknowledge him as our democratic Nigerian President. We never had that opportunity for three decades before his administration.

Each and every Nigerian can do something good no matter how small for which future Nigerian and African generations can be appreciative. Start to think about how you have saved or oppressed, helped or cheated your fellow Nigerians and your Nigerian Nation, uplifted or hurt Nigeria financially and economically, and see what changes you need to help lead Nigeria and future peoples of this great country into the Promised Land, the ElDorado.

It is better to be remembered as a peacemaker rather than a troublemaker. Nigerian money siphoned away and stashed into foreign banks is not helping your fellow Nigerians; such actions divest Nigeria of desperately needed investment for employment generation. You may own the whole of Abuja, the whole of Kaduna, Kano, Sokoto, Enugu and the whole of Niger Delta combined. Perhaps, you may be the most powerful person during your time; please start to think that one day when the end comes and God/Allah's time of judgment sets in, over which nobody has control, no matter how powerful and wealthy you are, how do you want to be remembered? How do you want to be judged?

Nigerian democratic dispensation ensures freedom of speech and expression as well as freedom of association and religion among others. Democracy is not licentiousness. The democratic experiment should not stupidify some Nigerians to disown invaluable African culture of dignity, decency and respectability to themselves, peers and leaders even when they disagree with one another's views, actions or governmental policies.

If you want to contribute effectively to policy changes in the best interest of Nigeria, you cannot do that successfully by being antagonistic to everything and everybody responsible for policy decision-making and implementation. Many times, authorities would bend backwards to accept opposition viewpoints, if such opposition standpoint is presented with civility, maturity, decency and understanding.

In this democratic experiment Nigeria needs civil, decent, respectable, dignified, knowledgeable, effective and efficient kind of opposition that healthily suggests workable, better alternative solution to Nigerian problems.

The ways some respectable Nigerian professionals, icons and luminaries argue and oppose everything do not make them sellable outside the confines of Nigeria. Those who are opposing unreasonably, unintellectually and unintelligently just for opposing sake are disappointing for they can do better. There must be responsible opposition and a press that may be liable criminally for deliberate falsehood that defame others.

If you want any policy changes, it is not decent, not dignifying nor civil to attack the personalities of persons in government with insults and name-calling without any justification. Why can't you be decent and civil if you are born and brought up decently in an African family with decent culture, tradition and values?

If you are a member or leader of opposition at local, state or federal level, or perhaps a member of the press, always relate to Nigerians your observations and provide better alternative suggestions with some decency, dignity, civility and high sense of responsibility.

If for forty years, any Nigerian continues to be too controversial, criticizing, attacking and attacking, bitter and bitter, nursing grudges, unforgetting and unforgiving, still having political enemies, boycotting reconciliation meetings and conferences, and never for once compromising socio-politically, then such Nigerian would need psychological evaluation to determine his/her mental capability to be part of a civilized democratic society. Turning down 'Nigerian Honour Award' is an intellectual absurdity which insults Nigerian institution, honour and highly held sacred tradition. Whoever the Nigerian president is, cannot be a tenable excuse to refuse the Nigerian Honour Award.

In civilized communities, members of the same household – the father, his wife and children – often belong to different political camps or parties with different political ideologies and they live happily together. If you have not been compromising, maybe you are the one who is not following Nigeria's progressive forward march, which began on May 29, 1999. You may need complete reorientation to fit into modern political life.

Hence, if you are not getting along as a socio-economic and political activist or for any other reasons, you may need a kind of selfappraisal or outside help in the form of psychological or psychiatric evaluation to determine what is wrong with you, and why you have been different for forty years from the majorityheld moderate opinions of over 140 million people.

In civilized communities, the work of the opposition group or party is not simple. Political gangsterism, political hooliganism or political talkativeness without any sensibility does not help. Nigerians need political maturity and sensibility, political savvy and sagacity. That is what helps the nation and Nigerians and not how insultingly you talk, write, do name-calling or oppose for no reason but just to be noticed.

Nigerian political system needs valuable and intelligent contributions rather than acts of provocation tendencies that disrupt and heat the polity. That is not why you are an elected representative, a pressman or a party in opposition. By your talks, writings, actions and deeds, you will be known and assessed. Remember, it is the empty vessel that makes the loudest noise. Always consider being a good example to those following.

People can be decent when they disagree and criticize. Whoever never sees anything good in others will definitely not be a decent, dignified, civil or civilized person. In a place of the blind, such oneeyed person may lead but what will you expect from his opposition other than negativeness! Nigerians must all change what they are doing wrong in the best interest of Nigeria, Africa and the Black Peoples of the world.

Whatever the grievances that exist, let Nigerians forget and forgive so that everybody can start anew during this Nigerian Fourth Republic. Whether you are a member of the Presidency, Legislature, Judiciary, Federal, State, or Local Officials, the Press, the Private Sector or Ordinary Citizens, remember to put Nigeria first in your daily endeavours and behave responsibly.

Nigerians must look at the fight against HIV/AIDS and other deadly diseases critically. Happiness, exercises and good food, rich in food values, help to build and strengthen one's immunity against diseases. So, the fight against HIV/AIDScan begin by stepping up agriculture to minimize reliance on chemicalized foods, which are being imported from overseas. People should get back to land and feed Nigerians with traditionally rich foods instead of overseas processed foods which are prime to depleting one's immunity and causing diseases.

Nigerians should think for a minute about the commercialization of HIV/AIDS programmes designed by advanced countries whether all the monies being voted reach their purported destinations or end up in private pockets of the donors' or the donees' countries. Eating the right food with proper hygiene, good moral lifestyle with good exercise as appropriate is an important part to prevent diseases by building and strengthening one's body immunity.

African traditional medicine with some modifications can cure the deadliest diseases which advanced countries assume incurable. It is not about shrines but herbs expertly mixed to enhance body immunity and cure diseases or prevent them. Medication with disease propaganda is commercialized in advanced countries, and it is expensive. Eliminate fake drugs. The Nigerian conventional medical practitioners should continue to explore the usefulness of traditional medicine for a good mix that cures Nigerians. The result could be cheaper and more effective.

Nigerian elites, academicians, the opposition groups, civil society groups, socio-economic and political activists, professionals, government functionaries, the Nigerian leadership and the generality of Nigerians should spend all their blessed energies positively to make what is good better, and then utilize the renewed powerful accumulated positive energy to change what is wrong and make it right harmoniously.

Nigeria will be a better place if Nigerian dissident elites stop crying wolf, wolf where there is none, stop condemning and complaining; stop being negative; stop being part of Nigerian problems and join hands to be part of the solution in the overall best interest of Nigerian nation and all Nigerians.

There is no excuse for violence if you are a person of God/Allah. Stop ethno-religious violence, which will not get you anywhere but hell fire with the devil because God/Allah is of peace, mercy, forgiveness, love and care. Stop being fooled and used by those who incite you into violence when their own wives and relations are protected and their children are graduating in European and American universities. If they incite you to go and cause violence, why not ask them where their own children are?

Your purpose on earth is to serve and promote mankind and humanity through which God/Allah will recognize your service to Him. Your sleeping in the church or mosque with so many times of prayers daily alone cannot take you to God/Allah or Heaven. Your service to mankind or humanity will be your gateway, path or avenue to God/Allah or Heaven. God/Allah does not need your favours, but mankind or humanity does. Start to do the right things now that you can, for you may not have another opportunity to pass through this world again.

On Saturday, November 19, 2005, the coronation and installation ceremony of Alake, the paramount ruler of Egbaland, Oba Adedotun Aremu Michael Gbadebo, Okukenu IV, took place. During the ceremony, ExPresident Obasanjo was said to have mentioned that the late Bashorun M.K.O. Abiola, winner of June 12, 1993 presidential election did not become president because of 'bad belle' – ill feeling. While reminiscing on the exploits of the Old Boys of Baptist High School (BBHS), Abeokuta, he said, "Only bad belle denied the school of producing three presidents for Nigeria." Chief M.K.O. Abiola and ExPresident Obasanjo were products of BBHS, Abeokuta, Ogun State, Nigeria.

In effect, the ill feelings of a few Nigerian elites robbed the entire Nigerian electorate of installing their choice as president on June 12, 1993 during the presidential election that was adjudged the fairest in Nigerian history. The few elites, who conspiratorially annulled the election, twisted and truncated the will of the Nigerian people. Those responsible were just not civilized enough to accept the practice and outcome of democratic processes.

The most unfortunate thing was that Chief Abiola died in prison mysteriously, and his wife, Kudirat Abiola, was assassinated by death squad purportedly sponsored by the succeeding dictatorial administration of 1993-1998. That is extremely wicked. Those responsible are answerable to God/Allah. They should be ashamed of their ignoble roles and tender unreserved apologies to Nigerians. They should ask for forgiveness from God/Allah.

Nigerian President and the Legislature should pass appropriate legislation that ensures that it was the last time that the democratic will of Nigerian people would be trampled upon with impunity by a few ethnocentric and egoistic elites. Such history should never repeat itself.

The conspiracy to deny Chief Abiola of the keenly contested and won presidency cut across elites from all Nigerian nationalities among whom were his best friends who were rich from inflated contract awards at the expense of Nigerian masses. We must all remember that there is a 'Judgment Day' after all our lives on earth.

If General Obasanjo as Military Head of State defied an overwhelming undue influence to install Alhaji Shehu Shagari as Second Republic President of Nigeria in 1979, Head of State General Ibrahim Badamosi Babangida should have defied the overwhelming misleading advisement, wrong influences and bad belle that made his administration to annul the free and fair presidential election of June 12, 1993 won by Chief M.K.O. Abiola.

The rhetorical questions to ask all Nigerians are: what if Chief Abiola were a Northerner, would he have suffered the same fate? Where was the empathy, contentment and Allahliness for which past Northern leaders were reputed? Unfortunately, it is the leader (IBB) who takes responsibility for actions taken on basis of misleading advisements, misdirected influences and bad belle. IBB was never a bad man, and he is not a bad man. Nigerian leaders must stay strong always above misleading advisement, wrong influences and bad belle. There should be equity and justice for all Nigerians.

Professor Humphrey Nwosu who was chairman of the Independent National Electoral Commission (INEC) should take responsibility for the confusion that caused the annulment of the June 12, 1993 presidential election as extensively discussed in this book – Chapter 16, Annulment of June 12, 1993 Presidential Election.

In this annulment case, General Babangida, General Sani Abacha and Chief Clement Akpamgbo were not the leaders to blame but the wrong advisement, actions, desperation and poor judgment of Professor Humphrey Nwosu to ignore the injunction order received from Abuja High Court on June 10, 1993.

Also, the letter from the Director of Information, Mr. Michael O'Brien of the American Embassy compounded the problems but it could have been regarded as an interference in the internal affairs of Nigeria and ignored. Unfortunately, Professor Nwosu did not cleverly see the handwriting on the wall but advised General Babangida against the majority opinion of members of the National Defence and Security Council (NDSC).

In October 2005, within few hours apart, Nigeria and the world lost two great women, First Lady Stella Omotola Obasanjo, great wife and great mother, and US Mrs. Rosa Parks, mother of Civil Rights Movement. Also, in January 2006, Nigeria lost two exemplary women, Mrs. Sa'adatu Rimi, wife of former Governor of Kano State, Abubakar Rimi, and Mrs. Buhari, wife of General Buhari, ANPP presidential candidate in 2003 and 2007. They were great supporters of the course and political aspirations of their husbands. May their souls rest in perfect peace. The world will always remember them for their 'behind the scene' contributions to Nigerian political system championed by their surviving husbands.

The harmonization of developmental programmes of National Economic Empowerment and Developmental Strategy (NEEDS) of Obasanjo regime with the Seven-Point Agenda of President Yar'Adua as basis for vision 2020 is in the right direction. The initiation of the development programmes coupled with socio-economic and political reforms confirms the seriousness of Nigeria to become an economic giant nation sooner than later. The country will surely be a better place for all.

GOD/ALLAH BLESS NIGERIA!

CHAPTER 5

THE GREATNESS OF NIGERIAN PEOPLE AND LEADERSHIP

On may 29, 2003, President Olusegun Obasanjo of Nigeria said, "We all have a stake in 'Enterprise Nigeria' and each of us stands a better chance of getting optimum dividends if instead of asking, 'What's in it for me?' we ask, 'What's in it for Nigeria?' to determine our choice of action when our sense of duty and service is called upon." Also, former President John F. Kennedy of the United States of America said over four decades ago, "Ask not what America can do for you, ask what we can do for America."

President Yar'Adua assured Nigerians on August 4, 2008 that a new era of good leadership was imminent. He identified leadership as the greatest problem facing Nigeria. He mentioned that the concept of leadership had been bastardized where people used leadership positions to show arrogance, oppress others and misappropriate resources meant for the generality of Nigerians, instead of serving them as directed by God.

President Yar'Adua reiterated, "The opportunity to lead in whatever capacity on its own does not confer leadership; instead, leadership is earned after the discharge of the responsibility honestly, sacrificially and to the best of one's ability. Only then can those beneficiaries of the service selflessly rendered recognize such a person as a leader."

He emphasized, "There is an urgent need for a serious national campaign on the concept of leadership and the futility of oppressors acquiring wealth through illegal means." He contended, "People must recognize the finite nature of such wealth, as well as the day of reckoning when the eternal consequences of oppression, abuse of office and trust of those they govern shall be visited on those who misuse such opportunities." He strongly believes in "Servant-Leadership."

It is essential to remind all Nigerian leaders at local, state, regional or federal level that not everybody will like you no matter how good you are, but make sure you continue to do your best in the best interest of your country so that your good work may be exalted, lauded and appreciated generationally and from generation to eternity just like the free education and developmental programmes initiated in 1950's by the sage and immortal Chief Obafemi Awolowo, first Premier of Western Region of Nigeria.

Nigerian leaders have a lot to learn from the strengths of American military superpower, economic wealth, sociopolitical experiment and expperience as well as her democratic principles and practices. The Nigerian leadership should also learn from the strengths, weaknesses and mistakes of other countries to guide them in their daily endeavours to be the best they can be and act in the best interest of Nigeria and Nigerians. With leadership behaviour modification toward Godliness/Allahliness, Nigeria can remain a model for Africa, the pride of the Blacks and a great nation to reckon with in the Comity of Nations.

The overwhelming problems of Nigeria are elitecreated, and as such, they can be solved easily and quickly, if the entire Nigerian elites and leadership adopt behaviour modification and change "business as usual".

Leaders must be exemplary, transparent, incorruptible, not fraudulent and honest. They must be unimpeachable, scandals free, accountable, service and nationally conscious, humble, God/Allah fearing, responsible, responsive and trustworthy. They must be hard working, visionary, knowledgeable, intelligent, inspirational and innovative.

They must be patriotic, nationalistic, effectively communicative, motivational, empathic, caring and loving, charismatic and productive. They must be people oriented, disciplined, assertive and possess research abilities for problem solving. They must be vast in conflict resolution strategies in order to quickly intervene in solving socio-economic and political problems.

Nigeria is blessed with cultures and traditions that influence the raising and nurturing of a great child from childhood to adolescence and then to adulthood, and later in life to leadership at local, state, regional or federal level.

Unfortunately, other external cultures have had great influence on the leadership Nigeria produced from independence in 1960 up to date who choose ostentatious living, greed, corruption, selfaggrandizement and dictatorship, and thereby abandon the care, love and welfare of their people as well as forget to remember whose sons they are. Their African sense of community is lost and forgotten.

Many chose to steal Nigerian government money and stashed it in foreign banks; some others collected full pay for contracts they abandoned; while others committed serious acts of shameful economic and financial crimes against their fatherland.

They squandered Nigerian limited resources and left their fellow Nigerians unemployed, poorer, stagnating and retrogressing. Their love for money, immediate gratification, ostentatious living and possession of all that glitters of the Western World, overpowered their sense of community, culture, tradition and great values for which Africans are generally known.

Unfortunately and regrettably, the military leadership between 1993 and 1998 committed serious acts of human rights violations cum economic and financial crimes, which attracted world community attention for which Nigeria was ostracized from the world comity of nations.

A lot of lessons were learned during those turbulent days, but how far can the leaders that plunged Nigeria into debt crises be made to account for their financial crimes against their native land? Nigeria must recover all of the loot that is identifiable and recoverable for national resuscitation and progressive development.

To earn the trust of the people, leadership exemplariness is an indispensability. Nigerian leaders should put the interests of the nation in particular and those of the people in general above their own personal interests. Leaders should be sound psychologically, mentally, physically, academically, professionally and morally to be able to perform their responsibilities successfully.

Nigerian leadership must consist of distinguished persons who could be described as generalissimos, men and women of profound education and professionalism. For the nation's nascent democratic experiment to mature and succeed, Nigeria needs most distinguished men and women to pilot the ship of state.

Nigeria possesses men and women of great savvy and sagacity in the Presidency, the Legislature and the Judiciary. Hence, with teamwork among the great persons of the Presidency, the Legislature and the Judiciary, Nigeria, may never regress and Nigerians may never regret again all things being equal.

To foster understanding between the leadership and the followership in Nigeria's nascent democratic dispensation, illiteracy and ignorance must be eliminated among the followership by using aggressive, businesslike educational programmes and enlightenment campaigns to achieve high level of understanding among the leadership and the general population of Nigeria.

There is greater need to focus on the westernized system of quality education in Nigeria as well as bridge the wide gap of literacy between North and South of Nigeria. It is a task that must be done.

Any legislator without the equivalent of a 4year college/university degree should give way and sponsor somebody else who qualifies within his/her locality. To make laws effectively in the Legislature, the equivalent of a Bachelor of Arts degree is the minimum requirement.

The present leadership must fully understand and appreciate that Nigeria of preindependence up to 1960 and from 1960 to 1990's is different from Nigeria of the twenty-first century. Presently, Nigeria practises westernized democratic system of governance which allows every 'Dick, Jack and Harry' to talk whether right or wrong, persuasive or provocative or nonintelligent.

There are bound to be more conflicts where everybody has equal opportunity to talk as he/she likes. Above all, there are more highly educated Nigerians presently who cannot accept to be deceived or trampled upon. Also the general population is much more enlightened and can no longer be blindfolded with impunity just as it happened during previous dictatorial regimes.

There will be insults and condemnations even from those who do not have the right sensibility, the African culture and great traditional values to know what is right from what is wrong. That is because the world is changing with some confusion, but good government must ensure that peace is maintained, and the people are carried along.

The President must be committed to make Nigeria great and make the people achieve great things. The Legislature and the Judiciary must cooperate and team up with him in the best interest of Nigeria.

For the good of Nigeria, the Presidency, the Senate, the House of Representatives and the Judiciary should establish a formidable, cooperative working relationship that is transparent and helpful for immediate solution of Nigeria's problems of elite corruption, health care, education, food security, infrastructural development, energy generation, full industrialization, safety and security, full employment, reliable transportation and communication, affordable housing, economic development and political stability.

Good governance that focuses attention on the deficiency needs of the people will effectively motivate them and ease their burden to ensure survival, growth, development and goaldirected behaviour. The need to change behaviour of 'business as usual' must start from the top hierarchy (the leadership) to the bottom (the followership).

The nation's problems must be seen to be vigorously addressed in action and solved with resounding accomplishment, but not just mentioning them in words and propounding theories for their solution without embarking words with effective, selfless, relentless and successful actions.

Effective governance will find out through extensive research, the deficiency needs of the people and provide for their needs. Such deficiency needs may be (1) psychological needs (2) physiological needs (3) sociological needs (4) health safety and security needs (5) esteem or ego needs and (6) self actualization needs.

On Thursday, March 25, 2004, ExPresident Obasanjo urged Nigerians to demonstrate the spirit of tolerance, patriotism, vigilance and commitment to democratic values and practices, always in all their spheres of activities.

He advised Nigerians to be guided by patriotic and nationalistic ideals and that they should always remember that the quality of governance, leadership and improvement of facilities, service and infrastructure available to them would usually be largely determined by the quality of the persons they elected into office to hold the reins of power as their leader and representative.

He warned emphatically, "Those who forget history often fail to know what to do with the present, much less how to organize and plan for the future, to avoid a decadent past. We must individually and collectively commit to ensuring that our painful past will and must never happen again. We must determine that it will never, never happen again."

He reminded Nigerians that democracy was about people, community, truth, justice, cooperation and collective efforts of building and nurturing open societies and institutions in the best interest of all. He made reference to adherents to constitutionalism as a means to protect all in society, guarantee citizenship and hold leaders accountable at all times as they serve the people. He enjoined all to nurture and defend democracy robustly all the time for it to work and be meaningful in the lives of the citizenry.

He explained, "We are building new structures and institutions for rehabilitation, reconciliation, regeneration and repositioning our country for stability, peace, growth, development and democracy." He added that his administration was encouraging the emergence of new leaders that would work in mutually beneficial cooperation, on all issues affecting Nigerians irrespective of their religion, region, class, gender or ethnicity.

He acknowledged that Nigerians were massively opting for dialogue, cooperation, consultation and reliance on due process and legal action to resolve disputes. He reminded Nigerians not to quickly forget the pains, deprivations, intimidation, insecurity and near hopelessness that characterized their lives and environment for years before 1999 and ensure in their daily actions that such dreadful years never come back again.

In his own vision of leadership and eldership, Senator Olorunnimbe Mamora representing Lagos East Constituency on the floor of the Senate said, "Senate ought to be the Council of Elders or the Biblical Sanhedrin. Elders, not necessarily in terms of chronological age, but in terms of maturity, conduct affairs with mental age, wisdom and reasoning of elders." He added, "The character, behaviour and utterances of Senators ought to be truly most distinguished as they are usually addressed, and they must maintain a modicum of behaviour compatible with decency and decorum."

The minimum leadership qualities requirement mentioned by Senator Mamora should be the minimum requirement expected from leaders or elders in all spheres of life and responsibilities in Nigeria. He added, "While the leadership may not be saintly, the followership is definitely not angelic as well." Senator Mamora's statement fully describes the reality in the life of all Nigerians whether a leader or those being led.

Where is the pride of leadership that is more prone to scandals, fraudulence, corruptibility, money laundering, greed, mischief, selfish radicalism, deceitfulness, irresponsiveness and irresponsibility! It is irresponsible to continue to think about state or region of origin, the religion and ethnicity of who should lead Nigerians instead of emphasizing on the prospective leader's qualities of character, empathy, professionalism, excellence, academics, responsibility, accessibility, acceptability and impeccability.

Where in the civilized democratic world is the election of a national leader made because of his state or region of origin? Where in the civilized democratic world is a person elected as president or prime minister especially in the USA or Great Britain because he or she is from the north, west, south or east?

When are Nigerians going to start to be like the civilized democratic world? The earlier the better and is best sooner than later for Nigeria as the leading black people's nation in the world.

Nigerian leaders at local, state, regional and federal levels should start to educate their people that in a democracy, everybody who qualifies constitutionally to be elected president, or any other elective position can seek mandate of the people and be elected irrespective of his or her ethnicity, religion, state or region of origin.

The importance of merit, qualification, experience and suitability of the candidate for the elective position being sought, should be the main consideration of the electorate. All acts of discrimination and exclusionism should be discouraged, made unlawful and unacceptable.

It is important to emphasize to all Nigerians especially the elites and leaders at local, state, regional and federal levels that disintegration of Nigeria or any other arrangement that encourages secessionist tendencies, polarization, balkanization or divisionism in whatever form or shape is not the best alternative lasting solution to Nigerian problems. The reason is because an indivisible, united, one Nigeria under God/Allah is bigger, stronger, more virile, more economically viable and better than any of its parts or a combination of some of its parts.

Any disintegration will adversely affect the image and the socio-economic and political influence, which Nigeria enjoys in the world generally and in the continent of Africa in particular. Nigerian political leaders should shelve their personal interests, differences and animosities and do only what is best for Nigeria so that history will praise and reward them .

They should refrain from doing what posterity will curse them for, and not forgive them. Always remember and be guided by the popular wise dictum, "United we stand, divided we fall." Any residence or nation that fails and falls shall become a liability for not only her present but also including her future generations.

Nigerian leaders and decision-makers should learn from the breakup of the second superpower, the Soviet Union, the USSR in the 20th century. The disintegration of the USSR is regretted today in many quarters because it offends against the balance of power between the Western and Eastern blocs with some attendant consequences. With only one superpower left in the world, it gives the only one superpower room for arbitrariness, abusive use of military power with impunity, flagrant violation and disobedience of international law, flouting of United Nations regulations and indiscretional application of the law of the jungle, "the survival of the fittest," when settling international disputes.

The tilt of balance of power to the West has left one "proverbial lion nation" in the forest with many other weak nations as preys. An unfavourable rearrangement of Nigeria may create more problems than are meant to be solved. An arrangement that keeps the United States of America together and indivisible, one nation under God, should be able to keep Nigeria together in the best interest of the nation and Africa's best interest because Nigeria has attained some remarkable successes as the peace and power broker in Africa and other black nations in the world.

It is regrettable that for over four decades, some Nigerian leaders and elders who have scores to settle among themselves or have axe to grind or wish to make paybacks have nursed grudges and fought among themselves to death irreconcilably as enemies, not because of political ideological differences or Nigerian best interests, but for personal animosity and selfish interests.

If every leader is working in the best interest of the nation, approaches may differ but that should not create any enmity. How long can Nigerian leaders and elders live as enemies of one another and for what? Are you fighting for Nigeria and Nigerians for benefits, which most Nigerians do not see for over forty years? Given that situation, it is Nigeria and Nigerians who are suffering for the leaders' wrongful actions, utterances, infightings, name-callings, frauds, corruption, crimes and other scandalous acts that heat the Nigerian polity.

Leaders and elders who are bitter, fighting among themselves for decades cannot nurse love, care and empathy, and cannot concentrate to do what is best for the nation and the people. There are leaders and elders who continue to play one part of the country against the other, groups against groups and individuals against one another by deception and pretending to be protecting their own people or ethnicities against nonexistent fears.

Such leaders or elders who cannot change but continue to sow seeds of discord, hatred, divisionism, tribalism and unpatriotism to heat Nigerian polity, should be set aside while the nation nurtures new leadership that would be exemplary to our generation and posterity. Nigerians should start to exercise their electoral power to recall leaders and representatives who are too controversial, confrontational and not beneficial to Nigerians.

Godfathers with money and influence who have little education should leave politics to their highly educated children and grandchildren and go back to their constituencies, their towns or villages. Nigeria is tired of political gangsterism and hooliganism especially at the local and state levels.

Modern politics is not for confusionists and semiliterates. Nobody is too old to learn. People at seventy or eighty still graduate in American universities. An American World War II veteran went back to school and finished his high school education at the age of 83. He passed his school certificate on a wheel chair at the age of 83 on May 29, 2008. He joined his 18year old classmates to celebrate at the graduation ceremony.

Wake up Nigerians and stop being used by leaders and elders for their own socio-economic and political gains or religious and ethnicity influences and enrichment while playing on your intelligence by deception and pretence. They may say they are fighting for you when they are actually inciting you against your fellow compatriots and the nation in order to secure their own socio-economic, political, religious or other selfish gains.

People from all nooks and corners of Western Nigeria benefited immensely from Chief Obafemi Awolowo's gigantic free educational and development programmes for which he will be remembered forever and ever. His footstep was followed by former governor of Lagos State, Alhaji Lateef Jakande, alias Baba Kekere, for which he will never be forgotten by all beneficiaries of free education and free healthcare in Lagos State.

Also remember the legends and champions of Nigerian independence like Sir Ahmadu Bello, the Sardauna of Sokoto, first Premier of Northern Nigeria; Sir Abubakar Tafawa Balewa, first Prime Minister of Nigeria; Dr. Nnamdi Azikiwe, Zik of Africa, first President of Nigeria; Chief Obafemi Awolowo, first Premier of Western Nigeria and many others mentioned in chapters one and two of this book.

Quoting from ExPresident Olusegun Obasanjo, "What sort of Nigerian are you?" As an appeal to all Nigerian leaders and elders, it is being asked, "For what are you going to be remembered eternally?" What conscience do you have when you corruptly acquired Nigerian government money and stashed it in overseas private bank accounts when such money could be utilized for investment, employment generation and economic development purposes in Nigeria?

What purpose is your enormous wealth of liquid assets worthy of billions of dollars in foreign developed countries when most Africans are hungry, unemployed, brain drained and exploited? Tell us what kind of conscience you have when a poor person steals a couple of naira to eat, he or she could face sentence of amputation of the offending limbs wherever such law applies, but those who have conspired to steal millions and billions of Nigerian government money and stashed them overseas are sacred cows and untouchables?

How long will that hypocrisy and deception continue with discriminatory application of the laws? Where is equity, justice and fair play? A man can commit adultery with impunity, but if a woman does the same thing, she faces death penalty. What kind of conscience do you have? Equal application of the law with justice and fair play is a requirement of Godliness/Allahliness whether you are rich or poor, man or woman. Nigerian laws must equally apply to all with equity, justice and fair play. That is the trend of global civilization. Stop cheating womanhood just because you are a man and nothing more.

The world has progressed by the Will of God/Allah beyond and better than how things were done before, during and after early centuries. Whoever cannot change for better is not capable of facing world realities. God/ Allah forbids cheating. Live and let live. Why not wish for others, those great things that you wish for yourself and your family? Let us be our brothers' and sisters' keepers irrespective of differences in ethnicity, religion or sex (man or woman).

Nigeria needs real transparent leaders and elders who can sit down together and deliberate healthily to move the country forward to greater heights without unnecessarily dwelling on their ethnicity, religion, culture, socio-economic, political and ideological differences. The main objective of harmonization is to talk out the differences and agree utilizing the spirit of give and take. Whenever there is any disagreement on policy decision or policy implementation, those who disagree should present better alternative suggestions persuasively without any confrontations, no name-calling and no call for violence, mass disruptive or destructive actions which hurt and heat the polity. Nigeria is sick and tired of political hooliganism.

Leaders and elders who cannot apply mature, nonviolence strategies to solve Nigerian problems should quit the stage or be sent out involuntarily. There are at present, capable, well-groomed, highly educated and professionally qualified Nigerians locally and internationally who can pilot the "Aircraft of State" to the Promised Land. Nigeria is blessed!

If you have not done Nigeria any good for forty years in politics since independence, you should quit honourably or be set aside if you are still causing trouble. Present world politics requires intelligence, maturity, relevant experience, education, professionalism, leadership qualities, political savvy and sagacity to achieve successes and not hooliganism, semiliteracy, religion or ethnicity background.

The diversities in Nigeria should be utilized as Nigerian strength. The Presidency and State Governors should set up programmes that encourage multiculturalism and multiethnicism development which should begin from school age and extend to leaders and traditional rulers participating fully in interethnic activities to include debates, seminars, conferences, friendly visits and games among various cultures, traditions and ethnicities of Nigeria.

The main objective of the programme is to enable Nigeria to build and nurture future leaders and citizens that would understand, appreciate and trust one another more than ever before and have nothing to fear about one another. Such programmes would enable Nigerians to identify themselves more as Nigerian citizens rather than emphasize their individual ethnic groupings.

May God/Allah please give Nigerian leadership the wisdom as received by the Biblical Solomon to captain the ship of Nigerian nation to greatness, excellence and economic prosperity without pain and suffering which were prevalent in past decades of military dictatorship (1966-1999).

It is worthy to refer to one of the comments credited to ExGovernor of Enugu State. Dr. Chimaroke Nnamani during his courtesy visit to Turakin Sokoto, Alhaji Shehu Shagari, former President of the 2nd Republic of Nigeria. He told former President Shagari, "You are an exemplary figure and represent a clear subjugation to the will of God. You represent nonaggressive pursuit of political power. You represent man surrendering to destiny and the will of God/Allah. You represent the good in our country which we want back." One wonders how Nigerians including leaders and elders can earn those kinds of accolades showered on former President Shehu Shagari! It confirms that everybody is making history every minute of one's life and people will reap what they sow individually no matter how long.

Nigerian leaders should share the following valuable thoughts and pronouncement of Dr. Martin Luther King, Jr. of the United States of America who declared, "The true meaning of achievement is service."

During one of his sermons, he said, "I want you to be the first in love. I want you to be first in moral excellence. I want you to be first in generosity. If you want to be important, wonderful. If you want to be great, wonderful. But recognize that he who is greatest among you shall be your servant."

Also, Dr. King adopted a strategy of nonviolence from Mahatma Gandhi, one of the greatest leaders of India, who served humanity with great spirit of love, humility, empathy, responsiveness and nonviolence. It must be remembered that Dr. Martin Luther King, Jr. was from a different race, different country and different religion from those of Mahatma Gandhi but they shared the same faith of nonviolence.

It is pertinent to mention the words of affirmation of commitment and patriotism credited to (Dr.) Mrs. Ngozi Okonjo-Iweala, ExFinance Minister, who was reported to have said, "How can you live comfortably somewhere else working in another country, helping to develop other economies while all is not well with your country? Your own country isn't working, but you are living abroad. To me, that isn't right."

There is a lot of wisdom in the statement credited to the ExFinance Minister, but if personal and possessional security issues are tackled successfully, and if equal opportunities are offered, Nigerians in the Diaspora love their nation, they will come home for nation building. "East or West, home is the best."

The Governor of Ogun State, Otunba Gbenga Daniel, should be praised and congratulated for embarking on a research system that exposed ghost workers, which enabled Ogun State Government to save 50 million naira monthly as reported in the Daily Independent Online of Friday, September 12, 2003. The research was said to have exposed somebody collecting 16 salaries, using four different accounts and 26 others who were still working after completing regulated mandatory 35 years of service.

What was the punishment meted to them as a deterrence to others? Such investigation should be conducted at all other local, state and federal government establishments which include the entire civil service, the parastatals, the military, police, navy, air force and the pensioners' accounts. If the exercise is carried out to eliminate ghost workers and pensioners, Nigeria will save a lot of money, which can be utilized to take care of essential projects for the benefit of the people. If all areas of wastes are eliminated, a lot of revenue will be saved and there will be less inclination to increase taxes on the people.

There should be greater emphasis on ensuring that the westernized educational gap between the North and the Southern regions is narrowed down considerably so that the whole country can always speak with similar, consistent and more coherent understanding. A lot of the old ways of doing things religiously without some flexibility is completely at variance with modern civilization and the New World Order.

The world is changing and Nigerians generally need higher education and enlightenment to follow and cope with the pace and trend of the changing world. The ways people used to do things are changing and people need westernized education at higher levels to understand and adopt the changes of the New World.

The contributions of Northern elders, leaders and governors are significantly indispensable in this case for the benefit of the people. They should embark on serious enlightenment campaigns that ensure that no child is left behind in the Universal Basic Education programme. It is better to initiate development programmes to enhance the people's standard of living than to leave them in penury only to resort to cutting their limbs if they steal a couple of naira to eat and live.

How many elites who stole millions and billions of money have had their limbs amputated? None! That is hypocrisy. The civilized world has shifted away from such capital punishment and discriminatory application of the law that punishes the poor and pats the wealthy at the back when they commit the same offence. It is barbaric.

It is heartwarming and appreciated to note that notable, eminent and most distinguished individuals in Minna, Niger State capital, decided to launch a massive campaign against illiteracy and ignorance. The activities of Minna Emirate Educational Foundation (MEEFO), a nongovernmental organization, comprising eminent citizens of the state, should be emulated by other groups in other parts of Northern Nigeria in particular and the whole of the country in general.

The membership of the MEEFO under the patronage of Emir of Minna, Alhaji Umaru Farouk Bahago, cuts across various professional groups of eminent Nigerians including Generals Ibrahim Babangida and Abdulsalami Abubakar who were two former Heads of State of Nigeria.

In the same vein, former Nigerian President, Alhaji Shehu Shagari called on well meaning indigenes of Northern Nigeria to wake up and contribute their quotas toward the development of westernized type of education in Northern Nigeria. Former Nigerian President Alhaji Shehu Shagari, who is the Chairman of the Sokoto Educational Development Trust Fund, mentioned that the 'FUND' allocated 5,000 naira to each student who was an indigene of the state pursuing university degree courses in Nigeria. The education fund effort was also backed by the Sultan of Sokoto, Alhaji Mohammadu Maccido. The effort is commendable, and it should be pursued more vigorously with more funds made available for the assistance of students.

It is significant to make references to the stand taken by the former Speaker of the House of Representatives, Alhaji Aminu Bello Masari on the leadership of Nigeria. In a statement credited to ExHouse Speaker Masari on Tuesday, August 26, 2003, he defined leadership thus, "Leadership is about service not arrogance or exercise of power. Power is transient. Position should not make us proud and arrogant such that when we have to go back to the society, it becomes impossible for us to assimilate."

ExHouse speaker Masari was said to have expressed displeasure at the proud and arrogant disposition of those in position of authority in the country, who were not demonstrating "selfless leadership associated with the nation's early leaders."

He was said to have lauded the sterling qualities of late Premier of Northern Region of Nigeria, Sir Ahmadu Bello, by saying, "His era was one of service for the people unlike what obtains in the country at the moment, and unless the present crop of leaders retrace their steps, their vaunted efforts at poverty alleviation would be futile." He added, "Let's fight corruption by setting good example."

ExHouse Speaker Masari was very empathic, and he was truly a man of the people on basis of his stand on most issues that affected Nigerians. He emphasized, "Addressing basic minimal requirement of life will go a long way in checkmating corruption, and unfortunately in this our country, we don't have what we call 'no go area'." He explained,

"There is corruption in developed countries but the level it is being practised has no direct impact on the ordinary citizens and that the minimum requirement of daily living is available to everybody."

He emphasized, "With everybody having at least the basic minimum requirement of daily living, there would be some peace. It is then that those who have can enjoy the benefit of what they have, because however rich you are, you can only enjoy your richness under peace and stability."

ExHouse Speaker Alhaji Masari added, "Fighting corruption is by setting example by the leadership. But what you find is that the system itself is structured in such a way that it produces corruption naturally, because the gap between the top and the bottom is so wide."

Your concern is shared, Mr. Speaker, but that is the trend all over the capitalist world where they talk and preach freedom and less about justice, fair play, and equitable distribution of wealth. How can there be peace? Serious inequity and wide inequality gap will always breed violence and destruction.

The above problems highlighted by ExHouse Speaker Masari are fundamental and not difficult to solve with exemplary leadership, transparency, honesty, economic and financial management savvy and sagacity; understanding of banking, monetary and fiscal measures, economic growth strategies, creating sound investment climate, creating full employment, ensuring price stabilization, narrowing inequality gap, ensuring political stability and applying sound welfarism strategies that uplift the generality of the people.

The inequality gap between the top (the rich) and the bottom (the poor) mentioned by ExHouse Speaker Masari is very crucial as it is the determining factor or the measuring rod of a nation's economic wellness or well being. Technically, the variance between the rich, the wealthy and the poor is referred to as the inequality gap. The wider the inequality gap in a country's economy, the poorer the country and the people become; but the narrower the inequality gap becomes, the better and greater the people's economic successes.

The best option for Nigerian leadership is to narrow or almost close the inequality gap as much as possible using micro and macroeconomic measures effectively and efficiently through open market operations. There must be economic liberalization and deregulation, increased capitalization, effective monetary and fiscal measures; stable demand, supply and price; reasonably low interest, inflation and discount rates; and by applying measures that steadily increase the growth rate of the gross domestic product (GDP) of the country.

There must be safety of lives, property and investment; political stability, industrial harmony and democracy, sound health programme, elimination of frauds and corruption; elimination of violent crimes, economic and financial crimes; maintaining peace and providing the right business climate for entrepreneurship.

The former Senate President Adolphus Wabara expressed deep concern and displeasure about illegal drugs as well as economic and financial crimes in Nigeria while inaugurating the Senate Committee on Drugs, Narcotics and Financial Crimes headed by Senator Shuaibu. He condemned the negative impact of illegal drugs.

He explained that high profile investment was not attracting to Nigeria as expected because Nigerians were being perceived negatively as untrustworthy crooks by international community as a result of nefarious fraudulent financial activities of a negligible few Nigerians.

Former Senate President Wabara reiterated that illegal drug dealing and financial crimes had: (1) seriously undermined the moral fiber of the nation's society; (2) created distortions in people's value judgment and promoted societal vices which were hindering economic development; and (3) resulted in illegal drugs proliferation and financial crimes which carried serious national security implications.

It is crystal clear that Nigerian government (the Presidency, the Legislature and the Judiciary) know, understand and are conversant with Nigerian problems and they are determined to solve them. Although there are overwhelming constraints, Nigeria needs to be cleaned permanently at all cost, with established deterrent measures that ensure the country is never again placed in a deteriorating, retrogressional, dictatorial, penurial or pariah situation at anytime throughout life.

The constraints, the bumps and impediments on the government's paths must be cleared decisively. Regrettably, possible casualties would include friends, associates and relatives but Nigeria must be sanitized for the present generation and posterity in the best interest of the nation without fear or favour and with justice and fair play to all her citizens.

After Obasanjo Administration preached against frauds, corruption, economic and financial crimes and established sound structures to root out these societal elitist evils, followed by Yar'Adua's zero tolerance for corruption, anybody who refuses to change cannot deserve to be a real friend, real associate or real relation. Whoever has not changed, should be replaced and sent into a reformatory, and all the ill-gotten gains recovered for Nigerian development. Members of any government that successfully clean Nigeria of corruption, other economic crimes and violent crimes will have their names written in gold, and posterity will forever say, "Thank you."

Hence, this government of the Fourth Republic cannot afford to fail the present and future generations about their expectations for a future prosperous and incorruptible Nigeria. If the government fails to act decisively now, knowing fully well that nobody wants to hear excuses anymore, it may be difficult for posterity to forgive the present leaders.

It is the greatest opportunity to make a difference in the lives of the present and future generations, so, the leaders in government must think, "What if the opportunity slips away and never comes back again; what will history say?" This may be an opportunity of a lifetime to salvage Nigeria. It is a task that must be done with cooperation, understanding and teamwork among the Presidency, the Legislature and the Judiciary. They can do it; they must do it in the best interest of Nigeria.

At the reception organized for 1949/54 alumni of Baptist Boys High School (BBHS), Abeokuta in December 2004, ExPresident Olusegun Obasanjo said that his incarceration on trumped up charges for attempted coup d'etat by late Head of State, General Sani Abacha was with God's knowledge, and it was for a purpose.

He referred to the vow of General Abacha that he (President Obasanjo), Chief Moshood Kashimawo Olawale Abiola and General Shehu Musa Yar'Adua would not come out of prison alive. He mentioned that the other two died in prison and that his being saved and brought out of prison by God was for a purpose. He referred to the Holy Bible and quoted the case of Esther, a maidservant who through divine intervention, married the Persian King Ahasuerus and utilized her position to save her kinsmen, the Jews, from extermination.

With the above revelation, Obasanjo Administration was not only symbolically ordained, it was providential. All he needed was the support of all to continue his good work that brought Nigeria out of chronic debt and pariah state to the path of honour, dignity and greatness in the comity of nations.

President Obasanjo as a human being was not perfect, but the country was in better shape than what it was between 1966 and 1998. Nigerians must thank God/Allah for His grace and pray for more. President Obasanjo fulfilled the purpose of humanity and human existence by leaving the Nigerian presidency on May 29, 2007 better than he met it during his inauguration on May 29, 1999.

It is recalled that in December 2004, during the ceremony marking the working relation between Leon Sullivan Foundation in Washington, DC and the New Partnership for Africa's Development (NEPAD), President Obasanjo was honoured for his commitment to transparency, peacekeeping in Africa and spokesman for Africa. The President of ChevronTexaco Petroleum, Mr. George Kirkland, described Nigeria as an example of transparency and good governance in Africa and hoped that Nigeria would continue to be a unifying factor in Africa.

While presenting the 2004 budget proposal to the National Assembly, ExPresident Obasanjo made some statements, which demonstrated an innovative style of leadership by encouraging consultation and full participation in government decision-making. He said, "We have consulted with the National Assembly on this reform programme and received valuable inputs for which I want to thank you. We have also consulted widely with the rest of the country including the organized private sector (OPS), governors, state and local government officials, civil society, religious leaders, traditional rulers, labour, academics and senior managers in our tertiary institutions, the political class, the military, police and paramilitary. The feedback has been good and valuable. It has enabled us to strengthen and enrich the programme."

The strategy of consultation and participation in government decision-making added some sophistication to policy making in furtherance of Nigeria's democratic experimentation. The strategy facilitated quick decision-making formulation, easy acceptance by all stakeholders and easy implementation of policies. Since all stakeholders' representatives were carried along, the possibility of dissension, condemnation of result or errors would be slim or nil, and the percentage of successful implementation of policy would be 99.9%. The decision to carry the people along was unique and was best to strengthen Nigeria's nascent democracy.

The government expressed conscern for workers all the time as demonstrated by the former Senate President, Adolphus Wabara, while inaugurating the Senate Committee on labour and productivity under the chairmanship of Senator Tawar U. Wada on September 30, 2003. The former Senate President, Adolphus Wabara, reiterated, " The only sure way to true national greatness is by paying very serious attention to workers."

He added, "Workers create the national wealth putting every hand and brain to productive use." He explained, "Workers must be primed for efficiency and the welfare of the workers must be paramount. Workers must not only be the subject of development but be the object of development as well." He advocated for better industrial relations, more human and safer work environment, less exploitation of workers and more commitment to workers' welfare in general.

Above statements of former Senate President Wabara showed great interest in workers welfare and development, industrial harmony and a workforce that is fairly treated and not exploited. The statements confirmed a leadership that cared.

Another leader of great thought, Ogun State Governor Obalofin Otunba Gbenga Daniel declared on Nigeria's forty-third independence anniversary, "We must wake up to the task of sustaining, deepening and strengthening all institutions that will guarantee the survival and durability of our democracy adding that by so doing, we must make truth our armour and unity our shield." He mentioned that his administration derived its mandate from the people's genuine and overwhelming yearning for good life, hence, its actions were firmly anchored on the tested and cherished progressive heritage of the people.

These glorious statements and actions of the leaders of Nigeria that emerged since 2003 showed empathy, love, care and concern for the people. Such magnanimity is completely different from the indignities and sufferings which Nigerians experienced during the era of dictatorship between 1966 and 1998.

The Nigerian leadership has persistently called on Nigerians to change from 'business as usual.' According to Gandhi, "We must become the change we wish to see." Therefore, the change expected by the leadership of the government (the Presidency, the Legislature and the Judiciary) must start from the top downward to the bottom.

Hence, leaders, elders and government functionaries must absolve themselves from frauds, corruption, economic and financial crimes to make it easy for them to sell the 'wish for change' to all Nigerian citizens. Leaders must be exemplary to be able to preach their good ideas successfully to the people. Good leadership is not, "Do what I say and preach according to the Gospel, but not as I do."

Confrontational style of leadership that heats the polity that also retards progress and disrupts teamwork is not good for Nigeria. In response to insincere critics of the former Senate President, Adpolphus Wabara, for those who namedcalled him a stooge, in the *Daily Champion* of Tuesday, April 13, 2004, he said to his pessimists, "I have been able to bring Julius Berger to rehabilitate roads in Abia, the Alaoji electricity project had been restored at more than 0.56 billion naira and the Aba-Owerri Road had been rehabilitated. You see, I'd rather remain a stooge and get things done than be a fighter who gets nothing done at the end of the day."

The above response of the former Senate President to his critics showed great statesmanship, great sense of responsibility and a wonderful team player that critics wanted to fail.

In his nationwide address of March 25, 2004 on the local government elections, ExPresident of Nigeria, General Olusegun Obasanjo, reminded Nigerians, "The quality of governance, leadership and improvement in facilities, services and infrastructure we get will be largely determined by the quality of the people we vote into power." The warning is very significant to all Nigerian voters. Remember, as you make your bed, so you lie on it.

The assertions of the former President of the Senate and Nigerian ExPresident Obasanjo are true to life, and they represent the realities of life. Any leader or representative of the people that is confrontational, and not teamplaying would achieve little or nothing for the people just like a rolling stone that gathers no moss.

On the other hand, a leader or people's representative with great understanding ability, who is accessible, compromising, cooperative, responsive, friendly with strong interpersonal skills and a teamplayer would be a great achiever.

Many times, those who want a leader to fail get disappointed, so, they will resort to spite him and call him names like stooge, fraud or rambo when he is performing successfully and creditably. Successful leadership is usually a big problem to people who are not partners in progress. An understanding and intelligent opposition will pull together with the government to share in the successes if the interest of the nation is put first. Some people often criticize to be noticed even when they cannot perform as good as the persons they are criticizing.

The ExVice President, Atiku Abubakar; former Senate President, Adolphus Wabara; and former PDP Chairman, Chief Audu Ogbeh; emphasized the imperativeness of good leadership during the "Leadership Awards" of *The Week Magazine* held at the main auditorium of the Nigerian Institute of International Affairs (NIIA), Victoria Island, Lagos in April 2004.

ExVice President Atiku Abubakar described leadership as a critical factor in the actualization of vision and in the realization of the goals of stability, peace and economic prosperity. He appealed to the media to continue to bear with political leaders to protect and develop Nigeria's fledgling democracy.

He contended that in the absence of good leadership, available human and material resources in the country would never be efficiently harnessed for the betterment of the citizenry. He expressed regrets that the media sector that fought vehemently for the enthronement of civil rule could engage in undermining the hard won democracy through unfair criticisms characterized by deep cynicism and negativism.

He added, "We love and care about the country as much as the media do, criticize us if we make mistakes, but do not dismiss everything we do." He explained, "The dividends of democracy may be slow in coming, but we have no alternatives to a system which guarantees choice, freedom, openness and the respect for the human person."

He advised, "When less informed segments of our society demonstrate impatience with democracy, the media should tell them that there are no quick fixes and that the leadership is being careful to get things right once and for all in this country."

In his own contribution to the imperativeness of good leadership, the former Senate President, Adolphus Wabara who chaired the occasion asserted, "Leadership is a critical factor which makes the difference in the world." He added that it was not enough to have abundant natural resources, good climate, brilliant and talented people, but there must be leadership to pull all the resources together in the right and proper mix to achieve the desired goals and objectives.

He explained that leadership was not limited to elected representatives and those appointed to positions of authority and influence alone, but included leaders in family, groups of friends, teams at work, community and in all activities of human endeavours where purposeful and inspiring leadership should apply.

He described leadership as a lifetime skill that must be tapped, nurtured and developed for the greater benefit of mankind. He amplified Nigerians' rights to demand good leadership from those who were at the helm of affairs and that leaders should make service their benchmark and watchword. He added that service was the essence of leadership but not avenue to feather one's nest, not excuse for plundering the nation's wealth and not a licence to oppress fellow human beings.

He further described leadership as a rare opportunity to uplift the society for the common benefit of all the citizens. He compared and equated the importance of leadership with that of the followership and described both as inevitably equal to each other and one unequivocally complementary to the other.

The former Senate President, Adolphus Wabara, pinned the socio-economic and political problems of Nigeria to bad leadership of the past. He quoted Harry S. Truman, one of America's greatest presidents and leaders of all times, who said, "The period where there is not leadership, society stands still. Progress occurs when courageous, skillful leaders seize the opportunity to change things for the better."

In his own contribution, the former Chairman of the People's Democratic Party (PDP), Chief Audu Ogbeh who was the guest speaker of the occasion, referred to certain irreducible minimum attributes, which a leader must possess in order to carry everybody along. Such leader, man or woman must exhibit an epitome of discipline as well as a sympathetic mind with some passion for the weak, the poor or the downtrodden.

He remarked, "Any individual who does not exhibit any of these attributes should not be part of the leadership process as well as democratization process." He assured that the government had renewed its bid to ameliorate Nigerians' problems by concentrating to tackle the shortage of water, light, housing and health facilities as well as solve agricultural, food and unemployment problems.

Eminent personalities who received awards for good leadership at the ceremony included ExGovernors Bola Ahmed Tinubu (Lagos), Boni Haruna (Adamawa), Peter Odili (Rivers), Sam Egwu (Ebonyi) and Abdullahi Adam (Nasarawa).

By assessing the speeches of Nigerian leaders, there is no slightest doubt that they know, understand and fully appreciate the imperativeness of good leadership. May God/Allah continue to give them the courage, the wisdom and the capability to practise what they say and preach for the betterment of Nigerian citizenry. Nigerian leaders could borrow a leaf from widely believed great examples of President Lee Kuan Yew of Singapore and Mohammed Mahatir of Malaysia who as a result of their visionary leadership, they were said to have succeeded in turning their countries into economic miracles.

Good decision-making is very important for leadership successes. Nigeria should take note of the problems in Iraq, the Middle East to fully appreciate the importance of not making any hasty, unwise decision, which could mar the entire nation.

Iraq was like a fly on the scrotum of the United States of America, the greatest and most powerful country in the world – the only super power both militarily and economically. This super power country used missiles to kill the fly on its scrotum and eventually created more problems than it wanted to solve.

Regrettably, the hasty decision to go to war in Iraq that toppled Saddam Hussein resulted in over 4,000 American soldiers dead and over 30,000 wounded, and more than quadruple those casualty figures happened to Iraqis. Eventually, the world witnessed more deaths, more terrorism, more suicide bombers, and the world became more uncertain about when the deaths and terrorism would end worldwide.

World elders and leaders cannot afford to abandon the world to the young but most powerful leaders of UK and US. World conflicts should not be only about victor or vanquished but about world lasting peace. World powerful leaders, who are interested in fighting wars to conquer, should condescend to seek advice and adjust policies as necessary for peace.

The forty-first President of the USA, the dad, George H.W. Bush, heroically drove the Iraqis out of Kuwait during her occupation by the Iraqis. He worked closely with the United Nations, and Iraq was contained. There was peace and no insurgents or suicide bombers. He did not call the UN all sorts of names nor denigrate the UN leadership as the son did. That is how elders lead completely different from the young and less experienced leaders with youthful exuberance. A word is enough for the wise. The world needs peace.

Continuing war means more deaths, more destruction of lives, properties and infrastructures; more devastation, economic downturn, more suffering for the poor and wider spread of hatred and conflicts globally. On the other hand, more war means more money for the rich, wealthy politicians and top government functionaries in the awards and execution of over inflated contracts for prosecuting war, reconstruction and oil prospecting.

More war means more budget deficit to be borne by posterity and more war means more budget-cut with less provision for human services and programmes that could alleviate the sufferings of the masses. Ironically, most rich politicians in authority tend to like war because they acquire more money and wealth and lose nothing with hardly any members of their families in the war front.

If the few wealthy and affluent do not want peace, the poor masses that are the afflicted, need and want global peace. Enough of war is enough. Lasting and enduring global peace is a task that must be accomplished. Greatest leaders are those who achieve peace, the greatest in modern times. They are awarded Nobel Peace Prizes in recognition of their contributions to world peace.

Suppose Nigerian General Sani Abacha who was accused of various crimes of human rights abuses and economic crimes, was to be forcefully removed just as it happened in Iraq, there would have been civil war that would have resulted in serious collateral damages close to what happened in Iraq.

Nigeria is peaceful and moving on because God/Allah worked out the sudden death of General Abacha who was regarded by the world community as a brutal dictator. A fly on your scrotum represents a time bomb or a suicide bomber on your scrotum. If you decide unwittingly to use crushing missiles to kill the fly in order to save the scrotum, you may end up breaking the scrotum while the fly escapes also. The result may be death.

Nigeria should always 'look before she leaps' and learn from others' mistakes when solving her socio-economic and political problems. With some patience, it could take time but Saddam Hussein of Iraq could be toppled and democracy entrenched in Iraq without the enormity of collateral damages as well as the insurrection from insurgents and suicide bombers, which the world witnessed unprecedentedly.

Therefore, Nigerian leaders should continue to utilize dialogue, diplomacy, consultation and peaceful conflict resolution strategies to solve her domestic and international problems rather than an act of confrontation or declaration of war. The same advice goes to the opposition groups, political parties and the press from whom much responsibility is expected. It is easier to start a problem than solve it or determine accurately how it will end.

The bottom line is that the world should be made safer and less prone to conflict each day of people's lives. Stop being a part of Nigerian problem; start being a part of the solution to the problems. Always put Nigeria first and act in the best interest of your country, Nigeria, your homeland. Nigeria is the only place you can call your own, if you are a Nigerian.

Most importantly, the Nigerian leadership should seriously start to measure the achievements and successes of the reform operations with the impacts they have on the ordinary people who are the masses. The more the masses benefit from the reform operations, the more successful they are.

The reforms should narrow down and bridge the 'inequality gap' in Nigerian society before the reforms can be said to be meaningful and successful. The feedback results will determine the level of successes of the NEEDS and Seven-Point programmes as well as the successes of the technical experts, presidential advisers and members of the Federal Executive Council socio-economically and politically.

The wealth of 'Enterprise Nigeria' dividends and opportunities should spread to the masses in all nooks and corners of the nation for their upliftment instead of being kept in the hands of few elites alone in the Presidency, the Legislature, the Judiciary, Governors, government functionaries, their relations and foreign partners. The overall priority objectives of government should be the survival and upliftment of the masses, full employment, economic prosperity, sociopolitical stabilization, low interest rate, transparency, accountability, exemplary leadership and good governance.

If Nigerian leaders between 1960 and 1998 (thirty-eight years) were able to accomplish as much as what Obasanjo regime achieved for Nigeria between 1999 and 2007, Nigeria would have become an economic giant in the world. Corruption and fraud would have been minimal in Nigerian society. The nation's march to the Promised Land would have been smoother and not more tedious. Nigerians should presently be enjoying the illuminations at the end of the tunnel with glorious songs of praises to God/Allah.

Those who should be closely watched are the young political leaders who were terribly critical of the old politicians for corruptly enriching themselves with hundreds and thousands, but when these young men and women became governors and political appointees, they buried themselves in corruption and fraud exceeding millions and billions of government money and hid themselves under the cover of constitutional immunity.

If anybody has not actually stolen from Nigerian wealth, he will not invoke the immunity clause in the constitution when he is called upon to account for missing and mishandled resources under his watch. Those who have been blocking the speedy amendment of the 1999 constitution may be 'chop and quench' politicians who should be watched and recalled.

Nigerian leadership can learn a lot from Britain, US, Russia, China, Japan, Canada, other African countries and the world in general by emulating what is best about those successful countries without falling a prey nor sacrificing Nigerian sovereignty and independence. Nigeria should not repeat the mistakes of those countries nor succumb to their neocolonization schemes. Remember, Nigeria was acclaimed the happiest nation in the world in 2004.

The dilemma of leaders and their advisers is real and should be recognized and appreciated. No leader has ever wished to fail, but as human beings, they are prone to human imperfections. There are great, wonderful, and successful leaders, but they are not infallible. Also, there are great dependable, honest and highly qualified advisers, experts, presidential aides, government officials, etc. but as human beings, they are not perfect.

According to late President Ronald Reagan, Fortieth President of the USA, "The greatest president is not the one who does the greatest things, but he who makes the people do the greatest things." In effect, the greatest President is the one who carries the people along and makes them accomplish great things. It therefore behooves on every President to listen not only to his closest advisers but also the yearnings of the generality of his people. The work of the President is usually the most difficult, Herculean task, but it must be done and done right.

The President's position in developing countries cannot be complacent in places prone to militarism and coups d'etat. In advanced countries, where coups are ruled out, the fear is terrorism and the citizenry that carry guns whom nobody knows when they can strike.

If the Head of State, General Aguiyi Ironsi, listened and took immediate preemptive actions in July 1966 when plans of military coup d'etat partially leaked to him, he could have foiled the coup, but he overtrusted advisement from some quarters which were not helpful. It therefore becomes difficult for a president or leader to decipher unequivocally whose advisement to trust when no adviser or expert is perfect.

If former President Shehu Shagari did not stop his former Minister of Transportation, Alhaji Umaru Dikko, from snooping into the suspicious movements of some military officers who were planning to topple him, he could have had enough intelligence report to enable him to preempt General Mohammadu Buhari from toppling the Second Republic. He overtrusted his General Officer Commanding, his kinsman, and thereby lost his presidency to General Buhari's dictatorship. As a leader, you cannot imagine that your closest relations, your best friends, your protector as General Officer Commanding or others you have helped are ready to overthrow you and take your exalted position.

The above two examples clearly analyze the precariousness of the position of the Presidency in determining who to trust and when. According to late President Ronald Reagan, Fortieth President of the USA, he said, "Trust but verify." As leader or president, therefore, your best friend, adviser or relation is the one who tells you the truth and frankly without biases nor personal interest, and the one that has nothing to hide. Even then, it is still difficult to determine who this best person is. That is what life is; it is full of uncertainties. In the midst of uncertainties one must try to spend a good life and be the people's person as president, leader or representative.

There are best experts, best advisers, best technocrats, best academicians and best professionals, but notwithstanding how highly rated these experts are, local or foreign, they are human beings with normal human imperfections whose innate abilities, education, personal interests and biases act as builtin control mechanism to direct their actions.

Experts, local and foreign as human beings have their personal biases, personal interests, personal impulses and personal constraints which would normally influence their thoughts, actions, reports, recommendations and advisements. In many cases, government functionaries, experts, advisers, aides etc. often commit unethical wrongs to satisfy their selfish interests, but unfortunately, it is the leader/president who is blamed vicariously, even if he/she has nothing to do with it personally.

Surrounded by all these uncertainties, how can a president build certainties around himself and succeed is a billion dollar question! The job of the president may be less difficult and less confusing if he/she is very sound, very intelligent, matured, experienced, not too rigid and not too flexible, as wise as Solomon, God/Allah gifted, original, transparent and respected. Above all, he/she must be the people's person.

These leadership qualities of the president will make advisers and aides careful, nervous and more hard working because they know that such president cannot be deceived, pushed around nor easily manipulated because he/she probably knows more than or as much as his expert advisers on many financial, socio-economic and political issues. He/

she would be the person who knows a lot, who can command respect and confidence, not controversial and acceptable to majority. He must be charismatic, look and talk presidential.

A person is addressed as an expert if he/she satisfies some accepted requirements, academic and/or professional, but such a person is still prone to human imperfections, which make him/her fallible. In real life situations, expert advisement has never turned out to be 100 percent perfect. For example, put three experts or professors with the same academic and professional qualifications in three separate identical rooms and give them the same socio-economic or political problem to solve under the same situational setting.

The end result may produce three different results, alternative solutions, recommendations and advisement. It is therefore possible that the three expert or professorial opinions on the same subjectmatter may create confusion instead of a perfect solution expected. It is therefore significant to harmonize expert opinions with real life situations before they are applied to minimize problems.

The above example is hypothetical to explain that the solutions to Nigerian problems do not rest entirely with experts, professors, technocrats, professionals or advisers alone but in conjunction with the generality of Nigerian citizens. Experts or professors often pretend they know what the people want without a thorough research and henceforth fail when their recommendations or advisements are applied.

Sometimes, local and foreign experts apply their foreign knowledge and expertise to African problems and fail because an African problem would best need an African solution. So, for Nigerian leadership to succeed remarkably, the authorities must listen to Nigerians and do what Nigerians want and not only foreign ideals that succeed in Europe and America.

Sometimes, expert opinions if not localized may be too sophisticated for Nigerian situations and would fail if applied prematurely. Leaders and advisers must be reminded that too much fertilizer and water to grow a plant may kill it, while the best medication if applied inappropriately may kill the patient that is intended to be saved.

'Enterprise Nigeria' in a democracy should reflect the aspirations of Nigerians as to what they wish and want and not only what the leadership and experts wish and want for Nigerians no matter how well meaning their intentions may be. Human beings are the most unpredictable resource, and to determine what is best for them requires great researchability, which most decision makers do not do because it takes time, may be expensive but perfect.

Researchability effectiveness is a major way of ensuring the meeting of minds of the leadership and the followership before decisions that affect the lives of Nigerians are reached. A government or leadership that develops full participation in the art of governance can never fail. That is food for thought to the leadership and advisers in Nigeria at local, state and federal government levels.

At this juncture, it may be worthwhile to consider presidential advice that failed, and its consequences so that Nigerians can learn from others' mistakes. It was announced on Thursday, June 3, 2004, that George Tenet, the United States Director of Central Intelligence Agency, resigned effective July 11, 2004 contentiously for personal reasons. George Tenet called his resignation, "The most difficult decision I have ever had to make." He added, "It is for the well-being of my wonderful family." He emphasized, "It is for the welfare of my high school son."

The reason given by George Tenet for his resignation was doubtful and contestable because the reasons overlooked American tradition, belief, culture and value, that duty for 'America, the USA' comes first.

It must be remembered that the fabricated report of the agency about Iraq's WMD was responsible for sending thousands of young US men and women into war front and harm's way in Iraq which resulted in over 4,000 deaths and over 30,000 wounded American soldiers as well as brought cries and sorrows to thousands of American and Iraqi families.

It was therefore ironical that he bowed out for the welfare of his own family after allegedly providing manipulated intelligence reports that put thousands of American and Iraqi families in jeopardy. It is true to life that the hangman never wants a rope close to his own neck. It later turned out that there were no weapons of mass destruction (WMD) in Iraq for which the US went to war.

In order to convince the world and Americans in particular that the US should go to war against Iraq, the intelligence agency allegedly manipulated intelligence reports that Iraq possessed unconventional weapons of mass destruction (WMD) which likely posed an immediate threat, and that an attack on America was imminent. The untrue message was echoed in the United Nations, the US House of Representatives and Senate (the Legislature) and in the British Parliament several times in order to justify a war against Iraq. It was also possible that George Tenet was being told what to say and write, but later made a scapegoat.

Nigerian advisers must learn from this episode too. The avoidable war has resulted in thousands of deaths of innocent lives, over six hundred billions of dollars expended and more terrorists than ever before have been created. Unfortunately, a policy meant to solve a problem, aggravated it and blew it up to a proportion that has made the whole world sleepless and worried.

There have been beheadings, extortion of ransom for kidnapped people, suicide bombings, chaos and killings at an alarming and uncontrollable proportion. All those atrocities result from manipulated advice and failed decision, and it seems a quick solution is not in sight to stop the killings and misery on both sides. Since Saddam Hussein was toppled, terrorism has struck Spain, London, Egypt, etc. causing many deaths of innocent people. Nigerian leaders must watch the decisions they make without being in a hurry to avoid Iraqi situation.

The above-mentioned example is an eyeopener for Nigerian leaders about expert advice, which must be thoroughly reviewed before implementation. Some foreign expert advice may be like the 'Trojan Horse' and leaders must be careful as to what advice to accept cautiously and what to reject outrightly.

Same goes with the purported US Intelligence Report on Nigeria released in May 2005, which predicted a kind of doom that would befall Nigeria and some West African countries within fifteen years. It is not real, but it is a serious warning sign for all Nigerians to watch movements in and out of Nigeria.

People must be accountable for their words and actions – no sacred cows and untouchables. Individuals and groups must be law abiding or face government action quickly, speedily and decisively. Nigeria's posterity is at stake as the report highlighted.

On August 15, 1986, during the White House Conference on Small Business, 40th President Ronald Reagan of the United States of America, said, "Government view of the economy could be summed up in a few short phrases: if it moves, tax it; if it keeps moving, regulate it; and if it stops moving, subsidize it."

Those who advised the President of Nigeria to impose fuel tax in 2004 had good intentions but the decision backfired. Imposing taxation on an essential product that has inelastic demand during high rate of inflation was an ill-advisement which abused the right application of open market operations strategy. A tax increase normally reduces money in circulation, increases prices, and rate of inflation is increased. That was not the best option during an economy that was not yet moving but was going through reforms for stabilization.

The ill-advisement eroded some of the President's popularity and caused some strikes and chaos until the increase was partially revised. The opposition seized the opportunity to regroup to embarrass the presidency. The government could have faced more serious chaos and worsening economic downturn if it did not softpedal.

To cushion the fuel tax hike effects, a palliative committee, headed by ExSenate Deputy President Ibrahim Nasir Mantu recommended magnanimous palliative measures of providing eleven billion naira as loan in addition to the reduction of taxes on buses and drugs to the barest minimum for the benefit of the masses.

It was observed that the recommendations were too good and generous, and as such, the elites hijacked them and did not allow them to work for the masses. The supervision of the implementation of the recommendations at state and local levels was difficult. Recommendations of advisers, experts or committees may not work as expected if there is shortage of researchability before decisions are made.

In similar circumstances, members of Cocoa Farmers Progressive Union of Nigeria (CFPUN) complained that 600 million naira approved by the Federal Government for farmers in 2000/03 to revive ageing cocoa trees was diverted and shared by nonfarmers described as ghost farmers, as highlighted in the *Guardian News* of Thursday, June 30, 2005. The Secretary General of the CFPUN, Mr. Sunday Adekunle, made the call to the Federal Government for investigation of the disappearance of the money. Membership of the CFPUN comes from Osun, Ondo, Ekiti, Ogun, Oyo, Lagos, Edo and Kwara States.

If government had been properly advised, alternative measures better than the imposition of fuel tax would have been applied, and there would not have been chaos, which necessitated the palliative measures that were not allowed to work for the masses that were meant to be assisted.

On February 8, 2005, the 'Independent Committee on Cushioning Measures of Fuel Price Hike' headed by former Deputy Senate President Ibrahim Nasir Mantu, was alleged to have accused the thirty-six State Governors and the Federal Capital Territory Minister of frustrating the Federal Government palliative measures as revealed in *This Day News*. The questions are:
1. Did the State Governors and other stakeholders contribute inputs to the decision on the palliative measures?
2. Were there any consultations with the State Governors about the workability or feasibility of the palliative measures before the decision they were being told to implement was reached?
3. Did the State Governors participate directly or indirectly in the decision they were expected to implement?
4. Was there any effective communication with the State Governors and all stakeholders during the process on the palliative measures decision?
5. Was there any research to discover the probability of any problems in the implementation stage of the decision reached and how to preempt such problems?

In a democracy, any federal committee set up for decision-making should do sufficient homework. It should take adequate steps that will enable it to arrive at rational decisions, which will not fail or be resisted during the implementation phase especially in cases where state and local authorities would be involved in executing the decisions.

The intention of the fuel tax was to fight the ills of the elites. As a result, the government advisers should have used alternative measures that could generate as much revenue comparable with what was expected from the fuel tax. The alternatives should focus on the elites who could afford them and not on the masses. Such measures include:

1. Imposing heavy fines on smugglers of petroleum products into neighbouring countries. Their products could be seized and sold by the government. Part of the money realized could be used to recruit college or university graduates and train them to man the borders to defeat smugglers. The same strict measures should apply at the seaports and airports.
2. Illegal oil bunkering must be fought to a standstill. A lot of money will be realized from that venture. Those captured should have their assets seized and sent to prison for a long time. According to Shell Petroleum Development Company's Corporate Affairs Director, Mutiu Sunmonu, "Nigeria loses at least $1 billion yearly because of oil theft in the Niger Delta Region." The information was passed to the Presidential Action Committee on Control of Illegal Weapons and Violent Crimes as contained in the *Punch News* of Thursday, February 3, 2005. That loophole for stealing oil should be blocked, turned into government revenue and utilized for national development.
3. The government should fight frauds and corruption as well as economic and financial crimes. A lot of money could be saved through that. Cases should be prosecuted speedily. Illegal gains or loot should be recovered.
4. The refineries should be resuscitated and saboteurs probed and punished. More refineries should be built to take care of the country's need of petroleum products. Reliance on importation of petroleum products should be eliminated or reduced to minimal level so that a lot of foreign exchange can be saved.
5. Countries that deal with illegal oil bunkerers and smugglers of Nigerian oil should be sanctioned. They should be forewarned.

Above measures would be fights against elites who could afford the penalties, and the gains realizable would be more than the proceeds from fuel tax which caused problems for the poor masses. For the reform measures to succeed speedily, the government must reduce rate of interest to below double-digit figures to stimulate the economy.

If the economy is stabilized and there is low rate of inflation and low interest rate, the masses will be happy under this situation that must have created the path to full employment. There and then, if the government introduces progressive fuel taxation, fully discussed and negotiated with all stakeholders, there will be no dissension.

It was the easy way out to just advise the President of Nigeria about the revenue advantages of imposing fuel tax without having done a research to show the cost benefit analysis and the implications of imposing fuel tax. An adviser's work is not easy, but it is full of glory, selfsatisfaction and self-actualization if it is done rightly. If it is done wrongly in a shoddy manner, the adviser's action could be catastrophic for his boss and the nation, and it could mar and diminish the adviser's personality and reputation.

In Vanguard News of Sunday, June 5, 2005, Dr. Brown Ogbeifun, former President of Petroleum and National Gas Senior Staff Association of Nigeria, mentioned that the truth about 'deregulation' was withheld from ExPresident Obasanjo. Its implementation was resisted with chaos until the NLC leadership met with the President personally and briefed him. With researchability, a lot of such avoidable problems would not arise.

Deregulation, privatization and liberalization are outstanding economic strategies, but they must be applied properly, and when appropriate, with caution by taking the right steps in full participation of all stakeholders. The possible impact on the masses should be a great consideration in socio-economic and political decisions.

Nigerians should be aware and careful of those who advise or incite them to violence, to stage mass destructive action for socio-economic, political or religious reasons. In most cases, those who incite you and your families to violence, suffering and dying, often secure their own lives and those of their families first before they expose you to dangers.

Some of the soldiers who fought on the secessionist side and were hurt and maimed over 40 years ago (1967-70) were neglected to be begging for alms by their own people and those who recruited them to fight. Some of them still live in Eastern Nigeria in 2005 begging for alms to eat. It is sad that successive Eastern States Governments could not house, keep and feed for life, these warriors who were led into war for the survival of the Eastern Region.

In the same wise, do not allow yourself to be fooled into violence anymore by people who use you to cause trouble but leave you in the lurch to face the music. Life is short but could be sweet, interesting, enjoyable, challenging and full of happiness, if people always seek compromises instead of violence.

It is therefore important to effectively communicate, discuss, dialogue and utilize diplomacy to settle issues harmoniously instead of rioting, destroying, killing, rampaging and breaking the law during a dispute with authorities. When dissidents incite you to commit these crimes against your country and less privileged Nigerians, simply because there is a dispute with the leadership, have you ever asked yourself, "Who suffers – yourself, the common Nigerian, Nigeria or the leadership you are in dispute with?" Remember, it is yourself, the innocent common people and your country that suffer and have a lot to lose and not the leadership. So, why not take due process instead of resorting to violence to solve problems?

Nobody gains from violence, which represents a two edge sword that cuts you, the violent person, and the innocent poor people who have nothing to do with the cause of your anger and the dispute. At best, you may allow the leadership tenure to run out naturally or by recalling them or by voting them out constitutionally during succeeding elections. Resorting to violence and hurting yourself with innocent people in order to avenge the wrongs purportedly done to those who incite you to cause trouble is unwise, stupid and dumb.

Remember to meditate in your life and be at peace. Have you ever had a second thought about the possible result of your resorting to violence? The person inciting you into riots and harm's way probably has his own family safe in America and the United Kingdom. Do not be fooled any more.

The advisers, aides and government functionaries who worked under General Sani Abacha did not see anything wrong with his regime even though the whole world was crumbling under his feet until he died. The comity of nations saw human rights abuses, frauds, corruption, money laundering, arrest, detentions and killings of opponents and innocent people by assassination squad, yet, his advisers, friends and others stayed by him until he died before they changed gear.

If his advisers had been frank and truthful to him, perhaps he could have softpedaled and changed to promote humanity instead of abusing and destroying humanity. If he did not listen to the advisers, what stopped them from quitting if they were advisers of merit? If a notorious leader and dictator loses his right hand people, he will think twice and change.

In this circumstance, where there were scores of advisers to one leader and Head of State, General Sani Abacha; it could be rightly said that there were many more bad advisers than there was a bad leader. On the other hand, Abacha's advisers, aides and government functionaries could have ended up in the gallows if they resigned or did not dance to his whims and caprices. As a human being, one cannot be too judgmental but leave everything to God/Allah to whom everybody is answerable during he last day – "God/Allah's Judgment Day"

One should look at how many Nigerian dignitaries were killed or assassinated during Abacha's regime (1993-1998) like Ken Saro-Wiwa, General Shehu Yar'Adua, Chief Mrs. Kudirat Abiola and other assassination attempts that failed. Then ask yourself, even if you do not believe in miracles, how General Olusegun Matthew Aremu Okikiolakan Obasanjo escaped from being dead in Abacha's prison and later became Nigerian President and Commander in Chief of Nigerian Armed Forces, and tell the world that it was not a miracle beyond human comprehension! How many like that have you seen in your lifetime or heard in the history of the world? Remember that Dictator Abacha planned that Obasanjo, Shehu Yar'Adua, Diya, Abiola and others would not come out of prison alive.

If instead of teaming up with the government for a better Nigeria, you are still antagonizing, why not do a selfappraisal by asking in your heart in the remotest part of your house, "What will you gain from testing the Will of God/Allah, by thwarting His work, setting back the hand of the clock of your country, Nigeria and becoming a clog in the wheel of Nigeria's movement forward enroute to the Promised Land?" Why not let Nigeria's leadership do all what they are supposed to do with your support, encouragement and honest healthy calls for redirection whenever it is extremely necessary to do so in the best interest of the nation without heating the polity? Please do not be the devil in Nigeria's period of salvation.

It was widely rumoured that General Abacha and some military officers were alleged to have planned to topple Babangida's regime in a couple of times. If it were possible for General Babangida to arrest, incarcerate and courtmartial them, he would have saved Nigeria from the horrors of Abacha's dictatorship of 1993-1998. Nigerian leaders should never hesitate to take decisive, preemptive actions in order to save the innocent people and preserve Nigeria's great future. A stitch in time saves nine. The law should be enforced always, justly and fairly, without discrimination.

In the *Daily Independent Online* of Wednesday, January 11, 2006, Cardinal Anthony Olubunmi Okojie said "Ours is a society that glorifies evil and applauds incompetence. If I may ask, who are the people receiving national honours in Nigeria, chieftaincy titles, honourary doctorate degrees, ministerial positions, appointment into plum government parastatals? In more decent societies than ours, many of these people would be behind bars, not standing at the podium receiving totally unmerited accolades."

He was 100% right; but the same thing is happening all over the world. There is no exception anymore. He agreed unequivocally that a revolution had started with the hitherto 'sacred cows' being called to account for their crimes against the nation. It is advisable for religious leaders to talk more about pedophilia, homosexuality, fraud and corruption among priests, bishops and pastors instead of partisan politics which can backfire on them because many church members may not want to be involved in partisan political views.

Cardinal Okojie, Professor Wole Soyinka, Nigerian Legislators, the Presidency and people of Nigeria should read further to know that Nigeria cannot be the worst when talking about corruption and fraud. Indicted lobbyist Jack Abramoff who created one of the worst US Congressional leadership scandals, told Judge Huvelle, "Your honour, words will not be able to ever express how sorry I am for this, and I have profound regret and sorrow for the multitude of mistakes and harm I have caused. All of my remaining days, I will feel tremendous sadness and regret for my conduct and for what I have done. I only hope that I can merit forgiveness from the Almighty and from those I have wronged or caused to suffer. I will work hard to earn that redemption."

Abramoff corruptly influenced top US Congressmen/Legislators and their aides and government officials by sponsoring their overseas trips, campaign contributions, meals and entertainments in exchange for congressional decisions and laws tailored to benefit his clients and businesses.

He allegedly collected over $80 million from the Indian tribes as bribes and fees with which he wined and dined with some top US Congressmen at his upscale Washington restaurant and flew them abroad for golf outings.

In exchange, he was able to influence Internet gambling legislation and postal rate increase among other things. He made plea bargains to reveal more. The wife of a legislator's aide was on his payroll up to the tune of $50,000.

When the scandal leaked out in 2005, some of the top US Congressmen involved started to donate part of the bribe money to charities in order to mitigate culpability and prosecution. Similar things happen all over the world, but the irony of it is that Western World countries where worse things happen are always quick to point accusing fingers at other less corrupt nations like Nigeria and other African countries. Nigeria is not worse than other countries. Those who have not resided in the Western World during the last ten years may not know that corruption is endemic worldwide without boundaries.

However, whoever cooperates fully with the EFCC, ICPC in the exercise of cleaning Nigeria of corruption and fraud should not regard himself/herself as finished nor a failure but as a patriot, a hero and a glorious pioneer for Nigeria's new and clean beginning. Nigerian elites crying foul and throwing stones at the sinners we know, might themselves be worse sinners not yet busted. Nigerian leaders who show remorse should be forgiven and given another chance provided they are very sincere and return the loot.

GOD/ALLAH BLESS NIGERIA!

CHAPTER 6

WHO SHOULD BE LEADERS IN NIGERIA

The main question to ask rhetorically is who should be a leader or who qualifies to be a leader in Nigeria as President, Senator, Member of House of Representatives, Governor, Local Government Chairperson, Councilor, Member of the Judiciary or any other leader in both private and public sectors of this great nation! To answer the question properly, one needs to consider the antecedents of some previous and present leaders of Nigeria and pick those whose antecedents are impressive for emulation.

The antecedents of some of the past and present leaders of Nigeria are briefly discussed in chapters 1 and 2 of this book for ease of reference. As a result, it becomes easy for Nigerians and other readers of this book to determine the kind of future leaders they want and whom they should look like in reference to some of the best past and present leaders whose antecedents are highlighted in this book.

Nigeria had leaders of leaders of great eminence like Sir Ahmadu Bello, the Sardauna of Sokoto, First Premier of Northern Region of Nigeria; Chief Obafemi Awolowo, First Premier of Western Region of Nigeria and Sir Abubakar Tafawa Balewa, First Prime Minister of Nigeria (1960-1966). They were among the Fathers of Nigerian Nationhood and Independence including Dr. Nnamdi Azikiwe, First Premier of Eastern Region of Nigeria as well as becoming the First President of Nigeria (1960-1966).

Nigeria has continued to have great leaders like Dr. Nnamdi Azikiwe, the Owelle of Onitsha, first President of Nigeria (1960-1966); General Aguiyi Ironsi, Military Head of State (January 15, 1966-July 29, 1966); General Yakubu Gowon, Military Head of State (1966-1975); General Murtala Mohammed, Military Head of State (1975-1976); General Olusegun Obasanjo, Military Head of State (1976-1979); Alhaji Shehu Shagari, Civilian President of Second Republic (1979-1983); General Mohammadu Buhari, Military Head of State (December 31, 1983-August 27, 1985); General Ibrahim Badamosi Babangida, Military Head of State (1985-1993); Chief Ernest Shonekan, Interim Administrator of Third Republic (August 1993-November 1993); General Sani Abacha, Military Head of State (1993-1998); General Abdulsalami Abubakar, Military Head of State (1998-1999); General Olusegun Obasanjo, Civilian President of Fourth Republic (1999-2007) and Mallam Umaru Musa Yar'Adua, Civilian President of Fourth Republic. With effect from May 29, 2007, Nigeria installed the first realist of a 'Servant-Leader' in the annals of the country.

The irony of leadership is that anybody who aspires to lead, wants to make a difference in the lives of people; be the best leader and leave a great legacy to posterity; but in most cases, leaders' dreams are hardly achieved and the opposite of their objectives has often happened. In addition to being gifted to lead, leadership must be learned through advanced management training, and great leadership, developed experientially.

Most leaders who raised the people's hopes during inauguration ended up with poor performance and approval ratings below 30 percent. In most cases, it goes on and on like that with majority of the people getting disappointed and frustrated. Leaders who succeed to get elected for the second or more terms may find their approval rating slipping to the lowest ebb at the time they are leaving office.

Leadership must imbibe service to satisfy the needs of the people who must also be carried along during the course of leadership. In most countries, leaders act as bosses and dictators and pretend to be democratic. Leadership exemplariness has no room for hypocrisy, but transparency, good governance and accountability.

The only panacea to dwindling performance rating of leaders is the establishment of a government that finds out the needs of the people, fulfills such needs and carries the people along using effective communication strategies.

The people's needs include: good democratic governance, provision of affordable housing, water, electricity, food security, safety, health care, buoyant economy, good transportation and communication systems, and fulfilling projects that focus on progress and development.

According to President Ronald Reagan of the USA, "The greatest leader is the one who makes the people achieve the greatest things." In most cases, that has never been the case. Most leaders often focus on their own benefits and care less about the people on whose backs they ride to leadership.

In effect, most leaders take care of themselves, their relations, friends, cronies, and associates first and foremost and invariably have few crumbs or nothing left for the people to eat and live year in, year out. Such inequitable distributions of resources and opportunities have created wide inequality gaps, increased poverty, hunger, anger, militancy, insurgency, war and suicide bombings.

In the choice of Nigerian President, Senators and House Representatives, President Olusegun Obasanjo advised Nigerians on Thursday, March 25, 2004 that they should be guided by patriotic and nationalistic ideals. Most importantly, he reminded Nigerians that the quality of governance, leadership and improvement of facilities, services and infrastructure available to them would usually be largely determined by the quality of the persons they elected into office as their leaders or representatives. His emphasis was on quality of leadership and not where they came from or their religion.

It must be highlighted that any policy of exclusionism which bars the most qualified and most suitable person to be leader, president or representative, often creates a problem for the masses, the majority not to receive the best services.

It is realized that there is no election, selection, nomination or allocation mechanism that is one hundred percent perfect, but the system that excludes or diminishes competitiveness is the most unfair and undemocratic. But in the search for peace, recognizing Nigerian prevailing political, ethnic, and religious situation, zoning may form an understanding within the political parties and not a matter that can be expressed in the Nigerian Constitution.

Nigerians had the opportunity to elect their leader, President Shehu Shagari, for the Second Republic from 1979 to 1983. Between 1960 and May 28, 1999, a period of thirty-nine years, Nigerian rulers were predominantly Northerners.

During the thirty-nine years after independence, Northerners were Heads of Nigerian Government for thirty-five years which was a great opportunity for the North in particular to have developed beyond what it is today, and Nigeria generally, if Nigerian resources were properly harnessed in the best interest of the nation. A lot of government money ended up in private pockets corruptly or got secretly stashed away in foreign private bank accounts.

Such action is at variance with service to God/Allah and humanity in the North that is acclaimed to be the most Allahserving region of Nigeria. The period from January 15, 1966 to May 28, 1999 was not different from the Biblical narration of the forty years situation of the Israelites in the wilderness. Up till today, Nigeria has not fully recovered from the untold maladministration and effects of dictatorship of more than three decades.

In the *Guardian News* of Thursday, April 29, 2004, the leadership of the Northern Unity Forum (NUF), Alhaji Mohammed Liman was quoted to have lamented, "Although the North had held power at the centre for about thirty-five years since Nigerian independence, the region had nothing to show for it in terms of education and economic empowerment.

He was said to have questioned how and why it was possible for the North to have been at the centre in control of the Federal Government and its apparatus for a period of thirty-five years out of forty-three years of post independence Nigeria, and the North was impoverished in commerce and materials educationally and economically.

The concern and lamentations expressed by Chairman Liman is the greatest concern the rest of Nigeria has about relinquishing the presidency back to the North. Where is the guarantee that Nigeria will not be subjected to another thirty-five years of travails, maladministration, economic pillage and regressional development? That is also one of the reasons for the clamour for the convocation of the Sovereign National Conference (SNC).

Fortunately, the Northern Youth Forum and many groups in the North are beginning to ask questions about why their elders and leaders ruled the country for thirty-five years and Nigerians have nothing to show for it except dictatorship, money laundering, economic downturn, unemployment and stashing of billions of government money in foreign private bank accounts. Why does Sharia law not work for these Northern leaders who are proven to have committed acts of corruption and other crimes? If Sharia can cut the limbs of poor people for wrongdoing, why does it not apply to the wealthy in order to be just and fair?

The fears about past sufferings created by leadership failures make it difficult for Nigerians to trust anybody outside their ethnicity, religion or region to be President of the country. That mentality is responsible for the clamour and agitation in respect of presidential successors in Nigeria.

Regrettably, forty-eight years after independence, Nigerians do not have the orientation that the best candidate should run the country irrespective of his or her ethnicity, religion or region of origin. The masses that represent Nigerian majority do not and will not care about where the president comes from if they are properly informed. The few Nigerian elites are the ones misinforming the followership and using ethnicity, religion and region of origin to score political points when it is in their favour to do so. What truly democratic and civilized country in the world still uses ethnicity, religion and region of origin to zone and elect its president?

Nigerian elites, who still talk about zoning and where the president should come from forty-eight years after independence without thinking about the most suitable Nigerian to be president, irrespective of his ethno-religious leaning, should be ashamed of their utterances and ethno-religious centricism. The use of religion, ethnicity and region of origin to elect a President is at variance with civilized world conviction that the best citizen who is the most qualified, suitable and acceptable candidate should lead irrespective of ethnicity, religion or region of origin.

Those who have been talking about where the president should come from are motivated by what they can personally gain from the arrangement and not what is best for Nigeria. Nigerians should be encouraged to talk and act more as Nigerians rather than their ethnicity.

Four and a half decades after independence, each ethnicity should have developed enough to be able to present its representatives to contest favourably with any other for Nigerian presidency.

The zoning, religion, ethnicity and region of origin considerations for the choice of the president are criteria for exclusiveness that are discriminatory and not democratic. They should be discouraged, legislated against and discontinued. A two or three-party system is best for Nigeria. The National Assembly should work hard to discourage the proliferation of political parties and reduce the number of existing political parties to two or three maximum.

One may wonder why Nigerian elites are not emphasizing on the best candidate, most qualified, most intelligent and most experienced person as president instead of bothering on ethnicity, religion and region of origin. It is argued that it is because Nigerians are too tribal or ethnicity conscious, and a lot of power are concentrated in the presidency.

It is believed that there is overcentralization of authority and national functions on the Federal Government. If more powers are given to the states, and the country is restructured to effect the decentralization of some of the powers of the presidency, the position may be less attractive to warrant the interethnicity struggles for the presidency.

Regionalization is gone, and it should be allowed to rest in peace. It is better for all of us to meet at Abuja (Centre of Unity) than first meet in the regions before going to Abuja to solve our problems. Regionalization elongates bureaucracy and it will make matters worse.

Under democratic dispensation, anybody who meets the requirements of the Nigerian 1999 constitution for the position of the President of the Federal Republic of Nigeria and wishes to contest for the position should be free to do so irrespective of his or her ethnicity, religion, creed, state or region of origin.

Freedom of speech as embedded in the Nigerian 1999 Constitution supports those calling for Igbo Presidency as well as the Northern Governors and others who have been calling for the zoning of the presidency to the North. They are entitled to express their wishes under the constitution, but that should not restrain any other Nigerian who wishes to contest if he or she is qualified to be president irrespective of his or her region of origin.

The *Punch News* of Thursday, May 6, 2004 reported that on Wednesday, May 5, 2004, Governors of nineteen Northern States resolved at their Kaduna meeting that the Northern Region should produce the next president. It was added that the Governors affirmed that the position of the North on the issue was nonnegotiable. They added that they would not leave any stone unturned to ensure that power shifted to the North.

The chief spokespersons of the Governors' Forum were ExGovernor Ahmed Makarfi, the host, and Governor Danjuma Goje of Gombe State, the Chairman. The ExGovernors should have concentrated energies on correcting thirty-five years of misrule of the North and how to uplift the people of the North socio-economically, politically and educationally, and always realize that everything is negotiable in a democracy.

In his own remarks like many other Nigerians, the Governor of Ogun State, Otunba Gbenga Daniel, was quoted to have commented that the constitution of the PDP did not preclude any section of the country from aspiring to the presidency.

The zoning system limiting the choice of the people and the span of democracy, may not promote the best candidate, may encourage reverse discrimination, promote mediocrity, stifle democratic process, and is therefore undemocratic. The Northern Governors' position declaration cannot break barriers of sectional, regional, religious and ethnic boundaries to promote overall national interest.

What if the most qualified and suitable person is from the South-South or South-East, will he/she be denied the presidency because of his/her region of origin? Is it ethical and professional not to support the best candidate purely because of his or her ethnicity, religion or region of origin? Where then is fairness that everybody has been talking about?

In his own extensive contribution to the presidential search for Niggeria, Mr. Emakoji Ayikoye in his article published on Wednesday, July 28, 2004 in *Nigeria World Message board,* described it as shallow thinking for those who thought that ruling Nigeria at presidential level should be based on regional consideration.

He was critical of the struggle among the HausaFulani, Igbos and Yorubas to clinch to the presidency and wondered whether only those three tribes constituted Nigeria. He then asked passionately where tribal occupancy of the presidency would lead Nigerians in the twenty-first century with its enormous challenges?

He reiterated that the Igbos had a taste of the presidency through late Dr. Nnamdi Azikiwe (1960-1966) as Nigerian leader and Vice President Alex Ekwueme (1979-1983) under Shagari Administration. He recalled that past Nigerian leaders misled, ruined and destroyed the country and wondered what was left of the nation to bawl about. He queried the moral justification of those calling for the presidency on basis of tribal and regional considerations.

He observed with deep concern, "If ruling Nigerians is a tribal thing rather than choosing the well deserving, refined, educated, noncorrupt, nonsycophant patriot, then I see Nigeria disintegrating into shards bearing in mind our diversity." He urged all Nigerian to refuse the ideology of politics based on tribal and regional sentiments, which he described as myopic, senseless and foolish.

He appealed to all Nigerian elites, intellectuals, religious leaders and all other Nigerians to disown tribal politics at presidential level. He reiterated that the future of Nigeria would not rest in the hands of the HausaFulanis, Igbos and Yorubas alone but on all Nigerians.

He then answered exhaustively the question of who should lead a unified and prosperous Nigeria in the future. He asserted that anybody with the underlying qualities specified below should rule:

(1) <u>A true Nigerian patriot should rule:</u>
    He defined a true Nigerian patriot as someone who would not be aspiring to the presidency just for the purpose of enriching himself and acquiring wealth illegally, but one whose priority would be for the empowerment of the people socio-economically, politically and religiously. He enjoined Nigerians to elect as president someone who would make Nigeria strong at home and respected in the comity of nations.

(2) <u>A noncorrupt, ethical Nigerian should rule:</u>
    He stressed that past leaders had entrenched corruption into the fabric of Nigerian society so much that Nigeria was stigmatized as one of the most corrupt nations in the world. He quoted two stunning United Nations assertions that firstly, Nigeria was 151st out of 177 nations that were not caring

for their citizens. In effect, Nigeria was regarded as one of the countries that were not providing or promoting welfare programmes that could socially and economically cater for the generality of the citizenry.

Secondly, that Nigerian elites had stashed away over $100 billion in foreign banks at the expense of their needy, downtrodden fellow countrymen. He recalled on Nigerians not to vote for leaders who would loot and launder Nigeria's economic resources and funds into their private bank accounts in foreign countries. He emphasized that Nigeria would not need any corrupt, unethical sycophants to rule the country any longer.

(3) A compassionate and Godfearing Nigerian should rule:
He described a compassionate and Godfearing Nigerian as one who would be able to feel and clearly perceive the needs of the people and treat them as he/she would want to be treated. He alleged that most Nigerian leaders since independence gluttonously looted away Nigeria's wealth abroad, and they became millionaires and billionaires overnight. He wondered how they acquired such enormous wealth when their followership faced penury and destitution. He clarified that Nigeria needed a leader who would not watch children and elders starve into their graves in a country that was blessed with enormous wealth of natural resources.

(4) An educated Nigerian should rule:
He prescribed that a person adept with great domestic and foreign policy expertise that would raise the standard of education and make graduates employable and employed should rule Nigeria. He lamented the criticism of a former Minister of Education that Nigerian graduates were unemployable and asked who should be blamed, the students or educators who were, most of the time, on labour strikes. He advised that Nigerian graduates could receive additional training on the job. He advocated for quality education, which would promote economic expansion. He reiterated that a leader (a) that would not provide social security for Nigerians; (b) that would not defend and stabilize education for the citizenry;

(c) that had no vision for the country; and (d) that would not protect Nigerians domestically and defend the nation's image and integrity should not be voted into power to rule the nation.

He concluded by emphasizing that only those who possess the above mentioned requirements should come forward and seek the mandate of the people irrespective of their Nigerian state or region of origin.

The above requirements from any Nigerian wishing to be considered for the position of the president are not exhaustive. Nigeria requires a person well-groomed in some of these academic and professional courses such as behavioural science courses, public administration, business administration, economics, financial management, general management, human resource and labour relations management, sales and marketing management, project management, international business, law and other related disciplines with over ten years of management experience.

Any aspirant who wants to be President, Senator or Member of the House of Representatives whether State or Federal including Local Council Chairpersons should possess an equivalent of 4 years university/college degree as the minimum verifiable educational requirement. Those who do not have the minimum educational requirement should go back to school and give way to others who qualify. What useful contributions will anybody make as a legislator, if he/she does not possess a 4year college/university degree or its equivalent? How can anybody lead successfully if the person does not possess the relevant academic or professional education? A half educated person cannot contribute significantly to lawmaking in the nation's legislature.

Any person who aspires to lead Nigeria in future should demonstrate his or her mission statement, political ideology, qualifications and relevant experience. The aspirant must tell Nigerians why and how he or she wants to lead the country and how he or she excels other contestants.

The requirements stated above will enable whoever successfully becomes the president to stay above board and vulnerability that results from poor advisement from advisers, aides, government functionaries, lobbyists and special interest groups whose selfinterests and biases make them misadvise leaders while in office.

For example, General Sani Abacha, former Military Head of State (1993-1998) was said to be large-hearted, misunderstood, misjudged and described to be a nationalist by his cronies, why and how did he go astray so badly in the eyes of the whole world and committed atrocities that caused Nigeria to be sanctioned by the comity of nations and ostracized from the international community? Where were his technical advisers and experts, aides and government functionaries?

Were all Abacha's advisers and wise men looking the other way and pretending nothing was wrong or that they were not seeing anything wrong in order to keep their jobs? What were they saying to him in secret and openly? What was their motivation to stay on when things were so bad? What kind of advice were they giving him? Why did many of them come in the open to dance, deride and disown him only after his death?

As a result of his limited education and experience in human resource management, limited international exposure, capability and experience in public service coupled with his highhanded temperament, he messed up his country regrettably from 1993 to 1998. Everybody who was telling him the truth about his misrule became his enemy and he subjected them to extermination. Even other world leaders like Pope John Paul II, African, European and American leaders failed to make him change his mind about the execution of Ken Saro-Wiwa, an activist and many others.

It is very significant that presidential advisers, aides and government functionaries tell the truth and nothing but the truth to any erring leadership instead of currying favours against the best interest of the nation. Nigeria needs an energetic and intelligent person who can continue on the path of national reforms, which will lead Nigeria to the Promised Land.

Under ExPresident Obasanjo, Nigeria achieved a horizon that was greater than the scope of boundaries of Nigeria by expanding her leadership beyond Nigeria to the African Union, the Commonwealth and the United Nations. Hence, any future leader of Nigeria must be a person who can maintain an equally high standing in the comity of nations.

Nigeria does not need a pupil president who will be under tutelage and manipulations of advisers that could make the country lose all accomplishments achieved so far. Nigeria cannot afford any small brat as president or vice president. There is a 'caveat' here for all Nigerians, the electorate.

Nigerians must act in the best interest of the nation and not only in the interest of what money can buy. Whoever wants to be president must be matured, look, talk and act presidential. He or she must prove himself or herself to be electable. The standard was raised by ExPresident Obasanjo's antecedent. The country should not go below his established standard.

Nigerian President or Vice President should not be any of those controversial youths and politicians who do not know how to talk with respect, dignity, decency and humility but keep on chasing money, business and women. Those who mix governance with ethno-religious bigotry and tribalism or those who mix state governance with private business and diversion of local council monetary allocation into private use in violation of Nigerian 1999 Constitution cannot be President or Vice President.

Within twenty-four hours, bad choices of president and leaders can overturn all the accomplishments made so far. Those who have fumbled as state leaders but want to be President or Vice President should be strongly told their limits and advised to go back to school and make necessary adjustments.

In the same vein, members of the legislature should be most distinguished men and women of 'timber and calibre' who are experienced, knowledgeable, highly educated and peopleoriented. They should be people who are above board, free from scandals, fraud and corruption. Nigeria is truly moving forward, and all eyes should be on the lookout for the right Nigerian leaders.

Nigerians should be seriously warned prior to holding elections that attempts to rig elections at either local, state or federal level would be contravening the Nigerian Constitution, and as such, offenders would face prosecution in the law courts. If convicted, they would be kept away from Nigerian society for a long time irrespective of their influence or status in society. There should be no 'sacred cows or untouchables' if the law is broken.

There was no Nigerian leader that did not love his country, even the worst of them. Even those who staged military coups d'etat gave reasons about their intentions, mission and vision. In effect, it is easy to want to be president, but what about education, experience, maturity, capability and leadership qualities required to be successful? Why has any leader failed when surrounded by so many advisers and technical experts? A leader that is very sound himself cannot be misled easily. So, in this twenty-first century, Nigeria needs great, dependable leaders.

The annulment of the June 12, 1993 presidential election won by Chief Moshood Kashimawo Olawale Abiola for which General Babangida was responsible as Head of State could not be his own making alone. Unreliable advisers and bad influences must have caused it. The example confirms that there are not many bad leaders as there are advisers. Leading Nigeria in this millennium is more difficult than ever before. Nigeria, therefore, needs the right person to lead irrespective of his/her ethnicity, religion or region of origin.

Nigerian government should never be handed over to an interim, unstable administration judging from what happened in 1993 when late General Sani Abacha toppled the interim transitional government, imposed himself as Head of State and maladministered the country, committed human rights abuses, economic and financial crimes and ran a pariah government from 1993 to 1998. Whoever wants to be president must satisfy the requirements of the Nigerian Constitution and receive the full mandate of the electorate in a free and fair, keenly and inclusively contested presidential election.

Events between January 15, 1966 and 2008 must have taught a lot of lessons and made Nigerian leaders wiser and ready to make amendments wherever necessary. Those who staged the January 15, 1966 coup d'etat said that they had good intentions and vision to redeem the nation but their actions backfired. If the January 1966 coup collaborators still living, knew before the coup d'etat, what they know today, perhaps they would have acted differently.

Similarly, perhaps General Buhari should not have truncated the democracy and civilian administration of the Second Republic. He had good intentions to rid the country of corruption, but his actions to redeem the country were transient. He deterred corrupt practices for which he incarcerated the politicians until proven innocent. If he has to do it again, perhaps he will do it differently for better results. A military dictatorship is not the best alternative solution to the problems of a democratically elected government. Those who toppled the First, Second and Third Republics of Nigeria were enemies of democracy.

In the same vein, perhaps General Ibrahim Badamosi Babangida (1985-1993) had the best intentions when he annulled the June 12, 1993 presidential elections and handed the government over to an interim transitional administration headed by Chief Ernest Shonekan. Perhaps, when he saw the misrule, the killings, the human rights violations, the economic and financial crimes committed by Abacha regime, he might have regretted leaving Nigeria in the mouth of the lion, devoured and torn to shreds. It is the man whose heart is made of stone that would not shed tears and profusely cry for Nigeria during Abacha's regime that was full of atrocities.

What if General Babangida had stayed a little bit longer in power, perhaps the history of Nigeria today would be different. Abacha's reign of terror might not exist; General Yar'Adua might have escaped death from HIV/AIDS virus injected into him; and Chief Moshood Abiola and his wife, Kudirat Abiola, Ken Saro-Wiwa and others imprisoned, hung or assassinated might still be alive.

On June 24, 2008, General Babangida expressed and accepted full responsibility vicariously for the annulment of June 12, 1993 presidential election won by Chief M.K.O. Abiola. He did not apportion any blame to his advisers, aides or military colleagues of the National Defense and Security Council (NDSC). He mentioned that Professor Humphrey Nwosu, the 1993 Chairman of Independent National Electoral Commission (INEC) did his job well. That is what great leaders do. They accept vicarious liability for whatever goes wrong under their watch without passing the buck.

It is observed that Professor Nwosu, INEC Chairman (1993) would have done a good job, if he understood the rule of law and due process; obeyed the court injunction that stopped the presidential election of June 12, 1993; cooperated with the Attorney General of the Federation, Chief Clement Akpamgbo to appeal the court order, or quash it by military decree as was advised by the AGF Akpamgbo.

Professor Nwosu would have done a good job, if he understood that advising, influencing and pressurizing the Military Head of State, General Babangida to take a unilateral decision at variance with his military colleagues on the NDSC was suicidal and could lead to a coup d'etat which later occurred, staged by General Abacha, who was then Chief of Defence Staff.

Professor Nwosu would have done a good job, if he was not desperately working against the majority opinions of the NDSC members, which led to the annulment of the presidential election on June 23, 1993, and the disbandment of his office.

Professor Nwosu would have deserved compliments if he stayed in his office and awaited NDSC decisions instead of jumping into Military Council Meetings to which he was not invited and was not a member and thereby made everybody in the NDSC uneasy, disturbed and mad.

He would have done a good job if he cooperated with the Attorney General and toed his line instead of engaging in fault-finding. Professor Nwosu was not a Lawyer and what was involved was serious legal issue, which was the responsibility of the AGF whom Professor Nwosu was undercutting and finding faults in his legal advice in order to discountenance the court injunction and satisfy the objections of Mr. Michael O'Brien, Director of Information of the US Embassy of June 10, 1993.

Professor Nwosu would have done a good job and be worthy of compliments if his advice, desperation and actions did not make him indirectly liable for all the problems that occurred as a result of the annulment of the election before and after the annulment up till today.

With foresight, Professor Nwosu should have understood that the problems that would have occurred as a result of a week or two postponement would have been less than the enormous problems created for holding the election on June 12, 1993 and its eventual annulment on June 23, 1993.

Who knows when the problems arising from June 1993 presidential election episodes would end after all the riots, assassinations, arson, imprisonment, and killings of opponents by General Abacha and the troubling remembrance events on every anniversary of June 12 since 1993 up to date?

The big problem which Nigeria has, is not as a result of bad leaders, but the poor advice and actions of leaders' advisers, aides, associates, cronies and government functionaries. That has been the big problem since independence from October 1, 1960 up till today.

Just like at the beginning of creation, Adam and Eve as husband and wife were not the problem but the advice given to Eve by the devil to convince her husband to eat the forbidden fruit in the 'Garden of Eden', created all the problems of the world up till today. In effect, General Babangida was not the problem, but the advice, pressure and opposing actions of Professor Nwosu which alienated all members of the NDSC during the second and third weeks of June 1993.

While General Babangida's colleagues in the NDSC and Attorney General Chief Akpamgbo were telling the Head of Military Government one thing, Professor Nwosu was in minority telling him something different reminiscent of backbitters and nonteamplayers. That was a dangerous game in a military rulership environment.

Professor Nwosu was trying to satisfy the wishes of Mr. Michael O'Brien, the Director of Information of the US Embassy, who wrote that any attempt to postpone the election was not acceptable to the US Government as if Nigeria was US Protectorate while members of the NDSC were infuriated and wanted to protect the Nigerian Sovereignty. Does the US ever base her electoral, internal affairs policies and decisions on what is acceptable or not acceptable to any other country including Nigeria?

It remains to be understood how Professor Nwosu should blame General Abacha and former AGF Akpamgbo instead of blaming himself for his indiscretion and poor judgment, for defying court order, committing contempt of court and creating confusion among members of the NDSC in particular and Nigerians in General. Professor Nwosu's actions byepassed due process and the rule of law.

Going through the Holy Books, the greatest rulers therein committed more serious mistakes. They were pardoned by God/Allah, and they became life's best examples to emulate to go to heaven. General Babangida exemplarily used due process of law to go to court to clear his name on a number of issues without heating the polity nor engaging in name calling. He did not call for violence, mass disruption, anarchy or ungovernableness even under extreme provoking circumstances.

On Thursday, August 19, 2004, the former National Chairman of the PDP, Chief Audu Ogbeh remarked, "When we blow the whistle, we want those who are contesting to tell us why they want to contest; what they are going to do; what they intend to improve on; and the innovation they will bring into the process of governance."

He added, "We are tired of just names and arguments about which zone's turn it is to produce the president. Let us hear from those who want to run, why they want to run because they have to govern." He emphasized that winning would depend on attractiveness of the programmes and their implementation. He reiterated that the party was experiencing a lot of anxiety and heat about early campaigning for an election that was three years away.

He referred to the case of the neighbouring country of Ghana where election would be coming up at the end of 2004, and yet, there was no frenzy and the kind of hype, which the 2007 Nigerian election had started to create. He promised that the party would halt it.

If political party members and supporters are fully employed and engaged in productive use in the country, they would not have time to start heating the polity with forceful arguments and campaigns in 2004 for an election that was fixed for 2007. An idle hand is dangerous, just like a hungry man is an angry man. Provide people with gainful employment and most of the problems of the country would be solved naturally.

Whoever can best solve the problems of the country and best serve the people should be president come 2011 and beyond notwithstanding his/her ethnicity, state or region of origin. May he/she not only be the choice of the people of Nigeria, but also the choice of God/Allah. Let it be said, "When I was hungry, you gave me food; when I was thirsty, you gave me water; when I had no clothing and shelter, you gave me clothing and housing; when I was sick, insecure and illiterate, you gave me healthcare, safety and quality education."

Such giver of great things that satisfy the needs of the people shall be our neighbour, brother/sister, leader and our chosen president, and it will not matter from where he/she comes from, whether East or West, North or South. Why can't all Nigerians irrespective of differences aim at electing the most befitting Nigerian person as President for the country come 2011 and beyond.

Speaking during the last week in November 2004, Chief Elvis Agukwe, National Coordinator of the Coalition for Democracy, and

Atiku Abubakar presidential support group and former National Director of Research of the PDP, told Igbo governors and other Igbos seeking the PDP presidential ticket in 2007 to wait for their turn. He advised them to recast their plans into a road map which could give the South-Eastern region the position of Vice Presidency in 2007, and eventually pick the presidential ticket come 2015.

He advised his Igbo kinsmen that presidential aspirants from the South-East zone lacked the capability to sweep presidential election. He added that he welcomed increased agitation to zone the presidency to the Igbos, saying that the agitation was the beginning of a journey that would end well. He explained with an analogy that if a person wanted to come first in class, and he ended up coming second, that would not be a bad deal. He advised the Igbos to utilize every opportunity available to negotiate for higher stake in the polity.

The Igbo Renaissance, a socio-economic and political organization, advised the Northern Region to wait for sixteen years after 2007 before they could qualify to produce the president of the Federal Republic of Nigeria. The group's national coordinator, Chief Pam Okafor, argued that Nigeria was structured on a tripod consisting of the Northern, Western and Eastern Regions of Nigeria. He asserted that the topmost post of the president should rotate among the three regions.

He added that since the Western Region would have had the presidency for two consecutive terms in 2007, the North should wait for sixteen years for the presidency to revolve around the South-East and South-South for sixteen years before it goes back to the North. He contended that the North had occupied the presidency for thirty-five years, the West for twelve years by the year 2007, while the East had it for seven months.

Chief Okafor omitted to let all those born after 1960 to know that the first President of Nigeria was an Igboman, Dr. Nnamdi Azikiwe, the Owelle of Onitsha, and he occupied Nigerian leadership topmost post from 1960 to 1966. His government was toppled on January 15, 1966 in a military coup organized by Ifeajuna, Nzeogwu and other Igbo collaborators who assassinated Western and Northern regional civilian and military leaders.

The Igbo coupists spared their Igbo leaders both civilian and military deliberately. Also, Chief Alex Ekwueme, an Igboman, was Vice

President of Nigeria from 1979-1983 under Shagari Administration. Invariably, it was the South-South that was left out of the equation since Nigerian Independence in 1960 until 2007, when Chief Goodluck Jonathan from South-South became Vice President Under Yar'Adua Administration.

In January 1966, Dr. Nnamdi Azikiwe was succeeded by another Igboman, General Aguiyi Ironsi from Eastern Region who became Head of State until he was toppled and assassinated in a retaliatory military coup d'etat organized by the Northerners on July 29, 1966 to avenge the killings of their military and civilian leaders on January 15, 1966 by Igbo military officers.

Considering other top positions in the Federal Service of Nigeria, the Igbos in coalition with the Northerners, always received more than their commensurate consideration at the expense of the Yorubas whose leadership were busy fighting among themselves while the North and the East were sharing the federal cake during their fragile coalition turned down by Yoruba leadership. It is therefore not honest to continue to preach that the Igbos were marginalized.

It is on record that between 1960 and 1975, and between 1979 and 1983, it was the Yorubaman that was relegated to the third place or hardly any place at all because Yoruba leaders were often antagonistic to the Federal Government. They were invited to participate in the coalition government of Shagari Administration, but they turned down all the hands of friendship to be partners in progress with Federal Administration. The intransigence of Yoruba leadership then robbed the Yorubas of their fair share of Nigeria's national opportunities. Regrettably, those who turned down Yoruba's share were not poor but living in affluence. The Yorubas were brainwashed.

Some other ethnicities, especially the Hausas and the Igbos, were misrepresented as enemies of the Yorubas just like some Igbos are presently misrepresenting some other ethnicities as enemies of Ndigbo. In national interest, all ethnicities have to work together as a team and put aside personal animosities and individual selfish interests.

It was the same wrongful notion that made the Yorubas to desert their kinsman, General Obasanjo, in the 1999 presidential election until they woke up and said, "never again" would anybody continue to mislead them into regarding other nationalities as their enemies. As a result, the Yorubas voted enmasse with their conscience in 2003 general, presidential and local government elections to support the mainstream political association that was widespread in Nigeria for the first time.

The Yorubas were always led astray to be in opposition for about three decades of Nigerian independence and when Chief Samuel Ladoke Akintola, former Premier of Western Region tried to change the tide by allying with the Northerners, he was made to pay the prize with his life by being assassinated by the IfeajunaNzeogwu led coup d'etat of January 15, 1966 masterminded by young Igbo military officers who had inordinate ambition to rule Nigeria.

In effect, the Yorubas suffered in the Union of Nigeria because of lack of cooperation from Yoruba leadership to be team players. The Igbos suffered because of the civil war which their leadership could have avoided through the use of dialogue and diplomacy knowing fully well that the terrible events that befell them after January 15, 1966 coup d'etat were retaliatory from the Northerners.

The actions of both the Easterners and the Northerners, which brought tribulations upon the nation, are condemnable, but the young Igbo military officers started it. For the overall benefit of the nation, finger pointing or pointing accusing fingers should stop for the nation to move forward.

Factually and without prejudice, the only region that has benefitted beyond its earning capacity and above its normal share of the national cake is Northern Nigeria, but its dictatorial leadership acted like the Biblical prodigal son such that the average Northerner and below, have not benefited as expected during thirty-five years that their leaders controlled the enormous wealth of Nigeria.

Regrettably, they cannot tell Nigerians generally, and the generality of Northerners in particular what they did with Nigerian wealth and where it is hidden in foreign private bank accounts. They left Nigeria insolvent/ bankrupt with overblown foreign debt, grave unemployment, corruption, economic and financial chaos and the country in a pariah situation. Hence, majority of elites became morally bankrupt and selfish.

Obasanjo Administration vigorously, embarked on corrective measures of past wrongs by pursuing socio-economic and political reforms. For the sake of posterity, few Nigerians cannot morally make the majority focus on breaking up the country instead of concentrating efforts on uniting it. Nigeria is a nation of the past, the present, the future and beyond.

The present Nigerians have no moral justification to break up Nigeria out of sheer selfish interest, so, the few elites should stop marring the nation no matter the weight of their anger. Aggrieved Nigerians should stop venting their anger on Nigeria, but blame the few Nigerian elites who are responsible for the problems in Nigeria.

In his own contribution to the aspiration to the presidency, Honourable Chinonyerem Macebuh emphasized competency rather than ethnicity or regional factor as prime qualification to be President of Nigeria. He described the clamour for zoning the presidency to the East or North as rubbish and as an instrument of deception of some people to grab power to steal money.

He reiterated that some of his Igbo kinsmen had very successful businesses in Ghana, Cote d'Ivoire, Republic of Benin and other West African coastal countries, and as such, they should help organize their people in Aba, Onitsha, etc. in business development. He frowned at how some Igbo leaders were busy organizing mass movement against the federal government unproductively instead of organizing their people for business development and economic prosperity by purchasing businesses being privatized by the government.

He added that some Igbo leaders did not relate well to those who held power, and they often snubbed those in power who made passes to accommodate them. What Hon. Macebuh just complained about was the same intransigence that the Yoruba leadership did between 1960 and 1975 and thereby lost their first place in Africa to become the third place in Nigeria.

That situation is reminiscent with the situation in which the Yorubas found themselves being led in antagonistic posture, at variance with the Federal Government of Nigeria three decades after independence for which they lost. The irony of the situation was that those who criticized the government loudest and posed in open confrontation against the government often went behind everybody's back to get their relations working in high places and benefitting immensely from government contracts and other goodies.

There were and still are many reference cases of incessant attacks and criticisms of the government because government turned down requests for favours for which some of them were not qualified. Obasanjo Administration was too magnanimous, always calling the dissidents to participate as if without them, Nigeria would not move forward. The best that can be done is vigilance to put any situation under check until their generation passes away. How can you change anybody who is used to confrontation for over fifty years?

There is utmost freedom in the USA, but nobody can intimidate the country, her leadership or any citizen with words, actions or by implication with impunity. A man cannot even intimidate his wife or children without suffering the consequences of serving terms of imprisonment.

Government should not focus on corruption alone. The focus should include societal discipline for the high, middle class and the masses. Nobody should be above the law of the land. There should be no sacred cows and untouchables if the law is violated.

Honourable Macebuh dwelled on the division among the Igbos and almost concluded that they were not ready for the presidency. He remarked, "The leadership that cannot effectively control their base may not be able to manage the nation successfully. We cannot entrust our nation's direction and future in the hands of those who are of the same ethnicity but always quarrelling among themselves."

He added, "When Dr. Alex Ekwueme was the Vice President, his governor gave him hell. When Anyim was the Senate President, he saw hell with his governor. This incumbent Senate President is also having hell. The others spent only a few months and got thrown out! In other regions of West and North, intra regional rivalries are not as serious as they are in the East. Given this background, an Igbo Presidency would not be able to sustain and resist a coup d'etat as the president has to readjust benefits and step on some toes."

He explained further, " A competent Igbo Presidency will face heavy threats; and we are not yet at the point where such a presidency can resist such threats. Time therefore is not ripe for an Igbo Presidency."

In addition to Honourable Macebuh's concern, the Igbos who have businesses nationally and internationally must reorientate their people generally to never forget their home base, towns and villages for development because East or West, Home is the best. There is no place like home.

It is recalled that before the Nigerian Civil War (1967-1970), the Igbos owned magnificent properties in Lagos, PortHarcourt, Kano, Kaduna, etc. at the expense of not developing their home bases, and when they were called back home for their safety in anticipation of the declaration of secession, a lot of them lost their properties, especially in PortHarcourt and elsewhere, and they had accommodation difficulties back home.

Although wherever any Nigerian citizen chooses to live in Nigeria should be his/her home, but never forget to help the development of your home base. It is in your home base that nobody can intimidate or discriminate against you. Your home base will always remain your primary stronghold. Your business successes in Ghana, Cote d'Ivoire, Benin Republic, Togo, etc. should be reflected on your home bases.

If a president emerges from a region that has not known peace for a long time persistently, it is most likely that the whole nation will be engulfed by chaos, confusion, unaccomplishments and retrogression. Therefore, the East must put its house in order and relate harmoniously with the rest of Nigeria. Without cooperation from other states or regions, no one state or region's votes can be sufficient to install a president of the Federal Republic of Nigeria?

If a presidential aspirant emerges from the North, it must be asked whether Nigeria will be better than the thirty-five years of Nigerian lives they wasted by overthrowing each other in incessant military coups d'etat. They also allegedly stashed away Nigerian government money in private accounts of foreign banks at the expense of innocent Nigerians riddled with grave unemployment, inflationary spiral, frauds, corruption, economic and financial crimes, human rights violations and maladministration.

On the other hand, if the East presents the president, can Nigerians be assured of peace, unity, and one nation under God, indivisible without tribalism, secessionist tendencies, frauds, corruption, economic and financial crimes and illegal drugs? As for the Yoruba leadership, we may ask whether they have learnt any lessons at all, to be president!

Has Nigeria started to develop a database that can provide useful information as to which states, regions or ethnicities produce indigenes that commit most crimes so that Nigerians can usually decide whether such states or ethnicities can represent the country's leadership?

In the same way, who is the governor of the year? Who is the Senator or House Representative member of the year? In a democracy, more information about leadership performance must be made available to the public to guide the electorate to make decisions in future elections.

Attempts by *This Day News* to pick the Governor and Senator of the year 2004, named the following personalities:

(1) Governor of the Year Nominees in 2004 included:
    (a) Obalofin Otunba Gbenga Daniel of Ogun State;
    (b) Donald Duke of Cross River State;
    (c) Sam Egwu of Ebonyi State;
    (d) Danjuma Goje of Gombe State;
    (e) Bukola Saraki of Kwara State: and
    (f) Umar Yar'Adua of Katsina State

(2) Senator of the Year Nominees in 2004 included:
    (a) Mamman Ali;
    (b) John AzutaMbata;
    (c) Uche Chukwumerije;
    (d) Olorunnimbe Mamora; and
    (e) Udoma Udo Udoma.

Nigerian leaders, elders and elites should remember and act on these wonderful sayings, "I shall pass through this world but once. Any good, therefore, that I can do, or any kindness that I can show to any human being, let me do it now, let me not defer it or neglect it, for I shall not pass this way again."

Contributing to search for the president, Alhaji Bashir Zubairu Usman, who was Speaker of the Kaduna State House of Assembly was reported to believe that the zoning system for the election of the President of Nigeria was undemocratic, pointing out that any Nigerian who had the right leadership qualities and interests in the unity of the country irrespective of his or her ethnicity or region of origin could be elected to the post.

He added that he would support the election of any Nigerian who had the unity of the country at heart. Speaker Usman's views ran counter to the declaration of the nineteen Northern Nigerian Governors at the end of their meeting who emphasized that the successor to the presidency in 2007 must come from Northern Nigeria, and that their declaration was not negotiable. His message was one of the most democratic and rare voices from the North in those days.

In the same wise, state governors, leaders and elders at local, state, regional and federal levels should be more conscious of their Nigerianness rather than their ethnicity, state or regional base. Each Nigerian state consists of a cross section of multiplicity of Nigerian ethnicities, and as such, state governors should stop making proclamations that are divisive and not in the best interest of one Nigeria.

It is childish and nonpolitical for Nigerian sectional leaders to come out of meetings, and then issue communiqué to the public saying. "It is not negotiable." Elected leaders should lead right in a changing and advancing world of democracy. To achieve progress and lasting world peace, everything must be negotiable. That is why there are no permanent friends but interests under democratic settings.

The former Chairman of the Peoples Democratic Party (PDP) Board of Trustees, Chief Anthony Anenih, was reported to have advised all campaigners bidding to succeed President Obasanjo in 2007 to hold their fire because only the president and not even the ruling PDP would determine his successor. He added, "Obasanjo ought to have continued as president because he is doing well, but the problem is that he is statute barred." Chief Anenih allegedly made the statement when he was addressing a closeddoor meeting of the stakeholders of the party from the South-West at Abeokuta, Ogun State. He reiterated that deference must be given to the president to choose his successor.

Chief Anenih had good intention, but the presentation was faulty under democratic setting. Nigerian ExPresident Obasanjo having done a great job would wield a lot of influence in the choice of a succeeding president which was quite normal, but he was not going to hand pick his successor for Nigerians.

It is recalled that the expresident had only one vote, which would not be sufficient to determine who succeeded him under democratic setting, but that one single vote could have sufficient weight to convince Nigerian voters that the candidate he supported would be the best for the country.

If Nigerian majority trusted the expresident, such trust would definitely extend to the candidate he admired. It was also possible for him to go out and campaign for the candidate he supported while the final choice rested with the entire electorate. Chief Anenih's statement demonstrated his great impressions about the good job the expresident did, and he was entitled to say his opinions in a democracy whether anybody liked it or not. In politics, there are not permanent friends, but permanent interests. Can Chief Anenih say the same thing since he lost the PDP BOT chairmanship? That is not sure.

Chief Elvis Agukwe, National Chairman of the Coalition for Democracy, a rabid nationwide proAtiku group, claimed that the original intention of the founders of the PDP was to rotate power between the North and South of Nigeria. He said that President Obasanjo's best option would be to support the aspiration of his deputy in order to sustain the continuity of the ongoing reform programmes of Obasanjo Administration. He also affirmed that it was improbable for the president to disappoint his Vice President Atiku Abubakar on account of the fastidious loyalty of Atiku to him.

He was emphatic that it was the turn of the North to produce the succeeding president in 2007. Chief Agukwe, an Igboman from South-East, dismissed the agitation from the South-East, his home state, for a president of Igbo extraction. He asserted, "There is no likelihood of any aspirant emerging from the South-East zone with the capacity to prosecute a presidential campaign in 2007."

Senator Bello (ANPP, Kebbi) expressed his opinion that the zoning principle, which helped the PDP to win the 1999 elections, was likely to destroy the party ahead of the 2007 elections. He regretted that the zoning strategy would help to preclude most qualified Nigerians from positions of authority. He said, "I believe that the principle of zoning the leadership of this country does not produce the best candidate that will rule the country, it only produces the best candidate in a section of this country which I feel should not be the case."

In the search for Nigerian Leader or President, it may be necessary for Nigerian leaders and elders to read and digest some statements of the former UN Secretary-General Kofi Annan during his address to AU leaders in AddisAbaba on Tuesday, July 6, 2004. He said:

> (1) "Let us pledge that the days of indefinite oneman or oneparty situation are behind us."
> (2) "There is no truer wisdom and no clearer mark of

statesmanship than knowing when to pass the torch to a new generation."

(3) "Politics must be inclusive, and a careful institutional balance must be preserved – including regular, free and fair elections, a credible opposition whose role is respected, an independent judiciary which upholds the rule of law and a free independent press."

(4) "Democracy is not perfect and democratization is not easy, but the more accountable governments are, the more likely they are to be responsive to the needs of their people."

(5) "Let us always remember that constitutions are for the long term benefit of society, not the shortterm goals of the ruler."

ExPresident Chissano of Mozambique, the 2004 outgoing AU Chairman urged his fellow African leaders to heed the advice of the UN Secretary-General. He informed the meeting that he himself would be stepping down and would be replaced in a democratic election. His example is worthy of emulation. The UN Secretary-General's statements above are significant for the guidance of African leaders.

The founder of Oodua Peoples Congress (OPC), Dr. Frederick Fasehun, was reported to have thrown his weight behind the Igbos for their quest for the presidency in 2007. He explained that with Nigeria standing on a tripod represented by the HausaFulani, Yoruba and Igbo, the presidency in 2007 should revolve on the Igbos because the other two major nationalities had had their turns. He stressed that to deny the Igbos the presidency in 2007 would be social injustice and that without social justice; there could be no peace.

Presenting Nigeria as a tripod represented by HausaFulani, Igbo and Yoruba does not show the true position of Nigerian nationalities. The establishment of thirty-six states in six geopolitical zones has changed the concept of the tripod in the twenty-first century Nigeria. Zoning leadership is a cheap, backdoor method of election.

The philosophy of the tripod excludes the minorities of the Mid-West, South-South and the Middle-Belt regions among others. Nigeria should also discard the zoning system, which is undemocratic and likely to cause reverse discrimination in presidential elections because the best candidates may fail to be considered for the post of the president if zoning system subsists.

The Igbo nationality represents one of the most talented, brilliant and enterprising group of people you can find on the face of the earth. The best Igbo candidate cannot be afraid of any competition with the bests from other parts of the country. That is what is done in most civilized communities in the world, and Nigeria should not be an exception to such acceptable democratic practice and norm.

Where is the pride of Nigeria if we cannot nurture our democracy to full status but continue to undermine it in the election of the president? When will that end? It must be now.

The best Nigerian candidates from all walks of life and all nooks and corners of Nigeria should go through their party primaries for the presidency, and whoever wins should be supported to govern no matter what, in the best interest of the nation. When will the Nigerian nation stop the misconceptions in some quarters that if they do not rule Nigeria or that if their turn is not assured, then the country should die, disintegrate, not breathe or become ungovernable?

According to Professor Ibrahim Agboola Gambari, "If people want to be president, we should ask them where they want to lead us to, their track record and vision. Their region of origin or ethnicities should not be the primary consideration for seeking the presidency." Some eminent people such as Professor Gambari feel that a person's military record as General or having served as Head of State before should not be the only criterion to get elected as President of Nigeria.

In his own comments as to who should not be president of Nigeria, Dr. Frederick Fasehun was reported to have declared on Thursday, August 5, 2004, that the Yorubas would never participate in the succeeding civilian government if former military ruler General Ibrahim Babangida emerged the winner in the 2007 presidential election.

He said that Yoruba people, especially the OPC, would resist any attempt by any politician or group to impose Babangida on Nigerians. He explained that General Babangida committed atrocities against the Yoruba race while he was in office, hence it would be difficult for him to have a smooth ride politically in the South-West. He added, "Yorubaland is nogo area for IBB."

He alleged that Babangida failed to honour an invitation to appear before a public hearing of the Human Rights Violation Commission. Dr. Fasehun was reported to have described those campaigning for General Babangida in Yorubaland as bastards who should be treated as lepers. He stressed that the Yorubas would not forgive Babangida until he showed serious remorse for his alleged atrocities.

Dr. Fasehun's speech did not recognize the spirit of democracy and the right of every Yoruba person to think, decide and act for himself/herself. Calling some Yorubas bastards for exercising their freedom of association was political intolerance, and asking them to be treated as lepers was inciteful, not exemplary and not acceptable in civilized communities in the world, where lepers are treated humanely and given the best medical attention in modern times. In a democracy, people have freedom of speech, expression, association and religious faith. As a result, those Yorubas allegedly campaigning for Babangida could not be rightly referred to as bastards for exercising their freedom of association, freedom of speech and expression as entrenched in Nigerian 1999 Constitution.

When speaking and pretending to be representing a whole ethnicity, race or nationality like the Yorubaland, such speakers should exercise restraint, courtesy and decency that are the greatest values of the Yorubas. Yorubas are individuals who are very intelligent and proud of their heritage and freedom to make their choices during elections. It is time to stop misrepresenting the Yorubas.

Judging from recent history, the only people that the Yorubas have followed enmasse was Chief Obafemi Awolowo who performed wonders that ensured the upliftment of the Yoruba race with his lieutenants like Governors Lateef Jakande, Ajasin, Bisi Onabanjo and so on. Since their exit, nobody has ever been able to win the hearts of the entire Yorubas except President Obasanjo whom the Yorubas supported enmasse and overwhelmingly during 2003 general, presidential and local government elections. Yorubas have the right to choose intelligent, polite, decent, respectful and respected spokespersons to speak and represent them.

Nobody or group(s) should usurp such rights and whenever a spokesperson is authorized to speak for the Yorubas, such person should talk with respect, dignity, decency and politeness in recognition of Yoruba's inherent cultures, customs and traditions of respectability, decency and discipline. There are too many impostors as Yoruba leaders.

In the same vein, some people pretend to be speaking for the Igbos or the North when in actual fact they do not have the authority to do so or the right followership that could make them speak for the entire race or nationality.

How can a body or one organization claim to be talking and taking decisions on behalf of the entire Yoruba race when the Egbados, Aworis, Egbas and all major units of Yorubaland are not represented in such organizations? Individuals or associations should be cautious and exercise restraint when arrogating to themselves, the power, authority or representation belonging to the whole Yoruba race which has not been properly delegated to those individuals and/or associations.

Some ethnic organizations spring up from different parts of the country and purport to be protecting their ethnic nationalities while committing atrocities and usurping the powers of the police, the judges and the juries. When will all atrocities being committed with impunity stop? Democracy is not licentiousness. People should get employed productively, stop anarchical tendencies and let the authorities do their work for a better progressive Nigeria.

In similar circumstance, the Campaign for Democracy (CD) was reported to have warned the PDP against fielding General Babangida as its presidential candidate during the 2007 elections. They alleged that General Babangida's Administration committed atrocities especially the annulment of June 12, 1993 presidential election.

The organization (CD) stressed that the apology demanded from General Babangida by Nobel Laureate Wole Soyinka would not reconcile the families who lost their loved ones of over 2000 people during the agitation for the revalidation of June 12, 1993 election results. They mentioned names of lost lives who represented the symbols of democracy like Chief M.K.O. Abiola, Rear Admiral Elegbede, Omoshehinwa, Pa Alfred Rewane and many others of over 2000 Nigerians allegedly massacred on the streets of Lagos, Akure, Ibadan, Aba, etc.

As a result, the organization promised to mobilize Nigerians, and to campaign against any political party that might field General Babangida as its candidate for the 2007 presidential election. The CD group can act freely as long as their actions are constitutional and in the spirit of the nascent democracy. The CD group cannot infringe on anybody's fundamental human rights with impunity.

In a democracy, people are free to make their points of opinion but cannot issue threats and intimidation with impunity. When will some Nigerians be made to know their limitations. Unfortunately, the News Media pay too much attention to the irrelevances from many individuals and organizations, and thereby give them unearned recognition and undeserved reputation.

Major Abubakar Umar (rtd.) was alleged to have urged Generals Babangida, Buhari, Marwa and Vice President Atiku Abubakar to forget their presidential ambitions. Umar argued that the military failed to solve the nation's socio-economic and political problems because of inherent limitations. He revealed that there were basic divergences in culture and orientation between the military and civilian leadership.

He explained that military rulers were bureaucratic and autocratic, oriented towards imposed order, command and nonpolitical approach to problems of governance culminating into a bane on democratic and economic development. He opined that a military trained person at the helm of affairs in a civilian administration would be like a round peg in a square hole.

He explained that political accommodation and the willingness to bargain collectively and compromise on conflicting positions which used to be indispensable in a civilian environment would be outside the purview of people with military background and regimental training of soldiering.

It must be remembered by all those who choose to exclude some others from being considered for the position of president that they should understand and accept that they do not have the final say about who becomes or does not become the president of Nigeria. Under democratic process, it is the electorate who decide. It cannot be right that no military personnel or General can succeed as head of a civilian administration.

That generalized philosophy propounded by Major Umar (rtd), cannot be right in all cases. The majority of all political leaders in the world's greatest and foremost democracy, the USA, have passed through various military trainings. It is easier for some people to adapt to changes and succeed more than others. The successful leadership of a retired Military General in a civilian administration depends upon his/her own character, exposure to life, education, training, development, civilization, background, upbringing, faith, religion and the possession of other leadership qualities. The best soldier or Military General can become the best civilian President of Nigeria as witnessed in American or European History.

It has been easy to condemn the military leadership and blame their dictatorship for Nigerian problems since independence, but what about the civilian advisers, ministers, commissioners, governors, government functionaries, permanent secretaries, general managers, directors, etc. who were in majority in the leadership of the country during the military and civilian regimes! Did the civilians who occupied positions of authority between January 15, 1966 up to date perform better than the military men who appointed them? NO!

They kept on moving from one regime to the other pillaging the country and helping their military masters stash stolen money overseas. The economics luminary and professor who served under General Abacha praised him for not travelling out of the country, but how was almost $5 billion government money stashed into his various private accounts with foreign banks without the assistance of his aides and advisers who were civilians? Yet, people kept on blaming the military leadership alone for Nigeria's woes.

Before his death, Honourable Wada Nas was reported to be leading a campaign for a South East Igbo Presidency. He said that the North should support the Igbo Presidency, so that the South Easterners who had been known as 'Northern Allies' could realize their dreams. He described the Igbos as among the most resourceful, intelligent, educated, imaginative and hard working people in Nigeria!

He mentioned that the Igbos were ahead in invention and industry and as such, they had the brains to produce a leader of the country. He queried, "Who is this active politician in this country today that is more qualified than (Dr.) Alex Ekwueme for the presidency of this country?"

The head of the presidency is a political appointment, which usually goes to the most acceptable person elected by the electorate. Such person in USA or Britain may not be the most qualified, most experienced or most educated, but must be the most acceptable to the majority of the electorate in order to win and become president.

It is the electorate that best decide who is the most acceptable to become the president under democratic setting. Chief Ekwueme should offer himself to the electorate and campaign for votes throughout the country in competition with others from other parts of the country that may offer to serve their fatherland. Chief Alex Ekwueme could be one of the best choices to represent the Igbos to contest for the presidency and perhaps have support from many Nigerians across all ethnicity boundaries.

When Chief Ekwueme lost his PDP nomination bid for the presidency in 2003, his overreactions soon after did not compare favourably with what happened in the USA in 2000, 2004 and 2008 which he should have emulated. There were comparable detailed records of what Al Gore, John Edwards, Howard Dean, Bob Dole, John Kerry and Senator Clinton etc. said and did with maturity, civility and patriotism in the spirit of their party and US national interest when they lost their presidential bids compared with what Chief Alex Ekwueme said and did in Nigeria under similar circumstances.

Chief Alex Ekwueme allegedly rejected all overtures from his PDP governing party and leaders, his colleagues and friends in the PDP and went to court to stop the party nominee from contesting the 2003 presidential election at the embarrassment of the PDP. As alleged, he abandoned the party and tried to split it in the midst of pending 2003 presidential election, which constituted antiparty activities. Such actions could have derailed the reelection of the PDP nominee in 2003. Nigerian leaders and leadership aspirants can always borrow from the best examples in Europe and America. He later played remarkable leadership conciliatory role in uniting the PDP and his committee succeeded in bringing back some dissatisfied leaders who broke away during the 2003 presidential and general elections.

Contributing to the search for the Nigerian President in 2007, the Marafan of Sokoto, Alhaji Umaru Shinkafi remarked that it was not decent for former Heads of State to go partisan again and to run for the presidency. He added that the constitution expected Nigerian exPresidents or exHeads of State to settle down and be useful members of the National Council of State and play their roles well.

Shinkafi reiterated what he would expect from a candidate for the presidency through contemporary experience as, "competence, performance, compliance with the manifesto, respect for the constitution, ability of carrying the nation along, offering real assistance and uplifting the dignity of the nation in the comity of nations." He added, "This is what is on record. All we need is somebody who is going to market us further."

It was reported that a joint meeting of members of Afenifere, a PanYoruba organization, and the Yoruba Council of Elders (YCE) was held at Ibadan to decide on a common candidate for the 2007 presidential election. A member of the body remarked, "We believe that the Yoruba nation cannot afford to fold its hands and watch things at the national level. We must participate."

The move for the Yorubas to speak with one voice is remarkable provided the forum is fully attended by representatives of all important and distinct units of Yorubaland. It would not be sufficient of representatives from few segments of Yorubaland to meet in Ibadan or Ijebu-Ode and pretend to be representing the whole Yoruba race. Any organization that talks for the whole Yorubaland must 'demonstrate Yorubaland character' and be fully representative of Yoruba spread of the South-Western geopolitical zone of Nigeria. Do the present Yoruba organizations speaking and purportedly representing Yorubaland, have Yoruba character and spread? That is food for thought!

Unlike the periods of losses, sufferings and marginalization, which Yorubas passed through before, as a result of their leadership intransigence, politicization and lack of cooperation with the federal authorities, any true Yoruba leadership from now on, must maintain and increase on the present gains and not let them slip away.

Such Yoruba leadership must be ready to cooperate, compromise, negotiate and fully realize Yorubas' fair share of the opportunities available in the nation. It cannot be a forum for antagonism or for venting personal vendetta against personalities in the federal government. Such forum must be able to account for its accomplishments for the Yorubas periodically. Nigerian leaders and elders act as bosses of the people and want to be acknowledged as bosses contrary to real leaders who serve with humility and accountability. In December 2008, Bishop Gbonigi allegedly described many of these impostors claiming to be

Yoruba leaders and Awoists as liars and confusionists. That is sad if true. What is the job description of Yoruba leader? Do Hausas, Igbos etc. have such designation?

The leadership of Nigeria, which has made so many strides in economic reforms and great struggles against corruption, cannot be rightly handed over to an amateur if Nigerians want continuity and a government that is not starting all over again. Therefore, Nigerian presidency must be in the hand of formidable leadership that can move forward quickly.

The choice of leadership should be strictly in accordance with the Nigerian Constitution, as it may exist after all necessary reviews being contemplated. Experience is the best teacher. Skill, capability, education, professionalism, transparency, energy, empathy and experience should be the first consideration instead of ethnicity, religion or region of origin.

The National Political Reform Conference (NPRC, February-July 2005) recommended a minimum of fouryear university/college degree or equivalent professional qualification for political office aspirants. Hence, any Nigerian without the minimum educational requirement should voluntarily stay out of competition for the presidency, governorship or the legislature. Nigerians are tired of mediocrity, fighting, slapping, confusion, inaction, regression, irresponsiveness, lack of initiative and maladministration in the public sector.

Borrowing some words from a renowned Akure, Ondo State politician in the Alliance for Democracy political party (AD), who served President Obasanjo for four years and served former Head of State Ibrahim Badamosi Babangida (IBB) for five years. He said, "If I were in his shoes, at some point in time, I will find a suitable way to say that I did not expect the nation to suffer the way it did under Abacha. We all suffered, even Babangida himself. The whole nation was regarded as a pariah state; the world related to you as a leper. It is true that we all suffered various degrees of personal discomfort."

He added, "What I like best about IBB (General Ibrahim Badamosi Babangida) is that he is the best historian I have ever worked with and the most polite boss I ever had. He is the best listener and the most polite. He is very appreciative of what you do for him. All the years I spent with him, I have never seen him shout down at a subordinate.

Other leaders I have worked with would shout you down and try to bully you."

When asked what he disliked about Babangida, he replied, "What I do not like about him is that he could change his mind ever so often. He is not as steadfast as I would have loved him to be; he changed his mind too often."

General Babangida's flexibility may be a problem as much as it can be an asset. It was General Babangida's flexibility and easiness to trust advisers, aides and associates that Professor Nwosu, 1993 INEC Chairman, unduly exploited by advising him to defy the court order of injunction as well as defy the majority opinions (a week delay by members of the NDSC), to hold the controversial presidential election of June 12, 1993, won by Chief M.K.O. Abiola which was annulled on June 23, 1993. The ability to trust people easily coupled with flexibility is a great leadership asset, but overtrusting can be a liability exploitable by advisers, aides and associates.

As to his personal regrets, the respondent said that later in his career, he started to see mediocrity being celebrated; that gave him concern. People were given undue advantages, even they themselves knew that they did not deserve. He added, "Merit is not always recognized." That is one of Nigeria's biggest problems!

As regards the Nigeria of his dream, he replied, "The type of Nigeria that joins the Asian Tigers where their economy is booming; where all our children abroad would come back home voluntarily to seize the opportunities being created. Where there is ethnic harmony; where all Nigerians feel free with one another. Where a Nigerian knows he will reap the reward of his handwork; that he does not have to be of your tribe or religion to get his fair share." Maybe future generations will seriously tackle these Nigerian perennial problems of discrimination; application of equity, justice and fairplay.

He referred to late General Murtala Mohammed, Military Head of State 1975 to 1976, as a hero because he was fair to all. He remarked that some Akure drivers were still carrying Murtala's pictures in their vehicles up to date. He added that Murtala was not from their ethnicity, but people still saw him as their fairminded hero. He commented, "A fair handshake, that's what Nigerians need."

The Democratic Party nominee, Senator John Kerry who was most favoured to win the 2004 US presidential election against the incumbent, Republican Party candidate George W. Bush, lost the election to the underdog because he was accused of being indecisive, flip-flopping, wishywashy and wavering on his votes on national issues requiring tough decisions during his many years stay in the US Senate.

As a result, any Nigerian who aspires to be President of Nigeria must promise the nation in his campaign that he will be consistent, assertive, firm, relentless in the fight against corruption and elites indiscipline; and that he will not be influenced by his ethnicity orientation, religious bigotry or political affiliation, when dealing with tough national issues.

Nigeria is tired of being wrecked by leaders being unduly influenced and taking dictations from Sokoto, Kano, Kaduna, Zaria, Enugu, Ibadan, etc. when major national issues are being decided upon just like the annulment of June 12, 1993 presidential election.

It was not a oneman decision, but the leader took responsibility. Soon after these influencing groups and individuals misled the leader, and the leader was gone ingloriously, they changed gear and joined the succeeding leadership pretending to be saints. Leaders must watch out. Do not be fooled.

In support of fiveyear single term tenure for the President and State Governors in Nigeria, Ambassador Mbadiwe opined that in a multiethnic set up of Nigeria, where the largesse of the nation was being rotated among the zones, two terms of four years each would be too long. He argued that the two terms of four years each would make people become impatient and start to see government as a means of selfaggrandizement instead of as a means of development. He asserted that if any zone took eight years, it might not reach the turn of some zones in forty years.

Ambassador Mbadiwe should be reminded that 40 years might be long in the life of a person but not in the life of a country, which has perpetual succession. Therefore, it is not the length of time or the number of years that matters but the quality of Nigerian administration at each time. It is not the masses or the majority of the people that are clamouring for zoning but the few elites who want to personally benefit from the arrangement.

The few elites think about the time it would take to be their turn to govern, while the masses think about good governance, because they are the ones who suffer from the maladministration by the few elites. Above all, the zoning strategy may not produce the best candidate and thereby result in reverse discrimination and lower quality of service to the people.

If there are employment opportunities, steady electricity, water, food, safety, health services, well supported educational system, good transportation and communication systems, housing, etc., the majority or the masses will not and have never cared about the length of tenure, ethnicity, religion or region of the president or governor.

The problems in Nigeria are not created by the masses or majority of Nigerians but by the few elites who are fighting among themselves for how they can personally benefit from the national cake. If the government provides the essential basic necessities of life with peace, transparency and progressive development, the Nigerian masses will not care where the president comes from, his ethnicity or religion.

For example, there is reliable information that some drivers in Akure, Ondo State still carry the photograph of General Murtala Mohammed, Military Head of State (1975-76) in their purses even though he was not a Yorubaman, but because he was transparent, consistent and disciplined. The masses loved his short administration assisted by General Obasanjo without caring about his ethnicity, religion or region of origin.

General Yakubu Gowon was Military Head of State for almost ten years (1966-75), but the masses did not care about the length of time, his religion, ethnicity or region of origin because there was money to spend on basic requirements. In effect, what Ambassador Mbadiwe should be emphasizing is the quality of those who would be future leaders or president and not from what region, religion or ethnicity they will come. What is very significant is good governance, getting the best and most suitable people to run the affairs of the country and not the length of time, zoning or religion of the leadership.

Sometimes, it takes some presidents about two years or more to find their feet. If he is gone after five years without much impact, it means that another one comes in to start all over again without settling down for two years or more.

The limited one single term of five years as recommended by Ambassador Mbadiwe gives the president or governor no incentive to perform better because he is always aware that at the end of five years, he becomes history. So, he grabs and grabs all that he can corruptly and leaves at the end of his term of five years. In this case, the incentive to work hard is not there.

On the other hand, a president or governor who has chance of coming back after four years would work hard to earn the possibility of another fouryear term. A good president who does well during the first term of four years, may do better when he comes back for the second term because he would have acquired a lot of experience. It is not all presidents and governors that would earn a second term, hence, the argument that eight years is too long is not tenable and not progressive.

Nigeria needs to find out why other successful democracies in the civilized world like the United Kingdom or United States of America choose two or more terms of four years each and not fiveyear single tenure for the positions of President, Prime Minister and/or Governor. US Senators have six (6)year tenure per term of unending terms until death or when voted out or in cases of voluntary resignation. In what other countries do presidents or heads of government spend fiveyear single term? The problems are the Nigerian elites and not the masses, time, ethnicity, religion nor the regions, but those who troubleshoot are the few elites. The masses that are in majority are not complaining. It is the few elites who are never satisfied that are always creating problems.

Nigeria as of today has produced some of the most brilliant intellectuals in the world and can no longer afford to be led by halfbaked leaders. Let all these great intellectuals emerge and compete from North, West, East and South and give Nigerians the best choice of leadership. The bookworms without the necessary leadership qualities and experience cannot solve Nigerian problems. Successful leadership needs more than book knowledge.

Youthfulness without the right education, experience, attitude and maturity cannot lead to successful leadership. Nigerians must watch carefully for the right candidates who will lead Nigeria to the Promised Land, the Eldorado. It must be remembered that a bad leader as president can truncate Nigeria's accomplishments of these past years within twenty-four hours of assumption of office, and everybody will be back to square one. You must always act and say, "never again" to maladministration or dictatorship.

It is worthy to remind those who are struggling for Nigerian leadership that they should familiarize themselves with the teaching of God/Allah as contained in the Holy Books thus, "Whoever desires to become great among you, let him be your servant, and whoever desires to be first among you, let him be your slave; just as the Son of Man did not come to be served; but to serve and to give His life a ransom for many." Matthew 20:2628.

On Monday, November 29, 2004, the former Governor of Abia State, Chief Orji Uzor Kalu affirmed his intention to contest and win the presidential election scheduled for 2007. He promised to make the difference in Nigerian citizenry. ExGovernor Kalu reiterated, "It is going to be a very difficult fight. It is going to be a very long fight. It is going to be a fight that will stand the test of time, and it is going to be a battle of all times."

He promised that he would return Nigeria to Nigerians and transform the economy so that Nigerians would enjoy the fruits of their labour. He was quoted to have said, "I know what I can do to restructure this economy; I know what the people of Nigeria need. I will not work alone; I will work with experts to do the job of turning around our economy for good. I will do for the Nigerian people what I have done for myself and for the people of Abia State."

Nigerians would want to know how successful Abia State people are to be able to determine how fit ExGovernor Kalu is for the highest post in the presidency.

When reminded that ExGovernor George Akume of Benue State remarked that ExGovernor Kalu was still young and that he could wait for eight years before he could contest, he replied that his youthful age was not material. He mentioned that President Obasanjo was Head of State at thirty-nine, and he said that his youth would be an asset. He mentioned that if the position of president were given to statesmen, they would not work thinking that they knew it all, but that he would work with people that knew how to achieve the desired results.

ExGovernor Kalu must remember that General Obasanjo became Head of State at thirty-nine as a result of a coup d'etat which killed General Murtala Mohammed organized by Lt. Colonel Dimka. He was not elected as president at thirty-nine. Also, one must use advisers and experts to govern, but as president, one must be matured, highly educated and experienced to be able to utilize the advisers successfully.

It must be remembered that not all advisers or experts are good and entirely dependable. Expert advice on Iraqi war made George Bush, President of the USA and Tony Blair, ExPrime Minister of Great Britain receive less than 30% popularity and job performance approval rating in 2006/07. To be successful as president, one must be very sound. It must be remembered that there is hardly any bad leader, but advisers, aides, associates and government functionaries who need to be watched and made to take commensurate responsibilities and blames for presidential failures.

When he was reminded that he would have to contend with Vice President Atiku and other power brokers and king makers in PDP, he replied that he would be equal to them in everything and do better because he cared for the future of the delegates and that of their children. He referred to the delegates as feepaying like himself and said that those power brokers and king makers had lost touch with present realities.

He mentioned that the previous Sunday, twenty-five thousand people wrote him promising to contribute five million naira each to his campaign and that they told him not to contribute anything. He added that his tribesmen, the Igbos in America had pledged to contribute "a huge chunk of money."

He emphasized, " you will not believe what you will see in terms of money, but I want to assure you, money will not be a hindrance to this noble ambition." At another occasion, it was hinted that money might come from major oil producing countries to assist his presidential campaign.

When he was reminded that some Igbos in positions of authority had said that it was not time for Ndigbo to occupy the exalted position of President of Nigeria, he replied that such Igbos were not true Igbos. He said that the Northerners occupied the post for thirty-five years, the South Westerners would have completed twelveandahalf years in 2007, and since the country was regionalized into North, West and East, it became logical that it was the turn of the Eastern Region to produce the President of Nigeria in 2007.

He emphasized that he was not contesting for Igbo President but Nigerian President and that he would be contesting under the PDP and not the APGA. When his attention was drawn to the problems in Anambra State, he said emphatically, "Nobody is using the Igbos. It is Igbos using themselves or allowing themselves to be used. Nobody has come from the North or South-West to partake in the crisis in Igboland, It is Ndigbo against Ndigbo. So, let Ndigbo and their leaders stand up and address the issues. We are our own enemies. Let the Igbo leadership address the Igbo problem."

He explained that people were suffering and that was why he was remaining in politics because he had something to offer. He said that the economic reforms in the country were necessary but that he would do better.

He promised that he would guarantee uninterrupted power supply within twenty-four months, and he referred to Malaysia, China and Indonesia as examples where there were uninterrupted power supplies which made them productive and sound economically.

He promised that if he became the president in 2007, Nigeria would not export a barrel of crude oil as all the oil would be refined in Nigeria and exported as finished products as well as its byproducts. By so doing, he would create jobs and impact on the country's economic system. He referred to the restiveness of the Niger Delta State and said that it was because there was no justice and fair play. He added, "There is problem all over the world today because everyone is talking about world peace, but none is talking about justice and fair play."

When asked what he saw about 2007, he replied, "God will intervene, and God will prevail. I see blood in all aspects of Nigeria if things continue the way they are." He concluded that he saw the fairest and freest election conducted by President Obasanjo, and he was sure that he would win.

The ExGovernor of Abia State, Chief Kalu, had a great hurdle and serious impediments to overcome in order to be nominated to contest for the presidency in the platform of PDP. His reliance on the Holy Bible was not sufficient because each aspirant had one and knew how to use it to scale through problems. Heaven helps those who help themselves.

ExGovernor Kalu needed a lot of help to be nominated to contest before he could talk of winning against the heavy-weights. He had to pass through the king makers and power brokers upon whose toes ExGovernor Kalu had stepped all the time. The presidential election winner could not be determined primarily by money alone nor by the Igbos in America but by certain criteria which were extremely challenging for ExGovernor Kalu to meet.

While answering a question in Maryland, USA during his visit, ExGovernor Kalu was quoted as saying, "See, there is no governor in Nigeria that has the courage to speak like I do. I am not afraid to speak the truth, but at the same time, I have two parents who are still living, and every time they accuse me of wanting to 'kill them,' then I slow down a bit, and also there is the party machinery and elders who work hard to make peace between me and the president all the time, and when they come to me and say, "O boy," how can we settle this thing; I let them prevail at times. Like in the case of Anenih, the Oba of Benin sent a plane to pick me up; he's some eighty years old; it was difficult to turn him down."

Also responding to why he was expelled from University of Maiduguri (UNIMAID), ExGovernor Kalu said, "Yes, I was suspended because we had disagreements with the school authorities, and they later called me back, but my conscience did not allow me to go back." ExGovernor Kalu should be able to see the childishness in his answers and then fully adjust presidentially for future presidential elections. As a presidential candidate, he must talk and act maturely and presidentially.

Above statements credited to ExGovernor Kalu might scare some people to elect him or any other in his situation as President or Vice President of Nigeria because Nigerians would try to avoid controversy in future leadership of Nigeria just like in the USA. Nigeria needs a President or Vice President that is matured, peaceful, not controversial, highly educated, experienced and exemplary to lead Nigeria and Africa.

Any controversial leader, President or Vice President, who cannot control his/her tongue which scares other leaders, traditional chiefs and including his/her own parents can plunge the country into civil and international wars. Given the situation, ExGovernor Kalu has a lot to learn and change if he is serious about future presidential bid.

He must grow up from being called 'O boy' and become a man in order to fit into presidential leadership position in Nigeria in the nearest future. Future presidential elections will be battle-royal among giants and not boys. The number of qualified presidential aspirants is increasing exponentially. He must start to talk and act presidential.

Age

In Yorubaland, it is often said that if a young man wants to act as an elder or leader, his age or youthfulness may be an impediment. Nigerian presidential aspirants should be matured, "act and talk presidential." During the 2004 presidential election in the USA, ExGovernor Howard Dean of the Democratic Party lost his presidential nomination simply because he did not act presidential during one of his campaigns.

Initially he (Howard Dean) was leading and everybody felt he would win the nomination, but he lost his place to Senator John Kerry. ExGovernor Kalu will need a lot of adjustment in this direction. A person can be young but talk and act with maturity; but that will depend upon one's upbringing, education, experience, role models, training and professionalism. There is still plenty of time for necessary adjustment in preparation for future presidential elections.

It might be true that Generals Yakubu Gowon and Olusegun Obasanjo were Heads of State of Nigeria at thirty-three and thirty-nine respectively, but they were matured and had gone through relevant trainings, promotions and experience before they led the country as dictators with the backing of the military. The situation is different and more difficult in a democracy. A young man leading a country under a democracy could easily lose his head. More so, Nigerian situation is different now from what it was in 1966 and 1976 when Generals Gowon and Obasanjo ruled the country respectively at youthful age without going through an election nationally.

If Nigeria is to lead Africa and be given the kind of recognition which she received in the world community under Obasanjo Administration, Nigeria would not need a pupil president but a matured leader, well educated and experienced to take the enormous responsibility of Nigerian leadership. It is cheap talk and cheap thought to feel that money alone from a bunch of American Igbo donors will do it. With proper campaign finance law, which is inevitable, the influence of money in elections may reduce in future. Above all, there will be many Nigerians who cannot be bought with money who will decide future elections.

There is another Yoruba proverb which says: if a young man wakes up everyday and says that when he gets old or becomes an elder, his staple food will be the head of pigeons. Yorubas believe that the spirit of pigeons may not let that young man grow up to live for long. In effect, if ExGovernor Kalu wants to be President or Vice President of Nigeria, he cannot afford to be as controversial as he was with the king makers and power brokers in Nigerian politics.

The way ExGovernor Kalu handled his problems with his deputy, Chief Anenih and ExPresident Obasanjo, did not look presidential or vice presidential. Nigeria can no longer handle confusion within the presidency or between president and the legislature or judiciary if a controversial person becomes the president. Ironically, it was believed that a lot of people controlling at state and federal levels need some growing up and tutelage to occupy their last previous positions and should therefore not be asking for higher positions.

It is still fresh in the minds of Nigerians, elders and leaders all over Nigeria that in 1966, some young military officers from the East with inordinate ambition to rule the country staged a coup d'etat that truncated the first Nigerian parliamentary democratic experiment on January 15, 1966.

As a result of callousness, inexperience, youthful exuberance, tribalism and immaturity, the January 15, 1966 coupists assassinated Northern and Western Nigerian leaders while they spared leaders of the Eastern Region and showed no remorse. As a result of their immaturity and youthful exuberance, they boasted about their treasonable crimes on pages of newspapers with impunity and complicated matters. That was the genesis of the problems that Nigeria has been through for more than 40 years without an end in sight. Hence, Nigerians will think twice before any young immature person becomes president of this great country.

Referring to the disputed US purported intelligence report on Nigeria that the country might break up within fifteen years, trouble-shooters must be seriously warned about the consequences of their actions. If anybody, group or ethnicity disrupts Nigerian democratic experiment as was done by IfeajunaNzeogwu and their conspirators on January 15, 1966, the rest of Nigeria will not forgive such person, group or ethnicity.

Nigerians must be prepared to defend the democracy earned after more than three decades of dictatorship, sufferings and dehumanization. The events that truncated the First, Second and Third Republics and their aftermaths must never be repeated. Nigerians have suffered enough as a result of youthful indiscretion at governance.

From all indications, it looks like the young ones who have been criticizing the elders, leaders and the old politicians have not performed better, but worse. Those who have committed money laundering, kept foreign accounts, diverted federal, state and local government allocations amounting to billions of naira, to private use in recent times are not the old politicians, but the young ones who criticized the old ones loudest. It must be remembered that the young Heads of State like Generals Gowon and Obasanjo whom ExGovernor Kalu quoted as examples were not elected but forced on Nigerians by circumstances in 1966 and 1976 respectively. Today, those two, Gowon and Obasanjo, rank among the greatest leaders in the world, and the world with Nigeria is happy and proud to have them.

Academic/Professional Qualification and Experience

Nigeria has produced highly qualified academicians and professionals with the right experience and maturity to be President of Nigeria, lead Africa and sustain Nigeria in her rightful position within the comity of nations. Nigeria is not just looking for any game player or moneybag as future president, but a leader of similar world class and reputation like ExPresident Obasanjo was. There are such people in the North, East, West and South-South. They should all come out and campaign all over the country in free and fair elections in 2011 and beyond.

As for those clamouring for zoning of the presidency, do they not have enough confidence in themselves to face other contestants from anywhere in Nigeria? In advanced countries, the presidency is not zoned. When will Nigerians be able to compete healthily among themselves without hindrances or exclusiveness? Any one who is involved in assassinating political opponents directly and/or indirectly should be prosecuted, convicted and made to serve capital punishment as a deterrence to others.

Any Nigerian presidential aspirant without twenty-five years postgraduate experience would need to prove himself to Nigerians to be elected. Nigerians cannot afford to revisit the mistakes of the past. Let Nigerians start to look for those candidates who can carry the burden of nationhood and move Nigeria forward in future elections. Wherever he or she comes from should not be the first consideration but his or her attributes, antecedents and excellence.

INEC must watch out for fake certificates and honourary doctorate degrees to disqualify candidates who are not qualified to run for high office. The minimum requirement recommended by NPRC must be observed as a minimum of fouryear college degree or equivalent. Whoever did not complete a minimum of four years university coursework or its equivalent should emulate John Ukechem Uguru who earned fouryear university degree at seventy-five years of age. Leadership and professional training courses in the armed forces and other professions at senior levels, combined with the right orientation and experience should be adjudged to be equivalent to 4year university degree. Book knowledge and bookworms alone cannot provide answers to Nigerian socio-economic and political problems

Nigerian 1999 Constitution

Those aspiring to be president must ensure they have never breached the Nigerian 1999 Constitution or else they should be disqualified. The Independent National Electoral Commission (INEC) should be more vigilant in future in terms of certificate forgeries, asset declarations, operation of foreign private bank accounts and criminal records declaration. Whoever has breached the Constitution should be eliminated.

A government functionary cannot open a parallel business in competition with the establishment he/she supervises and must not have committed fraud, corruption or received indictment for any criminal act. Nigerians should be more vigilant in future elections having learnt their lessons.

Bribing the electorate with money alone should not work. How will you be able to stop corrupt practices if you bribe delegates and the electorate to win presidential election? Selecting a successful, transparent leader or President will not be easy, but it is a task that must be done.

Above all, Abia Leaders Forum made astonishing, deadly and damaging accusations of corruption against ExGovernor Kalu in *This Day News* of Thursday, September 8, 2005, which were of interest to the EFCC and Nigerian leadership. Nobody has been able to quarrel with everybody, fight with everybody, act to defeat everybody and then successfully get elected in a democracy.

ExGovernors and other Nigerians should exercise their rights to sue for defamation just like President Yar'Adua did in October 2008, if anything embarrassing and denigrating published about them is not true. People and the Press should be made criminally liable for untrue publications intentionally made to defame their opponents. People should be made responsible and accountable for their actions to ensure a disciplined society.

Positivity

An aspirant to the presidency must be positiveminded, motivated and capable of motivating the people. He/she must be able to promise the people hope and help and not despair or negativity. ExGovernor Kalu acknowledged that for him to be elected the president would be a very difficult fight, a long fight, a fight that would stand the test of time, a battle of all times. To be more relevant and more positive, ExGovernor Kalu was emphasizing a difficult noble contest that was ahead and not a physical fight. There should be no physical fight but great use of intelligence and strong power of persuasion to win election.

ExGovernor Kalu also said, "I see blood in all aspects of Nigeria if things continue the way they are." That statement was belligerent and sent the wrong message or signal that was scary. Nigerians should be optimistic, not pessimistic, and stop being angels of doom. It is the prayer of most people that there will be no shedding of blood in Nigeria again. Never, never again will blood flow in Nigeria. All aspirants for leadership should avoid words of violence, intimidation and negativity. Nigerians aspiring to high offices should demonstrate a sense of civility, peace, knowledge, intelligence and other leadership qualities far above those they aspire to lead.

Nigerians expect their future leaders to be transparent, unimpeachable, smart, qualified, and highly intelligent and possess mastery in socio-economic, political issues and human resource management. Whoever does not possess these qualities and qualifications should go back to school instead of aspiring to the presidency or vice presidency. Abia Stateborn Elder John Ukechem Uguru earned resounding second class (upper) degree at the age of seventy-three from the University, and he hoped to continue for master's degree. Nigerians should congratulate and emulate him.

Exemplarily, General Gowon, Military Head of State (1966-1975) went to Warwick University, Coventry, Great Britain and obtained his doctorate degree after leaving office. Also, President Obasanjo, Military Head of State (1976-1979) and Nigerian President (1999-2007) went back to Nigerian Open University System of Education after leaving office as a great example to Nigerians for emulation. These two great exemplary leaders teach us that it is never too late to learn. Hence, age, position, wealth or high class of anybody in the society cannot be a barrier to advanced learning in universities.

In civilized, advanced economies and political environments, no politician ever comes out to say that he knows what the people need unless he actually finds out and relies on a research paper to show their responses about what they actually need. Leaders should first find out what the people need by operating an open, peopleoriented and fully participatory government and not assume what the people need without getting them to say what they actually need themselves. The people must be carried along to ensure excellent results in policy implementation. Nigerians have been sufficiently warned about the choice of their future leaders. Remember, as you make your bed, so you lie on it.

Nigerian elites are spending a lot of time clamouring for amendments to Nigerian Constitution, structure and type of governance from federalism to parliamentarianism. It must be remembered that Nigeria was practising parliamentarianism before it was truncated by IfeajunaNzeogwu military coup d'etat of January 15, 1966.

As at then, fraud, corruption, economic and financial crimes were limited, but today, these vices are practised more elaborately with unparalleled sophistication by the elites. How will any type of government succeed on such premises? The elites who are wrong are trying to blame the system instead of blaming themselves who are the wrong operators of the system that works perfectly in other places. It is a bad workman who quarrels with his tools.

It is wished that elites calling for changes spend sufficient energy to support the government to crack down on socio-economic, financial and political crimes and reforms so that any new constitution, restructure of Nigeria and type of government deemed best for Nigerians can stand on a formidable foundation.

What will those calling for sovereign national conference achieve if the elites among them and in other spheres of Nigerian society do not first embark on serious behaviour modifications? In effect, elites calling for changes and criticizing others should also look at themselves, criticize themselves, change themselves first and remove the 'speck in their own eyes' for Nigeria to be a better place.

Nigerians should realize that even if thousands of Sovereign National Conferences (SNCs), Pro-National Conference Organizations (PRONACOs) and the National Political Reform Conferences (NPRCs) combined; succeed to restructure Nigeria with perfection and make the Nigerian Constitution perfect, unique and infallible; the invaluable efforts and energies dissipated to achieve perfection may be in vain if Nigeria is not cleared of corrupt, fraudulent elites and economic saboteurs abundant in both the private and public sectors of the nation.

According to Yoruba proverb, "A house built with saliva will be pulled down by dew (moisture in the atmosphere)." Houses or solid structures built with formidable foundation will always last. The notation is confirmed by a popular song, which says, "Build your house on a rock, for the house built on sand will be washed away with the sand."

From the above narration, it is therefore imperative for Nigerians to support the relentless efforts of government committedly and determinately to ensure the success to rid Nigerian society of elite corruption and 'business as usual'.

If Obasanjo's regime was able to indict, prosecute and remove corrupt federal ministers, top legislators, top university administrators, top judges, Inspector General of Police, top government functionaries and top men within the ruling Peoples Democratic Party (PDP) unprecedentedly, the concern of all Nigerians should be how to find befitting leaders to continue such wonderful and courageous efforts in the future.

Who can step on toes of pathologically corrupt elites without looking back? How will the country not be back to square one? May God/Allah choose the rightful leaders for Nigeria who will continue to salvage Nigeria from the evils of corruption and economic sabotage.

If you ask some presidential aspirants why they want to be President of Nigeria, their first answer is, "because it is their zone's turn." Such an answer is ridiculous in the civilized world. Such aspirants cannot proudly and confidently say that they are the best and most qualified to be president and explain how they will fight corruption, economic sabotage, unemployment, inflation and establish exemplary governance based on transparency, accountability, responsiveness and be peopleoriented.

The effectiveness of anticorruption posture of President Obasanjo made former Senator Kennedy Waku (Benue), his arch critic 1999 to 2003, to wish that President Obasanjo stayed for life. Former Senator Kennedy Waku said in the *Daily Independent Online* of Thursday, April 7, 2005, "People said I used to criticize President Olusegun Obasanjo, but I never criticized Obasanjo. I disagreed with his policies until two months ago. I am beginning to write him letters, love letters, about the good job he is beginning to do."

He added, "But where were you all along? Were you waiting like Christ did at the wedding party where He was bringing wine at the tail end of the party?" He concluded, "If Mr. President can continue with this kind of assignment for the country and not for himself, so many years he needs to be there until the day death does him part. I support him."

In *Nigeria World News* of Tuesday, March 29, 2005, Mr. John E. Iyobhebhe expressed his concern and fear about who would succeed President Obasanjo in 2007. He said, "Let OBJ stay and complete the first stage of Nigeria's resurgence as a successful, strong, stable and proud nation." He added, "If OBJ does not stay, I doubt if any of the contenders to his office will have the will, desire or courage to tackle the biggest problem facing Nigeria today. It will be like starting all over again. It will be back to square one for Nigeria. May God/Allah help Nigeria."

With Mallam Umaru Musa Yar'Adua's emergence as President of Nigeria effective May 29, 2007 as successor to ExPresident Obasanjo, can we rightly say that Messrs Waku, Iyobhebhe, Anenih and many others have been proved right or wrong? Have Nigerians successfully replaced ExPresident Olusegun Obasanjo after the end of his second term in office? Nigerians should be optimistic, keep praying and support the government in the best interest of Nigeria.

Anybody who actually witnessed events in Nigeria before and after October 1, 1960, who passed through the dictatorial regimes and witnessed the behaviour of elites who committed economic and financial crimes, corruption and frauds and other felonies with impunity would be shaken and disturbed to miss ExPresident Obasanjo's fight against corrupt elites. He left the stage in 1979, and he left it again in 2007, succeeded by President Umaru Musa Yar'Adua.

In a country of over 140 million people, the best and right choice may be more difficult when emphasizing on zoning, ethnicity, region of origin, religion and not quality, capability, education, experience and transparency.

Is the fight against corruption holding at the local levels? Are things changing so that people do not have to bribe officials before obtaining their drivers' licences, their tags or plate numbers, birth certificates, court judgement transcripts, Nigerian passport and so on and so forth? Some police officers justified their collection of 20 naira from bus conductors as bribe on July 13, 2005.

The police officer that spoke in defence of his corrupt group justified their corrupt acts on poor condition of service and lack of funds for police budget. That is a ridiculous defence to continue to take bribe, and Nigerians should ask how the Police Chiefs and Inspector General of Police react to the revelation.

What deterrent measures have been established to stop corruption in the police force? These police officers should thank God/Allah for being employed while thousands of university/college graduates are unemployed. Corrupt officers should be replaced enmasse with unemployed university graduates.

Nigerians should watch and discourage the kind of impediment posed during the declaration of General Marwa's presidential aspiration in his home state (Adamawa) meted on him by the State Government.

The cooked up story of insecurity was reminiscent of the old, uncivilized, immature and undemocratic ploys of previous Nigerian regional governments when dealing with opposition candidates in 1950s up to 1965. There should be freedom and equal opportunities in a democracy.

Why are some Nigerian leaders and elders still intolerant, living in the past and paying lipservice to democracy? Where is the good example to the followership and posterity if presidential aspirants cannot freely declare their aspirations in their home states? Aspirants for the presidency, governorships, legislators (states and federal), local government chairmanships, political appointees and other leaders should be exhaustively screened to avoid the regrets and disappointments of the past.

Ironically and hypocritically, those who are involved in corruption, money laundering and other economic and financial crimes often turn around and complain of marginalization. Invariably, such complainants are the ones stealing Nigerian government money, stashing it in their private bank accounts overseas as well as marginalizing and impoverishing their own people.

Nigerian elites, government functionaries and politicians who commit acts of economic and financial sabotage against Nigeria and thus perpetuate generational poverty are nothing but economic and financial terrorists, who should be barred from leadership positions in the future. It is regrettable that many Niger Delta leaders were secretly behind widespread financial and economic crimes against the generality of their people who need investment, employment and development.

The ten million pounds sterling as alleged valued assets of the Bayelsa State former governor in London is sufficient to establish many small businesses for Ijaw youths who are unemployed. The average Niger Deltans are deceived by their own state elites to believe that they are marginalized and neglected by other ethnicities, whereas their own state and local elites who plunder and pillage their resource allocations and launder the money overseas are their worst enemies. The rest of Nigerians have always sympathized and empathized for them. Remember the Yoruba proverb which says, "Eyinkule lota wa, ile ni aseni ngbe", which means, "People's worst enemies are usually in their backyards, while the persons disrupting their lives are probably in their households closest to them."

Generals Buhari and Abacha appointed Niger Deltans as Ministers of Petroleum, yet their people continued to suffer. Chief Sam Edem, ex-chairman of NDDC allegedly gave ₦800 million to traditional medicine scammer. Niger Deltans should blame their states leaders first before blaming Yorubas and Hausas-Fulanis.

Elites are perpetuating economic and financial crimes in secret, complaining against it in the open and calling 'wolf, wolf' deceitfully and hypocritically while they incite innocent militant youths to fight and die for elite crimes.

It is high time militant youths started to question the rationale behind their fighting and dying while their leaders are involved in corruption, money laundering and amassing illegal wealth at the expense of militant youths' bloodletting. It is ungodly to incite militant youths to their untimely deaths through deception.

The youths are supposed to be nurtured to become the great leaders of the future and not to be manipulated and deceived to fight and die. The militant youths should start to ask questions in order to properly determine whether it is worthy to die fighting while their state leaders are manipulative and deep in corrupt practices.

GOD/ALLAH BLESS NIGERIA!

CHAPTER 7

NIGERIA'S FAST ECONOMIC GROWTH AND IMPEDIMENTS

Nigeria is one of the seven largest suppliers of oil in the world and one of the five largest suppliers of oil to the United States of America. Other Nigerian mineral resources include gas, zinc, gold, bitumen, iron ore, phosphate, tantalite, clay, etc., which make Nigeria potentially strong and sound economically.

Bitumen production in Nigeria will make her the second largest in the world next to Venezuela. Bitumen deposits are estimated at 42.74 billion metric tons covering over 120 kilometers of the coastal belts of Ogun, Ondo and Edo States of Nigeria. Bitumen is estimated to fetch Nigeria about ₦1.34 trillion annually.

Since the beginning of democratic governance in Nigeria on May 29, 1999, foreign investments have been pouring into Nigeria unprecedentedly. Oil accounts for about 40 percent of Gross Domestic Product (GDP), 90 percent of exports and 80 percent of government revenue. Serious efforts are being made to grow nonoil sector of 20 percent of government revenue at the rate of 10 percent annually. In August 2008, inflation rate reached 12%, interest rate 10.25% and foreign reserve over $60 billion.

Nigeria has experienced tremendous economic growth since the beginning of the twenty-first century. The progress was largely due to government's application of sound micro and macroeconomic policies as well as effective monetary and fiscal policies supported with myriads of economic reforms. The reforms are within the framework of the National Economic Empowerment and Development Strategy (NEEDS), the Millennium Development Goals (MDGs), the Seven-Point Agenda of Yar'Adua Administration coupled with the implementation of the Policy Support Instrument (PSI) fashioned by the International Monetary Fund (IMF).

The high rise of oil price consistently in the recent years has been a major factor sustaining the steady economic growth of Nigeria, which is regarded as one of the fastest growth in the universe. Hence, the government becomes unequivocally committed to make the Nigerian economy one of the largest in the world by the year 2020. To achieve this noble goal, the government is promising to fast track the key parameters of developmental paradigm outlined in the Seven-Point Agenda of Yar'Adua regime which is harmonized and in line with 'NEEDS' of Obasanjo Administration.

Nigeria's real Gross Domestic Product (GDP) growth is estimated at the rate of 7 percent, which ranks among one of the best in the world. The per capita income has risen from $ 400 to about $1,000 in 2007. It is estimated that about 50 percent of Nigerian population still live below the poverty line.

The Nigerian government of President Umaru Musa Yar'Adua focuses main attention on improvement of physical infrastructure with particular reference to power/energy, transportation, human capital development, the Niger Delta issues, safety and security, health, poverty alleviation, education, agriculture, water resources, debt servicing etc. Yar'Adua government has a 'Seven-Point Agenda' in harmonization with the National Economic Empowerment and Development Strategy (NEEDS), which is assessed as a laudable economic development programme initiated by Obasanjo Administration.

There is no doubt that the Nigerian economy is growing fast, but how much is the economic buoyancy reflected on the ordinary Nigerians? Is the rich getting richer and the poor getting poorer? Is the inequality gap getting wider or narrower? The answers to the questions can be the real determinant and best measurement of the effects of the NEEDS programme and the Seven-Point Economic Agenda. High sounding, well designed economic programmes/agenda on paper do not matter as much as the implementation activities which can have impact on the daily lives of the people. Past economic programmes failed because they were not implemented to reflect betterment in the lives of the people.

Laudable economic growth began to take shape in Ogun State (the Gateway State) of Nigeria. The great light of good old days of the sage and immortal Chief Obafemi Awolowo began shining in Ogun State again.

The hope for economic recovery, buoyancy, industrialization, employment generation, road development, concern for people's welfare, agricultural development, congenial business environment started being rekindled in Ogun State, the Gateway State of Nigeria.

In those good old days of 1950s and early 1960s, Western Nigeria was first in Africa in many great things under Chief Obafemi Awolowo's leadership. Remarkably, those great, wonderful days of great accomplishments have started to resurrect again in Ogun State under the governorship of Obalofin Otunba Gbenga Daniel.

The first trace of oil and gas in Ogun State was discovered over forty years ago, but the project was abandoned as a result of unfavourable political climate. As at then, Western Nigerian leadership being first in many things in Africa was not playing the political teamgame to be loved, admired and accepted to forestall political and economic strangulation by Nigerian majority in the North and the East who were in a coalition.

The western leadership was committing political suicide by forgetting the Yoruba proverbs thus, "When you are dining with the devil, you must have a long spoon; if you want to catch a monkey, you must act like one; if you are not very strong and having an effective weapon, you may not ask about the killer of your father."

Also, if you cannot beat them you either join them for the right reasons or minimize your confrontations using diplomacy and conciliatory strategies to ward off being crushed and destroyed. The wise man always plays the teamgame. You cannot be the oddmanout all the time if you are truly representing the people in a democracy, especially if you want your people to equally benefit from available opportunities.

Empirically, one of the most successful national politicians that Nigeria has ever produced was the first Nigerian President, Dr. Nnamdi Azikiwe, the Owelle of Onitsha, because he made remarkable and successful inroads into Yoruba, Hausa/Fulani and other nationalities beyond comprehension. He was not controversial. It was only his own people that did not treat him with the greatest admiration as the rest of Nigeria did with particular reference to events pre and post the civil war (1967-70).

Western Nigeria lost its first place politically and economically because it was not playing a flexible team game in Nigerian political setting. The leadership of the West (Yorubas) forgot that their sophistication, civilization, higher academic education, intelligence and professionalism were not the only qualities that would earn them the presidency of Nigeria in a democratic setting, and that they had to attract votes with diplomacy from the Northern and Eastern regions.

It is hoped that those wonderful old days and mineral discoveries that are back in Ogun State will not be allowed to slip away as it did in the past. This is an opportune time to better the lives of the people of Western Nigeria and Nigerians generally.

Unfortunately, Ogun State Legislators quickly forgot the problems of Western Nigeria State of emergency in early 1960s by starting random impeachment moves and disharmony with Ogun State Executive leading to allegations of poisoning the State Governor, Gbenga Daniel.

Also there was counter allegation of 2008 assassination attempt on the State Assembly Speaker, Tunji Egbetokun who replaced impeached preceding Speaker Titi Oseni. It is easy to start problems, but it is very difficult to accurately determine how the problems would end as well as who gets hurt, survives, wins or loses. All those concerned should beware!

On April 16, 2004, Ogun State residents woke up with the good news that their state government had secured $50 million financial assistance from PGS Exploration Nigeria Limited, a private firm to undertake three-dimensional seismic studies relating to oil, gas and some solid minerals. The study was undertaken jointly with the Nigerian National Petroleum Corporation (NNPC). The corporation's former Group Managing Director, Mr. Funso Kupolokun, expressed optimism about the progress made.

He was reported to have commended Ogun State Government for floating Gateway Oil and Gas Company and reiterated that construction work on proposed NNPC Mega Filling Station would commence in Abeokuta, Ogun State Capital. The areas of greatest interest for the exploration included Ogun Waterside, Tonegeji Island, Dahomey, Benin Embayment Basins and specifically, Ipokia metropolis and other shoreline areas.

On basis of the airborne geophysical survey report approved by the Federal Executive Council, it was confirmed that Ogun State was endowed with mineral resources. The potentials of the mineral deposits include oil, gas, zinc, gold, bitumen, phosphate and tantalite discovered in commercial quantities covering more extensive areas. The Governor, Obalofin Otunba Gbenga Daniel disclosed that there was some collaboration between his state and some European Union countries.

In similar vein, Ogun State has moved forward in agriculture and food production. The governor hinted that rice plantation was going on and that the Marriott people were being expected. He assured everybody of better days ahead that would be full of happiness.

Also on its path to economic prosperity, Ogun State Governor was reported to have signed a Memorandum of Understanding (MOU) with OBED Corporation of the USA to site a refinery at Olokola, Ogun State Waterside. The capacity of the refinery was expected to produce 150,000 barrels of oil or more per day. The project was expected to be completed in eighteen months. Governor Otunba Gbenga Daniel signed on behalf of Ogun State Government while Dr. James Garvin, Chief Executive Officer of Alabama US based company signed on behalf of OBED Corporation.

Disclosing the (MOU) information in the *Vanguard News* of March 24, 2005, the Managing Director of Gateway Oil and Gas Limited and consultant to Ogun State Governor on oil and gas, Mr. Wemmy Osunde, said that the investment was worth over $1 billion and that the site at Olokola happened to be an export processing zone proposed for the building of liquefied natural gas (LNG) plant. In effect, Olokola in Ogun State Waterside would represent a hub for energy projects.

Ogun State Government also secured the establishment of Free Trade Zones in Igbesa, Olokola and Kajola. The Government, the

Chinese Consortium and the Chinese African Investment Company were partners in establishing the projects. Nigerian Export Processing Zone Authority (NEPZA) approved the Ogun Guangdong Free Trade Zone (OGFTZ) after receiving the blessing of President Umaru Musa Yar'Adua.

Economic growth depends upon the size, quality, motivation, responsiveness, dependability and reliability of the labour force. To encourage increased productive capacity, representing the Gorss Domestic Product (GDP) of the nation, it is important to eliminate or minimize labour unrests, strikes and lockouts. Good government with great industrial policies, food management, good conflict resolution package and sound employees' reward system will be able to minimize tension on the job as well as create industrial harmony and enhanced productivity.

Fortunately, Nigeria is blessed with highly educated, intelligent, smart and professionally qualified people who are able to contribute immensely to the economic growth of this great nation if given the opportunity. Also, there are a few very wealthy Nigerians who stash their money overseas. Such Nigerians should be encouraged to repatriate their money back home for investment, industrialization and employment generation purposes to help build the nation's economy.

There should be a safe and enabling environment for personal and investment security, which must be guaranteed by acts of government. There should be deregulation efforts as well as governmental programmes that would motivate Nigerians, foreigners and investor companies to keep their businesses and money in the country. The dividends of economic growth must improve the standard of living and life expectancy of the masses. There must be just, fair, and equitable distribution and creation of wealth.

Machines, tools, equipment, computers and money represent capital resources critical to grow the economy. With low standard of living, it will be hard to forgo current consumption in order to save. As a result, the level of saving in poor countries is low, culminating in low capitalization and investment, low economic activities and growth. Labour must be appropriately combined with capital to enhance economic growth.

Low interest rate helps increase economic activity and growth. Nigeria's present double-digit, high interest rate cannot fully complement and sustain economic reforms going on in Nigeria. It is like a man applying the right medication to an illness but fails to abstain from conduct that can continue to worsen the sickness.

Financial lobbyists and special interest groups will not let low interest rate happen. The government must keep interest rate at 5 percent to ensure speedy economic recovery and development. Low interest rate will breed new small and medium size businesses, enable the old ones to survive, grow and generate employment.

Nigeria has abundant land resources that can support fast economic growth, like land surface, water, forests, minerals and all other natural resources. Abundant mineral resource alone cannot, on its own, constitute economic growth. It must be combined with labour (effective and efficient management entrepreneurship) and capital to generate economic growth. Undoubtedly, Nigeria has the potential to generate economic growth.

In addition, Nigeria needs technological knowledge, which represents the methodology of combining resources to produce output of goods and services. It is a key determinant of economic growth and development.

Technology improves and advances with new management techniques, scientific discoveries, innovations and new inventions. Technological advancement ensures that more output is produced with any given amount of resources.

In effect, technological advancement accelerates economic growth for any given growth rate in the workforce and the stock capital. Increased educational advancement provides greater potential for technological advances. Hence, Nigeria needs more funding for research and development coupled with technological advancement in order to promote growth appreciably.

It is ironical that interest rates are unduly high in developing economies like Nigeria thereby slowing down and stagnating borrowing, spending, business activities and economic growth. Also, it is ironical that banks are declaring astronomical profits with high interest rates at the expense of the poor majority and slowmoving economic growth. In the best interest of Nigeria and Nigerians, the present government should encourage increasing bank loans to Nigerians at low interest rates in order to encourage the formation of more small businesses, capitalization, employment generation and economic growth.

It is common practice in government establishments that huge sums of money meant for government or meant to be paid, as wages, pension, contract sum or other benefits are first deposited in the private bank accounts of government functionaries in charge for a few months to yield interest for them illegally.

Thereafter, the huge sums of money or part of it is moved to the appropriate government accounts or paid to the pensioners, contractors and other beneficiaries of the money. In effect, the interests yielded running into several millions of naira are fraudulently kept by the officers concerned.

There were serious allegations that huge sums of money running into billions of naira, approved by government and made available to be paid to Nigeria Airways pensioners and other categories of discharged employees, were first deposited in some personal accounts of government officials to yield interest, and delayed there, unpaid to the beneficiaries who needed their money for food, medicine and other essential requirements. The delayed payment caused many pensioners to die of hunger and disease because of lack of money to buy food and medicine.

In addition, there were ghost workers and ghost pensioners organized by government functionaries, and the huge money involved were going into private pockets. Similar incidents were perpetrated in many government departments and parastatals. The EFCC and the ICPC should help to stop this fraudulent and corrupt practice of illegal enrichment. Above fraudulent practice is sabotage on economic growth.

At the Indian Professionals Forum (IPF) in Lagos, the former President of the Nigerian Labour Congress, Mr. Adams Oshiomhole who later became Edo State Governor, was said to have wondered why the manufacturing sector was performing below expectation. He blamed the shortcomings on what he described as government insensitivity.

He then identified some constraints, which needed to be tackled decisively among other problems which hinder economic growth such as: (1) epileptic power supply; (2) unattractive interest rate; (3) dumping which reflected unbridled importation of goods; (4) inconsistency of government economic policies; (5) introduction and application of wrong industrial policies; (6) ineffective implementation of government Industrialization policies; (7) over dependence on oil at the expense of nonoil production sectors; and (8) unreliable hike in cost of production as a result of unstable price of oil and electricity.

He emphasized his concern about the nation's workforce, which was uniquely linked to industrial performance engulfed by the constraints mentioned above.

To help grow the economy, the SOLGAS Energy Limited was said to have planned to retain about 4,200 workforce of the Ajaokuta Steel Company Ltd. (ASCL) slated to be sacked during the takeover agreement. The American firm was purported to be injecting $36 billion (₦400 billion) into the company and was projecting to create 5,000 additional jobs between 2003 and 2005. Later it was said that the government determined the contract because of alleged overinflation of the contract sum.

Nigeria witnessed worsening economic waste and mismanagement, high rate of unemployment, hyperinflation, generational poverty, increase in crime rate, insecurity of persons and property, uncontrolled rural to urban migration, increase in health and safety problems, smuggling, human trafficking, illegal drug transactions, dumping, trans-border crimes, high rate of corruption, frauds, dictatorship, anarchical tendencies, human rights violations, incessant industrial confrontations and a great deal of family dysfunctionalization between 1966 and 1998.

There were many coups d'etat, and the last one saw Nigeria being ostracized by international community for human rights abuses and advance fee frauds '419' that placed the whole world at financial transactions displeasure, harassment and fear. Corruption and advance fee '419' fraudulent practices paralyzed local and foreign investment ventures in Nigeria, and Nigeria became rated as 101 out of 102 most corrupt nations in the world.

The good image of Nigeria became shattered, and all Nigerians abroad had it shameful and difficult to identify themselves as Nigerians especially where financial transactions were involved. The whole business world and private individuals were flooded with letters of advance fee frauds from Nigerian fraudsters seeking to dupe people. Lots of people of various nationalities were duped.

In addition to the above, there were serious deficit balance of payments problems and fraudulent stashing of Nigerian government money in secret banks in the Western world. As a result, the civilian government that was elected effective May 29, 1999, inherited many serious overwhelming national problems, which it battled relentlessly for four years.

Hence, ExPresident Olusegun Obasanjo had to travel to various world capitals to explain and talk to various Heads of State to convince them about the intrinsic good nature of Nigerians. He relentlessly sought debt cancellation, relief and debt rescheduling which initially yielded nontangible results until June 2005, but he was able to restore the good name of Nigeria within record time among the world bodies who cancelled the pariah status of Nigeria created between 1993 and 1998. President Obansanjo's contacts with the world leaders were fully rewarding with debt cancellation in July 2005 of over $18 billion.

The biggest problem was the intransigent economy which was shattered almost beyond repair, but with the determination and commitment of the government manifested in the initiation of economic and political reforms, there was assurance that Nigeria was seeing the light at the end of the socio-economic and political tunnel.

At the end of July 2005, after writing off over $18 billion Nigerian foreign debt by Paris Club, Nigeria was having $12 billion left to pay and Obasanjo Administration paid the balance in three spaced installments. Nigeria became foreign debt free when President Obasanjo left office on May 29, 2007. Before Obasanjo regime ended, strict regulations were made to curb abuses in obtaining foreign loan.

Hence, the succeeding government of President Yar'Adua should be careful of acquiring high interest foreign loan for executing Nigerian projects to avoid setting the country back to square one. Before July 2005, a substantial part of the country's Gross Domestic Product (GDP) was utilized for debt servicing at the expense of education, health, safety, agriculture, electricity, water etc. As at then, the foreign debt became unsustainable.

In 2008 budget provisions, the sum of ₦372.2 billion was earmarked for debt servicing, which was more than ₦121.1 billion provided for agriculture and water resources combined. Above all, ₦46 billionloan agreement concluded with the World Bank on Tuesday, July 8, 2008 for the maintenance of selected roads in Kaduna and some other states might be possibly generated internally to maintain Nigerian roads.

How are we sure that the money borrowed will not find itself fraudulently pocketed and the projects abandoned as usual? With over $60 billion foreign reserve, Nigeria cannot continue to borrow little sums of money from the IMF and World Bank at unreasonable rate of interest usually burdened with unfavourable conditionalities.

Nigeria should not go back into economic enslavement. Nigerian foreign reserves and other assets should be constantly monitored and protected to avoid their being seized and frozen by the Western World. It is difficult to comprehend how one country wakes up, seizes and freezes the assets of another independent country without going through the international court that has jurisdiction. The United Nations should regulate against such unilateralism in international relations.

ExPresident Olusegun Obasanjo arrayed a national economic revival, survival and development team during his second term in office beginning on May 29, 2003. The formidable team consisted of great economic and financial management professionals.

The team was made up of:
(1) The Minister of Finance, Mrs. (Dr.) Ngozi Okonjo-Iweala.
(2) Finance Minister of State, Mrs. Esther Nenadi Usman.
(3) Former Chief Economic Adviser, Professor Charles Chukwuma Soludo, later appointed Governor of Central Bank of Nigeria (CBN).
(4) Minister of Federal Capital Territory, Mallam Nasir el Rufai.
(5) Former Senior Special Assistant (Budget Monitoring and Due Process), Mrs. Oby Ezekwesili who later became a fullfledged federal minister.
(6) Director General/Presidential Adviser on Budget, Mr. Ade Augusto.
(7) Former Governor of Central Bank, Dr. Joseph Sanusi, succeeded by Professor Charles Chukwuma Soludo.

The highpowered team of economic and financial experts was constituted to provide advisement to the President of Nigeria on micro and macroeconomic policies as blueprinted in the national economic agenda titled, 'National Economic Empowerment and Development Strategy' (NEEDS).

Sound national economic policies should reflect:

(i) the creation of the right economic environment; planning, designing and implementation of right economic systems;
(ii) ensuring reasonable, price stabilization;
(iii) encouraging sound basis of aggregate demand and aggregate supply mechanisms;
(iv) ensuring inflation rate, interest rate, discount rate and foreign exchange rate are low and stabilized;
(v) providing 5% and above as annual growth rate of gross domestic product (GDP);
(vi) ensuring stable gross national and disposable income;
(vii) ensuring effective and efficient resources management, allocation and utilization;
(viii) encouraging sound bases of investment and capitalization mechanisms;
(ix) encouraging appropriate application of monetary and fiscal measures that grow the economy;
(x) ensures policy execution targeting full employment;
(xi) providing trade liberalization and appropriate application of trade protectionism;
(xii) ensuring national debt acquisition and redemption policies that support economic growth;
(xiii) ensuring effective budgetary administration;
(xiv) ensuring policies implementation targeting full industrialization, employment and economic prosperity; and
(xv) covers implementation of financial control systems that eliminate frauds, corruption, economic and financial crimes.

Many notable Nigerians showed concern but expressed remarkable optimism about their expectations for the speedy recovery of the nation's economy from its comatose state. The former National Chairman of the Peoples Democratic Party (PDP), Chief Audu Ogbeh, was credited to have remarked in London during the first weekend of August 2003 on the cultural day celebration of the Idoma Community Association thus:

(1) The socio-economic problem in Nigeria had increased the level of despair among Nigerians.
(2) Crime rate, unemployment rate and continuing migration from the rural to urban environment were increasing and worsening the situation.
(3) More local industries were closing down as a result of Nigeria's reliance more on foreign goods and the country's importdependent economy.
(4) The rural areas might become a social desert if rural migration continued without help.
(5) Graduates' unemployment was increasing at an alarming rate.

As former Chief Economic Adviser to Nigerian President but later appointed as Governor of the Apex Bank, Central Bank of Nigeria, Professor Charles Chukwuma Soludo held the view that organized private sector (OPS) held the trump card for Nigerian economic growth and that OPS should act as the pivot of growth of the Gross Domestic Product (GDP) and employment generation.

He emphasized that Nigerians had competent economic and financial management experts who would formulate economic policies which would be in the best interest of the country. He stressed that Nigeria would no longer take dictation from the International Monetary Fund (IMF) or the World Bank in the formulation of Nigeria's economic policies. He affirmed that the best interest of the country would take precedence in all economic policy formulation.

The Minister of Finance, (Dr.) Mrs. Ngozi Okonjo-Iweala explained that:

(1) The Federal Government had drawn up a 10year economic plan predicated on five percent plus as annual growth rate of the Gross Domestic Product (GDP)
(2) The tenyear economic agenda barred various ministerial

departments from initiating projects that were not accompanied by an 'economic and social impact analysis'.
(3) The objective of the blueprint economic agenda, 'NEEDS', was the attainment of micro and macroeconomic stability in relation to stable inflation rate, interest and exchange rates, gross domestic product (GDP), national economic growth rate of five percent plus, completion of abandoned projects, strict budget discipline, general public sector reforms and intensified efforts to contain the deadly HIV/AIDS spread.
(4) The main focus covered in the economic plan included education, agriculture, health, employment and increased industrial capacity utilization from forty percent to fifty percent.

For 'NEEDS' (National Economic Empowerment and Development Strategy) and Seven-Point Agenda of Yar'Adua to succeed, the following points must be taken care of. There must be:
(1) effective and efficient implementation of economic policies as may be appropriate;
(2) national interest must be placed above selfinterest, ethnicity, religious or political interest;
(3) efforts must be concentrated on nonoil product earning projects to reduce over reliance on petrol subsector earnings;
(4) attractive and enabling environment for private sector establishments and business investments;
(5) noncentralization of the economy towards the public sector in order to ensure greater emphasis on private sector expansion and development;
(6) discouragement of tollgates and rent seeking activities as appropriate;
(7) policy formulation and implementation in consideration of and in alignment with global economic trends;
(8) those responsible for socio-economic and political policy decision making and implementation should possess and exercise comprehensive knowledge, sagacity and vision to make and implement decisions in the best interest of Nigeria;
(9) economic policies of responsible protectionism for the survival of local businesses, guided globalization, reasonable

liberalization and helpful deregulation policies must be ensured.

The malaise of economic sabotage, which has adversely affected Nigeria, emanates in different forms and shapes. It ranges from tax evasion to frauds, corruption, economic and financial crimes including advance fee fraud419, money laundering and extortion, importers' malpractices, illegal oil bunkering and vandalization of oil pipelines, wrong governmental policies or ineffective and deficient implementation of governmental economic policies, vandalization of government infrastructures and utilities, violent robbery, violent crimes, price gourging, smuggling of banned products to defeat protectionism and strikes and lockouts resulting from incessant industrial disputes.

Tax is a major government revenue source. Amount of revenue collected by the government often determines government balanced, deficit or surplus budgeting. In effect, the amount of revenue collected usually determines what projects government can propose, embark upon and complete for the people. If government adopts progressive taxation strategy coupled with effective and efficient collection methodologies which ensure limited, minimal or nonexistent tax evasion and fraudulent practices, then the government may have maximized its tax revenue earning possibilities, 'ceteris paribus', all other things being equal.

In present time in Nigeria, it is very easy to evade tax payment. Hence, many individuals, groups, companies and businesses are not paying taxes in full with impunity. The present system of tax collection makes fraudulent practices possible. As a result, undercollection of tax revenue is very common, thus causing substantial revenue loss and limiting economic growth and development. The elites, small and medium scale businesses and big companies are able to bribe their ways with tax collection agencies to evade tax payment to the fullest.

It is therefore no gainsaying to estimate that about fifty-five percent of possible tax revenue is actually realized by government tax collecting agencies every year. In addition, government operational systems make fraudulent practices easy in the utilization of the fifty-five percent tax revenue collected. The amount of tax revenue that is utilized in the best interest of the people may not exceed twenty percent of tax revenue that is collectible.

In effect, if government is able to review the existing tax and collection systems in its entirety, the government would be able to augment its tax revenue base by forty-five percent. Such additional revenue can be used to grow the economy in the best interest of the people. The present tax and collection systems should have builtin control systems which help prevent, minimize or eliminate tax evasion and tax frauds. Tax evasion and frauds account for about eighty percent tax revenue loss.

In *Houston Chronicle* of May 8, 2003, it was reported that a Halliburton Company subsidiary, Kellogg, Brown & Root, paid bribes totalling $2.4 million to a tax official in Nigeria to obtain favourable tax treatment. It was said that the alleged bribery occurred between the years 2001 and 2002. It was received by a Nigerian official who held himself to be a tax consultant when he was actually an employee of a local tax office.

On June 18, 2003, the Netscape news reported that Houstonbased Halliburton disclosed to the U.S. Securities and Exchange Commission (SEC) that it might owe up to $5 million in taxes to Nigeria. It was confirmed that Nigerian ExPresident Olusegun Obasanjo gave an order for full investigation into the matter as part of a wider anticorruption crusade in the nation. What was the outcome of the investigation?

ExPresident Obasanjo added that those who were contributing to the bleeding of the Nigerian economy would be brought to book and that anyone who was found acting against the interest of the nation could not be seen as a friend of Nigeria. It was added that several employees were terminated after the discovery and that senior officials were not involved.

The assertion that senior officers were not involved and over $2 million was paid as bribe between the years 2001 and 2002 to evade paying $5 million tax was unbelievable. There must have been senior official(s) behind the scene who negotiated the bribery deal before Halliburton subsidiary company could installmentally pay such a heavy sum of over $2 million in a span of time between 2001 and 2002.

Such ploy of fraudulent practice of a continuing process for over a year could not have been perfected to succeed for so long without senior official(s) as accomplice(s). It was thereby easy to imagine that some of the junior ones terminated could have been scapegoats.

Similarly, the Nigerian House of Representatives Committee on Petroleum started to probe Chevron for $10.8 million tax evasion on Wednesday, August 17, 2005 as reported in *This Day News* of Thursday, August 18, 2005. "Many probes, but never an outcome!"

In countries like the United States of America, tax evasion is a felony punishable with severe penalties including recovery of evaded tax with interest and heavy fines and/or imprisonment and seizure or confiscation of the assets of the offender. All those involved should be prosecuted, convicted and made to pay severe penalties for tax evasion and tax fraud as a deterrence to others.

The companies that perpetrated the tax evasion and corruption as well as the employees involved should be prosecuted, convicted and made to pay severe penalties as would be done if it happened in the USA. There should be no sacred cows and untouchables. The companies and employees involved must be very powerful because the matter died down in the USA, and it did the same thing in Nigeria. Did Nigeria receive the evaded tax with interest? That is what US does for tax evaders.

On May 12, 2003, the Online Journal reported, "In last year's Corruption Perceptions Index, published by Berlinbased Transparency International, Nigeria ranked 101 out of 102 beating out only Bangladesh." The parameters used in the survey made the result unreliable, questionable, unreal and unacceptable.

With the establishment of the EFCC and ICPC, there is optimism about a fraud and corruptionfree Nigeria because corruption, fraud and other economic and financial crimes are being fought vigorously with commitment, strong determination and conviction that the malaise must be cleared from Nigerian society. First of its kind in Nigeria, many people who would have regarded themselves as 'untouchable sacred cows' are being arrested and prosecuted for corruption, advance fee frauds '419', and other economic and financial crimes.

Another inconceivable way of tax evasion is how importers sabotage government import policies at the ports. The laudable protectionism efforts and policies of government to protect local industries by promulgating wide ranging import restrictions are being thwarted daily by unscrupulous companies and individuals who circumvent the nation's import policies meant to resuscitate and grow the economy by conspiring with customs officials at the ports and borders (land, water and air).

In the *Daily Independent Outline* of Wednesday, July 30, 2003, it was reported that some dubious Nigerians were colluding with foreign companies for monetary gains to sabotage government import restrictions by importing banned goods into the country and getting them cleared by offering bribes to customs officials at the ports and borders.

The government regulated the import duty of five percent for completely knocked down CKD parts for assembly of new fridges in order to encourage indigenous entrepreneurs who were bona fide manufacturers of fridges to assemble fridges in Nigeria. Investigations showed that the five percent import duty concession was being abused by fridge manufacturers who imported fully built fridges into the country and cleared them under the five percent import duty rate.

Under normal circumstances, the import duty for fully builtup fridges should have attracted fifty-five percent import duty instead of five percent which the fraudulent importers paid. The government intention was that the five percent concession would enable fridge manufacturers to expand their businesses and thus generate employment for assemblers.

In another similar scenario, the government granted two and onehalf percent import duty for industrial machinery and equipment to encourage industrialization and sustenance of the manufacturing industry. Some fraudulent importers imported electronics and household appliances, motorcycles and various merchandise items which they cleared as industrial machines under the two and onehalf percent import duty concession regulated by the government.

It was also reported that there was collusion between government agencies responsible for enforcing import regulations and the fraudulent importers who abused government concessions.

The report further emphasized that preshipment inspection agents employed by government to protect government interest colluded with dubious importers. A shipper who was also an importer on becoming frustrated by dubious activities lamented, "It is very unfortunate that nothing seems to work in Nigeria." The pains of the shipper and his frustrations are not uncommon but there are better assurances that these abuses will not last for ever. ExPresident Obasanjo expressed optimism about Nigerians and the nation and provided some assurances that the government was bent on preventing, minimizing or eliminating economic and financial crimes in the country.

On May 29, 2003, during the inauguration of ExPresident Obasanjo's second term in office, he reiterated, "I cannot believe that Nigerians are innately corrupt. I cannot believe that Nigerians would in preference for a decent and civilized society, opt for one in which law and order is disregarded, and regulations are circumvented as the norm. I will continue to appeal to that good nature. My unshaken and unshakable faith, belief in and commitment to Nigeria is anchored in my equally strong belief in the intrinsic good nature of humans, and that given the right environment and impetus, man can change for the better." Nigerians can change for the better.

Nigerians can change with exemplary leadership that enforces discipline with strong sanctions that severely and deterrently punish offenders who commit economic and financial crimes as well as those who engage in the sabotage of government infrastructures and facilities. There should be no sacred cows. It will require the tripartite strong efforts, determination and teamwork of the Presidency, the Legislature and the Judiciary to eliminate corruption, fraud and economic sabotage in all facets of Nigerian socio-economic and political life.

In the forty-third independence anniversary speech on October 1, 2003, ExPresident Obasanjo reassured the nation that the leadership would be responsible, sensitive and transparent to deliver service while enjoining the full trust of the citizens. He reiterated, "Anticorruption efforts will continue until Nigerian society is rid of this major impediment, and there will be no sacred cows."

He declared, "There will be no condonement of foreign exchange manipulation, underinvoicing and money laundering which generally compromise our financial system." He added, "Financial Crimes Commission has full authority to identify and deal effectively with those who systematically abuse our financial system. No matter their declared investment intentions, they are not wanted."

The government should consider establishing reward programmes for informants whose information helps government to arrest, prosecute and convict fraudulent and corrupt people as well as economic saboteurs and violent criminals. The government should step up efforts for crime prevention, detection and deterrence as well as increase research and motivation efforts to help people change behaviour.

When Nigerians who work in the United States of America lose their jobs, they receive unemployment benefits which represent a reasonable percentage of their salaries for about six months or until they secure another job, whichever comes first. On the other hand, some Nigerian workers in their own country, work for more than six months without pay. There are pensioners who have not been paid for more than 2 years in their own country where they served meritoriously before retirement. Allegedly, some collapsed and died while waiting on the line to collect their pensions.

Unemployment rate is terribly high, and many graduating university and college students cannot hope for jobs because the money that could have been utilized for employment generation and economic growth were stolen and stashed away in foreign banks by the country's past leadership.

As a result of human degradations that happened in Nigeria in the past, there are fears, which make even the greatest optimist to naturally nurse some doubt about a new lease of life being promised all Nigerians. Remarkably, the changes desired are being noticed daily with strong fight pitched against corrupt leaders. A lot of progress was made to pay off many of the pensioners. It was remarkable. Those who remain to be paid, should be paid urgently to allay or mitigate their sufferings in their retirement age.

Nigeria is one of the seven largest exporters of crude oil in the world with an OPEC production quota of over 2.5 million barrels per day. In the *Guardian Online* of Thursday, July 13, 2003, Nigeria was said to be losing about 300,000 barrels a day to thieves accumulating to about $3.3 billion annually. The revelation was credited to the exGovernor of Niger Delta State, James Ibori. He was credited to have said that illegal oil bunkering was giving Nigerian government sleepless nights, and it was time to halt the activities of illegal oil bunkerers and pipeline vandalization before they bled the nation dry.

He was said to have confirmed that the federal government had identified the crude oil thieves and their customers, but he declined to name them. He added that the government would persuade some countries and individuals who were patronizing the crude oil thieves to desist. If the crude oil thieves and their customers are not named, exposed and sanctioned, they will not stop their illegal activities. Why were they not named since the exgovernor actually confirmed that the Federal Government had identified the thieves and their customers?

On August 8, 2003, it was reported in the *Vanguard* that crude oil thieves were selling a barrel of stolen crude oil at $7.00 against the official international price of $25.00 per barrel. It was reported that prominent Nigerians and even government officials were involved in the business, which explained why it thrived and became very difficult to be checked, controlled and stopped for good.

It was further alleged that the illegal activity involved highly placed Nigerians who were using the nation's security network outfit, and that those usually caught were stupid ones operating outside the syndicate as well as those who refused to play according to the rules of the illegal game.

It was pointed out that oil theft had been thriving in the Bakassi Peninsula in Cross River State since 1980. In 2005, the intensified fight against illegal oil bunkerers had yielded enormous dividends for government. As at June/July 2008, oil price rose to between $130.00 and $150.00 per barrel and illegal oil bunkering continued with greater intensity and sophistication. A lot of the money realized by the militants was utilized to procure weapons to fight the government. In December 2008, oil price dropped sharply to about $40.00 per barrel and made oil business less profitable.

In a presentation by a University of Port Harcourt Professor at the Society of Petroleum Engineers Conference in Abuja in early August 2003, it was reported, "If government is determined to check this act, the money siphoned from the country through illegal oil bunkering is more than enough to enthrone a sustainable development in the Niger Delta and put youths militancy and restiveness to rest."

It was suggested that government and the oil companies operating in the Niger Delta should establish agrobased companies and small-scale businesses to employ those unemployed militant youths of the Niger Delta region. Unless that was done, the trouble in the area would continue as Niger Delta fresh graduates from various universities who were unemployed would continue to constitute a nuisance to the oil exploration and production companies in the region. At the conference, no names of culprits were mentioned for governmental attention.

In *This Day News* of July 1, 2003, it was reported that the Nigerian Labour Congress (NLC) accused NNPC and exministers of sabotage by saying that the nation's oil refineries were not operating at optimal capacity due to what was alleged as a conspiracy between the Nigerian National Petroleum Corporation (NNPC) and oil marketers.

The NLC alleged that the NNPC and oil marketers had conspired to make sure that the refineries never worked and that whenever the Federal government pumped in money in the afternoon for necessary repairs, at night, the conspirators would use their agents to blow them up.

The NLC threatened, "We know the names of those involved. Some of them have been ministers until recently." The NLC did not mention names but insisted that the government must make the refineries work because taxpayers' money was used to set them up.

If the NLC leadership could compromise and did not name the government functionaries and others who were economic saboteurs, who else could and should? If Nigerian Labour Congress exleader Oshiomhole, Chief Gani Fawehinmi (SAN), Chief Anthony Enahoro, Alhaji Balarabe Musa, Dr. Frederick Fasehun, Gani Adams, Professor Wole Soyinka, the Nigerian Press and many others could not name the illegal oil bunkerers, who else could and should? What are they afraid of, judging from the level of their political activism? The world focuses on Governor Oshiomhole to compare his actions as Executive State Governor with his activism and criticism of government when he was leader of Nigerian Labour Congress (NLC).

Does it mean that even if any of them becomes Nigerian leader in future, there will be some toes of Nigerian saboteurs which they will not be able to step upon? Some people should be bold enough to expose the illegal oil bunkerers to Nigerians. Let the people know them for appropriate reprisals.

On Monday, August 4, 2008, the Chairman of Senate Committee on Gas, Senator Osita Izunaso complained that 1,260 oil spills were recorded in 2 years (2006-08) as well as a daily loss of $15 million (₦5.8 billion) as a result of gas flaring representing Nigeria's precious hydrocarbon product. It is pertinent to ask why this loss is condoned on a daily basis, knowing the weight of the economic value of this loss and the huge developmental benefits derivable, if the loss can be saved on a daily basis! This loss should not continue a day longer.

Furthermore, the activities of Niger Delta militants have resulted in great losses of revenue to Nigeria in general and the Niger Delta in particular. The serious shortage of oil production resulting in high price of oil has made the world to desperately continue to find alternatives to energy from oil production, and the world is reducing the demand and dependence on oil energy.

Sooner than later, the world especially the USA will achieve the alternative energy sources and drastically reduce the demand for oil. Hence, this is the time for Nigeria and other oil producing countries to make money; sooner than later, oil will worth less for the world is desperately looking for substitutes for oil. As at December 2008, oil price fell to less than $40.00 per barrel from over $140.00 per barrel in July 2008. Hence, sooner than later, those who have been fighting, killing, kidnapping and dying because of oil as well as other oil economic saboteurs and their mentors may find that their destructive actions are no longer worth it.

In the Guardian News of September 6, 2003, it was reported that the exPolice Affairs Minister, Alaowei B. Bozimo, acknowledged, "Apart from huge number of lives lost, the perennial crises in the Niger Delta State are costing the country ₦447.65 billion ($35 billion) annually, The region is hemorrhaging, bleeding. The economy is bleeding." He recognized that the interethnic crises in the region were better tackled through political dialogue rather than the use of force. He added, "What the government does not want to do is to appear to be fighting its own citizens."

He reiterated that activities like pipeline vandalization, oil theft, piracy, and hostage taking would not be condoned. He affirmed that there would be no foreign troops to help maintain peace and order in the region. He explained that ExPresident Obasanjo was reluctant to send in troops in a 'rambo' fashion, shooting their way through the Niger Delta, because that would only kill a lot of people for nothing, and the problem would still remain. The estimated loss calculated above was based on oil price at $25.00 per barrel in 2003. In 2007/2008, the price skyrocketed to between $130.00 and above $140.00 per barrel and the loss continued daily in greater dimension without an end in sight. Remarkably, with oil price going down to $40.00 per barrel in December 2008, crime rate in Niger Delta dropped considerably.

The government has continued to demonstrate concern for the people and complete understanding of Nigeria's problems. That in itself is praiseworthy. The resoluteness and commitment which the government leadership shows daily to tackle the problems is also complimentary and gives some hope to the people about a better future in the Niger Delta in particular and Nigeria in general.

In the *Netscape News* of August 9, 2003, it was reported that Nigeria closed its border with Benin Republic over concerns about increased cross-border crimes such as armed robbery, smuggling of contraband, guns and ammunition and human trafficking. It was also reported that NigeriaBenin frontier had been the main route for smuggling arms and ammunition, trafficking of young Nigerian girls to Europe for prostitution and smuggling of Nigerian subsidized petroleum products thus causing artificial fuel shortages in Nigeria. There was smuggling into Nigeria, products like frozen chicken, envelopes and other products banned to protect and encourage local production of Nigerian manufacturing companies.

On August 26, 2003, *This Day News* reported that more than 236 police officers were billed to face dismissal following their alleged involvement in extortion of money from drivers at police mounted checkpoints. The former Inspector General of Police, Tafa Balogun, was reported to have said that the exercise of dismissing corrupt officers would continue until the last cell in the corrupt clique was brought to book. He was also reported to have sought the cooperation of the leadership of the NURTW in the onerous task of stamping out corruption in the police force by telling their comrades to desist from offering bribes to police officers at checkpoint. He asserted that police checkpoints would be dismantled henceforth.

He directed that the use of siren which was constituting public nuisance daily in the country should be limited to the President, the VicePresident, Chief Justice, Governors, Deputy Governors, and Ministers among others that might be authorized to use siren.

Out of sheer hypocrisy, the former Inspector General of Police who was advising his officers against corruption was incredibly charged to court for corrupt enrichment up to the tune of ₦13.8 billion in 2005. One should not be surprised because it is the same hypocrisy that is happening all over the world including developed, developing and underdeveloped countries.

On August 25, 2003, the *Vanguard* reported that the Navy nabbed ten foreigners and six Nigerian collaborators over illegal oil bunkering on the Escravos and Forcados waterways in the Niger Delta State. The Nigerian Navy was also said to have arrested ten barges said to have contained about 1.2 metric tons of illegal products. The commander of the NNS Delta was said to have restated that the Navy would frustrate the activities of pipeline vandals. Regrettably, the condemned activities continued in greater dimension with sophistication.

On August 26, 2003, it was reported in the *Vanguard* that Nigeria and the Republic of Ivory Coast had concluded an accord to halt oil theft and illegal oil bunkering. It was mutually agreed that both countries would crack down on crude oil theft and the smuggling racket that had caused unrest and piracy in the strifetorn Niger Delta State. In pursuit of the agreement, the Ivorien refinery firm was said to have turned back three tankers which did not have proper documentation.

On August 27, 2003, the *Vanguard* reported that the government had retired twenty-eight top officials of the NNPC to reshape the company for repositioning toward government policy of full commercialization and partial privatization of the company. The government also approved the appointment, promotion and deployment of nineteen management personnel. From the above analyses, one could see the desperate and consistent efforts of government to tackle Nigerian problems on a daily basis. It is commendable that all stakeholders could cooperate to work together to ameliorate Nigerian people's problems.

During one of the weekend's presidential media chat, exPresident Obasanjo was reported to have hinted about government intention to further increase fuel prices as a way to curb the "seemingly intractable activities of illegal oil bunkerers in the country." Their activities had been causing fuel scarcity.

In their reaction to the purported line of thought of the President to increase fuel price, the NLC leadership felt that such line of thought to justify fuel price increase was traitorous and contemptuous of the Nigerian citizenry. The NLC representative wrote that fuel pricing could not continue to be subject to the whims and caprices of government leadership and that the presidency had failed to recognize the hyperinflation and suffering caused the people as a result of previous increases in the cost of petroleum products. The NLC contended that the government adopted importation of fuel products as religion describing the practice as a celebration of incompetence.

The NLC condemned and described the argument that the products were being smuggled out of the country because they were being low-priced as illogical, and asserted that the citizens of Nigeria could not be punished by arbitrary fuel product price increases because the government and its numerous security agencies were incapable of stopping smugglers. It reminded the government about its promises to ensure adequate supply of petroleum products and the functionality of the country's four refineries, and thereby expressed disappointment about government's failure to fulfill its promises.

The main objective of government is to always look for the best alternative solution for people's problems. Fuel price increase could be one of the solutions to the problems, but it is not the best alternative solution. Price increase often has dissatisfying and distasteful ripple and multiplier effects on the growth of Nigerian economy which is the priority objective of government.

Price increase could be counterproductive to socio-economic and political reforms and stability especially if the price increase targets essential products that form part of the necessities of life of the masses and particularly when demand is inelastic. Price increases of essential products are inflationary and would affect the masses more adversely. The government can make more money, but it should not be at the expense of the welfare of the masses. "Enterprise Nigeria" belongs to the masses more because they are in majority, and they have nowhere to go unlike the elites who have alternatives in Europe and America. In a democracy, the majority, the masses matter. There should be greater focus on the masses.

As for the palliative measures to help the masses, the elites have the resources to exploit the loopholes to their advantage. It is best to stick to policies that fight against the ills of the bad guys among the elites to save the masses from exploitation and manipulation. In the study of price mechanism, it has always shown that price increase may not be beneficial in the long run.

Nigeria was rated lower than Botswana, South Africa, Mauritius, Namibia and Tunisia in economic performance in Africa by the 2003 Economic Report on Africa (ERA 2003). The Economic Commission for Africa (ECA) reported that top performers had lower foreign debts, lower budget deficits and lower interest rates. They also had better market liberalization policies with few policy reversals, more effective legal systems on economic and financial crimes, better poverty alleviation policies, and high infrastructure of more reliable quality and greater accessibility.

In spite of the above, why is interest rate still kept at double-digit? Perhaps the work of lobbyists and special interest groups have been overpowering the good intentions of government. Interest rate at double digit is unwise economically because it retards national development.

The report highlighted key challenges to accelerate economic development. These are:
(1) poverty alleviation programmes;
(2) maintenance of fiscal sustainability;
(3) energizing bureaucracies;
(4) accountability and coherence; and
(5) institution building policies using an ECA designed expanded policy stance index.

It is hypothetical to assume that a problem is perhaps half solved where there is a realization that it exists and where there is genuine willingness, commitment and capability to solve it.

The best thing that happened to Nigeria and Nigerians effective May 29, 1999, was that the government leadership (the Presidency, Senate, House of Representatives and the Judiciary) were willing, committed and capable of delivering and redeeming Nigeria of the problems that bedeviled the country for four decades (1960-1999) out of sheer poor, misdirected dictatorship.

In effect, the leadership consistently demonstrated the will, the determination and ability to turn the comatose economy of Nigeria around, and they started laying a formidable foundation for the economy's speedy recovery by designing an economic growth plan of over five percent per annum projected for ten years. The government assembled a strong economic and financial management team of high calibre professionals who were fully determined, committed and working relentlessly to ensure Nigeria's return to the path of economic prosperity in a record time.

The Nigerian Senate, the House of Representatives and the Presidency worked hard to amend and put in place as was necessary, the 'Economic and Financial Crimes Acts' in line with the 'International Standards Requirement'. The EFCC Act helped to restore, enhance and perpetuate the world community's confidence in Nigeria's economic and financial administration thereby resulting in a subsequent rain of foreign investments into the country. The act helped to prevent, minimize and deter the commission of economic and financial crimes which were prevalent in the country.

The Senate commitment to rid Nigeria of economic and financial crimes was expressed on August 5, 2003 by the ex-chairman of the Senate Committee on Drugs, Narcotics and Financial Crimes, Senator Lawal Shuaibu, during the inauguration of his committee. He stated that the standardization of the Act was imperative to enable the Financial Action Task Force (FATF) of the 'twenty-nine member nation body' of the United Nations set up to fight financial crimes, review and drop the blacklisting of Nigeria.

It was observed that Nigeria was blacklisted by FATF because as alleged, there were no records of reported cases of money laundering and their prosecution. As alleged, FATF evaluation team received little cooperation when the members visited Nigeria on factfinding tour. Also, FATF conditionalities on legislation were allegedly not satisfied. The implication of the blacklisting in July 2003 carried grave consequences for the country being dubbed a country of fraudsters by the International Financial Community.

In her own reaction, the exMinister of Finance, Mrs. (Dr.) Ngozi Okonjo-Iweala said that the country was not sanctioned by the FATF but had only requested that Nigeria should upgrade her laws on financial crimes. To demonstrate responsibility, responsiveness and government's seriousness about the matter, a government delegation was dispatched to Paris, led by the ex-Chairman of the Economic and Financial Crimes Commission (EFCC), Nuhu Ribadu, for discussion. In addition, the National Assembly leadership organized meetings with exPresident

Olusegun Obasanjo to evolve strategies that could resolve the issues involved speedily.

The duo exChairpersons of the House Committee on Rules, Media and Public Affairs, Ita Enang and Abike Dabiri, expressed concern to see a quick resolution of the issues. The quick responsiveness of the government and the standard set by the FATF was a symbol for great incentive which attracted local and foreign investors. It was a great omen for future prosperous Nigeria and a step in the right direction toward economic prosperity.

The federal government passed a bill to effect the African Growth and Opportunity Act (AGOA) and continues to encourage the private sector to collaborate with it in the successful execution of the programme. The former Special Adviser to exPresident Obasanjo on African Growth and Opportunity Act (AGOA), Mrs. Modupe Sasore in Lagos wooed members of the Organized Private Sector (OPS) to collaborate with the government for the successful implementation of the AGOA programme in the best interest of Nigeria and the continent of Africa.

She emphasized the need for teamwork among the 'OPS', Ministry of Commerce, other government agencies, her office and all stakeholders to achieve success on 'AGOA'. She assured the 'OPS' that the government would provide the enabling congenial environment for business to thrive, and the programme to succeed. She hinted that trade revenue under AGOA in 2002 was over $9 billion for which Nigeria accounted for about $5 billion from oil and nonoil related products. She clarified that AGOA was established essentially to promote nonoil related products.

On the other hand, the OPS representatives who included Mr. Romeo Barberopolous, Chairman of the Export Group of Manufacturers Association of Nigeria (MAN) and Mr. David Iweta, President of Sapele Chamber of Commerce advised that the workability and success of AGOA rested on:

(1) The government should not pay lip service to the project like some other laudable ones, which were allowed to die for government inaction.

(2) The AGOA programme projected to generate two million jobs required one billion dollars guarantee from the government from which the private sector could borrow to procure equipment for increased production for export.

(3) Government should fund AGOA effectively from oil revenue and implement a two and onehalf percent dutyfree on equipment under AGOA.

On Saturday, June 19, 2004, at the View Valley Auditorium, Abeokuta, Ogun State, the former PDP National Chairman, Audu Ogbeh, told the South-West meeting of the party that the country could no longer rely on illdigested economic theories and warned that unbridled capitalism could be harmful.

Chief Ogbeh was alleged to have said, "The situation now is such that we appear to allow ourselves to be led by our socalled experts whose theories appear to be ill-digested and hopelessly out of tune with the dynamics of modern economic realities." He hinted that it was time to Xray concrete issues of economic significance and that the party would convene an economic summit to take far reaching economic decisions in the best interest of the nation.

He blamed the stagnation of the national economy on high interest rates, which had resulted in crises of poverty, diseases and backwardness. He emphasized that the interest rate should come down to encourage borrowing, investment and enhanced production capabilities. He explained, "More jobs and wealth are generated through production other than through contracts and trading."

He added that unemployment was the most dangerous threat to the nation's existence with 800,000 expected to graduate from universities, colleges and polytechnics in 2004, but with little hope of securing employment. Chief Ogbeh concluded realistically, "The economy is too serious a matter to be left to economists and bankers alone. We must discuss this because in the last analysis, we, not economists or bankers, take the blame, but we the politicians do."

High interest rate is a main restraining element in the drive forward to economic prosperity, microeconomics, employment generation and socio-economic and political stabilization. Lowering interest rate is one of the priority problems that the technical experts should have tackled, researched on, advised on and solved since the beginning of the Fourth Republic. Any socio-economic reform while high interest rate still subsists cannot fully achieve the desired results. High taxation can also be another impediment to rapid economic recovery and growth.

It must be remembered that in civilized communities like the USA, interest rate and taxation are constantly reviewed to stabilize the economy. The interest rate in the US is less than three percent and unemployment rate is less than 5.6 percent. In some countries with the best economies, the interest rate is as low as between one and four percent.

Highsounding theories designed by bookworms not backed by experience and not operating in the right implementation mode without human face may not achieve its desired goals and objectives. Presidential advisers, especially the 'NEEDS' team of experts and those of Seven-Point Agenda of President Yar'Adua should work on this area of national economic importance to achieve the best results.

In his own contribution to the PDP conference, the Governor of Ogun State, Obalofin Otunba Gbenga Daniel, reminded members to be law-abiding so that the party would not degenerate into a party that would be viewed as one with a "riotous conduct in the sharing of positions and patronage or in the intemperate vaulting of some of its leaders."

Chief Tony Anenih, former Chairman of PDP Board of Trustees, hinted that failed political leaders had ganged up against the PDP. He declared, "The way they have been carrying on is suggestive of the view that without them in public office, no one should be there, or better still, without them in public office, Nigeria could very well go to ashes."

Chief Anenih's observation must be great concern to all. Some people often wrongly feel that they are better than every other Nigerian. With arrogance and opinionation, they are never ready to benefit from others' opinions. Such attitude does not demonstrate the acquisition of the right education, political savvy and sagacity. Nobody knows it all.

The easy way to reduce tension and curb opposition excesses is for the government to be responsible, responsive, transparent, corruptionfree and carry the majority of the people along with good governance and great leadership. It is then that the opposition will have no reason to agitate and cause problems. In effect, the PDP leadership should look inwardly and see what is wrong that has fueled opposition's aggressiveness as well as what has helped them to regroup formidably from time to time.

ExPresident Obasanjo was reported to have said emotionally that corruption was hard to tackle because it was involving high, low, friends and those he respected. The expresident was very humane and empathic but those who have not changed from 1999 to 2007 and beyond cannot be friends or respected.

His assertion was a bold and honest truth and probably the majority of high, low, friends and the respected, involved in corruption, economic and financial crimes were in the governing political party (PDP). That revelation was well known to the opposition parties, so, if the PDP and the government failed to defeat corruption hands down quickly, it would be difficult to stop or restrain the breeding and invigouration of the opposition.

Secondly, the former PDP National Chairman talked about the stagnation of the economy, high interest rate, unemployment, poverty, diseases, backwardness and illdigested and hopelessly out of modern economic theories being propounded by technical experts, which do not meet the dynamics of modern economic realities. Realistically, the situation could assist the breeding, survival and expansion of the number and strength of the opposition.

It is hard, but the PDP must clean itself and speak the tone that supports government efforts and policies. The former chairman's statements demonstrated some frustration about some probable wrong steps, in act of governance which he was seeing, and was complaining silently about, but nobody listened. That is the way things are in the present world where almost everything is wrong and nobody listens. That is why the world is full of an accumulation of problems.

Thirdly, the PDP should also look at the indiscipline in the party, accusations of corruption against some governors, pocketing part of local government allocations, the modalities of the implementation of reform programmes, misappropriation of government funds, mismanagement of contracts, alleged corruption in PDP National Working Committee dissolved in June 2005, and many other grievances which helped the breeding, survival and expansion of the number and strength of the opposition groups.

In the light of the above, the more the government and the PDP put their house in order, the less significant the opposition parties become. Since the PDP had landslide victories in 2003 and 2007 general, presidential and local government elections, it should research into what has enhanced the strength and number of opposition groups and then make sweeping changes to contain the problems.

Neocolonialism is the new practice employed by developed countries of using their economic and political policies to indirectly maintain and extend their undue influence and control over the developing nations. Nigeria was colonized by Britain, but it achieved independence in 1960. In the same vein, Britain, France, Germany and Portugal colonized many other African countries.

The colonial masters ensured that the colonized countries adopted the linguae francae of their respective colonial masters in place of their own African languages. Invariably, the foreign languages from Europe were imposed on the African countries as a strain, ploy, string attached and incentive for development as if African continent, the cradle of world civilization, engineering, the art of writing and traditional religion, was not developing prior to colonization.

After independence of African nations, one expected that the influence from Europe would diminish and Africans would be left alone to channel their destiny without any undue interference and influence from their colonial masters who created and left a lot of unsolved socio-economic and political problems for all African independent countries.

The colonialists created and left disputes regarding to land and border demarcation, resource allocation, accurate population census, structural and relational problems between federal, state and local governments, and other constitutional problems that resulted in civil wars. Unwittingly, the colonial masters took sides in the civil wars which undermined the sovereignty of African governments and thus prolonged the civil wars unnecessarily.

Regrettably, the Western World has used debt issue as a weapon of neocolonization. The terribly disturbing aspect of the debt issue is the dubious nature of the composition of the debt and the corruption, recklessness and irresponsibility involved in the signing of the contracts relating to some of the questionable debts.

As at 1983, during the Second Republic of President Shagari, the foreign debt allegedly amounted to $3 billion but increased dramatically during the military regimes to more than $30 billion. That is incredibly irresponsible and unjustifiable. How did it happen?

Presenting a paper titled "Law and Economy – Challenges and Prospects for Law and Business" at a public lecture organized by the Centre for Law and Business on Wednesday, June 23, 2004, Prince Bola Ajibola, former World Court Judge and Chairman of the Nigerian Delegation to the Cameroon-Nigeria Mixed Commission on Boundary Disputes, mentioned that Nigeria had dispensed over $20 billion on interest and capital as foreign debt. He wondered why Nigeria as the sixth largest producer of oil globally could remain a debtor nation and underdeveloped.

Prince Bola Ajibola reiterated, "But this much I know, that these debts were owed because of our reckless, negligent and irresponsible acts, most due to the fact that we entered and signed bad contracts, which were heavily padded to our detriment, and in some cases, as a result of breach of those contracts by us in an irresponsible and dubious manner and without a thought of care for the consequences or negative impact on the common man."

He added that the nation's law and legal experts could not help the situation because most of those foreign debts contractual relations were entered into and executed with connivance and collusion of some of the same legal experts who, for the sake of corruption, compromised government position adversely.

Backing Prince Ajibola's assertions, it was regrettable that the unpatriotic acts of corruption committed by some unpatriotic legal experts bequeathed to Nigerians, crookedly contracted debts that economically enslaved, neocolonized and plagued Nigeria for decades until July 2005 when Nigerians breathed sighs of relief.

As a result of the biting effects of the national debts, the government at numerous times sought that the debts be cancelled and, as such, the creditor governments and their agencies demanded stringent economic reforms, which were often in bad taste to the citizenry.

Potential foreign investors have also made demands to influence governmental action in many cases regarding level of security, inflation, good governance, settled and peaceful political climate. They also demanded democratic setting devoid of violence, unrest or terrorism where law and order reigns supreme.

They requested high level industrial harmony, safety and effective control of frauds, corruption and economic and financial crimes. They often asked for special privileges relating to reasonable profit repatriation policy, sourcing of production materials, taxation relief possibilities, expatriate employment quota and adequate provision of enabling business environment.

Privatization is greatly encouraged by Nigeria, a process where public establishment or agency operated by the government is transferred or sold to the private sector. The objective of the exercise to transfer or sell a public company to the private sector is to move the services privatized out of bureaucracies, inactivity, business as usual, laziness, wastefulness, inefficiency, ineffectiveness, idleness, irresponsiveness, irresponsibility and defective services.

Privatized businesses move into areas of organized and rationalized business environment which ensures effectiveness, efficiency, transparency, business aggressiveness, responsiveness, greater sense of responsibility, accountability, cost minimization, profitability maximization, greater research and development.

Privatized businesses provide greater motivation to acquire, enhance and utilize skills, capabilities, and experience to the fullest. They often match productivity with commensurate compensation and benefits. Privatization often results in ideal management of resources acquisition and utilization, with ideal goals of profit maximization, business survival, expansion and perpetual management succession.

The privatization programme of the Federal Government of Nigeria represents a basis for fostering accelerated economic growth. The process creates enabling business environment, encourages and enhances private investment, ensures improved efficiency in productive sectors and enlists private sector participation in infrastructural development. Notable areas include electricity generation, telecommunications, health, agricultural and food production, research and development, housing, communication, transportation, mining of mineral resources, national resource development and all services that elevate the citizenry in the best interest of the nation.

The effectiveness and successfulness of Nigerian privatization programme can be measured or determined by how far it bridges or widens the gap of inequality between the rich and the poor in the country. The wider the gap of inequality, the poorer the generality of the people become. The narrower the gap of inequality among the citizenry, the more prosperous the people become.

Considering above hypothesis, a privatization programme that sells to foreigners and few rich Nigerians will increase the inequality gap and render the people poorer and poorer in a situation, which concentrates wealth in the hands of foreigners and few rich elites.

On the other hand, a privatization programme, which targets the generality of the people, creates and uplifts the middle class and bridges or narrows the inequality gap which will surely enhance the standard of living and life expectancy of the people and the Nigerian nation generally.

To be successful, national economic practice must encourage foreign investment to the fullest, but it is best when contracts with foreign investors, their implementation and obligations recognize the needs of the people and respond to them. Nigerian interests must be given first consideration and be fully protected.

The USA, UK and other developed economies do best with foreign investments. Nigeria should pursue similar policies that encourage foreign investment partnership aggressively by ensuring that old friends are kept while prospecting for new ones continues with greater tact than ever before. Do the foreign investments and privatization outcomes benefit the masses? For example, what lasting benefits accrue to the local farmers? What about organizing royalties or profit sharing for the local landowners? They can also be encouraged and provided with resources to engage in cooperative farming.

Privatization programme which targets sales to foreigners and few rich Nigerians ensures quick money available to the government for the execution of its projects, but the irony of it is that majority of the money may disappear into private pockets of elites through frauds and corruption at the detriment of the generality of the people if care is not taken. Such quick money generated by the government makes the government richer but that does not mean that the same effect is created in the people to whom the government is responsible.

Privatization programme should ensure equitable distribution of wealth to the people and not the concentration of wealth in the hands of foreign companies and few wealthy Nigerians in order to achieve its objectives. Domestic generation of investment resources and wealth is better than playing into the hands of foreigners in the interest of Nigerian National Security. In all life ventures, there would be merits and demerits, so, the government must lean more on areas that benefit the people most.

At this juncture, one can ask the executives in charge of privatization on how successfully the programme has contributed to the betterment of the generality of Nigerians! Is total revenue and expenditure properly accounted for? Executives should be moved around from seat to seat to detect and deter frauds. Heads should roll whenever necessary and speedily too for accounting malpractices.

It was reported on Wednesday, June 30, 2004, that the Bureau of Public Enterprise (BPE) scored poor marks from the World Bank as a result of the slow pace of the implementation of the privatization programme. It was said that the BPE encountered implementation difficulties as a result of which the privatization implementation progress received unsatisfactory rating. Have the heads of the implementation body taken responsibility for poor performance? Have there been corrective measures? What are the impediments and why have they lasted for over two years without remedial measures to ensure satisfactory rating? Have there been consequences and anybody replaced for being a clog in the wheel of progress? When can people proudly say, "Business as usual has stopped in the BPE?"

It was said that the BPE had drawn $21.59 million or 18.9 % out of $114.29 million that was set aside on June 14, 2001 for the privatization support initiative and that $2,571,525 was paid as commitment charges for an overall performance that received 'unsatisfactory rating' by the World Bank.

Four projects sponsored by the World Bank purportedly scored 'unsatisfactory' were:
   (1) the Second Health System Development Programme ($127.00 million);
   (2) HIV/AIDS Programme Development ($90.30 million);
   (3) Local Empowerment and Environment Management Programme ($70 million); and
   (4) Privatization Support Programme ($114.29 million).

The Nigerian leaders should be reminded: "The greatest leader is not one who did the greatest things, but one who makes the people do the greatest things," said by Ronald Reagan, Fortieth President of the United States of America. Therefore, the greatest leaders and elders of Nigeria are not the wealthiest ones who acquire wealth illegally and siphon money overseas, but those leaders who create wealth and economic prosperity among the generality of the people, are surely the greatest. Definitely, the greatest things which Nigerians dream about cannot be actualized through a public service described as having decayed very badly, full of inefficiency, waste, corruption and arrogance whose vibrancy and honour demonstrated a downward trend.

On Thursday, September 2, 2004, exPresident Obasanjo condemned banks charging high double-digit interest rates in the country as well as levies termed as legal charges on customers and borrowers describing the practice as criminal, anti-growth and anti-development. He added that there was no justification for banks to impose extra charges for administrative ledger.

He explained, "In developing countries like Nigeria, high interest rate stifles creativity, discourages investment, suffocates businesses and intimidates the ordinary person." He described high interest rate as generally inhuman and queried the kind of business anyone could establish at twenty-five percent interest rate. He asserted that in order to build a virile middle class, promote growth and development and expand the private sector, interest rate should be low.

Nigeria's reduction of interest rate from twenty-five to less than thirteen percent was a great improvement, but it was still double-digit. Compared with the world's most developed economies, which ranges between 1% and 5%, the reduction of interest rate to less than thirteen percent still needs further improvement.

ExPresident Obasanjo encouraged banks to demonstrate transparency, accountability, and due process in all facets of their operational roles as the engine of growth. He referred to the imperative reforms embarked upon by the CBN which he explained would strengthen the banking sector and empower the banks to restructure, redesign, be less susceptible to stocks and be able to reconceptualize their mission goals and objectives.

He envisaged that reforms would make the banks 'more focused, well-led, well-managed, confident, stable, energized and productive'. He implored banks helmsmen to take reforms seriously and to deploy their assets and productive capacity effectively and efficiently by ensuring that they 'modernize, retool, retrain, improve on technology and refocus' on their mission.

The Nigerian President asserted that banking institutions functioning only as foreign exchange and currency-trading institutions and rarely giving loans to agricultural and industrial programmes could not be adding value to the economy nor promoting necessary growth and as such, could not be proudly called a banking institution.

He added that instead of creating real jobs, many banks in recent times encouraged social criminality by imposing unrealistic deadlines on young ladies and men compelling them into all sorts of antisocial conducts in order to meet imposed targets on which the keeping of their jobs depended. Were these banks and officials sanctioned, indicted, prosecuted and convicted as deterrence to others to save workers from unnecessary exploitation? If any law is broken, the banks concerned should be prosecuted for the violation of the law.

In his own contribution through the exDeputy Governor, Operations, Mr. Shamsuddeen Usman representing the CBN Governor, Professor Charles Soludo, emphasized that structural weaknesses in banks had hindered their developmental roles as characterized by closedownership structure, weak capital base and dependence on volatile funds. Mr. Usman later became the Minister of Finance, but reassigned in 2008 cabinet reshuffle.

A proper diagnosis of Nigerian economic problems was carried out and properly analyzed. As a result, the capitalization base structure of banks was put at ₦25 billion, but what about the most important question of high, double digit interest rate which forms the fulcrum of Nigeria's economic stability and bane of business growth and development? How long does it take to fix the interest rate at a level enjoyed by civilized and developed societies like Britain, America and other countries, which are enjoying rapid economic emancipation and development with interest rate at below five percent?

The Chairman of the Federal Reserve System in USA, the equivalent of the CBN Governor, regulates interest rate periodically without hindrance in the best interest of the economy, the nation of the United States of America and the citizenry. The Federal Reserve System of USA, which is the Central Bank, regulates credit, monetary supply and formulates monetary policies. Its Chairman of the Board of Governors is regarded as the second most powerful person in the USA next to the President.

Economic trends and indicators, which are carefully studied responsibly and responsively dictate the quick need to regulate the rate of interest for economic stabilization, and it does not take months but few days without protocol to announce new rate of interest as may be appropriate.

On June 25, 2005, the Chairman of the US Federal Reserve System, Alan Greenspan announced new interest rate of 3.2 percent. Within the first six months of the year 2008, interest rate was reviewed downward more than two times depending upon the performance of the US economy which was stimulated with cuts in interest rates.

Considering the state of Nigerian economy, why has it been impossible to beat down the Nigerian interest rate to below five percent as it obtains in the most progressive world economies where special interest groups and lobbyists are not allowed to control nor dictate the level of the economy and the rate of interest? Lobbyists and powerful interest groups must be attempting to frustrate the nation's economic reforms by working against low interest rate.

The presidency must note seriously that no amount of economic reforms, nomatter how good intentioned and best executed, can fully succeed if the rate of interest is unduly high and at double digit. It should not be difficult for Nigeria to speedily tap the good examples in the world and apply them quickly to save and uplift the suffering citizenry even if the toes of elites, lobbyists, friends and foes who are clogs in the wheels of Nigerian progress have to be stepped upon. Nigerian leaders should be able to continue the fight against corruption effectively in Nigeria's best interest.

Anybody who has committed economic sabotage whether Nigerian or foreigner since May 29, 2003, does not deserve to be spared, respected or unpunished. Economic saboteurs should be indicted, prosecuted and convicted as deterrence to others. Whoever commits the crime against the nation must serve the sentence nomatter how highly placed or his influence in society.

In the *Vanguard News* of Tuesday, September 9, 2004, the former Minister of Finance, Mrs. (Dr.) Ngozi Okonjo-Iweala, was reported to have attributed the economic woes of Nigeria, the high levels of poverty among the people and poor socio-economic indicators to poor fiscal and accommodating monetary policies. She added that poor fiscal policy accounted for the volatility of Nigeria's revenue and expenditure.

She was critical of Nigeria's revenue, which depended on oil as the only determinant of the fate of the nation's economy. She advised strongly that revenue generation should henceforth diversify and equally focus on nonoil production sectors. She remarked that between 1971 and 2001, Nigerian national expenditure had followed a procyclical pattern.

She identified the following reasons as responsible for Nigeria's economic setbacks which paralyzed and rendered government efforts inconsequential, making it difficult to reposition, to have the desired impacts positively on the lives of the citizenry:

(1) lack of fiscal discipline;
(2) poor coordination of fiscal policy among the three tiers of government (the Federal, State and Local Governments);
(3) structural imbalance in the composition of public expenditure;
(4) weak revenue collection effort resulting in under collection;
(5) low tax compliance;
(6) corruption and lack of transparency;
(7) poor infrastructure;
(8) weak public service delivery;
(9) weak environment for private sector development; and
(10) weak public sector institutions and systems.

She revealed that Nigeria borrowed $13 billion at high interest rate, but because the debt was not paid back nor serviced as a result of poor financial discipline, the debt increased to $32.9 billion. She added that in spite of a lot of money that was paid to service the debt, the balance still remained enormous. As at April 2005, the debt was said to have increased to $38 billion. In June ending 2005, over $18 billion of the debt was granted to be written off by Paris Club.

She promised that the fiscal, monetary and public reforms would put the economy on a strong pedestal. Bureaucracies would be eliminated and consequently, avoidable wastes would be a thing of the past. On Monday, September 20, 2004, the *Vanguard News* carried a report about alleged threats to her life ostensibly on account of government economic reform efforts, which she championed. She promised that she would not succumb to the threats nor abandon the reforms. It was alleged that some people, hurt by government economic reforms had launched spurious attacks, hostility, blackmail and threats to her life with the main purpose of destabilizing government efforts to focus on the reforms.

She declared, "Anyone who has anything against me should come out in the open and say it. That is my style, very open. There is nothing to hide. There has never been anything to hide and never would be. You can trace everyone of my actions. I understand this, that this is a reform process; people feel hurt and threatened. I understand this, that the people will lash out anyway, at anyone they feel is doing this to them."

She acknowledged that the people in the villages were more appreciative and showing more understanding. She said, "Each time I want to receive inspiration, I go to the village. That is where the real people are." Just like in developed and civilized world, the best people live in the countryside. She emphasized that the reforms were not only on course but were yielding desired results beyond expected targets.

She explained that the inflation rate was falling, foreign reserves increased to $12 billion and that exchange rate had stabilized in the last few months. In JuneJuly 2004, inflation rate fell to fourteen percent, and there was a strong chance that it would fall further to ten or eleven percent with continued tight fiscal discipline.

In October 2005, the foreign reserve had moved to $30 billion, and foreign exchange rate had stabilized thus showing an improvement in the status of the economy. In 2008, foreign reserve moved to over $60 billion, interest rate fell to 10%, GDP growth was 7% and inflation rate fell to 9% thereby showing remarkable economic progress.

The former Minister of Finance, Mrs. (Dr.) Okonjo-Iweala, was reported to have said, "The second point is that low inflation rate will help to bring down interest rate. You know bankers never want to lend below the inflation rate because it will be eroding the value of money they have lent to you. If you bring the rate of inflation down, there will be no excuse for them not to bring the interest rate down. This is very important to the economy, and we are achieving it."

Above statement of the Minister of Finance is the usual argument of the bankers and lenders to keep interest rate high which is antithetical to the expected speedy success of the economic reforms. The statement ran counter to the good goals of government economic and political reforms.

One of the weapons or strategies of operations to control or check and stabilize inflation rate is the use of interest rate and possibly taxation in open market operations of the Central Bank or Federal Reserve System in the USA.

To allow inflation rate to dictate the interest rate is exploitative and is like placing the horses behind the cart to push instead placing them in front of the cart to pull. To rely on inflation to regulate interest rate is like government trying to shy away from its responsibilities, selfdefeating the purposes of its economic reforms, slowing down the pace of the reforms and hampering economic growth. That should not be the thinking of government but special interest groups, who become richer and richer while the masses become poorer and poorer.

In the USA, the Chairman of the Federal Reserve System, who is equivalent to the Governor of the Central Bank of Nigeria, regulates interest rate often without protocol and announces changes as many times as necessary in the year to check inflation rate and encourage borrowing to stimulate economic and business activities. Why should it be different in Nigeria? Why should the government wait for inflation rate to go down before interest rate can go down? Free market economic system practised in developed countries like USA does not mean that there are no subsidies, price floor, price ceiling, protectionism, marketing and economic regulations.

In fact, there is no completely free market economy, and for success of the deregulation policy of government, there must be regulation to check abuses or else, the economic system will be abused and it will eventually collapse. Economic reforms without building sound cushioning programmes will breed poverty, chaos, confusion and political instability.

The billion dollar questions to guide the present economic activists, technocrats and reformers in government are, "Why did economic reforms of previous Nigerian administrations fail? Why was there strong opposition to fuel tax? Was it popular? Are presidential advisers measuring popularity and problems of policies? What problems have been caused by present reforms, and how can they be solved to minimize the suffering of the masses? How can majority of the people be carried along in the reform process?"

In successful world economics, the interest rate is always below five percent. Why should Nigeria be different? High interest rate is exploiting and antithetical to economic development. The first exercise by the Presidency and the Legislature toward economic prosperity should have pegged interest rate to five percent or below. High interest rate is the whim and caprice of moneylenders, bankers and the wealthy elites operating at the expense of the poor masses.

The government must act with precision to put a ceiling of five percent as interest rate but reviewable whenever necessary as it is done in the USA to promote economic well-being. It is not progressive to let inflation dictate prevailing interest rate. It should be the other way round. The government should not bend to the whims and caprices of lobbyists and special interest groups on the issue of interest rate if it wants its reforms agenda to succeed quickly as planned.

In 2004, the Senate was vocal and working on nine percent interest rate and the CBN Governor mentioned nine percent, but in 2005, everything became silent except the announcement of thirteen percent interest rate. Were lobbyists and special interest groups in control or gaining upper hand? Give Nigerians low interest rate and see how the economy will grow faster than anticipated. To suggest that inflation should be allowed to regulate interest rate is to assume that the tail should better wag the dog; it should be the other way round for quick desirable results. If other buoyant economies operate more successfully at less than five percent interest rate, why is it impossible in Nigeria for the benefit of the people?

High interest rate widens inequality gap and thereby increases percentage rate of poverty and unemployment as well as decreases business and economic activities. It is antithetical to the spirit of economic reforms being vigorously pursued by the government. The wealthy people benefit more at high interest rate and get richer at the expense of the poor masses while the masses get poorer because high interest rate is inflationary, causes high prices and reduces monetary value.

What if Nigeria can reduce its inflation rate close to what it is in the USA, which was 1.9% in 2002 and 3.3% in 2004 and 2.9 in 2008? It is not easy, but government must take charge and continue to do what is best for the masses to uplift them. Ten percent interest rate in 2008 is not good enough even though it is better than what it used to be between nineteen percent and twenty-five percent. Double-digit interest rate is not progressive.

The banking system must be reviewed, reorganized and rationalized to serve the best interest of Nigeria and the people effectively and efficiently and not only the rich elites who exploit the masses by sharing heavy dividends from bank profits. The system allows banks to make easy money without working hard to earn it. They declare enormous profits, and the owners share dividends that do not spread to benefit the people. The banking businesses arrogantly act as bosses and not service providers who prioritize customer satisfaction in the first place.

Nigerian banks dictate their terms because there is no competition for customers nor the will and ability to serve people meritoriously, satisfactorily and beneficially. Nigerian banks should design workable visionary plans for a prosperous Nigeria that supports enhanced standard of living and increasing life expectancy of Nigerians. If they cannot utilize their high profits for business expansion to generate employment and attract tax incentive, they must be prepared to pay higher taxes to the government for national development.

Bankers should learn to apply the system of "Banking Made Easy" in Europe and America, embark on elaborate research, training and development, help stop all acts of foreign exchange violations, banking frauds and corruption, illegal money transfers and other economic and financial crimes. Ethically and professionally, they should generate funds from hardwork and other services rather than double-digit interest rate, which is not in the best interest of the Nigerian economy.

It was good news again that Nigerian external reserves moved to more than $60 billiion in August 2008, $30 billion in October, 2005, $26.6 billion in July 2005 from $24.37 billion in June 2005 and $23.5

billion in May 2005. The government must ensure that the gains reflect on the masses upliftment from poverty to above subsistence level toward higher standard of living, higher life expectancy and economic prosperity.

In conjunction with Organization of Private Sector, government must concentrate on rural development to help generate employment, create economic buoyancy, increase food production and selfsufficiency, increase capitalization and stop youth militancy, crimes, migration to urban settings and stop uncontrollable brain drain to overseas countries. Government must provide adequate infrastructures; research into community needs and help complement community efforts for rural dwellers to accomplish their dreams. One of the examples is as follows:

It is observed that Igbesaland residents of over 500,000, who are mainly farmers and businesspersons, have to travel a distance of over forty-five miles to transport their products and services to Lagos environs through Atan/SangoOta instead of less than eight miles through IgbesaAyobo/Ipaja /Agege Road if a bridge is constructed over Captain Davis River. Igbesaland can then become a hub for prosperous socio-economic activities for the benefit of Ogun and Lagos States in particular and Nigeria in general. The less productive and uneconomic merry-go-round of over forty-five miles instead of less than eight miles has continued in Igbesaland from time immemorial.

With abundance of fertile land for mechanized farming and other economic programmes in Igbesaland, a federal/state or privately sponsored project to construct the bridge over Captain Davis River is feasible and will yield enormous dividends for Nigeria. Igbesans' efforts and silent prayers of over half a century to secure government assistance to bridge the river have not been successful.

The community efforts to bridge the river in 1950s up to date were curtailed due to some deaths among who was Alhaji Aminu of Ogona Quarter, Igbesa, Ogun State. May his soul rest in perfect peace (amen). Igbesans should dedicate a day to commemorate the heroism of Alhaji Aminu and others who drowned in the river while working as volunteers, free of any remuneration to construct a bridge on the river, and to widen the IgbesaAyobo Captain Davis Road.

Igbesa community have continued to exert relentless volunteer efforts to bridge the river as far as their technical savvy and financial resources could carry them. The project deserves government attention and assistance. The government should help.

The construction of the bridge will enhance the economic standing of residents of Igbesaland and environs tremendously. Hopefully, the government will help Igbesa to construct a bridge over the river soon just as exPresident Obasanjo helped to construct bridges to connect Agbara Estate, Igbesa with Atan-Ota during his tenure as Military Head of State from 1976 to 1979. Igbesans remember the kindness and remain grateful to exPresident Obasanjo.

In the past, many Nigerians had to travel tens of miles to go to secondary/high schools, but in recent years, the establishment of many private universities, technical colleges and polytechnics in communities within reasonable and walking distance was a great credit to Obasanjo Administration.

The establishment of Crawford University, Igbesa; Ogun State Polytechnic, Igbesa and Technical College, Igbesa makes an invaluable difference in the development of the people of Igbesa community socio-economically and politically. Nigerians should support government's economic and political reforms in order to stop corruption, fraud, money laundering, illegal oil bunkering and other economic and financial crimes so that there will be abundance of money saved for project development in Nigerian localities. Nigeria is potentially strong and great.

GOD/ALLAH BLESS NIGERIA!

CHAPTER 8

REDUCING THE MENACE OF UNEMPLOYMENT

In Nigeria, there is no unemployment insurance cheque; there is no welfare cheque and there is no unemployment benefit. The situation is no work, no pay. Hence, unemployment or joblessness is moneylessness. How unemployed people survive in Nigeria is mysterious, puzzling and incomprehensible. Extended family system helps a lot. Friends also help.

There is no provision for governmental intervention. One expected that Nigerian leaders, legislators, ministers of labour and labour leaders since Nigerian independence in 1960, are fully aware of labour laws and benefits for employed and the unemployed in the USA and UK. They should have done something remarkable to help, but they never did. They often think about what will go into their own private pockets and not how to relieve the pains of the people on whose backs they ride to the top.

For decades, old laws were not reviewed and new laws are hardly enacted. The 1999 Nigerian constitution that is full of discrepancies remains unamended for years, year in, year out. Instead of planning about how to feed, house, educate and keep people safe and healthy; how people should and should not dress was given prominence in the legislative house for the sake of religious faith. How can anybody have true and genuine religious faith if the person is not of great service to the people and humanity?

Government functionaries know that government interventionist programmes exist in Europe and America, but nobody has ever suggested a way of assistance to the unemployed, senior citizens, unemployed parents of children, the disabled, the poor etc., not one time in forty-eight years. It is horrible to watch utter neglect of the needy in a country that is blessed with abundant natural resources.

Instead of utilizing available national resources to help the poor, elites often fraudulently enrich themselves, loot and launder government money overseas into their private bank accounts. It is sad to suffer neglect and deprivation in the midst of enormous blessed national resources.

Since there is no government subsidy, unemployment in Nigeria has a resultant effect of hunger, homelessness, suffering and humiliations. Hence, the unemployed are angry, ready to explode, revolt, commit crimes, arson, vandalize government infrastructures, sabotage government efforts, commit armed robbery, kill, kidnap for ransom, commit illegal oil bunkering and smuggle contrabands. The unemployed also traffick in human beings, commit illegal migration, involve in illegal drugs, commit fraud, corruption, become ungovernable, create gangs, form cults, insurgency, militancy, suicide bombing, damn life, become extremely violent and destructive at the least or no provocation.

Government functionaries mismanage the nation's wealth or resources. They pay in full for contracts that are not started but abandoned and they receive kickbacks for unduly inflated contracts with impunity. The practice of corruption and frauds pervades all spheres of activities of private and government operations by elites and nothing is left for the common people to start a good living.

If the masses are gainfully employed, everybody will be busy; crimes will be minimal and security of persons and possessions will be assured. If the government seriously embarks on programmes that encourage profitable investment and employment generation, the people's problems will be minimal and get easily solved.

On Monday, August 4, 2008, the Independent Corrupt Practices and other Related Offences Commission (ICPC) Chairman, Justice Emmanuel Ayoola announced that it snatched a fraudulent unemployment syndicate, which allegedly collected ₦22 million as bribe from about 140 job applicants who applied for jobs with the Nigerian Prison Service (NPS) and the Nigerian Immigration Service (NIS).

The Presidency, Legislature and Judiciary should view this case and similar cases seriously and apply deterrent measures that can eliminate bribery and corruption from Nigerian society. In a country with high unemployment rate, those who take bribe of this magnitude from applicants for jobs are merciless. Such offenders do not deserve any mercy.

The syndicate was said to be operating a special bank account into which each job applicant deposited hundreds of thousands of naira before being considered for government jobs. The bank account should be seized and government should encourage victims in this case and any other cases to come forward to facilitate the arrest, indictment, prosecution and conviction of offenders. The government should legislate against all abuses in job placement. Unemployment rate cannot reduce if bribery and corruption situation of that magnitude continues unchecked in job placements.

Unemployment rate in Nigeria is double-digit compared with the USA unemployment rate of about 5 percent in worst times. If it is true that only ten percent of National Youth Service Corps college/university graduates can be employed annually as mentioned by the former Minister of Labour, then it will be real to deduce that unemployment rate in Nigeria is very high at double-digit. Unfortunately, the former Minister of Education wrongly claimed that Nigerian university graduates were unemployable. Unemployment is the bane of evil deeds in many countries in the developing world.

Unemployment rate is the percentage of number of unemployed divided by the number of the labour force. The labour force represents all residents of the nation minus residents under 16 years minus adults that are institutionalized minus discouraged workers who are no longer looking for work because they are tired and frustrated of looking for jobs and they have given up for not finding a job.

Unemployment rate figures and adjustments should be compiled, reviewed and released daily by the Ministry of Labour and Productivity in comparison with what obtains in developed countries so that the

Nigerian government can constantly review and reduce the menace of unemployment periodically and progressively. The President and the Legislature should provide for those who are unemployed, senior citizens and the disabled in line with what governments do for their people in civilized communities of the world.

There is no unemployment insurance benefit in Nigeria at this time; maybe it will be initiated and implemented sooner than later by the government in the best interest of workers. There are a lot of benefits for workers about which the labour leaders should be talking and negotiating with the government amicably and peacefully instead of aligning with opposition political parties to confront the government on issues of politics. With friendship, dialogue, conciliation and understanding, more benefits can be achieved for Nigerian workers.

Labour union leaders should be involved in employment research and be partners in progress with the government on employment generation. Workers generally belong to different political parties; so, their leadership cannot afford to play partisan politics when they are still serving as labour union leaders. Labour leaders should work hand in hand cooperatively with the government to reduce illegal oil bunkering, smuggling, fraud, corruption, economic and financial crimes, strikes and lockouts because of their adverse multiplier effects on workers and employment generation.

Unemployment in Nigeria can be categorized under five main headings of (1) Frictional (2) Structural, (3) Seasonal, (4) Cyclical, and (5) Retrenchment. Government should identify, research, and minimize the ripple effects of these categories of unemployment in Nigeria. Find out what civilized countries do to help their people and just take actions to help Nigerians.

Career guidance, counseling, research, training and development should be provided at government expense for people without jobs. Different programmes should be available to assist laid off employees or those looking for jobs. There should be human resource centres where those looking for jobs can use the computers to go into the internet to view vacant positions in many companies, and they can use the telephones, faxes and copying machines free to assist them to secure jobs.

The federal and state governments of Nigeria should create resource centres. Reducing unemployment rate and increasing employees' welfare and benefits should be areas of priority of focus and research for labour leaders instead of involving in partisan political games. You can achieve a lot for workers only if you work closely with the government.

Unemployed Nigerians face a lot of odds. They face hunger and inability to pay for their rented accommodation. They face the risk of being ejected from rented homes as well as inability to provide essential basic facilities for themselves and their families. They live under terrible conditions without hope of assistance. This should be an area of concern to the President, the Legislature and the NLC.

They should find out what is done best in civilized countries and do the same for Nigerians. There were cases of those who had jobs but were not paid any salaries for over six months. There were pensioners who were not paid for over two years. It was observed that some pensioners, who were hungry, collapsed and died while waiting to collect part of their pensions. Given these situations, are Nigerian Leaders compassionate, empathetic and really sensitive to the plights of their suffering countrymen, women and children?

During the inauguration speech of ExPresident Obasanjo on May 29, 2003, for the beginning of his second term in office, he emphasized that unemployment problem was one of the main priorities of his administration. He mentioned, "We note with appreciation that our efforts to encourage small and medium scale industries has so far attracted substantial amount of funds from commercial banks. We will press ahead with our plans to make this sector of the industry a vital segment for jobs and income for a large number of Nigerians." The Nigerian Labour Congress (NLC) should constantly monitor and work for the progress of this government initiative with the banks so that more jobs are available for workers.

The high rate of unemployment in Nigeria has encouraged the commission of violent crimes such as smuggling, human trafficking, bribery, corruption, armed robbery, killings of innocent people, frauds, prostitution, economic and financial crimes and other illegal acts. High rate of unemployment has caused socio-economic and political instability, decreases in product demand, ill health, lower standard of living, decrease in quality of life and has reduced life expectancy in Nigeria.

Unemployment has encouraged illegal migration of Nigerian students, academicians and professionals thereby causing severe brain drain for Nigeria. In effect, unemployment has caused men and women who were trained in Nigeria, and whose education was subsidized by Nigerian tax payers, to travel overseas to seek greener pastures and the Golden Fleece, but only to be doubly disappointed.

They are disappointed because they cannot find jobs in their own country; and in overseas countries, majority of them can only find menial jobs for subsistence living quite below their qualifications, experience and expectations. They therefore have to suffer to make ends meet doing the dirtiest job that has no relevance to their academic attainments and professionalism. For example, many Nigerians overseas with university/ college degrees find themselves unavoidably engaged as taxi drivers, truck drivers, forklift drivers, security guards, nursing aids, dietary aids, clerks, cashiers or sales clerks in order to make ends meet.

In essence, many qualified Nigerians who find themselves in that situation are robbed of professional development personally, and they are at a loss to their country where they initially trained without job opportunities being provided for them. Employment generation in Nigeria is not difficult if those charged with the responsibility have the technical savvy, the right training and experience to accomplish the goals and objectives of full employment.

In civilized countries, unemployment rate is monitored daily to check and control its fluctuations. What are the labour leaders and the Ministry of Labour doing daily to reduce unemployment rate? That is a question that must be satisfactorily answered in order to reduce the menace of unemployment in Nigeria.

On January 17, 2003, about twenty-six Nigerians including a couple and their two children perished by drowning in the Atlantic Ocean while illegally migrating to Europe in search of greener pastures when they were passing through the coastal town of Tangier, Morocco, North Africa. It was said that the deceased clandestinely boarded an engine powered boat after paying huge sums of money to human trafficking barons in Morocco to arrange the journey. These illegal Nigerian immigrants continued to see Morocco and some other North African countries as transit centres and gateways to Europe through illegal routes.

The incident of January 17, 2003 was just one of too many accidents befalling Nigerian illegal immigrants to Europe and America. They died of exhaustion, cold, hunger and lack of medication. Some illegal Nigerian immigrants are even falling and dying as prey of fellow Nigerian illegal immigrants who constituted themselves into dangerous cults such as Yoruba Aso Rock, Ibo Stone Cold, Edo Delta Aso Rock, Eagle Square, etc. Usually, illegal Nigerian immigrants in Europe, America and other foreign countries often suffer untold hardships and humiliations living in hideouts trying to escape intensified police arrest, interrogation and eventual deportation.

Above all, their Nigerian accents subject them to various levels of discriminatory treatment, humiliation and lower ratings than their counterparts from the Western World even though these Nigerians may be more smart, more brilliant and better qualified academically and professionally. Sometimes they are ridiculously told that they do not understand English even though, glaringly, they speak classical English language, write, read and understand English language better than those who underrate them.

There is great need for government intervention to reduce unemployment rate. Unemployment has a multiplier effect of impoverishing families generationally. Such generational poverty breeds violence, promotes violent crimes of robbery and killings of innocent people. Unemployment kills initiative, intelligence and motivation; creates family dysfunctionalization, breaks marriages, impoverishes and lowers a person's personality, confidence, standard of living and life expectancy.

Unemployment could change a good, happy, middle class person into a bad, unhappy, poor one. As a result of unemployment, a good tenant could turn into a bad one; a lawful person could change into a criminal or unlawful person. It could destroy a person's total brilliant, prosperous life and make one suicidal and homicidal.

Unemployment could create anger toward oneself, the people and one's nation. Unemployment is a disease that could make a hungry man, an angry man. It could encourage militancy and revolution against constituted authorities of one's nation and the entire world. An unemployed person would hate the whole world and question God/Allah as to why he/she was ever born into the world to suffer.

Unemployment promotes idleness, cultism, gangsterism, illwill, illness, use and sale of illegal drugs, vandalization of national infrastructures and facilities, and it could lead the unemployed to commit economic and financial crimes. Unemployment of youths in the Niger Delta has been primarily responsible for the insurgency, militancy, kidnappings for ransom, trafficking in illegal drugs, weapons, illegal oil bunkering, arson, killings, anarchy etc.

To underestimate the problems and effects of high rate of unemployment in Nigeria is a disservice, a time bomb and a calamity in the making. The militancy and destruction of lives and property that have plagued the Niger Delta of Nigeria by youths is partially the result of unemployment.

Therefore, employment generation in Nigeria must be a priority. Full employment is not a difficult goal to accomplish in Nigeria if the rich, the elites, the leaders in government and the people are fully prepared to face the challenge to solve this national chronic malaise. The solution requires full cooperation of the government with the private sector as well as the provision of necessary facilities and infrastructures that are appropriate for full employment.

The government must fully fund and execute programmes that provide enabling environment for employment generation. Lower interest rate will increase borrowing, increase business activities, increase money velocity, create new small business owners, generate employment and uplift the middle class and the masses.

In one of the speeches of ExPresident Obasanjo in February 2003 when launching 'Africa Recruit' organized by the Commonwealth Business Council in London, ExPresident Obasanjo acknowledged that the main constraints inhibiting the development of Africa was the dearth of skilled perssonnel occasioned by massive emigration of academicians and professionals from the continent.

ExPresident Obasanjo also acknowledged and appreciated the quantum and quality of Nigerian professionals and academicians, resident and working overseas, whose expertise and services were direly needed for national development. He wished that African countries could be positively harnessed for the best interest of the continent of Africa.

He mentioned that 'Africa Recruit' programme gave practical vent and credence to the objectives of the New Partnership for Africa's Development (NEPAD). He urged Africans in Diaspora and the leaders in the private and public sectors to cooperate and ensure that Africa Recruit programmes and NEPAD succeed.

In his own observations at a workshop in August 2003, the former Minister of Labour and Productivity, Alhaji Husseni Akwanga represented by the Deputy Director, Mrs. Comfort Feyisetan, asserted that increasing social tension in Nigeria was causing slow pace and becoming a clog in the wheel of progress in the nation's economic development and prosperity.

In another vein, ExPresident Obasanjo made many trips to many foreign heads of governments soliciting for trade expansion and investment in Nigeria. A successful industrialization of Nigeria would eliminate or minimize the attendant problems of unemployment in the country. To minimize the effects of unemployment such as hunger and poverty, the President invited about 500 Chinese agricultural experts to Nigeria with emphasis that doors were open to Chinese pharmaceutical and construction companies. The main goal of his efforts was to achieve selfsufficiency in food production and accomplishment of full employment for Nigerians.

With full employment, the potential real gross domestic product (GDP) of Nigeria will be realized. Presently, the GDP gap which is calculated as potential real GDP minus actual real GDP is very wide because there are too many Nigerians who qualify, able and willing to work, but they cannot get jobs. In the interest of the nation, solving unemployment problems should be the priority of the government, the private sector and all stakeholders of employment toward full employment.

It is very important to increase oil and nonoil receipts by minimizing labour disputes (strikes and lockouts), civil strife and maintaining industrial harmony in order to generate and stabilize employment. It is also significant to maintain health and safety of persons and possessions as well as eliminate fraud, corruption, economic and financial crimes which can adversely affect employment if not checked.

The former Vice Chancellor of Babcock University, Ilishan Remo, Ogun State, Professor Adekunle Alalade was quoted to have said that so many things had gone wrong with the nation's education system that it made employers to become too skeptical to employ graduates of Nigerian universities. In the first place, where are the employers to absorb even the best Nigerian students where hardly ten percent of graduating students can find work yearly! That is one of the causes of brain drain from Nigeria to overseas countries.

At the sixth matriculation ceremony of the university, Professor Alalade was quoted to have said, "Until the nation's academic structures focus not only on needs but also on discipline, service driven as well as functional and holistic philosophy of education, the decay would persist." Professor Alalade was quoted to have lamented that pseudosystems had been established for the evaluation of knowledge, validation of learning and commendation of achievements.

He added, "Industry leaders and the Nigerian boardrooms are just about giving up on the hiring of fresh engineering graduates who have never touched an engine and Masters Degree of Business Administration who can hardly manage themselves."

The problems pointed out by Professor Alalade are hard to believe, but the students are not to blame even if there is no exaggeration by the Vice Chancellor. The problems highlighted are not difficult to fix if Nigerian educators work harder; stay on the job teaching instead of playing politics and soliciting for private business; review and redesign educational programmes to include more practical work of industrial attachment especially for students who are graduating.

What about academic democracy whereby students have a say in the running of the university? They should be able to see what is lacking or lagging and point it out without penalties. Professors and other educators should not see students as boys and girls and treat them as such, but the students should be regarded as young men and young women who should be respected and treated as future leaders of Nigeria.

Surprisingly, Nigeria students that are bashed daily, demeaned, condemned and put down all the time by their professors and so called employers, become the best performers among their colleague students and/or workers when they get to overseas countries at undergraduate,

graduate and post graduate levels, as well as when gainfully employed and trained in overseas industrial establishments.

When will the culture change among Nigerian elites and even those highly educated from being completely negative and seeing little or nothing good in Nigeria and Nigerians except themselves? Nigerian elites are bossy, proud and hardly see anything good in their subordinates except themselves. They like to put others down negatively. In civilized communities worldwide, the new trend is positive reinforcement and not the mentality of uncontrolled negativity.

In civilized environments, the situation is different where politicians, academicians, educators, professionals and others move from being positiveminded to completely change a negative situation into something completely positive and admirable. At what level will complaints stop for serious work within available limited time and resources?

Professors, educators, academicians and professionals of merit always motivate, inspire, impart knowledge and exemplarize positively instead of issuing outright condemnations all the time. Where are the good examples they are showing Nigerian students to emulate? A student who is never reinforced positively will go from good to bad and worse to worst.

Nigerian educators at all levels need complete reorientation in positive reinforcement programmes. Students need to be taught how to respect by giving them respect. African culture on tradition that makes the boss or fathers and seniors to first notice only what is wrong in everything and emphasize it without reinforcing what has been done right is an impediment to African rapid development. That must change.

Education presently receives substantial allocations and attention more than ever before, yet there are complaints everywhere and everyday because those who are in charge do not settle down on the job to fix the problems. It is a bad workman who quarrels with his tools. If educators do their work well instead of incessant strike actions for months yearly with the best designed curriculum coupled with effective supervision of its implementation, then all engineering graduates would have touched many engines before graduation and all holders of Masters of Business Administration degree would be able to manage themselves and get certified to manage businesses prior to graduation.

Where and what is the pride, commitment and knowledge of the teacher, instructor, lecturer, professor or vice chancellor if any of his/her engineering graduating students has never touched an engine and if his/her MBA graduating student cannot manage himself/herself nor manage a small business? That cannot be the fault of the student, the parents nor the government.

Educators should stop buck passing because these Nigerian students are best when they get overseas in the classroom or industry. Nigerian educators and the employers who condemn graduating students need to come to the USA to see how students are treated with dignity, decency and respect even though they are not better than Nigerian students that Nigerian educators usually condemn.

The Black Person is constantly abused, denigrated, stereotyped, put down, relegated to the background and inferiorized. The Black Person is psychologically and mentally tortured daily and always told to be unfit and not good by other races. Why can't Nigerian elites change the situation? According to President Obasanjo, "Those who do not see anything good in others, may not be good themselves. It is a bad workman who quarrels with his tools.

Free primary education of Chief Obafemi Awolowo, first Premier of Western Nigeria, and that of Alhaji Lateef Jakande of Lagos State, succeeded even though it started under sheds, huts, trees, etc. without any necessary infrastructure that are available as at today because the educators during the time of Chief Awolowo and Alhaji Jakande in the 1950's to 1980's were fully committed to make it work.

Why not first look for how best to help the students within available resources rather than looking for what the government should provide which is not available or how you can personally benefit most as educators? Student development should be first priority to educators within the resources available. If educators mix their profession with business and politics, then education suffers, and students will suffer too.

Pilots and Flight Attendants of a prominent airline in the USA gave up a high percentage of their pay and benefits to keep their jobs and their airline out of bankruptcy. That is a great sacrifice to the nation and the airline. Educators' incessant strikes for months yearly, resulted in many students spending many more years in the universities while many others who withdrew and went overseas as illegal immigrants have not been able to continue their education up till today for lack of funds.

Educators as professionals dealing with youth development should not have staged incessant strike actions of recent years, which jeopardized the upbringing of youths, the future leaders of Nigerian nation. Even if the government or education authorities are short of being completely responsible, strike actions which disrupt the lives of Nigerian youths should not have been an option or a solution to disputes within the academic community.

Where is the commitment and sacrifice for youth development, which can be heavenly rewarded without being engaged in business or politics when they should be teaching in the classroom? How many professors in America are in business and politics hardly any! American professors stay in the classroom and teach the students until they get it. Is that what is happening in Nigeria? No! Professorship is a school classroom appointment and not in business, politics nor money making adventures.

One expects education authorities in Nigeria to solve students' problems instead of condemning them. What about examination malpractices encouraged by some educators to make money? What about some educators who sell handouts to their students? Is it so bad that people just want to make money at all costs? Where is the conscience and national consciousness if everybody has to participate in fraud, corruption, economic and financial crimes or any money making gimmick?

Where else should people look for exemplariness, patience, endurance, hard work, transparency, responsibility, accountability, responsiveness, intelligence and above all, the desire for youth development without money being a first consideration, if one cannot vouch for education professionals?

If Nigeria should have any fraudulent and corruption problems, educators should completely stay out of them and be above board because they are the greatest humane professionals anybody can think of. It does not matter what anybody becomes, he/she must have passed through an educator. It is the greatest and most noble profession, and it must be treated as such. Those who cannot keep it noble and unblemished should be kicked out of it.

With effective supervision and constant performance appraisal, the profession can be made clean and honourable. All human beings are subject of human imperfections, but the highest standard is expected from educators. It is the most noble profession, which is underrewarded all over the world including Britain and the USA, but educators in the USA still do their work well because of the sake of the youths they handle to lead in the future.

Discipline in institutions of higher learning have relaxed to the extent that cultism has posed terrible problem of killings. Cults easily recruit members, and they are able to threaten school authorities and students that are nonmembers. If events in these institutions make students busy and secure, they will not establish cults or join cults. They will rather do something else that is productive instead of joining cults.

Students that bribe with thousands of naira before getting admission cannot be respectful to the institution and its authorities. If educators are hardworking, transparent, disciplined and make clear to the students the dos and don'ts and the punishment, and show determination to solve students' problems by reducing their burden and frustration, cultism would lose its significance and become self-disbanding. If educational system is operated with corruption that torments students, they will form groups as a defence mechanism. Educators have to be disciplined to be able to enforce discipline assertively, justly, fairly and consistently. What about using the right intelligence efforts that tell authorities about who is doing what, and what he is doing wrong?

An effective monitoring of activities with immediate follow up action will foil wrong thoughts and actions against established policies at source, preemptively and deterrently. First and foremost, educators must first put themselves and the institutions in order. Reformation from the top hierarchy can flow down easily and result in a total package of perfectly cleaned educational systems and services. Educators should encourage a decent, disciplined and exemplary learning environment and minimize complaints. Educators must be exemplary to the students in particular and to society in general.

The scandals within the education sector could have adverse effects on the students. If the education sector had to bribe with ₦55 million before its budget could be approved by legislative education committees, what then would be left for student development? These young students see that their educators (teachers, instructors, lecturers, professors, etc.) are doing wrong things corruptly, which make them demoralized, disappointed and frustrated.

Where are the good examples for them to follow if they have to bribe to obtain JAMB admission forms, bribe to pass examinations, bribe to be admitted to universities and bribe to secure hostels? Where are the incorruptible mentors and role models in the institutions for the students to follow other than joining gangs and cults as a defence mechanism? Nigerian students have suffered enough bashing and humiliations. School authorities should start to reform themselves so that Nigerians can have hope on the students who are future leaders of the country.

Something drastic must be done expeditiously to save the public service through reforms by structural reorganization and rationalization. Retire them en mass, train and support them on small business management so that they can utilize their gratuity and pension to establish small businesses and generate employment. They should be replaced with university and college graduates to close the chapters of nonperformers and clean the public sector of mediocrity.

Retiring people without paying them and supporting them to be better of is inhuman and is like sending them to their untimely death as well as enhancing generational poverty. The mass retirement policy adopted by previous regimes from the time of General Murtala Mohammed should be reexamined to ensure that retirees are treated as senior citizens honourably as in the USA and not like criminals for not paying them their benefits that are due.

There should be no excuses for not paying retirees except if those making excuses are not sympathetic or empathic and are not human beings. Paying workers, pensioners, and contractors for a good job promptly helps economic development, alleviates poverty and reduces criminal tendencies. Ironically, some of those withholding pensioners' emoluments are themselves pensioners in political offices who receive their own pensions regularly, while those of them who are not pensioners will one day join the bandwagon and chorus of pensioners.

At the award ceremony dinner to mark Nigeria Civil Service Day on Wednesday, June 23, 2004, ExPresident Obasanjo was said to have shown that he was appalled by the contents of the reports on the selfreview pilot studies conducted on some of the key government ministries. The report was said to have indicated that the existing civil service was decadent and corrupt.

As a result, ExPresident Obasanjo strongly felt there was a need for an 'efficient and precision-driven' civil service and that only young minds could accomplish the vision contained in his government's reform agenda. In order to effect sufficient changes in the direction of the public service, the president was said to have directed the Head of Service to recruit young graduates from tertiary institutions with first class performance into the civil service.

ExPresident Obasanjo believed strongly in the capabilities of the Nigerian tertiary institutions' graduates. He said, "With their ambition, motivation, creativity and capacity to learn, they will be the high flyers that will move civil service into the contemporary age of precision-driven efficiency and effectiveness." That line of thought is very true and motivational to Nigerian university and college graduates.

On Friday, June 25, 2004, at the lecture activities marking the seventy-fifth anniversary of the Government College, Umuahia, just a few days after ExPresident Obasanjo came out and said the nicest things about graduates from Nigerian tertiary institutions and raised their hopes, his former Minister of Education, Professor Fabian Osuji, was alleged to have said that Nigerian university graduates were not employable as captioned in the *Punch* of Monday, June 28, 2004.

The exEducation Minister's statement was quoted, "The present graduates from the nation's universities could not access productive employment because they were bereft of the required competence and skills." Perhaps Professor Fabian Osuji did not realize that no matter how much an academician had learned or was taught in the classroom, there must be an on-the-job training that would determine his/her competence, skills and capabilities.

Honestly, if Professor Osuji had also gone through a well-organized orientation, he would not come out to debase Nigerian graduates. Also, if the former Minister knew what was going on in the world in recent times, regarding education, he would know that Nigerian graduates could not be brushed aside. They are highly intelligent and smart. What they lack is their lecturer who is busy looking after business enterprise or the professor chasing after political office. They are rated first class when they get overseas where they are appreciated by their fellow students, lecturers and professors.

Nigerian graduates at work overseas are usually rated as among the best. Why are Nigerians never fully acknowledged and appreciated in their own country? Many elites in Nigeria in all spheres of socio-economic, political and educational sectors are very selfcentred and thereby have been disrupting Nigerian progress and development.

Chief Obafemi Awolowo started to implement his educational and developmental programmes under shelters and thatched roofs in Western Nigeria in 1950s without all the infrastructures necessary. Today many of those who started education under shelters have become academicians and professionals of high repute. It is a bad workman who quarrels with his tools. We are all living witnesses to the unflinching commitment of educators to educational development in the 1950s, 1960s and 1970s.

What about some educators who sell handouts, get involved in examination malpractices, those who concentrate on their private business interests instead of teaching their students and those who go on strike for months on flimsy excuses at the expense of their students? Who should be blamed, the students or the educators? Nigerian students study under terrible conditions, but they make it and come out comparable with the best in the world if not excel them. If any Nigerian educator has not seen that happening in United Kingdom (UK) and United States of America (USA), such people still have a lot to learn outside their small academic environment.

The former Minister of Education was also reported to have said, "Today, we produce graduates who have no competence at all, no skills. Our graduates are without employment because they are not employable." That cannot be true. It runs counter to ExPresident Obasanjo's views stated above.

If academic standard is a big problem that is not exaggerated, what are the professors doing in business houses and political positions instead of the classrooms teaching, instructing and conducting extensive research work in academics where they belong in national interest? In all advanced countries, professorship is a teaching, classroom position and not in businesses or political appointments where professors do not have working experience.

The statements credited to the former Minister of Education as highlighted above are demotivational and could have cost him his job in developed or civilized communities, which believe strongly in positive reinforcement to compliment students' efforts always. Nigerians generally and Nigerian students in particular are no pushovers in all spheres of their endeavours throughout the world.

The pertinent questions for pessimists about Nigerian students' academic standing are, "Where are the jobs, and how many Nigerian graduates went through job orientation and on-the-job training programmes but failed to make it? How many Nigerian graduates transferred to overseas countries but failed to make it in class or at work? What is the yardstick for measuring the academic standing of the students who graduated, but which they did not meet before they were graduated by the university authorities?" The bottom line is, it is difficult to comprehend why and where any graduating student shares any blame if the university authorities find him/her competent to graduate and he/she is graduated by the university.

Professors in civilized countries like the USA stay in the classrooms to teach and engage in extensive and intensive research work that helps students learning and development toward future great leadership. Professors, lecturers and teachers do not go about pursuing business enterprises, money and politics at the expense of their students and the detriment of their noble teaching profession.

Professorship is a promotional post in the teaching profession in college, polytechnic or university and not in practical politics. One can be promoted from lecturer I to Senior lecturer, then to Assistant/Associate Professor and Professor with Bachelor's or Master's degree with relevant years of experience without going through the rigours of doctoral course work nor writing extensive, intensive and exhaustive dissertation for the Doctor of Philosophy (Ph.D.) degree.

The Professor, Lecturer or Instructor's expertise is best utilized in the classroom under academic environment and not under partisan political climate. It is majority opinion that professors who undergo Doctor of Philosophy (Ph.D.) course work are usually more open-minded, accessible and less prone to arrogance. It is relevant real life, practical political experience and not book knowledge alone that can make professors fit for political offices.

Youth development in the best interest of the nation is more important and more glorious to most academicians than politics, which many regard as dirty, and full of deceit in developed countries. Educators/academicians are very unique people because nobody becomes anything without going through them for learning and development. It is a noble profession greater than monetary value.

Partisan politics and academics are two different professions at opposite ends of a continuum. The most successful political leader may not have gone beyond the four years college education or equivalent qualification plus all relevant life experience. Where such a person succeeds in practical politics, a political science professor may fail woefully.

For example, it is worthwhile to critically examine and compare the statements of three great Nigerians on graduate students' employment in Nigeria. The three men are (1) ExPresident Obasanjo, (2) former Minister of Education, Professor Fabian Osuji, and (3) Professor Adekunle Alalade, former Vice Chancellor of Babcock University, Ilishan, Remo, Ogun State.

(1) <u>President Obasanjo</u>

To effect sufficient changes in the direction of the Public service, ExPresident Obasanjo directed the Head of Service to recruit young graduates from tertiary institutions with first class performance. He said, "With their ambition, motivation, creativity and capacity to learn, they will be high flyers that will move civil service into contemporary age of precision-driven efficiency and effectiveness."

The President's statement is fatherly, positively directed, visionary, developmental, motivational, empathic, and it demonstrated unique political maturity. Above all, it opened the door of opportunity to graduating students.

(2) <u>Former Minister of Education, Professor Fabian Osuji</u>

He said, "The present graduates from the nation's universities could not access productive employment because they were bereft of the required competence and skill." He added, "Today, we produce graduates who have no competence at all, no skills. Our graduates are without employment because they are not employable."

That is an arrogant, outright condemnation of the entire Nigerian studentship, especially those who have graduated after satisfying college/university requirements for a minimum of four years and have been certified to pass out. One can see that the former minister's statement looks youthful, immature, antisociopolitical, judgmental and capable of breeding student dissatisfaction, frustration, disaffection and unrest.

If the former minister's statement is not an exaggeration, who should be blamed? Who are those represented by 'we' who are producing graduates who have no competence, no skills? Job competence or skill comes after job orientation and on-the-job training for freshers. That is quite normal for all no matter what highest level of education anybody brings to a new job.

The statement is hopelessly negative; it demeans and bastardizes all the graduating students' efforts of four years minimum; the money, time and energy spent by their parents, their hopes and aspirations deemed as a waste; and it shatters the students as if they are not good for anything. It is outrageous.

If a Professor/exMinister of Education denigrated Nigerian University graduates as unemployable, how employable was he if he masterminded ₦55 million bribery scandals, which implicated him and some most distinguished Senators and House Members of the Education Committees of the Federal Legislature? Nigerian elites in glass houses should stop throwing stones as well as stop playing 'holier than thou attitude' and hypocrisy, and stop making cheap talk. People should look at themselves first; remove the specks in their own eyes before they accuse others of having dirt in their eyes.

The world has changed. Nobody in political office dares condemn anybody of youths like that anymore in civilized communities. If it happens in the USA, the legislature and the people will enforce the officer's resignation or dismissal. It is good to learn from others' mistakes and be a positive leader. A mature politician holding a political ministerial appointment would not talk like that without a second thought about possible serious sanctions and consequences. From above statement of Professor Osuji, it is easy to see his limited exposure, inexperience in politics as well as his empathilessness, youthful exuberance and arrogance.

(3) <u>Professor Adekunle Alalade, ExVice Chancellor of Babcock University</u>

He was alleged to have said that so many things had gone wrong that made employers become skeptical of employing graduates of Nigerian universities. He added, "Industry leaders and Nigerian boardrooms are just about giving up on the hiring of fresh engineering graduates who have never touched an engine and Master's of Business Administration degree (MBA) who can hardly manage themselves."

If that statement is true and not exaggerated, it may be either the curriculum is not well designed or those implementing it still have more areas to cover, and yet they passed the students for graduation. Why should any student(s) be graduating when an important element remains to be covered in the programme? Who should be blamed given that situation?

This statement credited to Professor Alalade cannot be politically correct. It debases Nigerian students very badly. It cannot be imagined that it is not an overexaggeration. Does it mean that graduating students did not meet all course work, graduation requirements, all tests and evaluations administered by the respective universities before they were passed for graduation? Whose fault is it if such case(s) existed? If the university authorities were not completely satisfied about a graduating student's performance, why was he/she graduated?

If it is specified in the engineering curriculum that the students should have touched an engine before graduating and that an MBA student should be able to manage himseld or herself before completing the programme, so be it. Was any student ever graduated without meeting university requirements for graduation? If yes, how could it have happened under the watch of the university authorities? If it did not happen, why were people crying wolf, wolf when there was none?

The Professor and former Minister of Education who masterminded the collection of ₦55 million bribe from various top government educational functionaries under his supervision and the top ranking legislators who demanded, accepted and shared the bribe among themselves committed a terrible scandal. It is most likely that this is a pattern of behaviour, and more cases will likely leak out.

Those leaders involved in the bribery scandal knew that they were totally wrong, so they returned their shares intact when the scandal burst open. Regrettably, those who championed this bribery scandal were among those who hypocritically complained loudest about the shortage of education facilities, the pitiable condition of educational infrastructures and the quality of education and graduates.

If a professor/minister could not redirect the bribe takers by telling them no, who else should? From where and whom is the highest ethics, professionalism and morality expected other than a professor who teaches students, the future leaders of Nigeria? By just having the courage to say, "No," Professor Osuji would have saved the Legislature and the Ministry of Education all the embarrassment of the scandal.

The world is a learning process. Nobody knows it all. Presidents, leaders, elders, ministers, vice chancellors, professors, doctors, graduating students up to and including the ordinary people keep learning all the time. Whoever stops learning is as good as dead. In the USA, education curriculum is designed inclusively to leave no child behind. Whatever Nigerian students do not know, but ought to know, should be taught, and when they know it, they then graduate. Above all, professors must stay in the classroom and teach what needs to be known with empathy, commitment and responsibility.

In the USA, under the college/university quarter calendar of twelve or thirteen weeks, students are tested and evaluated every three weeks. Students are given copies of the result and report for their comments. If at the end of the ninth week, a student is not told that he/she is failing and his/her parents notified immediately for a conference, then the professor, lecturer or instructor will have a lot of explaining to make to the university or college authorities and the student's parents or guardian, if the student fails during the twelfth week in the final quarterly examination. Such educator would be risking his or her job. In effect, the educator-professors, lecturers, etc. are busy testing and grading students' performance while the students are busy learning and taking direction.

In the USA, there is effective supervision of what the lecturers, professors and other academic staff are doing. Students are also closely and effectively supervised for sightseeing, field studies and industrial attachments. Everybody works harder for every penny received. It is always no work, no pay. There is academic freedom as well as academic discipline.

At the end of every three weeks when the students are tested and evaluated, the students are served with questionnaires to comment on the lecturer, professor or instructor's work and relationship with the students without disclosing their names on their answers to the questionnaires. If the educator is scored low by majority of the students, he or she will be replaced at the end of the quarter or semester.

US academic systems are truly democratic. The professor evaluates the performance of the students, so also the students are opportuned to assess their professor's overall performance and relationship to the students. In democratic Nigeria, democratic academic process should strictly apply similarly to what obtains in the USA.

With many private universities springing up, there will be competition, and service will improve or there will be consequences. Nigerian universities and colleges should establish career guidance and counseling division and research, training and development division within the human resource department to help students on employment matters and other issues that may confront them.

An unemployment report allegedly published by the *Punch News* on Wednesday, March 3, 2004 was quite revealing. In it, the Kwara State Director of the National Drug Law Enforcement Agency (NDLEA), Mr. Soji Sodeke discovered that unemployment among youths was the major cause of increased trafficking in narcotic drugs. It was revealed that most narcotic drug offenders were fouryear college/university frustrated graduates who were suffering from the chronic effects of joblessness. Nigerian youths are not lazy if there is a job to do, but unemployment has increased over the years as a result of the nation's economic fluctuations.

Unfortunately, a lot of government money that could be used for investment, development and employment generation are stashed in private bank accounts of elites in overseas countries. Students are made the scapegoats. Hardly ten percent of college/university fouryear graduates who have completed the one year National Youth Service Corps (NYSC) get employed. About fifteen million youths are alleged to be unemployed according to the National Youth Council, a nongovernmental organization, yet, the elites do not care, and it is sad.

If school dropouts, deaf and dumb and those with other disabilities are employable and employed in the USA, then, it is sheer ignorance and lack of the right education of any person who says that Nigerian graduates are unemployable.

Joblessness has been identified as responsible for Nigeria's endemic social ills. Over one hundred thousand jobs were reported lost between 1999 and 2003. The Ministry of Labour and Productivity should be able to publish unemployment figures periodically to authenticate this well publicized report. Four industrial sectors were reported to be the most affected which were (1) food, beverage and tobacco; (2) chemical, rubber and leather; (3) nonmetallic products; and (4) textile industries, according to the United Nations Industrial Development Organization (UNIDO).

The private sector which is the largest provider of employment was reported to have suffered setbacks as a result of high cost of raw materials, high cost of energy and its epileptic supply, decrepit infrastructure, obsolete machinery, prohibitive cost of securing loanable funds, uncertain investment climate, safety and security problems, uncertain business environment, smuggling and dumping of cheap imported goods from other countries. Hence, where are the jobs for which the graduating students were tested, given job orientation and they failed? None! Those who have been blaming the students, graduates and the educational system have been blaming the wrong horse.

To help local industrialization and boost employment generation, the government has been seriously battling above-mentioned problems. It has prohibited the importation of majority of items that can be produced locally in Nigeria, but the protectionism and government's wise counsel increased smuggling activities, which the government must fight and beat decisively for its economic reforms to succeed.

Government must provide sufficient incentive to encourage youths who abandoned farming to return to the land to practise agriculture. Agriculture must be fully revived and equal emphasis must be placed on nonoil producing sector as done for the oil and gas sectors. Nigerian oil refineries must be revived, made to work at full capacity and expanded to eliminate the importation of petroleum products that can be produced locally. Such progressive step will save Nigeria some foreign exchange, strengthen Nigerian currency, increase foreign reserve and generate employment reasonably.

Nigeria is very rich in solid mineral resources, so, it must embark on their commercial exploration. Agriculture production must be given priority to enable Nigeria to feed her population selfsufficiently and minimize the importation of food items. The craze for fertilizer, its importation and impact on foreign exchange expenditure is heavy and ridiculous. Nigeria has fertile land naturally which can be boosted by local production of fertilizers using Nigerian available raw materials and resources to further generate employment.

The government must strongly pursue its deregulation policies but with focus on initially improving on necessary facilities and infrastructures that will create the right enabling business climate and make the deregulation process work in the best interest of Nigerians. The antiinvestment monopoly laws that restrain business entry into industries like the Nigerian National Petroleum Company (NNPC), the Nigerian Railway, Mining, Telecommunications, Land Use, and other similar acts should be reviewed to encourage the entry of local and foreign investments into these sectors.

What if the government embarks on establishing resource development centres in each Nigerian local government area which will conduct research into unemployment problems; train unemployed people and pensioners in entrepreneurship; help them with tools to establish small scale businesses and nurture them to success?

All these steps that give fillip to the private sector will generate employment; increase the opportunities for human development; reduce antisocial behaviours; reduce threat to national security; minimize or eliminate brain drain; curb illegal immigration and increase desired business, socio-economic and political attitude of Nigerians!

Above all, the government must fight and eliminate acts of fraud, corruption and economic and financial crimes prevalent among government functionaries at all levels of government to save its gains for national development. The conduit pipes for money laundering, stealing and stashing Nigerian government money in foreign banks must be blocked successfully. Illegal oil bunkering and oil pipelines vandalization must be stopped. The government must ensure socio-economic and political stability and maintain the security of persons and possessions to the fullest at all cost. These measures, if taken seriously and transparently, will become effective permanent panaceas for Nigerian employment problems.

In the USA, resource centres are established by government to help unemployed people find work. The resource centres provide career guidance and counseling, employers' contacts, research, training and development facilities, help draft resumes and prepare unemployed people for job interviews. They provide computers, papers, telephones, facsimiles and copy machines for free use on employment purposes.

They contact employers on behalf of unemployed people and arrange for vacant positions effectively. They help to arrange career change. They help unemployed to secure loans or grants to go for further studies in colleges or trade schools or to float small businesses. They arrange payment of unemployment insurance benefits to unemployed people for six months or until they find jobs whichever comes first.

There are over twenty human resources development centres established by government and private employment agencies spread out in Fort Worth, Texas alone, a town that is the size of Agege/Ikeja in Lagos State, Nigeria. What then is the work of the Ministry of Labour and Productivity if after forty years of Nigerian independence; above-mentioned services are not available closest to all unemployed Nigerians?

It is regrettable that some government functionaries buckpassingly blame students and graduates for being unemployable instead of blaming themselves for lack of initiatives to generate employment and fit students into work since over forty years of Nigerian independence.

It is also regrettable that NYSC graduates were told that only ten percent of them could find jobs after spending a minimum of four years in college or university plus one year of national service. Who is to blame for not sitting down, working hard, planning and fixing the problem of unemployment when even dropouts from high schools, colleges and universities in the USA and UK find jobs and earn a living? There are no jobs because the wrong people are still in the right places almost half of a century after Nigerian Independence of October 1, 1960. Chief Awolowo created jobs all over Western Nigeria and made education almost free in all sectors.

The primary purpose, objective and responsibility of any government is to provide services to the people. Government functionaries should stop acting as the people's bosses or acting as being superior to the people but as providers of services with humility and commitment to serve the people exemplarily. Where is the initiative to provide and expand such services as it is done committedly with sophistication in developed countries? Where is the researchablility to give Nigerians accurate rate of unemployment and its diminishing rate projection for short and long terms on basis of efforts toward employment generation now and in the future? What is the hope of the unemployed?

Government work can no longer be what it used to be or done how it used to be done, the same old way. It must be developing and moving to meet people's modern needs. Nigerian government services should be reorganized and rationalized to meet the collective aspirations of a rapidly developing Nigeria, the Blacks' greatest country in the world.

It is not sufficient to lay people off without providing avenues for alternatives for them by retraining them for the private sector with financial assistance so that, as human beings, they do not lose hope and rot away. Their retraining and financial assistance can make them employers of labour as entrepreneurs.

On November 5, 2003, it was reported in the *Guardian News* that Nigeria and some developing countries that were investment strapped, made a net transfer of $200 billion (₦25.8 trillion) to other countries with economically advanced status. The United Nations former Secretary-General, Kofi Annan remarked that such situation lacked common sense. He added that funds that could be promoting investment and growth in developing countries or building schools and hospitals were instead being transferred abroad. The situation was described as the paradox of the proverbial desert dweller that was shipping water to rain soaked forest region. It is like taking coal to Newcastle, which already has an abundance of it.

The government should do everything possible to discourage this 'capital flight' which could have been utilized for investment purposes to generate employment and boost the economy. With full employment, crime rate will be minimal and safety and security will be reasonably enhanced.

The challenging question to government, especially the Ministry of Labour and Productivity is, "When will Nigeria have an accurate count of unemployment rate that will be below six percent?" That is a task that must be done; it is a goal that must be accomplished. Labour Ministry officials must constantly reach out to employers of labour both private and public sectors, on employment generation as well as provide adequate facilities and necessary assistance to all those who are able and willing to be employed.

Unemployment rate must be monitored daily to see progress being achieved toward full employment. Much must be done to alleviate the sufferings of unemployed people, pensioners and senior citizens in Nigeria. The government should emulate the good things that are being done to humanity in the developed world to make life easier and better for Nigerians. No Nigerian should be left behind to rot in the forward march going on.

In the *Guardian* of July 26, 2005, some industry chiefs described the performance of Nigerian University graduates in recent years as abysmal. Mr. Keith Richards, the Managing Director and Chief Executive Officer of Guinness Nigeria Ltd. was reported to have said that on a visit to one of the country's universities, he discovered that it had no computers. If that situation is correct, what companies like Guinness in civilized nations usually do is to donate money generously to such institutions and communities or provide needed computers as many as required by such institutions and communities.

Civilized company executives do not go out to mock or denigrate products or graduates of such institutions. Guinness Company has made a lot of money in Nigeria with great profits, and as such, has moral obligations to engage committedly in educational and community development.

In similar fashion, if the foreign oil companies have not neglected their moral responsibilities to the oil producing areas of the South-South of Nigeria, the youth militancy that resulted in many killings would have been avoided. The oil companies have made a lot of profit and exploited the Niger Deltans without embarking on serious policies of employment generation, minimization of pollution hazards and the welfare of the people. What multinational companies get away with in Nigeria cannot happen in the western advanced countries without severe consequences and penalties.

Nigerian government should ensure that companies that make money in Nigeria fulfill their legal and moral obligations to Nigeria. Industry chiefs have a moral obligation to students before, during and after graduation, and they must stop their vituperations that denigrate Nigerian students and graduates. It is a bad workman who quarrels with his tools.

The Chief Executive of the UAC Nigeria Ltd., Mr. Ayo Ajayi, was reported to have described as embarrassing, the deteriorating quality of graduates from the country's tertiary institutions. He was said to have wondered whether the graduates seeking job opportunities actually passed out from secondary schools. It may be asked how many Nigerian university graduates the UAC Nigeria employed who were given quality job orientation and training but failed!

The mentality of many industry chiefs and others who never attained university degree qualifications other than honourary degrees is usually to denigrate those who worked hard to obtain a university degree for a minimum of four years. How many university graduates work for the UAC Nigeria since its incorporation? Except if things have changed for the better, UAC Nigeria was used to recruiting old hands with secondary school education. How many university graduates are in top management in the UAC (Nigeria) to make it easy to properly determine the true quality of Nigerian university graduates and whether they actually passed out from secondary schools? If the industry chiefs actually made the statements that put down Nigerian graduates, they must have spoken out of sheer empty arrogance and superiority complex. Did the industry chiefs get to the top without starting to learn on the job from scratch after graduation, if they ever attended universities?

The professors who continue to denigrate students and graduates should stay in the classrooms and teach their students what they need to know instead of negatively complaining and passing the buck. Nigerians should realize that whoever makes these denigrating generalization statements might be talking with pomposity, superiority complex, arrogance and little knowledge. Such people never see anything good in others except themselves.

Really highly educated persons do not indulge in denigrating others with emptiness and negative attitudes. In civilized communities in UK and USA, real industry chiefs help solve educational and community problems by using positive reinforcement and financing instead of mocking the people and denigrating students and graduates who are future leaders of this great nation, Nigeria.

Genuine problems identified included examination malpractices, cult activities, poor learning environment, incessant strikes by academic staff, poor teaching attitude, corruption in university/college administration, weak planning and poor implementation of educational programmes and policies, poor funding and poor infrastructure.

The university/college educators must focus on providing quality educational services and be able to generate funds for their institutions' continued existence and survival. Educators must work for their paychecks to earn them, and there must be thorough supervision of performance. There must be constant performance appraisal of professors and other faculty members by the university/college authorities as well as designed strategies to ensure constant feedback of learning and teaching attitude of educators. Students must appraise their teachers, lecturers and professors. There must be academic democracy fully entrenched in Nigerian educational system.

It is crystal clear that there is fraud, bribery, corruption, extortion of money and gratification within the educational community, which must be stopped. There is need for behaviour modification by educators and students regarding examination malpractices and other crimes. Standard code of conduct must be strictly enforced to clean the operators of the system. Educators must eradicate 'business as usual', and those who cannot modify behaviour and be exemplary should be sifted out of the system – no sacred cows and untouchables.

Reasonable part of the thirty-five percent return on investment in Nigeria widely acclaimed by international investors as the highest in the world should be applied for Nigerian national development, education, reinvestment, employment generation and increased welfare benefits for workers in particular and Nigerian people in general.

GOD/ALLAH BLESS NIGERIA

CHAPTER 9

WAR AGAINST CORRUPTION

Corruption pervades all spheres of activities in the universe. In most cases, corruption is as a result of high level of demand in the entire world faced with scarcity and acute shortage of supply to satisfy majority of people. If there is enough to satisfy everybody, corruption and its menace will be nonexistent, all things staying the same. Unfortunately, if some people who are pathologically greedy and selfish have the whole world in their hands, they will still not be content with what they have, but would still indulge in corruption. Some people go to acquire absolute power and thereby get corrupted absolutely. In the end, corruption brings down those who give and those who take corruptly.

Corruption is the act of being viciously immoral, depraved, capable of being improperly influenced, dishonest and capable of being bribed. Corruption embodies discontentment, greed, selfishness and insatiability. Corruption is like a two-edged sword that cuts the person who gives bribe as well as the person who receives the bribe that is given corruptly.

Regrettably, corruption may be difficult to stop because it is often created and nurtured by high class elites, the wealthy, the powerful, leaders, presidents, chairpersons, legislators, congress persons, the governing class, judges and topmost decision makers all over the world without exception. Usually, those who catch and punish corrupt people are capable of being corrupted as human beings.

Those who have powers to stop corruption are usually the ones who are deeply involved in it to increase their corruptly acquired wealth. Those who are condemning it in the open and those charged with investigating it are sometimes benefiting from it, accumulating wealth from it in secret and have their hands soiled in it. It subsists, thrives and perpetuates as a result of human imperfection.

Corruption thrives in all spheres of human endeavours including religion, politics, academia, professions etc. in both private and public sectors and pervades all social classes, poor, middle-class and highest ranks in all professions and all countries. The Holy Book conceptualized that all human beings have sinned and that whoever has never sinned should cast stone at the sinner standing trial, and everybody just dropped the stones. Nobody could throw the stones. If it is ordered that whoever leaders in the world that have never been improperly influenced and have never improperly influenced anybody should raise their hands; it is glaring that nobody would raise the hand.

Hardly any human being is saintly when faced with corruption-induced benefits and influences. Those who condemn corruption the loudest seem to be the greatest hypocrites and need to be watched. Corruption is endemic and twoway (the giver and the receiver; the giving and the receiving). Corruption has very powerful influence on humans because of its association with power, wealth, business, money, possession, materialism, affluence and weight of influence on people. Above all, corruption's correlation with money makes it the root of all evils.

Those who work hard at the alter usually eat from the altar. This hypothesis recognizes well-deserved, honest rewards, gifts and gratifications for appreciation of hard work, but not extortion, fraud, bribery and corruption which are dishonest and condemnable. Ironically, corruption knows no bounds in male, female, ethnicity, nationality, race, education or religion (Christian, Muslim, Traditionalist etc.). There are no human saints, but it is wise for Nigerian elites to stop being corrupt and/or corrupted or corrupting others, since Nigeria has established EFCC and ICPC to ensure zero tolerance for corrupt practices.

In developed countries, corruption is practised with civility hypocritically, but whenever it leaks, there are usually severe consequences; 'no sacred cows, no untouchables'. In advanced countries like the United States of America, when corruption practice leaks, those involved nomatter how highly placed often resign their appointments, demonstrate remorse, plea bargain and serve their sentences.

In Nigeria, when corrupt practice leaks, the highclass officials involved would deny it, fight it tooth and nail and bribe their way to the highest level of jurisdiction and get off the hook unscathed by exploiting all loopholes and applying all legal technicalities. The set up of Nigerian society makes things very interesting and laughable sometimes. Once you know your way, you can get anything – turn all stones on your path as impediments and cross all rivers that are said to be impassable. That is Nigeria, the microcosm of the entire world without exception.

Corruption comes in different forms and shapes. It is the bane of development particularly in the developing world where corruption is practised crudely and often difficult to be the 'oddmanout' as a result of how the entire system works corruptly under 'business as usual'.

Going back in history, there was abundant evidence to show that corruption was exported by Europe and America and planted into African race, and it has continued to grow thus enriching the elites at the expenses of the masses. It has been making the poor poorer, the rich richer, the developing countries less developing and the developed countries stronger and wealthier at the expense of underdeveloped nations.

Prince Bola Ajibola, former Attorney-General of the federation, former World Court Judge and the Chairman of the Nigerian Delegation to the Cameroon-Nigeria Mixed Commission on Boundary Dispute described bribery and corruption as, "Nigeria's grave and social menace, a huge devouring monster which has destabilized, distorted and destroyed Nigerian economy to a very large extent and a cankerworm which has eaten very deep into Nigeria's economic fabric." Prince Ajibola made the remarks while addressing a public lecture organized by the Centre for Law and Business on Wednesday, June 19, 2004, in his paper, "Law and EconomyChallenges and Prospects for Law and Business."

He traced the origin of modern day corruption to the period of post-independence when the government started to award contracts. He explained that as at early independence time, most contractors were foreigners who used to teach government executives how to load and pad contract sums with extra money, which was sufficient to open foreign accounts on behalf of Nigerian executives.

He humorously commented, "Nigerians have graduated by becoming experts in the field as they now tell contractors the sum of money they want as their padding or loading fee." He added that the establishment of the Independent Corrupt Practices Commission (ICPC) had not changed the situation of fraud and corruption.

He reminded Nigerians that the country maintained the position as the world's most corrupt country until it conceded the unenviable first place to Bangladesh. He advised that Nigerians should be able to tell any corrupt person to his/her face that he/she was corrupt. He said, "Let us call a spade, a spade. Anybody that is a thief should be told he is a thief." There should be no exception, no sacred cows.

When international financiers lend money to developing countries for project development, they impose stringent conditions that are not helpful to real development. Those who execute the projects would be mostly foreign contractors who inflate the project price and get their overblown quotations accepted by bribing Nigerian government functionaries. Usually, the kickbacks are stashed away in foreign banks thus leaving less money to complete the projects at required standard.

In effect, a considerable amount of the money borrowed for project development finds itself in private pockets. No matter how much of the money is stolen, the nation is indebted to the full amount of money borrowed at high interest rate. Invariably, the projects are half completed and abandoned. That notwithstanding, the debt created becomes compounded with high interest year in and year out.

As a result, the resources that should have been used for further development in other areas would be utilized to service such debts annually, thus making the country poorer and poorer and the creditor nations (the Western World) richer and richer at the expense of the poor masses of the debtor nation.

On Thursday, July 29, 2004, the *Punch Newspaper* reported that the Economic and Financial Crimes Commission (EFCC) found that some prominent Nigerians including former governors, senators and other top ranks were involved in land scam purportedly masterminded by one person named Success Amuchie in the Federal Capital Territory (FCT), Abuja. It was discovered that they acquired and developed plots of land in the FCT, Abuja without due process and diligence under questionable circumstances. The Nigerian big wigs allegedly bought the plots of land from Success Amuchie who was described as the kingpin and expert in forging titles, documents and certificates of occupancy.

The notable personalities purported to have been duped as a result of the land scam, fraudulently organized by Success Amuchie included a South-South exGovernor, exSenate President (1999-2003), former FCT Minister, a former Deputy Senate Leader, an expolitical adviser to the President, two former State Governors, a former Senator, two officials of the Nigerian National Petroleum Corporation (NNPC) and many other dignitaries.

The plots listed as acquired and/or developed without due process and under questionable circumstances included 1376, 1377, 1379 'C', 2444, 4551 'C', 1974, 1075, 291, 292, 480, 2505, 1379D, 774, 1117, 1037, 3343, 863, etc. Most of the plots were said to be acquired with forged documents, some were developed without approved building plans and others had forged certificates of occupancy. One of the victims admitted that he paid the sum of seven million naira to Success Amuchie, the alleged forger, for the plot and processing of building drawings.

It was unfortunate that all these prominent personalities in positions of authority in federal and state governments could be duped and cheated by land deal conmen without suspicion to the tune of several millions of Nigerian currency. If any of them had taken pains to follow due process as expected of them as Nigerian leaders, perhaps the fraud would have been detected long time. If these personalities in leadership positions failed to follow due process and were scammed, what do they expect from their Nigerian followership?

Leadership exemplariness is a great national asset that promotes orderliness, transparency, responsibility, accountability and a progressive polity. All these dignitaries who were victims of the land racket failed to follow due process, and therefore, suffered avoidable possessional losses. Proverbially, Yorubas believe that unearned money acquired through foul means could most probably disappear through similar courses. In most cases, money acquired corruptly and illegally would disappear fast and end into the pockets of scammers.

The government should embark on a serious campaign against fraud, corruption, economic and financial crimes and 'business as usual'. The laws of Nigeria should be strictly enforced; existing laws revised and amended appropriately to meet the needs of present time to deter wouldbe offenders. The laws should adequately punish offenders quickly, justly, fairly and proportionally without any discrimination.

In addition, the government can provide flyers in all public buildings, offices, schools, colleges, universities and all nooks and corners of Nigeria to orientate people and seriously warn everybody about the implications of its zero tolerance policy of corrupt and fraudulent practices.

The flyers should condemn and warn against fraud, bribery and corruption, economic and financial crimes, illegal oil bunkering, illegal drugs, illegal arms and ammunitions, economic sabotage, vandalisation of government infrastructures, business as usual etc. The flyers must promise reasonable rewards for informants who may remain anonymous when they report crimes to police (EFCC or ICPC).

In the continuing unprecedented policy to stamp out corruption in all facets of Nigerian society, about 131 contractors including elite businessmen, politicians and a company purportedly belonging to a former presidential special adviser were allegedly arraigned for prosecution by the Federal Government. They were accused of failing to execute contracts worth ₦7.086 billion after collecting mobilization fees, and in other cases, full payment.

The federal government was committed to recover the money. Various cases of fraud and corruption running into billions of naira are being probed in the Senate, the House of Representatives, the courts, ICPC, EFCC which involve sectors of energy, transportation, aviation, health, communication, housing, lands, FCT, agriculture, banking etc. As a result, many high ranking officials were forced out of their jobs.

In the same vein, the former governor of Osun State was asked to account for ₦126 million in respect of the implementation of the Bola Ige House Secretariat Complex Project. The money was allegedly paid to a consultant of the project. The case was investigated by the police who allegedly procured a warrant of arrest against the former governor. All these efforts being pursued went to confirm that the government was very serious about cleaning Nigerian society of fraudulent and corrupt practices.

On November 5, 2003, it was reported in the *Guardian News* that Nigeria and some developing countries that were investment strapped, made a net transfer of about $200 billion (₦25.8 trillion) to other countries of economically advanced status. As a result, the former United Nations Secretary General, Kofi Annan, remarked that such situation lacked commonsense.

He added that funds that could be promoting investment and growth in developing countries or building schools and hospitals were instead transferred abroad. The situation was described as the paradox of the proverbial desert dweller who was shipping water to rain soaked region. It is like carrying coal from countries not producing coal to Newcastle, UK which already produces an abundance of it.

ExPresident Olusegun Obasanjo was one of the founding fathers of Transparency International (TI) with the primary objective of fighting corruption within a country, as well as corruption encouraged by another country. It is on record that some developed countries and multinational corporations set aside some money to induce corruption in developing countries in order to receive favours in securing contracts corruptly and engaging in other businesses.

The parameter used for measuring corruption level of a country by Transparency International (TI) should take into consideration that the giver of a bribe and the taker are equally guilty of corruption, but that is not being done by TI. Also, there is need for TI to include corruption elimination effort index which is also overlooked. Corruption perception index and corruption encouragement index should be uniformly applied in all countries considered by TI in order to make the results comparable, authentic and acceptable, but that is not being done uniformly to all countries being monitored.

Different people have different perceptions, and as such, the result obtainable through using corruption perception index may sometimes be tainted by the biases of the researcher because people are most likely to perceive the same object or situation differently. Perception result may be different from the reality thereby ending up with a questionable result just like the corruption evaluation result given to Nigeria by the Transparency International.

If this index is not uniformly applied in all countries and in all cases, as it is usually the case, the Transparency International result may become questionable, unreal and unacceptable especially for rating Nigeria poorly as one of the leading ten most corrupt nations in the world when the indexes are not uniformly applied and are questionable.

For the evaluation result of Transparency International (TI) survey to be meaningful, authentic, reliable and acceptable, it must encompass a corruption fighting effort index, which will unequivocally define and measure the efforts of each country in fighting corruption. This index must consider the applicable corruption laws, the commissions established to fight corruption and their effectiveness, the results achieved and achievable by the commissions, the punishments meted out, the level of deterrence to commit corruption in each country and overall responses of the people to corruption fighting efforts of the government.

If Nigeria with a developing economy is ranked third corruptionwise by Transparency International, what positions do the European and American countries that breed, nurture and export corruption take in the ranking of corrupt countries? The Transparency International needs reorientation and specific guidelines of its 'modus operandi', which must be uniformly applied to all participating countries. The parameters to use in the evaluation must be well designed with scoring guidelines, which must be approved by majority of participating countries. In addition, TI must ensure that respondents to its questionnaires truly represent the diverse political groups and interests of participating countries. The process and results must eliminate biases that are expected from TI research personnel and the responding parties contacted in the participating countries.

Participating countries must understand that their scores in the corruption evaluation result have serious economic implications especially if the score is poor. Poor scores would tarnish the credit and investment worthiness and image of the country, and dissuade investors from doing business in such countries with poor results.

As a result, the activities of Transparency International must be monitored by participating countries to ensure that reliable and authentic results are achieved through the uniform application of approved parameters. The Transparency International (TI) must review and redesign its corruption measuring indices and retrain its operatives to apply them uniformly in all countries in order to stop embarrassing developing countries with its unrealistic and unreliable outcomes.

The billion dollar question for the government is whether the courts, the states and federal legislatures, the governors and local government council leaders/chairpersons, the police and government functionaries are demonstrating the same aggressiveness as the presidency to fight corruption! If opportunities abound to make the level of supply of amenities and essentials of living equal to demand for fairly decent living, corruption may die naturally among low and intermediate classes of Nigerians. If corruption cases are prosecuted with despatch, justice and fair play without discrimination (no sacred cows or untouchables), and immunity clause removed from the Nigerian Constitution, topmost Nigerians will be scared and deterred, and they will stop corrupt practices.

The Ex-Chairman of the House of Representatives Committee on Judiciary, Honourable Bala Ibn Na'Allah, being deeply touched and frustrated by the high rate of corruption among some serving state governors, reiterated that the National Assembly was determined to strip them of their immunity from prosecution for criminal and civil offences. He disclosed during the seminar on "The Role of the Legislature in the Campaign Against Corruption" held in Kaduna on Tuesday, November 23, 2004, the National Assembly's intention to amend the immunity clause in the constitution.

The present set of state governors are younger, highly educated and much more brilliant than what Nigeria ever had, but if some of them betray the Nigerian confidence bestowed on them, they should be made accountable for it. It is human to err, but corruption is usually a deliberate act. State Governors who represent the hope of the people should be transparent, reliable, decent, empathic, responsive, responsible, accountable and above board.

Mistakes made before May 29, 1999 may be looked with some consideration but not after then when the succeeding civilian government made its intention known to fight corruption hands down; and established the facilities and structures to do so. It is not wise not to know when to stop a bad act.

Governors may one day aspire to be president or vice president of the Federal Republic of Nigeria; they must be exemplary. Whoever is not, should not hide under the immunity of his office to commit criminal and/or civil offences. Hence, it is not doubtful that the intention of the National Assembly to strip governors of their immunity will receive overwhelming support of Nigerian citizens and international community. There have been cases of State Governors being prosecuted in courts for wrongdoings in the USA. Nigerian State Governors cannot hide under immunity clause to perpetrate economic and financial crimes as well as violate the Nigerian Constitution with impunity.

In the same vein, the Ex-Chairman of the Economic and Financial Crimes Commission (EFCC), Mr. Nuhu Ribadu, shared the view of Hon. Bala Na'Allah that the problem of immunity for governors was a clog in the wheel of progress in the war against corruption by hampering the work of the EFCC and ICPC (the Independent Corrupt Practices Commission). If the immunity clause in the constitution is being abused by those it is meant to protect, then, it may be rightly assumed that they do not deserve it. The ill-gotten gains must be recovered and ploughed back for national development.

In his own contribution, the Ex-Chairman of the House Committee on AntiCorruption, Hon. Nduese Essien, expressed utter disappointment for the rating of Nigeria as the third most corrupt country in the world by Transparency International (TI). He exclaimed that the root cause of Nigeria's development failure could not be attributed to lack of resources but to "widespread and deeply entrenched corruption." He said that he was becoming extremely worried about corruption in Nigeria which was becoming as problematic as the national debt burden which looked as if the more you repaid it, the higher the outstanding balance to service.

Looking at the deadly effects of corruption and its devastating consequences in the socio-economic and political life of Nigerians, one cannot disagree with the Ex-Speaker of the House of Representatives, Alhaji Aminu Bello Masari who described corruption as a weapon of mass destruction (WMD).

Former House Speaker Masari made the comment in Kaduna while opening the First Stakers Summit on corrupt practices and financial crimes in Nigeria on Tuesday, November 23, 2004. He exclaimed that the evils associated with corruption and financial crimes convinced the National Assembly to expressly endorse and pass the bills that established the AntiCorruption Commission as well as the Budget and

Due Process Unit in the Presidency. He described corruption as the weapon that the rich and the powerful employ against the poor and the weak to make the wealthy wealthier, the rich richer, the poor poorer and the weak weaker.

He added that no nation could endure and prosper in the atmosphere of injustice being promoted by corruption. He used strong language to further condemn corruption as reprehensible, unjust practice and conduct, capable of undermining the legitimacy and stability of any government.

ExHouse Speaker Masari assured all stakeholders that the National Assembly would continue to support all the institutions established to fight corruption and that all legislative proposals that could formalize transparency initiatives in governance would be welcome. He reiterated to the nation that the National Assembly would represent the foremost anticorruption institution and demonstrate the greatest stake in the survival of the Nigerian democracy and public welfare.

He reassured that the National Assembly was ready to effectively spearhead the battle against corrupt practices in the country. Contributing to the summit, the former Governor of Kaduna State, Ahmed Makarfi, advocated the dire need to establish internal mechanisms and structures that would effectively stop corruption and the looting of the national treasury.

Speaking about corruption on Friday, August 28, 2004, ExPresident Obasanjo admitted that it was difficult to absolutely eradicate corruption anywhere in the world but that he had seen countries where bribery and corruption was not a way of life. These vices of fraud, bribery, corruption, economic and financial crimes and many other crimes were not ways of life in Black African Continent where extended family system made every black person on earth his or her brother's keeper.

There are strict moral values of decency, dignity, respect, discipline, sense of responsibility and community as well as exemplariness and role modeling among Africans. Those great African values still exist, but they are mixed and messed up with Western World values where only what glitters is acceptable to be gold, and monetary values dictate life and existence. People want money and wealth at all costs, nomatter what and how, especially the elites worldwide.

These vices were exported by developed countries into Africa, and they continue to do so in wider dimensions as businesses grow between Africans and developed international communities. In present time, vices have assumed enormous proportion of various forms, shapes and great dimensions. Vices have eaten deep into the fabric of many Nigerian elites. It is serious. The adoption of some westernized lifestyles in replacement and preference to African culture, tradition and values has become the bane of Nigerian elites in recent time. Many elites are lost in the search for abnormal wealth at all costs, and only God/Allah can restore them to normalcy. They exist in all religions, ethnicities, academics and professions.

To eradicate fraud, corruption, economic and financial crimes and other vices in Nigeria, the government (the Presidency, the Legislature and the Judiciary) must be prepared to step on toes of all offenders irrespective of their influence and connections in society.

It may be necessary for government to call to order, friends, relatives, advisers, ministers, government high hierarchy functionaries, close associates and other elites, who mastermind criminal acts, especially economic and financial sabotage as a result of their belief that they have enough connections and influence to commit any crime with impunity. Some Nigerian elites believe that they are above the law. Such people need some reeducation and lessons to learn in a reformatory or penitentiary.

Tougher laws must be made and strictly enforced and cases of corruption and other crimes must be investigated and prosecuted expeditiously and convictions reached quickly with admirable and transparent justice and fairplay within ninety days.

There must be deterrent measures against crimes, but first and foremost, there must be well-organized and systematic motivational strategies applied by government to encourage behaviour change. To achieve behaviour modification in totality, there must be good governance that can relieve the pains and sufferings of the people. Unemployment rate must come down to less than six percent as it is in the USA.

On Saturday, August 28, 2004, it was reported in *Vanguard News* that stolen government money by government functionaries that was being stashed away in foreign banks had increases from $50 billion in 1999 to $170 billion in 2003. The information was alleged to be contained in World Bank document that was released to the Presidency. If the report was true, it meant government actions to curb corruption had not been fully effective, and more tightening actions were required to save Nigerian economy.

The poser for the government is, "Why can't these corrupt, economic and financial saboteurs stay under incarceration until they disgorge the ill-gotten gains back into the government purse for project development?" Democracy is not freedom or licence to steal government money. There must be tougher laws to deter economic and financial saboteurs. The government will be admired by the masses if fights against the elites to save the majority from abuses by the elites continue relentlessly without fear or favour. The masses will sing, "Hallelujah, the Messiah has manifested truly to redeem us."

The Nigerian masses cannot continue to accept governmental failures and excuses indefinitely after about fifty years of Nigeria's wallowing and wandering in the wilderness since independence in 1960 and IfeajunaNzeogwu coup d'etat of January 15, 1966, if problems still remain unsolved and Nigerians cannot breathe with a great sigh of relief of 'Never Again'.

The bad eggs, no matter who they are, should be sifted and placed in the reformatory to stop them from dragging Nigeria back into oblivion of the last fifty years. Whoever has not changed after December 31, 2008, is a danger to society. They should be set aside for reorientation in a reformatory while the remaining Nigerians move on. After they have served their terms in the reformatory, they can meet the rest by doubling their strides as clean and saved Nigerians. It is a task that must be done. If it is not done now, who is going to do it and when?

The practice of stealing Nigerian government money and stashing it in overseas private bank accounts has put Nigeria and Nigerians in terrible shape economically for decades, and it has created generational poverty among majority of Nigerians who previously enjoyed economic boom and lived in the midst of abundant human, material and natural resources.

Do elite Nigerians not realize that once they make substantial deposits into banks in the Western World, there is no way they can get all the money back and/or at death, high percentage of it evaporates as death tax? Invariably, the money deposited may be lost completely and irretrievably. Make no mistake about it. Such monies are better kept in Nigeria for development, investment and employment generation in the best interest of Nigerian people.

It was reported that security agencies including the Economic and Financial Crimes Commission (EFCC) and the National Intelligence Agency (NIA) were said to have been given the mandate to unmask the corrupt government functionaries at state and federal levels implicated in the World Bank report. From the report, it was deduced that just two government officials mentioned in the report could conveniently settle the total of Nigeria's foreign debt, which plagued Nigeria for about three decades. In the name of God/Allah, let those two people and others involved help Nigeria if not because of the present generation of Nigerians, but for the sake of humanity and posterity.

Nigerians ask unequivocally with tears in their eyes, "Who are these government officials mentioned in the report?" The people concerned should repatriate the loot, invest it in Nigeria and generate employment. What about using the money to help your community when you are still alive? Please do not forfeit Nigerian future prosperity and money to the Western World. Money in secret code operated bank accounts may not be easy to withdraw after the death, sickness or disability of the owner of the account if it is operated in foreign countries. The money may be forfeited to the foreign country. Please do not let that happen in the best interest of Nigeria, your children and posterity.

The World Economic Forum ranked Nigeria high in the diversion of public funds by being placed 97 out of 102 countries. Egypt was rated as the least public fund diverting country followed by South Africa. Nigeria was placed twenty-third out of twenty-five countries for public trust of politicians among others. These results are terrifying, and they are the handiwork of elites. When will it change if not right now and immediately?

The statistics were said to be disclosed by the former Minister of Finance, Mrs. (Dr.) Ngozi Okonjo-Iweala at a forum organized by the Nigerian National Petroleum Corporation (NNPC). The countries surveyed included Nigeria, Egypt, Tanzania, South Africa, Ghana and many others.

It was also disclosed that seventy percent of staff of the Ministry of Finance were secondary school certificate holders while fourteen percent were university/college graduates. She asserted that after some scrutiny, there would be retraining of personnel in order to equip them to be able to face the future challenges of the ministry. The likelihood of retrenchment was also emphasized. Will retrenchment of the workers be done transparently, justly, fairly and without discrimination or tribalism as expected? That is food for thought.

In civilized communities in the world, it is not unexpected that employers of labour would rationalize, reorganize, trim, retrench, retire or retrain employees with a focus that no discharged person is allowed to rot away without governmental support or redirection in form of providing welfare services and unemployment benefits. Employees considered not fit to continue on the job for one reason or the other are treated empathically, supported and redirected to stand on their feet in other spheres of life endeavours for which they best fit.

The rationalization exercise envisaged to be carried out in the Ministry of Finance and other government departments should be done with transparency, justice and fairplay devoid of favouritism, tribalism, discrimination or ethnicity consideration. In the past, tribalism played a big role in such cases; and where university/college graduation certificates are required, the authorities must thoroughly check for fake certificates and eliminate fraud and corruption in all its ramifications.

It was reported that the British Foreign Office made an unofficial complaint over the incessant breach of its foreign exchange laws by some state governors who used their aides as the conduit pipes to transport huge sums of foreign currencies into Britain without official receipts to back the transactions up from their home country. In *This Day News* of Friday, May 21, 2004, it was published that the money transfers undertaken by the governors' aides were procured from local finance houses in Lagos, Abuja and Kano contrary to established banking and financial regulations and procedures.

It was explained that an associate of the suspended governor of Plateau State was allegedly arrested in London over the contravention of British Foreign Exchange laws with over 1.3 million pounds sterling without valid bank documentation from the originating country. The governor also was questioned, released on bail and later was allegedly barred from entering Britain.

Before the above incident leaked to the public, the former Minister of State in the Ministry of Finance, Mrs. Nenadi Usman, accused some governors of illegal deals in foreign exchange transactions. The Finance Ministry observed that within a week after every FAAC meeting, exchange rates went up as a result of increased demand for foreign currencies because some governors were using part of their allocations to buy foreign money illegally.

It was further explained that few days after the FAAC meeting, some governors and their finance commissioners were often junketing abroad. As a result, the ExMinister of Finance, Mrs. (Dr.) Ngozi Okonjo-Iweala, called on State Legislators to take interest in finding out how State Governors expend their allocations from the Federation Account to curb misappropriation of state and local government funds. To the noble call, some individual legislators defended their governors and even commented that it was not their business to pry into how governors expended their allocations. Such remarks suggested some collusions might be going on. State legislatures should not abrogate their responsibilities to the electorate.

During the Third National Seminar on Economic Crimes on Monday, June 28, 2004, Alhaji Nuhu Ribadu, former Chairman of Economic and Financial Crimes Commission (EFCC) was said to have confirmed in Abuja that some state governors were indeed siphoning money overseas for their personal benefit despite their denials.

He also revealed that the Nigerian federal government had set up the Nigerian Financial Intelligence Unit (NFIU) within the EFCC with the objective of combating money laundering; and thwart the possibility of financing terrorist activities in Nigeria. In May 2005, he reconfirmed that twenty governors were keeping foreign bank accounts stashed with money in contravention of Nigerian 1999 Constitution.

He reiterated that the accusations levied against some state governors and their finance commissioners by the former Minister of State for Finance, Mrs. Nenadi Usman, and supported by the former Federal Minister of Finance, Mrs. (Dr.) Ngozi Okonjo-Iweala that some state governors and their finance commissioners were siphoning money abroad was true. Alhaji Ribadu accused the governors of perpetrating corruption, but he stressed that his commission was equal to the task of eradicating corruption, which had bedeviled the country.

The names of the culprits were not disclosed. Since the names of the culprits were not exposed, how would they stop their economic and financial sabotage against the nation? Nigerians heard several times that there would be no sacred cows in the dispensation of justice. Were those culprits whose names were kept secret and shielded, sacred cows? How will corruption be eradicated if the names of corrupt high government functionaries are kept secret and shielded?

Such policy or strategy is strange and would be ineffectual to deter those who are committing economic sabotage against the nation. Above all, it makes people keep suspecting all state governors including the innocent ones. Let the public know the names of the economic saboteurs so that they can face tough questions and embarrassment from the masses whom they have been cheating and deceiving.

Alhaji Ribadu brightened the hope of Nigerians when he revealed that his commission had secured the new amendment provided in the EFCC Act 2004 to facilitate the speedy trial of fraud and corruption cases. He added that over 500 suspects alleged to have committed economic crimes, money laundering and advanced fee fraud "419" were in detention waiting for trial, and about $500m worth of assets were seized and recovered.

He mentioned the case of a civil servant purportedly owning about 300 houses in Abuja and that top government officials committed and nurtured various economic crimes, but no names were disclosed as usual. Nigerians want to know the name of the civil servant who owns 300 houses in Abuja and whether he has been prosecuted, convicted and sentenced to long terms of imprisonment for economic sabotage against Nigerians, and if not, why? The ill-gotten gains must be discovered and recovered to be utilized for national development.

Alhaji Ribadu warned that financial and nonfinancial institutions that did not apply stringent internal financial control systems, but caused the public to be cheated, would be held responsible vicariously. Designated financial and nonfinancial institutions that were likely to facilitate the commission of "419" and other related fraudulent actions included banks, insurance companies, stake brokering firms, discount houses, financial houses, mortgage institutions, telecommunications, postal services, independent service providers, cybercafes and bureau de change.

He called for increased funding of the commission which he described as a critical success factor for curbing economic and financial crimes. He mentioned that as part of the funding, the Nigerian National Petroleum Corporation (NNPC) gave the EFCC ₦40 million while the Central Bank of Nigeria (CBN) had released ₦20 million out of ₦60 million that was promised the EFCC. He promised Nigerians that the EFCC was determined to clean "the street of all those who benefit from advance fee fraud by seizing their criminal proceeds as was the case of Fred Ajudua." Assets worth over $700 million were allegedly seized and recovered as at May 2005.

In his presentation at the seminar titled, "Advance Fee Fraud and Money Laundering in Nigeria: An Overview", Alhaji Ribadu hinted that the NFIU would function as an autonomous central national agency which would be responsible for the receiving and analyzing of financial information such as Currency Transaction Reports (CTR's) and Suspicious Transaction Reports (STR's) to be procured from financial and designated nonfinancial institutions for the purpose of disseminating intelligence information arising from the reports so obtained.

He added that information to be submitted to the NFIU would include Suspicious Transaction Reports (STRS's) and Currency Transaction Reports (CTR's) above prescribed threshold of ₦1 million or its equivalent in the case of one individual, or ₦5 million or its equivalent in the case of a body corporate and any other transfer to or from foreign country of funds or securities of any amount exceeding $10,000 or its equivalent.

The ExEFCC Chairman, Alhaji Ribadu, listed the following advantages derivable from the establishment of the Nigerian Financial Intelligence Unit (NFIU):

(1) It represents a veritable tool or mechanism for fighting economic and financial crimes in the nation.
(2) It is of great value to criminal investigation of economic and financial intelligence information of money trails.
(3) It facilitates the dissemination and sharing of appropriate financial intelligence information with other foreign financial

intelligence units (FIU's)
(4) It enhances the effectiveness and capability of the commission (EFCC) in the detection and prevention of financial crimes.
(5) It facilitates the development of an enabling environment for foreign investment inflow.
(6) The establishment of the NFIU would enhance the rating possibilities of Nigeria's financial control management by the Transparency International.
(7) The reports of NFIU would represent a credible resource input in designing authentic national policies that are in the best interest of the country.

The former Chairman of the ICPC, Justice Mustapha Akanbi, was said to have confirmed to the British Broadcasting Corporation expressing strong hope that with time, the hydraheaded problem of corruption, which had eaten deep into the fabric of Nigerian society, would be overcome. He convincingly pointed out that the ICPC was ready to "sacrifice all sacred cows." He explained that some "big fishes" such as former federal ministers, a serving minister who was dismissed with ignominy, permanent secretary and two chief directors of teaching hospitals, were being arraigned before the court of law. The antigraft panel (ICPC) was trying 72 suspects while the EFCC was keeping about 500 in detention.

Justice Akanbi said that before the ICPC was established, corruption had become endemic, and it had eaten deep into the fabric of the country. He commented, "I do not believe that Nigerians are foolhardy, that they will not realize that it is no longer business as usual."

He added that at a recent conference in Vienna, Austria, he met the Chairman of Transparency International, which rated Nigeria as the second most corrupt country in the world and demanded to know the parameters for the assessment. The antigraft panel boss disagreed with the Transparency International's perception of Nigeria wondering why the agency did not take into consideration the political biases of those who fed them with wrong impressions about Nigeria's corruption situation.

If Nigeria is the second most corrupt nation in the world, what position will the industrialized countries which export corruption into developing countries hold? The assessment cannot be accurate because the magnitude of fraud and corruption in the developed countries is unparalleled, but done in a secret way and usually covered up, but whenever it leaks out, heads usually roll without discrimination, with swift justice and fairplay.

However, Justice Akanbi reiterated that the rate of corruption was high, quite high, but since some elites, the 'untouchable sacred cows' were investigated, interrogated, arrested, detained, prosecuted and subjected to being convicted unprecedentedly, fears had been instilled into the hearts of prospective offenders. The zero tolerance measures taken against fraud and corruption will help clean Nigerian society.

The relentless fight against corruption in Nigeria is working like miracle. The results of the measures are positive and successful. The names of those who are relentlessly and fearlessly doing this reformation job in Nigeria at this time will be written in gold for the present and posterity to say, "Thank you for your noble acts of our redemption and salvation from corruption, poverty, economic chaos and insecurity. Your rewards are everlasting."

Corrupt Nigerian elites who have been siphoning ill-gotten Nigerian money overseas should stop and think because it is no longer safe to do so. The United Nations (UN) frowned against it and passed laws that would enable such corruption money to be intercepted, seized and returned to the country from which it was stolen. The Western World seriously took steps, especially the USA and Britain, to identify, seize and return such ill-gotten gains deposited in their banks to the countries from which they were acquired illegally.

The US government established the Department of Asset Forfeiture through its Attorney General's office that would ferret out and confiscate ill-gotten wealth stashed away in the country. By virtue of the Patriot Act and other US criminal forfeiture statutes, the Department of Asset Forfeiture will seize assets accumulated through criminal acts, which put the safety and lives of a population at risk or acts which are unethical in government or business.

It is gladdening to know that Nigeria is taking advantage of the statutes by compiling a list of suspected government functionaries having questionable fat accounts in American banks. The exercise was done by the Economic and Financial Crimes Commission (EFCC) under the chairmanship of Alhaji Nuhu Ribadu.

It is recalled that in the *Punch* newspaper of Monday, June 14, 2004, ExPresident Obasanjo was said to have renewed his campaign for debt forgiveness at the G8 Summit held in the USA arguing that most of the debts were dubious and could not be repaid by African nations including Nigeria. To Nigerians, the foreign debt most of which was dubious remained a very serious matter. Fortunately, God/Allah answered Nigeria's prayer in July 2005 as most of African foreign debts were written off.

Nigeria's foreign debt, about $35 billion in 2004 mainly derived from Multilateral Development Banks (MDB) for projects that assist economic development was criticized and disputed by the Institute of Chartered Accountants representative in 2003. Soon after, the ExMinister of Finance, (Dr.) Mrs. Ngozi Okonjo-Iweala, came strongly to defend the figure of the debt and its authenticity.

That notwithstanding, it should be of interest to Nigeria, the revelation of $200 billion scandal that allegedly rocked the World Bank, InterAmerican Development Bank (IDB), European Bank for Reconstruction and Development, Asian Development Bank (ADB), African Development Bank (AFDB), and other multilateral development banks. The scandal was reportedly probed. The scandal should be an eye opener for Nigeria and other African countries about the possibilities of fraud in their transactions with those banks.

The US Senate Committee hearing was told that multilateral development banks including the World Bank fraudulently used almost $200 billion meant for development projects in poor countries of the world including Nigeria. The US Senate Committee on Foreign Relations investigating the $200 billion scandal was allegedly informed by financial experts that the World Bank was allegedly involved in projects financing corruption in developing countries including Nigeria for up to $130 billion since it was founded in 1946 representing about twenty-five percent of the total bank loans of $425 billion made to developing countries.

The US Senate Committee Chairman of Foreign Relations was said to have commented that corruption in multilateral development banks operations must have robbed people living in poverty, the opportunity to improve their economic conditions. At the hearing, it was realized that people from developing countries supposedly poor were eventually saddled with paying back costs of funds as additional debts, which did not benefit them.

In effect, the Senate Committee on Foreign Relations observed that impoverished people of developing countries were not only being cheated out of development benefits, but they were also saddled with the responsibility of repaying the resulting debts to the banks. A lot of the debts were fraudulently cooked by the creditor nations and agencies to achieve economic neocolonization and enslavement of Africans in particular and developing nations generally.

In 2003, the World Bank and the multilateral development banks were said to have expended $18.5 billion and $35 billion respectively on projects in developing countries. But where and what are the effects of these purported expenditures? Why are the effects not visible? It is because misappropriation of funds occurs during implementation of projects meant to benefit the poor people. Eventually, funds of projects misused become debts repayable by the people who as a result, become poorer and poorer while servicing the loans, which they did not physically receive nor benefit from. There must be strict regulations for the acquisition of future foreign loans.

As reported in the *Daily Independent Online* of Tuesday, April 20, 2004, the World Bank Institute's research revealed that Nigeria was fingered in $185 million bribery scandal involving American oil firm, Halliburton and TSKJ Consortium for securing the contract to build Nigerian Liquefied National Gas (NLNG) trains in Bonny, Rivers State.

It was also said to be involved in another $2.4 million bribery scandal in the oil sector. Probes were established by Nigerian Legislature as well as the USA Congress, but since nothing is heard anymore about the investigations, one may conclude that the issues have been swept under the carpet after waiting for 4 years (2004-2008).

Corruption contributes a major obstacle to reducing poverty, inequality, infant mortality, diminishing standard of living and life expectancy. It kills incentive to work hard with honesty, increases unemployment, diminishes productivity, reduces per capita income, enhances poor governance activities and encourages criminal activities. World Bank Institute research confirms that improved governance results in high national income per capita and adherence to the rule of law. Tackling corruption is seen to provide a major boost to developing countries according to World Bank Institute research.

The battle against corruption, fraud, money laundering and other economic and financial crimes being fought vigorously and unprecedentedly by the government cannot be won speedily and completely unless there are severe laws and special courts that adjudicate on such cases speedily. Corruption is doing a lot of damage to Nigeria's international and national image. It constitutes the main reason why it is difficult for international community to consider Nigeria for outright debt cancellation in 2005.

The irony about the perennial nature of corruption in Nigeria is that many of those who are expected to enforce laws against corruption, frauds, and economic and financial crimes are dignitaries among government functionaries whose hands are deep in such crimes which impoverish the country and earn the nation international disrepute and condemnation. In reality, most leaders of the countries condemning Nigeria for corruption are hypocrites who know what they realize from kickbacks and inflation of Iraqi contracts and oil money.

In the *Daily Champion* newspaper on June 9, 2004, while addressing Local Government Chairmen Forum, ExPresident Obasanjo was reported to have given an instance where a state governor collected the monthly statutory allocation of a local government council of ₦57 million, remitted ₦10 million to the council instead of ₦57 million, and advised the chairman of the local government council whose mother died to utilize ₦1 million for burial ceremony out of the local government money. It was added that the President warned that both the chairman and his governor should be in gaol (jail) for their felonious acts.

Have both the governor and the local council chairman involved in this case refunded the people's money? Deterrent efforts and laws to stop such elite misbehaviour of financial malpractices should be strengthened. In civilized and developed countries, any shady deal involving amounts above one thousand dollars is a felony for which the chairman of the local government and the governor would be immediately impeached, advised to resign or removed from office and their case placed before a court of competent jurisdiction. Eventually, they could be imprisoned when convicted for about ten years.

In his own paper titled, "Returning Life to the Village", the former National Chairman of the PDP, Chief Audu Ogbeh, warned that any local government chairman who connived with the state governor to misappropriate the statutory allocation would be held accountable and brought to book. Chief Ogbeh mentioned a few instances where one chairman complained that out of ₦39 million published by the Office of the Accountant General, he received only ₦6 million while another claimed that out of ₦46 million allocated to his local council, only ₦10 million got to him. Over 500 local government chairmen attended the forum.

Chief Audu Ogbeh advised the local government chairmen to be guided by the philosophy of generating employment and developing infrastructure in their localities. If less than onefourth of the monthly allocations to local government gets to the chairpersons while the rest is in private pockets of governors, how can there be employment generation and development as advised by Chief Audu Ogbeh?

The office of the Accountant General of the Federation should continue to publish the monthly allocations in the newspapers so that local government chairpersons who receive less than their normal share of federal government allocations could complain. In addition, those involved in fraud and corruption should be constantly exposed, speedily investigated, prosecuted and convicted by special courts or tribunals as a deterrence to prospective economic and financial saboteurs.

Chief Audu Ogbeh enjoined the local government council chairpersons to bring the basic joys of life to their employers, the humble villagers who elected them into office. He referred them to the dilapidation, blown off school roofs, deskless classrooms, inadequate infrastructures and facilities, ungraded roads, broken bridges, substandard clinics and abundant glaring evidence of penury in the local communities, and hence, charged the local government council bosses to tackle them. How can they tackle problems if less than onefifth of their monthly allocations reach them? The rest is in the pockets of their governors. How can they function without money?

The Nigerian President Obasanjo advised the local council chairpersons to see their election as a call to duty to make a difference in the lives of their rural constituents. He added that they should focus on agriculture, small-scale enterprises and physical infrastructural development. ExPresident Obasanjo was said to have commented, "The electoral system as it is presently constituted, does not inspire confidence in the people."

He emphasized that unless Nigerians begin to feel confident that their votes would count in determining the election outcomes, the nascent democracy would be operating on slippery grounds. He referred to telltales about the local government chairpersons' elections that, "Some of them got into office in not too edifying circumstances." Why were those suspected of election wrong doings not exposed, investigated exhaustively and punished severely? Where is the deterrence for future election rigging?

On Saturday, June 12, 2004, the *Dallas Morning News* business column, page 1D, carried a report that the United States of America Securities and Exchange Commission (SEC), was investigating alleged bribes paid in connection with the construction of a Nigerian natural gas complex by Halliburton Company subsidiary and three overseas partners.

The SEC and U.S. Justice Department asked Halliburton for cooperation and access to information relating to millions of dollars in payments in respect of the Nigerian gas complex in accordance with the requirements of the Foreign Corrupt Practices Act which forbids bribing of foreign officials.

Nigerian elites should henceforth stop making illegal deals with foreigners because they do not keep secrets for long. "They are the ones who will encourage the thief to come and steal from the farm, and they will at the same time call the farm owner to arrest the thief." They have no shame doing illegal business. They will always use your illegal deals with them against you to subdue you. Nigerian elites and government functionaries should be warned.

The million-dollar question to Chief Audu Ogbeh and Nigerians generally is: "If as in the cases mentioned above, some governors give less than onefourth of local government allocations to the chairpersons with the rest in their private pockets or stashed away in their foreign private bank accounts, how can they perform, and with what balance? It must be remembered that some chairpersons would also line up their own private pockets with part of the less than onefourth of the allocation that was given to them. All erring elites concerned are perpetrating

Nigeria's underdevelopment and poverty of the masses. They should be dealt with severely.

Cries of SOS (Save Our Souls) against corruption and mismanagement of resources by some governors sounded loud and clear from the Kaduna Discussion Group (KDG) in accusatory tones against the Northern Governors as a sign of deep frustration and helplessness. It seems 2004 marked the year of renaissance in the North when the youths and some groups began to see, talk and question what their leaders had done to keep the North in penury and underdevelopment for four decades of Nigerian independence.

The awareness going on in the North looks ordained by God/Allah because it marks the genesis of a remarkable break from established northern culture, custom and tradition of the youth and less privileged northerners keeping quiet when leaders cheat them, wrong them and trample them. The Yorubas have similar accommodation for elders' wrongs with impunity, but the Igbos are naturally vocal.

Remarkably, northern youths and some groups and individuals are beginning to ask questions from their leaders on what the rest of Nigeria had criticized for over forty years. This new development in the North augurs well for Nigerian unity, Nigerian development and Nigeria's forward movement because the North, South, East and West of the nation now clearly see and understand together, what has been going wrong, which only the East and the West criticized for four decades. In the past, Northerners never criticized their leaders for wrong doings.

One would have thought that the North that is most religiously guided in Nigeria in the teachings of Allah and Sharia Laws, should have been an example and an embodiment of transparency, fraudless and corruption free, peaceful, caring and loving, accommodating and not hateful of their neighbours, especially those from other parts of the country who are in their midst for religious and economic development.

With the magnitude of corruption complaints against some northern leaders, why has the Sharia establishment not dealt severely with erring Northern elites who committed economic and financial crimes as a deterrent example to the rest of Nigerians? Rightful leaders and elders should use their good offices to act responsibly, responsively, with accountability and exemplariness.

It is hypocritical for leaders to acquire wealth illegally, stash stolen money in foreign banks and live ostentatiously at the expense of their people who face daily hardship of underdevelopment, unemployment, hunger, thirst, homelessness and ill health while these corrupt elites pretend that they love their people and their country, Nigeria.

The elites should in the name of God/Allah repatriate the money stashed in foreign banks back to Nigeria for investment, employment generation, national development and economic growth. The government should encourage Nigerians in the Diaspora to repatriate their money home for investment purposes.

The Kaduna Discussion Group (KDG) in a statement on June 20, 2004 accused the Northern Governors of misappropriation of federal allocations meant for the development of the North. As a result, the KDG enjoined the northern public for understanding, concern, support and cooperation in its determination to promote, enforce and demand accountability, good governance, anticorruption and leadership transparency in the north.

The KDG group members led by Ambassador Yusuf Mamman, former National Chairman of Alliance for Democracy (AD) and Governor of Niger State, Colonel Lawan Gwadabe (rtd.) include Malam Shehu Sani (President, Civil Rights Congress), Mallam Sani Zorro (former National President, Nigerian Union of Journalists), Mallam Suleiman Danzaki (former Chairman, National Union of Road Transport Workers), Mrs. Rifkat Sabo (former Kaduna State Chairperson of Nigerian Labour Congress) and others.

The KDG through its spokesman, Mallam Yusuf Mamman, complained that Northern Nigeria had degenerated to a state of animalism with particular reference to education, health, infrastructure and living condition. The group emphasized, "Our leadership, particularly the governors and local government chairpersons manifest utter irresponsibility, contempt and scorn for our people and seem to eternally perpetuate the culture of dependency and subservience, while the material condition of our people has degenerated to bare subsistence." The group queried, "Why do we blame others for our problems?" They added, "It is time for selfcriticism and selfappraisal. We must be forward looking."

The group recalled that the federal government arrested some ministers and permanent secretaries for allegations of corruption but wondered why northern governors had not done the same when it was crystal clear that corruption had reached an endemic proportion in the states and local governments in the North. Why have Sharia operators and executives looked the other way, pretending nothing has happened when northern elites are involved in fraud and corruption?

They demanded that the public wanted to know:

(1) What happened to Federal government allocated and released funds for state and local government development?
(2) Whether executed projects were worthy of amounts expended?
(3) Whether the projects were relevant and helped to solve socio-economic problems, enhanced quality of education at all levels, and whether they were channeled to critical areas for employment generation, economic empowerment, poverty alleviation and enhancement of social harmony?
(4) How was the forty-four percent of the federal account expended in the states?
(5) Why state government's officials were gallivanting in Europe, Asia and America for upwards of eighteen days spending public funds with impunity?
(6) The immediate and remote causes of not paying workers' salaries that were long overdue?
(7) Why infrastructural facilities in the North could not compare with what was obtaining in other parts of Nigeria? They asked whether it was as a result of paucity of funds or poor planning, and how to achieve effective prioritization possibilities.
(8) Why leaders announced high sounding goals without concrete actions to meet them and thus created frustration among the people?

The KDG (Kaduna Discussion Group) reminded Northerners in particular and Nigerians generally about past leaders thus: The KDG spokesperson said, "Our past northern leaders have led us creditably and selflessly. They bequeathed some lasting legacies to the North. We even invoke their names at will to give semblance of relevance to our present leaders and shore up their credibility. But their various performances on the ground leave a lot more to be desired."

The (KDG) spokesman went on, "Our past heroes earned our respect because they led us as the true servants of the people. We respected them because neither plunder nor manipulation was their watchword. We still remember them because they bequeathed enduring legacies of probity, accountability and harmony for us to cherish. But have our present crop of northern leaders built upon the legacies they inherited? That's the big question. That is also one question that we must collectively address to help the leadership."

The above line of thought is a milestone, a turning point and a challenge to northern leadership in the annals of the North which all Nigerians must praise, appreciate and encourage to generate more enlightenment in the North in their best interest in particular and the best interest of Nigeria generally. In defence of his own state, the former Kaduna State Governor, Ahmed Makarfi condemned critics' generalization that state governors were corrupt without specificity or mentioning names by the federal government and other critics. The Governor of Ogun State, Obalofin Otunba Gbenga Daniel criticized the generalization as well as former Governor Nnamani of Enugu State who also frowned at the generalization that governors were corrupt.

ExGovernor Ahmed Makarfi called on all critics of the governors to mention names specifically because it was like, "We are all rotten eggs, which is not the case." He explained that his administration published comprehensive audited reports of his government's accounts at the end of every financial year, and that he would publish a fiveyear financial summary of the state as audited and certified, adopted and passed by the legislature after every query would have been answered. He emphasized that his state was in the lead for funds accountability. He called on the federal government to always publish details of resources allocated to the ministers and heads of government agencies for effective monitoring just as they publish state and local government allocations.

On Thursday, June 17, 2004, in Lusaka, during a state banquet organized in his honour, ExPresident Obasanjo revealed, "It is not easy to deal with corruption. In it, you find the high and the low, your friends and even those you respect." He added, "There would be no witchhunting in the pursuit of officials accused of corruption, and they would be thoroughly investigated." Nigerians share the concern of Mr. President. It must be realized fully well that anybody who spent several millions of naira to win election might grab and grab to get his/her money back, and any honourable minister or official who pays ₦54 million before being cleared and confirmed by the Senate would grab to get his/her money back while in office. It is important to address these causes of corruption and tackle them as a priority.

Corruption is endemic in the whole world including the most civilized and developed countries, which recognize 'no go' areas while Nigerian elites do not. It is sad. The kind of corruption in US is never directed to perpetuate the poverty and oppression of the masses and whenever it leaks, whoever is involved resigns his position immediately and is punished appropriately.

Mr. President, the situation can be ameliorated with a well-designed campaign finance law that would relieve elected representatives of enormous financial burden and debt. There must be deterrent laws and well-organized, effective law enforcement agencies and a trusted judiciary to dispense justice, speedily and in a fair and just fashion. The immunity coverage of the governors should be reviewed and adjusted appropriately.

African parenting, culture, tradition, custom, values and sense of community that taught Nigerians to be their brothers' and sisters' keepers never had a place for fraud and corruption. Economic and financial crimes were exported into African midst to divide, rule and break the protectionism long embedded in African precious, enviable extended family system and neighbourliness.

African value system encourages dignity, honour and respectability for the head of the family, and it has always taken a whole village or community to raise a Nigerian child. Nigerian elites who get infested with corruption and other crimes would find it difficult and uncomfortable to go back home to live in their towns and villages where innocence and great qualities of transparent life abound.

Any government official who awards a contract without strictly observing approved necessary guidelines or due process leaves room for corruption, and the contractor who obtains money and not perform but beats the system is corrupt. He or she must be made to disgorge the ill-gotten gains. The same thing must apply to all who are involved in ill-gotten gains including government functionaries whether high or low, foe or friend or those we respect.

There is nothing wrong if a contractor performs satisfactorily as expected and makes gains. The main purpose of business is profitability. Performing the contract and successfully completing the project would benefit the citizenry, and the contractor himself/herself would be happy with the gains, expand his/her business, generate employment and help the economy to grow.

Whoever cannot perform creditably to uplift Nigerian Administration is not Nigerian friend. Whoever cannot put the corrupt past behind him/her and change from being corrupt to uplift Nigerian government must not be respected anymore. Whoever may be a clog in the wheel of Nigerian progress to achieve Nigerian laudable objectives should be replaced and put in a reformatory.

If any corrupt person has not learned any lesson between 1960 and 2008, let the police do their work by prosecuting him nomatter the relationship of such corruption element to the presidency. Maybe it is the penitentiary that will make such people better Nigerians. Whoever wants to be respected should stop being corrupt. Whoever wants to promote relationship or be friendly to the presidency must stop being corrupt so that Nigerian Administration can succeed and be a model for the rest of Africa and the world.

ExPresident Obasanjo emphasized, "Our aim is not to fill the jails, but to recover and fill the treasury with what we need to develop." Whoever is ready to cough out the stolen money, and if he or she actually does so, may be given lighter sentence or probation. The nation should not be dragged into the ridiculous game played by Abacha family who broke the gentleman's agreement concluded to help recover the Nigerian money stashed in foreign banks.

A cooperating and patriotic legislature should be able to pass stricter and deterrent laws against fraud, corruption, economic and financial crimes and sabotage. An effective and efficient judiciary should be able to try economic saboteurs speedily and convict them appropriately as deterrence to others.

The fight against fraud, corruption and all forms of economic sabotage requires the teamwork of the Presidency, the Legislature, the Judiciary, State Governors, Local Government Chairpersons, the

Councilors, government functionaries, elders, leaders, religionists, traditional chiefs, academia, professionals and all Nigerians.

After several months of negotiations, Switzerland government transferred $50 million out of General Abacha's loot to the coffers of Nigerian Government on April 23, 2004. The government promised to deploy the money for the funding of social, health and educational projects. The government also trailed $100 million of Abacha's loot to Kenya, but the money was said to have ended in eighteen "nostro" accounts of several European banks.

The efforts to recover illgiven gains should continue relentlessly to all nooks and corners of Nigeria while the hunt for traditional rulers who allegedly got money and materials worth millions of naira from corrupt politicians and government officials should serve as a lesson to all.

This Day News of April 24, 2004, reported that in April 2002, Switzerland, Britain, Luxembourg, Liechtenstein and Jersey Island agreed to release $1 billion in a deal which would facilitate the release of Abacha's son from prison and that Abacha's family might keep $100 million in an arrangement aimed at helping the government to discover other assets stolen by the late dictator.

It was said that soon after Abacha's son was released, he reneged the gentleman's agreement and refused to cooperate to keep the family's part of the bargain. Unfortunately, Sharia Establishments often close the eyes when 'sacred cows and untouchables' are involved in economic and financial crimes. That is hypocritical and sad.

So far, the government must be credited for recovering some of the loot which some of Abacha's lieutenants, aides, advisers and close associates pretended to know nothing about. It was out of sheer magnanimity that Abacha's family should have been allowed to keep $100 million.

Such concession or grace out of illegally acquired Nigerian money was too much. It was partial condonment of illegality, which was better because it helped to end the endless case, and government could concentrate on governance of the country. Continuing the case would have meant heavier legal fees, which would have been more than $100 million, promised to leave for Abacha family.

The money siphoned away could have been utilized for:

(1) local investment;
(2) to develop the Niger Delta;
(3) generate employment;
(4) fund social, health, housing, agriculture and educational projects in Northern Nigeria.

In the *Daily Independent Online* of Wednesday, April 21, 2004, it was reported that the Special Assistant on Special Duties to late Head of State, General Sani Abacha, late Alhaji Wada Nas said that he agreed with Professor Sam Aluko that Abacha's loot was exaggerated. The statement itself, if true, was an admission that there was Abacha loot by the two eminent Nigerians (late Hon. Wada Nas and Professor Aluko) who served in the top hierarchy during Abacha regime.

Patriotic Nigerians who know where the loot is, especially those who participated fully in Abacha's government as advisers, aides and top government functionaries, should assist government efforts to recover the loot in the best interest of Nigeria and Nigerians. Why have Northern Nigerian socio-economic and political groups not stood up to condemn Abacha's loot in the name of God/Allah?

In civilized communities in the world, withholding such vital information is an accessory to the crime; it is prosecutable, and if convicted, such person is liable to prison sentence. It must be understood by all well meaning Nigerians that if the loot is recovered from Abacha and many others, the money can become a veritable way of reducing massive unemployment, youth restiveness and criminal tendencies.

In the *Daily Independent Online* of Wednesday, January 19, 2005, it was reported that ₦1.96 billion was recovered from exInspector General of Police, Tafa Balogun for corruptly enriching himself as confirmed by the Economic and Financial Crimes Commission (EFCC). It was further alleged that he had $150 million in Swiss bank accounts, $200 million (London) and ₦500 million in Nigeria. Some sources alleged that he had more than was discovered. He was said to be facing ninety-five counts on the charge of stealing about ₦13.8 billion. In the end, the matter was settled in court using plea bargains and political intervention.

In the *Vanguard* of Sunday, May 1, 2005, Senator Nuhu Aliyu, former Deputy Inspector General of Police, was said to have confirmed that some members of the National Assembly included those people he had arrested in the past for grave criminal offences including '419' advance fee fraud.

He further remarked, "Now that former Inspector General of Police is facing trial in court, I hope and pray that he will be able to convince Nigerians that he had no hand in any criminal activity, especially when it relates to siphoning funds. Don't forget the amount of money being mentioned, ₦13 billion. ₦13 billion is a hell of money that could turn the police into an active service and that could provide the wherewithal for good performance. But if it is true as alleged that he took away the money, it is unfortunate." In early July 2005, it was reported that the EFCC had recovered ₦17.7 billion from the former Inspector General of Police.

What simply came to mind was the plight and sufferings of thousands of low cadre police officers who did not receive their salaries for months and thereby resorted to collecting ₦20 as bribes from bus conductors while their boss was allegedly filthy rich in corruption. It will be recalled that some bus conductors who would not part with the ₦20 bribe were shot and killed by desperate policemen at police check points.

A police commissioner was reported to have said, "He, Tafa Balogun (ExInspector General of Police) allowed himself to be used recklessly by Obasanjo who dumped him like used toilet paper." Such a comment was very unfair. The ExInspector General of Police dumped himself when he corruptly enriched himself to the tune of the amounts specified above, which was more than the annual budget of some developing countries. There are some countries in the world that would hang such corrupt people for economic sabotage.

An Assistant Inspector of Police who asked for anonymity said, "The former Inspector General of Police got what he deserved, and it was long overdue. He was an epitome of corruption. His fall will be followed by disgrace." He was said to have accused the ExInspector General of Police of high profile corruption, and that he had not given satisfactory account of ₦1.4 billion he collected on behalf of police to conduct the 2003 elections. The EFCC Ex-Chairman, Nuhu Ribadu and his men should be commended for doing a wonderful job to rid corruption out of Nigerian society.

The EFCC Ex-Chairman and his staff were also reported to have foiled a ₦55 million bribe, which involved the committee leadership in the Senate, the House and some members of the Legislative Education Committee. Did any of the bribery conspirators in this case ever think about the multiplier, damaging effects on students, their parents and Nigerian educators if ₦55 million was used to bribe the legislature education committee members in order to manipulate the education budget? Only God/Allah knows how many legislative committees have committed similar offences. The Ex-Chairman, Federal Capital Territory Administration (FCTA) Mallam ElRufai, made similar complaint that two senators demanded ₦54 million bribe from him to facilitate his Senate confirmation as minister. He almost lost his job for speaking out. Unfortunately, ElRufai himself was declared wanted in December 2008 by the EFCC for frauds worth billions of government money. See how the pot was calling the kettle black!

Honourable Haruna Yerima (Borno) was alleged to have complained about some of his colleagues in the House of Representatives Committees who were alleged to be involved in corrupt practices, but before his complaint was investigated, the House of Representatives members were alleged to have voted to suspend him for a month and even threatened him with expulsion.

He complained in February 2005 that some of his colleague legislators were extorting money from Ministers and government parastatals bosses to allocate more funds, inflate and pass their budgets. ₦55 million was collected from former Minister of Education, Professor Fabian Osuji. The Central Bank was said to have coughed ₦50 million and later ₦20 million to legislative committee. The practice was extortionism and not an acceptable way of asking for and receiving donation to assist legislative performance. As an example to others, the Legislature must operate within its annual budget passed into law.

In order to receive more revelations, the president can offer immunity to government functionaries who can come out to reveal how legislators extorted money from them. In addition to that, the ICPC, EFCC and the presidency should operate a reward system to benefit those who provide information that leads to the arrest, indictment and conviction of corrupt and fraudulent Nigerians as well as other criminals. The names and identities of such informants must be kept confidential.

Whoever has not stopped corrupt practices after all the past warnings, persistent or desperate calls for transparency and exemplary leadership, should go to prison.

It was unfortunate that Professor Fabian Osuji, former Education Minister, fell with some topmost Senators and others into this corruption mess, but if it was their first time of doing it, their compromise time to commit the felonious corrupt practice would have been longer during which some of them might have had a second thought to decline and say, "No". It was also unfortunate that while the electorate were wallowing in poverty, in various localities, some of their elected legislators were sharing millions of naira corruptly extorted overnight instead of making laws that would help Nigerian citizenry.

If the legislators concerned did not ask for ₦55 million from Professor Osuji, he would not have desperately borrowed money from many sources. He was made the scapegoat. How would the ministers, departmental heads, and contractors, etc. from whom money was extorted recover their money without resorting to corrupt practices? Regrettably and invariably, the extortion situation would create an extended corruption network, a ripple effect from the legislators to the ministers, the heads of departments, contractors, etc. who would in turn pass it to the next layer down the line to the masses to recover the bribes given out because nobody wants to lose his/her money.

The burden of bribes that companies, businesses and people give out are passed to consumers in the final analysis for replenishment. Such extortion, bribery and corruption would indirectly hike prices and become inflationary to the disadvantage of an economy that is attempting to stabilize. In effect, the extortion scenario, if unchecked, would glorify corruption as a business venture per se, nurtured from the top hierarchy of elites (the legislature) to the downtrodden masses.

The Legislature has its annual budget within which it must operate as an example to others. Asking for bribe and money from ministers, departmental heads, contractors, etc. by lawmakers is breaking the law. Such extortionist tendencies and actions should stop to revive legislators' good personal images as most distinguished personalities as well as overall images of the Senate and the House of Representatives.

The irony of the corrupt situation was that it was deliberate and those involved knew that what they were doing was wrong and shameful judging from the way the House Legislators allegedly reacted to slap Hon. Haruna Yerima with a month suspension when he tried to blow the whistle about corrupt practices in the Legislature. Was Hon. Haruna Yerima punished for speaking the truth to correct an ugly situation of corruption in the Legislature? Was punishment a good example or an intimidation to cover a wrongdoing of the Legislators? Was that not obstruction of justice by the Legislators?

The system was so vulnerable that Professor Osuji applied for ₦20 million loan from National Universities Commission (NUC) and got the cheque out the same day as part of the ₦55 million used for the bribery of Senate and House Committees on Education. What reason was stated for the loan on the application form, and how would it be paid back into the coffers of NUC that was raising hell and complaining about lack of funds? According to Daily Independence Online of Thursday, March 24, 2005, the payment voucher for the loan was NUC/URC/1132/12/04 issued in cheque number 31417062 on December 3, 2004.

Some of the legislative members were accused of:
(1) receiving financial gratification from ministers and contractors in their oversight functions;
(2) demanding money before confirming political appointees;
(3) demanding money regarding the ₦25 billion equity capital requirement by the banks; and
(4) demanding money from heads of ministries before approving their departmental budgets.

Those who were involved in the above acts if proven guilty would be better for a reformatory instead of the Legislature. With hands full of millions of money from corrupt practices, and minds full of how to hide the money and cover up the deals from leaking out, how can such legislators have time to initiate and make laws in the best interest of Nigerians and Nigeria?

Those who voted to suspend Honourable Hassan Yerima before investigating the corruption charges he levied against some of his legislative colleagues included both sexes (male and female), Christians and Muslims. Is such hasty suspension action justifiable and right ethically, professionally, morally and spiritually? Traditionally, if men would not listen to your complaint because of their nature, impatience and fatherhood, women usually and normally do listen because of their motherhood, patience, love, care, nature and femininity.

Religionwise, those who do not call God/Allah daily nor attend churches and mosques regularly may not listen to people's complaint about corruption before passing judgment because of their limited spiritually, but Christians and Muslims as they abound in the Legislature should first listen because of their devotion to the teachings of God/Allah and their level of maturity as most distinguished personalities. Was Hon. Yerima's suspension true and justified, and for blowing the whistle or what? The story was and is still incredible.

Regrettably, in the corruption charge levied by Hon. Yerima against his colleagues in the House, both men and women, Christian and Muslim legislators allegedly retorted with suspension and intimidation without first investigating his complaints. What will those who took part in the suspension action tell their constituencies and their enlightened children who know what justice and fairplay means and entails? Are these distinguished men and women no longer thinking, "What if their children, families, friends and constituencies hear their involvements with injustice, unfair decisions and corruption practices?" How would they explain their actions?

The suspension and intimidation of Hon. Yerima by men and women, Christians and Muslims simply confirms that injustice, illegal gains and corrupt practices know no boundaries in sexes, religions and ethnicities.

It is likely that elected representatives (president, governors, legislators, councilors, etc.) face serious financial embarrassment from creditors and godfathers after having spent many millions of naira out of borrowed money to be elected into office. Also, the local inhabitants and the entire constituencies want some financial benefits from elected representatives all the time.

People's mentality is that legislators are going there to make money. For example: the former Senate President Wabara may have spent millions to be elected Senator going by the controversies that followed his election as well as how he became the Senate President. If he would not grab and extort, how would he be able to get back or recover all the money taken from him within four years from his salary, which would not be enough? In effect, the system creates corruption and must be reviewed.

Secondly, ExGovernor Kalu of Abia State was said to have mentioned that he gave ₦100 million to the PDP to assist 1999 presidential election campaign. Politicians who spend such money always want their money back in so many folds using different means while in office. Nigerians, when you took their money and sent them into debt before you elected them into offices what justification do you have to blame them when they steal the money back after being elected? You are all equally guilty of corruption.

Civilized and advanced democracies have registered lobbyists and special interest groups who offer bribes to manipulate legislative votes and decisions as well as presidential advisers' and experts' reports, recommendations, decisions and advisement. It should not be condoned for being morally wrong, and it is not a viable excuse to say it happens all over the world.

What was extremely sad, wrong and condemnable was for some Nigerian Legislators to extort ₦54 million from each presidential nominee before the Senate confirmation of his/her appointment as well as demanding ₦55 million from each Minister before his/her departmental budget was inflated and approved, and extorting money from contractors at places where they exercised oversight functions.

Such acts are unconscionable, egregious, felonious, uncivilized and represent a great disservice to Nigerians. It is serious act of indirect robbery. Fortunately, these scandals have stopped which is great credit to the Legislators. It looks like they learned their lessons in the hard way. If elites modify behaviour, Nigeria will be better for it.

In the civilized world like the USA, Legislators/Congressmen are not poor, they make their extra money with decency and dignity. Scandals are rare but they happen. Nigerian legislators should find out how things are done differently in advanced, civilized communities to stay out of trouble and scandals, and avoid disgracing our nascent democratic experiment. They have been using the wrong method to solve genuine financial problems created by the system, and they never thought it would backfire because Nigerian politicians in the past had done the same corrupt practices for over forty years (1960-2003) with impunity as sacred cows and untouchables. Now, it is different.

Regrettably, some most distinguished ladies and gentlemen, the sacred cows, the untouchables, people of timber and calibre, the moneybags and the most influential Nigerians had forty years of grace (1960-1999) to change their corrupt practices and business as usual, but they failed. They also had additional four years of transitional period (1999-2003) to change their corrupt habits, which have become pathological, but they have not.

Hence, whoever has not changed should be filtered from Nigerian society into a reformatory because enough is enough after more than four decades of grace (1960-2003). In a situation where traditional rulers are not spared for receiving gifts traceable to corrupt enrichment, then if you refuse to change, you may appropriately end up in the penitentiary.

It looks more certain that God/Allah is the One cleaning Nigeria with ExPresident Obasanjo and President Yar'Adua as His first and second messengers. Hence, Nigerians should all rally round to be part of the crusade to salvage Nigeria from the snakehead and nemesis called corruption.

The financial burden of legislators and others who pass through electoral process to hold office is overwhelming, but that cannot be justification for corruption and extortion. The legislators should work with the Presidency to make laws that relieve them of the burden instead of being defensive and quarreling with the President. The presidency and the legislature should cooperate fully to enact campaign finance law that can save them from the burden of debt resulting from the electoral process.

Changing when it is time to change is part of being clever as elected representatives and leaders of the people. Even God/Allah cannot give anybody forgiveness especially if his/her repetitive, inappropriate, inexcusable, corrupt behaviour is deliberate and not accidental. Corruption is one of the deliberate felonies that cannot attract forgiveness because it has plagued Nigeria for over forty years and has devastated its citizenry. All must fight it hands down at all costs and from now on. Please heed the warnings to avoid being corrupt and/or being corrupted by others.

General Mohammadu Buhari, Military Head of State (1984/85) placed elected representatives and political appointment nominees of Shagari Administration in incarceration until they proved that they were corruptfree. The onus of proof of innocence rested with the detainees. They remained there until General Ibrahim Badamosi Babangida overthrew his regime in 1985.

Politicians suspected of corruption, who fled overseas were pursued. Shagari's Minister of Transportation, Alhaji Umaru Dikko, was pursued to London, kidnapped, drugged, made unconscious, caged and tagged "Ambassador Luggage" to be placed on a plane en route to Nigeria to answer corruption charges, but fortunately for him, the airplane was halted by British police on a tipoff, and Alhaji Umaru Dikko was rescued. Prominent among those detained was Alhaji Balarabe Musa, the impeached governor of old Kaduna State.

Empathically and in consideration of the financial commitments of elected representatives (president, governors, legislators, local council chairpersons and councilors, etc.), which outweigh their total emoluments under the present system, the President and Legislature, should work hard in unison to enact a campaign finance legislation which can help reduce the financial burden, commitment and embarrassment of elected representatives.

Such helpful law will minimize the tendencies for corruption, dependence on godfathers and creditors as well as help elect the best candidates who may not be financially strong enough to face the 'money bags'. Instead of facing the realities of the wrongs and damages which corruption scandals have caused and cost the Legislature and taking responsibility, some members felt aggrieved, bitter and defensive in ways that could make bad matters worse.

It is disingenuous for some elite legislators to embark on slanders, witchhunting, fault-finding and wildgoose chasing expeditions as was alleged for paying Israeli Accountants $250,000 to trace ExPresident Obasanjo's funds in order to nail him for corruption, an episode which was said to be unsuccessful. It was also misguiding for some legislators to allegedly start to look for impeachable offences of the President of Nigeria because he was fighting corruption relentlessly, an exercise that stepped on many toes including those of some leaders of the Legislature.

The best thing is for all to work together to stamp out corruption in all facets of Nigerian society. Whoever falls in this corrective exercise which is unprecedented in the annals of Nigerian nation, should accept it as a necessary lesson learned the hard way, and for the sake of posterity, stop contemplating a revenge possibility and help spread anticorruption messages and implications to all nooks and corners of Nigeria. Such evangelism is a task that must be undertaken by all.

ExPresident Obasanjo made the following statements among many others:
(1) "The Presidency in its totality is united in this war against corruption."
(2) "We cannot stand for confusion in this anticorruption exercise."
(3) "There are no sacred cows."
(4) "We are going to be focused."
(5) "In this anticorruption crusade, whether you are friend or foe, the battle must go on. The war must continue."
(6) "My family knows where I stand on this issue. They all have a code of conduct. If they don't follow, they will be treated like anyone else."

About 2,309 applicants for college admissions were reported by Vanguard News on Sunday, June 12, 2005 to have presented fake certificates for admission to Ibadan Polytechnic Higher National Certificate programme. The applicants were from various parts of the country. The certificate forgery racket requires thorough investigation to smash the mentors and perpetrators of certificate forgery. Those involved directly and indirectly should be arrested, prosecuted and convicted as deterrence to certificate fraudsters. The sources of forged college certificates for sale should be exterminated.

It is in the best interest of Nigeria if Nigerians in all their spheres of life endeavours can seriously and patriotically assist the presidency to fight corruption. Can the Governors, Legislators (state and federal), the Judiciary, the Police (top to bottom), Local Government Chairpersons and Councilors, Obas and Chiefs, Elders and Leaders, etc. proudly talk and act against corruption?

Is anticorruption message with its implications being carried to all nooks and corners of Nigeria including schools, churches, mosques, social clubs, the private and public sectors? Anticorruption crusade cannot be left to the presidency alone. All hands must be on deck to fight corruption to a logical conclusion. Nigerian image, her fate, her sociopolitical and economic prosperity and the fate of Nigerian posterity hang on the outcome of the fight against corruption. Nigerians cannot afford to fail this time and onwards.

The greatest apprehension of most Nigerians in the Diaspora and in Nigeria is how to find the right leaders and government functionaries who will continue the fight against corruption in Nigeria relentlessly. Fighting corruption as it is, may be like cutting the branches of a big menacing tree and destroying the leaves. In essence, if the taproots are not attacked and destroyed, the tree will always grow back. In the same manner, if the causes (taproots) of corruption are not attacked and solved, the present fight against corruption may not yield lasting dividends.

Corruption cannot be fought haphazardly to achieve the objectives of exterminating it. To kill corruption, the causes (taproots) must be annihilated and burnt to ashes. If not, corruption may grow back, assume more enormous proportion under new leaders who care less or can be easily manipulated by foreign interests.

To exterminate corruption, it must be fought scientifically, philosophically, motivationally using positive reinforcement persuasively, spiritually, and aggressively with some human management sophistication and legally, which relates to negative reinforcement as the last resort. Using these modern management strategies will require a master plan of short and long terms, which will make Nigeria corruptionfree and become a model society for the whole world.

Corruption envelops the whole world. Corruption is endemic, and the world is pathologically corrupt. Even those who preach against corruption using the Holy Books daily are not saints. It has become a disease, which has eaten deep into the fabric of society. What is being done in Nigeria at the moment is fighting corruption aggressively by cutting the branches and destroying the leaves of the menacing tree by arresting, indicting, prosecuting and convicting corrupt government functionaries at federal, state and local levels. Such actions are deterrent, but the causes (taproots) of corruption are still intact. The following examples are worthy of consideration:

(1) If 100,000 graduates are looking for jobs, and there are 1,000 vacancies, corruption will subsist under that situation.
(2) If 100,000 students qualify for university admission, and there are only 1,000 places coupled with shortage of hostels,

corruption will subsist under that situation.

(3) If an elected representative has to borrow several millions of naira from godfathers and other creditors to spend in order to win election, corruption will subsist.

(4) If demand for any essential product far outweighs supply thus creating shortages, corruption will subsist.

(5) If corruption laws are not enforced deterrently, equitably, justly, fairly, nonselectively, nondiscriminatorily; if there are sacred cows and untouchables, corruption will grow back and thrive.

To exterminate corruption will require short and long term master plans which should contain exhaustive corruption diagnosis, hypothesis, prognosis, execution, supervision, verification, assessment, feedback and adjustment strategies, and above all, there must be effective plans for law enforcement against corruption as well as motivation, rewards and benefits for good services in all nooks and corners of Nigeria.

With corruption elimination crusade going on at Federal Government level, how much are the state and local governments involved? The fight against corruption must place all Nigerians on board. The sanitization should be top-down and bottom-up to be effective and achieve the desired results. It should not be selective or discriminatory. Accountability and transparency should be encouraged within economic, financial, sociopolitical and other groupings.

The alleged ₦2.9 billion fraud within the PDP culminating in the dissolution of its National Working Committee as revealed by the *Punch* newspaper of Friday, June 10, 2005 was disturbing. Other political parties should crosscheck what their officials are doing because they are not saints. Thorough investigation should be conducted, and those found fraudulent should be brought to justice as deterrence to others.

Those leading militant youths as well as sociopolitical activists are alleged to be getting richer and richer at the expense of the people. That is not the right way to fight for the people. Who are the owners of illegal oil refineries in the South-South States? Do the local and state government functionaries and elected representatives not know them nor suspect anything about their illegalities? Nigerians should stop being fooled.

Where are the billions according to Mrs. Ogbebor and how did they become millionaires and billionaires as wondered by Professor Tam DavidWest? Are people leading just to make money? Militants are becoming millionaires and their secret mentors among leading politicians and other leaders in the South-South zone are becoming multibillionaires. How will corruption, illegal oil bunkering, oil pipes vandalization, kidnappings and militancy stop without deterrent measures when these illegal activities have become big time businesses and profitable sources of wealth? They are not fools.

Fraudulent and corrupt practices occur in all shapes and forms everywhere in the world without exception. Corruption in Nigeria is a childplay compared with what happens in advanced and developed countries. Corporate frauds and corruption are very common in the USA running into billions of dollars.

Bernard Madoff of New York, USA was arrested in December 2008 for $50 billion fraud. Bernard Ebbers, former Chairman of WorldCom, was sentenced to twenty-five years imprisonment in New York, USA on Wednesday, July 13, 2005 for corporate fraud of $11 billion, which resulted into the loss of about 30,000 jobs. Further examples of fraud and corruption existed in corporations like Enron, Halliburton, Anderson and so on and so forth, running into billions of dollars. Chevron was allegedly investigated by the Senate for $10.8 million tax evasion. That is how it is all over the world. It started from developed countries, and it will not end or stop easily because the world elites are benefiting from corruption just like illegal drugs war.

Nigeria is on the right path in its fight against fraud and corruption. The fight against corruption must be conducted and spread to all nooks and corners of Nigeria to rid the menace out of Nigerian society. It is a task that must be done, and the fight against corruption must be won.

Nigerians must give ExGovernor Kalu of Abia State every opportunity to defend himself against allegations of corruption levied against him by the group called Abia Leadership Forum as well as the accusation of keeping a foreign account while in office. He must be assumed innocent until proven guilty by the court or tribunal with appropriate and competent jurisdiction. The petition purportedly signed by Kalu's former Deputy Enyinnanya Abaribe, Chijioke Nwakodo and

Ekekwe John Egu alleged that Governor Kalu established the following businesses while in office:
(1) The *Sun Newspapers* in late 2003;
(2) Slok Airlines which commenced operations in 2003;
(3) Acquisition of over 100 houses and hotels in Abia, Lagos and a $1.7 million mansion in Potomac, Maryland, USA in June 2003;
(4) Marina International Bank in late 1999;
(5) Other interests in several banks, financial institutions and the gas and oil sectors;
(6) Possession of eleven ships worth $33 million, etc., etc.

The case was being handled by the EFCC as reported by This Day News of Thursday, September 8, 2005. In the same manner, all the State Governors and other government functionaries facing probes and indictments should be given every opportunity to defend themselves. The President and the Legislature should speed up to review and amend the immunity clause in the Nigerian Constitution. All ill-gotten gains should be recovered and utilized for national development in the best interest of Nigerian masses.

The former Governor of Bayelsa State in the oil producing Niger Delta, Chief Diepreye Alamieyeseigha, was on bail and house arrest in London, UK for money laundering of 1.8 million pounds sterling. He allegedly jumped bail and smuggled himself back to Nigeria on Sunday, November 20, 2005. It was revealed that he dressed as a woman and forged travel documents to pass through both United Kingdom and Nigeria airports security undetected. How could somebody on bail and house arrest with his passport seized, manage to leave the house and travel out of London to Nigeria undetected? The episode looked impossible.

He addressed a news conference at the state capital, Yenagoa, in the government house. It was said that as he drove into town, the streets were lined with crowds of people waving white handkerchiefs in jubilation. It was revealed that he knelt down and prayed while thanking the Ijaw people for bringing him back.

Wrong value judgment with 'human vanity worshipping' is still common in Nigeria. If it were in the USA, an electronic movement equipment monitor with alarm would be stuck to his leg to prevent his escape. He complicated his case by jumping bail, forging travel documents and escaping to Nigeria. He relied on very bad advisement and used very poor judgment. He made a bad case worse. That is what youthful exuberance does to people. At last, he was impeached, lost the governorship and immunity and had to face prosecution for stealing N124 billion.

The former Chairman of Economic and Financial Crimes Commission (EFCC), Nuhu Ribadu, described the case of the fugitive governor thus, "It is a tragedy; it is a challenge to us and to our justice system." How much has this criminal behaviour tarnished the image of Nigeria? It was the second time that a Nigerian state governor was declared wanted by the British police for money laundering. Plateau State ExGovernor, Joshua Dariye, committed the first case. The President of Nigeria and legislature must amend the immunity clause as a priority to be able to prosecute governors who commit crimes.

It must be realized that the ethnicity to which any governor or government functionary belongs is not a licence for him/her to commit money laundering, forge travel documents and jump bail from British prosecution. In this case, all Ijaws in particular and Nigerians in general should condemn the felonious acts of the former Governor of Bayelsa State and any others who have broken the law. There must be thorough investigation of the case and all accomplices prosecuted and convicted appropriately as deterrence to others. What is the need for pride or jubilation if someone commits money laundering of 1.8 million pounds sterling, forged travel documents and jumped bail from London court? How are we sure that the money laundered was not part of the allocation for the development of Bayelsa State of Niger Delta?

The exgovernor should have repatriated the ten million pounds sterling representing his allegedly valued assets in London for purposes of investment in Bayelsa State on small businesses in order to generate employment for Ijaw youths. Nigerian politicians and leaders should discourage money laundering, capital flight and brain drain in the best interest of Nigeria. Elites should stop robbing Nigerians instead of investing in them.

The money taken overseas can never be fully recovered. Stop being fooled. Nigerians should utilize their wealth to benefit their fellow Nigerians in Nigeria. Your wealth in overseas bank accounts does not make you to become your brother's keeper in Nigeria. Always remember, "East or West, Home is the best. There is no other place like Home!"

GOD/ALLAH BLESS NIGERIA!

CHAPTER 10

POLITICAL STABILITY AND TOLERANCE

Nigeria emerged united and stronger after a troubling civil war (1967-1970) and over three decades of dictatorship. Before the civil war, there were two bloody military coups d'etat on January 15, 1966 and July 29, 1966 respectively which resulted into killings and widespread violence. The war was completed with the spirit of no victor, no vanquished followed by a period of rehabilitation, reabsorption, reconstruction and reconciliation.

After the civil war, there were periods of successive coups d'etat resulting in dictatorships and political instability for decades. The events before and after the civil war taught Nigerians a lot of lessons, which made many Nigerians to say, "Never Again to Dictatorship; Never Again to War and Divisionism."

During the civil war and dictatorship (1966-1999), there were killings, riots, high inflation, economic downturn, economic fluctuations, hunger, disease, illhealth, insecurity of lives and properties, unsustainable foreign debt, high rate of unemployment, high interest rate of double digits, high rate of fraud and corruption, low rate yield of Gross Domestic Product (GDP), human rights abuses, high crime rate, high rate of migration, vandalization of government infrastructures, illegal oil bunkering, smuggling of contrabands, illegal arms, drugs and human trafficking. Nigeria was declared a pariah state and ostracized by the international community; it was a period no Nigerian ever wants to revisit, never again.

Military rule ended on May 29, 1999 with the emergence of a democratically elected civilian President Obasanjo in compliance with the Nigerian 1999 Constitution. There and then started a new era for Nigeria and her people. Within a few years, Obasanjo Administration was able to restore and enhance the image of Nigeria considerably.

Nigeria's pariah status was cancelled, her ostracization was annulled by the United Nations; foreign investments poured in; socio-economic activities improved; frauds and corruption were seriously fought and Nigeria became the peace and power broker in Africa. Normalcy was restored to Nigeria and people enjoyed enhanced political stabilization for the first time in decades.

Nigeria moved from being a pariah state to become a beloved country and the greatest one to be reckoned with in Africa. The Nigerian President Obasanjo became the Chairman of African Union and the Chairperson in Office of the Commonwealth. Nigeria hosted conferences of Commonwealth Heads of Governments, ECOWAS, AU etc. Archbishop Anthony Olubunmi Okojie of Lagos became a Cardinal, Nigeria launched its satellite into space, and Eyimba made Nigeria proud by winning the CAF soccer cup and Cardinal Arinze became one of the final nominees being considered for the papacy. The Paris Club cancelled $18 billion of Nigeria's foreign debt and the balance of $12 billion was paid in three installments.

The successor of President Obasanjo was President Umaru Musa Yar' Adua effective May 29, 2007. President Yar'Adua believed strongly in the rule of law, due process and service to the people as 'Servant Leader'. His administration moved very cautiously to reverse some decisions hurriedly taken by his predecessor's government functionaries during the last couple of weeks of his successorship to the presidency. He has been leading with the best examples and he deemphasized the indispensability of office holders in his administration. He replaced the EFCC Chairman, Nuhu Ribadu with Mrs. Farida Waziri. He has been able to demonstrate sincerity, transparency and humility as well as infuse discipline in his administration. He reshuffled his cabinet after a year in office.

Nigeria possesses enormous wealth of human resources scattered all over the world who have experienced best socio-economic and political practices and are ready to apply them for the advancement of Nigerian people. In terms of mistakes of the past, Nigerians have vouched, "Never Again, Never Again!" Nigeria will never allow unpleasant history to repeat itself. Nigeria has decided to settle down and become a great and wonderful example to the world. Nigeria has become a remarkable leader in Africa.

If Nigeria does not settle down to lead and thwart the neocolonization, marginalization and discrimination efforts being perpetrated against the Blacks all over the universe, who would?

If Nigeria does not settle down to lead the efforts to save the Blackman socio-economically and politically, who would?

If Nigeria does not properly harness its resources to lead black people's collective efforts for the total emancipation of the black world out of poverty, illhealth, disease, hunger, impoverishment, socio-economic strangulation and enslavement, intertribal and religious wars, political destabilization, fraud and corruption, who else would?

If Nigeria, the pride of the Blackman continues to allow the pervasion of political intolerance and disintegrates or fails, who else would lead the Blackman to the Promised Land?

It is therefore, in the best interest of Nigeria in particular and the black people of the world generally for Nigerians to maintain political tolerance and stability, peace, economic well-being, religious tolerance, transparency, democracy, true federalism and good governance.

Nigerians have a lot to learn from the outcomes of the 2000, 2004 and 2008 presidential elections in the USA; which were conducted without bitterness or threats of national disasters from those who lost. Nigerians should start to approach the act of losing with grace, dignity and maturity and not as an end to life. Winning an election should not become a do or die game. Crude and brazen rigging of elections should stop.

Nigeria is not an exception to election rigging, but the new democratic nation must be an example for the world to emulate. Each major political party rigged the 2007 elections in its stronghold with contemptuous boldness and shamelessness. It was therefore highly hypocritical for any political party leadership in opposition to be acting as the pot calling the kettle black. It happens everywhere in the world too, but with some civility. Election rigging must stop.

As a democracy, Nigeria has a lot to learn from the political life of the USA. After the 2004 presidential election in the USA, the incumbent, President George Bush (the winner), joined Senator John Kerry (the loser) who was more favoured to win by most other countries worldwide, in calling for understanding and national unity without bitterness in a spirit of no victor, no vanquished. During the campaign, which was very contentious, the exit polls were very tight, and it was difficult to predict a winner.

George W. Bush, the winner, declared, "We have one country, one constitution and one future that binds us." He added, "And when we come together and work together, there is no limit to the greatness of America." The first thing that both candidates focused on was national unity and the greatness of America.

Given similar situations in Nigeria in 2003 and 2007 the losers called on Nigerian people to stage massive disruptive and destructive action that might render the country ungovernable. A nationalistic, patriotic, matured, gracious, gallant or tolerant loser does not utter such words, which may be interpreted as treasonable. When some Nigerian elites talk and act as if they are above the law, one wonders whether such people talk and act out of sheer empty arrogance, ignorance or lack of civility!

Senator John Kerry, without being bitter for losing, told his supporters that President Bush (the winner) and himself (the loser), "had a good conversation" and "talked about the danger of division in our country and the need – the desperate need – for unity." Senator Kerry added that he chose to concede in order to avert a "protracted legal fight which was not in the best US national interest." President George Bush accepted his opponent's telephone call conceding victory to him at 11:02 a.m. on November 3, 2004. In 2008, Senators McCain and Clinton conceded victory to Senator Barack Obama with praises, grace, decency, dignity and patriotism in the best interest of the USA.

During the conversation, President Bush told his opponent, Senator John Kerry, "I think you are an admirable, worthy opponent." He added, "You waged one tough campaign." Senator Kerry gave his supporters who felt dejected and disappointed, a message of conciliation, reiterating that Americans must join hands together in common effort, without bad feelings of defeat or recrimination, and without anger or rancour to move the country forward in the right direction.

The unity that emerged between President Bush and John Kerry and their supporters after a hardfought political battle for the presidency is worthy of emulation by Nigerian politicians who need to place Nigeria first above any other consideration. The 2004 US presidential election was not without some complaints about the creation, distribution and counting of provisional ballots, voting machine glitches, some absentee voters who did not receive their papers in time to vote and many other complaints which could have resulted in a protracted legal tussle if Senator Kerry had not conceded victory early in the name of US national interest.

Independent monitors including Common Cause members and the Lawyers Committee for Civil Rights reported complaints of lost absentee ballots, machine malfunctions, shortage of provisional ballots and other resources, but the common sense of patriotism of Senator John Kerry, his advisers and the Democratic Party leadership prevailed to end any situation that might cause further divisionism that could have plunged the US into any political uncertainties.

On the other hand, Nigerian presidential aspirants who lost nominations or contested and lost election predicted doom for Nigeria. Can't they learn from American experience where everybody focuses on national interest and unity even when election imperfections exist?

According to the *Fort Worth Star-Telegram* of Thursday, November 4, 2004, page 15A, the executive director of the lawyers committee, Barbara Arnwine, was alleged to have said, "Voting is under-funded in many areas, and it needs fixing." She added, "We harangue people to vote, and then we don't have the capacity to handle the crowds."

On the other hand, if above election complaints of 2004 and those of Florida 2000 happened in Africa, Russia, China, etc., the Western World Governments and their Press would have hypocritically treated them in terrible light, would have rained abuses on the leaders of those countries and would have called them dirty names. They would have described any governments and leaders emerging from similar situations to be illegal and worthy of economic sanctions. Other countries seem to understand the hypocrisy in the politics of the Western World and their Press reports, and so, they care less.

As a result of human imperfections, complaints happened in the election, but the stakeholders accepted them with good spirit without resorting to violence and name-calling, as would have been the case in any Nigerian election.

In developed nations, there are many cases whereby both husband and wife in the same house share different political ideologies and belong to top ranks of different political parties. In that same family, the children share different political views and align with their mother or father without any bitterness, rancour or acrimony. On many occasions, husbands and wives appear on television on opposite sides of the table to answer questions and argue healthily on the differences in their political leanings, political liaisons, beliefs and orientation.

Given above situation, playing politics to win is not a do or die game. It is made funny, amusing and interesting within such nuclear families that entertain different political ideologies. Politics is played with civility in this situation, which is completely different from the way Nigerian elites behave during and after national elections. Some elites often act as if it is their birthright to be Nigerian President, and if they don't, Nigeria is doomed. That is ignorance. It is dishonest to play politics as a do or die business for corrupt enrichment.

From the *Fort Worth Star-Telegram* publication of Saturday, November 6, 2004, page 4, it was reported that J. Quick, Professor of Organizational Behaviour at the University of Texas at Arlington, said, "But we as Americans have a strong history of reaching out to those who have been defeated." Robin Jarrett, Professor of Psychiatry at University of Texas Southwestern Medical Center at Dallas said that disappointment was a part of life. She added that like the Rolling Stones said, "You can't always get what you want." We all have disappointments and are exposed to situations that cause grief and sadness."

The State Governor of California, a Republican, is married to one from the Kennedy family who are first class, staunch, lifelong Democrats. When will Nigerian political elites learn to be civil, peaceful and contented, socio-politically and economically?

After the 2004 US election, people comforted each other and got along. For example, in Georgetown, Delaware after Election Day, some reveling in victory and others reeling in defeat met in timehonoured tradition whereby winners and losers assembled to demonstrate goodwill and unity and put the rhetoric of campaigning behind them. They called that day, Thursday November 4, 2004, "Return Day."

The tradition began since early nineteenth century. It used to include a parade of carriages and convertibles in which winners and losers rode together. During such ceremony of Thursday, November 4, 2004, Governor Ruth Ann Minner, a Democrat, was reported to have sat perched atop the first carriage smiling and waving, while her unsuccessful challenger, Republican Bill Lee and Independent-Libertarian, Frank Infante, were relegated to facing backward in the rumble seat of Minner's carriage.

In effect, both winners and losers at the election with their supporters assembled two days after the presidential election, and they all had fun and decided to move forward without bitterness. Such practice is good to emulate by Nigerian politicians and their supporters. Winning in politics should not be a do or die affair in the interest of the nation, which everybody must put first above all other considerations. Nigerians can do it if the leadership and elders lead by example.

In the *Fort Worth Star-Telegram* of Saturday, November 6, 2004, diehard Democrat Theresa Hudgins, surrounded by Republicans at home and at work, especially her husband who is a Republican, said, "I was just bawling. Everyone is so happy – my husband has got a real spring in his step because Bush won; but I am just really sad. It is going to be a very long four years."

It is natural to feel disappointed if one loses an election, but losing does not provide sufficient grounds to call for violence to make the country ungovernable. Such calls are unpatriotic against the nation, much more than against the winners that you intend to hurt. Always remember that people (winners) come and go, leaders come and go, but Nigeria, your country, your native land, your fatherland, the only country you can call your own, will always remain perpetually. Don't hurt Nigeria no-matter-what; keep talking using diplomacy, dialogue and due process to solve Nigerian problems.

Remember that Nigeria belongs to over 140 million people. They are the ones who choose their ruler. If you do not win this time, you may win another time provided you are not slammed with treasonable offence charges and incarcerated for life. All Nigerians should be encouraged to be at peace. Stop inciting Nigerians into violence. It may be treasonable.

Hypocritically, election rigging in the Western World is treated with civility and described simply as election complaints resulting from human imperfections, and the highest courts of their countries help to perfect the rigging most usually by ruling in favour of the political party of the president that appointed them into office respectively. The Western Press will not make any noise or publish any adverse reports about their countries' election complaints and riggings as they unfairly do aginst other countries.

On the other hand, similar election complaints in other countries are automatically treated loudest as rigging by the Western Governments, their sponsored election monitors and their Media with threats of sanctions and name-calling to incite the opposition to engage in violence, as if the same election complaints which are underreported and covered up, have not been happening in the Western World countries and their allies.

It is all hypocrisy and holier than thou attitude. The opposition parties resorting to violence, killings and arson often forget that it is their country that is being destroyed and economically set back when they are incited to cause mayhem for election imperfections, malpractices or riggings.

Whenever there is election complaint as it is termed in the Western World or election rigging as the same complaint is usually called in other countries, all stakeholders concerned should go to election tribunal or court as provided in the nation's constitution and stop anarchical actions usually sponsored by outsiders who pretend they love the opposition groups in order to embarrass the government.

Nomatter what problems you have, always behave responsibly in the best interest of your country. It is unbelievable that some Nigerian elites, academicians and politicians go outside Nigeria to Europe and America to address congressional conferences and condemn their country, Nigeria ignorantly, not knowing that those people they talk to, will never come to Nigeria to expose their own countries in bad light nomatter what happens.

At this juncture, the leadership of the Nigerian Labour Congress (NLC) and its affiliated unions has a lot to digest from the publicized statement of Dr. Frederick Fasehun, founder and leader of Oodua People's Congress and former labour activist. In the *Daily Champion* of Friday, October 29, 2004, Dr. Frederick Fasehun was quoted as saying, "Strike is a legitimate weapon that can be used by the working class to make a deaf government listen." But he contended that incessant strikes were damaging to the economy. He stressed that incessant strikes could lead to a depressed economy.

He exclaimed, "Who suffers from a depressed economy? It is the common man. That is why I have said in the past that one or two strikes a year to call the attention of the government to the suffering of the masses; there is nothing wrong in it." He called on the Nigerian Labour Congress to say that instead of a strike, the NLC should be the arrowhead of the civil society concerning the agitation for the staging of a Sovereign National Conference (SNC).

The call on the NLC to limit the incessant strike action, which has serious consequences for the economy and the masses, is commendable, but to make the NLC an arrowhead for political agitation is to politicize the organization and make it less credible. The opposition groups should not use the NLC to confront the government on political matters pertaining to the SNC, which presupposes that a legitimate Nigerian government is not in existence. The NLC leaders' primary responsibility is to get the best for the workers and not use their offices to gain political prominence at the expense of workers they lead. The NLC leadership represents the workers and is financed by workers who share different political views.

Different workers belong to different political parties numbering about twenty-seven in Nigeria. In a democracy, the labour leaders can form a political party after obtaining the workers' mandate, but they cannot ride on the backs of workers who do not share their political decision to join the political parties or civil society groups that oppose the government. In addition, membership of any labour union that forms a political party should not only be voluntary, workers who choose not to be members of such emerging political party cannot be forced to finance it.

Alternatively, labour leaders who want to join political parties may resign their posts in the unions and let workers champion their course constitutionally instead of coercing them to team up with nonunion members, nonunion workers and other political parties in opposition to attack and embarrass the government that employs them.

The government increased workers and pensioners emoluments without strikes and lockouts. If the NLC leadership can stop compounding the problems of the masses by limiting strikes and keeps talking, negotiating, compromising, not dictating terms, listening, making useful suggestions, and positioning as partners in progress with the government, maintaining some neutrality and not taking sides with the opposition, perhaps workers will achieve more, and the masses will understand and suffer less.

In most developed, industrialized and advanced economies, workers aggrieved with their management do go on strike, but not all workers in the country have to join with the so called civil society groups to plunge the whole country into darkness, personal and possessional insecurity, and chaos. For example, workers of a particular airline in the USA went on strike briefly but not all aviation workers in the USA.

Why is it that if one industry's workers have a dispute with their management, then all Nigerian workers would be called upon to participate, or when one university's employees have problems with the universities authorities, then all Nigerian universities have to be closed down? Such path to economic peril and perdition of the country should be stopped by all who wish the country well or the government has a responsibility to do something about it once and for all.

Skyrocketing fuel prices and loss of two million jobs could have cost President George W. Bush of the USA his reelection bid for the presidency in November 2004, but people lived with it and survived it without chaos or calls for indefinite strike action, which could put the country into jeopardy. The love of one's nation should be above all other considerations. That is a lesson Nigerians should learn especially elites sponsoring incessant strike actions.

The government approved relief measures on fuel price hike, which unfolded ₦11 billion loan for transporters, as well as slashed import duties on buses and drugs from twenty-two percent to ten percent and from twenty percent to five percent respectively for the benefit of the masses. It seemed that the loan was hijacked by the elites and manipulated against the masses it was meant to benefit.

Majority of Nigerians living in the rural areas use kerosene and other oil and gas products daily at high price, while a very negligible percentage of them use buses and drugs, hence, many of them would hardly benefit from the ₦11 billion loan meant to cushion the effects of the fuel price hike.

If money meant for local government development was diverted by some state authorities, who could vouch that ₦11 billion loan meant to help the masses would reach its desired targets? Already, there is a long persistent cry for help in the Niger Delta State by Rita LoriOgbebor publicized in the *Vanguard News* of November 9, 2004, saying, "Where are the billions?" The chorus that is being sung in many states of Nigeria is, "Where are the billions allocated by the federal government to local councils for development? Where are the checks and balances? Where is accountability?" Why are State Assemblies not asking questions? Are they colluding?

How effective can the supervision of the implementation of the report of the palliative committee, on fuel price hike, led by former Deputy Presdent of the Senate, Alhaji Ibrahim Mantu be, as approved by the National Economic Council? All stakeholders should keep talking, negotiating, listening and compromising with great sense of responsibility to the Nigerian masses.

A protracted strike action called by the NLC was not the best alternative panacea to cushion the effects of high price of fuel. Any indefinite strike action planned by NLC would not hurt the elites nor the leadership in government, but the masses. Such strike action planned nationwide, was therefore, not only a disservice to the nation, but a stagnation of the people's desire for economic emancipation.

The government can strategize an effective intelligence gathering and effective information feedback system possibly using informants who are promised commensurate financial rewards complemented by efforts of law enforcement agents. Such effective intelligence gathering network will stop at source, frauds, corruption, money laundering, smuggling, illegal oil bunkering, oil pipeline vandalization and other financial and economic crimes which hinder Nigeria's move towards economic prosperity. With such economic and financial security network in place, a lot of money will be saved, and there may be no need to raise taxes.

Also, effective revenue collection modalities will boost government income and enhance the implementation of projects that help the people instead of relying on tax increases, which raise prices. There and then, there will be less hardship on the masses. Furthermore, the stoppage of above acts of 'business as usual' would be core steps to assist the success of economic reforms embarked upon by the government which the masses consider to be stressful. In effect, the government would be seen to be fighting the abuses of the elites, which will make it difficult for the NLC, the Civil Society Groups or the opposition groups to manipulate the masses to stage any violence against government interests.

If government blocks the conduit pipes of Nigeria's financial and economic wastes and mismanagement, it will not need to raise taxes in order to fulfill its obligations to Nigerian masses because resources would always be available for development. The watchword is tolerance by all stakeholders in the interest of Nigerian nation, the most populous and richest black people's country in the universe.

In the Vanguard News publication of Friday, March 11, 2005, the President of the Middle-Belt Progressive Movement (MPM), Mr. Potter Dabup, former Deputy Inspector General of Police (DIGP), was reported to have criticized the Arewa Consultative Forum (ACF) for threatening war over the alleged lopsided composition of membership of the National Political Reform Conference. He warned that no ethnic or religious group in the country had a monopoly of violence.

He was said to have reminded the ACF at the news conference in Kaduna that heavens did not fall when the HausaFulani oligarchy was in power for about forty years. He questioned whether the ACF had become the mouthpiece of only the Northern Muslims. Potter Dabup added, "We the people of the Middle-Belt want regionalism because we have been marginalized for upwards of fifty years. We want the Middle-Belt to be carved out."

The statements credited to MPM President Dabup showed elements of bitterness for past oppression and maladministration. Nigerians should continue to forget and forgive the past, be at peace, practise mutual tolerance, love and care and focus on developing the new Nigeria that has emerged to an appreciable level where no person is oppressed with abundance of opportunities, equity, justice and fairness to all the citizenry. Nigeria can be a great, glorious and prosperous nation of our dreams.

It is all right to connect the past with the present and project the present to the future, but if people dwell too much on past wrongs, there may be no room to think and plan for a brilliant, prosperous future. According to a Yoruba proverb, "If we do not forget about the wrongs done to us yesterday, including the past, we may not have friends to play with." For the sake of the great country (Nigeria), the people must move on in solidarity, unity and oneness with the spirit of brotherhood and indivisibility to enhance and solidify the strength and blessings acquired from the opportunities provided by our diversity.

Pessimists, sadists, angels of doom and those who cannot make their points for consideration without making intimidating statements are just not civilized but also ignorant because Nigeria will live beyond all her present people as it lived beyond her past inhabitants. The Nigerian nation will live forever.

On Tuesday, March 22, 2005, the purported leader of Niger Delta Volunteer Force (NDVF), Alhaji Mujahid Dokubo-Asari, was reported to have said that he was battle ready against the Oodua Peoples Congress (OPC), and that thousands of Yoruba souls would go if the Ijaws were attacked.

Alhaji Dokubo-Asari was allegedly banned from Yorubaland by OPC for calling Chief Obafemi Awolowo, first Premier of Western Nigeria, a devil. The OPC leadership, Gani Adams and Dr. Frederick Fasheun, have since faulted the purported ban of Alhaji Dokubo-Asari from Yorubaland. Professor Wole Soyinka and Chief Anthony Enahoro had also assured Alhaji Dokubo-Asari that the alleged ban was not real.

In a democracy, where there is freedom of speech and expression, Alhaji Dokubo-Asari cannot be stopped from expressing his opinion. In the same vein, those who thought that Alhaji Dokubo-Asari's opinion was wrong had the same right to express their opinions. What is greatly needed is tolerance to hear each other and harmonize the opinions expressed without a fight. Alhaji Dokubo-Asari should have been given the opportunity to explain why he called Chief Obafemi Awolowo a devil. He is a human being; he must have his reasons. It is left for others to prove him wrong without causing any bad blood under democratic setting.

Even though Chief Obafemi Awolowo was the greatest Yoruba elder and leader during his time, and he did wonderful things to uplift the status of the Westerners, yet, as a human being, he might have stepped on some toes, and except you allow such people tot talk, how can you know!

What matters is what the majority of Nigerians and God/Allah call Chief Obafemi Awolowo and not what any young person acting on secondhand information calls him. Many Nigerians born after 1955 are in haste and do not learn Nigerian history. It is possible that Alhaji Dokubo-Asari based his opinion about Chief Awolowo on secondhand information because he might be too young when the sage was first premier of Western Nigeria.

It is an act of intolerance if it is true that Chief Ebenezer Babatope dismissed the NDPVF leader as a senseless and misinformed youth leader without listening to his reasons for demonizing the immortal sage, Chief Obafemi Awolowo. Hey, Chief, the era of nobody should or can talk is gone. The world has changed and is still changing fast. Every Dick, Jack or Harry talks in a democracy, and it does not matter whether what is said makes sense or not.

There must be tolerance. It is hard for the old school of thought to swallow, but that is the new world. If Dokubo-Asari knew the struggles, the accomplishments of Chief Awolowo and what he suffered in order to make Nigeria a great country, he would have called him a saint instead of a devil. The free primary education which Alhaji Dokubo-Asari went through was the handwork of Chief Obafemi Awolowo. The youths need to know their history and learn about respect for elders from their parents.

The government has a strong part to play to reorientate all those who are making threats, intimidating, initiating and inciting people to violence, South, North, East or West, to know there are consequences for breaching the constitution, and nobody is above the law.

It is doubtful whether the government has done enough in this area that borders on personal and national security as it is successfully doing in the arena of fighting corruption. It is getting clearer that there are no 'untouchables' in the arena of fighting corruption. It is getting clearer that there are no 'untouchables' in the fight against corruption. The same thing should now apply in the enforcement of law and order.

For example, in the USA, you can call people names up to the President, but you cannot intimidate or threaten the smallest person, your child or wife, and above all, the country without severe consequences. You cannot intimidate anybody with impunity no matter who you are. Do Nigerians including the activists, youth militants and their sponsors know their limitations under the law? Safety and security must be guaranteed. All stakeholders must act in the best interest of the nation. The government, religions, elders and leaders in all spheres of activities should infuse discipline into Nigerian society, so that a model great country can be bequeathed to posterity.

The government must realize that with full employment, all the militant groups, activists and youths will be self-disbanding if they are not idle. It is not difficult to achieve full employment if you can step onto some more toes to drastically reduce interest rate and give tax incentives to small scale and medium based companies as well as efficiently utilize all monies recovered from corrupt elites for investment and employment generation.

The government must seriously consider enacting antiterrorism act like the Patriot Act of USA to put those who intimidate the country, cause, stir or incite ethno-religious conflicts in incarceration under lock and key until they successfully pass through a beneficial reformation programme.

Unfortunately, the monetary allocations to the police that should have been utilized to develop a virile, effective and efficient police system for Nigeria are allegedly lodged in the private pockets and bank accounts (local and foreign) of exInspector Generals of Police and other top ranks of police.

Instead of the police assuring Alhaji Dokubo-Asari of his safety, that assurance had to be given by Gani Adams, Dr. Frederick Fasheun, Professor Wole Soyinka and Chief Anthony Enahoro. Can the reform system Nigeria is going through please assure the entire citizenry of their rights and limitations under the law? Any system that allows people to trust militant and dissident groups for their safety instead of relying on the police, encourages anarchical tendencies. The ability of any person or group in Nigeria to cause trouble must be constantly observed, watched and contained.

It is neither safe nor acceptable for some individuals or groups to assume and freely exercise the power of the police, prosecutor, judge or jury with impunity. To allow them to continue is condoning anarchical tendencies and the breaking of the law. They will continue if not challenged and restrained to remain within the limits of the law. The laws of the land must be effectively enforced without fear or favour to remind all Nigerian residents about their limitations and rights under the law. That is what ensures safety of persons and property.

Alhaji Dokubo-Asari was reported to have mentioned that nobody could stop the Niger Delta from its agitation, but that should be as long as such agitation conforms with the rule of law and the Nigerian Constitution. It was also reported that Alhaji Dokubo-Asari warned, "If Pro-National Conference Organization (PRONACO) fails to find solution to the problem of Niger Delta Region, the people know how to solve their problems." Majority of intelligent Nigerians can see a lot of misconception, misinformation, and pseudosense of invincibility in his speech similar to what made the Eastern leadership to drag Nigeria into the civil war (1967-70) for which about two million people were direct victims among those dead and those displaced.

If Nigeria won then, to keep the country together, it will always win, again and again, if the situation arises. Does any Niger Deltan who was old enough to witness the horrors of the civil war (1967-70) wish such events for their own people? Maybe the purported militant youths in Lagos, Port Harcourt, Kano, Kaduna, Warri, Enugu and other parts of Nigeria were too young or not born to personally or physically witness what happened during the civil war.

Then, they need to seek advice from those who love and care about them and not those who may be inciting them and using them for their own selfish motives and gains. It is being rumoured that some of the militant youth leaders, their godfathers and some politicians in Niger Delta Region are getting richer and richer at the expense of their followership. If that is true, such wealth is from corruption and other crimes, which must be condemned.

PRONACO is not a legalized Nigerian or State Assembly to solve the Niger Delta problems as misconstrued by Alhaji Dokubo-Asari and some others. It is like going the wrong way for salvation. How will PRONACO decisions be implemented and by whom if they are at variance with the concepts of existing government of Nigeria?

PRONACO that needed and collected about ₦400 million arising from a minimum of ₦20 from groups and individuals to enable organizers stage their conferences, should better utilize the money to organize orientation programmes of 'waste to wealth' for Nigerian masses. If PRONACO organizers spend ₦400 million on the conference, how will their recommendations be implemented for immediate benefit of the people who are yearning for immediate results and changes in their situations? Their recommendations may be well meant, beautifully tailored and constructed, but the results may be efforts in futility if they cannot be implemented immediately.

Hence, the movement should concentrate on improving the lots of the masses who need food, housing, healthcare, education, employment, safety and security. The people want the above fulfillments before bombarding them with problems about the structure and constitution of Nigeria. That is the job of the President and the Legislature. Let them do their job, which if they cannot do their jobs successfully, they should be changed constitutionally and not by force of arms or anarchical actions. The rule of law must be maintained absolutely.

PRONACO may make a difference only if it focuses and implements developmental strategies that uplift the Nigerian masses. PRONACO's trend and focus on Nigerian Structure and Constitution is a secondary requirement for the masses. It is an elitist programme for those looking for government positions, and it is a duplication of the NPRC set up by the government. PRONACO representatives should have attended the NPRC at government expense, recorded their views, kept and utilized the ₦400 million collected locally and internationally to improve the plight of the people.

Solving the people's problems should always come first before embarking on elitist programmes, which cannot benefit the suffering masses immediately. What Nigeria needs is not antagonism but cooperation and understanding among leaders to promote the best interest of Nigeria. Some leaders usually emphasize differences rather than what unites Nigerians. Such acts are unpatriotic and selfish.

Nigerian masses need counselors, role models, mentors, etc. that can show them how to establish small-scale businesses, cooperative organizations, how to procure bank loans and how to make them great through positive redirection. Nigerian citizens will gain a lot if PRONACO directs its efforts toward evangelism that helps the people permanently and spends less time criticizing the government and leaders who have temporary tenureship of four years.

What about teaching the people about the importance of their votes, the census and how the people can be vigilant to avoid rigging of elections? What about teaching the masses their rights to recall elected representatives who cannot perform to their expectations? What about teaching them about mechanized farming and moneymaking strategies?

It is great for PRONACO to meet and recommend great ideas on Nigeria's structure, resource control and derivations, etc.; but how do you get them implemented quickly for the benefit of the people who need immediate help, and how soon? Did PRONACO recommend anything different from what we have been hearing and know with ₦400 million? Is the end result worth the expenditure? PRONACO should strategize to spend its time and money on what benefits the people most. Do not promise the masses heaven when you have no control of heaven.

If the discovery of secret airstrips for smuggling illegal arms and ammunitions into the country is true, then Nigerians must be vigilant to preempt any insurrection. But for God/Allah's sake, Nigeria should not let the militant leaders and activists who incite and mastermind violence or insurrection escape to Europe and America with their wives, children and relatives. They should be placed in the forefront of any trouble they cause. The experience of events of the civil war (1967-1970) is still fresh in people's minds when those who orchestrated the war fled with their families and left the ordinary masses in the lurch to suffer death, hunger and deprivations.

Remember not to be fooled twice like it happened during the civil war (1967-70). Some recent cases of accomplices or mentors deserting you during difficult times are worthy of mentioning thus:

(1) Senator Chris Adighije was reported in the Daily Independence Online of Thursday, April 7, 2005, to have said, "I regret that

I tried to mediate between the committees and the minister. But what has shocked me is that the people I call distinguished men, who personally came to my house, are now walking away from the truth. It is shameful that they can lie like this." In the ₦55 million bribery scandal affecting some Senators, former Senate President Wabara allegedly described Senator Chris Adighije thus: "He is not a friend of mine in the Senate. Since I became Senate President, he has been looking out for ways to bury me. Adighije is being used, and they have succeeded in pulling me down.

(2) ExPresident Obasanjo sacked the former Minister of Housing and Urban Development, Mrs. M. Osomo, for poor handling of the sale of Ikoyi property. It was reported that instead of bidding for the houses and before the release of advertisement for bids, some elites had been given allotments and some had actually paid for the houses. Those who received allotment letters included some State Governors, Federal Ministers, some past and present top government functionaries, exmilitary generals, some top military and police officers and some highly influential elites, their friends and relations. When ExPresident Obasanjo heard about this practice of 'business as usual' he felt highly disturbed and embarrassed especially when he learned that some of the houses were allocated to his inlaws. He then directed that the allocations be cancelled, and he sacked the Federal Minister, Mrs. M. Osomo.

A close aide to the sacked minister said, "She feels humiliated and has been so lonely and depressed and would not just talk to anybody. Yesterday alone (Monday), she broke down twice and complained that she was so shocked how the same people she took as friends would betray and reject her at such a crucial moment when she needed them most."

(3) Similarly, those who encouraged ExVice President Atiku Abubakar to run against his boss, ExPresident Obasanjo in 2003 presidential election when ExPresident Obasanjo really needed his support for his reelection as president, set Atiku Abubakar on a collision course against his boss, ExPresident Obasanjo.

Although he did not cave in at the last minute, who knew what interpretations were given to his movements and meetings with delegates and governors to the PDP national convention to nominate the party's flag bearer for the 2003 presidential election! Such people, acting as 'devil incarnate' who advised him (Atiku Abubakar) to bid for the 2003 presidential ticket might have done some damage in the relationship between the two of them, and most regrettably, they might not stay with him in 2007 to help him in his presidential ticket bid when he needed them most.

Since when in the 'History of the World' did a Vice President pitch himself for nomination to the presidency against the President seeking reelection, and there was no damage done to the relationship between them? Devils in human clothings are always around on both sides. Nigerians, do not let the sugar-coated trouble-shooters and nonconformists fool you anymore because as soon as you get into trouble, they will leave you in the lurch. In this regard, history has always repeated itself. The consequences of allowing yourself to be fooled even once are clear and always there. Do not get hurt and later deserted by those who incite you to fulfill their own selfish interests.

(4) The former National University Commission Secretary, Peter Okebukola, who was persuaded to cough out ₦20 million to former Minister of Education, Professor Fabian Osuji, as loan was named in the 'Senate Education Committee Bribery Scandal'. It is terrible to find yourself where you do not belong and later deserted by those who led you there. Professor Osuji was deserted by those who demanded the usual ₦55 million from him. He thought he was saving a course to get his ministerial budget padded and approved. He thought he was promoting his job, but those people he trusted put him into trouble and deserted him. If he sought presidential advice initially, he could have been saved. His action put innocent Okebukola into trouble for which he was left on his own to tackle.

The four incidents mentioned above are warning signs not to allow yourself to be fooled by being incited to cause trouble or do wrong things because those who push you into it would desert you when there is a problem.

The Federal Government should not bequeath youth militarism, cultism, group gangsterism, hooliganism, mediocrity, unemployment, sociopolitical intolerance and violence to posterity. Just as it is fighting corruption and fraud relentlessly, so it must focus serious attention to youth and societal indiscipline. Nigeria needs a clean and disciplined society where people understand how to give and earn respect and understand their limitations under the law. Nigerian laws must be strictly enforced.

Above all, Nigerian leaders must first of all ensure that the people get all the good things they deserve; and the leaders must be exemplary, transparent, empathic and not corrupt. Nigerians must be motivated socio-economically to be lawa-biding, patriotic, life loving, hopeful, inspirational and encouraged to be able to make the right value judgment about all things that surround them. They must be able to ensure optimism about their prospects for higher standard of living, increasing life expectancy and economic prosperity.

In calling for the Sovereign National Conference (SNC) in midMay 2004, the leader of the Northernbased Islamic Group Concerned Muslim Organization, Alhaji Datti Ahmed was alleged to have said, "It is either we stay together in peace and harmony based on equity and justice or we go our separate ways. It is Sovereign National Conference now or we go to war, because the Federal Government has failed and the system has collapsed."

Alhaji Datti Ahmed's frustration was expressed as a result of the ethno-religious crisis, which broke out in Kano aimed at killing nonMuslims in retaliation for the killings of Muslims at Yelwa in Plateau State during the previous week. It would be recalled that ExPresident Obasanjo effectively arrested the situation in Yelwa, Plateau State and Kano State following a declaration of a State of Emergency in Plateau State with severe warnings to other trouble-prone spots and those planning to cause trouble.

Nigeria is a secular state as provided in the Nigerian 1999 Constitution. As a result, it cannot dabble into the practice of any religious faith or activity other than provide national safety and security for all citizens to practise their religious faiths without disturbance.

To ensure the safety of people to practise their religion, it does not require the convocation of SNC to achieve peace. The government should enforce the existing laws provided for troublemakers whether Christians or Muslims. It does not need the SNC to enforce law and ensure peace.

The thought about separation because of ethno-religious conflict called for by Alhaji Datti Ahmed is not the best alternative solution because Christians or Muslims abound and cohabitate in all states of the Federation of Nigeria. The States of Nigeria cannot be separated on account of religion because there is no state that is entirely Christian or Muslim inhabited. The only solution for ethno-religious conflicts is to make and enforce severe and deterrent laws and penalties against ethno-religious conflicts, their sponsors and operators. Those responsible including their mentors and collaborators should be treated as terrorists whether Christians or Muslims. They should be pursued vigorously, aggressively and ruthlessly, caught and punished severely without exceptions – 'no sacred cows and no untouchables'.

Nigeria's intelligence apparatus should be strengthened sufficiently with the right sophisticated equipment and training with the support system capable to nip crimes and crises plans in the bud before they are hatched. There should be moving cameras to take pictures of arsonists during riots so that criminals can be identified, pursued, caught and punished appropriately even after the riot has ended.

The complaints lodged by the Emirs against Kano political leadership during their one-day emergency meeting summoned by the President of the Supreme Council of Islamic Affairs, the Sultan of Sokoto, Alhaji Muhammadu Maccido should be investigated and culprits brought to book no matter how highly placed so that the innocent lives lost should not be in vain.

At the Northern Emirs and Muslim meeting, it was alleged that the political leadership of Kano State stoked the reprisal attacks on nonMuslims by inciting the militant youths to avenge the killings in Yelwa, Shendam, Plateau State. Such revelation is troubling, and it should be thoroughly investigated. Those responsible should be appropriately punished and severely warned against any repetition of ethno-religious violence and crimes in general.

Alhaji Datti Ahmed's anger, outburst and threats about separation or war if SNC was not convoked was a miscalculation. It must be unequivocally understood that it is a long painful journey for Nigeria to go from disintegration or separation and war with grave consequences to prosperity. On the other hand, it is short time, easier and comfortable to journey from peace, solidarity, unity and strength to prosperity. Nigeria's terrible experiences on January 15, 1966 and July 29, 1966, culminating in the civil war (1967-70) and events thereafter have made it difficult for Nigeria to settle down completely.

Does Alhaji Datti Ahmed want Nigeria to start the vicious cycle with separation and war all over again by making such inciteful statements about separation and war unless there is SNC? Does he understand the implications of convening an SNC and under what circumstance it could happen, perhaps, if there is no legitimate sovereign government in existence? Does he understand the implications of Nigeria separating or disintegrating, and Nigeria being at war? Is that what Alhaji Datti Ahmed, leader of Northernbased Islamic Group Concerned Muslim Organization, want for Nigeria and posterity-separation and war?

As leader of a respectable and responsible religious organization, it is always best to move from positive thoughts of peace, conciliatory tone, patience and good temperament to solve Nigerian problems instead of issuing empty threats that could complicate matters. If other opposing religious leaders made similar threats then Nigeria could start to burn. Any true and exemplary leader of a household, family, city, local council, state, federal, business or religious organization should be most humble, peace loving and exemplary to always talk about peace and not war, unity and not separation or divisionism, hope for successes and not despair; loving and caring and not hateful; always optimistic and not pessimistic; Godly/Allahly thinking and not devilish.

If elites calling for SNC or else, there would be war, succeed to create a war, are they going to be in the warfront with their wives and relations or escape with their relations to Europe and America reminiscent of events during the Nigerian civil war (1967-70)? How many of these elites talking about war have actually witnessed war and participated in the war front? Majority of them were too young or not yet born to witness the sufferings, deaths, hunger, illhealth, homelessness, destruction and horrors created before, during and after the Nigerian Civil War (1967-70). Hence, they talk to orchestrate separation and war without any understanding and reservation.

The President of Federal Republic of Nigeria should constantly repeat his warnings to all states prone to ethno-religious riots, arson and killings. If there are any violations, he should work with the legislature to declare a state of emergency to save innocent lives. The President should start to teach lessons so that the elites can become disciplined, less swollen headed and law abiding. In fact, the highest elites should be the most humble, respectful, law abiding and exemplary.

All the ethno-religious and political extremists who are causing arson, killings and serious violence should be treated as terrorists whether they are Christians or Muslims. A true Christian or Muslim cannot be involved in violence, chaos, arson and killings directly or indirectly. Those who participate in arson and killings of innocent people in the name of religion are religious thugs and murderers. God/Allah sees them and would award befitting severe punishment to them.

The stand, words and actions of any Godly/Allahly religious leader whether Christian, Muslim or Traditionalist should be divine, exemplary and not belligerent so that peace can reign supreme throughout Nigeria. Any decisions that Nigerians make today in haste and in anger may be a curse for future generations, and they may not forgive us.

Nigerians of the past till the present time are smaller in number compared with Nigerians of the future to eternity. Therefore, Nigerians of today should not take decisions that can jeopardize the future, which is bigger and greater than the past and the present put together. It is therefore selfish for any leader(s) to preach separation or war in Nigeria under any guise. Separation or war could result in sufferings, deprivations and untimely death. A lot of Nigerian families have not fully recovered from the effects of the Nigerian Civil War of 1967-70 and the succeeding reigns of dictatorship, terror and maladministration.

It must be realized that any pain or suffering in any part(s) of Nigeria would affect the whole 'Enterprise Nigeria' socio-economically and politically. Disintegration or war solves nothing but could complicate Nigerian's problems.

The President of the Middle-Belt Progressive Movement (MPM), former Deputy Inspector General of Police, Potter Dabup, told the *Vanguard News* on Thursday, March 10, 2005, at a Kaduna news conference, "We the people of the Middle-Belt want regionalism because we have been marginalized for upwards of fifty years. We want the Middle-Belt to be carved out."

Considering the regime of General Gowon (1966-1975) who originates from the Middle-Belt, the creation of states, the holding of many topmost positions in the armed forces, the civil service, government parastatals and the private sector by many Middle Beltans, the claim of Middle-Belt marginalization for fifty years cannot be true. The Military, the Air Force, Police, the National Airline, Government Parastatals and the Civil Service were occupied by a lot of Middle-Beltans at top levels during the thirty-five years that the North ruled Nigeria.

What did Yorubas get when Middle-Belt got all that? What did South-South get? The Middle-Belt suffered the effects of oppression and domination by Northern leaders before the creation of states, but not for fifty years. The main objective of the creation of states by General Gowon was to help selfdevelopment and reasonable level of self-determination within the confines of one Nigeria under the Nigerian 1999 Constitution. If the above is true and indisputable, then it may be said that the Middle-Beltans have been recognized and rewarded for their sufferings and those of the indormitable Joseph Tarka. Things should be better now in the Middle-Belt than those days when Chief Obafemi Awolowo and Senator Joseph Tarka were pulling together to survive and help their people inspite of overwhelming political stratagem mounted against them by the governing leadership who did everything possible to suppress them.

With the above narration, if there is anything the Middle-Beltans have failed to accomplish between 1966 up to date, they should ask their leaders and representatives who took part in running this country and her organs from 1966 for thirty-nine years. They should ask, "Where are the billions?" Ms. Ogbeboh asked that in Niger Delta. Have leaders of the Middle-Belt, past and present, been team players in the Federal system and has anyone of them stashed wealth in foreign bank accounts? The question is very important to determine the welfare of the average Middle-Beltans and whether they were marginalized by their own leaders or by outsiders. Who marginalized whom, when the whole country suffered? Nigerians must forget the past wrongs and move on.

The glaring problem of the Middle Beltans is how they can utilize their Christian or Muslim faith to maintain religious tolerance and nonviolence with their counterparts in the North. As true believers of God/ Allah, Christians and Muslims may be asked, "For whom and for what are you causing religious violence, arson and killing of innocent Nigerians, and why, if it is realized that God/Allah is always for peace, mercy, love and care and not violence, arson and killings of religious opponents? To eliminate religious violence in the North, local and state leaders must be made accountable for any breach of peace. They cannot entirely deny knowledge and responsibility.

The demand for regionalization of Nigeria as some Yoruba and Igbo groups are requesting including Potter Dabup may not be the best alternative solution to Nigeria's socio-economic and political problems. Regionalization of Nigeria to be headed by Deputy Prime Minister under a parliamentary system will be creating additions to the existing bureaucracy in the art of governance of the nation.

Parliamentarianism of the First Republic was truncated by the military coup of Ifeajuna and Nzeogwu on January 15, 1966. Nigerian problems are elitemade and not much related to the structure of Nigeria or the system of governance, as people are being deceived to believe. Regionalization may create a new gang up of the majority against the minorities within a region and may result in their oppression as was experienced before the creation of states in Nigeria.

Corrupt politicians under federal system will still be the same under parliamentary and regional grouping unless if they are removed and replaced with transparent ones. A new structure and better constitution will only work under transparent leaders. Hence, reform leaders, leadership aspirants and Nigerian society before handing over a restructured Nigeria with a new constitution in order to achieve the best results for Nigeria – "New wine in new bottle."

If the resources allocation system recognizes and rewards each state according to its productivity, and if each state reaps what it sows, then every state will work hard and be nonoverdependent on the federal purse. Babysitting states that can be hardworking and be productive but are not, should not continue forever. It is buckpassing to talk about marginalization when you are not productive.

Resources allocation on parameters that do not strictly relate to productivity is not equitable. If your state population is large as well as your land area, then you should be producing more in relation to your large population and large land size. State leaders should generate employment and make their people employed and productive to enhance their standard of living instead of everybody waiting to share the oil resource from the Niger Delta.

The Presidency and the Legislature should emphasize 'no work, no pay' and people do not reap where they do not sow. The nonoil producing states can productively develop their potentialities toward businesses and professions that can make them earn resources, which will make them as much economically viable as the oil producing states.

If oil is found in commercial quantity in Ogun State, there must be oil and valuable minerals in Lagos State and the States in the North. Explore the possibilities to the fullest.

On the other hand, the oil producing regions and their leaders must realize that the oil wealth became a reality as a result of the sweat (the initial and continuing investment) of 'Enterprise Nigeria' and not that of the South-South alone. The whole of Nigeria invested money from cocoa of the old Western Region, coal from old Eastern Region and cotton, groundnut, hides and skin from the old Northern Region for the exploration of oil in 1950s and 1960s.

The development of the oil fields by 'Enterprise Nigeria' and not South-South alone has continued ever since. With such realization, it may be morally wrong and wrong businesswise or investmentwise for the South-South to wake up one day and effect the annexation, seizure or acquisition of the assets of 'Enterprise Nigeria', and thereby exclude majority participation of the rest of the country and expect to be at peace. To be at peace, the people of the oil states must be partners in progress with the rest of Nigeria. The militancy from the South-South is making the world to find alternatives to oil and reduce its demand. Certainly, there will be regrets.

The contribution of the South-South Oil States to the investment of 'Oil Enterprise Nigeria' if measured could not be more than twenty percent. In effect, it will be appropriate to compromise with the rest of Nigeria for derivation allocation that is reasonable and responsible.

It is easily arguable that the oil fields or oil wells are in South-South geopolitical zone, which is Nigerian land, and the oil business enterprise is owned by Nigeria. It is Nigerian investment.

The environmental problems and abuses must be properly addressed by the Federal Government in partnership with the affected state governments, but the rest of Nigeria should not be divested of the dividends of their investment on oil exploration, which began in 1950s up to date.

The companies that operate in the oil producing regions must also bear responsibility for environmental pollution. The problems can best be solved through negotiations, conciliation and compromise, and not kidnappings, killings, fightings, violence or infrastructural vandalization which may cause the need to declare a State of Emergency throughout the South-South zone. Oil money must no longer be stolen and stashed overseas by South-South governors, and the leaders must not condone illegal oil bunkering which helps the militants to procure illegal arms and ammunition.

It is better to nurture the oil wealth business to greatness in peace with reasonable percentage derivation for South-South States than all parties to lose the whole oil wealth in war and regret. It must be remembered that the rest of Nigeria will not tolerate secessionist tendencies nor unconstitutional seizure or acquisition of 'Oil Enterprise Nigeria' by any ethnicity, state or region without a punch.

It must also be remembered that individuals, groups, people's representatives, government functionaries, legislators and governors, whether North, South, East or West who are not compromising, may be the first to fly to Europe and America with their wives, children and relations if there is war. The civil war of 1967-70 is a reminder. Everything must be done to keep them in the country to face the music which they create.

Nigerian people and leaders are reminded that there are international adversaries in the corner who will reap from their problems, confrontations and nonconciliation. They are listening, hearing and seeing with their ears and eyes wide open to take advantage of Nigerian leaders' mistakes and capitalize on them for their own benefits. Some of Nigerian bookworms and others born after 1955 that have not learnt any practical lessons are talking and propounding unworkable derivation theories out of sheer real life inexperience, especially about the civil war (1967-70). They are also boasting that they cannot be intimidated by sticking to between fifty and one hundred percent derivation.

If you, South-Southerners want to eat it all when the whole country invested in the exploration and development of the oil industry for over four decades, how do you become your brother's keeper and not being seen as greedy? How are you contributing to equitable development of Nigeria? Elders should restrain all those concerned who are fomenting troubles from North and South, East and West for redirection.

Their youthful exuberance of winner takes all coupled with their arrogance is not helping a united, indivisible, strong Nigeria, which we cherish. Nigerians must always consider the best interests of over 140 million people and not their personal or sectional interests alone when dealing with Nigerian issues. United we stand; divided we fail and fall.

Regionalization will take the country back to square one as it was in early 1960s. What will be the fate of state(s) that will be minorities under the ethnic regional groupings if there are disagreements? Such regroupings create room for oppression, enhance bureaucracy, cause limitation of opportunities and increase tendencies for collective disagreement with the central government, which would encourage secessionism. It extends the distance to federal administration for assistance, and the regional authorities can limit states' self-determination, which is counter productive.

It is being reemphasized that individuals, groups, states and regions should stop excessive reaping from where they do not sow, and continuous babysitting of states that are not ready to work hard for their development should stop. Nonoil producing states can become prosperous by specializing in areas of business activities where they have best comparative advantage.

It is ridiculous to rely on culture, tradition or religion to refrain from business activities that make money but expect to share from the sweat of others who engage in such business ventures. Even culture, tradition or religion teaches contentment with what people have and working hard conscientiously to make more.

If resource derivation is never one hundred percent in other countries like the USA, UK, Russia, China, Japan, Canada, etc., then there is no justification for some groups in South-South asking for one hundred percent resource derivation. Nigeria can adopt the average of resource derivation percentages in USA, UK, Russia, and China so that the country can move on progressively.

Every Nigerian ethnicity or nationality resents being dominated by any other as was allegedly done to the South-South by the core Easterners, the Middle-Belt by the core Northerners and the Mid-Westerners by the core Westerners in 1950s and 1960s before the creation of states. It is not unlikely that those who benefitted a lot then during regionaliztion at the expense of minorities quickly forget the demerits and implications of occupation, domination and exploitation in the system of regionalization being proposed for Nigeria by them.

The system that gives the existing thirty-six states continuing development at their own pace without any regional encumbrances within the context of one Nigeria in the democratic fashion similar to what obtains in USA will be best for Nigeria. Nigerians should respect one another's culture, tradition and religion devoid of extremities. The world is changing, and Nigerians must change with the changing world.

All stakeholders in Nigerian polity comprising the government (Presidency, Legislature and Judiciary), the opposition parties, the NLC and its affiliates, the elites, public and private sector practitioners, other interest groups and the masses should observe the following steps for peaceful conflict resolution in the best interest of the nation. These steps are not exhaustive, but they are useful guides. They represent the twelve commandments for conflict resolution.

(1) Each individual or group must respect one another as well as honour the right of somebody to agree or disagree. Respect begets respect.
(2) Stakeholders must be free to express their concerns without coercion, fear or favour. Provide an environment conducive for full discussion and honest negotiation.
(3) Each person or group must share common goals and aspirations. Explore areas of common interest and stay positive.
(4) Participants must be open-minded to accommodate others' points of views.
(5) Listen carefully to all proposals and contribute to discussions

open-mindedly and positively. Expunge any complexes during discussions and negotiations.

(6) Each participant must demonstrate great understanding of the issues involved. It is best to discuss and settle safe areas first and foremost, and then gradually move courteously to knotty areas of the negotiation.

(7) Examine, analyze and passionately consider the consequences of all inputs and outcomes. Be empathic all the way. Do not use majority view unwisely, unjustly and unfairly. Majority opinion may not be right all the time. Minority opinion must be respected, recognized and taken into consideration.

(8) Imagine, compare and contrast several alternative solutions with focus on the best and most agreeable alternative solution. A boycott or walk out is not a solution. Stay and get your views recorded. You cannot be a quitter considering national interest.

(9) Positively offer reasonable compromises. Remember, you represent 'Enterprise Nigeria' of many interests, so, your personal interest and biases cannot override the nation's best interests.

(10) Ensure you negotiate virtually reasonable, cooperative agreement that is legal, performable, enforceable and most beneficial to the nation and all citizens.

(11) The best interest of the country must be paramount in your decision-making.

(12) Be proud you are part of the solution that places your country in the best shape and not part of the problem that jeopardizes your fatherland. Be national conscious from the start to the end. By the time you finish, be happy and contented that you have served humanity, Nigeria, your homeland, creditably and deserve God /Allah's enormous blessings for a job well done.

During half of 1960s, when Dr. Nnamdi Azikiwe, the Owelle of Onitsha was Nigerian Leader and First President, with his illustrious Igbo teammates in the NCNC who were men of timber and calibre, Nigeria was a great and respected country. Contemporarily with Sir Ahmadu Bello, the Sardauna of Sokoto, First Premier of Northern Nigeria; Chief Obafemi Awolowo, First Premier of Western Nigeria and leader of the Yorubas; Dr. Michael Okpara, Premier of Eastern Nigeria and Sir Abubakar Tafawa Balewa, Nigerian First Prime Minister under parliamentary democracy, Nigeria excelled most other countries and was a model within the international community.

Those were great days with great people who were founders of Nigerian nationhood and independence. They did not steal and stash billions of Nigerian government money in private bank accounts in America, Britain and Switzerland at the expense of impoverished Nigerians, as it is the vogue with Nigerian elites and politicians of present time. There was mutual respect and dignity for all. They served the people and put the people first before any other consideration.

As at then, secessionism or Biafranism was never an option. There was healthy competition between the Yorubas and the Igbos as well as abundant opportunities for all Nigerians to become the best they could be. It was never contemplated that people from one ethnicity of Nigeria (Easterners) could collaborate to arm themselves, and could kill the national and state leaders of other ethnicities (Westerners and Northerners) while they safeguarded their own ethnic leaders (Easterners) as IfeajunaNzeogwu and other conspirators did on January 15, 1966.

The unfortunate events and circumstances that followed IfeajunaNzeogwu coup d'etat, the retaliatory coup of July 29, 1966 and the modes of handling the situation brought about secessionist tendencies and realities which dissolved after the civil war (1967-1970). Nigeria resumed and cemented its oneness and indivisibility with the spirit of general amnesty, no victor, no vanquished, followed by rehabilitation, reabsorption, reconciliation and reconstruction. It is difficult to forget and forgive the horrors of the civil war era and over three decades of dictatorship, but for the sake of posterity, Nigerians must move on together in solidarity forgetting and forgiving one another.

Adults of 1960s up to 1976 who actually witnessed events before, during and after the civil war (1967-1970) would understand that not every Igboman at that time supported secessionism or Biafranism as the best alternative solution to Nigerian problems. The handing over note of the secessionist army to Federal Government by General Phillip Effiong, commander of the Eastern forces, confirmed that assertion. Hence, the statement credited to State House Assemblyman, Hon. Ben Chuks Nwosu was not entirely accurate.

The Daily Independent Online of Thursday, September 22, 2005, recorded that Hon. Nwosu said, "Every Igboman, dead or alive today, is part and parcel of Biafra and its connections, connotations and its struggles. It is therefore inconsistent with history for any Igboman to deny Biafra in any way." Was the statement pressured out of Hon. Nwosu thirty-five years after the circumstances and realities that led to secessionism or Biafranism dissolved? Perhaps it was made to satisfy, discredit, dampen or neutralize his political opponents' accusations during the World Igbo Congress (WIC) held in USA in September 2005.

How much do views and expressions about Biafranism and allegiance to it hurt 'Igbo Presidency Project'? Those who want to rule Nigeria must identify with Nigeria without any ambiguity. They must look, talk and act Nigerian; look, talk and act presidential without any doubt about their faith in one Nigeria and her indivisibility. The same requirements go with the position of Vice President of Nigeria. Nigerians cannot afford disloyalty to the course of one Nigeria, united and indivisible under God/Allah, a semblance of the United States of America, the world's greatest democracy, economic giant and military super power.

ExPresident Olusegun Obasanjo visited foreign Heads of Governments several times and unprecedentedly secured over $18 billion debt cancellation for Nigeria. He also successfully restored the good name and image of Nigeria by changing its pariah status and its ostracization by the comity of nations for human rights violations and economic and financial crimes, which occurred between 1993 and 1998 during General Abacha's regime.

During the process, PRONACO leadership accused ExPresident Obasanjo of junketing the globe for impossible and unachievable debt forgiveness. Contemporarily, the leadership of PRONACO travelled overseas many times to solicit for funds of about 400 million naira ($3.5 million) donation to stage their conference but ended up disagreeing and factionalizing for reasons of embezzlement and/or misplacement of priority in the disbursement of funds by its leadership. There is never smoke without fire. Given the two comparable scenarios above, PRONACO (both leadership and followership) should ask themselves whether they can honestly do better than those government functionaries whom they have been criticizing!

Relating to the kidnapped USA journalist Jill Carroll and many others, it was foolhardy to argue not to negotiate/talk with terrorists/rebels when the lives of innocent Americans were on the line for beheading. One wonders if the policy would change if the close relatives of any of those in authority were the ones kidnapped and facing death by beheading. The world needs gradual departure from extremism and insensitivity in all forms and shapes when the lives of innocent people are at stake in the hands of terrorists/ rebels.

African leaders represented by Nigerian ExPresident Obasanjo talked to coupists/rebels in Sao Tome and Principe, and they reinstated their overthrown president and government without killing anybody. Talks with rebels in many African countries like Nigeria, Liberia, Togo, Sierra-Leone, Congo, Sudan, Ethiopia, Eritrea, Zimbabwe, Uganda, etc. have saved lives. Why can't the lives of innocent Americans, British, French etc. be saved at all costs given similar circumstance? National pride and military superiority should never overshadow diplomacy when the lives of innocent people are at stake.

Nigeria used diplomacy to free many oil workers who included Americans and British citizens kidnapped by militants in January 2006 and there after. Similarly, many lives in the hands of militants continue to be saved by talking to them. Leaders faced with problems of militancy/insurgency should closely look at the causes of dissidency, talk, negotiate and narrow the gap of misunderstanding, perhaps the world can become one large extended family, united and peaceful.

GOD/ALLAH BLESS NIGERIA!

CHAPTER 11

NIGERIAN STATE SECULARITY AND RELIGIOUS TOLERANCE

Traditional religion existed in Nigeria before the advent of Christianity and Islam from the Middle East into Nigeria, and people lived in harmony and at peace with one another. The religion traditionalists still exist in very large numbers and they believe in the existence of the Supernatural Being Whom they represent with what they believe would channel them to God/Allah, the Supernatural Being, the Omnipotent, Omnipresent, Omnisapient and Omniscient – The Almighty.

About fifty percent of Nigerians do not go to church or mosque and/or are not practitioners of the Muslim or Christian religion. Most Nigerian names reflect the Christian, Muslim or Traditional religion of their parents or grandparents into which they were born, but it does not mean that they practise the religion reflected by their names. In effect, majority of Nigerians are not religious practitioners for not attending churches or mosques regularly.

Many Nigerians are very religious and godfearing without attending churches or mosques regularly. A group of Nigerian religious elites insisted that Nigerians should identify their religions during the 2005 census count. Nigeria is a secular nation. People should be free to serve God/Allah in any way they choose. Unfortunately, many advocates and leaders of religion worldwide may not go near Heaven or God/

Allah because of their hypocrisy of, "Do what I read and say from the Scriptures (the Holy Books), but not what I do that are imperfect and sinful."

Many Nigerians chose and converted into either Christianity or Islam in the urban areas while the rural settlements were dominated by the religious traditionalists. In effect, Christianity, Islam and Traditional religions existed laterally without violence, and people lived in harmony and at peace with one another as fathers and mothers, brothers and sisters, as one another's keeper and neighbour.

The religionists did not preach violence initially but peace, respect, dignity of life and tolerance. In fact, God/Allah stands for peace, mercy and all the great things of life. Can anybody truly represent God/Allah or truly call himself/herself a person of God/Allah if the person has no peace, mercy, tolerance or the general actions that truly depict the Personality of Almighty God/Allah? No!

These days, a lot of things are done in the name of religion or God/Allah to serve personal interest contrary to the teachings of the Almighty God/Allah. Watch out for whoever is preaching religious violence or perhaps talking too tough about it to cause trouble. He must have vested interest in making money or gains out of religion and other people's miseries. That is not the way of God/Allah. Many people who call God/ Allah's name loudest have turned to be hypocrites.

The Nigerian 1999 Constitution allows freedom of speech, freedom of association, freedom of religion, and it is very emphatic on state secularism. In effect, the government does not interfere with individual's religious faith – Christianity, Islam or Traditional religion.

Each religion recognizes the Supernatural Being, the Almighty God/Allah, the Omnipotent, Omnipresent, Omnisapient, Omniscient, the Alpha and Omega, Maker of Heaven and Earth, the Merciful and the Peaceful.

Each religious denomination therefore calls God/Allah different name(s), but each denomination has the same Supernatural, Almighty God/Allah in mind when using different names in different languages to pray to God/Allah.

Each religion, nomatter what or whichever, teaches morality, humility, humbleness, good neighbourliness, peace, harmony, coexistence, kindness, respect for one another, alms giving to the poor and tolerance.

Anything different from these peaceful life characteristics is irreligious, humanwishful thinking and devilish.

Nigerians will stop being fooled as soon as they are provided with gainful employment, because they will be too busy to listen to deception from some discredited religious leaders who may be fake; as revealed in and/or warned by the Holy Books.

God/Allah is a peaceful Supernatural Being and Father of all. Each religion leads to Him. It is, therefore, incredible and unimaginable that some people could create chaos under any guise using the name of God/Allah, the Peaceful, to cause unrest, arson, killing and other actions resulting in destruction of lives and property contrary to the teachings of God/Allah. Each religion teaches, "Thou shall not kill." Yet, people kill and preach hatred while falsely using the name of God/Allah.

In the *Daily Independence* of Tuesday, August 26, 2004, former Vice President of the Federal Republic of Nigeria, Atiku Abubakar said, "Incessant religious crises in Nigeria during the last four years were caused by people with ulterior motives who had something to gain." That is, such people encouraged or caused religious riots using the name of God/Allah out of sheer selfish interests contrary to the teachings of Almighty God/Allah, the Peaceful. It is incredible that some people could commercialize the name of God/Allah for personal gains contrary to the tenets of religion that lead people to God/Allah.

No religion teaches or preaches violence by itself, its leaders and/or followers do. Hence, the leaders of the various religious sects have a lot of work to do to ensure that both themselves and their followers remain God/Allahfearing, peaceful, neighbourly, tolerant, caring and loving. Some religious leaders who nurse superiority complex and/or preaching hatred and religious supremacy over other religions are not serving the best interest and wishes of God/Allah. Such religious leaders are confusionists serving their own selfish interests for personal gains.

All people are equal before God/Allah and all approaches to God/Allah through religions become the responsibility of God/Allah and not human beings to determine which way is good or better. It is also the responsibility of God/Allah to determine who is right or wrong and who goes to heaven or hell.

Therefore, the unhealthy rivalries between religious denominations and claims of one religion being right or wrong, superior or better than the other depict human arrogance, and ignorance of the way of God/ Allah. The Almighty God/ Allah may accept or reject people because of their actions and not as a result of their religious denominations as long as they are serving the tenets and wishes of God/Allah.

A person's service to help and uplift humanity shall count more, and be more rewarding than sleeping in the church, mosque, synagogue etc. and/or praying to God/Allah every hour of the day. A person's primary purpose on earth is service to uplift humanity.

Therefore, the advice of ExVice President Atiku Abubakar to the delegation of the Association for Muslim-Christian Mutual Relations is worth a billion dollars. ExVice President Atiku Abubakar said, "All leaders of conscience must be worried about these emerging conflicts and do something to bring them to an end." He also cautioned against involving the government in religious matters. He reminded the Association, "Religious violence was an alien factor in Nigeria because Christians and Muslims lived peacefully and cohabitated with one another in the country."

It is equally sad to involve religion in politics and preach hatred against any other fellow when the teaching of God/Allah says, "Love thy neighbour as thyself." He added, "I believe in peaceful coexistence in my actions and deeds." His assertions should be a great lesson of instruction to all acclaimed leaders and followers of religion in Nigeria, that they should cohabitate in peace and harmony with one another.

Practitioners of religious faiths must emulate Dr. Martin Luther King Jr. of the USA, who adopted a strategy of nonviolence from Mahatma Gandhi, one of the greatest leaders of India who served humanity with great spirit of love, humility, empathy, responsiveness and nonviolence. It was remarkable that both Dr. Martin Luther King Jr. and Mahatma Gandhi belonged to different religious faiths, different races and different countries, but they shared the same faith of tolerance and nonviolence.

One cannot see any verse in the Holy Books that supports killings of people of other religious faiths or causing chaos in the name of religion. If any such verse that encouraged violence inadvertently existed in the Holy Books, perhaps it might be applicable in the early world and centuries when religions were in rivalry against one another during their gestation period. Such verses would not fit into modern times and should be revisited and reviewed to fit into the twenty-first century and beyond so that we do not bequeath confusion and violence to posterity on issues of religion.

At the time immemorial, human beings were offered as spiritual sacrifices in all religions, but the barbarism and cannibalism changed to making use of ram, other animals, birds, other creatures and material things as sacrifice. In the same manner, people's orientation for religious violence should change, not sooner or later, but now.

Hence, most of what was good up till those early centuries even if documented, expressed or implied, may not be good for now, and should be reviewed, adjusted, changed or discarded as may be appropriate. It may require great scholars and religious practitioners of each religious faith to put heads together and give their followers what is practical and modern in the changing world. The advent of Jesus Christ changed a lot of things during His 33 years on earth as a symbol that appropriate changes could continue.

If God/Allah does not approve of changes for better, perhaps all of us would be living today at the Gulf of Aden, the Horn of Africa or along the Red Sea. God/Allah changes situations for better, and human beings in 'His Image' should do the same when it is worth it to change laws, conceived ideas, customs and tradition whether religious or otherwise as soon as it is appropriate to do so. The world is changing, so humanity must change with it in the spirit of God/Allah. The world is too large these days for everybody to belong to one or two religions. People must respect the religious faiths of others and vice versa, and people must live together and interact in peace and harmony. That is the Will of God/Allah.

It is surprising that Nigerians base their entire spiritual existence and practices, on what is dictated from some other countries that are not as God/ Allahfearing as they are. Nigerians are practising democracy, and not oppressing their people. They are changing developmentally and operating an open system of governance appreciated by international community. If you want to copy anybody, group or country, you must ensure that such individual, group or country is better spiritually, socio-economically and politically.

Unfortunately, these countries are not the best examples that Nigerians can copy hook, line and sinker because they are never at peace with themselves and their neighbours. God/Allah, the Supernatural

Being, the Omnipotent and Omnipresent is in Nigeria too. He was in the past; He is in the present and He will be in the future, and so, human beings must change with time and modernize in the spirit of God/Allah. If anybody calls God/Allah rightly in Nigeria, He will answer the prayers just like people in any other part(s) of the world. If the countries in the Middle-East cannot settle their differences, be at peace, love their neighbours as themselves and stop the killings and sufferings of their innocent people, then, they cannot be said to be an example of Godliness/Allahliness which the world can emulate.

The fact that you know, memorize and can say every word or verse in the Holy Books – Christian, Muslim or other religions, does not make you a better religious practitioner and servant of God/Allah than others unless you apply your knowledge relatedly to benefit humanity in modern times devoid of violence and hate.

Do not be deceived and misled into committing ethno-religious crimes against humanity anymore, contrary to the ways and teachings of God/Allah, the Peaceful and the Merciful. Always remember that you will be judged on the 'Judgment Day' by what you do to humanity while on earth.

Your words and actions will be examined to judge you and not simply because you are a Muslim, Christian or Traditional Religious Practitioner. The number of times you stay in church or mosque is not what will save you before God/Allah but your words, actions and deeds to humanity, the images of God/Allah.

Another example that is worthy of emulation is the cooperation, which made Protestant leaders share stage at Muslim convention in Chicago, USA as reported in the *Fort Worth Star-Telegram* of Saturday, August 30, 2003. It was reported that the Southern Baptist leader said at the Muslim convention that not all Baptists agreed with recent statements of evangelicals 'demeaning Islam'. Thousands of American Muslims assembled on Friday, August 29, 2003 for their three-day annual convention organized by Islamic Society of North America. They stressed their desire for closer relations with other faiths to counter evangelicals who wrongly accused Islam of inciting terrorism.

The organizers invited moderate and liberal Protestant leaders to address participants. Reverend Daniel Vestal of Cooperative Baptist Fellowship representing moderate Southern Baptists reiterated that not all Baptists agree with recent statements credited to evangelicals like Reverend Jerry Vines of Southern Baptist Convention, Reverend Franklin Graham and Reverend Pat Robertson who made untrue statements critical of Islam.

He appealed to the Muslim Convention that many other Baptist Christians did not support the demeaning statements of Rev. Jerry Vines, Rev. Franklin Graham and Rev. Pat Robertson. He demanded understanding, community and common cause with the Muslims.

Replying on behalf of the Muslims, the Secretary General of the Islamic Society, Sayyid M. Sayeed, extended their appreciation that when Muslims were migrating to US in large numbers in 1960s, it was the Christians who provided campus ministries for Muslim college students with space to worship.

Rev. Bob Edgar, who headed the National Council of Churches representing thousands of mainline Protestant and Orthodox Christian congregations, drew loud ovation when he said that his group opposed the US led war on Iraq. He condemned the hate speech of the reverends that were speaking evil of Islam. He said that he believed that God was calling Christians at that moment in the USA to model and practise good behaviour. About 35,000 people participated in the convention.

The Nigerian Christians and Muslims should emulate such religious cooperation and tolerance in the USA. All religions serve the same God/ Allah, so, religious practitioners should be at peace, in harmony and be tolerant. God/Allah, the Almighty, the Peaceful, the Merciful, the Redeemer, the Omnipotent, the Omnipresent, the Omnisapient, the Omniscient, the Alpha and Omega, Maker of Heaven and Earth will ask individuals to account for their actions and activities while on earth. Their type or denomination of religion will not be the deciding factor on the Day of Judgment.

The service and worship of God/Allah, the Almighty, is conducted by Christians, Muslims, Traditionalists, Jews and Gentiles as well as other conventional and traditional religionists in different forms and languages throughout the universe. In effect, religious conventionalists and traditionalists give service and worship to one and the same God/Allah in different forms, methods and languages with prayers for God's answers and solutions to problems. God/Allah is often described as the Merciful, the Peaceful and the Father of all. If God/Allah is Peaceful and Merciful, those who are directly and indirectly committing arson and killing people in the name of religion, should be devils incarnate.

With above realization, what are religionists fighting for, and why are they fighting among themselves if not for selfish interests? God/Allah does not fight, so they are fighting for their own selfish interests. If the interest is God's and how to enter the Kingdom of God in Heaven as proclaimed by religionists, there should not be such grave divisionism, antagonism, hatred, fighting and killing, which represent various acts of the devil and ungodliness.

Why is there widespread hatred and fighting or rancour among Christians and Muslims, Catholics and Protestants, Jews and Gentiles? Are all the wranglings, fightings, killings and hatred among religious denominations about God or for God? No, because God is God/Allah of love, peace, care and mercy. Is God/Allah's interest responsible for the incessant religious conflicts, riots, arson and killings? No! People reach God through service to humanity with worship and prayers to God/Allah.

Therefore, if prayers are not heard or answered, people should reassess their relationship with God/Allah by adhering to His teachings, reevaluate, review and redirect their practices and activities. Human sins usually envelop and block prayers from reaching God/Allah. The question for all religious spiritualists (Christians, Muslims and Religious Traditionalists) is, "Why are prayers not being heard anymore?" It is because there are too many sins.

According to NAIJANET.com *News Headline* of Monday, November 1, 2004, many religionists, Muslims, Christians and others, sought divine intervention to oust US President George W. Bush during November 2, 2004 US presidential election. The publication confirmed that Nigerian religionists were bombarded by mobile telephone text messages urging people to pray for US President George W. Bush's defeat. The message read thus, "Join us in praying for the defeat of Bush, an arrogant, bigger evil and enemy of Islam and Muslims."

A thirty-four year old tyre mechanic in Kano, Northern Nigeria, Mallam Nasiru Abdullahi, was alleged to have said, "Nobody needs to tell me to pray for Bush's defeat in the US election in this holy season when prayers are most answered." It was added, "I have been praying for the defeat of Bush since Ramadan started, and I will not stop until the elections are conducted. I am confident Allah will answer our prayers because it is a prayer against His enemy."

A forty-six year old textile trader, Mallam Adnan Habibu was claimed to have reiterated, "I have received the text message four times, but the sender doesn't need to waste his time because I have included Bush's defeat in my list of requests to Allah this month. It is among my five top requests to Allah this month. It is among my five top requests to Allah, which I recite day and night. I can't imagine the destruction Bush will bring to Muslims in his next four years as president."

On the other hand, a banker, thirty-one-year old Sadiq Yanus, was said to have emphasized, "Whether Bush wins or loses, nothing will change in the US policy toward Islam and Muslims because the problem is not Bush 'per say' but the American mentality." It was added, "Kerry may be right in his criticism of Bush's hawkish approach to global issues, but that doesn't mean he will be any better. Just let Kerry be at the White House, and you see what will happen."

The prayers to God/Allah that President George Bush should not be reelected cut across many religious denominations in the world. On November 2, 2004, at 11:00 p.m. Central Standard Time, it was becoming crystal clear that God/Allah was not hearing nor answering the prayers of these majority of the people in the world both Christians and Muslims who prayed, fasted and fought spiritually and relentlessly against the reelection of President George W. Bush.

Have people sat down these days and asked why their prayers are not being answered? It is because there are too many sins, halftruths, arrogance, lies, cheats, frauds, corruption, boldface deception, selfishness and no justice in the world anymore. Ironically, some opposition activists trying to cast stones at the authorities, performed worse when they were elected and/or appointed into governorship, commissionership and ministerial posts in the past, but they cry loudest now as if they are saints. People of all religions whether Christians, Muslims or Traditionalists must change behaviour for world prayers to be heard by God/Allah. There are too many sins.

In the BBC news of Tuesday, November 2, 2004, captioned Nigerian prophets see Kerry win. It was revealed that spiritualists and church prophets told the *Daily Sun Newspaper* that it had been decreed in the spiritual realm that President George W. Bush would lose. It added that Satguru Maharaji said, "His (Bush's) chances of retaining his White House seat are very slim because of his antecedents." Why was it impossible for anybody to predict that President George W. Bush would be reelected in November 2004 US presidential election? Nigerians should stop being deceived with fake predictions.

It is common knowledge that some Nigerian spiritualists who claim to possess power to predict the future through spiritual guidance make fake and vague predictions about their members' health and wealth. Most predictions from the socalled religious spiritualists, which in most cases are never specific, have helped to recruit many people, especially those facing difficult time caused by poverty, rising unemployment, inflation, ill health, insecurity and other problems possibly at home, work or one's business. If there is full employment, the fake spiritualists will have nobody to lie to because most problems that draw people to fake religious spiritualists will disappear naturally.

Those actually chosen by God/Allah in churches, mosques and traditional medicine houses are able to heal, redeem and predict accurately. But these days, there are many fake spiritualists who take advantage of people's vulnerability to exploit them in many ways. If none could predict the victory of President George W. Bush, the result of the election should be 'caveat emptor' (buyer beware) for all those who believe in the predictions that they usually pay heavily to purchase.

Ironically, armed robbers, corrupt and fraudulent people, financial and economic saboteurs, smugglers, illegal oil bunkerers and dangerous criminals often go for spiritual prayers before they start their operations.

Also, the former Chairman of NDDC, Chief Sam Edem was allegedly duped to the tune of eight hundred million naira by a traditional spiritual scammer. Less than one third of the money was recovered from him by the EFCC in October 2008. The money could have been utilized for the development of the Niger Delta of Nigeria. It is sad.

Sometimes, fake religionists and traditional medicine practitioners are arrested by police for armed robberies, killings and deceptive money doubling acts and pranks. Given this situation, how can prayers be heard, and how can predictions be true and real? What will the head or other parts of a dead person do to make you rich? Stop being deceived.

Stop killing innocent people for spiritual use of their body parts. Dead men don't bite; they cannot make you rich either.

Stop being fooled by those who falsely claim to be money doublers. If a person claims to be a money doubler, ask why he/she is as poor as a church mouse and poorer than those whom he/she wants to help! If the person cannot make himself/herself rich through money doubling, how can he/she make you rich?

The police should offer rewards to informants who can provide information, which can lead to the arrest and conviction of all collaborators who use buses and taxicabs to kidnap unsuspecting passengers to slaughterhouses of shrines. The fake spiritualists who kill people and those who sell human body parts should be arrested and prosecuted to promote safety. Any amount that could make the country safe should be spent as a priority. ExGovernor Lucky Igbinedion of Edo State (The Heart Beat) who offered ₦100,000 reward for tips on information that could lead to the arrest and prosecution of criminals should be commended and emulated by others in authority.

At the Shehu Kangiwa Square, Sokoto, which was venue for the grand durbar marking the bicentennial of the Sokoto Caliphate on June 20, 2004, ExPresident Obasanjo asserted that Nigerian leaders had strayed away from the virtues of truth, justice, social engagement and care for the followership for personal gains contrary to the preachings, teachings, principles and practices of late Sheik Uthman Dan Fodio, the Founder of Sokoto Caliphate.

He described the late leader, Dan Fodio, as an organizational strategist, an administrative genius and a reformer who believed in dialogue, persuasion, openness, focus, truth, justice and social engagement as well as the welfare of his people. Dan Fodio was said to preach peace, love, compassion and tolerance.

He wondered why many present leaders had strayed away from Dan Fodio's values because of their crave for personal, material and political gains. He condemned religious bigots and fanatics who as infidels engaged in burning down churches or mosques, the houses of worship of their religious opponents.

He asserted that both Islam and Christianity believed in the "dignity of man, nonviolence and care of the aged." He emphasized that the basis of both religions of Islam and Christianity was the belief in one

God/Allah. He clarified that the removal of corruption, dishonesty and other vices abhorred by both religions would require the inevitable stepping on toes of some people. That is a task that must be done in the name of God/ Allah.

In his own contribution, the Sultan of Sokoto, Muhammadu Maccido Abubakar III, enjoined the people and their leaders to live by the values of Islam and the examples of the Caliphate, and steer clear of intolerance. He added that his people should continue to preach peaceful coexistence irrespective of religious or cultural differences.

In his end of Ramadan message to all Muslims in 2004, ExPresident Obasanjo reminded them, "The Sallah celebration provided another opportunity for all Nigerians to imbibe and practise the virtues of discipline, dedication, sacrifice and piety which the Ramadan embodied." He advised, "Exhibit the spirit of brotherly love, tolerance and patriotism which are vital to the maintenance of unity, peace and stability in the country."

Governors, other political and religious leaders also urged Nigerians to embrace peace, and need to embrace values, which would be beneficial to national development. The governor of Kwara State, Saraki said, "As taught and practised by the Holy Prophet Mohammed, I urge all faithfuls to continue on the path of selfdenial, complete devotion, piety, fellowship and caring for our neighbours."

ExGovernor Ibrahim Idris of Kogi State in Lokoja urged all Muslims to adopt the spirit of brotherhood, peace and patience, which the month of Ramadan preached. He emphasized on the need for religious tolerance and peaceful cohabitation among all tribes and people of different religious persuasions.

ExGovernor Nnamani reminded all Muslims, "The hallmark of any religion is the virtue of tolerance, peace and selflessness. Islam is a progressive religion that must be practised by the individuals in an atmosphere of peace and selfdenial." He called for smooth coexistence between Muslims and their Christian brothers. He explained, "The two religions are basically the same and preach similar messages." He explained further, "The messages are the same. They teach the same thing about the Almighty, Maker of all things, and the Great Author of the Universe. The minor difference is that the messages come through two different Messengers."

The governor urged all Nigerians to emulate the humility of these two Messengers who lived exemplary lives of piety, devotion, honesty and holiness. He asked all Nigerians to eschew acrimony, avarice, violence and all vices capable of upturning the gains made so far to entrench democracy. He urged religious leaders to preach tolerance and virtuous living to their followers to avoid relapsing to the sordid past of "religious bigotry and ethnic jingoism."

Ogun State Governor, Otunba Obalofin Gbenga Daniel charged Muslims to use the lessons of Ramadan period for unity and sustenance of the current democratic government in Nigeria. He reminded them to use the lessons of Ramadan to guide their daily activities. The governor's exspokesperson, Niran Malaolu noted, "Islam is a religion of peace." He enjoined Muslims to continue to live in peace with themselves and others. Governor Gbenga Daniel charged the Muslims to eschew violence and show tolerance and love to all in the spirit of EidElFitri celebration.

Dr. Lateef Adegbite, the Secretary General of the Nigerian Supreme Council for Islamic Affairs (NSCIA) urged government to evolve measures that would alleviate the suffering of the masses, plan properly and avoid waste. He pleaded with Nigerians to live in peace, harmony and love with one another while leaders should have the fear of God/Allah and avoid corruption. He urged Muslims to endeavour to stay in clean living and avoid lapsing into impurities of mind and body. He added, "We must also maintain the fellowfeeling and spirit of give and take which Islam teaches us."

From the Christian community, the Vatican advised, "Peace is an edifice resting on the four pillars of truth, justice, love and freedom." Archbishop Michael L. Fitzgerald, President of the Pontifical Council for InterReligious Dialogue, remarked that truth was marked out as the pillar of peace because it included the recognition that human beings were not their own masters but were called to fulfill the Will of God, the Creator of all, Who was the 'Absolute Truth'.

He emphasized the need for respect for human rights and dignity of every human being. He added that lack of justice in individual, social and international relations had caused a lot of unrest and violence in the world. He pleaded, "We all belong to one human family and should see our fellow human beings as brothers and sisters. It gives the capacity to share both in sorrows and joys, makes allowances for weakness and the ability to forgive. Forgiveness is essential to the restoration of peace during conflicts."

The Archbishop of the Lagos Catholic Archdiocese, Cardinal Anthony Olubunmi Okojie, reminded Nigerians, "No one individual or groups could fight for God. It is God, the Creator of all beings, Who is in a position to keep and defend His creation." He called on Muslims to live together in peace and harmony with all since the country belongs to all Nigerians irrespective of religious affiliations and that each person will one day give account of his/her actions to God.

In his own message, the coordinator of NasruLlahFathi (NASFAT) Society of Nigeria, Lokoja Branch, Mallam Jamiu Abdulraheem, reminded political leaders of the hardship in the country and called on them to address the situation in the spirit of brotherhood preached by Ramadan.

The Chief Iman of Abuja, Ustaz Musa Mohammed, urged Muslims "to spare a thought in these hard times for their brothers who do not have anything to eat and to avoid ostentatious living but to live modestly." Christian and Muslim elites involved in corruption scandals of millions of naira should desist. In his goodwill message, the President of the Nigerian Supreme Council for Islamic Affairs and Sultan of Sokoto, Alhaji Mohammadu Maccido, called on Nigerians to be united and peace loving.

On Wednesday, April 14, 2004, the News Headline reported that Muslim militia killed three Christians as a result of religious feud bringing the total to 226 in two months of titfortat violence. It was said that the Muslim militia comprising HausaFulani ethnicity attacked the villages of Rwang, Doka and Jenkur in Southern Plateau State killing three and destroying several houses as a reprisal attack in the ongoing communal crisis in the state. It was reported that the crisis displaced over 6,000 people across three states as confirmed by eyewitnesses.

It was reported that the Muslim HausaFulani in the area who were mostly cattle herders had lived in relative peace with their counterparts who were the Christian Tarok farmers for decades until 2001 when fighting broke out. Since 2001, about 1,250 inhabitants of the area were reported killed as a result of incessant religious feuds. It was also reported that the Christian leader from Kaduna State alleged that the

Islamic extremists in the region were being funded by foreign militant groups but Islamic leaders denied that.

On Friday, April 16, 2004, the *Daily Independent Online* quoted the former National Security Adviser, Lt. General Aliyu Mohammed to have said that various terrorist groups with independent agenda or with links to international networks were seeking havens and new recruits in West African subregion. It was reported that the impacts of terrorist groups were being felt in Mali, Chad and Niger Republics during the opening ceremony of the first West African International Security Conference (WAISEC) in Abuja. Nigeria must enact terrorism act similar to the Patriot Act of the USA in order to effectively deal with terrorism and ensure national security.

In their contribution, ExPresident Olusegun Obasanjo of Nigeria and former Chairman of the National Transitional Government of Liberia, Gyude Bryant, called for a united front in the global fight against terrorism. There was concern for arms proliferation in West Africa, which posed a major security threat with the presence of illegal lethal weapons in large quantities that have fuelled civil wars and communal clashes in the subregion.

On Monday, July 5, 2004, President Olusegun Obasanjo met with a delegation of the Sokoto Caliphate that came to thank him for attending the bicentennial anniversary of the great kingdom. He revealed that some allies were plotting to see to the disintegration of Nigeria because they considered the country potentially too big and strong. He added that the great human and natural resources the nation was endowed with had become a source of envy and jealousy for which the enemies were working hard to pull the country down at all costs. He warned that Nigerians had the responsibility not to allow the wishes of the enemies to succeed.

He urged Nigerians to consciously embrace the noble, enviable and invaluable legacies of past leaders who contributed immensely to the "unity, development, upliftment and sustenance of one indivisible Nigeria." He reminded the delegation that Sokoto Caliphate was a 'symbol of influence' covering an overwhelming large territory under the sovereignty of the Caliphate. He commended the Sultan, Alhaji Muhammadu Maccido and his people for successfully conducting the bicentennial anniversary of the Caliphate.

In his response, the Sultan of Sokoto, Alhaji Muhammadu Maccido told ExPresident Olusegun Obasanjo that northern rulers and leaders had initiated new strategies to make the region free of ethnic and religious crises. The strategies, he explained, included their moves to "revive the spirit of brotherliness, tolerance, mutual understanding, respect and peaceful coexistence among people of diverse background living in the northern states" of Nigeria.

He made allusions to the initiatives packaged by the Conference of Northern Traditional Rulers, Clerics and Leaders of Thought to distribute to the people, the literature compiled on the bicentennial anniversary celebration. He explained that the literature would act as a source of 'inspiration and enlightenment' to the people who would imbibe the virtues of past leaders of the Caliphate.

He assured ExPresident Obasanjo of the Federal Republic of Nigeria, "We are confident that with dedication and unity of purpose, we can once again be our brothers' keepers and be good neighbours wherever we reside to make a living in our great country, Nigeria." He presented gifts to the ExPresident and former Vice President, Atiku Abubakar who was in attendance. The delegation included the Emir of Kano, Alhaji Ado Bayero; Emir of Zazzau, Alhaji Shehu Idris; and Emir of Gwandu, Alhaji Mustapha Jokolo among others.

The Rt. Rev. Simon Bala, Bishop of Diocese of Gusau called on leaders not to use their position to give unfair preference to any interest group anywhere in the country. He called on Zamfara State government to give all religious establishments equal opportunities to operate schools. He also called on the state governments to respect the fundamental freedom of worship as enshrined in Nigerian Constitution. He deplored the situation of insecurity in the country and appealed to the federal government to improve on the level of security of lives and property in Nigeria.

On Friday, July 2, 2004, former Minister of Federal Capital Territory (FCT) and All Nigeria Peoples Party (ANPP) chieftain in Plateau State, General Jeremiah Useni, remarked that the suspended ExGovernor Joshua Dariye should not be allowed to return to office after the expiration of the state of emergency declared by the Federal Government as a result of ethno-religious riots. He advocated for fresh governorship elections in the state to elect the people's governor. He commended ExPresident Olusegun Obasanjo for declaring a state of emergency as a result of sectarian violence, which claimed several lives and destroyed property worth millions of Nigerian money.

General Jeremiah Useni insisted that the suspended governor Joshua Dariye did not win the state governorship election in the first instance. He emphasized that it was won by ANPP's candidate, Commodore Jonah Jang. He opined that the local government chairman in the state should be sacked and fresh elections held. He refuted claims that military officers in the state were against the suspended governor. He maintained that they did not have any personal animosity against the state governor.

On the other hand, the former governor of old Kaduna State, Alhaji Balarabe Musa, suggested that the federal government should embark on steps to prosecute perpetrators of religious violence to serve as a deterrent to others. He stressed that it was wrong for the federal and state governments to allow those who caused and instigated ethno-religious riots that resulted in loss of lives and extensive property damage to go free without prosecution. He emphasized that such crises were bound to reoccur incessantly if those responsible were never pursued, caught, prosecuted and appropriately punished.

He reiterated, "One of the fundamental things is that persons who were found to have been involved in organizing the violence should be arrested, prosecuted and punished. Once this is done, then we will be on the path to peace." He complained, "Some powerful persons in the society were responsible for recruiting unemployed youths to unleash terror on innocent Nigerians with impunity." He accused the government of not doing enough to arrest the situation. He attributed the cause of violence to the failing economy and the gripping poverty which deprived some Nigerians of the basic necessities of life. He appealed to the federal and state governments to muster the political will to arrest and prosecute the arrowheads of disturbances.

On Wednesday, December 1, 2004, the Northern Governors Forum convened the Northern Unity Conference to find lasting solution to the incessant cases of ethno-religious conflicts occurring in Northern Nigeria. The Conference was held in Kaduna under the chairmanship of Alhaji Saminu Turaki, ExGovernor of Jigawa State who was also the Chairman of the Northern Governors Forum. He promised to forward any resolutions and agreements reached at the meeting to the nineteen Northern States Governors for implementation.

The twoday summit was planned to: (1) identify the causes of crises in Northern Nigeria; (2) sensitize Northerners on the harmful effects of crises; and (3) find ways to unite leaders and their diverse ethnic nationalities.

At the meeting, the Chairman of the Christian Association of Nigeria (CAN), Most Reverend (Dr.) Peter Jatau, Catholic Archbishop of Kaduna Archdiocese, was represented by Catholic Bishop of Kafanchan Diocese, Chairman of Kaduna State Chapter of CAN, Right Reverend (Dr.) Joseph Bagobiri. Dr. Jatau's Archdiocese consisted of the nineteen northern states and the Federal Capital Territory (FCT), Abuja.

He blamed the disunity and ethno-religious problems in Northern Nigeria on the northern state governors whom he accused of blatant favouritism and discrimination in favour of one religion against the others. He emphasized, "Unless and until the various levels of governments in Northern Nigeria learn to treat adherents of the two major religions equally, peace will continue to elude the region."

In his own presentation, former Head of State and presidential candidate of the All Nigeria People's Party (ANPP), Major General Mohammadu Buhari (retired), was said to have blamed some of the invitees from the North for their attitude and the performance of the northern governors. He blamed their economic performance, which he described as failing. Former Vice President, Atiku Abubakar and former speaker of the House of Representatives, Alhaji Aminu Bello Masari, hinted that ethnicity and religious bigotry was the 'twin evil' responsible for progress retardation in Northern Nigeria.

ExVice President Atiku observed that in spite of differences in language, ethnicity and religion, their people were brought up as brothers and sisters and wondered inconceivably how in three decades, the people in the northern states could have become so terribly divided and in conflict. While emphasizing that the solution to the incessant crisis lay with northern leaders, he reiterated that the crises continued to drain the muchneeded human and material resources for development. He described the crises as wanton and senseless.

He explained that United Nations Development Programmes (UNDP) attributed human development to the management of diversity and emphasized, therefore, that diversity could not be an excuse for disunity. He emphasized the philosophy of the world becoming a global village with borders collapsing and communities getting closer to each other. He urged northerners to adopt the concept of globalization because it was no longer possible to live like the forefathers in a changing world.

In his own submission, the former Speaker of the House of Representatives, Alhaji Aminu Bello Masari affirmed that unity and peace were at the heart of the problems of Northern Nigeria in particular and Nigeria generally. He emphasized that without peace, it would be difficult to serve the people and provide the indispensable leadership critically needed to transform Northern Nigeria from the "scourge of poverty and restiveness to serenity of prosperity and peace."

He condemned the politically and criminally motivated gangsters masquerading in ethnic and religious garbs who had been causing wanton destruction of lives and property to ordinary peace-loving and law-abiding citizens and called unequivocally for concerted efforts to expose, arrest, prosecute, convict and punish the culprits severely.

In his own contribution, the Sultan of Sokoto, Alhaji Mohammadu Maccido, enjoined participants to act in unison to ensure peaceful coexistence in Northern Nigeria. He commended the concerted efforts of the Northern Governors Forum that convened the peace summit. It was observed that many distinguished, eminent Northerners were reported to be conspicuously absent at the peace conference. Those reported to be physically absent included Alhaji Shehu Shagari, Second Republic President of Nigeria; former Head of State, General Ibrahim Badamosi Babangida; former Minister of Defense, Lt. Gen. Theophilus Yakubu Danjuma; and former Head of State, General Abdulsalami Abubakar.

To curb the crises in the North, the laws and their enforcement against ethno-religious conflicts should be strengthened and made deterrent federal felonies. Governors that cannot maintain peace and unity in diversity risk the declaration of state of emergency by federal authority. Offenders and their mentors must be hunted and sought without time limitations, pursued until arrested, prosecuted, convicted and sentenced for capital punishment or long terms of imprisonment as may be appropriate and proportional to the offence.

Preemptive action to foil ethno-religious offences using increasing intelligence gathering should be stepped up. Those who preach hate should be apprehended and prosecuted for inciting ethno-religious violence. Discrimination laws should be enacted and enforced.

There should be enlightenment campaigns against ethno-religious violence which is antithetical to security of investment, industrialization, economic prosperity, national security and security of life and property. There should be zero tolerance for ethno-religious violence and similar crimes throughout Nigeria. The responsibility of maintaining peace, law and order rests fully with federal authorities using the resources at their disposal. If no leader incites ethno-religious violence at local or state level, there would be none.

The laws should go after the mentors and planners of violence and crimes as well as the operatives to incarcerate them. To kill a tree completely, the taproot must be attacked and destroyed. If northern leaders cannot agree among themselves, then the Federal Government cannot rely on that source to solve ethno-religious crimes. The government should therefore act decisively and consistently each time there is ethno-religious peace violation in the North or any other part of the country.

The Christians and Muslims at all levels fanning ethno-religious violence are not fighting for God/Allah or about Him because God/Allah does not need such help; and violence is not the way of God/Allah – the Peaceful, Merciful, Omnipotent, Omnipresent, Omnisapient, Omniscient, the Alpha and Omega, the Maker of Heaven and Earth. Therefore, those who should be dealt with first and foremost are the 'big guns' in religions inciting ethno-religious violence. They are not fighting for God/Allah but for their own private pockets and selfish interests.

On Thursday, May 6, 2004, the *News Headline* reported that about 300 Muslims were killed by ethnic Tarok Christians in the central town of Yelwa according to information received from Justice Abdulkadir Orire, Secretary-General of the Jama'atu Nasril Islam who described it as genocide. The conflict between Christian Tarok and the Muslim Fulani was deeprooted in competing claims to a fertile land over which the two groups claimed ownership.

The Christian Tarok who are farmers believe that the Muslims who are cattle raisers are alien and not indigenous to the area while the Fulanis claim that they have grazed cattle there periodically for many generations. The conflict in this area is incessant, and it has claimed hundreds of lives each time. The perpetrators of the crimes seem to have mentors who incite them and protect them from the arms of the law.

The enormity of the problems of deadly conflicts between Muslims and Christians makes it imperative for government to take serious actions of preemption, prevention and deterrence to eliminate ethno-religious crimes. Why does secular state of Nigeria become powerless in cracking down on religious troublemakers who commit the most heinous crimes of killings and arson with impunity every time with or without the slightest provocation? Those who commit arson and killings in the name of religion including their mentors are criminals, vandals and are terrorists who should be incarcerated in a penitentiary or put away in a reformatory whether they are Christians or Muslims, indigenes or foreigners.

In order to ensure Nigeria's survival, there is need for special acts of legislature that establish federal special courts to deal quickly and decisively with economic sabotage and ethno-religious conflicts especially when they result in killings and arson. These vandals should be pursued, arrested and prosecuted to the last person and including their mentors for the safety, well being and economic survival of Nigeria and Nigerians. Conflicts, killings and arson destroy enabling environment for investments, and retard government efforts to attract foreign investments.

In the end, the same people who disrupt peace and create capital flights would blame government for underdevelopment and marginalization. Ethno-religious confrontation is two-edge sword, which causes collateral damages and scares away investment and development. It chases away business and prosperity. Those perpetrators of ethnoreligions violence should stop or be stopped and put away in a penitentiary for a very long time to ensure that the peace-loving Nigerian society is no longer violated by the devil-sponsored criminals.

As a result of Yelwa killings in Plateau State, representatives of various Muslim organizations allegedly ended a one-day emergency meeting in Kaduna on Tuesday, May 11, 2004, with a pledge that

Northern Muslims would take up arms against Christians in a fight-to-finish.

In Kano, Muslim youths protesting the killings in Yelwa, a Muslim town in Plateau State, descended on nonMuslims and committed various acts of arson and killings. They burnt down churches, houses, properties, vehicles, police patrol vans and injured many people.

Muslim organizations allegedly met under the auspices of 'Concerned Muslim Organizations of Nigeria (CMON), chaired by Ibrahim Datti Ahmed, National President of the Supreme Council for Sharia in Nigeria (SCSN). The meeting decided that the government should convene Sovereign National Conference (SNC) urgently to discuss the fate of Nigeria in order to avert anarchy.

A lot of people were pulled out of their vehicles and set ablaze. A lot of people took refuge in the police barracks and stations. Candidates writing their May/June 2004 Senior Secondary Certificate Examination of West African Examinations Council (WAEC) were allegedly invaded at the examination centres while female students were reportedly raped. Is that fighting for God/Allah or the devil? Is that fighting in the interest of God/Allah? Is killing innocent people, committing arson, disturbing students at examination centres and raping female students the Jihad that sends any vandal to paradise if he dies? No!

Religious leaders should be able to control those who are fighting their Jihad against innocent people who were pulled down from their vehicles and killed. Looting, burning property, killing innocent people, stealing, raping students at examinations centers and committing crimes against God/ Allah and humanity cannot be Jihad and not in the interest of God/Allah.

Two students of Bayero University, Kano heading toward the old campus were allegedly forcibly removed from the commercial vehicle and killed. Is that Jihad to go to paradise? It is important for law enforcement secret intelligence agents to infiltrate into the various secret meetings being held by groups of Christians and Muslims and detain all collaborators who want to plunge the country into religious war and unnecessary chaos. They are trying to pull the country back to the deadly events of preNigerian civil war. Foreigners with religious extremism and violence should be accosted and deported.

The mentors (directly and/or indirectly) of above-mentioned atrocities of arson and mayhem should face quick justice. Maintaining the security of Nigerians regarding ethno-religious confrontations cannot be left in the hands of state and local authorities that discriminate against other religions and ethnicities. Any state or region that encourages, incites or fans ethno-religious violence should be declared a state of emergency by federal authorities to protect the innocent and law abiding citizens anywhere in the country.

Those who are most guilty of religious and ethnicity violence are the planners behind the scene, the mentors, the preachers of hate who brainwash one set of religionists against the other as well as those who incite the unemployed youths to commit acts of arson and killings. These masterminds of ethno-religious violence represent the source and snakehead of the major problems which can be attacked and smashed at source through enlightenment campaigns, diplomacy and the use of force decisively as a deterrence whenever necessary. There must be effective intelligence gathering mechanism for the derailment and preemption of ethno-religious and political uproars before they are hatched.

If any Nigerian has not changed 'business as usual' and continues to act detrimentally to Nigerian national security and prosperity, he or she should face the full weight of the law irrespective of his or her influence in society. If the elites steal millions and billions of money, they are treated as takers, sharing the national cake, but when the poor, less privileged people take the crumbs from the cake, they are treated as having stolen, then prosecuted and convicted. Where is justice? What is Sharia doing? Such inconsistency cannot clean the country of fraud, corruption and other violent crimes that jeopardize the progress of the country.

Nigerian leaders (Presidency, Legislature, Judiciary, State Governors, Local Government Chairpersons and Religious Leaders), have great responsibilities to protect the innocent people in the society from these misguided ethno-religious lunatics in human skins and clothings who organize killings and arson in the name of religion and ignorance; and if you do not, on whose heads will the blood of these innocent souls rest? No true religion should encourage killings, arson and violence. Religious intolerance should be fought to a standstill by government as corruption is being seriously fought without 'sacred cows or untouchables'.

What happened to those Christian and Muslim masterminds who planned arson and killings at secret meetings and incited youths to carry them out? What happened to youths who carried out the killings? What happened to the victims and their families in terms of compensations? These terrorist acts must be countered with the severity they deserve so that the dead victims would not have died in vain.

If those who attend churches and mosques do not want to be at peace, they should be made to understand that majority of Nigerians do not go to churches or mosques, but they need and are entitled to peace. Majority of Nigerians do not want to be bothered by these violent religious hypocrites. What were the behaviour examples of tolerance and Godliness/Allahliness, of those leaders and followerships who attended churches and mosques but held secret meetings, planned and executed killings, arson and violence? Sincere and true religious leaders and followerships would preach and encourage peace according to the teachings of God/Allah, but not incite youths to commit killings, arson and violence on religious opponents.

The government must do its job decisively to protect innocent Nigerians who outnumber the evildoers in their midst. If it requires combing all nooks and corners of cities and villages to hunt, arrest, prosecute and convict these culprits, it must be done no matter how long it takes in the best interest of the nation's peace, tranquility, security and safety. People who get away with one crime always have the tendency to commit more crimes with false notion of invincibility.

The Rt. Rev. Simon Bala, Bishop of Diocese of Gusau, was said to have appealed to the Zamfara State government for equal opportunities to establish and operate schools. What is the excuse to restrain the establishment of more schools to help the development of the people? How can the people develop if there are not abundance of schools, and those who want to establish schools are artificially restrained and not encouraged by the government that should be partners in progress to do so? If every benefit possible is not encouraged to reach the people, then what is the purpose of governance in a democracy?

In a secular democratic Nigeria, religious belief cannot be a genuine excuse to restrain development. Right leadership embraces development always, and does not restrain it because of ethnicity or religion in a secular nation under democratic setting. Adverse religious indoctrination makes some leaders, bigots and people get everything wrong about what religion is, what it should be and its purpose. That is unprogressive and sad.

It is hoped that the next set of Nigerian leaders will not include anybody who is not accustomed to changing time, civilization, modernity and development. Regrettably, some elites are leaders when they should still be in schools, colleges and universities learning about human resource management and development, political science, managerial economics and finance, sociology, psychology, etc. To be successful, leadership must acquire the right education and experience, which can help the socio-economic and political emancipation and development of their people. God/Allah does not restrain development, so also religion does not, except those who deliberately and selfishly misinterpret religious teachings. May God/Allah give Nigeria the right leaders who will not discriminate against any Nigerian citizen irrespective of ethnicity, sex and religion.

The Federal Government and political party leaderships should be able to overrule obnoxious, retarding policies that limit and regress the people's development in the states. Periodic reorientation of the leaders through seminars, conferences and workshops coupled with exchange visits to other states will help state leaders to selfreappraise their performances and do better in the best interest of their people.

Nigerians have already lost about forty years of their valuable lives due to coups d'etat, dictatorships, maladministration, corruption and other leadership indiscretions and vices. No Nigerian in West, East, North or South wants any more waste and retrogression because life is too precious and short.

Foreign and local investments and economic prosperity cannot occur in disturbed, unsafe and violent areas. Hence, perpetrators of ethno-religious crimes, kidnappers of oil workers, violent militant groups and their mentors are not helping the development of Nigeria. They should find peaceful means to solve their problems with diplomacy, consultation, conciliation and compromise and never take the laws into their own hands. A good leader in a democracy will tolerate all religions without discrimination and also encourage private participation in state or national development.

The Holy Books talk and teach in parables but human beings often deliberately and intentionally misinterpret the parables literally to suit their selfish, personal and group interests. Jesus Christ said that the devil would usually quote the Holy Book to suit its purposes. When the Holy Books talk about separating the offending limbs from the body, it does not mean physically amputating the hand or leg or plucking off the eyes or blocking the ears that facilitate a crime. The parable simply teaches and encourages people to separate themselves from sinful acts.

Unfortunately, some governments in the world still supervise amputation of arms, legs, hands or fingers of those who steal a couple of dollars to eat for survival while their elites who steal millions and billions are regarded as sacred cows and untouchables who take from the national cake. Such elites are not regarded and treated as thieves like the poor persons. That is double standard. Elites who commit fraud, corruption, adultery, economic and financial crimes and other serious crimes have not been having their limbs amputated except poor people who steal bicycles, a couple of dollars etc. Sharia does not encourage hypocrisy and discriminatory practices.

It is reported in the Holy Bible that Simon Peter cut off somebody's ear with his sword in support of Jesus Christ, but Jesus warned Peter to sheathe his sword because whoever killed with the sword would fall by the sword. He then took the cut off ear and pasted it back perfectly. He advised his apostles to turn the right cheek if they were slapped on the left cheek. These parables meaningfully emphasized to the apostles the need to maintain peace and tolerance in all their transactions and interactions. He told them that wherever they were not received, they should shake off the dust on their shoes there.

He did not tell them to create religious violence, kill or cause arson if they were not well received as they carried on their teachings and preachings. Hence, it is difficult to understand where religious leaders and followers fighting, killing and burning houses of religious opponents got their own learning and knowledge from, perhaps from the devil and not the Prophets Who were forebearers of religions. There should not be thugs and hooligans in religions meant to serve God/Allah, the Peaceful and Merciful.

Unfortunately, renowned US Evangelist Pat Robertson allegedly preached that the US government should use its resources to assassinate

President Chavez of Venezuela contrary to the tenets of the Lord, God/ Allah and the Holy Books, which say, "Thou shall not kill." Religious leaders, Christians, Muslims and others, should stop dabbling into partisan politics and making dangerous and inciteful political statements. They should leave to "Caesar what belongs to Caesar and to the Lord, God/Allah what is His" in accordance with the Holy Books.

If religious forerunners preached peace, mercy, love, care and good neighbourliness at early times, what justifications do followers both Christians and Muslims have to engage in violence, arson and killings of religious opponents? After all, the many different religions represent avenues, gateways, paths and routes to get to the same one God/Allah and His Kingdom.

The Holy Books emphasize the existence of the 'Promised Land' symbolically and parabolically as the destination(s), goals, objectives and targets of highest and greatest actualizations of individuals, groups or nations, but may not necessarily be physical landspace for anybody, groups or nations to go and grab on conviction that the Holy Book says that it belongs to the individual or group. God/Allah will rather give you what nobody owns instead of make you take forcibly what belongs to somebody else. Such situation can result in chaos, which God/Allah does not support. What the world needs is peace, tolerance, contentment, good neighbourliness, kindness, mercy, love and care, friendliness and Godliness /Allahliness.

Most religious problems in the world are borne out of greed, fraud, corruption, hypocrisy, selfaggrandizement and other devilish actions at variance with the tenets of God/Allah. The Holy Books warn about the emergence of fake prophets and that not everybody who calls Him God/ Allah shall reach His Kingdom. Hence, what are you fighting, killing, committing arson and inciting religious violence for? What is your gain? Violence is not the way of God/Allah. Stop being fooled by those who incite you into ethno-religious violence.

It is unthinkable religious intolerance and extremism for a country leader to think/talk about wiping off another country from the face of the earth. Is such thought/talk the wish/way of God/Allah or the devil? Is that how to reach paradise, heaven or hell? People of different religious faiths and beliefs should be able to live together in harmony, and countries should be able to exist side by side in peace. People must be able to freely choose their religion, and only God/Allah, the Almighty, the Merciful, the Peaceful can appropriately determine who is rightly and actually serving Him and doing His wishes.

Those who purport to be fighting for God/Allah whether Christians, Muslims or Traditionalists are confusionists who are misguided because God/Allah does not need anybody's favours. If Western countries derive their power from possession of nuclear weapons and keep on intimidating, bullying and occupying other countries, how can you effectively, justifiably and morally check the proliferation of nuclear weapons which the weaker countries are seeking to acquire in order to be powerful, become recognized and able to protect and defend themselves.

"Vox Populi, Vox Dei" (the voice of the people is the voice of God/Allah). Hence, religious leaders and scholars should evolve a reformation that expunges all acts of inhumanity to humanity pretentiously done in the name of religion. Up till present time, some groups and countries have relied on archaic practices, parables, customs and punishments of periods before Christ and Prophet Mohammed including early centuries to kill, behead, maim, commit arson, hang people, flog and stone offenders to death, execute and amputate offenders' limbs for minor offences and justifying suicide bombing operations with their religious faiths and teachings. Religionists both leaders and followers need reorientation, redirection, selfappraisal and selfdiscipline.

Corrective, nonviolent and nonmilitary solutions should form major missions of the superpower(s) instead of chasing oil in exchange for obsolete weapons of war, F16s and other weapons of war, as well as manipulating intelligence, lying and bullying everybody around the world and ending up being hated by all. All acts of socio-economic, political and religious inhumanity to humanity should not continue to posterity unending. 'The buck must stop here' with this generation.

Religious leaders at all levels should confront and stop pedophilia, homosexuality, corruption, frauds, hypocrisy, deception, adultery, discrimination, illegal wealth, violence and other crimes that thrive among them and religious environment.

GOD/ALLAH BLESS NIGERIA!

CHAPTER 12

IMPRESSIVE INTERNATIONAL RELATIONS

Nigerian foreign policy concept is 'nonalignment' which suggests a 'via media' course of neutrality from the political ideologies of the West or the East – Far Right or Far Left. The nonalignment policy enables Nigeria to take a stand in her best national interest without being compelled to yield to pressures from other nations seeking to impose their political persuasions and ideological leanings. Africa is the centrepiece and main focal point of Nigeria's foreign relations.

Nigeria of over 140 million people occupies an enviable position in the comity of nations. The nation is well represented in the United Nations (UN), African Union (AU), Economic Commission of West African States (ECOWAS), New Economic Partnership for Africa's Development (NEPAD), Organization of Petroleum Exporting Countries (OPEC), the Commonwealth of Nations and most other distinguished international agencies. Nigeria as a leading African country makes Africa the centerpiece of her foreign policy.

It is on record that Nigeria had hosted the whole black world at the National Theatre, Iganmu, Lagos, where there were displays of rich black cultures, traditions and dances lasting two weeks in 1979. It was fully attended. The gathering was highly successful, and General Obasanjo as Military Head of State (1976-1979) deserved great commendations for bringing the black people of the world together. Blacks need more of that initiative that brings them together in their motherland.

In his inauguration speech of May 29, 2003, to mark the commencement of his second term in office, ExPresident Matthew Okikiolakan Olusegun Aremu Obasanjo referred to contemporary events in the world and commented that it appeared a new paradigm was evolving for a new world order whereby the hope, confidence and security assumed by all nations big or small were undergoing significant changes.

He advised Africans to recognize the change and prepare adequately to curtail the serious risks of the effects of marginalization continually suffered by African nations or else, the situation would become complete 'delinkage'. He emphasized the need to cultivate new friends while cherishing the old ones; but he reminded Nigerians that they should not forget to remain "masters of their own fates, captains of their own destinies and architects of their own fortunes."

He expressed deep concern over the issue of national debt relief campaign, which he stagemanaged vigorously for six years. He added with deep emotion that there was great inequity and injustice in the debt issue totaling $30 billion as at 2005. Fortunately, the President laughed last for his remarkable accomplishment of getting about $18 billion of the debt written off by Paris Club at the end of June 2005 with promises for further debt relief and more aid to Africa. The conditions for the debt relief were met speedily, and the balance left was paid instalmentally without any hesitation so that Nigeria could start on a clean slate debtfree for the benefit of posterity.

The president's campaign for debt relief and debt rescheduling could have been less difficult if the lenders did not know that a lot of the borrowed money was misappropriated by many Nigerian leaders of the past. The president's observation about the inequity and injustice in the debt issue was very true to a great extent, but those Nigerian leaders and politicians who borrowed money for the nation's development but squandered it corruptly and fraudulently for their ostentatious living to satisfy their personal interests instead of national interest should be blamed.

Some Nigerian leaders even succeeded in recycling part of the money borrowed for projects of national interest back overseas and stashed it in foreign private bank accounts. The corrupt and fraudulent politicians and government officials who facilitated such economic and financial crimes committed greater inequity and injustice against Nigeria as well as the lenders who benefitted from the corruptly contracted debts at high interest rate.

Nigerian debts did not surface without valid written contracts between the lenders and Nigeria. The lending practice in the Western World is a kind of neocolonization economically as it makes the borrower poorer and more subservient to the lender forever especially in situations where the money borrowed was not utilized productively like many Nigerian foreign debts. Borrowed money that is not productively utilized will usually be very difficult to pay back as the high interest on it continues to accumulate annually without any benefit or revenue as usual from uncompleted and abandoned projects.

The present leaders (the Presidency, Legislature and Judiciary) should work cooperatively to recover all ill-gotten gains that put the country into debt for which Nigeria spent over $1 billion annually for debt servicing, otherwise, posterity may not forgive those corrupt leaders as well as those who had the opportunity to recover the ill-gotten money but never did.

It is hard to prove and hard to recover the ill-gotten gains, but the President in full cooperation with the Legislature and the Judiciary should continue relentless efforts to recover ill-gotten gains that put Nigeria into debt and penury for decades. The conditions for acquiring foreign loans should be made strict and there should be effective supervision to ensure that foreign loans are strictly applied productively for the purpose for which they are acquired.

The Nigerian authorities should therefore evolve programmes of persuasion, prevention and deterrence to Nigerians that are likely to commit economic and financial crimes. All Nigerian money known to have been illegally acquired should be recovered without fear or favour. Nigeria should build reformatories in which to keep persons who fail to refund their proven ill-gotten gains. There should be no sacred cows.

If the Presidency, Legislature and Judiciary work as a team to stamp out fraud, corruption and other economic and financial crimes in Nigeria, they will succeed to give Nigeria a sanitized, clean and transparent society. The cleanliness must be from the topmost persons in Nigeria to the lowest. It could be done in good faith, nonselectively and without discrimination.

In the *Daily Independent Online* of November 25, 2003, the former Abia State Governor, Chief Orji Uzor Kalu, said, "Before corruption can be reduced in Nigeria, the fight against it must start from the top, especially senior government functionaries." He added, "Those who allegedly mismanaged ₦300 billion should be taken to anticorruption panel, because we must start to deal with the menace from the top now." He also said, "Bold steps had not been taken to prosecute those who stole billions of naira at the anticorruption panel. But it is only those who steal ₦5,000 that face the anticorruption tribunal."

Judging from recent events, a lot of the exgovernor's concerns must have been taken care of. Whatever remains should be investigated thoroughly and acted upon fairly and judiciously. The exgovernor should assist the authorities by mentioning names and incidences of suspected corrupt practices by politicians and government functionaries. He should fully cooperate with the EFCC to disprove the damaging allegations of staggering corrupt enrichment levied against him by Abia State Leadership Forum published in *This Day News* of Thursday, September 8, 2005.

Borrowing money at lowest interest rate to prosecute infrastructural projects or capitalization to promote national development is a good idea if the money borrowed is utilized effectively, efficiently, prudently and judiciously, and not diverted to unproductive use into private pockets or for personal interest instead of national interest. If productively utilized, the benefits derivable from completed projects would be more than sufficient to pay the debt and any accruing interest.

It is ironical to ask lenders for debt cancellations, relief or debt rescheduling when the lenders know that part of the money borrowed for national development projects often finds itself into the private pockets and bank accounts of a few politicians and government functionaries. Invariably, such corrupt politicians stash back the money into their hidden foreign accounts, which Nigerians may not know but are well known to the foreign creditors. Nigerians will everlastingly be grateful to ExPresident Obasanjo for getting almost all of the debt written off unprecedentedly and also for his initiative to ensure that procurement of foreign loans was regulated before the end of his tenure.

Foreign creditors were saying it loudly that few Nigerians who acquired money illegally thereby throwing the country into debt had enough money to bail Nigeria out of indebtedness if they were patriotic. It was gratifying to note that ExPresident Obasanjo of Nigeria travelled overseas many times with his economic team trying to negotiate for debt relief, debt rescheduling and giving encouragement to foreign investors to come and invest in Nigeria to boost the nation's economy. Regrettably, one crisis after the other in form of ethno-religious violence coupled with insecurity of lives and property limited the successful invitation of foreign investors in 2003.

Later, sweeping national reforms embarked upon seriously and transparently by ExPresident Obasanjo dramatically changed the whole situation for Nigeria. It was on record that no lender would give any reasonable debt relief or rescheduling as long as Nigerian environment was infested by perpetrators of corruption, frauds, economic and financial crimes with impunity.

At the Commonwealth Business Forum in Abuja, it was reported by Vanguard News on Friday, December 5, 2003, that the Canadian Prime Minister, Jean Chretien, told the Nigerian President to forget about the debt forgiveness from Canada because Nigeria had enough resources to pay back. It was revealed, "Nigerians have as much as $170 billion stashed in foreign private bank accounts with a debt stock currently put at $31 billion."

He emphasized that Nigeria could not be considered a poor nation needing debt forgiveness. He added that what Nigeria needed was transparency and good governance to ensure that a few people did not hold on to the wealth of the country at the expense of majority of Nigerians as was the case. He also announced that Canada would no longer give foreign loans to Nigeria but would provide assistance in the form of grants.

It was appreciated how Obasanjo Administration worked hard to turn the country's economic mismanagement around. The law against economic and financial crimes was passed and updated in line with international standard requirements. Many cases of fraud and corruption were prosecuted in court by the ICPC and EFCC far beyond the total number that was ever recorded for forty years of independence.

Many important personalities regarded as sacred cows and untouchables in the past were investigated, indicted and prosecuted. It looked like the concept of 'no sacred cows' was followed to a reasonable extent. Also, the security position was tackled seriously resulting in temporarily closing borders and engagement of talks with some heads of governments over cross-border crimes and economic sabotage.

Nigerian elites who abused the opportunities available to them to commit economic and financial crimes against the nation should learn a lesson of remorse from a 'thief of conscience' who in December 2002, thirty-four years after stealing a gold wedding band and earrings from Sarter Hamann Jewelry Store in 1968, mailed them back to the store owner, Hamann, with a sincere expression of apology. Anonymously, the thief said, "Enclosed are two items that I stole from you in 1968. I am very sorry, and I should not have taken your property. The pieces belong to you, NOT me. I was wrong, and I want to apologize for my actions."

In the same manner, those who illegally benefited from Nigeria, thus plunging the country into debt and economic jeopardy for over forty years of independence should return their loot voluntarily with anonymity. Those whose fraudulent cases are provable should be persuaded by meeting them oneonone to refund the illegally acquired money or assets. Those who refuse to cooperate should be prosecuted, convicted and sent to a reformatory while their assets are confiscated up to the amount proven to have been stolen with added interest.

The Nigerian leaders should employ all strategies including payment of rewards of up to 0.1% of recovered loot to people who provide information that leads to conviction of fraudsters and recovery of their loot. This 0.1% of ₦1 billion payable to an informant when recovered is ₦1 million.

If any government leadership, the Presidency, Legislature and Judiciary, fail to recover Nigerian money and properties proven to be illegally acquired by elites, who put present and future Nigerian generations into penury and suffering, it may be difficult not to charge them of connivance and as accomplices by future generations.

It may be recalled that many Obas and Traditional Chiefs from Ogun State paid a courtesy visit to ExPresident Olusegun Obasanjo in September 2003. They expressed similar concerns by urging the

President of Nigeria to take measures to stamp out corruption in Nigeria and recover ill-gotten gains. The cases of silent looters who are not detected, and do not return their loot willingly should be left to God/Allah for adjudication.

Nigeria was in the forefront of ensuring economic integration of the West African subregion as well as strong advocate of regionalization of African Economy. A lot of focus was placed on the smooth flow of foreign investments into Nigeria, in spite of mitigating problems, which include:

(a) safety of personnel and investments;
(b) economic and financial crimes which were rampant;
(c) corruption, frauds;
(d) armed robbery, especially cross-border types;
(e) epileptic type of power supply;
(f) infrastructural vandalization – electricity cables, oil pipelines, etc.;
(g) hostage taking in Niger Delta;
(h) incessant labour strike actions – labour law of 2005 regulated on any possible abuses;
(i) ethnicity and religious disturbances resulting in killings and arson;
(j) unfavorable business climate and poor infrastructure; and
(k) insufficient information and wrong perceptions obtained through media and press reports.

Government actions demonstrated strong commitment and determination to deal with the problems enumerated above. The government closed the Seme border with the Republic of Benin temporarily to check cross-border armed robbery, smuggling, dumping and importation of banned products. The government action was reported to have yielded significant results leading to the repatriation of over thirty criminals and returning of over one hundred stolen vehicles to Nigeria from Benin Republic.

On the waterside, the Nigerian Navy arrested ships with over 15 expatriates and some Nigerian collaborators. The ships were laden with stolen crude oil. The Navy then stepped up efforts to stop the illegalities being perpetrated in the coastal areas. The unwholesome activities of the criminals included illegal oil bunkering, oil pipeline vandalization, hostage taking for heavy ransom and sea piracy. The illegalities are being seriously contained.

As of September 2, 2003, the operatives of the Economic and Financial Crimes Commission (EFCC) had intensified the search for suspected fraudsters who had gone underground following the arrest of their ringleaders who were prosecuted in the law courts.

It was reliably revealed that some of the followerships of the core fraudsters fled out of Nigeria, and they were hunted internationally by International Police Organization. In the past, the '419 Advanced Fee Fraudsters' had terrorized the world community with fraudulent letters and duped many people out of huge sums of money. The ringleaders of the fraudsters who were arrested, were refused bail by the courts, and at least one of them died in incarceration.

With the same determination, the Federal government should decisively tackle ethno-religious violence by enacting antiterrorist acts like the US Patriot Act of 2002 to smash the networks of ethno-religious militants and their mentors, whether Christians or Muslims, who are inciting people or militants into violence. They scare investor with their violence, killings, arson, kidnappings, and vandalization of oil infrastructure.

RELATIONS WITH CHINA:

The relationship between Republic of China and Nigeria is based on the policy of "One China" – the unification of China and a united, indivisible, one Nigeria. While welcoming the Chinese, Deputy Minister of Foreign Affairs leading a ten-man delegation on a courtesy call to his office, the former Vice President of Nigeria, Atiku Abubakar, requested the Chinese Government to accept to be a major player in the New Economic Partnership for Africa's Development (NEPAD). He added that Chinese contributions to NEPAD would have positive and tremendous economic impact on the new economic agenda of the African Union (AU) and the West African subregion represented by the Economic Commission of West African States (ECOWAS).

The ExVice President explained that within two years, the West African subregion would witness the emergence of a single currency and market with the objectives of enhanced economic developments, employment generation, poverty alleviation and poverty eradication.

China never showed any doubt in supporting Nigeria and Africa for permanent seats in the United Nations (UN), foreign debt cancellation and helping to launch Nigerian satellite.

In his response, the Chinese Deputy Minister of Foreign Affairs, Mr. Qiuo Zonghai, expressed appreciation of Nigeria's support over the struggles for the reunification of China and human rights efforts. He praised both countries for their wonderful cooperation in the areas of telecommunications and energy, which had progressed beyond expectations. The relationship between the Federal Republic of Nigeria and the Republic of China is excellent and on the right course.

China entered into a 'Memorandum of Understanding' with Nigeria in oil business and its business investments in Nigeria is unparalleled. China is involved in establishing a trade free zone in Igbesa, Ogun State and planning to build a general hospital there.

RELATIONS WITH LIBERIA:

Liberia, a member of ECOWAS and African Union (AU) was torn apart as a result of civil war started in 1989, which killed over 200,000 people and made many Liberians as refugees in Europe, America and other African countries especially Nigeria.

To broker peace in Liberia, Nigerian ExPresident Olusegun Obasanjo, Chairman of African Union (AU), provided asylum for Liberian ExPresident Charles Taylor who stepped down in a bid to end the fierce fighting in Monrovia, capital city of Liberia. Nigeria also provided a safe haven for Liberian refugees in Ogun State of Nigeria as well as sending about 2,000 Nigerian soldiers to Liberia as peacekeepers.

ExPresident Obasanjo was cheered as a hero by thousands of Liberian citizens as he was driven through Monrovia, the Liberian capital city, for playing a central role in ending the civil war, fighting and bloodshed in their country. The citizens waved the micromini green and white Nigeria flags chanting, "We want peace, no more war." The Nigerian President was accompanied by Liberia's caretaker President Moses Blah in a motorcade of military jeeps with mounted machine guns and armoured personnel carriers. They waved back and blew kisses of love and affection to the people. With clinched fist raised up, ExPresident Obasanjo replied to the waving Liberians, "You will have peace."

It would be recalled that a Liberian, Earnest Smith who was riding a bicycle along side the President's motorcade, raised up one hand in victory sign chanting, "I am very happy today, and I am very grateful to Nigerian ExPresident Obasanjo. He is trying to bring peace to our country." An agreement was concluded in Ghana between the Liberian rebels and the government. As a result, Mr. Moses Blah handed over power to neutral businessman Gyude Bryant in October 2003. Peacekeepers were organized from ECOWAS countries. As agreed, Interim President Bryant's administration paved the way for Liberian general elections in 2005.

There was nothing more graceful than Nigeria and other ECOWAS countries helping a brother nation, Liberia, restore peace and governance during her darkest days of anarchy, killings, hunger and devastating rebellion, which took the lives of about a quarter of a million and displaced many from their homes into refugee camps arranged inside and outside Liberia.

To show appreciation, the Liberian Transitional Government delegation led by the Chairman Elect, Mr. Gyude Bryant, arrived in Nigeria, Abuja, Federal Capital Territory, at the State House in midSeptember 2003. They thanked ExPresident Obasanjo and the great people of Nigeria for their invaluable and tremendous contributions in terms of human and material resources, which ensured the return of peace to their country, Liberia.

Mr. Bryant, a businessman who ascended to Liberian Interim Presidency from October 14, 2003 until October 2005, revealed that Nigerian troops were doing an excellent job in his country and that he looked forward to a new beginning in the relationship between his country and Nigeria. He reassured that he would be going back to Liberia to "calm anger and unite a divided country."

In response, Nigerian ExPresident Olusegun Obasanjo revealed that Nigeria would continue to support the peace efforts in Liberia. He praised Mr. Bryant for his successful businessmanship and his deepest concern about the progress and development of his country, Liberia. He advised that Mr. Bryant would be able to attract international assistance for rebuilding his country. He called on the international community to assist Liberia not only in areas of disarmament and demobilization, but to revitalize the crumbling economy of Liberia.

The world forgot too soon how Charles Taylor, exPresident of Liberia, got to Nigeria in exile to secure Liberian peace and stop further bloodshed. The world should therefore be reminded that it was the agreement of understanding that Nigeria should provide asylum for exPresident of Liberia, Charles Taylor that brought peace, tranquility, stoppage of continuing bloodshed and the emergence of a caretaker/transition government into Liberia. The agreement was the handiwork of the United Nations, the African Union, ECOWAS, European Union, the United States of America, Nigeria and representatives of Liberian warring parties in full participation and consent to achieve peace.

Taylor's case must serve as a deterrence to any other African leader(s) who are troublemakers that send innocent citizens to their untimely deaths. The precarious violent situations in some African countries are becoming too long to settle and should no longer be treated with kid gloves.

It was gratifying to African leaders for their genuine and relentless efforts, which channeled the Republic of Liberia back to peace, polls and constitutional democratic governance in mid-October 2005 after fourteen years of civil war. The international observers praised the peaceful votes and remarked that it was free and fair. It was a great achievement for Africa, Africans and the Black Peoples of the world; it was a further confirmation that with Africanness, the wonderful Black People of the world can solve their problems successfully and peacefully.

Eventually, peaceful Liberia emerged as the first African country to elect a female as President, Ellen SirLeaf Johnson and she has performed excellently and remarkably with exemplariness.

RELATIONS WITH SAO TOME AND PRINCIPE:

In July 2003, while President Frandique de Menezes of Sao Tome and Principe was attending the Leon Sullivan Summit in Abuja, Federal Capital Territory of Nigeria, his government was toppled by a group of military officers led by Major Fernando Pereira. Nigerian ExPresident Obasanjo who was Chairman of African Union (AU) immediately rallied other Presidents of African Union member states to condemn the putsch. It was universally held that the rest of democratic Africa would no longer brook military takeover in the continent. He then opened initial consultations with the coup leaders and later dispatched a negotiation team to Sao Tome and Principe.

In addressing the coup leaders, the former Nigerian President bluntly reiterated that he was addressing them on behalf of Africa. He emphasized that as a soldier himself, he was aware of the paramount importance of the welfare of officers and men of the military, but that would not be sufficient justification to topple a democratically elected government. He added that soldiers were not trained to take over government. He described the situation as victory for the people, if not for their president or the military. He reemphasized that African leaders would no longer tolerate coups, and that countries where soldiers interrupted democratic governance would be attacked by the rest of Africa.

The coup leader, Major Fernando Pereira, gave his word of honour that there would be no more military intervention in his country. He emphasized that the coup was to draw attention to the problems of the military and that he took note of ExPresident Obasanjo's offer to contact him in case of any future problems. Major Pereira further added that in a country where development was hampered by corruption, social and economic decline, directionless rulers and misdirected state institutions, the army could not indefinitely stand still watching when the destiny of the people was being undermined.

Nigeria and other African nations brokered an agreement with the coup leaders for the reinstatement of the President of Sao Tome and Principe, and he was reinstated with a provision of general amnesty to all the coup members.

Reinstated President De Menezes praised the leadership roles of Nigerian exPresident Obasanjo, other African leaders and members of the international community who helped to end the coup nightmare. He promised to work together with the coup leaders to rehabilitate his country's image. He added that he would honour the agreement reached with the coup leaders to reorganize his cabinet and grant amnesty to the coupists.

It was extremely gratifying to exPresident Obasanjo, other African leaders and members of international community who helped to reach an acceptable settlement in Sao Tome and Principe without loss of lives and property throughout the period of one of the shortest military governments ever recorded.

RELATIONS WITH CAMEROON:

In the Republic of Cameroon, there are over four million Nigerians resident there. It is therefore imperative for Nigerian government to ensure and promote their safety as well as protect their interests so that they can live and work in their host country in an atmosphere of freedom and dignity. Nigeria and Cameroon have had longstanding dissonance over their border areas stretching from Lake Chad to the Atlantic Ocean, a land boundary of about 1,700 kilometres. The major problem areas include the Bakassi Peninsula and the maritime boundary. During the colonial era, Cameroon was part of Nigeria and both nations were inseparable twin brothers.

In the 1960s, there was over 25,000 kilometres of water, which dried up to about 2,000 kilometres. Nigerians kept moving into the dry land as there was no demarcation then to determine whether the drying land belonged to Nigeria or Cameroon. The bulk of the area being disputed was shared by the colonial masters among neighbouring countries of Nigeria, Cameroon, Niger, Chad, and to some extent, the Central African States without definitive demarcation or delineation. The area occupied by Nigeria had an administration, the police and military establishments.

As of 1993, the demarcation of the disputed land was completed, and it was delineated. The necessary documents were ready to be signed and ratified by Nigeria, Cameroon, Niger and Chad, but before the documents were signed and ratified, Cameroon took Nigeria to the World Court, the International Court of Justice (ICJ) at The Hague, Netherlands in 1998.

On October 10, 2002, the International Court of Justice (ICJ) gave its judgment, which ceded large portions of the South-South, especially the oil rich Bakassi Peninsula, and part of Northeastern Nigeria to Cameroon, which also lost a portion of its NorthEastern land to Nigeria. Nigeria immediately showed her displeasure at the judgment, and it appeared that its implementation would be difficult, not hitch free.

Also, it might trigger renewed hostilities between Nigeria and Cameroon. It might even result in war between the two neighbouring, brotherly countries. In the past, the border dispute had resulted in several skirmishes, which the judgment of the International Court of Justice was likely to fuel.

As a result of African brotherhood, which is very strong among all African countries, exPresident Obasanjo of Nigeria preferred to meet President Biya of Cameroon under the auspices of the former United Nations Secretary-General, Kofi Annan, to find a political solution to the crisis. The anticipated peaceful political solution was also the expectation of other African nations and the international community. Nigeria as the 'big brother' persisted to explore all avenues and opportunities for a diplomatic settlement of the imbroglio and logjam created by the ICJ judgment for two brotherly African nations.

Dramatically, the two countries agreed to resolve the border dispute amicably, peacefully and diplomatically. As a result, a Nigeria-Cameroon Mixed Commission was set up to demonstrate the political will to overcome all obstacles to peace arising from the maritime and land borders separating Nigeria and Cameroon. The Mixed Commission's assignment was to look into the border dispute and make recommendations for settlement, which would ensure lasting peace, tranquility and good neighbourliness.

The two countries, Nigeria and Cameroon, demonstrated wonderful commitment in their contributions of human, material and financial resources toward the success of the Mixed Commission. By their actions, the two countries manifested political maturity and goodwill to solve the problems of brotherly people of common origin separated by artificial borders by using peaceful and diplomatic means. Thus, the two countries set a right model of behaviour, which other African countries in particular, and the world in general could emulate during troubled times to ensure peace, tranquility, progress, good neighbourliness and prosperity for Africa, the world and humanity.

The Nigerian government agreed to hand over to Cameroon, the civil administration as well as withdrawing the police and military forces from the Lake Chad area as decided in accordance with the International Court of Justice judgment of October 10, 2002. The Mixed Commission set up by the two countries under the auspices of the United Nations former Secretary General Mr. Kofi Annan made tremendous progress.

In one of his happiest moments, exPresident Olusegun Obasanjo asserted that one of his greatest achievements in office was "not going to war with Cameroon." This wisest decision portrayed the Nigerian Presidency as a model of excellence worthy of emulation by other world leaders, especially the powerful ones who believe only in their military might and in the law of the jungle, the survival of the fittest.

The NigerianCameroonian border dispute was thrust upon the two countries by their respective colonial masters who mixed up things before they left after the independence of the two countries. If the dispute developed into war, the former colonial masters would take sides and sell weapons to both warring sides at exorbitant, prohibitive prices and make brazen profit at the expense of two brotherly countries. Fortunately, the two countries, Nigeria and Cameroon, approached the dispute with great sense of responsibility, reconciliation and diplomacy without concocting stories and lies reminiscent of Iraqi war as justification to go to war. There was no bullying, intransigence or unhealthy aggressiveness by either Nigeria or Cameroon in tackling the dispute.

A war would have derailed the two countries' focus on economic survival, growth and development pursuits. Many innocent lives would have been lost or dislodged into refugee camps, and a war would have shattered the lives and economy of both countries.

Both ExPresident Obasanjo and President Biya deserve commendations for taking the path of honour, diplomacy, dialogue, conciliation and peace instead of war to solve their border dispute. They avoided causing collateral damages, which could have left indelible scars in the lives of the people. With that noble example from ExPresident Obasanjo and President Biya, Africans should always hold one another's hands and move forward watching the back of one another with love, care and affection for one another in the spirit of Africanness and African brotherhood.

On Tuesday, June 8, 2004, President Obasanjo demonstrated great statesmanship by reiterating strongly and vehemently that Nigeria would not be led into a needless war with any of its neighbours even while trying to resettle about 26,000 persons displaced as a result of the International Court of Justice (ICJ) judgment of October 10, 2002, on Nigeria-Cameroon border dispute.

When Governor Ali Modu Sheriff of Borno State as Chairman presented the second situation report of the Presidential Committee on the ICJ judgment to Nigerian President Obasanjo, he stressed emphatically, "Nigeria's role in Africa means, we must assume a peaceful posture." He enlightened, "The peaceful resolution of the differences between Nigeria and Cameroon should send positive signals to the world and provide useful lessons worthy of emulation by other countries." Such wonderful line of thought for world peace and understanding, emanating from one of Africa's greatest leaders is not only commendable but also invaluable to all members of the United Nations.

Somebody else as leader who might be youthful, inexperienced and immature could have miscalculated the military strength and power of Nigeria; could have started a war with Cameroon; and could have thrown Africa into chaos, confusion and in jeopardy. Hence, Nigeria should be careful in electing only future leaders who are really mature, experienced and qualified to lead. Nigeria does not deserve further problems after over forty years of independence, the majority of which was under military dictatorship. It must be remembered that a future Nigerian leader must be the one that can be capable and acceptable to lead Africa and be greatly respected in the Commonwealth of Nations and the United Nations. According to ICJ judgment of October 10, 2002, Bakassi Peninsula was ceded to Cameroon in 2008.

RELATIONS WITH BENIN:

The Nigerian government had to close its border with Republic of Benin in August 2003 as a result of concerns about increased trans-border criminal activities of armed robbery, car snatching at gun point, killings, smuggling of contraband, smuggling of subsidized petroleum products out of the country, thus creating artificial scarcity, and human trafficking especially girls for prostitution in Europe. Prior to the closure of the border, Nigerian Government officials were said to have held meetings with their Beninoise counterparts over the imperative need for cross-border crime fighting, but the Republic of Benin officials did not follow up as urgently as required.

The Nigerian government discovered and confirmed that the Republic of Benin border area was being used as haven by cross-border hardened criminals, and that the border was porous and notorious for smuggling arms and ammunitions into Nigeria as well as being a popular route for trafficking of young Nigerian girls to Europe for prostitution. Also, it was discovered that Benin border was being used for the smuggling of subsidized petroleum products thereby causing fuel shortages in Nigeria.

The border was also being used to bring banned vehicles and other products into the country thus jeopardizing the protectionism established for the benefit of local manufacturing businesses. Banned products ranging from frozen chicken, bottled water, to envelopes as well as used cars of more than eight years old were finding their ways through Benin Republic border into Nigeria. The border was being used for economic sabotage activities against Nigeria.

As soon as Nigeria closed the border with Benin Republic, the crime rate fell incredibly as there was no case of car snatching reported in Lagos, Ogun, Oyo, and Kwara states respectively. That was proven indication that the criminals came from across the border. The economic reality of the border closure started to hurt trade activities in Benin Republic. As a result, the authorities in Republic of Benin then took the matter seriously and arrested some of the trans-border crime suspects.

About mid-September 2003, the Beninoise authorities were reported to have extradited the car robbery kingpin suspect, Ahmadu Tidjani and about thirty other notorious criminals and armed robbers believed to be members of his gang to Nigeria to face trial. In addition, over one hundred exotic cars and other vehicles believed to have been snatched at gunpoint at various places within Nigeria were recovered in Republic of Benin and brought back to Nigeria by the police with Ahmadu Tidjani and other trans-border crime suspects.

There was clamour for quick trial of the criminals as well as canvassing for a comprehensive probe to fish out their collaborators in the Army, Customs Department and the Nigerian police. Without conspiracy and help from border police, military and customs officers, it could not have been possible for the cross-border criminals to succeed in going in and out of Nigeria with the numbers of cars stolen and successfully taken across the border without being caught.

In order to eliminate, prevent or minimize trans-border criminal activities, a committee of security officers was set up from the Nigerian Police and Republic of Benin Gendarmes to review performance of joint endeavours between Nigeria and Benin Republic, as well as deliberate on operational strategies, logistics, new initiatives and recommend modalities to encounter any challenges that might be posed by trans-border criminals.

The responsiveness of Obasanjo Administration to solve the cross-border problems was appreciable, completely different from 'business as usual'. The government demonstrated zero tolerance for crimes and it received full support of all Nigerians. Above serious case was solved diplomatically and peacefully between two sister countries showing tremendous understanding and cooperation. This is a great pointer that through dialogue, most problems can be solved. It is the cheapest, least costly and safest way of conflict resolution rather than adopting belligerent methods to solve problems. African examples can be models for the world.

The responsiveness of President Kerekou of Benin Republic in arresting and extraditing the suspects was equally commendable because as soon as he realized the whole picture of what was happening from his country to Nigeria, he acted decisively in the best interest of the two countries, Republic of Nigeria and Republic of Benin.

President Kerekou of Benin Republic said, "I was not even aware of the existence of that man (Tidjani) until after the closure of the border. When I heard it myself, I told the Solicitor General to go and get him, dead or alive, and take him back into custody. I often say that I would prefer to abandon ECOWAS and unite with Nigeria because when somebody is big and strong, you have to respect him. ECOWAS without Nigeria is zero. I have said it." This exemplary model of solving African problems through cooperation and understanding should be emulated by the world at large.

As a follow up, it was reported that Beninoise President Matthew Kerekou sacked about thirteen security chiefs over the trans-border robbery kingpin Alhaji Hammani Tidjani matter. Those sacked included top military officers in the country's presidency and the Ministry of Defence.

It was reported that investigation showed that Alhaji Hammani Tidjani, the kingpin, gave a Peugeot 406 to a top security official in Benin Republic while he gave large sums of money to others and promised them more when the problem was over. All those known to be connected with the case who received gratifications from the kingpin were sacked by the Beninoise President.

It was also reported that Alhaji Hammani Tidjani had very close relationship with all cadres of Beninoise police, other security agents, government officials and the high and mighty in Republic of Benin. He must have had a lot of connections and influences with some Nigerian border security agencies to be able to successfully commit all the trans-border crimes for which he was charged to court.

In the same wise, the Nigerian police authorities should conduct serious investigation over all officers of the Nigerian security agencies at the NigeriaBenin border who must have collaborated with the activities of the trans-border criminals. It is recalled that on Easter Sunday, April 19, 2003, five persons in the entourage of Dr. (Mrs.) Iyabo Obasanjo-Bello, the daughter of Nigerian exPresident Obasanjo, were murdered by unknown gunmen around Ifo, Ogun State on the Lagos-Ota-Abeokuta road most likely by trans-border criminals.

Definitely, the criminals overstepped their bounds when they attacked Nigerian dignitaries and elites. When these criminals were attacking and robbing poor people at gunpoint, snatching cars and killing non-elites, the authorities and the Nigerian police looked the other way and pretended nothing serious was happening until the President's daughter became a victim.

The pertinent questions for the police, the customs, the military and others charged with NigeriaBenin border security are: Why did they not fight trans-border criminals seriously when they were killing, smuggling, snatching cars at gunpoint and committing violent crimes against ordinary people until the murder of five people in the entourage of the President's daughter who was lucky to escape to safety? Did no Nigerian connive with those trans-border criminals?

The Beninoise authorities sacked military officers, police and high government functionaries who collaborated and received gratifications to protect the trans-border kingpins. What punishment did Nigerians who conspired with the kingpins receive like their Beninoise counterparts? Nigerians need to know the names of those who aided and abetted such heinous crimes and the punishment they received as deterrence to others. It is never too late to teach them lessons.

RELATIONS WITH SUDAN (DARFUR):

The Darfur crisis in Sudan has posed serious problems to Africans in particular and the entire international community in general. The crisis there, which has killed and displaced hundreds of thousands of innocent people, has been a great concern to Nigeria, especially when President Obasanjo was the Chairman of the African Union. African leadership unanimously requested from the world body that any problem in Africa be allowed to be resolved in African way by Africans. As occasion or situation may warrant, assistance may be sought from outside Africa for necessary tools to succeed. It appears that the request is being respected by the world to let Africans settle and solve their problems with Africanness, the African way.

The US has continued to regard the situation in Darfur as genocidal, but African Union (AU) has maintained that there is need for more investigation and proof to establish the truth. So far, Africa maintains that the Sudanese government intention is to quell a rebellion for which it armed the Jan Jaweed, the Arab militiamen.

Sudan was accused of mobilizing and arming the Jan Jaweed to attack Darfur villagers in retaliation for the rebellion that the two nonArab Darfur rebel movements launched against the government since February 2003. All warring parties in Sudan must give peace a chance to end the sufferings and killings of innocent people. The world is tired of atrocities in any part of the world, especially in Africa. It must end sooner than later at all cost.

Reporting on Darfur in September 2004, the United Nations former Secretary-General, Kofi Annan, said that Sudan government in Khartoum had not made desirable progress to restore security, implement ceasefire, stop attacks on civilians, disarm the Jan Jaweed, arrest and prosecute those who were perpetrating atrocities.

The African Union has been working tirelessly to give Sudan crisis an African face that requires African solution. A special African Union (AU) summit on Darfur was held on October 1517, 2004 in Libya attended by Nigerian ExPresident Obasanjo, Egyptian President Hosni Mubarak and leaders of Libya, Sudan and Chad. Remarkably, African leaders organized the deployment of African troops to help end the twenty-one-year old civil war in Southern Sudan as well as settle the Darfur crisis.

It is remarkable that during the regime of ExPresident Obasanjo, Nigeria made wonderful sacrifices in men, material and finance to solve African problems by Africans. Additional Nigerian soldiers were said to be added to the number serving in Darfur (Sudan) at the beginning of July 2005. Some Nigerian soldiers died during their peacekeeping operations and some died in accidents. Darfur atrocities subsided as soon as Sudanese President Bashir faced indictment proceedings for genocide at the International Criminal Court in 2008.

EVENTS AT THE UNITED NATIONS:

Having tremendously improved Nigerian image in the world with particular reference to the country's leadership role in Africa, ExPresident Olusegun Obasanjo addressed the United Nations General Assembly on Thursday, September 23, 2004, and declared that Nigeria was qualified to be a permanent member of the United Nations Security Council.

In his address to the UN General Assembly, he reiterated that Nigeria, and indeed the African continent, held the strong view that the UN Security Council should be expanded both in the permanent and nonpermanent categories for it to be fully representative of the world community, become effective and acceptable. He asked that the regions of the world that were not yet represented in the permanent category should be considered for membership.

He amplified that African issues constantly occupied substantial part of the time of the Security Council, and as such, Africa should be accorded priority consideration for permanent membership portraying Nigeria as well qualified candidate for the position. He emphasized the expectations of the African continent for institutional reforms and expansion of the United Nations.

He intimated the United Nations about the Darfur peace talks in Abuja scheduled for October 21, 2004, which deliberated on socio-economic and political issues. He commended the United Nations for its determined engagement in crisis resolution and peacekeeping with particular reference to Africa. He impressed upon the Untied Nations on the need to pay more attention on socio-economic challenges, which inevitably faced countries emerging from conflicts, stressing that they got into such crisis situation initially as a result of socio-economic problems.

He expressed Africa's unflinching support to the United Nations for the commencement of negotiations for an international legal instrument that would enable states to identify and trace illegal small arms and light weapons globally. He assured that such legally binding instrument would bring peace, stability and security to African continent. He condemned unequivocally, the roles of mercenaries and their sponsors in Africa mentioning that the attempted invasion of Equatorial Guinea by mercenaries was unacceptable. He added that such acts of introducing mercenaries into the continent would be hampering every imaginable rational effort to promote peace, stability, security and democracy in the continent.

On behalf of African Union (AU), he appealed to Africa's partners to uphold and demonstrate the shared common global interests, interdependence and common humanity by assisting with adequate resources to enable the continent pull its populace out of poverty and misery. He emphasized that Africa required genuine partnership anchored on mutual benefits to attain sustainable development especially in areas of external debts, which had created serious negative economic impact on the lives and development of the populace of Africa.

He advocated that Africa's external debt crisis if resolved comprehensively and innovatively would brighten the prospects of development in the continent. This prayer of ExPresident Obasanjo spread and caught the heart of all the rich nations in the world thus resulting in unprecedented debt cancellation for most African countries including Nigeria by the creditor nations in June/July 2005.

The Nigerian ExPresident hinted that the continent of Africa remained committed to fight HIV/AIDS and that Nigeria, Chad, Sudan, Cameroon, Niger Republic, Burkina Faso and Cote d' Ivoire embarked on an immunization programme for polio that kicked off in Kano State, Nigeria on October 2, 2004. He informed the UN General Assembly about the hear-trending cheerful news that Somalia had constituted its national assembly, but unfortunately, over one hundred and fifty persons were massacred in the refugee camp in Burundi, regretting that the Great Lakes Region remained a flash point of acts of violence as exemplified by the killings there.

Remarkably, the talk all over the world was how to rid Africa of poverty, debt, deadly diseases and underdevelopment. The G8 meeting in the United Kingdom in July 2005 made the increase of African aid a priority as well as debt cancellation for African countries.

In similar mode and mood of empathy, the G8 meeting held in Japan in early July 2008 made food aid to Africa and other developing, poor countries a priority as a result of high rise of prices and inflation that enveloped the world because of astronomical rise of price of oil which almost abrogated the purchasing power of the masses in the world. In July 2008, oil cost was $147.00 per barrel while in December 2008, the price fell to below $40.00 per barrel causing budget deficit problems for oil producing countries including Nigeria.

RELATIONS WITH HAITI:

Former Foreign Affairs Minister, Bolaji Akinyemi in an interview with the Daily Independent News of March 2004, described Haiti as the "first and only successful revolution by Africa against slavery, against slave owners, against oppression and against humiliation – the first and only representation of blacks." He added that African states should have ensured that the former Haitian leader, JeanBertrand Aristide, was helped substantially to quench the rebellion that sent him into exile in February 2004.

Professor Bolaji Akinyemi stressed that the failure of African governments to help President Aristide quell the insurgency in Haiti was not only a disappointment to the Haitian people in particular but the entire world of blacks. He said that the failure recorded in Haiti represented a setback in the struggle of the black people, which Haiti typified in the Caribbean subregion. He emphasized that it was the responsibility of African nations to make sure that Haiti was not in a mess.

Professor Bolaji Akinyemi, an expert in international relations, reiterated that Nigeria and South Africa should have provided President Aristide with financial and military resources to confront and defeat the rebellion that drove him out of his country. He argued that the insurgency was orchestrated by a band of thugs who had access to illegal drug money and weaponry.

He dismissed the reasons of election rigging and dictatorship advanced by the Western World for the removal of Aristide from power as unfounded. He queried whether the American election of 2000 was not rigged. The problem of political instability, poverty and hunger still lingers on in Haiti, and the country needs the collective assistance of their black brothers and sisters in African countries as suggested by Prince Bolaji Akinyemi.

RELATIONS WITH SIERRA-LEONE:

Nigerian soldiers' participation in the peacekeeping mission in Sierra-Leone under the United Nations Mission was remarkable, and there was praise for them all over the world. Their mission in Sierra-Leone involved disarmament, demobilization, and rehabilitation of excombatants in the Sierra-Leonean civil war and provision of physical security for Freetown, Sierra-Leone's national capital.

Over seven hundred officers and soldiers of the Third Battalion who left the country in October 2003 for Sierra-Leone returned to Nigeria in November 2004 to receive a warm welcome. Major-General Abdulhafeez Adewuyi, the General Officer Commanding (GOC), Eighty-Second Division of Nigerian Army, Enugu who welcomed them to their barracks in Takum, Taraba State, congratulated them on their wonderful accomplishments during the Sierra-Leone mission, which according to GOC Adewuyi, made Nigerians and Nigeria proud of them. He remarked that various reports received from leading United Nations officials, force commanders and diplomats in Sierra-Leone were full of compliments for the quality of soldiering and discipline demonstrated by Nigerian soldiers during the Sierra-Leonean mission.

He added that news reports emanating from local and international sources continued to shower praises on Nigerian troops for successfully winning the hearts and minds of Sierra-Leoneans who were appreciative of their unique contributions to community relations projects which they executed in Sierra-Leone, their West African brotherly country.

He told them to fully apply the lessons learnt and experience gained during their peacekeeping mission in SerraLeone to security duties at home for which the Nigerian army was being called upon to contribute. Responding on behalf of the Third Battalion, their Commanding Officer, Lieutenant Colonel Stephen Ovadje summarized that though their mission was full of tension, it was successfully conducted without any casualty or any recorded incident of misbehaviour.

RELATIONS WITH CONGO AND RWANDA:

The relationship between Congo and Rwanda headed by Presidents Joseph Kabila and Paul Kagame respectively became strained as a result of Hutu extremists from Rwanda who were alleged to have committed genocide on Rwandan Tutsis and moderate Hutus but fled to occupy the jungles of Eastern Congo after killing over 800,000 Rwandans in 1994.

Rwandan President Paul Kagame complained that the Hutu rebels from Rwanda occupying the jungles of Eastern Congo continued to threaten his country by allegedly claiming that they would advance on Kigali, the Rwandan capital. He said that under threat to his country, he would not rule out the possibility of sending troops to Eastern Congo to flush out the Hutu rebels. President Kagame added that if the Rwandan army entered the Eastern Congo, their mission would be to destroy the Hutu rebels and not to occupy the Eastern half of Congo as he did in 1996 and 1998.

On his return from the Francophonie Summit in Quagadougou, Burkina Faso, the Rwandan President mentioned that the threat against his country still remained, and so, they reserved the right to retain the flexibility to defend themselves. He added that Rwanda could and would strike Rwandan rebels in Congo if little were done to disarm them as envisaged by the United Nations Security Council. He confirmed that he met President Kabila of Congo at the Burkina Faso summit.

On the other hand, Congo's Foreign Minister, Ramazani Baya, described Rwanda's threats as provocation, which might force Congo to respond. He asserted that his country, Congo, did not deserve Rwanda's provocation, which if pushed too far might force Congo to react to protect its citizens and its borders.

As a result of the dispute between Congo and Rwanda, exPresident Olusegun Obasanjo of Nigeria and Ex-Chairman of African Union (AU), waded in to douse the tension and resolve the crisis diplomatically in an African way. The two African countries and neighbours were reminded that war often resulted in destruction and killing of innocent people and the disruption of the peace of mind of their citizens. They must listen to mediation like Nigeria and Cameroon or face UN, EU and AU sanctions.

War causes retrogression of national development, and as such, leaders that cannot bring about peace and development lastingly to their citizens are just not fit to lead in the twenty-first century and beyond. Any sensible leader will not encourage war under any guise before exhaustive diplomacy. Africans do not need justification for war among African countries. African problems must be settled the African way by leaders using diplomacy, consultation, conciliation, persuasion or sanctions as the last resort.

The African custom and tradition of the big brother nation coming in to settle disputes between colleague brotherly African nations worked wonders in the past, and there is no doubt that the dispute between Congo and Rwanda (two brotherly neighbours) will be resolved amicably and permanently through African leaders intervention using best peaceful conflict resolution strategies. As a result of escalation of war, killings and refugee problems in late 2008, the United Nations appointed ExPresident Obasanjo to go to the region to broker peace.

RELATIONS WITH TOGO:

Togo, a West African coastal country situated between Ghana and Republic of Benin on the Gulf of Guinea, gained independence from France in 1960. Togo is a member of the African Union (AU) and Economic Commisson of West African States (ECOWAS).

Veteran President Gnassingbe Eyadema ruled the country unchallenged for three decades. At 69, he died while being flown to France for emergency medical attention. Less than twenty-four hours later after the announcement of his death, the country's military leadership unconstitutionally swore in his son, Faure Gnassingbe, retroactively amended the constitution to make the action technically legal and sealed the border with Benin Republic. That allegedly prevented the Parliamentary Speaker, Fambare Natchaba Quattara who should have been named the Interim President, from entering Togo.

After his swearing in ceremony as President of Togo, Faure Gnassingbe was told frankly to go and return Togo to constitutionality by holding election for the post of president. Thereafter, the ECOWAS, AU and EU put pressure on Togo to return to constitutionality or face appropriate sanctions and severance of ties with Africa, the European Union, the Americans and the United Nations. The imposition of sanctions created problems in Togo and made the leadership reconsider their actions.

ExPresident Obasanjo said that the African Union would not accept any "unconstitutional transfer of power" in Togo. He called for respect for the nation's constitution in the provision of interim presidency for Togo that would lead to the democratic election of a President of Togo in accordance with her constitution.

In the same vein, the South African ExPresident, Tabo Mbeki, expressed condolences for the death of President Eyadema and urged the country to return to constitutional provisions governing succession of the Head of State. On the other hand, the African Union Commission President, Alpha Oumar Konare, described the Togo situation as a seizure of power by the military. He said, "It is a military coup d'etat." The stand taken by African Union was supported by the world including the French who gave Togo their independence in 1960.

As a result of continued pressure diplomatically and economically on Togo leadership by West African leaders in particular and African leaders, the European Union, the United States and the United Nations in general, Faure Gnassingbe, the imposed leader, agreed to step down and he opted for election in the interest of the nation.

He offered to be a contestant for the presidency, so, he lifted the twoweek old ban on political activity and allowed demonstrations and events, if plans were first submitted to the government and approved. An election was scheduled for April 2005, and the Deputy Speaker, Bonfor Abbass, was named Interim President until an elected president took office. Faure Gnassingbe won the presidential election controversially. He then formed a unity government to douse national tension that erupted.

OTHER RELATIONS:

During the Kenyan and Zimbabwean presidential elections, which resulted into mass killings and arson because of allegations of brazen riggings, the Nigerian President, Umaru Musa Yar'Adua played remarkable mediation role by talking to the stakeholders concerned to maintian peace and form a unity government. The South African ExPresident, Thabo Mbeki played a leading role to establish peace in Kenya and Zimbabwe.

The important lesson taught and learnt in this case is that African Union has succeeded in demonstrating that the continent will no longer tolerate unconstitutional takeover of governments in any of its fifty-three countries. Also, an African solution to the problem avoids violence, killings, arson and civil war. It helps Africans generally to seek to enforce their constitutional rights and leaders to stay within the constitutional provisions of their nations. It warns that Africa will no longer tolerate coups d'etat and dictatorship in any part of the continent.

At the twentieth anniversary lecture of the Guardian Newspaper in Lagos on December 4, 2003, the South African ExPresident, Tabo Mbeki, an illustrious African leader, was reported to have said, "It is the expectation of peoples of Africa that Nigeria and Nigerians will do all they have to do to ensure that we change history of our continent and disprove the view expressed by Dr. Henry Kissinger, former American Secretary of State, that we are a festering disaster of our age."

South African President Mbeki quoting Dr. Kissinger said, "Henry Kissinger has described our continent as a tragedy because of what we and others have done to the peoples of the continent." He added, "It is a tragedy because we have had a history of military coups and dictatorships. It is a tragedy because we have waged the most merciless wars against one another, including the commission of genocide, as though African lives were worth nothing."

He also explained, "Africa's tragedy will turn into the festering disaster of our age because I see a continent that is steadily getting more and more impoverished." He concluded, "Because we have failed ourselves in the past, we will never succeed in the future unless those who benefit from our crippled positions extend a helping hand to us, to enable us to walk."

While sharing the conclusion of the South African President, it is true that African leaders and elites had failed Africans in the past, but recent leadership, emerging in Africa raises hope of a great continent emerging strong, formidable and inspirational. The bright light, which started shining in Africa under the leaderships of leaders like ExPresident Obasanjo of Nigeria, ExPresident Tabo Mbeki of South Africa, and other leaders of African Union, is making a big difference in the continent. The African continent of the dreams of former Presidents

Kwame Nkruma of Ghana, Dr. Nnamdi Azikiwe of Nigeria, Julius Nyerere of Tanzania, Emperor Haile Selassie of Ethiopia, Nelson Mandela of South Africa and many others are coming through.

The reconstitution of the African Union, its focus, goals and objectives, and its pursuits are beginning to make a difference. The insistence of African leaders to pursue 'Africanness' is yielding recognition and acceptance worldwide and it is making a big difference and moving Africa forward in the right direction despite overwhelming impediments created by outsiders. We are succeeding.

Africa is blessed with enormous resources. The people are very strong and very resourceful. What Africa needs is a change from 'business as usual' by the elites. Such behaviour modification by the elites will stop brain drain, stop stashing of African government monies into private accounts in foreign banks in Europe and America, stop fraud, corruption, economic and financial crimes and sociopolitical instability. The elites and leadership of African governments should start to do their best in the best interest of the continent and all black people of the world. Africa should stop accepting high interest rate loans as well as economic advice from financial agencies that do not have the best interest of the continent at heart. Detrimental high interest foreign loans promote neocolonization which can lead the continent into perpetual economic enslavement.

The outsiders who benefited from the African continent's crippled positions would not extend a helping hand to enable Africans to walk except in situations where they will make more profits and reap more than commensurate dividends and benefits, much more than the helping hand they lend. Their hidden understanding is that the ripping off of African economy is the assurance of their (foreign agencies) own prosperity.

Africans have to shake off the shackles put on their feet by the colonial and neocolonial masters to rise, stand up and walk by themselves. Africans can do it, and they will do it successfully judging by the present enlightenment, the awareness, and collective realization of what is wrong, and how the continent and her people have been wronged.

The ability, willingness and determination of the leadership will ensure Africa's success. The cooperation coupled with great sense of brotherhood among African leaders leaves nobody in doubt that a new dawn has risen in Africa through the AU, NEPAD, ECOWAS and other African groups. African leaders should stop brain drain, fraud, corruption, wars, money laundering and stashing of government money into private bank accounts in Europe and America. Promote full employment and investment.

The extension of a helping hand desired and fervently prayed for by South African ExPresident Mbeki occurred miraculously in June and July 2005 when the continent's creditor nations unprecedentedly wrote off majority of the continent's foreign debts. Beyond expectations, they also determined unanimously to increase foreign aid to ensure African development at the G8 meeting in Scotland, United Kingdom in early July 2005. They demanded transparency, corruptionfree Africa, democratic governance, prudent resources management, political stability and socio-economic and political reforms in the best interest of African peoples. The creditor nations frowned at part of aid money meant for project development ever corruptly finding itself in leaders private pockets as used to be the case.

In Nigeria, the EFCC headed by Chairpersons Farida Waziri and the ICPC by Justice Emmanuel Ayoola are doing a wonderful job to eradicate fraud and corruption from Nigerian society, especially among elites from both public and private sectors of Nigerian economy. ExPresident Olusegun Obasanjo, Ex-Chairman of the African Union, said, "While we cultivate new friends and cherish old ones who have supported us, we must never forget that our objective is to be master of our fate, captain of our destiny and architect of our fortune."

The African Union should earnestly start to consider the establishment of an African Common Market (ACM), African Court of Justice (ACJ) and an African Security Council (ASC) so that Africans can solve their problems as members of the same large African family. The ACM, ACJ and ASC will exist without undue influence, dictation, divide and rule constraints from those who created most African problems through enslavement, colonization and neocolonization, and they that ridicule, humiliate, marginalize and economically neocolonize Africans but pretend to be friends and benefactors of Africans.

After the establishment of the ACM, ACJ and ASC, African countries will still remain members of the International Court of Justice (ICJ) and the United Nations (UN), and hold their positions of influence in these other international bodies, but solutions to African problems need domestication and treatment Africanly using African values, traditions, strength and power.

Africa appreciates the debt relief granted by the creditor nations in June and July 2005 as well as the elaborate promise for increase in aid to Africa by the G8 nations at their summit in Scotland, UK in July 2005. The undaunted efforts and commitment of the former British Prime Minister, Tony Blair, which ensured that Africa received debt relief, and increase in aid for African development are fully appreciated.

It is high time African leaders embarked on socio-economic and political reforms that say, "never ever again" to corruption, fraud, economic and financial crimes, money laundering, political oppression, coups d'etat, dictatorship, stashing of African government money in European and American private bank accounts, human trafficking, brain drain, illegal drugs and all acts that debar African development.

African leadership focus should be on prudent management of resources, poverty alleviation, increasing standard of living and life expectancy, safety, health and welfare, agriculture and mass food production. There should be more attention on affordable housing, provision of essential infrastructures and facilities, clean water and regular electricity supply, economic prosperity, sociopolitical stability, democracy, constitutionality, education and national development.

African governments should be united, watch each other's back, be partners in progress and become their brothers' keepers. Always remember that the greatest leader is the one that makes his people achieve the greatest things. In actuality, the greatest leader is not the one that achieves the greatest things for himself but for the people.

Americans prefer positive reinforcement to encourage behaviour modification, and it has worked better and achieved greater results than applying negative, punitive and aggressive actions. Such persuasive strategy that has worked wonders in America should have been applied in the Middle East to save the lives of innocent people that were lost during the Iraqi war.

The objective of establishing democracy in the Middle East is achievable by using peaceful means. Those who believe that if they die fighting for their faith would go to heaven, bliss or paradise do not have to be killed to effect changes to democracy. They need counseling, love and care using diplomacy, persuasion, conciliation, consultation and effective conflict resolution strategies. They need humane treatment not force of arms and war. They need evangelization.

The war was a terrible mistake and those responsible directly and indirectly should be condemned by the United Nations, the American People and the Iraqis. African Leaders should ensure that the mistakes and atrocities committed in the Middle-East, Darfur, Liberia, Rwanda, Sierra-Leone, Congo etc. never happen again in Africa!

If God/Allah changed Biblical Paul, David, Solomon and others and made them the greatest benefactors to humanity as well as giving Abraham a ram to offer as sacrifice instead of his son, the same only God/Allah, the Almighty could change Saddam Hussein if given time and opportunities to change instead of the US prematurely starting the regrettable war based on deliberately manipulated intelligence reports that resulted in the loss of thousands of innocent lives, and hundreds of thousands disabled and/or displaced.

If God/Allah took away the life of General Sani Abacha of Nigeria, acclaimed the notorious dictator, in his sleep, untimely and suddenly to save the lives of many dignitaries in Nigeria from 1993 to 1998, then given time and applying the right and transparent diplomacy, the Middle East can become the custodian of democracy beyond the world's comprehension without firing shots that killed thousands of innocent souls in Iraq.

If Libya convincingly abandoned her weapons programmes that the US termed offensive without firing a shot, the world can change for the better and be at peace if the US follows diplomacy and not 'power or might is always right' in solving international problems. If progress was being made in IsraeliPalestinian peace initiative as well as North Korea disarmament of nuclear weaponry in June 2008, then, there are no problems that transparent diplomacy cannot solve. With God/Allah everything is possible.

It is hoped that the lessons from Iraqi war will guide decisions to diplomatically solve the Iranian nuclear programme dispute. The United Nations (UN) experience should be utilized to the fullest this time without manipulated intelligence reports from UK and US. The Israeli war of Januray, 2009 which killed over one thousand Palestinians and less than twenty Israelis was a regretful defiance of world opinion. Perhaps it was waged to beat the advent of a new US Administration expected to take office on January 20, 2009 which might not favour such aggression supported by the preceeding George Bush Presidency. With Barack Obama Presidency, the world will witness peace again.

The alliance put together by the forty-first US President Bush (the daddy) to save Kuwait from Iraqi occupation army was solid and admirable to the whole world. The alliance put together by the son, Forty-third US President George Bush was like a kangaroo type of arrangement to deceive the world. African leaders should watch out for one another and be vigilant. Always be your brothers' and sisters' keepers. There is no other place we can call our own, but Africa as Africans.

The Superpower(s) should give Africans the resources to protect their people, lands and waters by themselves instead of planning to station foreign troops on African soil and/or water to protect them as a ploy of neocolonization. Africa should unanimously say, "NO! ENOUGH IS ENOUGH

GOD/ALLAH BLESS NIGERIA!

CHAPTER 13

THE NEED TO ELIMINATE DISCRIMINATION

Discrimination is the act of demonstrating biases, passing unfair judgment or unfair treatment of people just because of their age, sex, ethnicity, national/state of origin, religion, disability, lifestyle or colour of skin.

In civilized and developed communities in the world like the USA and UK, discrimination attracts severe penalties especially in employment, promotions, discipline, contract awards, other benefits and the sharing of opportunities, in respect of sex, colour, national origin, ethnicity, religion and disability.

In the USA, highpowered governmental commission, known as the Equal Employment Opportunities Commission (EEOC), oversees the enforcement of laws barring discrimination. The Commission (EEOC) assists victims of discrimination to pursue their cases in law courts and often provides attorneys to help them. Discrimination actions often attract stiff financial penalties, which cover reparation for actual and punitive damages. The Equal Employment Opportunities Act and the Civil Right Act Title VII of 1964 recognize equal opportunities for all and provide severe penalties for violations.

Dr. Jubril Olabode Aka (DMS, MBA Aviation, Ph.D.)

AGE DISCRIMINATION:

Citizens of sixty-two years of age and above are regarded as senior citizens. In many business establishments, they enjoy special discounts in their daily purchases and other financial transactions. At retirement age, senior citizens are highly regarded and treated with dignity and respect for having accumulated tremendous wealth of experience and having served their country working for decades. They are paid social security benefits to augment their pay cheques. Senior citizens are also regarded to be retrainable and reemployable, and in most cases, they are reabsorbed into employment on lighter duties to make them engage in physical and mental activities that prolong their lives. Retirees qualify for medicare/medicaid at the age of sixty-five.

In Nigeria, it looks as if it is a sin to reach the retirement age, judging from the neglect and the way retired persons are treated by government functionaries who do not regard that payment of their pensions is a priority and some of them die while waiting on line, expecting to be paid their several years of arrears of pension and other benefits. Retirement age is 55 involuntarily or thirty-five years of service whichever comes first. There is no provision for healthcare, medicaid or medicare.

Nigerian problems are not difficult to solve if leaders join hands together and identify those who are misleading for personal interest instead of leading for success and assisting the government to achieve its laudable objectives in record time. There are bumps and impediments, but they must be identified quickly and removed decisively. The Nigerian leadership should watch out to discourage and condemn acts of discrimination that do not provide equal opportunities for all Nigerian citizens.

On Saturday, March 20, 2004, *The Guardian News* carried the news that six envoy nominations forwarded by ExPresident Olusegun Obasanjo to the Senate for approval were allegedly recommended for disapproval by the Senate Standing Committee on Foreign Affairs because they were nearing the age of retirement. It was alleged that the six nominees had earlier been turned down for the same reason.

The six nominees were said to have cleared six other important criteria thus? (1) meeting minimum standards; (2) candidate's character:

(3) federal character principle; (4) equity; (5) special knowledge/skills; and (6) endorsement by home state senators.

If the six nominees successfully crossed above six hurdles, how does age close to retirement age become the main deciding factor for their disqualification when there is no constitutional provision that bars them from achieving their lifelong career of self-actualization as their country's ambassadors.

The six envoy nominees according to the report were: (1) Mr. O. I. Udoh (Akwa Ibom); (2) Ambassador G.B. Preware (Bayelsa); (3) Mr. A.N.C. Nwazumudah (Delta); (4) Mr. E.O. Olusanmukun (Ekiti); (5) Ambassador C.N. Umelo (Imo); and (6) Ambassador S.A. Adekanye (Osun).

In order to clear this hurdle, the six envoy nominees chose to voluntarily retire from public service just to additionally qualify as noncareer appointees whenever their names were represented by the president. Yet, some members of the Senate Standing Committee on Foreign Affairs were still unyielding to approve the nominations according to reports. At that point, it became glaring to many Nigerians that some members of the Senate Standing Committee on Foreign Affairs who were against the nominations might be nursing ulterior motives which were most likely to create a confrontation with the Presidency and heat the polity unnecessarily without any justification.

The Ex-Chairman of the Senate Standing Committee on Foreign Affairs, Senator, Professor and former Ambassador to the USA who commanded enormous wealth of experience and wise counsel, was said to have argued, "Most of the nominees were already approaching the age of retirement; as career diplomats, they ought to be allowed to give way to younger ones." He pointed out that their renomination amounted to frustrating the hopes of youths in the country. The reason adduced amounted to age discrimination and sent the wrong message, which made people feel that ageing was a disease instead of being an invaluable virtue and asset as realized in advanced, developed and civilized communities in the world.

The Ex-Chairman of the Senate Standing Committee on Foreign Affairs might have nursed honest and good intentions, but his alleged remark had a connotation of age discrimination, which would have incurred lawsuits and stiff financial penalties in civilized, developed and

Industrialized countries where there were discrimination laws. Ironically, it was argued by many Nigerians that the committee chairman was himself appointed as Ambassador to the USA at the age of sixty years in 1999 by the same ExPresident Olusegun Obasanjo who nominated and renominated the six names for Senate confirmation. Sixty years old is above the retirement age in Nigeria.

The questions agitating the minds of many enlightened and educated Nigerians in the Diaspora included:

(1) If Professor, Senator and former Ambassador to the USA, Jubril Aminu, became Ambassador at above the age of retirement, why should the six ambassador nominees who were said to be nearing the retirement age of 55 be recommended for disapproval by his Senate Committee because of their age? What was the justification for differential treatment?

(2) Nigerians quoted many precedents whereby some Nigerians, both career diplomats and political appointees, had been appointed and reappointed ambassadors well over the age of sixty years. They included Chief M.T. Mbu (Germany, 1994-95)); Chief Arthur Mbanefo (New York, Permanent Mission, 1999); Ambassador George Dove Edwin (London, 1988); Ambassador Abubakar Udu (Cairo, 1999); and Ambassador Sanusi (Deputy High Commissioner, London, 1999). If any or all of the precedents are correct, then the disapproval recommended becomes questionable and discriminatory.

(3) Why is what is good for the goose not good for the gander? Could the recommendation for disapproval of the six names be motivated as a result of state or regional discrimination?

(4) What if any or all of the six ambassador nominees were Northerners like the Chairman of the Senate Standing Committee on Foreign Affairs, would the Committee recommendations for disapproval be different?

(5) Were there any ulterior motives behind the first and second recommendations to disqualify the six ambassador nominees after they successfully crossed six other rigorous hurdles that qualified them to be Ambassadors of Nigeria? Even when they adjusted their status to qualify as appointees, they were still allegedly turned down. Why?

(6) Where was the display of consistency, equity, justice and fair play by the Senate Standing Committee on Foreign Affairs to recommend the disapproval of the six ambassador nominees judging from the precedents mentioned in (2) above?

(7) How can the rule of Nigerian Public Service on compulsory retirement age be allowed to undermine the supremacy of the 1999 Nigerian Constitution in respect of Presidential prerogative to appoint ambassadors in accordance with Article 171, Chapter VI, Subsection D on Presidential Appointments? Where is the understanding that if any rule conflicts with constitutional provision, the rule becomes negated since the constitution is supreme? In this case, the nominees had not reached the retirement age, and they had not completed the thirty-five years of statutory service.

(8) What else did the rejected envoy nominees need to do for easy confirmation? Did they not cooperate or not have reliable godfathers?

The Chairman of the Senate Standing Committee on Foreign Affairs, who was Nigerian Ambassador to the USA and lived in the USA for many years, fully understood the implications of age discrimination in developed and civilized societies. His wealth of international experience should have been shared with Nigerian people for their benefit generally and the Senate in particular during decision-making. If Senate Committee recommendations are questionable, then where is Nigerian salvation? On basis of available facts, the Senate Committee's recommendation for disapproval was most likely based on sentiment and not the rule of law.

It is not out of place for the youth to take their turn patiently while learning, gaining experience and maturing to take over in future without being too much in a hurry. There is a Yoruba proverb, which says, "Bi omode ba fe se bi agba, ojo ori re ko ni je." It means, "If a young person wants to act like an elder, his or her age, youthfulness and inexperience will act as an impediment."

Nigerians must be reminded that it was the hurry and impatience of the Eastern Nigerian (Igbo) youthful military officers to take over democratically elected government of Sir Abubakar Tafawa Belewa on January 15, 1966, that became the genesis of all the problems that Nigeria faced for more than forty years up-to-date. It was the Ifeajuna/Nzeogwu military coup d'etat of January 15, 1966, staged by young officers of Eastern Nigerian extraction, who brutally, selectively and discriminatorily killed military and civilian leaders of Northern and Western Nigeria that generated retaliations, mistrust, killings, divisionism, secessionist tendencies, death, horror, suffering and displacement of about two million innocent people.

It led to dictatorships, which bred untold hardships of violence, killings, fraud, corruption, money laundering, etc. for almost four decades from which Nigeria has not fully recovered. Some of these youths parading themselves as leaders with forged identities, fake certificates/diplomas and illegal enrichment who did not complete their academic studies should be advised to go back to school before aspiring to be President, Vice President, Governor, Senator, Member of the House of Representatives etc.

Democracy allows freedom of competition among young and old, men and women and let the best person win after due consideration. The challenging question repeated again is, "Would the recommendation to reject the six envoy nominees be different if some or all of them were from Northern Nigeria?" In the civilized world, there are cases of people recalled from retirement and appointed to head foreign missions. Nigerians in the Diaspora need answers to the questions above to clear the issue for all Nigerians and avoid a repetition of discriminatory practices by legislative members who are supposed to protect existing laws, review them for necessary amendments and make new ones.

On the other hand, if those who took decision to reject the six envoy nominees because of being close to retirement age were the ones nominated by the President under similar situations, how would they feel if so rejected on flimsy excuses? Does any provision of the 1999 Constitution expressly or impliedly disqualify them?

To minimize tension, bad blood, disharmony, bad belle, and the heating of the polity, Nigerians need better reasons for one arm of the government to reject what the other arm of the government recommends. Nigerians need more understanding, unity, oneness, empathy, cooperation and exemplariness which must start from the leadership of the three arms of government – the Presidency, the

Legislature and the Judiciary, and roll down graciously to the bottom for the citizenry to emulate.

The fact that the elder politicians disappointed Nigerians does not mean that the youth can or will do better and must be placed in positions without really maturing. Some youths in leadership positions have also more seriously disappointed Nigerians. They have done the worst in fraud and corruption. Youthfulness makes people prone to a lot of temptations, which Nigeria cannot afford anymore. What about the way some of the youths in leadership steal government money, talk and act detrimentally contrary to the nation's interest? Nigeria needs the right leaders; Nigeria needs elders; and Nigeria needs the youths.

Nigerians must take their turns and prove themselves to be really qualified for leadership whether young or old, but conclusively, the elders are better focused than the youths. The ExGovernors and their Finance Commissioners who committed money laundering and stashed away Nigerian money worth millions and billions of naira into their private foreign bank accounts are young and not the older Nigerians.

Early in the first term of ExPresident Olusegun Obasanjo, some youths including some youthful state governors, met and decided that anybody above fifty years old should not be President of Nigeria. In effect, they met gunning for the positions of Nigerian President and Vice President when it was glaring that some of them had not actually performed creditably as governors. They committed the most shameful corruption scandals in the annals of Nigeria. Nigerians must no longer be fooled anymore.

In *This Day News* of March 21, 2004, Alhaji Shehu Shagari, former President of the Federal Republic of Nigeria during the Second Republic (1979-1983), referred to what the young military officers did in 1966 as: "It first started on Saturday, January 15, 1966, when Major Chukwuma Kaduna Nzeogwu, after he and his accomplices had murdered our civilian and military leaders, announced the forceful takeover of power, from the democratically elected government, for what later turned out to be spurious reasons. Similarly, subsequent coup leaders, Ironsi, Gowon, Joe Garba, Murtala Mohammed and Bukar Dimka, variously interrupted the status quo. Each, after having overthrown his own military superiors, started to proffer reasons and/or excuses for snatching political power from his victims. In almost each case, the gullible

Nigerian public accepted the reasons announced, and sometimes even cheered the newcomers only to turn around sooner than later to start complaining and ardently praying for another change of government. This was our Nigeria of turbulence and instability; a country blessed with great resources and potentialities, yet marred by what looks like a spell of ethnic rivalries and highly politicized and ambitious armed forces."

He added, "Since January 1966, most of the senior members of the Nigeria Armed Forces have been more concerned and more heavily engaged in the business of coupplanning and/or running governments than in the task of protecting the territorial integrity of the country. Even the civil war in which they fought so gallantly to keep Nigeria one was itself the direct result of the infighting between power seeking coup and countercoup leaders. The cost to Nigeria is incalculable, considering among others, the number of valuable lives lost and the talents and skills wasted in the process of incessant changes in the command structure within the military as well as among the civilians." He commended the decision of Murtula/Obasanjo regime to hand over power to civilians, which he described as wise, honourable and magnanimous.

The facts and wise saying above are what the exuberance of youthful military officers caused and cost Nigeria. Nigerians have learned their lessons in the hard way that it becomes difficult to totally trust anybody young or old, but definitely, the elders and older ones are better, more reliable and more focused than the youths who are prone to many distractions.

How can it be explained that those below fifty-five years, the retiring age in Nigeria who are elected into offices as leaders, become grossly involved in money laundering, illegal oil bunkering, frauds, corruption, stealing, stashing millions of government money in their foreign private bank accounts, and engaging in business and contracts that run counter to the best interests of their posts and responsibilities?

Older ones are not as sophisticated in committing economic and financial crimes as the young ones. In those days, the older politicians were stealing hundreds and thousands while these younger leaders steal millions and billions. The younger politicians have terribly disappointed Nigerians by committing serious economic and financial crimes against the nation. Being young does not make a person a better politician than the old ones.

How can it be explained that these young leaders who vehemently criticized their predecessors for wrongdoings, but when they got elected, they did worse than their predecessors whom they used to condemn? How can it be explained that a lot of the money provided to state and local government functionaries for development of their states and local governments became traceable to private pockets and young governors' foreign private bank accounts? These situations of fraud and corruption are worse and done more sophisticatedly in greater dimensions than what the old politicians did. When accused of glaring economic and financial wrongdoings, they turned round and claimed constitutional immunity, and talked of marginalization.

Nigerians can easily excuse the mistakes of the old man who has fewer years to live than tolerate the deliberate wrongdoings of the youths who have failed to learn from the old politicians' mistakes, but continue to plunge their country into economic and financial mess much more destructively, unprecedented in the annals of Nigeria. How are they better than those whom they have been criticizing?

The Presidency must start to record, compile, analyze and publicize data periodically on the number of Nigerians below fifty-five compared with those above fifty-five who commit economic and financial crimes, frauds, corruption, 419 advance fee frauds and other crimes against the nation. Such publication should reflect their state of origin and locality so that Nigerians can know the sources of Nigerian bad habits. If there are too many crooks, criminals and drug traffickers from any state or region, then Nigerians should be careful not to elect the President or Vice President from such family, state or region in future elections.

ETHNICITY DISCRIMINATION:

There is ethnicity discrimination among Nigerians referred to as tribalism. It happens in all spheres of Nigerian activities, especially at the workplace where it occurs during recruitment, promotion, training and development of employees, awarding of contracts and allocation and distribution of other federal government benefits. Nigerians have often felt more comfortable when they are working close to members of their ethnicities with whom they can speak their native dialects.

It has always happened that most heads of departments want to be surrounded by their ethnic nationalities that they trust, and as such, many Nigerian workers have been passed for promotion, recruitment, salary increases and admission into institutions of higher learning because of their ethnicity.

To solve some of the abuses of tribalism at government establishments, the government introduced the federal character system, which reflects an ethnic quota in government activities requiring equal distribution of benefits and equal share of the national cake among all ethnicities as much as possible.

The federal character practice is meant to ensure that all ethnicities are equally represented in government settings and parastatals. The intention is great, but the result is often flawed with reverse discrimination. Some people are recruited or promoted above more qualified candidates because they are filling their ethnic quota within the federal system. It has encouraged mediocrity, mistrust and disunity in federal workplace completely different from government intentions for adopting federal character system. Notwithstanding the flaws, federal character experiment allows equal distribution of development and equal share of opportunities among ethnic nationalities when transparently executed by the leadership.

The Zamfara State government was alleged to have introduced discriminatory fees in its school system whereby nonindigenes have to pay prohibitive fees. The policy drew the attention of federal authorities because nonindigenes started to withdraw their children from the state public schools. It was alleged that the state set up a committee to screen out nonindigenes from the candidates shortlisted for admission into post primary institutions in the state. Alhaji Aliyu Mohammed, the State Commissioner for Science and Technical Education, explained that the objective of the policy was to meet the educational needs of the indigenes of the state.

In his reaction to the complaints, the former Attorney General and Minister of Justice, Chief Charles Akinlolu Olujimi, said that discrimination against other Nigerians was unconstitutional and could be treasonable if proven to be true. It was said that segregation policy was clear violation of Sections 18, 41, and 42 of the 1999 Constitution. Section 18 provides that government is to ensure equal and adequate educational opportunities for all Nigerians. Section 41 provides that every citizen of Nigeria is entitled to move freely throughout the country and to reside in any part thereof. Section 42 states that all Nigerians are guaranteed the right to freedom from discrimination.

Chief Olujimi allegedly remarked that it was unconstitutional to bar citizens from attending public schools because of their places of origin. It might not mean that Zamfara State government was directly barring Nigerian students of other states of origin from Zamfara State public schools, but it was applying prohibitive discriminatory school fees for students from states other than Zamfara.

SEX DISCRIMINATION:

Sex discrimination in Nigeria needs immediate attention to meet up with world trends. What a man can do, a woman can equally do it. That is the progressive world trend. Paying men more remuneration than women for the same job is discriminatory. Refusing to employ women for most technically and physically challenging jobs is wrong. The workplace should reflect a fairly competitive environment for men and women with equal opportunities. Refusing to give one's children (boys and girls) equal developmental opportunities to be educated under any guise such as culture, tradition or religious faith is inhuman and grossly discriminatory.

Cases where men hide under tradition or religious belief to treat women with levity is morally wrong and should be challenged and changed. In a situation where man can commit adultery and some other marital offences with impunity while the woman is capitally punished for such offences does not show equal treatment for men and women, and it is discriminatory.

It is wrong to assume that you are right all the time because you are a man while the woman is assumed wrong all the time in similar circumstances. Men should give up their false ego centricism, which debases women in the background. The menfold should give up chauvinism and face the real world challenges of equal opportunities for men and women, boys and girls, ladies and gentlemen.

More enlightenment campaigns and education at local, state, regional and federal levels will help stop sex discrimination. The legislatures at state and federal levels can send the right message through appropriate legislations. Some states are more behind than some others in tackling sex discrimination. They should all buck up because sex discrimination retards development and civilization. The world has continued to move, change and modernize. Nigerian leaders should move, change and modernize with the progressive world.

What was right and best in the olden days up till yesterday, may be wrong and not good enough for today in recognition of the changing world, development and continuing civilization. The New Testament recognizes the need for a change from old or past behaviour in many aspects in line with the changing world. In actuality, to be a living person, one must follow the changing world trend.

When both man and woman pass through the same academics, professionalism or training, where is the justification for society to treat the female lower than the male if they can both equally perform in a business environment or in a marital situation? At the beginning of the slavery era, it served some people's purposes who benefited and considered it right, but with the passage of time, the world condemned slavery. The situation changed to freedom for all.

At a time in the world, dictatorship and colonization served some purposes, and the perpetrators benefited and thought they were right, but today, the world trend is decolonization and democracy. In the same way, sex discrimination that is prohibited in all civilized and developed societies in the world will change with time in Nigeria, sooner than later, with continuing higher education.

Any sex discrimination law must provide safeguards that ensure Nigerian women do not become too powerful to be able to drive their husbands out of their homes, seize all the property or organize homicide to receive insurance benefits as often witnessed in developed countries like the USA. Power sharing must be equitable and not tilted against men. In some developed countries, most men or husbands are treated by their women or wives like pets – domesticated animals, which are kept for pleasure and can be thrown out at will. That is very common in the USA!

It was reported that a young lady was kidnapped in Pakistan for three days and later released by her captors after many pleadings from her family members. With the thought that she might have lost her virginity in the process of the abduction, her family disowned her and felt that she should be dead because what happened to her was regarded as a disgrace to the family. Hence, her older brother took a gun and killed her with impunity.

Also in Pakistan, a father, Nazir Ahmad, was said to be very angry because his twenty-five year old eldest daughter married for love. As a result, he slit her throat when she was asleep and killed her. He then went ahead and killed his three other daughters aged four to twelve on the assumption that he feared they might follow in the footsteps of their oldest sister. The *Fort Worth Star-Telegram* of Sunday, December 25, 2006 reported that Ahmad surrendered to the police in Eastern Pakistan.

On Friday, January 6, 2006, the Punch Newspaper reported that forty-five commercial motorcycle operators were convicted by magistrates for violating Kano State law of Northern Nigeria, which bans them from carrying women. It may be asked whether adequate provision has been made to transport all women who need transportation in Kano State of Nigeria and any other place(s) where such law applies.

Above kind of law is not only discriminatory and petty, but it retards commerce and development as well as restricts ability of women to make choices like men to move freely. It is not only unprogressive but also undemocratic and could be challenged up to the highest court of the land to determine its constitutionality. Constitutional lawyers and women's organizations should help challenge these convictions as well as state laws and actions of government officials, which are not civilized or acceptable in this millennium.

The three cases above call the need for the overhauling of the awkward thoughts, culture, tradition and beliefs of some people in the world who are still living in the past for they cannot see the best of the best qualities, inherent in women and females generally, and their equality with the menfold. Religious leaders (Christians, Muslims and Traditionalists) and heads of governments should rise up to change the hearts of men who are likely to commit violence against women because of their odd beliefs about men being superior to women. Chauvinism must be condemned by all.

World leaders, legislators, governors, local leaders and all those who underrate women and support laws that repress, oppress and regress women are chauvinists living in the past. It is remarkable that women have been heads of governments of Britain, India, Liberia, Chile,

Germany, Argentina, Isreal, etc and the USA elected its first female Speaker, Nancy Pelosi in 2006. When will Nigeria elect its first female president? In 2007, Nigeria installed her first Female Speaker of the House of Representatives, Mrs. Olubunmi Etteh.

The menfold did not let her stay as Speaker of the House for up to six months before they dug up excuses and forced her to resign or face arrest from the EFCC. The leadership that succeeded her bought an expensive car for each legislator, so, they let him live. Some legislators allegedly received cars but traded in their cars for cash and pocketed the money. That is men's world. You cannot beat them. So, unfortunately, you may have to join them for the right reasons in order to survive and continue to live. Men can play the team game; most women cannot, but they are very compassionate and easily misled.

CHILD ABUSE:

Child abuse exists in all parts of the world. It exists as excessive discipline in Nigerian society, but in most cases it does not happen deliberately. Child abuse must be differentiated from child discipline. Nigerians love their children but discipline them to straighten them up. Appropriate and proportional discipline makes children grow up the best they can, and should be, and become grateful to their parents at adult age.

In Nigeria, neighbours help, and teachers do discipline children appropriately to build up a great child. It takes a whole village or community to raise a Nigerian child. Even plants, trees, flowers, hair and fingernails, if allowed to grow wild without appropriate trimmings periodically, will pose terrible problems just in the same way as children will grow wild if there is no effective redirection, supervision and discipline. Hence, it is not wrong to impose proportionate discipline, which does not harm the child. The best interest of the child must be the controlling factor. The child must in no way be put in dangerous or harmful situation.

The Legislatures at state and federal levels have a great responsibility in this situation by enacting laws that eliminate excessive, inappropriate discipline and child abuse. As a step in the right direction, a Nigerian, Professor Onyekwere Ebigbo, was said to have been appointed as a member of African Committee of Experts on the Rights and Welfare of a Child. Child enslavement or child labour must be eliminated.

It must be realized that any law that sends a parent, teacher or an adult to prison for child abuse must compel the prosecutor to prove his/her case beyond any reasonable doubt. It is on record that some children in developed countries of the 'Western World' were induced to lie against their parents, teachers or other adults who were sentenced to prison for twenty-five years to life imprisonment, but in later years they were released when the truth came out that the children had lied. Nigeria cannot afford such mistakes. Any law to be promulgated must provide checks and balances.

GOD/ALLAH BLESS NIGERIA!

CHAPTER 14

UNITY IN DIVERSITY

Nigeria is a wonderful nation of many ethnicities, languages, dialects, cultures, traditions, religions, beliefs, and dozens of political ideologies and party affiliations, all embodied in 36 distinguishing States and a Federal Capital Territory, Abuja, Centre of Unity. Though tribes and tongues may differ, in unity and brotherhood Nigerians stand as passed on by the Fathers of Nigerian Nationhood and Independence.

The fathers of Nigerian independence, Dr. Nnamdi Azikiwe, the Owelle of Onitsha, first President of Nigeria; Chief Obafemi Awolowo, first Premier of Western Nigeria; Sir Ahmadu Bello, the Sardauna of Sokoto, first Premier of Northern Nigeria; Sir Abubakar Tafawa Balewa, first Prime Minister of Nigeria, and all great Nigerians before them, envisaged Nigeria to be one great nation under God/Allah, indivisible like the United States of America.

These forerunners of Nigerian existence and independence had their socio-economic, political, ethnic and religious differences, yet, they never doubted the unity, oneness and indivisibility of their great nation, Nigeria. Chief Awolowo declared that if the Eastern Region was allowed to secede in 1967, the Western Region would follow. Dr. Azikiwe exemplarily abandoned the secessionist enclave and crossed over to Nigerian side in 1969.

The Nigerian civil war (1967-1970) was fought to keep Nigeria one and indivisible. At the end of the war, the objective of keeping Nigeria together was achieved and each successive military government created states to encourage selfgovernance to allay the fears of domination of minorities by majority ethnic nationalities. The creation of 36 states helped more focus on selfgovernance and selfdevelopment under the umbrella of one Nigeria.

Dr. Nnamdi Azikiwe (an Igboman of Eastern Nigeria) was highly respected all over Nigeria, and he had many political supporters in Lagos and Western Nigeria. His political party, the NCNC, won many elections in the West and Lagos, the heartland of Yoruba nationality. He was loved, admired and highly respected by majority of Nigerians, North, West and Eastern Regions of Nigeria. Eventually, he became the first President of Nigeria showing that the first Nigerian leader after independence in 1960 was an Igboman until the first coup d'etat of January 15, 1966.

The Igbos made the best use of the opportunity to hold many top positions in government civil service and the parastatals more than any other ethnicities. They spread conveniently all over the country for entrepreneurial ventures. They were the most enterprising nationalities. In entrepreneurship and academics, the Easterners (Igbos) were unparalleled, enviable and second to none during the lifetime of Dr. Azikiwe and his formidable team of Igbo politicians before the civil war (1967-1970).

Instead of the spirit of teamwork and conciliation to negotiate insider positions for the Yorubas in federal government setting, Yoruba leaders were usually at loggerheads with one another and confrontational to the federal government. As a result, the Western Nigeria that was always first in Africa became relegated to the third position in Nigeria. Confrontation has never yielded any good dividend without indelible scars. Nigerian leaders of all nationalities should have learnt their lessons for a greater Nigerian future. Western Nigeria witnessed a state of emergency declared by the federal government under Northern and Eastern regional coalition, which the Yorubas did not join but stayed in opposition. Such decision could not have been the best alternative decision.

The emergence of Chief Samuel Ladoke Akintola, the greatest Yoruba orator, as Premier of Western Nigeria, who was regarded as the most eloquent Yorubaman that ever lived, would have changed the position of the continuing humiliation of the Yorubas in the Federation of Nigeria controlled by the Northern and the Eastern Regions because of his friendship, diplomacy, alignment and conciliation with the Northerners. Unfortunately, the Ifeajuna/Nzeogwu coup d'etat of January 15, 1966, assassinated him as well as the political leadership of Northern Nigeria to destroy the rapport, which Chief Akintola of Western Nigeria was building with Northern Nigeria. The coup wrested power from the Northerners and gave it to the Easterners led by General Aguiyi Ironsi (an Igboman).

It is recalled that Dr. Azikiwe as the first President of Nigeria was a ceremonial head, while executive power rested with the Prime Minister, Sir Abubakar Tafawa Balewa of Northern Nigeria. The Igbo leadership especially the young Igbo military officers of January 15, 1966 who staged the Ifeajuna/Nzeogwu coup d'etat did not like that structure and so, they changed it by force and assassinations of Northern and Western regional leaders unwittingly.

Regrettably, the young Igbo military officers who staged the coup d'etat made Nigeria lose her democratic path for military dictatorship as a result of which the country was wandering in the wilderness and groping in darkness for more than thirty years. Presently, events are showing that Nigeria is moving faster to the shining light at the end of the tunnel. Nigerian elites should change 'business as usual' so that the wandering in the wilderness and groping in darkness will not extend beyond the year 2010.

It is not true to suggest that Nigerians hate Ndigbo as claimed by Chief Ralph Uwazuruike in the *Guardian News* of Saturday, September 25, 2004. He was quoted to have said, "The issue of Ndigbo in Nigeria is that of hatred. Nigerians hate Ndigbo. God knows why." Between 1960 and 1970, Chief Uwazuruike and many others like him were too young to have physically witnessed the genesis of Nigerian problems visàvis the problems of the Igbos of those years compounded by Ifeajuna/Nzeogwu coup d'etat.

Chief Uwazuruike needs to do some research about the causes of the civil war starting from 1959 followed by IfeajunaNzeogwu coup d'etat of January 15, 1966, which killed Hausa/Fulani and Yoruba military and civilian leaders but protected the Eastern leadership both military and civilian. This was followed by the retaliatory military coup of July 29, 1966, and then the civil war from 1967-1970. The research should extend to the era of reabsorption, reconstruction, rehabilitation and reconciliation, and the kindest gesture of 'no victor, no vanquished'. His research should determine who started the war by throwing bombs on innocent Lagosians from the air. Every person is the architect of his or her own fortunes or misfortunes. There is no reason to pass the buck.

At the age of nine years during the civil war, Chief Ralph Uwazuruike could not understand that if his Igbo heroes assassinated the leaders of other ethnic Nigerian nationalities contrary to Nigerian ethnic traditions, they must expect reprisals, and that it is best not to start a fight because you may not be able to accurately predict how it will end. All Nigerians have suffered terribly because of the indiscretion of young military officers of Eastern Nigeria extraction of January 15, 1966.

Chief Ralph Uwazuruike agreed that in order to avoid the chain reactions which had devastated Nigeria, the Nigerian problems preceding 1966 and thereafter should have been resolved through nonviolence, diplomacy, dialogue, consultation and conciliation in good faith to save about two million Nigerians who either died or were displaced from their cities, towns, villages, homes, businesses and their farmlands.

Chief Uwazuruike was reported to have said, "Then, I started questioning myself why didn't Ojukwu use nonviolence instead of fighting?" That is what every wellmeaning human being would say preferring nonviolence to war in solving all socio-economic and political problems.

It must be remembered that Mahatma Gandhi and Dr. Martin Luther King, Jr., who propounded and practised the doctrine of nonviolence to solve sociopolitical problems, did not preach or encourage acts of secessionism. Nobody should envisage the success of any secessionist activity without violence.

Secessionist tendencies and activities unequivocally breed dissension, confrontation, violence, nonconformity, civil disobedience, sufferings, war and death of innocent people. Secessionism, which Chief Ralph Uwazuruike purports to be championing through nonviolence hardly ever succeeds that way without any confrontation in the annals of the world. It will be difficult to succeed in Nigeria without throwing a punch.

Chief Uwazuruike was reported to have said, "What you should understand prima facie is Nigeria is no good. How Nigeria is being administered is not good, and that is why some people are even calling for sovereign national conference, and that is why some people are calling for Biafra. Others say self-determination."

It is not Nigeria that is not good but the few bad elite Nigerians of questionable characters who can be found in both the leadership and the followership; among Igbos, Yorubas, Hausas etc., East, West, North and South of Nigeria. If Chief Uwazuruike is advocating secessionism with the belief that the whole of Nigeria is not good, then he must reexamine himself very closely because someone who sees nothing good in all others may have problems being good himself. Bad people abound all over the world including the most advanced, developed and most civilized communities. Hence, as there is no saint, people must be careful of being judgmental.

Considering the Eastern Region that Chief Uwazuruike wants to secede, what will happen if bad people exist within the leadership and the followership as they normally exist in all societies? What will be the fate of any eastern state and individuals who do not support secession? The plan for secession may lead to chaos, deaths and economic disaster. Invariably, it is the innocent and poor people and their families who suffer and get killed. The elite troublemakers often flee and escape to Europe, America and other African countries.

The utopian nation state of Chief Uwazuruike's wildest dreams is an illusion in the world that is full of human imperfections. Therefore, the right solutions to Nigerian problems are not the calls for secession, Biafra, sovereign national conference or self-determination. Such ignoble calls that are prone to confrontation, civil disobedience, unconstitutionality and violence will further complicate Nigerian problems by raising more problems than the advocates for secession, Biafra, SNC or self-determination want to solve.

Chief Uwazuruike's actions of purportedly sponsoring MASSOB (Movement for the Actualization of Sovereign State of Biafra) are treasonable and may not be tolerated for long by Nigerian authorities. As a lawyer, Chief Uwazuruike cannot claim ignorance of the implications of his actions regarding MASSOB. There are several other ways to bring salvation to your ethnicity peacefully other than through anarchy, war and deaths.

May it be asked of Chief Ralph Uwazuruike and his adherents if there are not better alternatives to help the Igbos other than nursing secession in twenty-five stages well into the future as claimed by him! The twenty-five-stage plan of growing MASSOB is nothing short of prospectively and potentially growing and breeding confrontation, confusion, misdirection, chaos and rebellion against Nigeria and her constituted authorities. How much will Chief Uwazuruike's thought further alienate other Nigerian nationalities? Does he want to repeat the terrible history of 1966-1970? Does he understand where he is going and the tragedy he is calling for? Does he want more deaths and sufferings for innocent Nigerians who cannot escape to Europe and America like himself and his teammates when trouble starts.

How much does Chief Uwazuruike's concept of MASSOB contradict and complicate the vision for Igbo Presidency and derail the focus of the Igbos for the project in 2011 and beyond? Is the establishment of MASSOB as constituted in Uwazuruike's revelation not like shooting the Igbos on the right foot? Countries that share borders must be friendly with one another to avoid prolonged war and hostilities. How does Chief Uwazuruike's plan for MASSOB guarantee peace for the South East posterity if it secedes? Will all the Igbos presently in other parts of Nigeria have to apply for visas or permits to stay and/or carry on their businesses in Nigeria?

It is hoped that MASSOB and its mentors directly, indirectly and secretly, are not repeating the mistakes of 1966 and the civil war (1967-70) which placed the Igbos on a collision course with their colleagues in the West, North, South-South and majority of well-meaning Igbos who did not and may not support secessionist tendencies and activities.

The vital question is, "What are the concerns of Chief Uwazuruike and MASSOB, and how can they be addressed?" Chief Uwazuruike was reported to have said, "Let every ethnic nationality go; let Yoruba be on their own; let Hausa be on their own; let Igbo be on their own; let Niger Delta be on their own." With this request, Chief Uwazuruike was not limiting the secessionist advocacy to his own region, the South East. He is suggesting a complete breakup of Nigeria. His ideas are full of hate and intolerance. He should have limited his ideas to his own people, the Igbos, and let the Yorubas, the Hausas and other ethnicities talk and decide for themselves.

This line of thought is very dangerous for Nigeria if Chief Uwazuruike is not stopped for preaching hate and divisionism. He admitted that he had his supporters spread all over the country pursuing a twenty-five-stage longterm plan, which may take years to execute. If Chief Uwazuruike were an adult during the civil war (1967-1970) and actually experienced the evils of the war, perhaps he would not pray for any situation that can bring about the memories and horrors of secessionist attempts and failures to break up Nigeria.

Chief Uwazuruike was bitter about what he described as robbing Peter to pay Paul by sending Niger Delta people's resources to the North to establish Abuja, the Federal Capital Territory, and building refinery in Kaduna. If there is any case here, it is best handled by the Niger Deltans, and not sufficient for an Igboman to use it as an excuse for the call for secession.

Abuja is the Federal Capital Territory (Centre of Unity) designated as no man's land thus belonging to the whole of Nigeria and made centrally located in the heart of Nigeria. A 2005/06 investigation revealed that over 50% acquisitions of Abuja land belonged to the core Easterners. Does Uwazuruike have a cost benefit analysis of his actions? No!

Building a refinery in Kaduna is not an offending project. If there is any problem about it, the Legislature and the Presidency can be appealed to in order to correct it. The Presidency and the Legislature as well as the Governors of the oil rich regions have been working hard on acceptable resource allocation, resource derivation and control policies, which eventually can take care of Chief Uwazuruike's concern.

Above all, projects for the building of more oil refineries as well as renovation and maintenance of existing ones are being vigorously pursued by the government. Hence, this complaint of Chief Uwazuruike is not sufficient to call for the break up of Nigeria.

What is the guarantee that any state that breaks away will not have internal problems as much as there could be external problems militating against such break away state? Will it continue to break up for every internal problem or solve it through dialogue, consultation, diplomacy and conciliation?

Chief Uwazuruike should conduct research into events and socio-economic and political problems, which emanated from the domination of minorities when the South-South geopolitical zone was under the rule of the Igbos of the old Eastern Region. At that time, the South-South was always complaining about socio-economic and political domination of their resources by the Igbos of East Central, but later in life, the problem was solved by the creation of more states, peacefully and not by secession, which could have caused a civil war.

In effect, there is no problem that cannot be resolved peacefully with good intentions and great spirit, if all stakeholders concerned use the best peaceful conflict resolution strategies compromisingly. A brilliant lawyer, academician and professional like Chief Uwazuruike should help Nigeria to subsist, not break nor kill it for future generations yet unborn.

Nobody nor groups should be so bitter, unforgiving and unforgetting to be so prepared to plunge Nigeria into an alert situation while hatching secessionist tendencies progressionally with twenty-five-stage plan which no one knows when and how it will end. In what civilized countries do groups exist which usurp police, judge and jury functions, pass and execute sentences with impunity?

Nigerian Government should make sure that such undisciplined group activities are not bequeathed to future generations. The fears being generated by these groups should be tackled from their sources and taproots. If dissident group members have gainful employment, it is most likely that the groups will be self-disbanding, especially educationally qualified members in their midst who are being exploited for being unemployed and have no alternatives.

Chief Uwazuruike said, "You remember that if on August 26, 2004, I had lined up tanks and all the arsenals on earth, I wouldn't have compelled all Igbos on earth to stay at home, but by word of mouth only and voluntarily." It is a wonderful self-actualization for one just trying to gain prominence to have successfully told the Igbo nation to stay at home, and they all did. Such wonderful power of persuasion if applied positively rather than negatively could uplift the Igbos to the first place, which they occupied in Nigeria before July 29, 1966 and the civil war of 1967-1970. The Igbo withdrawal from work was a negative approach at a time when there should be collective efforts and teamwork to uplift and move Nigeria forward with her citizenry. An order to stay at home promotes economic stagnation, diminishing productivity and confrontation, which may not help the well-deserved project of Igbo Presidency.

There are still living Igbo elders, leaders and most distinguished traditional rulers just like the great days of Dr. Nnamdi Azikiwe in Igboland who should not be quiet but constantly call to order those erring Igbos who were below teenage years during the regrettable civil war (1967-70), and who want to repeat the mistakes of the past when Nigeria witnessed its darkest days. Secession does not do anybody any good. But if anybody should ever start a rebellion again, the people should ensure that the rebel(s) do not escape with their families while leaving the ordinary, innocent people in the lurch, realizing what happened when Chief Uwazuruike was below teenage years and could not fully appreciate the horrors of the civil war (1967-70).

The Igbos in particular and Nigerians generally will appreciate it if Chief Uwazuruike uses his education, legal professionalism and experience in India, Nigeria and internationally to help provide food, health, shelter, safety, education, development, growth, economic upliftment, peace and political stability for Nigerian people instead of twenty-five stages of planned agenda for secessionism.

Secession failed then, it will also fail if it ever rears its head. Its perpetrators may not be able to escape judgment the next time. Chief Uwazuruike should attend to the needs of the Igbos, disabled as a result of the civil war instead of nursing another rebellion. Those disabled soldiers and fighters during the war should have been catered for and not abandoned on the streets to beg for alms to eat.

Chief Uwazuruike complained about the nineteen Northern governors who challenged the thirteen percent derivation policy of government in court and added that the Northern States would not allow the consumption of alcoholic beverages but would collect the lion's share of value added tax (VAT) out of such federal revenue from other states of Western and Eastern Nigeria because they have more local governments and more land space.

He added that the derivation percentage was 50:50 before 1966 when there were groundnut pyramids, palm oil and cocoa, but as soon as oil was discovered in the East, the derivation percentage was slashed down. He further complained about the Land Use Decree, which he described as meant to confiscate people's lands and resources.

He asserted that if those resources were discovered from the Northern States, northern politicians would not have supported lower derivation percentage and the enactment of the Land Use Decree. He reiterated that northern people would not have allowed anyone to cross over to their place to take or share their resources nor talk of one Nigeria. He added that it was funny for somebody to try to perpetuate a forced marriage. He said it would not work, so let the people go.

He should have addressed his concerns formally to the National Political Reform Conference (NPRC) for consideration and appropriate decision. The President and the National Assembly should wake up and correct the wrong situations highlighted by Chief Uwazuruike. His complaints are genuine and reasonable, but the solution is not secessionism, which he is advocating.

Chief Uwazuruike's concerns mentioned above should be looked into seriously by the Presidency and the Legislature. A lot of injustices need to be addressed and corrected. New Nigeria should evolve a system that motivates productivity and limits cheating when people reap where they do not sow. Uwazuruike's argument is easily convincing, but Nigeria cannot be allowed to break up as a result of issues that can be discussed, harmonized and settled amicably without resorting to violence, rebellion or treasonable acts.

The North must take responsibility for ruling the country for thirty-five years and yet, Nigeria still remains in the wilderness trying to correct the wrongs created by dictatorship. It is the spirit of God/Allah that believers of God/Allah in the North should ask themselves what they may be doing wrong that is making enlightened and highly educated Westerners and Easterners to call for the sovereign national conference and a restructuring of the country.

The power of the majority in the North cannot continue to be exercised indefinitely to oppress or regress the highly intelligent minorities that constitute the former Eastern and Western Regions of Nigeria without problems. The North must be ready to move with the trend of world civilization and adjust to the changing world. The South-East, South-West and South-South feel they are not moving forward fast enough because the North is not moving to catch up with them. They also feel that the North is using its majority to 'rule them from behind' which is regressional for them in particular and the whole of Nigeria in general.

These are problems that the North must fully recognize to keep the country together by changing behaviour of business as usual. It is not wrong to want to lead, but you must have all it takes to lead right. Life is too short. Nigerians cannot continue to accept leaders who perform below expectations after more than 40 years of their lives have been wasted by dictators and leaders without the rightful directional abilities.

On basis of world experience generally and Nigeria in particular, secession complicated problems instead of providing solution, and it brought mistrust, divisionism, war, sufferings, deaths, hunger, displacements, socio-economic and political wreck, dictatorship, anarchy, regression and other untold hardships. Secessionism is not the best alternative solution to solving national problems.

It shows selfdefeatism; it creates a quitter; it breeds precariousness, confusion, confrontation and war. It should not be encouraged, not even as a last resort. Disintegration is not good for Nigerian future generations who also have the right to determine their own future associations. Chief Uwazuruike's addiction for secession demonstrates the mentality of a quitter who does not properly weigh the implications of his actions on the innocent majority of people.

Chief Uwazuruike should direct his full energies to exploring the strength possibilities of 'unity in diversity' to reap the full benefits accruable from the inherent differences of peoples who are united. The results will be better than turmoil from secessionism, divisionism, disintegration and disunity. Together, Nigerians can make the country a better place for themselves as well as future generations yet unborn.

If Chief Uwazuruike successfully made the Igbos to stay at home on August 26, 2004, he should use the same magic wand and energy positively to unite the Igbos to bring out one most acceptable and electable Igboman to contest for the Nigerian presidency come 2011. There are many highly educated, matured and experienced Igbos who are qualified to be President of Nigeria, but the utterances of Chief Uwazuruike and many others are undermining the trust and confidence which other Nigerians repose in Igbos that will help an Igboman to be elected as President or Vice President of Nigeria in 2011 and/or thereafter.

Nigerians should not make the mistake of allowing dissidents or those who advocate secessionism and their mentors who are not patriotic to be elected to the Presidency or Vice Presidency position. Anybody who has no patience, endurance or true love for the oneness and indivisibility of Nigeria, or whoever has breached the Nigerian constitution should not be eligible to be President or Vice President. Nigerian leadership should not condone fire that can burn future generations of Nigeria. Whoever breaks the law now must serve the punishment as deterrence to others. Whatever will break the unity and strength of the country must be resisted at all costs now and stamped out to keep future generations safe from threats of secession, the vagaries of war, confusion and insecurity.

The problems of the 1960s created by young Igbo military officers who staged coups that threw Nigeria into the wilderness and darkness for almost forty years started clandestinely from the Eastern Region. It should not be allowed to rear its head again. It is ironical that while a great majority of Igbos are working hard to contest for the highest positions in Nigeria, a few ones are jeopardizing the great efforts and promising success of Igbo leadership by orchestrating a twenty-five-stage plan to break up Nigeria.

The Igbos should stop believing that they are hated. Those who want to find out the truth should study the wonderful accomplishments of the Igbo leadership before the civil war (1967-70) especially the life of great Igbo leaders like Dr. Nnamdi Azikiwe and many of his Igbo contemporaries. The present bickering that exists among the Igbos was never like that in the past. The Igbos used to speak with one voice during the Premiership and Presidency of Dr. Nnamdi Azikiwe. The problem of the Igbos is no longer caused by outsiders. The Igbos should look more inwards for solution by themselves and treat their problems as an internal affair. It must be done quickly because any prolonged problem in any part of Nigeria will definitely affect the whole of the country as time goes on.

Nigerians must be united to make the nascent democracy wax stronger, forget and forgive the past wrongs and build a great country for themselves and posterity. In togetherness, Nigerians can solve any problem, climb any mountain, cross any river, turn any stones on their paths and bequeath a great and prosperous nation to their children and great-grand-children. A united, indivisible and prosperous Nigeria is a task for all to accomplish in togetherness.

Nigerians at all levels and classes should never quit when there is a problem to solve, especially if you are placed in charge to represent your ethnicity, nationality or the whole country. If the Head of State, General Ibrahim Badamosi Babangida (IBB, 1985-1993) did not quit for Sonekan's Interim Administration (1993), Abacha's Administration with all its attendant atrocities of human rights abuses, killings, corruption, fraud, money laundering, economic and financial crimes of stashing about $5 billion Nigerian money in foreign private bank accounts, would not have happened to the country.

Also, the country should not have been declared a pariah state ostracized by international community if Abacha's regime did not come into being. In addition, Nigeria's great sons and daughter like General Shehu Musa Yar'Adua, Chief Moshood Abiola and his wife Kudirat Abiola, Ken Saro Wiwa and many others would still be alive today contributing their quotas toward the development and upliftment of our great country, Nigeria!

On Tuesday, June 7, 2005, the Chairman of National Political Reform Conference (NPRC), Justice Niki Tobi was reported to have averted a walkout by Igbo delegates for alleged uncomplimentary remarks made by a Northern delegate, Alhaji Usman Farouk, retired Commissioner of Police and former Military Governor of the defunct North Central State. Alhaji Farouk was representing Gombe, Northern Nigeria at the conference.

The alleged disparaging comments by Alhaji Farouk were, "In the past six years of democracy, leadership of number three (Senate President) in the country has changed hands five times among the five states of the South-East geopolitical zone. Therefore, in my view, if they (Igbo) are allowed to become the President of this country, chances are that they will put the nation in serious crisis as a result of which the much sought foreign investors would be scared of coming to invest in Nigeria." He later apologized, but he said that there was nothing new in the comments he made.

Alhaji Farouk's comments made Igbo delegates uncomfortable but challenged. The world knows that the representatives of South-East at the conference consisted of highly intelligent people like former Commonwealth Secretary-General, Chief Emeka Anyaoku, President General of Ohanaeze, Professor Joe Irukwu, Chief Chima Okafor and other Igbo delegates who were very competent to give a befitting remarkable response.

As men of 'timber and calibre', they should not have been shaken by the comments of Alhaji Farouk who was throwing stones from his glass house. These great South-Easterners should have thanked Alhaji Usman Farouk about his observation, but they should have reminded him about the thirty-five years of maladministration of the country which fell between 1960 and 1998, and that if the Igbos had the opportunity to rule the country for onequarter of that period of thirty-five years, Nigeria would have better stories to tell today.

The Igbo delegates could have used the opportunity to promise the country that if given the presidency, they will ensure that any of the atrocities that occurred between 1960 and 1999, which included when Alhaji Farouk was Military Governor and Commissioner of Police, would never happen in this country. With such simple statement, the message from Alhaji Farouk would have been counterbalanced and neutralized.

Above all, the five times change of hands of the Senate Presidency was not as bad as overthrowing the federal administrations of Gowon, Murtala, Shagari, Buhari, Babangida, Sonekan followed by Abacha's reign of terror – all kinsmen of the same Northern Region like Alhaji Farouk.

There were cases of election boycotts by some political parties which never resulted in cancellation of the whole election but rather gave the participating party an advantage to win unopposed and run the government without effective opposition. As a result, boycotting a meeting, conference or election, or staging a walkout in a democracy does not solve any problem. It is better to remain, be counted and be recorded even if you have minority opinion. Always remember that if you boycott or walk out, the conference, meeting, election, etc. will continue without you and any decisions reached will be binding on you and the people you represent.

In effect, a befitting response from the South-East delegates would have turned the table against Alhaji Farouk, and every delegate would have laughed. Everybody would have been happy, and the NPRC forum would have been livelier and more congenial. Ethnic Nigerians should not meet at meetings and talk or act like enemies. When will Nigerian leaders start to laugh with one another and show the right examples of peaceful coexistence that can be bequeathed to posterity?

The rebellious actions of kidnapping oil workers, blowing up oil pipelines, seizure of oil vessels and continued increase in youth militancy that killed federal soldiers and civilians in Niger Delta are bound to attract serious consequences. Each part of Nigeria needs the other(s) for full development. The destructive actions of the youth militants surely have economic consequences on the South-South subregion in particular and Nigeria as a whole.

Global price stability of petroleum products becomes adversely affected as a result of violence caused by the youth militants of Niger Delta and threatens the security and the unity of Nigeria. But with patience, understanding, love and care for one another, mutual respect, transparency and continuation of socio-economic and political reforms, Nigeria will get to the Promised Land sooner than expected. Let us be our brothers' keepers as one large extended family.

Nigerian leaders and representatives should try to crack jokes among themselves, smile and be happy. Past and present US Presidents cast jokes and create laughter, also US Congressmen from different political parties do. During official businesses they criticize policies, proposals and decisions but not personalities. They do not boycott meetings and conferences. Nigerian leaders should copy the best in the world and be exemplary. Periodic short orientation courses can make Nigerian leaders the best in the world.

GOD/ALLAH BLESS NIGERIA!

CHAPTER 15

NIGERIAN PATRIOTISM

Nigerian patriots are Nigerian nationals who are capable, willing and have demonstrated love for their fatherland, Nigeria. There are various ways of showing love for one's country. The love for one's country may include paying the maximum price of dying for the country in her defence, if her existence or survival is being jeopardized. Nigeria is the only country, which all Nigerians can call their own.

Nigerians do not need visa to go back to their country and it is the only place where nobody can discriminate against you or treat you as a secondclass citizen without facing some problems. East or West, Home is the best. Nigeria, which is our homeland, is the best. Nigerians have always loved to be taken back home (Nigeria) even when they are dead. There is no place like home (Nigeria) for Nigerians. Nigerians love their country unequivocally and would be prepared to pay the maximum price with their lives, to preserve Nigeria's perpetual succession, her integrity and survival.

On May 29, 2003, ExPresident Obasanjo requested Nigerians to be patriotic. He said, "We all have a stake in 'Enterprise Nigeria' and each of us stands a better chance of getting optimum dividends if instead of asking, 'What's in it for me?' we ask, 'What's in it for Nigeria?' to determine our choice of action when our sense of duty and service is called upon."

Dying for Nigeria does not mean dying for any past, present or future leadership of Nigeria in their personal or private capacities.

Nigeria as a corporate entity should not be confused with or mixed up with her leadership and her leadership behaviour. Nigeria is a completely separate and different entity from her leadership whether good or bad, transparent or not, exemplary or not. Leaders will always come and go, but Nigeria will remain forever.

Leadership performance could be an important secondary factor to determine your love for your country, but it should not be the primary element for any reasonable person to denounce and discount his or her fatherland, his or her nativeland, his or her birthplace, Nigeria, which the Black People of the world hold very dearly and are very proud of.

Nigerian and secessionist soldiers of the civil war (1967-1970) died for Nigeria trying to save the course of a great nation. The former Military Governor of Western Nigeria, late Adekunle Fajuyi, a Yorubaman, could have escaped but he stayed and died while trying to save and prevent the assassination of General Aguiyi Ironsi, an Igboman who was Head of State of Nigeria during the July 29, 1966 retaliation coup d'etat. So also, many distinguished Nigerians died in the course of championing the great course of a better and prosperous Nigeria, their birthplace.

What about the Fathers of Nigerian Independence? Would they not have lived, fought, hoped and died in vain for Nigeria if their successive generations cannot say patriotically with pride that they love their country, their fatherland, their nativeland, their birthplace, Nigeria, and will save and protect the nation at all costs? If you have problems with the leadership, blame yourself for what you may have done wrong that brought the military to power or the leaders you did not approve of and try to make amendments constitutionally in ways that do not heat the polity.

Ironically, those who are making the loudest noise and critiques today about Nigeria had opportunities and were brought in to serve the country in leadership positions, but they did not perform better than those they were criticizing. What did they do better for Nigeria when they served in the past military and civilian administrations? They failed to make a difference and Nigerians' sufferings continued. Despite that, Nigerians are patriotic; they love their country, Nigeria without a doubt.

Some Nigerians died and the world mourned for their deaths like Chief Obafemi Awolowo, Dr. Nnamdi Azikiwe, Sir Ahmadu Bello, the

Sardauna of Sokoto, Sir Abubakar Tafawa Balewa, Chief S.L. Akintola, Chief Moshood Abiola, General Shehu Yar'Adua, Senator Joseph Tarka, Ken Saro-Wiwa, Mallam Aminu Kano, First Lady, Mrs. Stella Obasanjo and many others because of their good work to humanity when they were alive.

On the other hand, it must not be forgotten that while some others were still alive, Nigeria and the world community were praying hard for their demise because of the killings, pain, suffering, human and civil rights abuses, corruption, economic and financial crimes, stashing Nigerian government money in foreign banks, money laundering, other heinous crimes and havoc which they caused humanity and the country, Nigeria.

The problems that Nigerians had suffered under civilian government and military dictatorship for over four decades were not caused by Nigeria, your country, but by a few misguided Nigerians who constituted her leadership and eldership, trusted with the reins of power but failed to deliver.

Therefore, if things go wrong in Nigeria, who do you blame: (a) Nigeria – your country and birthplace; (b) yourself who assisted the poor leadership to power; or (c) the poor leadership that jeopardized the prosperity of Nigeria and Nigerians? There are still so many pots calling the kettle black in Nigeria for which Nigerians should be aware and keep on moving Nigeria forward at all costs. The best answer to the question is either 'b' and/or 'c' while 'a' is eliminated. In effect, Nigeria as a country does not do the wrong things but Nigerians and the leaders do.

If Nigeria were occupied by foreign aggressors, it would become the duty of all Nigerians to stay together and repulse the aggression and the aggressors at all cost irrespective of the rating of the leadership performance. In effect, you are not fighting for the leadership of your country but for the survival of your country. Given that situation, Nigerians should be fully prepared to defend their country, Nigeria, their motherland, their birthplace, at all costs, including dying for it.

If there were disintegration or secessionist tendencies or actions in any part of the country including a serious breach of the Nigerian Constitution, Nigerians should be ready to fight at all costs to keep Nigeria together, united and indivisible, not because of any past, present or future leadership that might have primarily disappointed Nigerians since independence in 1960, but for the sake of Nigeria 'per se', future generations and the wish to see that Nigeria maintains her perpetual succession possibilities without any hindrances. The legacies that could be bequeathed to future generations of our great great grandchildren will be a great, prosperous and wonderful Nigeria, united, strong, indivisible and incorruptible.

It is true that Nigerians and Nigeria have been terribly hurt by the elites through corruption, frauds, economic and financial crimes, maladministration of the enormous wealth of resources which God/Allah gave Nigeria since independence without remorse, but Nigerians must stay strong behind Nigeria, their country, at all costs knowing fully well that no matter how long, the leadership, past, present or future, would pass but Nigeria will always remain. Nigerians must differentiate between Nigeria, their country, their fatherland, their nativeland, their birthplace; and the Nigerian leadership, who represent the elites that hurt the hearts and consciences of most Nigerians.

Nigerians should never allow the indiscretion and maladminstration of any leadership, past, present or future to make them feel that they could not love their country, their nativeland and their birthplace to death.

Do not let the evils of any human being be the decider of how much you love your country. Do not love your country, Nigeria less because of your disappointment about what or who somebody else was or is in Nigeria. Do not hate your country perpetually because of leadership failures. Naturally, leaders will go and other leaders will come but Nigeria will remain forever. Always love your country.

The problems of Nigeria are not caused by the innocent or ordinary citizens; the masses in majority, but by the few elites who are corrupt and not transparent. They pretend to be friendly with the leaders and the presidency when in actuality they are the worst enemies of the country. If some elites cannot assist the good work of the government transparently and exemplarily, but continue marring it with fraud, corruption and violence, then, their homes and offices should be in the penitentiary and not outside among Nigerians.

ExPresident Obasanjo remarked that corruption was hard to fight because some of those involved included some friends and some of those he respected. That is natural, but with the need for continuing relentless and unprecedented efforts to crush corruption in Nigeria, anybody who does not get the message to change 'business as usual' cannot be a friend of the presidency, and such persons cannot be respected.

Every rightthinking and wellmeaning Nigerian locally and internationally must support the initiative and efforts to stamp out corruption as well as economic and financial crimes from Nigerian society. Nigerians at home and abroad should start to change their value judgment of honouring rich elites who got their wealth through dubious means.

Nigerians should start to accuse, blame and provide helpful information to the police about their brothers, sisters, uncles, relations, and others who were entrusted with positions to manage Nigerian resources but wrecked the country since independence. Covering up corrupt people will not eliminate the crime nor help Nigeria, your adorable country. But then, would you stop loving your country because of some misguided elite politicians who misdirected and maladiminstered Nigeria?

The fight for Nigeria must continue with love, diplomacy, persuasion, consultation, dialogue and conciliation without heating the polity or hurting Nigeria. The aggrieved group should differentiate between the endless love for one's country, which enjoys perpetual succession naturally, and the love or hatred for the past or present leadership that has limited tenureship. The leadership of Nigeria will change constitutionally after the end of its tenure, but no Nigerian by birthright can change his or her birthplace, Nigeria, to any other country. Your birthplace is your home and most probable resting place. "East or West, Home is the best." The leadership of Nigeria will continue to come and go, but Nigeria will always remain.

Professor Wole Soyinka, the Nobel Laureate, was reported to have said, "I never allow myself to be hopeful or pessimistic; I take Nigeria as an ongoing project." When asked whether he would die for Nigeria, he replied that it would depend upon the circumstances. He added, "But I am not setting out to die for any obtuse concept, especially an artificial concept like Nigeria."

The love for one's country should not be based entirely on leadership performance. The irony of leadership is that human imperfections in decision-making have often robbed the society of their great expectations. But that notwithstanding, who should be blamed for electing leaders who cannot perform, yourself, Nigerians or Nigeria? You can only blame yourself or Nigerians for making wrong choices of leadership. You cannot rightly blame Nigeria, your country for that. A lot of factors constrain individual's judgment when choosing the leaders. The national process of making the best choice among the best alternative choices is a complicated process beyond human comprehension. Only God knows the best choice and can accurately pick the best while human beings cannot.

Hence, to be at peace, Nigerians must accept the realities of human limitations and make do with what they have, and do not despise it or quarrel with it. It is a bad workman who quarrels with his or her own tools. With patience, cooperation, understanding, peace, goodwill, solidarity, love and care for one another and the country irrespective of socio-economic, ethno-religious and political differences, Nigeria will become great without any iota of doubt.

It is recalled that Chief Gani Fawehinmi (SAN), Chief Anthony Enahoro, Professor Wole Soyinka and some other sociopolitical activists had continuously risked their lives several times fighting for the courses they believed were best for their beloved country, Nigeria. Luckily, they survived in prison for trumped up political charges where some others died. Their pains and sufferings and unjust incarcerations were not meted on them by Nigeria but by the leadership. Should they love their country less for what happened to them? No! If they relent showing unqualified love for their country, their past efforts and sufferings would be in vain.

But Nigerians ask all critics and pessimists of Nigeria, "Are you always right in your approaches to solve Nigerian problems?" If not, in a democratic Nigeria with over 140 million opinions, progress can only be made through harmonization, cooperation, consultation and conciliation using peaceful conflict resolution strategies. Extreme opinionation and boycotting talks or conferences are not exemplary for Nigeria's progress and future generations. Name-callings and personal attacks on leaders should stop in the best interest of Nigeria.

In effect, the amount of sacrifice Nigerians should continue to make toward accomplishing national goals should not be dependent entirely on their love or hatred for the leaders who are human beings and fallible like themselves. Nigeria is not an abstract, obtuse nor artificial concept, but God/Allah's own country with enormous blessings of human, material, and natural resources of invaluable dimensions, which make Nigeria proud and respected among the Comity of Nations. Many people in the world today would love and want to be Nigerians. Nigeria is a God/Allah given entity, an innocent natural entity that has perpetual succession.

Never say, "What is wrong with Nigeria?" Instead, please ask, "What is wrong with Nigerian elites who make the leadership of Nigeria?" What good is it if you are blaming, complaining and doubting your love for your fatherland instead of blaming the elites who have lost their African great values of transparency, incorruptibility, graciousness, respectability, responsibility, accountability, responsiveness, empathy, impeccability, unparalleled sense of community, decency, dignity, humility and Godliness/Allahliness?

Out of sheer frustration, the weak minds may compromise their love for their country, but Nigerians should stay strong for the end of their sufferings is in sight. Nigerian hour of salvation has come when no son of man would be able to halt the forward march to the Promised Land, the Eldorado. Get ready to be counted as one of the faithful who will get there.

Nigerians must start to ask questions maturely, peacefully and responsibly from the past and present leaders and those aspiring to be future leaders to tell Nigerians whether the country has ever benefited from their services and how! The present leaders are fighting corruption and other ills that have been the bane of Nigerian society, and they deserve to be supported. Their tasks are Herculean, and they must be encouraged to succeed. They need to be commended for what they are doing right, and positively reinforced to adjust areas that need improvement through dialogue; friendliness, cooperation and conciliation from all, including the opposition groups.

Remember, you cannot successfully and effectively solve human socio-economic and political problems by using negative attitude, force and condemnation only, without fully understanding the problems through extensive and intensive research efforts. Those who are clamouring for changes and results must be prepared to make sacrifices and show understanding. Regrettably, majority of those criticizing loudest held political appointments between 1960 and 1999, and yet, they did not make a difference. What difference other than confusion did they make?

There is always room for improvement, but presently, Nigeria is far better administered now than the past when the nation was ostracized from the Comity of Nations for human rights violations, killings, corruption, frauds, rampant economic and financial crimes, money laundering, staggering foreign debt, unemployment and all acts of evil against humanity. There were incidents of stashing Nigerian money in foreign banks and injecting General Yar'Adua with HIV/AIDS infected needle. That was barbaric dictatorship, and Nigeria should continue to say, "Never again; never again!" Nigeria is now almost foreign debtfree. Let us thank God/ Allah for his mercies.

Nigerians should love their country, Nigeria, their birthplace with the greatest concentration of Black People in the world and immensely blessed with human, natural, mineral and material resources. There are many foreigners who want to be Nigerians. Always remember that anybody who does not see anything good about his or her country to be proud of, may not be a good person himself or herself. Nigeria is a worthy country to live and die for. "Enterprise Nigeria" is a separate, perpetual, corporate entity, completely different from her leadership. If past and present leadership cannot be fully accountable to Nigerians because they are 'sacred cows and untouchables', they must realize that they will be answerable to God/Allah for any misdeeds. Hence, Nigerians should not be shaken in their love for their great and promising country.

A really intelligent, highly educated and patriotic person would be humble, compromising, persuasive, conciliatory, not troubleshooting but problem solving, exemplary, respected, respectful and peace-loving in his/her words and actions. Some elites are still using their outdated old influences to confuse Nigerians by being antagonistic to everything that the Federal or State authorities do, by posing as if they know it all, and that Nigeria should be run according to their thoughts and wishes or else, the country should not be governable, exist or function.

For example, the government set up a National Political Reform Conference (NPRC) and invited Nigerian representatives from all shades of life and interests in the country to discuss and shape the future of the country. Some of those invited to participate in the NPRC turned down their invitations and formed another conference, called Pro-National Conference Organization (PRONACO) and thus divided the focus and attention of Nigerians. At best, the dissenting group could have joined the government efforts, make their points known and recorded at the NPRC, and later form PRONACO to monitor implementation of decisions reached at the NPRC cooperatively.

If the PRONACO group honoured government invitation, they would still be free to contribute their dissenting voice, issue minority reports and highlight areas of harmony with the NPRC overall report. Such approach would keep Nigerians focused in one direction of reforms. Those who form the PRONACO have the democratic right to do so, but the approach did not show compromise, conciliation, respect for national authority and readiness to keep the nation unheated socio-politically as it is done in developed countries.

After PRONACO must have fully participated in the NPRC, and the reports are implemented fully or partially, the PRONACO could surface to press for more areas of the NPRC report that need more attention with civility and not as if they are running their own country that is different from 'Enterprise Nigeria' which belongs to all of us (Nigerians).

In conclusion, Nigerians should love their country as they love themselves or more and ensure that leadership performance, which is temporary, does not diminish or discount their love for their country. Nigeria will be our legacy to posterity perpetually while the leadership, which is of limited tenureship, will periodically come and go in quick succession. It is worthy to live or die for Nigeria no matter who the leader is.

The problems you do not like about Nigeria are not created by Nigeria, our blessed nation, but by the elites. Nigeria is not the problem but the elites in leadership are. Nigerians should stay strong, united, patriotic and hopeful for a greater and prosperous future. The new dawn has arisen for Nigerians. It must be remembered that there is no perfect country or utopia in the world. The most developed countries of the Western World have more homeless people, more mentally retarded, higher crime rate, higher corporate fraud and corruption, higher health problems and greater fear of insecurity than Nigeria. You cannot know the problem if you have not lived in developed countries where all that glitters deceptively is regarded as gold. The consolation is that Nigeria has abundant resources for development. The trends of events show that Nigeria is catching up fast with the leading countries in the world. Let every Nigerian work hard to achieve greatness and prosperity by the target year of 2020.

GOD/ALLAH BLESS NIGERIA!

CHAPTER 16

ANNULMENT OF JUNE 12, 1993 PRESIDENTIAL ELECTION

The revelation on June 12, 2008 by Professor Humphrey Nwosu, Chairman of the defunct Independent National Electoral Commission (INEC), claimed that General Sani Abacha and former Attorney General, Chief Clement Akpamgbo should be blamed as principal actors in the nullification of the presidential election of June 12, 1993. He also revealed that Chief Moshood Kashimawo Olawale Abiola won the election with 8,323,305 votes while his opponent, Othma Tofa had 6,073,612 votes. Chief Abiola contested on the platform of Social Democratic Party (SDP) while Othma Tofa represented National Republican Convention (NRC).

The revelations came too late after fifteen years of silence on issues that daily tormented and destabilized the country. The presidential election of June 12, 1993, annulled on June 23, 1993 caused deaths, killings, arsons, sufferings, human rights abuses, widespread violence, pressurized voluntary resignation of Babangida military regime and haunted Abacha's military palace coup that shook the foundation of the country. Nigeria became a pariah nation, ostracized by the international community. Professor Nwosu's silence for fifteen years was cowardly and condemnable, but it was better late than never.

According to the evidence presented by Professor Humphrey Nwosu, there was a court order of injunction received on June 10,

1993 against the decision to hold the presidential election on June 12, 1993. Thus, without successfully appealing and/or quashing the court injunction order, holding the election was contrary to the rule of law and a contempt of court order could have fetched Professor Nwosu a prison sentence with eventual court declaration that the election held in defiance of court injunction was illegal, null and void.

Unfortunately Professor Nwosu did not use the right judgment by continuing to advise General Babangida to ignore the court order, against the wishes of majority of the members of the National Defence and Security Council (NDSC).

It would be less problematic to postpone the election for one week other than defy court order, defy majority opinions of the Military Council members (NDSC) and not carrying all the stakeholders along before the election was held defiantly. Regrettably, Professor Nwosu continued to advise General Babangida to defy the rule of law and due process, to unilaterally authorize the holding of the presidential election in defiance of all odds. The advice brought serious consequences to all stakeholders. It could lead to a military coup, which it did in the end.

In effect, all the problems of national instability which Nigeria has experienced in relation to June 12, 1993 presidential election up-to-date could be associated to the wrong advice and indiscretion of Professor Nwosu for not properly assessing the legal and sociopolitical implications of holding the election stopped by court order without first quashing the court injunction. It was better to delay the election for a week or two rather than hold it in defiance of all legal and sociopolitical odds and subsequently have the results annulled.

Professor Humphrey Nwosu was not a member of the Military Council, yet, he desperately bursted into their meeting to advise the Military Head of State, General Babangida against the majority decision of the Military Council. Professor Humphrey Nwosu was not a lawyer; yet, he would not allow the former Attorney General, Clement Akpamgbo to do his job. Chief Clement Akpamgbo, the Attorney General advised that the court decision could be quashed with a military decree or through an appeal before the election could be held, but Professor Nwosu advised and did everything different in defiance of all odds and blamed others for his misdirection and poor judgment.

Professor Nwosu, the INEC Chairman in 1993, should have allowed the Attorney General, Chief Clement Akpamgbo and members of the Military Council to take the lead and decide on the situation harmoniously and rationally for him to comply. Instead of that, he (NWOSU) continued to work against the NDSC majority decision and he continued to advise the Military Head of State against the wishes of his military colleagues which resulted in 'bad belle' and possibly led to the annulment of the presidential election, the pressurized exit of General Babangida, the emergence of an Interim Administrator and the palace coup of General Sani Abacha. The advice and actions of Professor Nwosu led to the awful and unpleasant chain of reactions that followed anarchically.

Presidential advisers, aides, associates, government functionaries and all appointed officials should always properly gauge the mood of their work environment in order to minimize the possibility of creating tension and heating the polity. It seems to hold true that there are not many bad leaders, just watch the advisers. General Babangida was too humane and flexible, so, Professor Nwosu took advantage of that and never realized that he was wrong.

In similar fashion, General Abacha was advised by his cronies to convert from his military dictatorship to civilian presidency. He did everything unethical to achieve the objective until his death. He established an assassination military squad that killed and wounded many of his opponents. The country was declared a pariah state and ostracized by the comity of nations. Advisers and aides did all the dirty and criminal work associated to his administration but it was General Abacha that was blamed for everything.

Similarly, presidential advisers, aides, government appointees, associates and some government functionaries selfishly pushed the efforts for the proposed third term tenure of ExPresident Obasanjo. They did a lot of wrong and unethical things within few weeks to the end of his tenure, which almost dampened his great and unique period of accomplishments in office. There are not many bad leaders, but advisers who must be watched very closely. They often do wrong things selfishly only to say in defence that the president gave approval.

It is not a good defence to say that the president approved it, if the adviser, minister or government functionary responsible for obtaining the approval did not make sure that it was the right thing to do before committing the president to approve the submission.

The 'caveat' is, "Those who are in positions of final authority must be careful about what their advisers, aides, associates, ministers and other government functionaries commit them to approve." Advisers, experts, ministers etc. are human beings who have their own selfinterests, biases and personal commitments, which always affect their recommendations presented for approval. Unfortunately, they never want to take full responsibilities for the approval of their recommendations when the leader's approval is faulted and there are problems.

In the year 2000, there were controversies in the presidential election held in the USA, especially in the State of Florida, the 'Sunshine State'. Democrats requested for court intervention and every stakeholder had to wait patiently until the related cases were processed and finalized by the courts up to the Supreme Court. Even though the Supreme Court decision was not popular, and fell short of majority expectations, it was accepted as the final settlement to give peace a chance in the interest of the nation.

Mr. Michael O'Brien, Director of Information of the American Embassy, Lagos wrote to Nigerian Government that a postponement of Nigerian presidential election of 1993 would not be acceptable to the USA despite the injunction order issued by Abuja High Court to stop the election. It may be interesting to ask whether any country's embassy in the world wrote to the US Government to complain about the 2000 US presidential election and the step by step approach/process taken by the courts to clear complaints up to the Supreme Court! It should make sense to Professor Humphrey Nwosu, former Chairman of the Independent National Electoral Commission (INEC) that court orders must be obeyed; due process and the rule of law must be maintained to prevent anarchy, which his actions encouraged.

Professor Nwosu should have allowed the rule of law to work instead of advising the Nigerian Head of Military Government, General Ibrahim Badamosi Babangida to ignore the court injunction contrary to majority opinion from members of the National Defence and Security Council (NDSC). It looked as if Professor Nwosu was pursuing an agenda that conformed with the contents of the letter from Mr. O'Brien of the American Embassy without consideration for 'Nigerian National

Security Interest', the rule of law and the implications of disharmony among members of the Supreme Military Council headed by General Babangida.

If the court order of injunction was not quashed by military decree or a successful appeal against the court order obtained, did Professor Nwosu ever think that other stakeholders might later go back to court to ask for the nullification of the election that was held in defiance of court injunction? What did Professor Nwosu stand to lose personally if the election was postponed for a week in order to cool off and solve all the problems that warranted court intervention? With his level of education and experience, Professor Nwosu should have visualized and concluded that holding the election without clearing the immediate problems surrounding it and impeding its success might complicate matters, and create more terrible chains of problems and consequences than were meant to be solved.

The letter purportedly received from the Director of Information in the US Embassy, Mr. Michael O'Brien said, "We are awaiting the Federal Government's reaction to the court decision. However, any postponement of tomorrow's election is unacceptable to the US Government." The letter was regarded as an undue interference in the internal affairs of Nigeria by majority of the members of the NDSC, but Professor Nwosu chose to advise the Head of State differently and pursued a conflicting agenda desperately at the expense of Nigeria's National Security, the painful outcomes of which still live with Nigerians up till today.

It came up to a point when members of the Military Council (NDSC) stressed the sovereignty of Nigeria by saying, "We are not banana republic. No one should tell us what to do. Postpone the election at least for a week to prove that we are sovereign nation." Yet, Professor Nwosu seemed not to see the handwriting on the wall. He underestimated the problems that were brewing and he continued to advise the Military Head of State to go a different direction and eventually making him the oddmanout. That is not how best to be part of a military administration, which is vulnerable and susceptible to being overthrown by a military coup for minor disagreement among members of the military ruling council.

At another serious juncture, General Sani Abacha who later staged a palace coup shouted with anger on Professor Humphey Nwosu and uttered, "Who do you think you are? You conducted a presidential election the court prohibited. You helped to cause the current political confusion without the support of the members of your commission." Furthermore, the members of the NDSC complained that they wondered why their military colleague (General Babangida), the Military Head of State "should be listening to a civilian official (Nwosu) who was not even a member of the ruling council."

Yet, Professor Nwosu did not realize the enormity of the problems his advice and actions were causing, and about to cause the Head of State, General Babangida; the National Defence and Security Council (NDSC); the two contesting political parties (SDP and NRC) and the entire nation. He did not understand that not even the US Government would have ignored or disobeyed a court order but would pursue an appeal to its logical conclusion contrary to what Professor Nwosu was pressurizing General Babangida to do.

Most people who do not go beyond 4year college/university degree know that one must obey a court order or appeal it, if one is not satisfied. There are consequences for ignoring a court order or if somebody contemns a court order. General Abacha who was not an academician was furious like many others about Professor Nwosu's actions of contempt of court.

The former Attorney General, Chief Clement Akpamgbo advised that the Abuja High Court injunction order should be obeyed, be appealed or perhaps a new military decree could be promulgated to override the order of the court. He did his job well in line with the rule of law and due process, but Professor Nwosu who was not a lawyer advised differently and continued to do so with impunity because somebody listened to him. He (Nwosu) complicated the problems and passed the buck by blaming General Abacha and Attorney General, Chief Akpamgbo instead of blaming himself for the problems he caused the nation from June 12, 1993 up till today, and lasting for as long as there would be June 12 (Remembrance Day) in every year to come.

Also, General Sani Abacha as Deputy Head of State and member of NDSC did his job well by complaining, castigating and redirecting Professor Nwosu about the implications of his persistent advice to

General Babingida, which was contrary to the majority decision being reached by the NDSC. Unfortunately, it was only Professor Nwosu who did not see and appreciate the damages he was causing.

The big lesson to learn from this episode is that Nigerians should start to blame presidential aides, advisers, appointed officials and other government functionaries directly for wrongs committed by them instead of putting all the blames on the president or leader. Presidents or leaders cannot see everything that their delegates handle.

Also, Presidents and leaders should always look closely and suspiciously at the advice they are given realizing that presidential advisers, aides, experts and other officers who work for them have their own interests, agenda, biases and human imperfections which always direct their reports, recommendations and policy implementations. Professor Nwosu should take responsibility for his wrong advice actions and poor judgment in the events culminating in the annulment of June 12, 1993 presidential election and the terrible outcomes that followed.

Whenever there is no choice in avoiding to pick any of the evils confronting oneself, the best alternative choice would be to choose the one with the least problems and implications. Professor Nwosu did not do that, but simply passed buck. May God/Allah always give us the 'Wisdom of Solomon' to enable us pick the best alternative choice.

Undoubtedly, Professor Nwosu's counsel and actions failed to unite and harmonize the deliberations of the members of the NDSC headed by General Babangida and thereby precipitated crises and his exit. His exit was followed by the appointment of an Interim Administrator, Chief Ernest Shonekan and his overthrow by General Abacha in a palace coup. Above all, the presidential election was annulled on June 23, 1993 and the Independent National Electoral Commission (INEC) headed by Processor Nwosu was disbanded, rendering him jobless.

The big lesson is that the unpleasant chain reactions could have been avoided with the best professional advisement that would have united but not divided and compounded the sociopolitical and national security problems of the country. As a result of impatience, mistrust, disunity, and inability to make rational decisions, everybody lost individually and collectively. The nation (Nigeria) regressed into dictatorship, vindictiveness, human rights abuses, assassinations of political opponents, money laundering, fraud, corruption, economic downturn and sociopolitical instability which were avoidable.

Above all, ExSenate President Nnamani's alleged activities to become an Interim President as revealed by INEC Chairman Iwu were dangerous, unpatriotic and condemnable.

CHAPTER 17

OPTIMISM ABOUT NIGERIAN FUTURE

It is becoming clearer than ever before that Nigeria with her great people of over 140 million has wonderful hope for a brilliant and prosperous future. All socio-economic and political indicators show that Nigeria is rising to become one of the twenty greatest countries in the world within the first three decades of the twenty-first millennium.

Nigeria, the most populous and richest nation of Black People in the world is blessed with enormous wealth of natural resources of oil, gas, bitumen, gold, tantalite, iron ore, zinc, phosphate etc. In terms of human resources, highly qualified Nigerians, both academically and professionally can be found all over the world in various spheres of world endeavours. Nigerians in general are second to none in smartness, brilliance, intelligence and enviable accomplishments.

With the rule of law and due process coupled with financial, economic and sociopolitical reforms being vigorously, selflessly and relentlessly pursued, the Nigerian nation has become more stable, responsible, transparent and accountable more than ever before. The new shining image of Nigeria has attracted both foreign and local investments beyond expectations.

The foreign reserve rose from nothing to over sixty billion dollars, inflation was down to single digit and the Gross Domestic Product (GDP) had a progressive annual increase of seven percent, which was favourably comparable with most of the best records in the world. The

Nigerian economy is improving at a fast rate, but requires single digit interest and inflation rates of below 5% to perform best.

Also, unemployment rate has continued to go down remarkably. Impressively, the Nigerian foreign debt has become little or nothing after $18 billion was written off by creditors and the balance of $12.6 billion was paid off by Obasanjo Administration in the year 2006. Foreign debt was calculated to be less than $4 billion in 2008. Acquiring additional foreign loan by Yar'Adua Administration is poisonous to Nigerian posterity. It is hoped that the government understands the implications and listens to Nigerians to avoid being neocolonized.

From 1960 to 1999, Nigeria was confronted with plethora of problems that only God/Allah could solve because of their enormities. Many Nigerians died in the problems, many migrated to Europe and America in search of greener pastures, while others who had no resources to make a choice remained. As a result of prolonged sufferings with the end not in sight, many Nigerians became the doubting Thomases about a change in their situation and worried about their survival.

Many people assumably believe that nothing good can come out of Nigeria. There are people who reach that conclusion honestly on basis of their past horrible experiences built up between 1960 and 1999. The evils that befell Nigeria for forty years of independence included coups d'etat, the civil war, corruption, frauds, smuggling of contraband, arms and ammunition and petroleum products, human trafficking, anarchy, killing of innocent people, robberies, money laundering, illegal oil bunkering, vandalization of public infrastructures, and economic and financial crimes which were committed with impunity.

Most Nigerians looked hopeless and helpless because of leadership failures and irresponsiveness for almost four decades. Sometimes, those entrusted with power and authority to stop, control, prevent and deter crimes were the ones who condoned them. Some of the criminals were described as elite ones who were regarded as sacred cows and untouchables. Above all, the image of the country was tainted by human rights abuses, which earned Nigeria the label of a pariah state by the International Community between 1993 and 1998.

Anyone who witnessed above-mentioned situations in Nigeria for so long without changes in forty years can honestly say that nothing good can come out of Nigeria but there is still hope. Nigerians who actually suffered for forty years would be fifty-five years old and above who must have spent over half of their live expectancy without any hope of change for the better. In such circumstances, one cannot blame such honestly pessimistic Nigerians. At such age, most people who suffered indignities for four decades would have resigned to fate and conceded defeat. It is natural.

On the other hand, there are hardcore pessimists who see nothing good in Nigeria unconsciously, and who are happy about Nigeria's situation because they gain from it and wish the ugly situation continues. Many times, derogatory statements about Nigeria are made by political opponents to undermine the leadership at the helm of affairs in government even when considerable and relentless efforts are being made to change things for the betterment of the people.

Sooner than later, it is expected that a new dawn would have risen full of hope and optimism for Nigerians with a leadership that is visionary, imaginative, energetic, responsible, accountable, responsive, promising and committed to clean Nigeria of corruption, fraud, crimes and all acts that are inimical to the best interest of the nation. The machinery set up to return Nigeria to civility, dignity and respect within the comity of nations yielded wonderful dividends. Nigeria has been able to host renowned international conferences of heads of governments, the Commonwealth, African Union, African Games, NEPAD, ECOWAS, and Nigeria has established herself as the peace and power broker in Africa.

There are pessimists or skeptics who simply want to settle personal scores or want cheap popularity by criticizing and insulting the leadership who are performing Herculean tasks of rebuilding Nigeria that was systematically vandalized, sabotaged and destroyed year in and year out for about forty years by the elites, especially the military. Surely, it takes time to resuscitate any structure that was gradually vandalized, sabotaged and destroyed day in and day out for four decades.

Never, never again shall Nigeria retrogress into those terrible days. To solve the people's problems, Nigeria does not need calls for mass destructive action, calls for ungovernableness, calls for general protests or calls for strikes and lockouts. Such calls are retrogressional and not in the best interest of Nigeria's peaceful existence, growth and development, economic survival and prosperity.

Nigeria's democratic experiment should be fashioned, guarded and guided to ensure freedom of speech and expression but not licentiousness to malign, provoke or defame the leadership with untruth or sensationalism that abuses the right of free speech. Where is your culture, ethics, tradition of respect and dignity for the truth, true speech and true reporting? If you are a patriot, a nationalist with leadership potential, you do not need to insult, provoke or put any leader down to make your point clear or to be recognized with your potential or your standing in society.

Hence, the 'Freedom of Information Bill' must contain provision that makes all publishers responsible and accountable for the information they disseminate. Character assassination must be a crime. You can be constructive and objective but civil and not provocative in your criticism. Everybody must be made accountable and responsible by the system we operate as Nigerians equally guided by the rule of law.

Also, remember to offer brilliant suggestions for policy improvement without calling any government official a fraud or a rambo. At the age of forty and above, any Nigerian who cannot control his/her tongue, anger, temperament and general disposition should explain his/her benefit to present and future Nigerian generations. It must be of great concern to you as a Nigerian about what legacies you are leaving to future generations with your attitude of intolerance, divisionism, poor temperament and arrogance.

Some elite Nigerians, especially outdated academicians propounding unworkable theories and causing confusion should cool off and calm down, recognizing that what was best yesterday or yesteryears may not be good enough for today. They need to adapt to new learning and adopt new changes, which manifest daily. Nobody knows it all. Higher education and professionalism should make you humble, respectful and intelligent, not arrogant. Nigeria has been able to produce many brilliant academicians and professionals today more than ever before. Perhaps what you accomplished at fifty plus, a twenty-five year old Nigerian now has more. Hence, it does not pay to be arrogant for what elites think they have achieved in this country. Nigerians are tired of unhealthy rivalries and obstinacies in politics that dominated early post-independence era, which bring the nation into the unusual predicament. Yet, unfortunately, most elite Nigerians have not learnt their lessons.

A Nigerian Professor, Tam David West, was reported to have said the following as published in the *Vanguard News* of Monday, June 13, 2005: "If the University of Ibadan gives my son full scholarship to come and study here, I will not support it. It is as bad as that. The education system should make the bright, brighter and the less bright, bright. Our system makes the bright, mediocre and the mediocre, a failure." This statement is extreme pessimism, which cannot be the best judgment of the learned Professor with the great antecedents that we heard about.

To be taken seriously, Professor Tam David West should have highlighted the real problems in the educational system of Nigeria and provide suggestions for solution. There cannot be a mediocre among Nigerian university graduating students and graduates. Interestingly, this particular Professor's son, a new breed, may be optimistic about everything Nigerian, completely different from his father's pessimism quoted above.

Even if this Professor's statement is five percent right, who is to blame besides the operators of Nigerian educational system? You cannot blame the students nor the system but educators who design, execute and supervise academic programmes. The statement that generalizes the entire products of Nigerian universities as mediocres must have emanated from a terribly negative mind, which sees nothing good in good and hardworking Nigerian students and educators. Regrettably, many of the old minds that achieved a lot in the past but stopped learning, cannot appreciate the changing, progressive world. To them, everything about the New World and new breed is condemnable because they stopped learning, stopped changing and stopped moving with the progressive world.

Although Nigerian educational system is not perfect, but people should better speak positively on how to improve it other than waste valuable time condemning everything that is Nigerian. It is a bad workman who quarrels with his tools and whoever sees nothing good in others should reexamine himself/herself.

Most colleague academic authors and real professors in America attain the Doctor of Philosophy (Ph. D.) Degree with many years of teaching experience and they continue in extensive research work daily, publishing books and not immersed in chasing money and political offices, but additional knowledge in their fields of expertise. They stay in schools/colleges/ universities and teach, thus imparting knowledge. Why is it different in Nigeria where it is difficult to know who the real professors are?

Unfortunately, many elite Nigerians who should positively contribute to move the country forward progressively, waste valuable time in condemning everything that is Nigerian, and they take delight in fault-finding to justify their pessimism. With their 'holier than thou attitude', they pretend to be the best and perfect guys. Such elites who are pessimistic about everything Nigerian, are not only part of the problems, but they contribute significantly to the problems. Sadism makes them unhappy when Nigeria progresses because they do not like being proven wrong about their pessimism.

If you love your country, Nigeria, help make the difference through nonviolence and nonprovocation in your actions, thoughts and writings. Heating Nigerian polity unnecessarily and hurting the country simply because people belong to different political camps is not in the best interest of this nation, the only country you can call your own. Constructive, objective, genuine, healthy and honest criticism of government or leadership policies and activities should be presented in a way that helps the country to grow, to develop and to move forward without heating it.

At the PDP convention of December 2003, the ExSenate President, Adolphus Wabara, hinted that the National Assembly had resolved to work with the Executive and Judiciary to further the course of democracy. He added that previous antagonism between the Executive and the Legislature made a mockery of the concept of separation of powers. He clarified that past antagonism overheated the polity unnecessarily and frustrated attempts at development.

He emphasized, "Our people and the country were the worse for it." He also said, "We are also resolved to exercise our power of legislation, representation and oversight with responsibility and maturity for the glory of the party, the people and the country." To show concern for the people's suffering, as a result of economic reform measures embarked upon by the Executive, the ExSenate President said, "The National Assembly has resolved to give adequate support to the reform agenda of the Executive while putting in measures to cushion some of the painful effects of the reform."

His assertions above are full of concern for the people, the country's growth and development in peace and full cooperation with the Presidency and the Judiciary. There are a lot of great things in stock for Nigeria, if the people are united and are at peace with one another.

In the same wise, the Ex-Speaker of the House of Representatives, Alhaji Aminu Masari, expressed concern for increasing rate of poverty and disease in the country, the continuing depreciation of Nigerian currency and the increasing difficulty of the people's survival. He recognized that hunger and unemployment had contributed to high rate of crime. He then showed appreciation of the President's efforts to change the tide of poverty in Nigeria. Empirically, Nigerians today are favourably competitive and comparable with the best in the world academically and professionally. With the focus of the present Nigerian government, there is no doubt that there will be a great Nigeria to bequeath to future generations.

From the inauguration speech of the ExPresident Olusegun Obasanjo on May 29, 2003, Nigerians can draw the greatest inspiration and optimism from his speech which expressed a "vision of a united Nigeria, a strong Nigeria, a prosperous Nigeria, a peaceful Nigeria, a just Nigeria, indeed a great Nigeria." ExPresident Obasanjo acknowledged that the Nigerian situation was transitioning from "the darkest episode of our history to the dawn of hope." He expressed optimism about Nigeria thus, "The nation is getting stronger and the future is looking much, much brighter."

He described corruption as the antithesis of development and articulated government determination to "fight this evil to a standstill." He expressed his strongest belief that Nigerians could change. He reiterated that he had repeatedly called for moral rectitude and that he would continue to repeat the message.

He said, "I simply refuse to accept cynical view that Nigerians prefer chaos to order. I cannot endorse the view that Nigerians are innately corrupt. I cannot believe that Nigerians would, in preference for a decent and civilized society, opt for one in which law and order is disregarded and regulations are circumvented as the norm. I am a firm believer in the good nature of the Nigerian, and I will continue to appeal to that good nature. My unshaken and unshakable faith, belief in and commitment to Nigeria is anchored in my equally strong belief in the intrinsic good nature of humans, and that given the right environment and impetus, man can change for the better."

Above philosophical statements of ExPresident Olusegun Obasanjo should form the bedrock of all Nigerians' hopes and aspirations and help them channel their behaviour toward achieving a greater Nigeria for future generations.

During the commemoration of the 69th birthday ceremony of a revered religious leader Cardinal Anthony Olubunmi Okojie, on Wednesday, June 29, 2005, Lagos, he purportedly declared that Nigeria did not deserve a debt relief because of her affluence. He argued that an affluent Nigeria that could raise ₦6 billion in twelve hours for the construction of a presidential library did not deserve such a gesture. He was alleged to have said that the gesture to relieve Nigeria of foreign debt should be delayed until Nigeria had a better government.

In the Punch News of Thursday, June 30, 2005, the religious leader allegedly said, "What have they done with the excess oil revenue? If such gesture is granted us now, I am sure our leaders will not be able to account for it. The time has not come for debt relief. It is not fair for us to embark on this campaign now."

It is noted that presidential library is not new in the civilized and developed world and the six billion naira said to be donated for the presidential library is less than fifty million dollars compared with almost twenty billion dollars 'debt writeoff' granted to Nigeria by the Paris Club within twenty-four hours of Cardinal Okojie's speech calling for delay of debt relief to Nigeria. The statements quoted above do not seem to be in the best interest of Nigeria.

It is unfortunate that a man is never honoured in his own community, state, country or among his own people. It was the same way that the Lord Jesus Christ was badly treated by His own people. The United Nations (UN), the Commonwealth, the African Union (AU), ECOWAS, NEPAD, the World Bank, IMF, Nigerian Creditor Nations, ExBritish Prime Minister (Tony Blair), British Prime Minister Gordon Brown, who was Chancellor of the Exchequer, and others that matter in the world praised the Nigerian government for unprecedented national reform activities and the relentless fights against elite fraudulent and corrupt practices.

Unfortunately, some lucky and wealthy Nigerians who nurse personal animosity against government leaders often close their eyes and pretend to see nothing good in Nigeria. American and other world religious leaders have not been denigrating their home governments unnecessarily. It is hoped Nigeria, a secular state, will not be an exception. Religious leaders who make partisan political, derogatory speeches all the time may be running the risk of knocking their heads against politicians. That is religious suicide because different churchgoers have different political affiliations. Church leaders must play 'partisan political party neutrality'.

With commendations flowing into Nigeria from the world leaders unprecedentedly, it was most unbelievable that Nigerian pessimists still existed in 2005 up till present time. With the great efforts of ExPresident Obasanjo, ExMinister of Finance (Dr.) Mrs. Okonjo-Iweala, and the overseas tours of some members of the Legislature to plead for debt relief, it was inconceivable that any Nigerian existed in 2005 that could advocate for the postponement of Nigeria's debt relief and the enormous benefits attainable therefrom.

If Obasanjo Administration bailed Nigeria out of pariah status, for which Nigeria was known between 1993 and 1998, to become the beloved country and leader in Africa in particular and loved by the world community generally, then, it might not be easy to expect a government that surpasses such administration.

If Obasanjo Administration succeeded in national reforms and had unprecedentedly fought fraud and corruption among elites, it might not be easy to expect a government that would surpass such administration.

If Obasanjo Administration succeeded to secure a cancellation of over sixty-seven percent, $18 billion of its foreign debt from Paris Club as at the end of June 2005 with promises for more relief, then, it might not be easy to expect an administration that would surpass such accomplishing administration.

The result of the cancellation of almost all the foreign debts of Nigeria demonstrated that God/Allah worked in a mysterious way and confirmed that the work of God/Allah was incomprehensible. It showed that God/ Allah brightened the hopes and aspirations of Nigerians in a miraculous way. Yar'Adua Administration should avoid taking Nigeria back to square one in the way his regime is hobnobbing with World Bank and IMF to acquire foreign loan. It is like obtaining credit cards which can be disastrous for Nigerians yet unborn.

President Obasanjo emphasized, "Nigeria got out of this debt quagmire by resolving and working hard to break with the past by identifying new voices and new leaders, by rejecting business as usual and voting for new values of accountability, transparency, fair competition, social justice and the upliftment of the living standards of Nigerians."

He referred to the pessimists, the doubting Thomases by saying, "I can only say for those that doubted that we would ever get debt relief or those that felt that we were junketing around the world doing nothing, history and events have vindicated us. We are challenged by their position. But we urge them all to change their attitudes and join hands with other Nigerians to build a new society that all Nigerians can enjoy."

President Obasanjo salvaged the image of Nigeria from being a pariah state, which was ostracized from the international community for human rights abuses, corruption and fraud. Nigeria rose to greater heights of respectability, dignity and honour in the eyes of the world in record time. It is expedient to ask, "What good things did those falsely crying wolf, wolf, do for Nigeria before, during and after Obasanjo Administration?"

For how long are you going to be pessimistic about your country, Nigeria, especially when you deliberately close your eyes to all the great world events that were hosted by Nigeria since May 29, 2003 – the All Africa Games, the Conference of Commonwealth Heads of Governments, the NEPAD, AU, ECOWAS, etc. If the image of Nigeria were not great, all those international events would not have been staged on Nigerian soil.

> (1) If you think Nigeria is the worst because of human imperfections in the last general elections (presidential, federal, state and local legislatures), then think about violent election events in other parts of the world. You will realize that Nigeria is not as bad as you think.
>
> (2) If you think that Nigerians are the most corrupt and

fraudulent, then look at the magnitude of US corporate frauds, the financial malpractices that occurred in Enron, Anderson, world.com, Halliburton and many other establishments in the world, you will realize that Nigeria is not as bad as you think.

(3) If you think that Nigerians are among the poorest people in the world, then visit most American and European cities at 6 a.m. in the morning to see the number of the poor, homeless and jobless people on the streets and under the bridges that have just been released from temporary shelters. Then you will realize that Nigeria is not as bad as you think.

(4) If you think that educational standard is falling in Nigeria, please visit American and European classrooms to see the level of students' response to academics despite the provision of the best academic infrastructure anybody can imagine in the world. Then you will realize that if Nigerian educators reduce the tendencies and actions of incessant strikes and lockouts, then, it may not be worth it to go overseas to study. Nigerian educators must be effectively supervised to do their work. That being so, Nigerian educational standard ranks at par with the best in the world with improved infrastructure.

(5) If you think that Nigeria is the worst for killings, crimes and gangsterism, then find out the activities and number of serial killers and other serious crimes daily in America, Russia and other countries. You will thank God that you are safer in Nigeria than in any of those other countries mentioned. Statistically, daily murders, armed robberies and other serious deadly crimes in each of fifty states of the USA are more than what happens in Nigeria in a year of 365 days. Crimewise, Nigeria is safer than most parts of the world.

(6) One of the most terrible things that some misguided Nigerians did differently that was very shameful was the '419 advanced fee frauds' which tormented the whole world unabatedly for years. Fortunately, the responsiveness of

the Nigerian government is crushing this menacing evil.

How anybody in his/her right senses could fall for these fraudsters beats every imagination. For example, when I was faxed three consecutive letters from the 419 fraudsters from Lagos addresses to the US, I responded that instead of asking me for advance fee, they should send me advance money for travel tickets to and from Geneva, Switzerland, as well as money to cover initial expenses which could be deductible from the huge commission which they promised. Then, they stopped bothering me because they realized that I was not stupid.

If in reality, there were millions of American dollars stashed in three boxes at Geneva Airport by Abacha family, why would the fraudsters not go and get the boxes themselves? Those who give out their money to 'advanced fee fraudsters' are about forty percent guilty of greed, encouraging the commission of fraud and taking part in illegal business.

It was also easy to know that Mohammed Abacha would not be stupid to let his father's money lie in Geneva Airport just for anybody to grab. We thank God/Allah that the menacing snakes of the syndicate of 419 fraudsters were decapitated when the leaders were arrested and detained while being prosecuted. With the same determination and teamwork among the Presidency, the Legislature and Judiciary, Nigerian problems of corruption, fraud, insecurity, economic and financial crimes and other vicious felonies can be surmounted and stamped out of Nigeria.

It is unfortunate that those who are not honest about their criticism and pessimism of Nigeria and her leadership want to make people believe that Nigeria is the worst and cannot change. It is recalled that more serious fraud plaguing the USA presently is 'identity theft fraud' and electronic scams spreading like wild fire all over the country.

These fraudsters find out people's Social Security numbers and drivers' licence numbers, which they utilize to empty their victims' bank accounts as well as make credit purchases, which often put their victims in debt for the rest of their lives. Identity theft fraud in the USA has caused a lot of havoc, and it knows no bounds. It is very sophisticated and very hard to detect and arrest the perpetrators of the fraud. The US authorities are seriously cracking down on the perpetrators of 'identity theft fraud'.

There are similar fraudulent groups that have bases in Spain, United Kingdom and most other countries. They write individuals and tell them that they have won lotteries worth hundred thousands of money in euro currency and ask for one percent of the winnings as administrative and agency commission in advance before the winnings can be deposited into winners' bank accounts. There are serious fraudulent practices all over the world; Nigeria's case is not an exception, but thank God/Allah, the crackdown on corruption and fraud by Nigerian government is very effective, and it is yielding remarkable dividends.

The problems of corruption, frauds, economic and financial crimes, which Nigeria has, are imported and alien to Nigerian culture as far back as early years of Nigerian independence. Every Nigerian is brought up with strict discipline at home, at school and in society. It takes a whole village or community to raise a Nigerian child. Every Nigerian child has a family name to keep sanctified and make the family proud. Every Nigerian child is taught to know whose son/daughter he/she is. It is not Nigeria that has anything to change but some Nigerian elites who forget their family ideals, forget godliness, are ostentatious and shameless, live above their means, forget their birthplace and whose sons/daughters they are.

Nigerians simply need to reeducate themselves about their value system, and stop honouring vanity. They should realize that there should be no sacred cows and no untouchables in the dispensation of justice, and that nobody is above the law. It is unfortunate that some Nigerian elites have gone astray. They continue to devalue Nigeria and Nigerian lives, but Nigeria is blessed and remains very strong.

The challenge before Nigerians generally and the leadership in particular (the Presidency, Legislature and Judiciary) is, "What legacy shall they bequeath to the unborn, the future generations? What Nigeria shall they hand over to the future? What do they want Nigerian children, grandchildren, great-grand-children and great-great-grand-children to be? Nigerians must all act in the best interest of Nigeria whether they are in government or opposition so that history may judge us fairly and rightly. If we fail to act when we are bestowed with the power and authority to clean Nigeria and set it in the right direction of economic growth and prosperity, it may be difficult for posterity to forgive the present Nigerians.

To continue to say that Nigeria is poor is demonstrating ingratitude to God/Allah about what Nigeria has compared with many other countries in the world. Some past and present government functionaries wasted Nigeria's talents and resources by acting as the Biblical prodigal son. Nigeria is blessed with abundant resources of human, material, mineral, natural and fiscal resources that could make Nigeria one of the wealthiest in the world, but they were mismanaged, wasted and stashed away in foreign private bank accounts by some elites and leaders.

An alleged $170 billion flight capital from Nigeria to foreign countries could have sponsored investment, employment generation and economic growth and prosperity in Nigeria. The huge capital flight described as unreasonable and senseless, just like carrying coal to Newcastle or sand to the desert was great insensitivity committed by a few Nigerian elites who hypocritically called themselves leaders, elders, patriots, nationalists, etc. at the expense of the generality of other less privileged Nigerians on whose backs they rode to positions of trust and political power which they eventually betrayed.

The resources that can make Nigeria one of the wealthiest nations are prevalent in Nigeria. The elites and leaders only need to explore, tap and manage them effectively and efficiently. Why have some Nigerian elites conspired with foreigners to cheat and make Nigeria lose millions of naira daily? Can Nigerian elites and leaders patriotically stop wasting Nigerian resources and save the money for national development? Elites connections, business intrigues and constraints will make it hard and difficult to clean Nigeria completely, but Nigerian leaders should continue the fight against corruption and frauds relentlessly because majority of Nigerians, posterity and history support them unequivocally.

Fortunately, Nigeria does not face year in year out natural disasters, challenges and risks of earthquakes, icebergs, hailstorms, volcanoes, tornadoes, winter, wild fires, suicide bombers, serial killers, sniper suspects and the kind of mental disease epidemics prevalent in developed countries, which are never widely reported. Without checking and opening up their closets, developed countries often deceive their people by making them believe that the diseases in their midst emanate from Africathe Blackman.

In the developed countries, there are worse cases of illnesses in their hospitals and mental health, mental retardation establishments than what occurs in Africa and other developing countries. What about the number of diseases that are said to be incurable, which traditional doctors can handle perfectly in Nigeria? Fidson Healthcare Limited, an indigenous Nigerian firm, started to manufacture AntiRetroviral Drugs (ARVs) – Virex for AIDS treatment at low and affordable price. The company and its chairman, Fidelis Ayebae, deserve hearty congratulations. Nigeria should encourage and fund more medical researches.

Nigeria's disaster is that some elites and past leaderships were not appreciative of what God/Allah has done for the country. As a result, they embarked on frauds, corruption, civil war, coups d'etat, economic and financial crimes and sabotage culminating in the devaluation of Nigerian lives. As a result, many Nigerians unavoidably resorted to risky migration to seek solace, green pastures and the golden fleece overseas where there is none but a lot of hardship, suffering, discrimination and inclement weather conditions which are strange in African continent. The situation is comparable with journeying from Lagos (South Western Nigeria) to Sokoto (North Western Nigeria) when what you are looking for is in the pocket of your trousers (Sokoto).

One of the first things to do to save Nigeria is that Nigerians should stop worshipping vain human beings for their wealth if the source is questionable. There should be less emphasis on people's state of origin, ethnicity, religion, connections and relations but recognize people on basis of their productive capabilities, responsibility, transparency, ingenuity and exemplariness that suit the aspirations of Nigerians in their march toward political stability and economic prosperity.

Why do the elites conspire with foreigners to cheat and make Nigeria lose billions of naira daily? Can't that be stopped and saved for national development? Nigerian authorities must closely monitor for conspiratory external and local influences, which are usually responsible for the wrongful management, distribution and utilization of Nigerian resources. Deregulation and liberalization of Nigeria's business ventures will also help if the policy is geared to the best interest of the people of Nigeria with safeguards that can eliminate abuses from foreigners and local elite conspirators who scam Nigerians.

Money saved from eliminating corruption, frauds, economic and financial crimes, money laundering, smuggling, and vandalization of infrastructures, etc. can be utilized for national growth and development toward national prosperity. The country requires effective and efficient management that can contribute immensely to uplift the standard of living of Nigerians and enhance their life expectancy.

In Mid-December 2003, ExPresident Obasanjo asked the Nigerian media to "help in building a new Nigeria where the entrepreneurial, patriotic and resilient spirit of the Nigerian will be brought to the core." He called on the media to help the people rekindle their 'can do' spirit for the benefit of posterity. He remarked, " Let us not shy away from the fact that some sections of the media have failed to appreciate the value of our democracy. Indeed, they at times appear dedicated to undermining our democratic enterprise. They seem to have forgotten so soon where we were just a few years ago. They give the impression that they are capable of seeing and reporting only the negative. This is not fair to Nigerians. A person who sees no good in others may have no goodness in himself."

He emphasized that the Guild of Editors should check the infiltration of quarks into the media profession, and that quarks were ruining the reputation of the profession and its practitioners. He enjoined them to set "high standards, monitor the profession, encourage retraining and expand opportunities for refresher programmes."

It is not unlikely that a person might find himself or herself aggrieved and in the opposition at any time. The love of and interest in one's country should be paramount and always override all other considerations, which should ensure that the opposition becomes a part of the solution of Nigeria's problems, rather than become a part of the problems because leaders will go and other leaders will come, but Nigeria shall forever remain.

A notable example was the US presidential election, which ran into similar problems in 1999/2000. The stakeholders (Democratic and Republican Parties) followed due process without calling for mass action, name-calling or resorting to any treasonable tendencies. They proceeded to the Supreme Court, which ruled in favour of the man who ostensibly did not win the majority or popular vote.

The decision given by the court had a lot of doubts, yet the Democrats accepted the Supreme Court verdict without calling for mass violence that would render the US ungovernable as the losing parties did in Nigeria. The Democrats in US accepted the verdict that was not in their favour because they put the interests of their country, the USA first above all other considerations and allowed peace to reign supreme. They did not consider winning as a 'do or die' game. They did not consider ruling the country as their birthright.

Expresident Obasanjo admitted passionately that Nigerians witnessed harsh life realities, despair, gloom, bleakness, setbacks, darkness, rotten infrastructures, frustrations, serious maladministrations resulting in social disarray, tyrannical rule and human rights abuses which traumatized Nigerian national psyche. He pleaded that it was time to rise and put all impediments aside and work together.

Contributing further to discourage pessimism, he referred to hard core pessimists as prophets of doom who were loud and clear with their predictions of an impending Armageddon when they predicted post events of the 2003 presidential and general elections. He said that they were proved wrong. He described Nigerians who are pessimistic as those who could not see anything good or have anything positive to say about their fellow citizens and their country at home or in the scheme of things in the world. Pessimists included those who never gave government policies a chance to work and those who always begin their analysis and comments with negative ideas and posture.

He elaborated, "I have in my short span of life, seen tangled lives made straight, wrongs righted, marriages remade, friends reconciled, families reunited, businesses and business relations revived, desolate structures rehabilitated and refurbished, faith rekindled and despair turned to hope. It is all in the mind; it is a matter of attitude and a touch of God. Any situation and any person can be changed. Even Nigeria can be changed, and it is changing."

He challenged Nigerian pessimists thus, "If you cannot love Nigeria and be positive about your country and make constructive contributions to its sustenance, unity, development and growth, I should ask, what sort of a Nigerian are you?" He added, "The measure of patriotism and dedication to common and collective good is not to become pessimistic and cynical, but to join hands to work hard for the nation, the community, family and individual. That is how to build a nation."

He continued, "I am more optimistic Nigerians can change and be changed to see the glass as half full rather than half empty. What we need is faith and belief in God, in ourselves, in Nigeria and in what is Nigerian." He added, "I believe in the innate goodness of an average Nigerian which should be developed and utilized for building a peaceful, stable, secure, just, equitable, prosperous and corruptfree society." He warned, "Nigerians should look back and ensure that now and in future, the mistakes of the past are never repeated."

He directed, "Our vision, our sight and our attention should be placed on a high pedestal and on high horizon such that by the end of the first decade of this century, Nigeria reaches its trajectory for sustainable development, stability and growth." He emphasized, "This is not a pipe dream. It is an attainable objective, and I challenge all Nigerians to join hands, leave the frustrations of the past behind, and be part of this robust movement for a greater Nigeria. Together, in such a spirit of confidence in ourselves, faith in God and dynamic optimism, we can make the difficult easy, the impossible possible, and miracles to happen."

Some elites misguidedly described the unprecedented foreign debt relief to Nigeria as fake. Such pessimism is not only unpatriotic but also sad and unfortunate. It looks crystal clear that any progress Nigeria makes while moving forward is a problem to some sadists. Such elites are just not civilized nor possess the right education and value judgment. Those who see nothing good about Nigeria may not be good themselves.

In appreciation of the unprecedented debt relief, Nigerians must be reminded of what the Ex-Speaker of the House of Representatives, Alhaji Aminu Bello Masari said, "There has never been debt relief, either original or fake." It is very true that the July 2005 debt relief was unprecedented, and those who worked hard for it to happen should be commended. Nigerians in the Diaspora fully appreciate and commend the relentless and selfless efforts of the Presidency, the Legislative Leadership and Nigerian groups who demonstrated publicly to request for debt relief. May God/Allah continue to answer Nigeria's prayers (amen).

Nigeria could have gone to International Court of Justice (ICJ) or could have repudiated the debt as suggested by some legal luminaries and wellmeaning Nigerians, but such steps are not without serious implications. By going to court (ICJ), Nigeria would spend millions of dollars as legal fees for years, and the result would be unpredictable. By repudiating the debt, Nigeria would have been branded a financial risk and unworthy of further credit by international creditors. Such action would scare foreign investors away.

ExPresident Obasanjo deserved a commendation for his wellcalculated fighting spirit as a soldier, which ended the civil war in 1970 and stopped further sufferings as well as his almost six years peaceful pursuit of debt relief which yielded incredible results beyond easy comprehension. The lesson is that with patience, steadfastness, forthrightness, determination, good spirit and prayer as ExPresident Obasanjo did, one can move a mountain.

The critics of ExPresident Obasanjo called him loner, rambo, fake, etc. They distorted his leadership qualities of excellence, transparency, discipline, consistency, assertiveness and business acumen, and changed them to stubbornness and opinionation, which have nothing to do with his wonderful and invaluable achievements for Nigeria. A great leader, Obasanjo like Ronald Reagan of the USA and Tony Blair of UK, must be stubborn and opinionated. It is the duty of great advisers to work harder to provide better expert opinions in order to change the leader's opinions for better governance. May God/Allah always give our leaders the right, honest and capable advisers. Remember, there is hardly any bad leader without many bad advisers!

On Tuesday, January 31, 2006, at the Second Economic Conference in Abuja, international investors asserted that the thirty-five percent return on investment in Nigeria was the global highest. Fitch, the international rating agency, confirmed the report. With all these great records of economic and political accomplishments in Nigeria, it should not be difficult for the most diehard pessimists to understand that Nigeria is moving forward at greater strides, better and faster than ever before.

In most cases, if one has a tough decision to make that has nationwide implications, it is better to consult with one's elders and not coactivists alone for fear of being misled by their group exuberance. These real elders who may not have chains of university degrees have acquired enormous wealth of life experiences and wisdom that can have more successful real life application than what can be obtained from academic authors and books in Europe and America.

For example, the parents of Abia State former Governor, His Highness, the Oba of Benin and some real elders helped former Governor Kalu out with wonderfully rich advisement during his problems with Chief Anenih and some PDP leaders. The elders who helped him were not university professors or political activists whose advice might have made matters worse. There are still real elders in abundance in all Nigerian nationalities in most towns and villages, but many elites who feel they know too much often ignore them until they run into trouble.

Nigerians should be reminded about events that made the Western Nigerians of the 1950's and 1960's who were first in Africa in most things to become relegated to the third place in Nigeria because of leadership confrontation with the federal authorities, which led to the declaration of the 'state of emergency' in Western Nigeria. The Yorubas suffered a lot of humiliations, indignities and degradation during the time, perpetrated jointly by the North and the East coalition primarily because of Western Nigerian leadership disunity, divisionism, intransigence, obstinacy and lack of political diplomacy to be team players at the time.

How on earth could Western Region (the Yorubas) at that time beat a combination of the political trickery and stratagem of the North and East coalition to subjugate Western Nigeria and relegate it from being first in Africa to becoming third in Nigeria? So, it was simple diplomacy and condescension that Western Nigerian leaders needed to overcome the onslaught from the North and the East, but they failed out of sheer obstinacy, and were crushed by the federal government using divide and rule strategy and state of emergency powers in the constitution. It was brute politics. Yoruba leaders were arrested, detained, tried for treasonable felony and imprisoned. Sooner than later, the Igbo led IfeajunaNzeogwu coup d'etat came up on January 15, 1966 and finished what was left by assassination. It was sad and bad.

With a strategy of condescension like if you cannot beat them, you join them for the right reasons, the history of Western Nigeria, the Yorubas and Nigeria, could be different from what it is today. The Western Nigerian leaders were divided, disunited and fighting among themselves, so, it was possible for their common enemies to penetrate their ranks by dangling the 'carrot of benefits' in their faces and planting the 'Trojan Horse' in their midst. As a result, they played into the hands of their adversaries, and Western Nigeria became relegated to the background for over three decades until the advent of General Olusegun Obasanjo as civilian president on May 29, 1999.

The marginalization of the Yorubas and their sufferings for over three decades made them so badly hurt and disillusioned that they could not believe their eyes that one of them could ever be President of Nigeria. They could not believe that the North and the East could vote for a Yorubaman to be president, but as ordained by God/Allah, it happened on May 29, 1999 and May 29, 2003 by landslide majority votes. In the same wise, Nigerians should strongly believe that with God/Allah, everything is possible and Nigeria can change for better.

During the period of the sufferings of the Yorubas, there was a saying planted among the Yoruba populace, which gave them some consolation and helped them to stand strongly and defiantly: "Kaka ka dobale fun Gambari, ka roju ka ku," meaning, "Instead of bowing down or condescending to Northerners' wishes, we better endure till death." Fortunately, that mentality has since disappeared, and the Yorubas presently cooperate fully and graciously at all levels of government including socio-economic and political activities with all Nigerian ethnicities without exception. Such mentality of superiority complex often leads to selfdestruction. Nigerians in general must learn from their own experience and from what happened to the Yorubas for noncooperation and confrontation of the past with the federal government.

Nigerians generally, must realize that every Nigerian ethnicity has bitter stories to tell about having suffered killings, arson and one indignity or the other at the hands of other ethnicities as a result of ethno-religious violence and coups d'etat. But who started the killings? The IfeajunaNzeogwu coup d'etat and their collaborators started the killings with the assassinations of Hausa/Fulani and Yoruba military and civilian leaders on January 15, 1966. The chain reactions and retaliations, followed by civil war (1967-1970) and incidents of mistrust and divisionism, which marred the whole Nigerian situation have continued up till today. When will these distractions and destructive tendencies stop? Enough is enough!

Nigerians generally should understand that individual citizens or groups couldn't continue to obsess or dwell on the past wrong things meted on them, if they want to make progress. A mind full of obsession for the past wrongs and evils cannot open up to accommodate progressive plans and activities for the present and the future.

Knowing the quality and resourcefulness of the Igbos and their heroism, it cannot be completely refuted that some of those who should participate in Ndigbo leadership are made to act as spectators of their young leaders' corrupt practices without having a say. Most of those talking loudest do not even match forty-five percent of the wisdom of Zik of Africa and his Igbo team members that we used to know, admire and respect. It is the same in Yorubaland, Hausaland and other lands in Nigeria, when we make references to Chief Awolowo, Sir Ahmadu Bello, Sir A.T. Balewa etc. The Nigerian electorate should change that situation by electing the best leaders for best services in future elections.

Given the Western Nigerian situation analyzed above which was ten times more serious than the crisis in other parts of Nigeria, yet, Chief Obafemi Awolowo, first Premier of Western Nigeria, the sage and architect of first place rating in Africa for Western Nigeria, accepted Nigeria's highest national honour award presented by Second Republic President Shehu Shagari, his arch political rival in two presidential elections. Chief Obafemi Awolowo struggled for over two decades to become the President of Nigeria, but he failed each time, blocked by Northern and Eastern coalition employing political stratagem.

Judging from Chief Awolowo's antecedent, he was one of the most quailfied for Nigerian presidency during his time, and yet, he only smelt it for over two decades and never had it. He went through the rigours of state of emergency, and he was imprisoned for treasonable felony. He was tortured physically and psychologically for many years. His Yoruba race and Yoruba leadership were disorganized, detained, imprisoned, humiliated, coerced and intimidated by using federal might, yet, he did not give up on Nigeria.

With diplomacy, tolerance and accommodation for others' opinions and some flexibility, he could have been trusted with the presidency. Nigerians should learn from others' past mistakes and adjust. Unequivocally, the Igbos need Nigerian majority's trust to achieve Igbo Presidency in 2011 or beyond.

Despite all the above physical and psychological torture of over twenty years, Chief Obafemi Awolowo was decorated with the highest national honour award by 2nd Republic President Shehu Shagari, a Northerner who was one of his toughest political rivals, and he accepted it with honour, dignity, respect and decency knowing fully well that it was Nigerian honour award and not the personal award of former President Shehu Shagari. It is time for Nigerians to unite and find solution to Nigeria's problems in togetherness.

All Nigerians at home and abroad have suffered terribly from one indignity or the other within over forty years after Nigerian independence of 1960 without exception. All past and present presidents, heads of state, leaders, elders and traditional chiefs have suffered as well as the followership in different shapes and forms. Can anybody imagine the devastating pains, which Nigerians of all grades, classes and levels have suffered as a result of unfulfilled dreams? Starting from the founders and champions of Nigerian independence to the present leadership and the entire citizenry of Nigeria, all Nigerians have suffered untold hardships in different forms.

Have you found out how terribly the First, Second and Third Republics were truncated, and how some leaders were killed, disgraced or humiliated? Have you found out about the pains and humiliations which the Fourth Republic President Obasanjo went through during the trumped up charges of coup attempt, the mockery military trial and life imprisonment commuted to fifteen years in prison by General Sani Abacha's regime? Many other Nigerian leaders suffered similar fate. Some elites were assassinated.

What about the military heads of state; they all suffered judging from the way they left office? If General Babangida were complacent in office, he would not have left the office for an interim civilian administration 'ceteris paribus'. He must have watched the excesses of Abacha's regime of 1993-1998 with regrets and helplessness unable to save Nigerians. Generals Aguiyi Ironsi, Yakubu Gowon, Murtala

Mohammed, Chief Odumegwu Ojukwu, the secessionist leaders and General Buhari suffered in one form or the other in their positions while playing leadership roles in Nigeria.

Economically crushing circumstances and dictatorship as well as national political instability forced many Nigerians overseas, away from their relations, culture, traditions, value system and traditionally rich foods they were used to. Many could not see their families for decades while living as undocumented, illegal aliens in foreign countries where they encounter discriminatory practices daily from their host countries of Europe and America.

These sets of Nigerians in overseas countries suffer under terrible vagaries of inclement weather extremities of either too cold or too hot, which are never known in Nigeria. During these periods of weather extremities, Nigerians overseas shed tears and wonder why they ever left their great country, Nigeria, where they never ever have to go through any weather hazards seasonally. Their host countries use them and pay them discriminatory wages.

On the other hand, Nigerians who could not travel overseas suffered severe economic hardship for decades after independence. They went through military dictatorships, human rights abuses, maladministrations, high rate of unemployment, high rate of inflation, hunger, violent crimes, insecurity, socio-economic and political instability, illhealth and assassinations of some prominent political opponents. Many innocent people lost their lives. Both sides suffered during the war.

Since every Nigerian, high or low, rich or poor, leader or follower, may have suffered, the wisest question to ask is, "When will the sufferings end?" For the sufferings to end, Nigerians generally, the elites and leadership in particular, should rededicate themselves to change for a better Nigeria. Nigerians should forgive, forget and accept that there is no victor and no vanquished because everybody has suffered seriously, socio-economically, politically, physically and psychologically. Nigerians nurse a common goal of a prosperous Nigeria, achievable with different approaches which must be harmonized in peace, cooperation and understanding.

There should be a new beginning in all nooks and corners of Nigeria in the North, South, West and East, and the new status should affect all spheres of Nigerian endeavours. It should be an example for the rest of the world. Nigeria as God/Allah's own country is closest to the Promised Land. All hands should be on deck to get Nigeria there. With the right focus by all Nigerians, the sufferings would end sooner than later.

ExGovernor Kalu, a prominent Igboman, young and virile who lived and governed Abia State (1999-2007), one of Igbo heartlands, said on Monday, November 29, 2004, "Nobody is using the Igbos. It is Igbos using themselves or allowing themselves to be used. Nobody has come from the North or the South-West to partake in the crisis in Igboland. It is Ndigbo against Ndigbo. So, let Ndigbo and their leaders stand up and address the issue. So, we are our own enemies. Let the Igbo leadership address the Igbo problem." In effect, Nigerian problems are manmade for which the elites should feel guilty, change behaviour and be their brothers' keepers.

During Obasanjo Administration, it was glaring that foreigners saw Nigeria in better light more than some Nigerians see their country with unjustified pessimism. For example, there are cases of American, British and other foreign nationals who naturalized as Nigerians citizens. United States Congresswoman, Carolyn Cheeks Kilpatrick from Detroit, Michigan who led a twenty-five-person US Trade Mission to Nigeria in August 2004, said, "What we want to do is help build our motherland strong because we know who we are as Africans in Diaspora; when Nigeria is strong, we are strong."

When asked about her impression of Nigeria, she replied, "I have been coming to Nigeria for twenty years now, and I am really excited about the people. They are the strongest, most resilient, friendliest family that I have anywhere. I am optimistic, just as US has problems; there are also problems here. Nothing is perfect, but I think when we work together to build a new world, a new African World with strong leadership and good services for the people, education, healthcare; then, they will grow too, and that is our mission."

When asked whether she was amazed that Nigeria being the sixth largest oil producer in the world and yet the country remained poor, she replied, "There are numbers of reasons for that, one of which is that your past leadership looked out more for themselves than the people of Nigeria. I am glad to say that they are gone and that you have the most wonderful and strongly committed president in person of Obasanjo who will make the difference and be the leader the African World needs. He is the number one African leader in the world today, and I think his relationship with Mbeki in South Africa and so many others as the Chairman in the African Union will be a plus for Nigeria."

If foreigners can see Nigeria in great light, the citizens need to rally round the government positively to solve problems, instead of constituting themselves as problems for the government and Nigeria.

At the Second Economic Conference held in Abuja, international investors reported on Tuesday, January 31, 2006 that the thirty-five percent return on investment in Nigeria, as confirmed by Fitch, the international rating agency, was the world's highest. The government must ensure that investors plough back a substantial part of the high profit for national development. Overall, Nigeria has been making tremendous economic progress.

May God/Allah give us the 'Wisdom of Solomon' to always make the right choices.

EPILOGUE

Nigeria is one of the world leaders in the production of oil, gas and other essential mineral resources. With vision 20/20 backed by 'NEEDS' and 'Seven–Point Agenda' programmes of Obasanjo and Yar'Adua regimes respectively, Nigeria has become a country to reckon with by the Comity of Nations. Nigeria is great with great people and great leadership potentialities.

Some people see Nigeria's cup as half empty, but I see it optimistically as more than three quarters full.

Some pessimists wrongly see Nigeria as the most corrupt nation in the world, but with more than two decades of residency in America, and partially in Europe, I have not seen any country, which is entirely free of corruption, discriminatory practices and election rigging. Bernard Madoff of New York, USA was arrested in December 2008 for committing $50 billion fraud, which is one of the highest ever in the world. He is not a Nigerian.

Many people see Nigeria as the most difficult to rule, but I see Nigerians as the smartest, highly intelligent, highly educated and most blessed compared with many other countries. Nigeria could be the easiest to rule if the leaders are transparent and exemplary.

Transparency International's report on Nigeria as being the most corrupt nation was wrong, flawful, and unreliable for overlooking Nigeria's corruption fighting efforts and tremendous progress accomplished.

An international social scientists group, Europe based, who released the result of their fouryear survey in 2006 reported that Nigeria was the happiest country in the world, but placed the USA, Britain, Russia,

Japan etc. outside the first ten happiest nations in the world. The report is a further testimony and confirmation that happiness is not determined solely by the amount of wealth an individual, group or nation possesses.

Nigeria's democratic experiment is one of the youngest in the world fashioned in the paradigm of the United States of American democracy after being subjected to over three decades of military dictatorship. The government is made up of the Presidency (Executive), the Legislature (the Senate and House of Representatives) and Independent Judiciary. The Nigerian Legislature has limited time in office, made up of a maximum of two terms of four years each, just like the President and the State Governors. Nigeria is very rich in mineral deposits, which include oil, gas, bitumen, iron ore, gold, zinc, phosphate, tantalite, etc. The latest discoveries make Nigeria a promising economic giant if her wealth of resources are properly harnessed and judiciously managed and expended in the best interest of the country.

Nigeria is one of the seven largest suppliers of petroleum products in the world and ranks among the five largest suppliers of oil to the United States of America. Nigeria is close to becoming the largest supplier of gas in the world and the second largest producer of bitumen in the world on basis of its latest discoveries coupled with extended efforts at developing and expanding its mineral wealth.

Nigeria's business contact with the Asian and American continents has expanded tremendously in petroleum, telecommunications, steel mining and agriculture. The country has become very attractive to foreign investors because of its wealth of resources and its democratic values. Nigeria's remarkable location around the Atlantic Ocean, the Rivers Niger and Benue, the Chad Basin, the Jos topography, Olumo Rock at Abeokuta and the Zoos, makes Nigeria very attractive. Also, the Abuja Federal Capital Territory (Centre of Unity) undergoing wonderful world class development, the hospitality of Nigerians generally, their wonderful culture, sense of community, traditions, the world class Tinapa Tourist Centre and the development of many other places of interest act as great attractions to tourists.

Nigerians now know the menace and sufferings attached to poor leadership and dictatorship and are saying, "Never Again. Never, Never Again." Above all, the government has staged the fiercest battle against fraud, corruption, economic and financial crimes, and it is winning. It has embarked on infrastructural development to provide enabling environment for business, education, food production and security. Nigeria is the darling of the Black People's World, and she has been receiving tremendous world support in her quest for permanent membership of the United Nations Security Council.

This book critically presents the thoughts of many individuals and groups about Nigeria, and as such, it makes an excellent reading for students in particular, the youths generally and all others who want to rekindle their knowledge about Nigeria's past, the present and the way forward to the future.

Those who allegedly took $170 billion legally or illegally as flight capital out of the country into foreign banks, if true, should be persuaded to repatriate the money back into Nigerian economy for investment purposes, employment generation, economic growth and development. Building a strong investment climate will diminish the incidents of capital flight.

It is important that Nigeria's economic policies are not dictated by the IMF and the World Bank and that their agenda are not accepted hook, line and sinker without modification to suit Nigeria's economic development purpose. The two foreign organizations have their interests and biases, and as such, Nigerian government must look inwards more to adopt only policies that suit Nigeria's development, culture and status. The red signal is 'caveat emptor' to avoid accepting the 'Trojan Horse' whenever considering the IMF and World Bank gestures and conditionalities.

In the words of a member of the Nigerian Bar Association, Ilorin, he reiterated thus, "All these monitization, fuel tax and what have you are foreign to us. Nigerians don't deserve all these pains. Our democracy is home grown, so our leaders should look inward and give us a homegrown economic policy that will cushion all these pains, not another policy that will further pauperize ordinary Nigerians." He added, "Federal Government should stop rolling out economic policy that will kill Nigeria and please the international community." It must be realized that the IMF and World Bank are financial agencies of the Western World with vested interest to make money and be profitable like all businesses.

Out of curiousity, Nigeria and other countries of Africa should start to ask questions about how the Western Governments that have controlling interests in the IMF and World Bank get money to spend at will in spite of their growing very high deficit balances without the kind of control that are dictated to Nigeria and other African governments as to how and what to budget, spend, have or not have and what not to do. They can dictate to other countries, but nobody can tell them what to do. It is hypocritical. Nigeria must be truly free from neocolonization and shady foreign debts.

What Nigeria needs are practical economists with valuable, relevant experience about Nigerian economic culture and operations. If Nigeria can stop corruption, frauds, economic and financial crimes, money laundering and capital fight, smuggling of contraband, vandalization of development infrastructures, illegal oil bunkering, etc., Nigeria will be able to occupy her rightful place in the world economy. Double-digit interest rate is antithetical to speedy economic recovery, growth and prosperity.

Nigerians, ExPresident Obasanjo and 2005 members of Nigerian Legislature should be congratulated for securing foreign debt cancellation of over $18 billions unprecedentedly as well as promises from G8 nations to increase aid to Nigeria and other African countries. It was a big success for Obasanjo Administration's relentless and selfless efforts to move Nigeria toward economic prosperity.

This outstanding, interesting and thought-provoking book cannot be complete without mentioning 'terrorism', an area of greatest concern to the present world. It must be realized that terrorists abound in different parts of the world sponsored in various forms and shapes by individuals, groups and states or governments.

Terrorism represents the systematic application of the courses of action that inspire intense fear, fright, panic, killings, arson, destruction, consternation, coercion, threat and violence which terrify, alarm, startle, dehumanize and abuse human rights. Dictatorial regimes or democratic governments that eliminate opponents by assassination with secret military squads and commit human rights violations can be charged for acts of terrorism. Individuals who hijack planes commit acts of terrorism. Military invasion and occupation of a country by another country illegally is an act of state terrorism. Militants or insurgents involved in arson, killings, bombings, vandalization, kidnappings etc. are involved in acts of terrorism.

Between 1967 and 1970, Africa helplessly watched Nigeria going through a civil war fought to keep Nigeria one by two young leaders below the age of forty years (General Yakubu Gowon and Chief Odumegwu Ojukwu) who conducted the war against each other for Nigeria and the secessionists of Eastern Nigeria respectively. An estimated two million victims were displaced with a lot of collateral damages. The war ended in the spirit of no victor, no vanquished. There was declaration of general amnesty to the secessionists followed by an era of reabsorption, rehabilitation, reconciliation and reconstruction.

The spirit of humanity, empathy, kindness, goodness, love, care, no victor, no vanquished and forgiveness (amnesty) made the war to stop and end in actuality and not prolonged too unduly. If the Nigerian approach to the civil war was only to fight indiscriminately and win, there would have been more collateral damages, more destruction and other atrocities, which would have left indelible scars that would be difficult to forget and forgive. Nigerians should learn from their mistakes and never repeat them.

Nigerians are best at whatever they lay their hands on. They are classy and class conscious. Their rank consciousness enables them to aim high, emulate and practise the best examples, keep their families' good names untarnished and endeavour to be the best they can be in all their spheres of activities locally and internationally.

The social class stratification in Nigeria makes many at the top feel some kind of superiority complex. Hence, the elites including government functionaries, elected representatives and political appointees often feel and act as bosses of the electorate instead of serving the people. Such mentality of superiority complex is antique, ridiculous, absurd and uncivilized.

Nigerians should take the time to know their rights fully guaranteed by the constitution and always exercise such rights peacefully and intelligently. Nigerians must stop electing into office, those who cannot serve them best, and if anybody is mistakenly elected, he or she must be recalled in accordance with the provisions of the Nigerian constitution. Mostly, some top rank citizens feel they are above the law and correction.

They look down on others below their ranks with arrogance. The mentality should change because 'pride goes before a fall.'

In the first time in the annals of the nation, young military officers and their collaborators from South-Eastern region led by Ifeajuna and Nzeogwu reigned terror on Nigerians on January 15, 1966 by brutally assassinating military and civilian leaders of Northern and Western regions and overthrew the democratically elected government of the First Republic of Nigeria. They took over the government, protected their own military and civilian leaders from Eastern Nigeria and ruled the country dictatorially for six months before they were overthrown.

After forty years of suffering, groping in darkness in the wilderness, Nigeria should not tolerate any acts of terrorism and anarchy on its soil again. Hence, Nigerians should be extremely vigilant to save their hardwon nascent democracy. It should be zero tolerance for anarchical tendencies and incitement of youths to militancy, their untimely deaths and selfdestruction.

Elites who deceive and incite others' children and relations into militancy, nurse theirs in overseas colleges/universities; steal, launder and stash Nigerian government money meant for local government development into overseas private bank accounts at the detriment of the citizenry should be condemned, indicted, prosecuted and convicted. Nigerian youths should be aware of leaders and elders who are hypocritical.

According to Ronald Reagan, the fortieth President of the USA on January 20, 1981, he said, "As for the enemies of freedom who are potential adversaries, they will be reminded that peace is the highest aspiration of the American people. We will negotiate for it, sacrifice for it; we will not surrender for it now or ever." In similar fashion, Nigeria cannot succumb or surrender to the blackmail, intimidation, vandalization, killings and kidnappings by the militant groups, young or old, Christian or Muslim, wherever they may be in the country.

Nigeria should double efforts to generate employment to the fullest nationwide and encourage rapid development of the oil producing regions. The government should encourage deurbanization whereby people will go back to the rural areas and work productively in their villages, instead of being hired, incited and used as militant youths and thugs for destructive purposes.

The world must learn from the examples of Nigeria and Cameroon who settled their border disputes peacefully. It must be realized that socio-economic and political benefits derivable from world peace are immeasurable and invaluable.

Leaders who talk about war, war, war and win, win, win only, as well as those who constantly instill fears about state and personal security in the citizenry in order to win votes in elections cannot succeed for long in manipulating the people. Such leaders would need reorientation about the enormous advantages of maintaining world peace through the spirit of give and take and respectability for world majority opinions. Win or lose a war, there will be collateral damages. So, there is no better choice than peace through diplomacy.

On the other hand, the spirit of consultation, conciliation, diplomacy, honest truth, no victor, no vanquished, empathy and mutual respectability among leaders without displaying any superiority complex is the only catalyst that wins permanent and enduring peace coupled with dignity for humanity.

The greatest world leaders before 1950s were warriors who won wars, but thereafter, greatest leaders of the world are the ones who win hearts, achieve and maintain peace and make their people achieve the greatest things. Modern greatest leaders use diplomacy, intellect, maturity, academic education, professionalism and socio-economic and political savvy and sagacity to solve national and international problems rather than military hardware and political deception.

Unfortunately, the USA leadership from 2001-2009 believed in military force and war rather than diplomacy and peace because the defence industries became extrememly profitable and a lot of money was made from inflated war contracts.

Nigerian leaders should be well guided by this philosophy about 'greatest leadership and achievement' in order to be the greatest. The process of zero tolerance for fraud and corruption, economic and financial crimes and terrorism coupled with unsustainable foreign debtfree status that began under Obasanjo Administration is the catalyst, the pivot, the fulcrum and aircraft that will successfully pilot Nigeria to greatness en route to the Promised Land. With patriotism, peace, unity and solidarity among Nigerians irrespective of ethnicity, religion or political differences, the end of the journey to greatness is pretty close.

It is great news that Mrs. Ellen JohnsonSirleaf has been elected as President of Liberia (West Africa) after almost two decades of civil war, which killed thousands of innocent lives and rendered many more as refugees in many parts of Africa, Europe and America. Mrs. Ellen Johnson-Sirleaf has thus become the first woman president of an African nation in the history of black peoples of the world. President JohnsonSirleaf, a Harvard University graduate and an economist, can be described as the harbinger of peace, unity, good governance and eventual socio-economic prosperity and political stability in Liberia. A new dawn has arisen in Liberia for emulation by Nigerian women.

People do not become cultists, gangsters, hooligans, thugs, miscreants and militant youths overnight. Miscreants do not overnight resort to criminal activities like: vandalizing oil and gas pipelines, destroying government infrastructures, committing arson, illegal oil bunkering, economic and financial crimes, armed robberies, creating mass civil disobedience and carrying arms and ammunition illegally.

These crimes cannot happen and be staged with perfection without organized mentoring and incitement by some local leaders, elders and politicians. The mentors and leaders of militant groups often acquire illegal money by inciting and using their followership to commit crimes. By kidnapping oil workers and collecting ransom, their leaders acquire money worth millions and become filthy rich illegally by extortion. Their followerships, who hardly receive any benefit, are often misled to fight and die for nothing. Those of them who get caught and face prosecution are often abandoned to fend for themselves.

Some militants facing treasonable charges may likely have acted criminally with stupidity by relying on false protection from godfather politicians who are not reliable. Their attorneys should guide them on their rights and limitations under the law so that they do not continue to utter inciteful inappropriate statements that selfincriminate them and make a bad case worse. Where are those who nurtured them in criminality, protected them, gave them arms and ammunition and assured them of invincibility with false promises? Remember to stop being fooled. When your sweat and blood make them wealthy, they will dump you when you get into trouble for carrying out their criminal intentions.

It is not real or true that the Igbos have enemies/adversaries in Nigeria outside their own ethnicity or nationality as suggested by the statement credited to Chief Ojukwu in the address read on his behalf by Chief Ugochukwu Agballah.

It is no gainsaying that in most countries where women have led, they have led well with good governance, empathy, responsibility, responsiveness, accountability, honesty and transparency as mothers of their respective nations. Some of them have been described as iron ladies. They include exBritish Prime Minister, Margaret Thatcher; exPrime Minister of Israel, Ms. Golda Meier; exPrime Minister of India, Ms. Indira Gandhi; etc. Women politicians worldwide have not been known to be as corrupt, fraudulent and manipulative as many of their male counterparts.

Nigerians can no longer afford to support outdated/expired/lapsed, already overspent, tired, exhausted, frustrated, semieducated, troubleshooting, unproductive and corrupt politicians of over three or four decades who have not done Nigeria any good. Some young politicians are just not good while great and experienced old ones remain indispensable. Productivity and not age matters. Some politicians live on borrowed and expired influence with little knowledge about the realities of modern world. They keep on fighting among themselves and heating the polity unnecessarily. They should go and rest.

Regrettably, menfold in all world spheres of activities including religion of all kinds, have deliberately discriminated against women for more than twenty centuries. There must be a change of heart among men and religions whether Christian, Muslim or Traditionalist. The trend must change now. Nigerian women should come out and contest during elections. They are as good as men, if not better. Women femininity is an embodiment of motherhood, peace, humility, responsibility, trustworthiness, transparency, respectability, exemplariness, quality leadership, accomplishment and good governance which the world needs indispensably now.

If Nigerians think that some of their politicians are the most corrupt ones in the world, then read about the United States Republican eight-term Congressman, sixty-three years old, Randy Duke Cunningham. He was a Vietnam War fighter pilot who pleaded guilty to graft and tearfully resigned on Monday, November 28, 2005. He admitted remorsefully that he took $2.4 million in bribes mostly from defence contractors in exchange for government business and other favours.

He said, "The truth is, I broke the law, concealed my conduct and disgraced my office." He added, "I know that I will forfeit my freedom, my reputation, my worldly possessions, most importantly, the trust of my friends and family." He was a member of the House Appropriations Subcommittee that controlled defence dollars. He was said to have secured contracts worth tens of millions of dollars for those who paid him off. He was accused of federal charges for committing bribery, fraud and tax evasion. He accepted that he was wrong.

The difference between Congressman Cunningham and most bursted Nigerian corrupt elites is that he was remorseful, he tearfully resigned his enviable position, and he seriously apologized to his friends and family for breaching their trust in him.

He did not defensively threaten the presidency or heat the polity with inciteful statements. He did not become violent to slap any other congressman or dress as a woman to jump bail and claim immunity from prosecution. He did not launder the money to other countries, and he took responsibility fully for his wrongful acts. He did not pass buck nor accuse anybody of causing his downfall in order to divert attention and wield unearned and undeserved sympathies.

He courageously condemned himself for his corrupt actions. He acted with civility and did not make a bad case worse. He fell from grace to grass but maintained remarkable decency, gallantry and responsibility to the end. He regretted his acts of impropriety. He made an atonement. Nigerian indicted corrupt politicians never showed any remorse.

With Nigerian democratic experiment, some politicians and political office holders who commit more serious economic and financial crimes against their country, Nigeria, still remain in office protected by the immunity clause contained in the Nigerian 1999 Constitution. The immunity provision should be reviewed to ensure equitable justice before the law of the nation for all Nigerians.

It was great and wonderful news that Nigeria concluded an agreement with Paris Club of Creditors to take the country out of debt trap of about three decades. By the agreement, Nigeria secured a debt cancellation of $18 billion while the balance of $12.1 billion was payable as $6.4 billion being the first tranche. The second tranche payment was $1.3 billion while the last tranche payment was about $4.4 billion to set the country free of over $30 billion foreign debt by March 2007. It was a great unprecedented achievement creditable to Obasanjo Administration.

In the spirit of united, indivisible, one Nigeria, ethnic militarism does not augur well for present and future Nigerians. The militia groups usurp and perform the civil functions of the police, prosecutor, judge and jury without any legal authority. They pose anarchical problems. They illegally possess illegal weapons. Clashes between groups have resulted in the deaths of many innocent people, which made the government to proscribe and clamp down on them. They do not exist or operate freely in the most civilized democracies in the world.

Elites who are encouraging their existence, using and inciting them, have their own children in colleges and universities in Europe and America. They place their own relations in higher socio-economic and political class. Nigerian dissident group leaders should realize that using other people's children and relations for militarism and insurgency while theirs are safeguarded in colleges/universities is unGodly/unAllahly.

The peaceful resolution of the border adjustments between Nigeria, Cameroon, Chad and Niger Republics should be an ideal model for the rest of the world. Nigerians should continue to strive for the best and get it. The successful and peaceful negotiation in January 2006 for the release of four foreign oil workers who included an American and a British after two weeks of being kidnapped by militant dissidents in Niger Delta is another miracle the world should copy from Nigeria, the leader of the black people's world. Nigerians are very smart and really gifted. It is wonderful to be a Nigerian.

At Akore Village, Igbesa, Ogun State, the first Nigerian rural settlement, poverty alleviation scheme was launched by World Malayalee Council (WMC), an International Humanitarian Organization on Sunday, February 5, 2006 with a borehole. The Chairman of Ado-Odo/Ota Local Government Council, Dr. Gboyega Salami and His Royal Highness, the Oloja of Igbesaland, Oba (Dr.) Samuel Olushola Banuso, graced the occasion. The entire people of Igbesaland are grateful to WMC, an Indian nongovernmental humanitarian organization as well as the Federal and Ogun State governments of Nigeria.

Lastly, the author reminds Nigerian government and leaders that to have peace, development, socio-economic and political stability, they must win the hearts of Nigerians with good governance, exemplary leadership, love, care, empathy, transparency, accountability and responsiveness. The war against corruption must be won and there must be religious, political and ethnic tolerance. Nigerian elites can do better; they must in the best interest of Nigeria.

In conclusion, 'Nigeria the Beautiful' has become a great country to reckon with among International Community for her socio-economic and political progressiveness. The consistent pace of development at all fronts endears Nigeria to the Comity of Nations unequivocally. Nigerians are great with enviable accomplishments; the leaders are daily striving to achieve greatness and exemplariness; and the country, Nigeria, a potential world class model, the greatest Blackman's nation in the universe is wonderfully blessed by incomprehensible 'Acts of Providence'.

GOD/ALLAH BLESS NIGERIA!

APPENDIX

ACKNOWLEDGEMENTS

I hereby express my gratitude to God Almighty for the great and wonderful successes which I have recorded in my life in Nigeria (West Africa), the United Kingdom and the United States of America. I also want to thank God exceedingly for giving me life, strength, sound health, abundant resources and right judgment that fostered the writing of this book titled, "Great People, Great Country, Nigeria The Beautiful." The purpose is to tell the world that a prospective economic superpower nation (Nigeria) is being nurtured for realization before the end of the third decade of the twenty-first millennium.

In 2007, I published a book titled, "A Female US President Is Salvation, Blessing, Peace and Prosperity" to promote the dignity of women as well as the equality of sexes. My other published book titled, "Blacks Greatest Homeland Nigeria Is Born Again" demonstrated a wonderful endeavour to appreciate and promote humanity, especially Black People who are marginalized, denigrated, discriminated against and abused daily before Barack Obama, a Blackman, providentially became the President of the United States of America effective January 20, 2009.

Barack Obama represents the harbinger of 'Change and Hope' for the Americans in particular and the whole world in general. Events about the incomprehensibility of the emergence of a Blackman politician as the USA President in the White House symbolize that the Messiah has come or He is close to the world, ready to impact the world with 'Change and Hope'. We thank God/Allah for making the Blackman happy and proud. We are further reminded that the Lord Jesus Christ did not come from among the aristocrats and not from the Whiteman!

I also thank God, the Almighty for giving me four wonderful and lovely children, Ms. S. Olubunmi Aka, Ms. Z. Olayide Aka, Mr. I. Femi Aka and Miss Makayla Tokunbo Aka. All of them are exceptionally brilliant children with wonderful accomplishments that make me happy and proud. Olubunmi Aka holds B.Sc Mechanical Engineering and Masters Degree in Geographical Information Systems while Olayide and Femi hold college degrees in Computer Science and Estate Management respectively. The baby of the family, Miss Makayla Tokunbo Aka is a second grader with extraordinary brilliance. I thank God for giving me such wonderful children in my life. I wish all of them God's enormous blessings (amen).

My inestimable gratitude goes to my father, Chief R. Akindele Aka and my mother, Mrs. A. Aka, devout worshippers of God/Allah who never missed praying and serving God/Allah many times daily. I used to wonder how they got such incredible energy to be so prayerful. My father was a traditional doctor and healer who held tight to his traditional religion. People used to come to him for traditional medical cure and healing from many works of life endeavours. He was very good at his job for which he became a chief and a leader of traditional medicine practitioners. My both parents lived exemplary lives.

My two most blessed, distinguished father and mother gave birth, raised and nurtured a wonderful child by giving me abundant love and care with all the encouragement and enabling environment which provided a formidable foundation that made me sail through very sound, moral, academic and professional education with considerable ease and minimal difficulty.

My parents were always prayerful for successes, trusting, supportive, confident and proud of me for always coming out as one of the best and second to none among my peers. Without their relentless efforts that saw me succeeding, my happy experiences, songs of praises and narrations of success today might be different. They did exemplary parenting in need and in deed. They were always there for me. May their souls rest in perfect peace with the Lord (amen).

Most precious was my grandmother, Chief Oku Ashamu Aka, Iyalode (meaning the first mother) of Igbesa. She loved and cared for me so much that she shielded me from all afflictions. She loved my mother and her children exceptionally beyond easy comprehension, and she used to provide us with all facilities that gave us the joy of life. Tough as my father, Chief R. Akindele Aka (alias Baba Egun) was, he dared not discipline me whenever my grandmother was visible. As leader of all females in Igbesa, she was generous, kind, loving, caring and exemplary. She was elderly and respected, and usually consulted by the Oba (the King) when dealing with traditional issues that affected females. I miss her. May her soul rest in perfect peace (amen).

I wish to thank Ms. Rachel Williams who helped to type my book, "A Female US President Is Salvation, Blessing, Peace and Prosperity", as well as this book. She is a great aunt to my beautiful daughter, Makayla Tokunbo Aka. I have known Rachel since 1993 when my friend and mother of my daughter Ms. Stephanie Yvette Williams was living with her in Fort Worth, Texas. Mrs. Danyell Edwards, sister to Rachel and Stephanie, has helped to keep my daughter several times. They all belong to a great wonderful family. May God bless them, their parents and their entire family. (Amen)

My constant contact with Principal Felicia Donaldson and her Assistant Principal Ms Cheryl Estes of Dan Powell Intermediate School, Everman is great and inspirational. Ms. Donaldson tells her students every time that failure is not an option and she works hard to achieve remarkable goals for her school. She is exemplary and very enthusiastic about her job and principalship. Ms. Tania Lewis is exceptionally wonderful. The entire faculty members of the school are nice and friendly. I thank you all.

I want to thank Ms. Laura Vasquez, Secretary of Shelby Alternative School, Everman, Texas, who helped me all the time in my secretarial needs without accepting any compensation. I did not know how to be thankful enough for her kindness to me. May God Almighty reward her family with blessings in so many folds (amen). Her friend, Ms. Kate Silva was also very admirable and hard working. I used to be very happy whenever I was in their midst. Ms. Silva is a very beautiful woman and very much liked by her students.

I always remember Ms. Cecilia HolmesBuckner, her sister, Bernay Jackson and her children Andrea, Angelica and Ariana Buckner who are great African Americans. Cecilia and Bernay have wonderful Christian values. I admire them a lot and wish them God's enormous blessings (amen).

My thanks also go to Mr. Saminu Ayinde Ajo (deceased) who provided me with the necessary guidance, mentorship and private coaching that used to make me come first in my class since I was a little boy. May his soul rest in perfect peace (amen).

I also remember my cousin, Chief Amusa Tijani Odofin who taught me A, B, C to Z even though he never attended the four walls of any school classroom to learn to speak, read or write in English. He provided me with food, farm crops and products that supported my childhood education. I thank him exceedingly.

I remember to thank late Chief Alhaji Braimoh Agemo of Ogona quarter, Igbesa who picked both Deacon A. Yode Aka and myself on a bicycle from Igbesa to Ado-Odo and enrolled us into Ado-Odo Secondary Modern School as student members of the second set of the commencement of the institution. May his soul rest in perfect peace (amen).

Ironically, I may never have had basic secondary high school education if my uncle, Chief M. A. Aka, the Olupana of Igbesa did not enlighten and pressurize his uncle (my father) to withdraw me from the secondary modern school and send me to Badagry Grammar School, Badagry because he was convinced beyond any reasonable doubt that I was a material for higher education. It was then that I took the common entrance examination, came first and won six years Western Regional Government Scholarship initiated by Chief Obafemi Awolowo, first Premier of Western Nigeria. Without his (Chief Olupana) advice, I could not have utilized the educational opportunities available in Western Nigeria at that time. I thank Chief Olupana exceedingly. May Chief Awolowo's soul rest in perfect peace. Nigeria remembers him always, especially Yorubas who enjoyed free educational and scholarship programmes, which he initiated.

I cannot forget Chief E. K. Akinde, the Ajiroba of Igbesa who provided me with a Mathematics teaching job at his missionary secondary modern school. It was my first salaryearning job in my life. He stood by me ever since then, as my mentor and surrogate parent. May God Almighty bless him and his family (amen).

I should not forget my mother's uncle, Chief Honourable Dada Elero, the Asiwaju of Igbesa who in conjunction with my uncle, Chief M. A. Aka, the Olupana of Igbesa talked to Chief Aromire of Ota, Ogun State who was Nigeria Airways Personnel Manager during the Nigerian Civil War to facilitate my employment into the national airline on August 27, 1967. Messrs H. K. Dada and R. A. Akomolafe facilitated my employment paperwork. I thank them exceedingly.

The opportunity made me a great careerist in Airline Management with a master's degree in aviation management from Embry-Riddle Aeronautical University, Miami Graduate Division, Florida, USA, 1979. Thus, I became the first employee to be sponsored by the Nigeria Airways for such aviation graduate degree overseas. If Chief Dada Elero and Chief Aka did not talk to Chief Aromire who employed me as a personnel clerk, I may not have become a university aviation management degree graduate as at today. I thank them all from the bottom of my heart. I always remember my great cousins – Folabi Ade Dada, Biodun Dada, Lanre Dada and the youngest girl, Jaiye Dada, who is presently a reputable attorney in London, UK. They are now grown men and women with chains of academic and professional university degrees from the USA and UK respectively. I thank God for them. I am proud of them.

How can I forget Kabiyesi Oba Ashafa, the Onijanikin of Ijanikin, who in recognition of my mother's ancestry from Ijanikin, gave me a reference letter to support my application for Lagos State Scholarship in 1975 when I was to go to Brighton University (Business Graduate School, Brighton) for the postgraduate degree in Management Studies 1975/76. It was one academic year programme.

Before the approval of the scholarship was announced, I had completed the programme and personally paid for it in full with the arrears of salaries collected as a result of Udoji Salaries Award granted by General Gowon's Military Regime (1966-1975). Hence, Lagos State did not reimburse me but the scholarship was approved. I thank Kabiyesi

Oba Ashafa for giving me the letter of reference without hesitation when Mr. and Mrs. A. A. Ajo introduced me to him in 1975. May the soul of my cousin, Mrs. Suwebat Abebi Ajo, nee Olakisan rest in perfect peace (amen).

In effect, a lot of my family members and distant relatives contributed immensely to my development from childhood, then adolescence to adulthood and to them all, I say, "Thank you and may God bless you" (amen).

It is also very important to thank national figures that assisted my development directly and indirectly like Chief Obafemi Awolowo, General Yakubu Gowon (rtd), Airline Captains Thahal and Allwell Brown, Mrs. Nike Ogunade and General Olusegun Obasanjo (rtd).

I benefited from Chief Obafemi Awolowo's free primary education for one year, the secondary modern school education for one year and utilized the Western Nigeria Regional Government Scholarship established by Chief Obafemi Awolowo for six years granted purely on merit and competitiveness without any undue influence, bribery or corruption.

Is it possible in Nigeria today for any student in the country to win a regional government scholarship without bribery and special connections with topmost government officials? The answer is 'capital no'. Although the world declined from good old days morally, reforms are reshaping Nigerians to be the best. The unprecedented reforms that started in the annals of Nigeria were a big credit to President Olusegun Obasanjo and his cabinet. Nigerians must glorify God for the unprecedented 2005 debt relief for Nigeria in particular and Africa in general under ExPresident Obasanjo's leadership.

Nigerians have to do a rethinking and stop "business as usual", bribery, frauds, corruption, economic and financial crimes, and all other crimes that are inimical to the best interests of Nigeria and Nigerians. Such rethinking and adjustments should start from the topmost hierarchy of Nigerians to all others at the bottommost part of the ladder. I thank Chief Obafemi Awolowo for his contributions to my educational development. He also created technical schools and generated employment. There was abundance of everything and life was worthy of living in Western Nigeria during his time when his tribesmen (the Yorubas) were first in Africa.

I also benefited from "Udoji Salaries Award" of the mid1970s and utilized the fantastic arrears to fund my postgraduate studies at Brighton University (Business Graduate School, Brighton), Sussex, UK. I am extremely grateful to General Yakubu Gowon, the Military Head of State, who granted the "Udoji Salaries Award" for the opportunities that the award opened to me, which I seized and utilized for my development.

I was on study leave in Brighton, 1975/76 when I heard that General Yakubu Gowon was overthrown; but thank God he concentrated his time and energy on his doctoral programme in Political Science at Warwick University, Coventry, UK. What a great leader to emulate during difficult periods! I doff my hat for Dr. Yakubu Gowon, former Nigerian Head of State who encountered and overcame the physical discipline of the course work of doctoral program in UK without waiting for honourary university doctorate degrees, which are often commercialized.

To emulate, appreciate, meet and thank General Gowon in Coventry in 1976, I applied from Brighton to Warwick University for the Master's Degree in Business Administration, but I had to return to Nigeria because I did not have enough fund to finance the programme.

I recollect that during the Udoji Award, all electrical appliances and equipment, musical, refrigeration products and house furnishing materials were cleared from Mushin shops and markets. People were happy and grateful to General Gowon all over the country. One also remembers the time of Chief Okotieboh, Finance Minister, when there were songs and praises all over the country for the arrival of new Nigerian currency notes. Those were good old days when Nigerian currency was stronger than the US dollar and Nigerians were respected all over the world for Nigeria's strong economy. Most unfortunately, majority of the new breed type of politicians are 'jeun jeun, that is, eat and quench', who acquire illegal wealth at the expense of suffering masses. That is sad!

I am extremely grateful to Captains Thahal and Allwell-Brown and Mrs. Nike Ogunade who were Nigeria Airways Managing Director, Director of Flight Operations and Secretary to the Director of Flight

Operations respectively. In 1978, when I was Principal Airline Management Instructor at the Nigeria Airways Ground Training School, Ikeja, the Managing Director, Captain Thahal and Captain Allwell-Brown, Director of Flight Operations and his Secretary, Mrs. Nike Ogunade assisted me a great deal to obtain Board and Management approval for my sponsorship for the Master's Degree in Aviation Management at Embry-Riddle Aeronautical University (Miami Graduate Division), Florida, USA, 1979.

There were strong overwhelming oppositions, openly and secretly, against the approval from my closest friends, colleagues, peers and boss of the same Yoruba ethnicity like myself who were officers in the Personnel Directorate, but despite all that, Captains Thahal and Allwell-Brown, who were not Yorubas like myself, stood firmly and supported my application for sponsorship to the end. It was unbelievable; similar to how Blackman, African American Barack Obama emerged as the President-Elect of the USA on November 4, 2008 and became the 44th President of the USA on January 20, 2009 providentially.

I remember vividly the last emergency top management meeting that was convened purposely to review and cancel the approval. Captain Thahal as chairman arrived at the fully attended management meeting after ensuring that every participant was seated and ready to hear his final decision on the approval which antagonists described as unprecedented and should be reversed. It came to a stage where Captain Allwell-Brown threatened to resign as Director of Flight Operations if the approval was reversed. He exclaimed, "This is my time to help a young man actualize his educational goal. I have to help today when I can because I may not be in this post tomorrow."

After being inundated with arguments pro and con, Captain Thahal, the Chairman of the meeting simply reconfirmed the approval of the training and sponsorship of Mr. J.O. Aka. He told the extraordinary management meeting that he personally took responsibility for the approval. He added that he would not be at peace in his mind if he cancelled the approval he gave to train Mr. J.O. Aka.

In the circumstance, Captains Thahal and Allwell-Brown were my angels without any ethnic or religious considerations. Without any further deliberations on the subject, Captain Thahal, who was scheduled to captain his Boeing 707 flight to London, left for his waiting plane already boarded by passengers.

I never had any previous interactions with either of the two airline top captains who were not Yorubas like myself but they helped me transparently. Only God knows how many people these two wonderful good Samaritans have helped in their lifetime. I did not meet Captains Thahal and Allwell-Brown before 1978, and I have not seen them since then to say, "Thank You." May God, the Almighty, the Omnipotent, Omnipresent, Omnisapient and Omniscient bless them with members of their families wherever they may be (amen). May God Almighty reward them abundantly. I look forward to the day when I will meet them personally and say, "Thank You; You Are Exemplary Nigerians."

How many Nigerians today can do their jobs honestly and responsibly without considerations for money as bribes, ethnicity/tribe, religion, relationship or connections with them? Nigerians should recall and do as much and/or even better than the good old days for the sake of posterity.

There is a great lesson to learn from above narrations by all Nigerians. Nigerians should start to deemphasize their ethnicity leanings and address themselves more as Nigerians. Just like the "Biblical Good Samaritan", Captain Thahal, a Northerner and Captain Allwell-Brown from South-South of Nigeria, held me, a Yorubaman, up and firmly to succeed while some of my Yoruba closest friends, peers and superiors were severely antagonistic, secretly and openly, and doing everything to frustrate the approval of my sponsorship for the master's degree in aviation management, but God's good wishes prevailed.

It is better for Nigerians to think more about themselves as Nigerians rather than their small ethnic groupings because one indivisible Nigeria is bigger, better, stronger and more influential in the comity of nations than any of Nigeria's parts or combinations of some of her parts put together. As Nigerians, united we stand, divided we fail and fall.

I also remember sharing the same classroom for the Aviation Master's Degree Programme at Embry-Riddle Aeronautical University, Miami Graduate Division, Miami, Florida, USA in 1979 with Andrew Agom, Julius Aiyede, Ibraheem Allison and a host of great Nigerians of various ethnicities working hard together as Nigerians and not as belonging to different Nigerian tribes. There was no discrimination. There was no tribal or ethnic sensationalism or sentimentalism.

I doff my hat for Nigerians generally for they are masters of their destinies, struggling hard to achieve at highest possible levels in all spheres of academic and professional endeavours in many parts of the world. May Andrew Agom's soul rest in perfect peace (amen). If riding with the State Governor by Andrew Agom could not guarantee safety, who else is safe? The Federal Government should review existing safety laws and enact stringent ones to ensure safety of lives and properties.

Permit me to ask this hypothetical and controversial question for wise Nigerians to ponder upon. Whose interests are the regional elder clubs or organizations protecting with their policies of exclusiveness? Maybe future Nigerian generations would be broaderminded to break the artificial barriers of regional or subregional exclusiveness being practised by these organizations. I look forward to days when my own Yoruba children and children's children would be welcomed by Arewa Consultative Forum (ACF) of Northern Nigeria or Ndigbo top hierarchy organization of Eastern Nigeria and vise versa. These regionbased organizations promote ethnicism rather than Nigerianism. They are exclusive and tribal conscious.

My strong philosophy for Nigerian oneness arises from the fact that, if Captains Thahal and Allwell-Brown, who are not Yorubas, did not help me in 1978, I may not be a doctor of philosophy today. Nigerians gain more in a larger family of one united Nigeria other than in its fragmentation. Whoever is truly working in the best interest of Nigeria will put Nigeria first rather than his/her ethnicity. I appeal to all Nigerian leaders whether local, state, regional or federal to search their minds and ensure unequivocally that each step, action or utterance they make every moment is inspirational, transparent and puts Nigeria first. The same appeal is extended to all other categories of Nigerians.

Also very importantly, I benefited immensely from "Operation Feed the Nation" (OFN) programme initiated by General Obasanjo's Military Administration 1976-1979. I became a renowned farmer in my locality and hometown, Igbesa, Ogun State, until I travelled to the United States of America in 1989 for the doctoral programme. General Obasanjo's OFN programme afforded me unique opportunity to go back home every weekend to my people in the rural society where I witnessed and learned from the rural community, great lessons about the intrinsic nature of the real Nigerian.

In the rural areas, I saw appreciable evidence of the best Nigerianhood with great humanity, portraying inherent wisdom, originality, innocence, humility, transparency, morality, hospitality, untapped wealth, genuine love and care, security, trust, faithfulness, empathy, kindness, godliness, undisturbed people, nonmoney mongering, peace, contentment, honesty, good neighbourliness, respect and dignity for one another.

Within the rural community, we all knew one another very well and there was no faking. The situation so described was completely antithetical to what was happening and still happening up-to-date in urban settings with seats of governance where there are elites and the leadership of the country, who care less about basic amenities for their parents, elders, brothers, sisters, uncles, aunts etc. in the rural locality.

Government monetary allocations meant for rural development to provide drinkable water, electricity, health care, education, roads and other essential facilities are usually, heartlessly laundered into private bank accounts overseas by Nigerian elites. It is terrible and shameful that most Nigerian elites have magnificent properties in Europe, America and other African countires while their Nigerian localities lack basic facilities for subsistence living.

Every weekend, my movement from Lagos to the rural area for farming gave me wonderful lifelong experience. It changed my orientation and made me a better person to serve humanity. Great Nigerians in rural communities all over the country form the majority of the Nigerian population who represent our fathers, mothers, brothers, sisters, uncles and aunts. The rural settlers represent the bestbehaved, bestcultured and most ethical Nigerians usually marginalized and treated as less civilized by the elites who live in the cities. Fortunately, the government that evolved from May 29, 2003 changed such erroneous misconception by giving the greatest attention possible to rural development especially in agriculture, rural electrification and rural industrialization.

Within the rural community, I saw happiness, contentment and selfsufficiency in the faces of those who had less material wealth than the affluent and insatiable elites in the cities. The OFN was an eyeopener, which provided food security, selfsufficiency, and money with which

I proceeded overseas in search of 'Greener Pastures' and the 'Golden Fleece' in the USA.

Ironically, the greener pastures for which I was going to the USA were available in my farms in Igbesa, Ogun State. I did not realize that until I got overseas and started struggling, working and studying. Overseas was very fair then, it is worse now. I wish I had stayed at Igbesa to mechanize and develop my farms for full commercialization, and did not travel out, knowing what I know today that the best and wealthiest Europeans and Americans live happily in the rural communities often described as countryside. I thank and applaud General Obasanjo for the OFN initiative when he was Military Head of State of Nigeria. I wish the programme were fully resuscitated in the best interest of all Nigerians who dream to fully engage in food production as well as cash crops for foreign exchange earnings.

Life in overseas countries for Africans in particular, who are naturally black and beautiful, as well as other nationals from the Eastern Bloc and the Middle East, is usually disturbed by discriminatory practices meted on them by nationals and governments of their host countries. Hence, living overseas cannot be sweeter than living in one's own country thus confirming the popular dictum, "East or West, Home is the Best. There is no better place like one's Home."

Hopefully, Nigerian government will design and evolve laudable programmes which will provide the right, safe, secure and congenial environment that will encourage Nigerian professionals, academicians and others abroad to come back as well as repatriate their wealth home for national development.

The death of my cousin and best friend, His Highness, Kabiyesi Alhaji Oba Sikiru Ishola Yussuf, the Onikogbo of Ikogbo, Igbesaland, has left a vacuum that is difficult to fill. He left for the Lord, God/Allah at the time when he should have continued to reap the dividends of his great life. He is greatly missed and will be remembered for a life well spent in the Air Force and later as leader of his peoplehis subjects. The greatest honour to him will be to successfully carry out his last wishes until we meet again in the Lord, God's Kingdom. We will always remember his kindness, philanthropy and exemplary leadership for the rest of our lives. Despite his wealth, kingship and dignity, he used to call me uncle and bow as a sign of humility. One of my Guiding Angels is gone. May his soul rest in perfect peace (amen).

I cannot forget the kindnesses of my brother A. Idowu Aka; my baby sister, Victoria Idayat Abebi Aka; Lamidi Aka, Sabitu Aka, Alhaji Chief Bola Olagbaye, a great achiever and accomplisher both academically and professionally in business, finance and law; Chief Adewale Gbeleyi, the law; Chief Mohammed Odu, a successful businessman; Mr. Folorunsho Aina, the kindest man; Prince A. Fagbemi; Chief Yemi Odunsi, Babameto of Igbesa, the Philanthropist; Dr. Samuel Adedeji, the best friend and realist; Chief S.A. Buraimoh; Professor Yushau Sodiq, his wife and children, the nicest and very religious family, friends in need and in deed; Dr. Sherian Smith, my Professor at Tarleton State University, Stephenville, Texas, very kind and empathic; Mrs. Florence Idowu FashinaHaastrup; Alhaji Ganiyu Jimoh and his son, Saheed Jimoh are great friends of mine in need and in deed; Mr. Krishna Pant (my greatest friend from Nepal); Chief Nusirat Saula, the law and the judge; Pastor R. A. Akomolafe and his brother, Reverend Akomolafe of CAC and family; Mr. Reginald L. Moss of Human Resource Center, a very kind man; Mr. Atanda Bankole, a great cousin; Mrs. M. Titilayo BelloAka; Chief S. Agboola Aka, a most Igbesa distinguished chief of great personality; Ms. Latisa Franklin; Alhaji A.A. Ajo and Abebi; Abibu Fagbayi; Adesina Samuel; Sikiru Salami (Olaiya); Ms. Constance Jones; Madam Juanita Perkins, my Godmother; Police Officer Ladipo (Badagry); Engineer M.A. Akingbade; Deacon A. Yode Aka; Tunde Onabanjo, Ohio, USA; Ms. Candace Tuck; Funke Akingbade (Miami, 1979); Remi Eniafe (Miami); Police Officer Raheem Yakubu; Mr. Ade Ogede; Ms. Mitchel Jones; Ruth Ann Dickson, Assistant Manager, Oakwood Terrace Apartments, Everman, Texas; Princess Ayinke Gbeleyi; Prince Tunde Gbeleyi; Ms. Tawa Akinde; Mr. and Mrs. Sonola (Baba and Mama Remi); Mr. R.A. Olayinka; Ms. Agbeke Odu; Biliaminu and Ramonu Akindele; Ramonu Odu of Ado-Odo; Alhaji Busari (Baba Isiaka); all descendants of Olupana Chieftaincy Family; all members of Igbesa Club; all great residents of Igbesaland and distinguished chiefs and a host of others who are best of family and friends during all times, hot or cold, great or challenging, easy, tasking or difficult. I remember a great Igbesan, Philanthropist Martin Olusola Aina and his wife Megan Anita Aina from UK, now in New York, USA.

I always remember that Chief Yemi Odunsi, Babameto of Igbesa trusted me with $5,000 in 1989 when I was travelling to the USA with the understanding that I could return it whenever it was comfortable for me to do so. He wished me well in the USA. It took about 2 years hard work in the USA to save enough money before I paid it back with exceeding gratitude. I will forever remain thankful to him. May God bless him and his family (amen). Chief M.A. Akinogun, Okanlomo of Igbesa, former President of Igbesa Club is blessed with admirable personality. These wonderful testimonies are challenges to individuals to always be the 'Good Samaritan'. God will bless you in multiple folds, if you are kind and helpful to the needy.

I remember Cecilia Bailey, Jane Obodo, Toyin Okunade, Olagbemileke Oke, Rossy Egbusin, Bunmi Ajayi and his wife Olubisi Stella Ajayi, George Okeke, Leye Charles (New York), Paul Odofin, Eddie Osa, Asad Javed, Walter Ihebinike, Capt. Carlene Morrison, Capt. Charles Shakleford, Bill Knight, his wife and young daughter Hope Knight. They are all great and wonderful friends. Ms. Kelly Meyer, the payroll icon, Supervisor Anthony Hopkins, Allen Cameron and Ron Roik of Allied Barton Security Services were very helpful, accessible and responsive. God Bless Them!

I had the golden opportunity to meet Ms. Tonya Jackson (Director), Ms. Opal Barrett, Housing Programme Manager and Ms. Erica Alcala, the Leasing Specialist as well as some of their residents – Wanda, Lynn McDaniel, Babara, Lynda, Ray, Martha Gonzalez, Margarret, Ellen, Milton etc. at Casa Inc; Catholic Charities, Diocese of Fort Worth, Inc. They are wonderful people who made me very happy always. I miss them. God Bless Them!

I cannot forget Igbesa Club; the premier social club of Igbesa whose members include illustrious academicians and professionals like educators, professors, lawyers, accountants, auditors, doctors, engineers, architects, businessmen and political giants. One of the accomplishments for which the club is excelling is the periodic award of scholarships to some university students. The club also engages in the provision of drinkable water from wells to some villages in Igbesaland. It is a great joy for my membership of the club for over three decades for which I am very proud.

Local, State and Federal authorities, leaders and politicians should emulate the philanthropic examples of Igbesa Club instead of engaging in money laundering, corruption and stashing Nigerian government money in their foreign private bank accounts. They should please invest on Nigerians and Nigeria, for their properties worth millions and billions of dollars overseas are not benefiting Nigerians, their great countrymen. Long live Igbesa Club; God bless members of Igbesa Club!

How can I forget the kindness of Mr. Kehinde Dada of Arlington, Texas who picked me up at DFW International Airport on November 4, 1989, and my free accommodation for two years provided by my junior cousin, airline pilot, Adam Dayo Aka and his girlfriend Jane Iwuchukwu. I thank them exceedingly.

Also important was the kindness of Mr. Jimmy Oyenekan and his wife Irene who rescued me from the Arlington temporarily abandoned apartment by my cousin after three days. They also accommodated me for nine months for a very small amount of money. I'll remember their kindness always. They introduced me to Festus Oyewo who helped me with a sales job in Fort Worth in 1991 and became one of my best friends.

One cannot forget Senior Evangelist Michael Obayangbon (alias Baba Tosin) and his lovely wife (Mama Tosin); Senior Evangelist Henry Fakunle and Senior Evangilist Francis Olagoroye of the Celestial church of Christ in Irving and Arlington, Texas, USA respectively for their kindness and usual prayers. May God bless them and their families (amen).

Constantly remembered is Versie R. Taylor whose family and friends destroyed our great marriage. She was everything to me. May God Almighty give her sound health and reward those who directly and/or indirectly destroyed our marriage. I also remember Dr. Matthew Talabi of Ado-Odo; Isreal Orisharinu; Mercy and Pricilla Uju; Mojisola and Kemi Osuji; Ojuolape Oyeneyin of Ondo; Jimmy Adebiyi of Miami (1979); Mr. Art Tribble and Mr. White former and succeeding Principals of Shelby Alternative School, Everman respectively; Mr. James King, former Principal of E. Ray Elementary School, Everman; Mr. Herman Norris, Assistant Principal, Everman High School; Ms. Sharon Tidwell, Personnel Officer, Everman I.S.D; Mrs. H. Baker, Asst.

Principal, Everman Jr. High School; Ms. Williams; Samson Ahmed, Badagry; Tunji Akapo, a genius from Badagry; Mr. Faramola, U.K.; Yemi Folarin and Latundun Folarin; Haruna Bankole and family; Mureni Aka and family; Rali, Nike, Kudi Aka and their families; Salim Amin AbiSaid, Brighton, 1975/76; Chief and Mrs. Adedokun; Hadji M.A. TiamiyuBamgbose; Rev. Pastor S. Obanla; Akanke Lapite (nee Gbeleyi); Mrs. Lola Phillips (nee Odagi); Opeyemi Olajumoke Lawal, Toyin Lawal and Abu Ogunola (Ike Baba Adija) of Ado-Odo.

I cannot forget my best friend, John Ejiogu, his wife and Chike Asiodu who are the most wonderful Nigerian Igbos I have ever met. They are kind, nice and not tribalistic. I also remember Alani Kamoru, Akanni Shonola, Rashael Nwokobia, Shomade and his niece, Ayo who have been great friends since youthful days.

Great American, Carol Stanford was responsible for typing my doctoral rationale, term papers and dissertation for over three years. She took the pains to convert all British/English spellings and words to American /English spellings and words, which was remarkable kindness for utilizing her extra time and energy to do that for me. In the same vein, her partner and friend, Sue Carden whom I have known since 1990, typed my book, "Blacks Greatest Homeland Nigeria Is Born Again" under great strain trying to figure out the spellings of most Nigerian names and clearing the confusion between British/English spellings and American/English spellings and words. It was not an easy task coupled with her busy schedules, but she did it with utmost zeal and remarkable enthusiasm.

Unfortunately, when Nigerian "419 advance fee fraudsters" faxed several fraudulent letters to their company in Fort Worth, Texas 2005/06 demanding money to retrieve Abacha's loot from Geneva, Switzerland, I had to take time to explain to them to disregard the fraudulent letters and I assured them about the arrests and prosecution of the ringleaders by Obasanjo Administration. These two ladies, Carol and Sue, and their husbands are exceptionally some of the greatest white Americans I have met who are accessible, accommodating and not discriminating against Blacks. They have travelled extensively outside the borders of the USA, which makes them open and broadminded to accept all people. Extensive travelling educates and reorientates people to the changing world and it exposes them to the benefits of globalization.

For God's sake, I remember those interesting youthful days I spent with these great Nigerians and pray for a reunion in my lifetime. They include: Chief Akin Odu, former President of Igbesa Club and son of late Chief Odu of Igbesa and Headmaster of CMS School; Chief Oluwole Ayinde Ajo in London, UK; Deacon A. Yode Aka; Jubirila A. Aka (Baba Kabiru); Amuda Aka; Brother Lateef Jimoh and Uncle Lati Kasumu of Ado-Odo; Prince Adebayo A. Banuso, a recognized genius, unbeatable in his class; Kabiyesi Oba Olu Banuso, the Oloja of Igbesa, Jimmy Odunsi, Taiye's husband; Akanke Bolaji (Gbeleyi) Lapite; Commissioner Ayoka (Aina) Akinde; Celina Jaiye (Odagi) Amore; late Aminu Bola Aka; Beloved Saidat Aka; Kamoru Elegbede, very brilliant guy; Honourable Mufutau Ajibola very brilliant, studious and steadfast; Honourable Timothy Akojenu; Badagry; Chief Jimmy Fadun, a prospective Senator; Funmilayo (Salu) Aka; Tola Bimbo Aka; Biola Aka (Alado); Tayo Aka; Commissioner Tebun Fagbemi; Gregory and Aite Dalmeida; Snr. Phillip Akintoye of Ado-Odo; Snr. Hameed Dada; Snr. Tawa Kolawole Giwa, the Senior Prefect and neatest, best dressed student of our time; Benjamin Ashade, Alias Biggy; Samuel Ogunyemi; Bode Ajasa; the Salakos from Ota:Labaika, Bastu, Hakeem, Azeez, Muse and others; the Durosinmis; Owoyele Akinwale; Christiana Biodun Ayeni; Awoleke Setonji Ayeni; Chief and Snr. Whenayan Ayeni; Ibrahim Alafia; Lateef Pedro and his sister; Eric, Ali, Muse Hundeyin and others; Folorunsho Akin, very brilliant and neatest student; Professor Sunday Ajose, mathematical genius of North Carolina State University; Salami Eniafe, the fastest runner, and his sister Suwebat; Commissioner Miminu Badmus, a great personality; Mrs. Lola Salaam; Senior Evangelist Abiodun and Lola Fagbamila; Dr. Johnny Arije and Phillip Arije; Tola Taiwo Akapo; Godfrey Okay Nwosu of Brighton, Sussex, UK 1975/76; Menase Oteje and Folabi; the Arogbokuns of AkungbaFestus, Jonah, Samuel and others; Jide Apantaku; Snr. Sandy Emmanuel Orebote; Tosin and Sunday Orebote, the OsijosYomi and Co.; Chief Accountant Julius Odeniran; Felicia Ibe, Miami 1979; Rosemary Umoren of Brighton and Middlesborough, UK (1976/77); Deborah Gilmore 1979; Miami; Deborah Layide Erinle; Akin Erinle and Co; Chief Jubril Ojugbele, Chief Oba Jide Ojugbele; Isiaka Ojugbele; Mr. Raheem Ojugbele (Baba Kadija); Chief Oba Akanni Bamgbose; Chief Isiaka Bamgbose; Sunmola Oshunbiyi; my favourite teachers, Rev. Euler Ajayi; Mr. B. S. Hundeyin; Mr. A. A. Idowu and Mr. Oladipo of Badagry.

Nicole Ann Alexander and Sharon Dixon were great neighbours at Oakwood Terrace Apartments in Everman, Texas, USA after my wife forced me out of my house at 5224 Trail Lake Dr., Fort Worth and planted her boyfriend Clarence Herron in my house from 2004-2008. I thank them exceedingly. In the end, my exwife (Versie) was awarded my house and all my property of 15 years. That is America especially if you were not born here and your accent is different.

I nurse a lot of admiration for Ms. Nilliah Chadwick and her son, my friend, De'Ryian. Nilliah is hard working, highly educated, brilliant and majestic. People talk nice about her. She is wished complete recovery from her car accident of mid2008 with God's blessings (amen).

I always remember Yinka and Adeola Akinjomo and their big sister Fumbi. I will forever be grateful to Grace Yinka Akinjomo of OdeIrele who stood by me in need and in deed during my darkest moments. May God reward her and her family in so many folds. I thank Mama Bade, the law, for her kindness in 1985/86. May God bless her and her family. My brother Alani Aka is a great religious leader. I am very proud of him and his entire family.

Always remembered are my nephews and niece in London, UK, Kazeem Aka, Olawale Aka, Olatunji Aka, Gbolahan Aka and one of the most precious girls of the family, Ojuolape Aka. All the above past and present friends and family members give me extremely wonderful gracious memories for which I am grateful to God for His mercies and blessings.

Chief Jaiye Olatokun (nee Akinde), Iyameto of Igbesa and Mrs. Kehinde Showunmi (nee Akinde) were very kind to me. Chief Jubril Ojugbele formerly of Ministry of Health, Ikeja employed me the same date that I joined Nigeria Airways. The mother of Chief W. Apesin (Mama Alasan) took me to Badagry and accommodated me free to attend Badagry Grammar School. Ms. Shade Akinde, Chiefs R. A. Dada, Dada (Baba Yisa) and R. T. Agemo were nice to me. I can never forget the kindness of these great Igbesans.

Judging from the above, a lot of great Nigerians tremendously contributed to my development from childhood, adolescence to adulthood and to them all, I say, "Thank you and God bless you all." I am a symbol of a great Nigerian that it took a whole country of diverse Nigerian ethnicities to raise for which I am extremely grateful. All the assistances in different forms and shapes given to me directly and indirectly are appreciated. You all made commendable difference in my life; you all make me great and proud as a beloved Nigerian and a lover of Nigeria and Nigerians. You have all shown me how to put Nigeria first and I will continue to emulate that in all my spheres of activities. No matter what, it is worthy to live and die for a great country, Nigeria and Nigerians. My home! My home! My home! Nigeria (West Africa) is my home. I will be back to my home sooner than later to contribute to Nigeria's forward march to the Promised Land. In togetherness, with genuine faith in God/Allah, patience, peace, understanding with love, care and respect for one another, we will all get there. May God/Allah bless you all (amen).

Lastly, I happily acknowledge, appreciate and recognize the support and encouragement from the members of the Board of Directors of Global Community Enhancement, Inc. USA as well as the importance of its services for the benefit of humanity.

The incorporation of the Global Community Enhancement, Inc. USA represents a great step in the right direction. Its mission to promote development, upliftment, welfare, education, healthcare, counseling, progress and other essential human services for communities in need is invaluable.

The pioneering members of the Board of Directors who have done marvelous job for the enhancement of humanity include:
1. Mr. Michael Stanislous, President
2. Mr. Martin Olushola Aina, Vice President
3. Dr. Jubril Olabode Aka, Director
4. Mr. Christopher Ishaku, Director
5. Ms. Arinola Aina, Director

With the headquarters in New York, USA, the organization aims to expand and internationalize speedily to provide needed services for development of African countries beginning with Igbesa community, Ogun State, Nigeria, West Africa.

In similar fashion, the Champions for Nigeria (CFN) Organization is developing to become a premier organization that nurtures and promotes the best interest of Nigeria and her people. Members of the organization abound in Nigeria, United Kingdom, United States of America, Canada etc. I appreciate my membership of the CFN whose membership include most distinguished ladies and gentlemen of great academia and professionalism.

Undoubtedly, Nigeria is a great country rich in human, material and mineral resources of oil, gas, bitumen, bauxite, coal, lead/zinc, ironore, gold, limestone, phosphate, tantalite, clay etc. All hands must be on deck to make Nigeria become one of the economically great superpower countries before the end of the third decade of the twenty-first millennium. It can be done. It must be done. Yes, We Can! Yes, We Can! Thank You?

GOD/ALLAH BLESS NIGERIA!

MAP OF

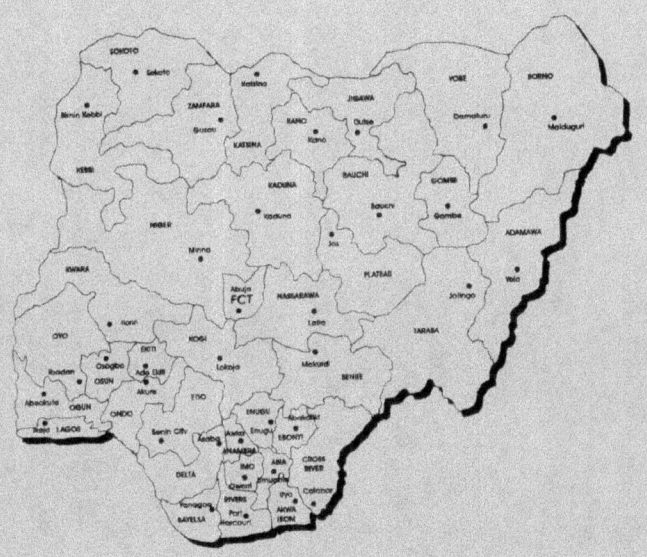

NIGERIA

THE NIGERIAN NATIONAL ANTHEM

Arise O' Compatriots, Nigeria's call obey
To serve our fatherland
With Love and strength and faith
The labours of our heroes past
Shall never be in vain
To serve with heart and might
One nation bound in freedom, peace and unity.

O God of Creation, direct our noble cause,
Guide (thou) our leaders right,
Help our youth the truth to know
In love and honesty to grow
And living just and true
Great lofty heights attain
To build a nation where peace and justice shall reign.

The final words of the national anthem were formed from the entries of the best five picks: **John A Ilechukwu, Erne Etim Akpan, B A Ogunnaike, Sotu Omoigui and P. O Aderibigbe.** *A total of 1499 entries were submitted in a competition organized by the National Publicity Committee on the Draft Constitution/Return to Civilian Rule.*

The National Pledge

I pledge to Nigeria my country
To be faithful, loyal and honest
To serve Nigeria with all my strength
To defend her unity and uphold her honour and glory
So help me God.

The Nigerian Coat of Arms

The coat of arms is represented by a shield, two wavy bands, two horses, an eagle and some plants at the foot of the shield.

The shield, which is black, stands for the rich and fertile earth the country is endowed with.

The wavy bands represent the River Niger and the River Benue which flow through Nigeria.

The two white horses represent dignity and pride.

A common wild flower (Coctus spectablis) in Nigeria covers the ground on which the symbols stand, and it stands for the beauty of Nigeria.

The motto of Nigeria "Unity and Faith" is written on the Coat of Arms.

The wreath is in the national colours (Green and White) and the eagle represents strengths.

NIGERIA

STATE	CAPITAL	TITLE
ABIA	Umuahia	God's Own State
ADAMAWA	Yola	
AKWA IBOM	Uyo	Land of Promise
ANAMBRA	Awka	Home for All
BAUCHI	Bauchi	
BAYELSA	Yenegoa	The Glory of All Lands
BENUE	Markurdi	Food Basket of the Nation
BORNO	Maiduguri	Home of Peace
CROSS RIVER	Calabar	The People's Paradise
DELTA	Asaba	The Big Heart
EBONYI	Abakaliki	The Salt of the Nation
EDO	Benin City	The Heart Beat
EKITI	AdoEkiti	Fountain of Knowledge
ENUGU	Enugu	Coal City State
GOMBE	Gombe	
IMO	Owerri	Land of Hope
JIGAWA	Dutse	The New World
KADUNA	Kaduna	Liberal State
KANO	Kano	Centre of Commerce
KATSINA	Katsina	State of Hospitality
KEBBI	Birni Kebbi	
KOGI	Lokoja	The Confluence State
KWARA	Ilorin	
LAGOS	Ikeja	Centre of Excellence
NASARAWA	Lafia	The Home of Solid Minerals
NIGER	Minna	The Power State
OGUN	Abeokuta	The Gateway State
ONDO	Akure	The Sunshine State
OSUN	Oshogbo	State of Living Spring
OYO	Ibadan	The Pace Setter State
PLATEAU	Jos	Home of Peace and Tourism
RIVERS	Port Harcourt	Treasure Base of the Nation
SOKOTO	Sokoto	Seat of the Caliphate
TARABA	Jalingo	Nature's Gift to the Nation

YOBE	Damaturu	The Young Shall Grow
ZAMFARA	Guasau	
FCT	Abuja	Centre of Unit

NIGERIA IS BORN AGAIN
The Poem

(1)
Nigeria Is Born Again!
Nigeria Is Born Again!
Congrats, Our 1999 Democratic Nation, 4th Republic, Reborn May 29, 2003.
The Mystery Date, Representing Milestone of CiviliantoCivilian Transition.
When President Matthew Okikiolakan Olusegun Aremu Obasanjo Launched,
A "United, Strong, Prosperous, Peaceful, Just, And Indeed A Great Nigeria."
We Envisage Numerous Bumps Ahead; But United, We'll Triumph Gracefully.
Wake Up All Nigerians; Glorify God/Allah, Credit Obasanjo for Debt Relief.

(2)
Nigeria Is Born Again!
Nigeria Is Born Again!
Wake Up Nigeria, The Federal Republic Of Nigeria, "Our Fatherland."
Nigeria Stands On Quadruped Pillars: Presidency/Senate/House Reps/Judiciary.
Toe Traits of Obasanjo, Yar'Adua, Mark, Bankole, CJN Kutigi & CJ Ade Alabi.
Let Nigeria's Interest Reign Supreme: Presidency, Legislature & Judiciary.
With TeamWork, To Wax Nigerian Polity Stronger & Unheated.
Wake Up All Nigerians; To Turn Stones Unturned & Cross Rivers Uncrossed.

(3)

Nigeria Is Born Again!
Nigeria Is Born Again!
Wake Up Nigeria, The Federal Republic Of Nigeria, "Our Fatherland."
The Only Country On Earth, We can Call Our Own, "Our Motherland."
The Black Peoples Nation of Nobles, Kings And Queens, "Our Homeland."
Though Tribe, Tongue, Religious Faiths & Political Affiliations May Differ,
In Brotherhood We Stand, Indivisible, In Godliness, Forgiving & Forgetting.
Wake Up All Nigerians; Change Business As Usual and Trust Our Leadership.

(4)

Nigeria Is Born Again!
Nigeria Is Born Again!
Wake Up Nigeria, The Most Populous African Nation Of 140 Million People.
Shun Ethno-religious Riots, For Godliness Is Peace, Mercy, Grace and Love.
With Tolerance As Key To God/Allah, The Peaceful, Omniscient, Omnipotent.
Let Us All In Togetherness Patriotically Strengthen Our Nascent Democracy
For Democracy Is Catalyst, Pivot, Fulcrum & Aircraft To Our Promised Land.
Wake Up All Nigerians; Be Selfless Best In Serving Nigeria And Humanity.

(5)

Nigeria Is Born Again!
Nigeria Is Born Again!
Wake Up Nigeria, The Benevolent, The Peace And Power Broker In Africa.

Place Nigeria First & Change Behaviour Inimical To Nigeria's Best Interest.
For That's What Guarantees Our Economic Survival, Growth And Prosperity.
Translate Our Diversity Into Unity, Strength, Trust, Oneness & Greatness.
Like LegendsAhmadu Bello, Awo, Zik, Balewa, Gowon, Obasanjo & Shagari.
Wake Up All Nigerians; March On Relentlessly To Greatest Heights.

(6)

Nigeria Is Born Again!
Nigeria Is Born Again!
Wake Up Nigeria, The Blessed And Wealthiest Black Nation On Earth.
Stop Corruption, Smuggling, Money Laundering & Illegal Oil Bunkering.
To Sustain And Enhance Nigerian Dignity And Respect In Comity Of Nations.
Always Strongly Emphasize Your Nigerianism More Than Regional Ethnicities.
Because One Nigeria Is Bigger, Stronger & Better Than Any/Some Of Her Parts.
Wake Up All Nigerians; Say, "Never" To Dictatorship, Divisionism & Terror.

(7)

Nigeria Is Born Again!
Nigeria Is Born Again!
Wake Up Nigeria , Our Wonderful Land Of Rich Cultural Heritage.
Ask Not, "What Nigeria Can Do For You" Ask, "What We Can Do For Nigeria".
Be Righteous, Faithful, Empathic, Responsive, Accountable, And Peace Loving.
For Blessed Are The Righteous And Peaceful; The Kingdom Of God Is Theirs.
Help Disadvantaged And Less Privileged; Your Reward Is Abundant

& Eternal.
Wake Up All Nigerians; Support Fiscal, Socio-economic & Political Reforms.

(8)

Nigeria Is Born Again!
Nigeria Is Born Again!
Wake Up Nigeria, Land Of Abundant Human, Material And Natural Resources.
Keep The Nation Indivisible With Freedom, Where No One Is Oppressed.
That The Independence Struggles By Our Nationalists Are Not In Vain.
Protect Niger Deltans From Vandals, Exploitations & Illegal Oil Bunkering.
For They Are Our Great Kiths, Kins and Hens That Lay The Golden Eggs.
Wake Up All Nigerians; It is Honourable To Be Keepers Of All Our Nationals.

(9)

Nigeria Is Born Again!
Nigeria Is Born Again!
Wake Up Nigeria, Beautified By Atlantic Ocean, Rivers Niger and Benue.
Let Educators Stop Resorting To Incessant Strikes And LockOut Tendencies,
For Those Who Suffer Most Are Students, The Future Leaders Of Our Nation.
Please, Ponder More On Students' Plights And Less On Earthly Gratifications.
For Your Heavenly Rewards & Blessings Are Invaluable, Abundant And Eternal.
Wake Up All Nigerians; Invest Positively And Qualitatively In Nigerian Youths.

(10)

Nigeria Is Born Again!
Nigeria Is Born Again!
Wake Up Nigeria, Land Of Hope & Opportunities For Economic Prosperity.
Help Students Shun Cultism, Gangsterism, Killings & Other Violent Crimes.
For Youths Are Our Hopes And Legacies To Glorious Nigeria Of Our Dreams.
Always Follow Due Process & Rule Of Law Instituted By President Yar'Adua.
For If You Are Not Exemplary, Your Prospective Leadership Chance Is Slim.
Wake Up All Nigerians; Give Our Youths Enabling Environment For Success.

(11)

Nigeria Is Born Again!
Nigeria Is Born Again!
Wake Up Nigeria, One Of The World's Seven Largest Suppliers Of Oil & Gas.
Ask, "What Kind Of Nigerian Are You?" Exemplary, Transparent, Optimistic!
Or Pessimistic, Corrupt, Fraudulent, or Economic And Financial Saboteur?
Who Suffers For Labour Disputes, Strikes And Lockouts? The Masses Do!
Evolve Dialogue/Consultation, Conciliation, NonViolence Of MLK & Gandhi.
Wake Up All Nigerians; Stop Strikes Jeopardizing Nigeria's Prosperity Goals.

(12)

Nigeria Is Born Again!
Nigeria Is Born Again!
Wake Up Nigeria, Blessed God/Allah's Land Flowing With Milk & Honey.

In 2003 Blessings, Obasanjo Became AU Chairman & Okogie Cardinal.
Nigeria Rose From Pariah Status In 1998 To Most Beloved Nation In 2003.
Hosted 8th African Games & Won, CHOGM & Became Chairperson In Office.
Enyimba Surprised CAF & Universe; We launched Our Satellite Into Space.
Wake Up All Nigerians; To Champion Nigeria's Advancement To Prosperity.

(13)

Nigeria Is Born Again!
Nigeria Is Born Again!
Wake Up Nigeria, The World's Largest Concentration Of Black People.
Where One Out Of Every Ten Blacks In The World Is A Nigerian.
Whose Soldiers Sacrifice And Ensure African SocioPolitical Stability.
On Peace Missions In Congo, Sierra-Leone, Liberia, Sudan, Lebanon etc.
Engaging In Disarmament, Demobilization, Rehabilitation & Security.
Wake Up All Nigerians; You Are The Pride Of All Blacks In The World.

(14)

Nigeria Is Born Again!
Nigeria Is Born Again!
Wake Up Nigeria, The Most Resourceful Nation Of Black Peoples On Earth.
Emulate Ogun State Governor, Otunba Gbenga Daniel, Obalofin Of Ijebuland.
Who Possesses Strong Interpersonal Skills, contented With God's Endowment.
An Achiever And Trail –Blazer, Our Pride Who Eliminates Ghost Workers.
Is Constructing Roads, Wooing Investors And Generating

Employment.
Wake Up All Nigerians; Toe Ogun State Footsteps, Where New Dawn Has Risen.

(15)

Nigeria Is Born Again!
Nigeria Is Born Again!
Wake Up Nigeria, The Blessed Land Of Rising Hope For Prosperity.
Where Oil And Gas Flow In Abundance, With Steel And New Discoveries Of
Oil, Gas, Bitumen, Gold, Phosphate, Etc. In Ogun (Gateway) State, Home Of
Awo, Obasanjo, Gov. Daniel, Aka Olupana, Olagbaye, Odagi, Ajo & Akinde.
With Kings Awujale, Alake, Olota, OluIlaro, Onigbesa & Alado Of Ado-Odo.
Wake Up All Nigerians; March Fast To The Promised Land – The El Dorado.

May God/Allah bless The Federal Republic Of Nigeria!
Long Live Nigeria!
By
Jubril Olabode Aka (DMS, MBA Aviation, Ph. D.)

GREAT IGBESA FAMILIES

There are great and most distinguished pioneering families and names in Igbesa, Ogun State of Nigeria that are to be remembered forever. They are families that have contributed to the beginning and development of Igbesaland.

The wonderful families and names include: Olupana (Aka, Aduloju, Osho Obodi, Akingbade, Olakisan, Falola, Agesin, Tabeloju etc.), Kabiyeses, The Excellencies Oba Aluko, Oba Salu, Oba Gbeleyi, Oba Banuso, Oba Asiri of Ilamiro, Oba Yusuf of Ikogbo etc; Oku Ashamu (Iyalode of Igbesa), Omoseke, Akinde, Odagi, Aina, Ajo, Olagbaye, Dada Elero, Ojomo, Odu Head Master, Ajana, Bamgbose, Gbeleyi, Akomolafe, Saula, Ajose, Adedokun, Jolaogun, Ojugbele, Apesin, Eniafe, Erinle, Obanla, Odunsi, Kaka, Durojaiye, Odunfa, Akinbode, Tijani Owolu, Ajayi, Olaiya, Olaotan, Tiamiyu Bamgbose, Akinogun, Akinosi, Padayeri, Abatan, Buraimoh, Badiru, Bankole, Tanisewu, Irawo Osan Bagbaleru, Akeran, Ekerin, Adesola, Salawu, Sadiku, Lesanmi, Agemo, Olorun Ero, Fagbayi, Alagbole, Oridami, Abumo, Adegun, Osolo, Sanni Etedi, Amuda Etedi, Akapo, Odu, Okedeyi, Masha, Fadun, Alebe, Bada, Adalemo, Ojulari, Salami, Odegbile, Adepoju, Adeosun, Kilani, Dada, Alegun, Deji & Great Descendants of Ogbomoso at Igbesa, Jimoh Egbun, Fagbemi, Owolabi, Itabiyi, Adenle, Amosun, Talabi, Ajayi, Adedoyin, Eniosi, Olaotan, Olaitan, Shitu, Oladega, Ojo, Lamina, Omotowu, Omoloto, Akinola, Oke Pefi (Idanyin), Animashawun, Ogunbiyi, Ogundipe, Ogunlabi, Ogundele, Abore Ilamiro, Ajagona, Akindele, Akinyele, Akinleye, Fuwape, Oriyomi, Ambawi, Yaya Keke, Akintan, Odesile, Adesina, Jonah, Michael Idowu, Sanni, Sibotini, Odu Onipere, Johnson, Liadi Ariyo, Ogboni Ayo of Ogona, Ajanlekoko, Adigboluja, Olusesi, Inakoju, Dada Oro, Baba Akeju (Iwaro), Baba Saula Olopa Oba, Lemomu Taibi, Saka Gbagi (Baba Olopa), Ajanaku, Itu, Sanni Rekete, Fagbenro, Oke Ekun, Owolabi, Falohun, Fagbohun, Ogbe, Oforan, Osoja, Arowolo, Jojo, Ejose Ojanjan, Fakayode, Awele, Ilari Opa, Agagu (Ilemo), Kosebinu, Kosewon, Aribilu, Anigilaje, Dada Ekun, Aina Akibon, Odu Ake, Dadabiro, Salami Akebioro, Aina Abe, Aina Ebe, Arile, Osanyinbi, Dosumu, Logun, Oguntoyinbo, Inakoju Falohun, Otena, Bada Arowojobe, Aina Jasere, Agbanijoriadan, Olomide Akinogun, Ilo, Awile (Itolu), Ojugbele Onadi, Oyede, Latoye,

Ijan, Isiba, Owo Ogun, Ogungbile, Imosu, Senikoro, Akera, Olakijena, Fafunmi, Adoga, Oyewun, Jinadu Onibembe, Fuwape Aruposi, Alabe Onibembe, Lani Lemuse Alaponran, Oje Yo Alakuba, Oje Mambo, Sule Awelu, Dada Awunju, Agboluaje (Ida Ose), Aduro, Asoko, Asuko, Agunbiade, Aina Ori, Sanni Akeran, Egunjobi, Orokele, Olowokere, Esipa, Adalemo, Odeale (Baba Muniru Opeloyeru), Oga Ona, Otade, Inakoju, Adokunrin, Aminiawo, Ajoga, Ogunbewon, Ebiora, Ajenifuja, Obanla Alufoge, Shakoto, Ejikale, Afofu, Amilaka, Adegbe, Ayato, Amure, Bello Keke Iyawo, Agbokotarale, Laari, Awoyo, Atobajaiye, Dada Ofa, Ilu Ogbelasan, Atunrase, Aniyan, Okara, Felenge, Oyawenu, Jigan, Aseperi, Awogi, Agbona, Oforan, etc. The list is inexhaustible..

May the Souls of the Departed Rest In Perfect Peace (Amen)!

GOD/ALLAH BLESS IGBESALAND!

IN MEMORIAM

To the Memory of Three Great Black Women
Mrs. Stella Omotola Obasanjo (Nigeria, W. Africa)
Mrs. Rosa Parks (USA)
Mrs. Coretta Scott King (USA)

The author reminds the world about three great women, Nigerian First Lady, Mrs. Stella Omotola Obasanjo (1945-2005); Mrs. Rosa Parks (1913-2005) of the USA, a pioneer and mother of the Civil Rights Movement both of whom departed the world to the Lord in late October 2005; and Mrs. Coretta Scott King (1927-2006), widow of the slain civil rights activist and leader Dr. Martin Luther King, Jr. of the USA.

Mrs. Stella Omotola Obasanjo lived an exemplary life as Nigerian First Lady, a great mother, a great wife and unifier in Nigerian democratic, sociopolitical dispensation. Her unifying force created wonderful impressions among varying Nigerian nationalities, especially during periods of political crises.

Her innermost connections and influences saved her husband, General Olusegun Obasanjo, from being liquidated by General Sani Abacha in a trumped up case of coup d'etat. Her husband later became Nigerian President, Commander in Chief of Nigerian Armed Forces, Chairman of African Union and Chairperson in Office of the Commonwealth.

If she had not made the timely secret telephone calls and connections to American and European leaders to abort the desperate plan of Abacha to hang/execute/kill her husband and many others, General Obasanjo might not have lived up to 1999 to become Nigerian President on May 29, 1999. Above all, Nigeria and Africa would have lost all the accomplishments of General Obasanjo as President of Nigeria and Chairman of African Union. Her miraculous intervention that saved her husband was angelical. It helped to save many Nigerian dignitaries who were incarcerated by Abacha dictatorial administration. She will be remembered to eternity—Great First Lady, Stella Omotola Obasanjo, Adieu.

On the other hand, Mrs. Rosa Parks (1913-2005) of the USA said that enough was enough to segregation and humiliation of the Blacks in public means of transportation by refusing to give up her bus seat to a white man for which she was arrested by Montgomery, Alabama Police on December 1., 1955. Her nonviolent action resulted in 381day boycott of public transportation and the formation of the Civil Rights Movement of Dr. Martin Luther King, Jr.

According to Rev. Barry Black, the US Senate Chaplain, who eulogized Mrs. Parks said, "By sitting down, this Mother of Civil Rights Movement enabled millions to stand up in a better world." Mrs. Rosa Parks became the first woman to lie in honour in the Capitol Rotunda where the bodies of great American Presidents like Abraham Lincoln, John F. Kennedy and other US national leaders have been paid tributes after their deaths. Rosa Parks would be the first black woman represented in Statuary Hall where many American States have statues honouring notable people in their history. She changed America and Americans.

The world also mourned Mrs. Coretta Scott King (1927-2006), widow of slain civil rights leader Dr. Martin Luther King Jr. and the first lady of the Black Civil Rights Movement in the United States. She founded the King Center, a teaching facility, archive and museum as tribute to her husband's work.

Reverend Jesse Jackson described her as a "freedom fighter who provided stability for her husband, Dr. Martin Luther King Jr." The US President George W. Bush described her as a "remarkable and courageous woman and a great civil rights leader." Former Atlanta Mayor who was US Ambassador to the United Nations, Andrew Young, said that Mrs. King's fortitude rivaled that of her husband and that she was strong, if not stronger than her husband was. She was formidable and steadfast in the successful struggle that established a national holiday approved by President Ronald Reagan in 1983 for her husband who was regarded as a martyr. She was a great wife of fifteen years, a great mother and a great widow for almost forty years.

Mrs. Coretta Scott King's burial ceremony of Tuesday, February 7, 2006 was attended by four US Presidents; Jimmy Carter, the thirty-ninth; George H. W. Bush,the forty-first; Bill Clinton, the forty-second; and George W. Bush, the forty-third; three governors, three planeloads of most distinguished Congress members and many celebrities of the civil rights movement.

President George W. Bush, the forty-third president, described her as, "A woman who worked to make our nation whole. She not only secured her husband's legacy, she built her own and having loved a leader, she became a leader, and when she spoke, Americans listened closely." President H. W. Bush (forty-first) said, "Our world is a kinder and gentler place because of Coretta Scott King."

President Carter referred to Dr. And Mrs. King thus; "They overcame one of the greatest challenges of life, which is able to wage a fierce struggle for freedom and justice and to do it peacefully." Forty-Second President Bill Clinton said, "They understood that the difficulty of success does not relieve one of the obligations to try."

Adelaide Tambo representing a delegation from South Africa said, "South Africa salutes her for her role in building an alliance that served to make freedom a reality for so many of us from around the world. Coretta's spear has fallen. It is now our duty and our responsibility to pick it up." May her soul rest in peace, adieu.

These three great women, Nigerian First Lady Stella Omotola Obasanjo, Mrs. Rosa Parks and Mrs. Coretta Scott King of the USA, left the world in a better shape than they met it. Nigerians and entire peoples of the world say 'adieu' to First Lady, Mrs. Stella Omotola Obasanjo; Mrs. Rosa Parks, pioneer and mother of Civil Rights Movement and Mrs. Coretta Scott King, first lady of the Civil Rights Movement.

May Their Souls Rest In Perfect Peace With The Lord (amen).

ABOUT THE AUTHOR

Dr. Jubril Olabode Aka (alias Bode Endurance), the author of "Great People, Great Country, Nigeria The Beautiful", 2009 is also the author of "Blacks Greatest Homeland Nigeria Is Born Again", 2006 and "A Female US President Is Salvation, Blessing, Peace and Prosperity", 2007. He holds a Ph.D. in Business Administration (USA, 1992), MBA in Aviation Management (USA, 1979) and Postgraduate Degree In Management Studies (Brighton, UK, 1976).

I am an Awori, Yoruba Nationality from South-Western Nigeria. My father was from Igbesa, Ogun State while my mother was from Ijanikin, Lagos State, South-Western Nigeria. I was one of the pioneering students of Baptist Day School, Igbesa and later transferred to the CMS School, Igbesa. I attended Ado-Odo Secondary Modern School as one of the second set of its commencement for one school session after which I transferred to Badagry Grammar School, thus becoming one of the third set of its commencement.

Having scored the highest point in the state organized entrance examination, I was awarded the Western Nigeria Regional Government Scholarship for six years under the gigantic educational programme initiated by the sage and immortal Chief Obafemi Awolowo, first Premier of Western Nigeria. I have always shared the view that Chief Obafemi Awolowo was one of the presidents Nigeria should have had during our life time, perhaps the Nigerian nation would have been far better than what it is today, and Nigerians would be having a more pleasant history than what it is at present time. During Chief Awolowo's Premiership in Western Nigeria, the accomplishments of Yoruba Nationality were first in Africa. He will be remembered eternally.

I attended graduate business school, Brighton of Brighton University, Sussex, UK, 1975/76; Embry-Riddle Aeronautical University (Miami Graduate Division), Miami, Florida, USA, 1979; Century University, New Mexico, USA, 1990/92; and Tarleton State University, Stephenville, Texas, USA, 2001. I also, attended Management Development Programmes at the Centre for International Management, Geneva, Switzerland, 1978, and Urwick Management Center, Slough, England, UK, 1978. I hold memberships of British Institute of Management (1976), Nigerian Institute of Management (1977) and Institute of Personnel Management of Nigeria (1977).

Dr. Jubril Olabode Aka is an Economist, a Management Consultant, an Educator and a Trainer. I was Airline Assistant Chief Management Instructor, Economics Instructor and a Business Executive of many years standing both in Nigeria and the USA. I have lived in Texas, USA for 2 decades. I am now ready to participate fully in African development toward socio-economic prosperity and political stability.

My special interest areas include global community enhancement, management consultancy, industrialization, labour management, sales and marketing management, and in particular, projects that help youth and leadership development toward socio-economic prosperity of developing countries. I am greatly interested in working relentlessly by evangelizing against discrimination to ensure equal opportunities for all irrespective of ethnicity, religion, sex, age, state or region of origin. I am particularly concerned to see an end to abuses meted on women, youths, students and children.

I am a member of the Board of Directors of the Global Community Enhancement, Inc., USA. The mission of the organization is to promote development, upliftment, welfare, education, healthcare, counseling, progress and other essential human services for communities in need. The organization aims to expand and internationalize in record time to developing countries with particular reference to African countries beginning with Nigeria, West Africa.

Lastly, it is highly significant to clarify that this book is addressed to African, European and American readers as well as other nationalities from East, West, North and South in the world. Therefore, readers may experience differences in spellings such as labour for labor, jeopardise for jeopardize, actualise for actualize, honour for honor, centre for center, behoves for behooves, travelled for traveled, advisor for adviser, ones for one's, judgement for judgment, offense for offence, practise for practice, programs for programmes and so on and so forth. Any of the spellings whichever is applied should be accepted as correct as long as it conveys the author's message clearly.

God/Allah Bless Nigeria, My Home, Sweet Home!
Thank You!

Jubril Olabode Aka (DMS, MBA Aviation, Ph.D.)

BIBLIOGRAPHY

1. Dr. Jubril Olabode Aka, Ph. D., Blacks Greatest Homeland Nigeria Is Born Again. New York Lincoln Shanghai, iUniverse, Inc. 2006. ISBN13: 9780595832750 (ebk)
2. Dr. Jubril Olabode Aka, Ph.D., A Female US President Is Salvation, Blessing, Peace and Prosperity, New York Shanghai, iUniverse Inc. 2007. ISBN: 9780595449972 (pbk); ISBN: 9780595691517 (cloth); ISBN: 9780595893164 (ebk).
3. Usman Dan Fodio: Salaam. co.uk, Biographical Dictionary.
4. K.A.B. Jones – Quarterly, A Life of Azikiwe, 1965
5. Dr. Nnamdi Azikiwe, My Odyssey: An Autobiography (1971); ISBN: 0900966262.
6. Paden, John N., Muslim Civic Cultures & Conflict Resolution, Brookings Institution Press (2005), p. 240. ISBN: 0815768176
7. "Abacha Sani" Encyclopaedia Britannica, February 3rd, 2007.
8. Nigeria Recovers Abacha's Cash, BBC News, November 10, 1998; Retrieved on October 21, 2006.
9. Isaac B. Thomas, Life of Herbert Macaulay (1948).
10. Tamuno, Tekena N., Herbert Macaulay; Nigerian Patriot, London: Heinemann Educational, 1975.
11. Oxford University Press: A Dictionary of Contemporary World History, Awolowo, Obafemi (b. March 6, 1909, d. May 9, 1987).
12. Dosumu O.A., His Truth is Marching on: a Pictorial Biography of Chief Obafemi Awolowo, 1997. ISBN: 9789782218001.
13. Olusegun Obasanjo, My Command, Heinemann, Ibadan/London/Nairobi, 1980, p. 267, 35.

14. Ahmadu Bello, My Life, Cambridge University Press, 1962
15. Nigeria Year Book, 1962. Daily Times of Nigeria, 1962, pp. 112 (Abubakar Tafawa Balewa).
16. James S. Olson, Robert S. Shadle, Historical Dictionary of the British Empire, Greenwood Press, 1996 (Abubakar T. Balewa).
17. Shehu Othman Classes, Crises and Coup: The Demise of Shagari's Regime. African Affairs, Vol. 83, No. 333, 1985.
18. Shehu Shagari, Beckoned To Serve: An Autobiography.
19. Gowon's 1967 Speech Creating 12 Nigerian States.
20. Gowon's January 12, 1970 Speech Welcoming Biafran Surrender.
21. US Library of Congress – The 1966 Coups, Civil War, and Gowon's
22. Daily Trust, Yar'Adua Interview, March 3, 2007.
23. US Library of Congress: Country Studies – The Babangida Government.
24. Dibie, Robert A., Public Management and Sustainable Development in Nigeria Military Bureaucracy Relation, Page 51, Moshood Abiola, 1998.

JUBRIL OLABODE AKA & CHILDREN

Dr. Jubril Olabode Aka, Ph.D. (The Author)

Ms. S. Olubunmi Aka

Ms. Z. Olayide Aka

From left to right:- Ms. S. Olubunmi Aka Ms. Z. Olayide Aka Mr. I. Olufemi Aka.

Miss M. Tokunbo Aka

www.ingramcontent.com/pod-product-compliance
Lightning Source LLC
Chambersburg PA
CBHW071358230426
43669CB00010B/1381